COEXISTENCE AND COMMERCE

Guidelines for Transactions
between East and West

COEXISTENCE AND COMMERCE

Guidelines for Transactions Between East and West

SAMUEL PISAR

McGRAW-HILL BOOK COMPANY

New York Toronto London Sydney

COEXISTENCE AND COMMERCE: GUIDELINES FOR TRANSACTIONS BETWEEN EAST AND WEST

Designed by Christine Aulicino

Library of Congress Catalog Card Number: 79-112842

First Edition 50190

To Nachman

1904–1952

The spirit of commerce has a tendency to soften the manners of men and to extinguish those inflammable humors which so often have kindled into wars

Alexander Hamilton, 1787

ACKNOWLEDGMENTS

Several teachers of international renown have left an indelible influence upon my thinking and writing: Professors Zelman Cowen of Melbourne, Peter B. Carter of Oxford, René David of Paris and Harold J. Berman, my mentor at the Law School and the Russian Research Center of Harvard University.

Two individuals have made direct contributions to the substance of this work: the late Leon M. Herman, Senior Specialist in Soviet Economics at the Library of Congress, long the nation's foremost expert on East-West trade, supplied a constant stream of precious materials for Book One; Jeffrey M. Hertzfeld of the New York Bar collaborated in the long, arduous, multilingual research and in the drafting of Book Two. Their wives, Augusta Herman and Geneviève Hertzfeld, shared the drudgeries and joys of authorship in the Loire Valley during the summer of 1967.

Few possess a better understanding of America's political and legislative processes, or wield a more incisive blue pencil, than Norman I. Gelman of Washington and Milton S. Gwirztman of Washington and Paris. Both have read and improved large segments of the manuscript.

Many friends and acquaintances from different countries, West and East, have helped over the years in discussions, correspondence and numerous other ways. They include Liliana Archibald, Murray Feshbach, Paolo Gori, John N. Hazard, Tedd Joseph, Judith Kipper, William C. MacMillen, Jr., Lawrence C. McQuade, Melville B. Nimmer, Cornelius Pope, Myer Rashish, Jean-Pierre Saltiel and Robert B. Wright.

Without underestimating the yeoman labors of others, Carla Lewis, who typed reams of illegible script, and Pierre Sauvage, who proofread successive drafts, should be cited for unflagging patience and devotion.

Special thanks are due to the editors of the *Harvard Law Review* for permission to draw upon my articles published in their illustrious journal.

An undertaking of this scope in the midst of a demanding professional life has meant virtual withdrawal from other extracurricular activities. For this I owe an apology to partners, associates, relatives and friends.

My wife Norma (who was restricted to practicing her lieder pianissimo) and my daughters Helaina and Alexandra have stoically endured the book's intrusion, wondering in silence, I suppose, whether coexistence and commerce should not begin at home.

S.P.

CONTENTS

BOOK ONE

Second Part: The Commercial Setting

BOOK TWO

Second Part: The Settlement of Disputes

INTRODUCTION: KEY ISSUES

To attempt a book on the subject of East-West commercial relations one must be a guarded optimist, and I am. I have proceeded on the assumption that the economic systems of both communism and free enterprise will survive into the indefinite future. Neither side will voluntarily dismantle its own social structure or try to overwhelm the other with military force. This stalemate between the two contending spheres of our politically divided world holds the relatively cheerful prospect of coexistence and, with luck, constructive cooperation and competition.

I see this pattern as developing simply because the alternatives are unacceptable to anyone. To move toward an ultimate test of strength would be to court mutual annihilation. To reject the option of ampler economic intercourse would be to invite needless waste. But to accept, with due caution, the challenge of broader contacts is to enhance the prospects for evolutionary change and adaptation, in the interest of each system.

Efforts to expand economic dealings between the two will remain controversial, for in the background lie potent and legitimate concerns. East-West relations have continually been in flux. Proponents of international détente, constantly looking forward to a disintegration of military blocs and a blurring of political and economic divisions, too often mistake a temporary improvement in the weather for a fundamental change of climate. The Warsaw Pact's military crackdown on Czechoslovakia, for example, came precisely when the cold war seemed about to thaw into oblivion, with sobering impact on both segments of the European continent, as well as on the world beyond. Such events offer a sharp reminder rather than a new lesson: commercial transactions between East and West take place in a highly complex and volatile environment, subject to recurrent cycles of conflict and accommodation.

The nineteen-seventies will not necessarily be more stable than the two previous decades, but the checkered course of postwar events should by now have convinced most reasonable men that increased exchanges of peaceful goods and skills can be mutually advantageous. The arduous task of bridge-building is periodically interrupted; yet a common interest in survival and prosperity demands that the process go on.

Soviet attitudes on trade with the capitalist world have gone through several contradictory stages. Initial revolutionary nihilism gave way to an aggressively outward-looking New Economic Policy,[1] followed once again by a quest for national self-sufficiency. After the Second World War Russia embarked upon a strategic effort to divert the foreign commerce of the adjacent eastern European countries from their former trade partners in the West toward its own economy. It soon became apparent, however, that such traditional exporting states as Czechoslovakia would suffer material damage as a result of arbitrary confinement to a regional trading zone, ruled by an artificial doctrine of socialist preference. Today the Soviet Union itself is engaged in external commercial operations on a larger scale, in terms of volume, variety and geography, than at any time since the revolution. And it has given official endorsement to the law of comparative advantage in the international exchange of goods, services and ideas.

The world market has both political and economic attractions for the Soviet Union. Procurement of Western plants and technology, licensing of industrial know-how, disposal of surplus domestic production, development of new sources of raw materials and a diplomatically oriented drive to cement relations with less developed areas are all important aspects of current Soviet policy in the sphere of commodity trade. Though less apparent because of social convulsions, similar influences are coming into play in the case of China. Evidently, "command economies" can no longer immunize themselves from world market forces. While it is far too early to speak of a disposition toward economic interdependence, the practical value of the international division of labor has been recognized at the highest levels of communist leadership. This represents a significant change in state policy as well as in party dogma and opens a wide range of opportunities for interested Western firms; for the communist world offers a vast and rapidly expanding market to outside suppliers, and the conventional sale of goods is being increasingly supplemented with lucrative prospects for industrial, technological and managerial cooperation.

Business dealings between Eastern and Western countries have continued even in the absence of diplomatic relations, and when political tensions have been high. Governments which recognize neither the East German nor the Peking regime, West Germany and Japan, for example, have found pragmatic ways to stimulate trade with both. The quest for profitable economic exchange seems strong enough to transcend ideological barriers.

Nonetheless, the variable international atmosphere is a central obstacle to the normal growth of East-West commerce. The flow of goods is often at the mercy of state policies which subordinate economic to political considerations. Notable examples are the severe export restrictions, import discriminations and credit limitations which the United States still applies on a world-wide basis in order to inhibit dealings with the Soviet and Chinese orbits. Milder counterparts of such controls exist elsewhere. In addition, a dwindling measure of coordinated regulation is enforced multilaterally, under the auspices of allied organizations concerned with collective defense. Clearly, one cannot ignore the political, diplomatic and strategic environment in which antagonistic societies pursue their economic advantages. But it is equally obvious that if East-West trade is to know stable growth the institutional framework in which it is currently transacted must adapt. The intrusion of factors extraneous to normal commerce cannot but give newcomers to this area of activity the sensation of wandering in the wilderness; those initiated in the arcane mysteries of the subject have learned of necessity how to improvise makeshift solutions for recurrent difficulties. This is particularly evident with European businessmen, who through experience have far outdistanced their American counterparts in the East-West economic arena. Makeshift improvisations, however, cannot provide a permanent or satisfactory framework for flourishing trade.

Moreover, the communist system of state-directed and conducted commerce poses a long-term challenge to the international business community as a whole and to its traditional modes of operation. In 1961, while on a congressional fact-finding mission to Moscow, I was startled to hear a Soviet deputy minister say: "Your Attorney General, Robert Kennedy, should give me a medal for the way I compete with the major international oil trusts." Considering the aggressive Soviet forays into world aluminum, tin and oil markets during the late fifties, the remark was not entirely in jest. But even in the pursuit of legitimate commercial gain government monopolies have a propensity to dislocate the normal course of trade. When employed as outright instruments of state policy such monopolies may become politico-economic weapons against which the Western businessman is helpless. Because the volume of communist exports and imports is still limited, this danger appears distant. But, given the steady upward trend in trade with the East, it is high time to consider means of safeguarding the established channels and methods of international business from unregulated intervention by state-operated institutions.

The U.S.S.R. long ago began outwardly to adapt its trade to external requirements, employing both dialectical rationalization and hard-headed pragmatism. In order to acquire respectability in the preponderantly capitalist scheme of world commerce, its state monopolies have made a noticeable attempt to conform to the great body of mercantile law and practice which is the common heritage of capitalist traders. Communist officials speak the normal language of the market place, profess the sanctity of contractual obligations and employ most of the standard techniques to which businessmen are universally accustomed.[2] Undeterred by Marx's dogma that "business is theft," the Russians and their imitators have found it expedient to adopt, wholesale, many traditional institutions, laws and practices conceived and perfected by private merchants over the centuries. They have done this not only in their business arrangements with the outside world, but also in commerce among the planned economies themselves.

It has been suggested in the West that there is a general trend everywhere to move away from restrictions of national legislation toward a universal conception of the rules of international trade.[3] Communist commentators have found support in their own legal systems for the proposition that commercial law tends inexorably toward global uniformity. They, too, endorse the view of Lord Mansfield, the great eighteenth-century English jurist, who, in the best rationalist tradition of his period, held that the theoretical foundations of mercantile norms were nothing more than universal common sense and reason in action—a manifestation of the natural law of mankind.[4]

My personal inclination is to dissent from this verdict, at least in regard to communist foreign trade practice. I believe it can be demonstrated that the East's adherence to widely followed principles of the "law merchant" is more apparent than real. The dissimilarity between Eastern and Western economic organization, the divergent frames of reference in which domestic commerce is conducted and the absence of a common core of legal concepts all create a unique environment. That which is standard and conventional tends to become distorted in a manner never anticipated by the founders of ground rules responsible for the orderly functioning of international business. In their adaptation, both token and real, to established Western patterns, the communist systems have created many novel institutions, fashioned in the Soviet image by a group of nations which encompass one-third of the globe's population in one-fourth of its land mass and which carry on an annual exchange of more than $25 billion worth of goods with the rest of the world. These institutions cannot be denied recognition, nor can they be judged solely from the traditionalist vantage point of our own ideas of social structure, economic organization, property and law. Just as England, in her own time, gave form to a body of practices which acquired universal repute as a *jus gentium* of international commerce, so the Soviet Union and its allies can justifiably claim the right to forge original methods for the more convenient conduct of trade with similarly and differently organized economies. An example of how the new communist institutions are winning acceptance abroad can be seen in the role played by the special foreign trade and maritime arbitration tribunals which today dispense justice to merchants of the West.

These developments have been a natural by-product of the Soviet Union's evolution as a major trading and seafaring power and a pacesetter for likeminded nations. To a certain extent, however, they have also been a function of the absence of a coordinated Western policy. America's crusading anticommunism and the intense export-consciousness among her allies have operated at cross-purposes, thus hampering the establishment of a unified position.[5] Western Europe, Canada and Japan were long ago persuaded by the argument that increased trade helps the East to evolve into consumer societies, that "a fat communist is a peaceful communist." Only the United States has remained preoccupied with the extent to which Western supplies build the biceps rather than the midriff of the communist system. As a result, commerce has tended to develop along lines chosen largely by the East, under a proliferation of bilateral arrangements with individual, often weaker market economies. At a time when emergent nations are searching for social and economic models to emulate, the political contest over which rules should govern this vital component of practical international coexistence has been allowed to go by default.

Any effort to devise an enduring normative framework is conditioned by the overriding fact that in East-West trade time-honored practices universally employed by merchants become distorted. Even if state monopolies were slavishly to observe the prevailing customs, laws and techniques of international business, such observance would not, in my opinion, automatically bring about the required accommodation.

The distortions are not a result of malicious communist deliberation, nor are they caused by the continuing conflict between socialist and capitalist societies. By and large, they developed spontaneously from the intrusion of peculiarly structured, state-operated monopolies into world commerce. If international tensions could disappear with the wave of a magic wand, many of the technical difficulties that now afflict this sphere of exchange would remain.

The geographic and political limits of East and West are, of course, imprecise, even flexible. A sale from France to Japan, unquestionably an Eastbound export on the evidence of the compass, in this book's usage becomes strictly "Western" trade. Similarly, a shipment from Singapore to Warsaw is Westbound only in a physical sense. For our purposes it falls under the rubric of a sale from West to East. Subtler analysis is needed in the case of transactions between, say, Hungary and Austria, or between Yugoslavia and Cuba. I deem the former East-West trade; the latter, by the same standard, becomes purely "Eastern" commerce.

Both communism and capitalism exist within changing orbits. Though it is a customary oversimplification to treat them as precisely defined social categories, internal differences in history, religion, law, ethnic composition, geography, size, resource endowment, industrial development and dependence on foreign trade, all conspire against uniformity and lend each orbit a complex coloration. Among the several communist countries, disparate national pressures are caused by unequal progress toward the proclaimed goal of communism, varying degrees of economic centralization and nationalization, divergent patterns of structural reform, and so forth. At the two extremes are the U.S.S.R. and Yugoslavia. The latter, engaged in an experiment without parallel in East or West, can no longer be considered as centrally planned economy; nor can its foreign trade be viewed as a state monopoly on the Soviet pattern. Historical links as well as ideological and political affinities best explain that country's frequent classification with the Eastern sphere. Again, although in its social philosophy Sweden may be nearer to Yugoslavia than to the United States, for our purposes it remains firmly within the West.

Once we move beyond geography and social doctrine, it becomes even more hazardous to label modern nations "Eastern" or "Western" by reference to their political affiliations. The East today is no more monolithic a "bloc" than is the West. Consider, for example, the political postures of the Soviet Union, Rumania and Albania. The split between Russia and China over the stewardship of authentic Leninist revolution appears to have irrevocably shattered the idea of a single, world-wide communist camp.

A more practical distinction between East and West lies in each segment's economic orientation. True, the communist world prefers, for the present, to style itself as "socialist." But uniform allusions to "socialist countries" and "socialist law" might convey the misleading impression that transactions with advanced welfare states of the West are also under discussion. For this reason, and to alleviate the monotony of repetition, I have elected to speak alternately of "Eastern," "communist," "socialist," "collectivist" and "centrally planned" systems.

While the main points of divergence between the two types of economic organization are obvious, we must not lose sight of the similarities. Today, several Eastern countries are experimenting with administrative decentralization, profit incentives and market-oriented production, while free enterprise systems are succumbing to large-scale government intrusion. In western Europe the concept of a mixed economy is widespread. One-third of Italy's business life has passed into the hands of the state. In France the public sector's importance is comparable, and economic planning is accepted as an appropriate technique for the conciliation of individual initiative and state priorities.

Even the American ideal of pure private enterprise is bending visibly under the weight of public needs. In the process, the heresies of a managed economy are being transformed into respected scripture. Few realize that the Federal government of the United States, with its substantial dealings in military hardware, foreign aid and surplus agricultural commodities, ranks only after the Soviet government as the largest international trader, that one-third of the U.S.'s land is held in public ownership, and that almost one-quarter of its gross national product is expended by national, state and local authorities on the purchase of goods and services.

Though contrasts can certainly be seen between the stereotypes of the United States as the citadel of free initiative and the U.S.S.R. as the fountainhead of communist doctrine, our analysis must go behind the simple polarities, for these obscure a vast twilight zone of systematic planning and concession to market forces. Institutionally and conceptually, the Eastern structures often deviate from their Soviet model as much as they differ from one another. The same is true of the United States and the countries of western Europe.

Jan Tinbergen, the eminent Dutch economist, has suggested that the Eastern and Western systems are gradually developing common institutional structures.[6] Even among the Soviet elite there is an undercurrent of belief that, far from moving apart, capitalism and communism are actually creeping toward convergence.[7] My own observation of the intensely practical field of East-West business contacts lends support to this hypothesis.

As the collectivist economies falter beneath the burden of excessive regimentation and the liberal economies brace themselves for the onslaught of social disorder, freer interaction between them, and the experience of one to the other, become steadily more relevant. For the West this affords opportunities which are at once materially attractive and helpful in strengthening the fragile fabric of peace. Since time immemorial, merchants venturing into remote markets have somehow managed to develop flourishing and friendly relationships and to overcome the obstacles of religion, race, nationalism and witchcraft. What they are presently facing in the East is no more than the hesitant resistance of an ideology, one that is in awe of their accomplishments, willing to employ their techniques, but unable to embrace certain of their objectives. The challenge requires patience, ingenuity, adaptability and, above all, diplomatic sensitivity to the verbalism in which communist philosophy is couched.

In the last few years Eastern economies have given ample evidence of their desire to become integrated into a single world market. National leaders and business executives of communist countries have scarcely disguised their admiration, even envy, of Western production and marketing efficiency. In the interest of mutually beneficial ventures there has been an unmistakable willingness to embrace capitalist methods both at home and abroad, although euphemistic devices have frequently been needed to disguise the common, profit-oriented objectives. Indeed, in the course of day-to-day negotiations, I have often been led to wonder whether among its own "faithful" communism is still considered a viable economic system, rather than a political arrangement held together by vestiges of dogma.

Be that as it may, certain fundamental differences between a capitalist and a communist economic structure must be kept in mind. In the former, despite the growth of far-reaching governmental participation, regulation, incentives and controls, the primacy of the market remains the basic motivational factor. At home and abroad, trade is carried on predominantly by private firms functioning in a comparatively free economic environment. In the Soviet-type economy, on the other hand, the moving principle is the supremacy of the state plan. The national means of production are concentrated in government hands, and commerce is conducted exclusively by public instrumentalities. Domestically and in world markets, the omnipresent sovereign operates on a gigantic and monopolistic scale as owner, trader, investor, banker, moneylender, insurer, shipper, retailer, airline operator and supplier of financial and technical assistance.

Bearing in mind the foregoing observations, I propose to regard the following areas as belonging to the communist sphere: the U.S.S.R., Poland, Czechoslovakia, East Germany, Hungary, Rumania, Bulgaria, Albania, Cuba, Communist China, North Korea, North Vietnam, Outer Mongolia and Yugoslavia. Despite the prevalence of mixed economy syndromes, the free enterprise world is deemed to encompass primarily the industrialized member nations of the Organization for Economic Cooperation and Development:[8] Canada, United States, Japan, Austria, Belgium, Luxembourg, Denmark, France, West Germany, Greece, Iceland, Ireland, Italy, Netherlands, Norway, Portugal, Spain, Switzerland, Turkey, United Kingdom and Finland. Occasionally the less developed countries of Africa, Asia and Latin America will be discussed in comparison with or contrast to the East, although most of these areas clearly do not belong with the West in either an economic or political sense.

To be immediately useful, this work addresses itself to the day-to-day needs of those who have an interest in trade with the East, but who are unfamiliar with its opportunities, pitfalls and techniques. Ideally, it approaches a more basic challenge as well, and one which remains to be met by policy-makers on both sides of the political frontier: how to devise a framework which would ensure the orderly assimilation of communist state monopolies into a stable pattern of international commercial activity, and thus enable East-West trade to realize its full social and economic potential. The great Western trading nations which are at the heart of world commerce have, in fact, the responsibility and the means to establish proper norms. Conceived in an atmosphere free of ulterior political objectives, such norms may also win adherence in the East.

If they are to be constructive, proposals for joint or separate action must reflect a spirit of compromise and tolerance toward divergent social patterns. It would be neither realistic nor just to demand deep structural changes within the Eastern-type economy or its foreign-trade apparatus. I submit that the former approach, undertaken in a favorable political setting, can yield answers to the broader question of how the West might learn to live peacefully and productively with the durable phenomenon of institutionalized communism. A corresponding lesson could, hopefully, be learned in the East as well.

Within this volume the reader will find two largely complementary books. The first deals with the complex ideological, political, strategic, economic and commercial factors at work and seeks to identify the basic obstacles to business activity between free enterprise and state enterprise countries. The second deals with the empirical evidence of negotiated, performed or litigated transactions and addresses itself to the peculiar legal and procedural problems involved. The conclusion offers a proposed code of fair practices designed to eliminate anomalies at all levels of East-West trade.

My subject cuts deeply across several disciplines. To give it adequate treatment (in terms which are representational rather than exhaustively descriptive) I have had to stray more freely than I like from the proper preserves of the international lawyer, to those of the economist, banker, business manager, diplomat, political scientist and public servant concerned with foreign policy and military defense. These trespasses occur because none of the institutions and concepts in question can be adequately understood apart from the amorphous and essentially alien environment in which they are required to operate.

BOOK ONE

FIRST PART

THE ECONOMIC AND POLITICAL CONTEXT

1

THE CONFINES OF THE EASTERN MARKET

A. The Promise of Intrabloc Preference

One of the consequences of Germany's defeat in the Second World War was the creation of an economic vacuum in eastern Europe. The Soviet Union, as the new dominant power in the region, moved quickly to fill this vacuum with its own presence, hoping thereby to block the possible return of Western commercial interests. In order to achieve this objective, the smaller communist states were invited to enter into comprehensive bilateral trade agreements with the U.S.S.R. These pacts reflected an ambitious effort to commit a maximum of available resources to exchanges with the Soviet Union. A network of similar commercial pacts was, in due course, established among the other Soviet-oriented states of the region.

By 1946, a strongly inward-looking commercial community was visibly taking shape in eastern Europe. In that year, the socialist countries of the area already accounted for 55 percent of the total foreign trade of the Soviet Union. Two years later, their share rose to 60 percent.[1]

The move to establish a regional economic organization in eastern Europe was made on January 30, 1949. The Council for Mutual Economic Assistance, announced on that date, came to be known in the West under the shorter name of Comecon. One of the main functions to be carried out by the Council was "the task of exchanging economic experience, extending technical aid to one another, and rendering mutual assistance with respect to raw materials, foodstuffs, machines, equipment, etc."[2] The coming into existence of Comecon was followed, in October of the same year, by the accession to power of a communist government in China. Three small states in Asia, and (at a later stage) one in Latin America, were in time accepted by the Soviet Union into the orbit of its economic interest: North Korea, Outer Mongolia, North Vietnam and Cuba. The socialist market was thus extended to three continents and more than one billion people.

The consolidation of such a vast population and expanse of territory under a communist form of government was quite understandably received by the Soviet leadership as a development of great historic significance. In pondering the shape of things to come, Soviet leaders foresaw the emergence of two world-wide competing political systems: one based on the abhorrent principles of capitalism, foredoomed to decline; the other embodying the values of the new socialist epoch and, therefore, assured of steady advance and ultimate triumph.

On the economic plane, in particular, the potential benefits to the socialist grouping of nations promised to be immediate and far-reaching. Characteristically, Stalin hailed the vastly enlarged sphere under communist rule (with Cuba, of course, still on the outside) as a phenomenon of profound qualitative significance to the future of the world economy. The international realignment, in his opinion, had given rise to a new economic reality, namely a "socialist" world market, "parallel" to and competitive with the old, "considerably shrunken," capitalist market. Stalin was certain that this remarkable development had fundamentally redirected the course of history. "The disintegration of the single all-embracing world market," he wrote, "must be regarded as the most important economic consequence of the second world war." Not only did it improve greatly the economic and political outlook for the communist countries; in addition, he believed, "it has had the effect of further deepening the general crisis of the world capitalist system."[3]

As a consequence, the capitalist world market came to be regarded in eastern Europe as little more than a supplemental source of supplies that happen to be at any one time physically unavailable within the region. The countries making up the socialist market were expected, in due course, to develop the needed capacity to produce all, or virtually all, the food, raw materials and industrial equipment required to sustain a viable economic community. Long-range planning remained oriented toward the eventual attainment of effective, if not absolute, regional self-sufficiency.

One way to build such an economic order, as the highly doctrinaire leadership saw it in the early fifties, was for each member state to devote a preponderant share of its foreign trade resources to the creation of an enlarged, parallel, and self-contained "socialist international division of labor." Under the benign influence of such a policy, the communist countries would not only become one another's principal trade partners; they would also become participants in a great enterprise of mutual economic integration. Such systematic integration, in turn, would promote an ever higher degree of national specialization in production and thus pave the way for still more active commerce within the political bloc, as well as a more efficient utilization of domestic resources.

The early performance of the new "world market" provided abundant support for the official view that the communist countries of Europe and Asia were engaged in a uniquely successful venture in economic cooperation. On the evidence, the drive for massive commercial intercourse had gotten off to a good start. Soviet trade turnover with the other Comecon countries increased six-fold between 1946 and 1953, from $777 million to $4,773 million.[4] It was also discovered along the way that the same administrative procedures which had been worked out to maximize the exchange of goods within the East tended to restrain trade with the outside world. By 1953 only 17 percent of Soviet foreign commerce was devoted to the world market at large.

After the first few years of active intrabloc trading, therefore, Soviet spokesmen were sufficiently encouraged by the progress achieved to be able to report (much too hastily, as it turned out) that all their original sanguine assumptions about the innate superiority of the "socialist world market" were validated by subsequent experience. The great expansion of intraregional trade was represented as being, in effect, the objective judgment of history, providing "irrefutable proof of the historic progressiveness" of the new, parallel world market.[5]

With the passing of Stalin from the scene, the degree of concentration on intrabloc trade came to be viewed by Eastern policy-makers as excessive. By 1957, the percentage of Soviet intrabloc trade declined from the earlier high point of 83 percent to 73 percent. Since then, China's and Albania's harsh political quarrels with Russia have sharply reduced the role of these two countries in the "socialist world market." More and more the Soviet Union found itself compelled to scale down previous ambitions for the preeminence of its economic sphere. Eastern Europe as a region and Comecon as an institution became the main theater of its commercial operations.

As experience exposed the wholly planned economies to the realities of international trade, many intractable problems began to overshadow the theoretical promise of a socialist international division of labor. For the same reason that internal economic practices are now subject to serious reexamination, leaders throughout Eastern Europe are also currently inclined to view the utility of the socialist market in a more sober light. A number of difficulties confronting these countries in their day-to-day trade exchanges have come to be ventilated in public with increasing candor. In the case of Czechoslovakia and Rumania, in particular, an attitude of skepticism toward the economic efficacy of present-day intra-Comecon commerce gradually rose to the surface. Hungary and Poland also began to share this attitude, while Bulgaria and East Germany continued in their strong orientation toward the concept of a closely knit economic bloc, with the Soviet Union as its center of gravity.

B. Obstacles to a Socialist Division of Labor

That there has been a measurable decline in enthusiasm for socialist preference in foreign trade is quite evident. Official opinion in east Europe frankly admitted that the increase in commercial exchange within Comecon during 1961–1965 was the smallest in recent history, namely 55 percent, as against a growth of 71 percent for 1956–1960 and 85 percent for 1951–1955.[6] This poor record cast an obvious cloud over the announced plan to increase intra-Comecon trade by another 45 to 50 percent during 1966–1970. Nor does the recent statistical evidence offer any more cause for comfort. Imports into the U.S.S.R. from the other socialist countries of Europe actually declined between 1965 and 1966. Between 1967 and 1968, they increased slightly, from 4.6 billion to 5.1 billion rubles. In the same period, Soviet exports to the Comecon region increased from 4.7 billion to 5.2 billion rubles.

By the early sixties it was no longer possible to suppress the glaring fact that conflicts of national interest can, and do, occur among countries with similar political and economic institutions. The inherent contradictions of capitalism seem to have found an echo in the inherent contradictions of socialism.

Czechoslovakia's situation demonstrates one aspect of the problem. Before the war that country enjoyed a fine world reputation for the diverse engineering products manufactured at the Vitkovice ironworks and Skoda automobile plants, and for the high grade of its textiles, shoes, china and glassware. Having been put to work largely for the Soviet market, one that is vast in scope and variety but easily satisfied in matters of quality, the Czechoslovak export economy not only lost ground at the level of comparative advantage, but also found itself out of step with the technological advances and more exacting standards of the West. Without doubt, this was one of the main factors which inspired the aborted "springtime of Prague."

The first major Comecon dispute to come to the surface involved the question whether each country in the region should develop its own fully diversified industrial structure or whether some countries should be required to concentrate on the production of raw materials and farm products, thereby leaving their neighbors free to specialize in the manufacture of finished goods. As could be expected, the more developed countries, the U.S.S.R., Czechoslovakia and East Germany, lined up firmly on the side of national specialization. While the others adopted a policy of discreet silence, Rumania chose to espouse the cause of diversification. Although it was assuredly not planned that way, this particular dispute turned into a direct challenge to Russia's authority within the region.

The Premier of the U.S.S.R. at that time, Nikita S. Khrushchev, strongly favored competition in the international arena. His political antennas were normally turned westward, ready to receive signals of economic distress among the "unstable" capitalist societies, especially those constituting the principal competitor of Comecon, the European Economic Community. The more he waited, however, the more cause he had to be disappointed. The late fifties and early sixties showed a steady average rise of 7 percent per annum in industrial production by the Common Market group of nations and a growth rate of 14 percent in their mutual trade. The implication of this unique phenomenon was quite obvious to the Soviet leader. It reflected improved opportunities for trade, based on more efficient, large-scale production for a multinational rather than a local market.

Against the background of what he called the steady "internationalization of production within the aggressive bloc of Common Market nations," Khrushchev opted for more active measures of integration within Comecon, among them a scheme of supranational planning of production for the region as a whole. The proposals, placed before an extraordinary session of the organization assembled in Moscow in June 1962, were met with open resistance rather than enthusiasm. Inasmuch as Comecon (like the E.E.C.)

was organized to function on the basis of unanimous decisions, it was sufficient for the opposition of one power, Rumania, behaving like a Gaullist France of the East, to scuttle the entire design. When the wrangling was over, Comecon remained, as it was before, a regional forum for periodic consultations aimed largely at improving the climate for bilateral commercial exchanges among the member states.

The next major round came in April 1969. Once again the Kremlin's integrationists were countered with the Rumanian brand of national-interest communism, this time somewhat less timidly supported by other states, notably Hungary. Greater economic cooperation and closer coordination of foreign trade plans were generally acceptable. But most of the smaller countries preferred to build their own economies ahead of any fundamental commitments to the bloc.

Although the controversy was papered over as much as possible, the stakes in these debates were high: was Comecon to become an organization of the Common Market type, with supranational powers, or a much looser grouping in the spirit of the European Free Trade Association? For the time being, the argument seems to be drifting in favor of the latter. The most unanimous message which emerges out of the current disarray is an aspiration toward expanded trade with all countries of the world, regardless of their social systems.

These incidents illustrate the unique difficulties involved in trying to achieve integration within the socialist orbit. One of the obstacles is, in fact, almost insuperable. As long as each nation remains free to plan its national economic life, the less developed members will seek to acquire the whole spectrum of modern industrial techniques rather than agree to specialize in producing, say, minerals, fuels and raw materials to be processed by their more advanced trade partners. Conversely, the route toward specialization will continue to be blocked by the strong desire of the same "late bloomers" in the group to retain the right to plan and manage local economic affairs in accordance with their own perceived national interest.

To the outside observer, this inability to create an effective incentive for state enterprises to produce for a regional rather than a national market stands out as a fundamental weakness of the existing system. It suggests, in fact, that if the countries of eastern Europe have shown relatively less economic progress, this has been due primarily to the political failure of Comecon to induce any sizable international specialization of production.[7]

To be sure, there have been a number of notable achievements in regional cooperation. The member countries have agreed, for example, to the multinational construction of an oil pipeline leading from the Volga-Ural area to several outlets in eastern Europe; to the link-up of some of their power systems into a unified electric grid and, in May, 1970, to the establishment of a mutual investment bank (without Rumanian participation). Aside from these publicized joint projects, initiated at the political level, the attempt to attain a division of labor in the realm of industrial production has not succeeded. "It is no secret," in the words of a Polish commentary, "that the degree of interest shown in various forms and scopes of cooperation within Comecon is not identical in all member countries. This arises from many causes, but the principal reason is the divergent degree of economic development of the individual countries."[8]

Turning to another source of difficulty, we find that the wholly planned economies have been unable to work out an effective pricing scheme. They were compelled, to their own palpable distaste, to fall back upon "world," *i.e.,* capitalist, prices in the exchange of goods within the region. Yet as long as they remain in this predicament, the Eastern countries find that they cannot avoid reciprocal charges of unfairness which, in turn, tend to impose a strain on mutual trust.

The nature of the complaints that come from the highly industrial member states, such as Czechoslovakia and East Germany, has been known for some time. As discreetly stated by one East German economist, the situation is simply this: "In certain cases the limited scope of the existing international division of labor (within Comecon) leads to a situation in which production is not always equipped with modern techniques, especially in machine-building." The Soviet Union, the most important consumer of industrial equipment, very often orders small batches of machinery items. Serious trouble for manufacturers thus arises from the fact that "the proportion of mass production is at present still unsatisfactory. Some types of output are produced in very small quantities, using a wide variety of principles of design."[9] In other words, the scale of machinery production is all too often very modest. In addition, output is based on haphazard design; and costs are, therefore, high. But the price received from the Soviet Union is the "world" price, which is generally based on the more efficient, mass scale system of manufacturing practiced by the major producers of the West.

A new kind of complaint has begun to be heard from the other end of the exchange. The economic press of the Soviet Union has offered evidence to the effect that its own Comecon trade, based on world prices, is in many respects rather unprofitable. As presented, the analysis seems plausible enough. The U.S.S.R. provides its partners with an enormous volume of fuels, minerals and other raw materials for use in industry. In order to meet the growing demand for such commodities, an ever larger amount of capital has to be fed into the mining branches of industry. Yet, the mounting cost of this vast outlay of funds is not adequately covered by the prices received from socialist clients. By contrast, the export of machinery is much more profitable, at least as far as relative capital costs are concerned. It has been calculated that in order to obtain one foreign exchange ruble from the sale of standard raw materials, the U.S.S.R. has to invest between five and eight times as much capital as in the case of exported machinery items.[10] The economic inertia which governs intrabloc trade is such, however, that the Soviet Union continues to absorb a flow of imports heavily weighted on the side of machinery. It further emerges from these candid discussions that the machinery is of rather dubious quality, as measured by prevailing world standards. On this delicate issue, Soviet trade experts have stated their case in the ginger terminology which governs public discussion of sensitive regional affairs: "Some socialist machinery could be resold on the world market only at sharply reduced prices." [11]

C. Erosion of the Concept of Two Separate Trading Zones

A variety of sharply discordant notes has progressively found its way into the once monotonous debates that tended to suffuse the subject of "fraternal" trade among communist countries. Today, Soviet officialdom can no longer ignore the salient fact that an exchange of goods with ideologically compatible partners is not always a good economic bargain. The desire to obtain concrete, measurable benefits from all external commerce is gaining ground throughout the socialist world. The policy-makers of the U.S.S.R. are no exception in this respect. They have come to recognize that the commodity composition of current Soviet foreign trade is essentially an outgrowth of the cold war which bears little relation to the country's present structure and performance as an industrial producer.

As a matter of record, the pattern of commodity exchanges between the U.S.S.R. and the other socialist regimes began to assume its present shape about two decades ago, under pressure of political tensions that developed between the major powers of East and West during the late nineteen-forties. In that highly charged atmosphere, the state of mutual distrust led, step by inevitable step, to a harsh commercial estrangement. As a consequence, the basic pattern of Soviet foreign trade, based on the exchange of abundant raw materials for advanced production equipment from the industrialized countries of the West, was severely disrupted.

Faced with so drastic a change in the nature of its commerce, the U.S.S.R. had little choice but to look elsewhere for imports, especially machinery and other finished goods urgently needed to rebuild the demolished industrial plants of the country. It was indeed rare good fortune that a substitute source of capital equipment could be found so close at hand, in the two small but industrially mature countries of East Germany and Czechoslovakia. Given its dominant political position in the region, Russia experienced no difficulty in carrying out this adjustment to the unfolding cold war.

To compensate for the abrupt loss of free access to the machinery markets of the industrial West, Stalin had the more developed nations of Comecon restructure their manufacturing systems so as to be able to respond to the Soviet demand for imports. In effect, Czechoslovakia and East Germany were required to convert the orientation of their production plants from light to heavy industry. Within a matter of a few years, these two highly versatile "industrial colonies" began to produce a wide variety of basic equipment for export to the U.S.S.R. Soviet imports of machinery from Comecon as a whole rose rapidly as follows: from $7.5 million in 1946 ($212 million from the West) to $208 million in 1950 ($99 million from the West), and to $733 million in 1955 ($181 million from the West).

The Soviet Union managed to keep its own export pattern unchanged; it began to ship to its new trade partners roughly the same range of minerals, forest products and foodstuffs that it had exported to its Western suppliers in the past. On the surface, therefore, the substitution was a conspicuous success. The highly politicized climate of the period enabled the leadership to profess that the industrial equipment supplied by the small industrial countries of east Europe was an adequate replacement for the entire range of advanced machinery formerly obtained from the major nations of the West.

Today, the same movement of trade no longer appears rational. An annual exchange whereby, for example, in 1968 the Soviet Union exported to Hungary some $140 million–worth of machinery and equipment while importing from this semi-industrialized country more than $263 million in the same category of goods can be explained only by economic inertia.[12]

With the passing of time, these conditions of exchange have become so mutually burdensome that each of the Comecon members may be observed seeking to find some measure of relief through the world market.

Small wonder, then, that the economic incentive to continue to expand production for export year after year, in order to meet the growing internal needs of Comecon, has visibly faltered. Most of the Eastern countries now appear inclined to the view that present arrangements for production and exchange within the region are in need of a searching reappraisal. It is openly acknowledged that the approach to the problem of specialization had been too simplistically conceived: raw materials in exchange for finished products, farm produce for industrial goods. In the future, specialization would presumably be more selective, following a pattern in which a given member country exchanges goods within the region on the basis of a clear comparative advantage.

Ways are currently being sought to reach agreement on a scheme of specialization by country, within, rather than between, individual branches of industry: with regard to, say, size of steel-plate, types of farm machinery, capacity of power generators and so forth. In addition, Soviet economists recommend a greater concentration of effort by other Comecon members on the production of minerals and other primary materials for use in industry. In particular, they would like to encourage their socialist trade partners to develop the capital-intensive mining industries, in the hope that this would relieve the present burden on the U.S.S.R. or, according to the official formulation, make it possible "to increase the two-way exchange of raw materials among Comecon members." [13]

No doubt, such a drastic modification of the pattern of commodity trade will require a long and painstaking process of consultation, negotiation and administrative adjustment. Meanwhile, it is already possible to discern a general disposition in the area as a whole to use rigorous economic calculation as the basis for production decisions. One clear implication is that henceforth, in cases where no Comecon member can be shown to have appropriate capacity for production, the trade authorities would readily turn to the world market to find the commodities best suited to meet their needs.

The economic planners of the region are no longer disposed to labor against heavy odds. They now know that they have tried in vain to simulate the existence of a world-wide market within the compass of a region that produces less than 30 percent of the current industrial output of the world. Specifically, Soviet policy has begun to show a new appreciation for the value of broader contacts with the international industrial community. One of the first concepts to lose ground has been the idea of separate world markets, which had allegedly emerged from the successful establishment of a contiguous domain of communist-ruled states in Europe and Asia.

Today, the prevailing view rejects the notion of two hostile, noncommunicating economic orbits as not only untenable, but downright harmful to the interests of the East. Such a notion only discourages the study of world market conditions and hinders the development of practical business contacts based on scientific knowledge of the economic facts. "Some economists," asserted a Soviet writer in 1963 in the official journal of the Ministry of Foreign Trade, "repeat the mistaken proposition on the question of the world-wide market upheld in the essay by Stalin." Nowadays, he affirms, the U.S.S.R. is engaged in "purging Soviet foreign policy of all harmful encrustations that have come to be associated with the Stalinist cult." [14] Presumably the correct Leninist course has again been rediscovered. The accent was placed once more on economic cooperation with all states, socialist and capitalist.

D. The Search for Economic Efficiency

It is not necessary to chronicle the major turn of events in recent communist economic history to arrive at the conviction that, at the present juncture, the makers of public policy in the U.S.S.R. are demonstrably facing two ways. They have good reason to look back on the many successes that have come their way since the revolution of October 1917, including the emergence of new institutions for the management of social and economic affairs. From this point of view they derive a strong feeling of confidence that the basic development method they have pursued since the late twenties has been validated. The administrative economy created by the use of trial and error techniques has won them membership in the big league of industrial powers within the span of a few decades. Simultaneously, they are peering even more intently into the future, trying to perceive the answer to a critical question: can their highly centralized system continue to perform effectively in the competitive arena of modern production under conditions that will assuredly involve greater reliance on the rapidly evolving disciplines of science and technology? In this direction, the view is becoming clouded by hitherto unknown doubts. The Soviet leaders have been wondering publicly for some time whether the vast corporate structure in which they have welded together all production and distribution units in the country has not reached a phase of diminishing returns.[15]

During most of the sixties, the U.S.S.R. and several of the other countries of eastern Europe have been engaged in an earnest search for new techniques to improve the competitive position of their economies. The immediate frame of reference has been the industrial community of the West. Whereas a few years ago the dynamic character of Western production had been the main object of Eastern envy, in the present drive for efficiency the accent has, quite clearly, shifted to the qualitative dimension of economic performance.

The planners of the East do not, of course, need to be reminded about their own unique assets in the economic competition with capitalism. They are quite proud of the fact that their distinctive method of development has a built-in, rather effective mechanism for maintaining a high and stable level of saving and investment. It is most common for the Eastern command economies to plough in excess of 25 percent of the national product every year into new plant equipment.

Another prominent feature of the Soviet type economy is the full employment of the human and physical resources available for production. The manufacturing enterprises in every communist state are at all times under government instruction to raise their level of output. For that purpose, they are provided with new capital funds to expand plant capacity so that they can accept still higher targets in the future. On the basis of this policy of systematically forced growth, the planning agencies have been able to respond to persistent political pressure requiring them to raise their economic sights ever higher, especially in the industrial sector. The central political authorities, for their part, have generally provided the large investment funds and the new manpower needed to meet these increasingly ambitious aims. Yet, in recent years the ruling establishment has evidently been beset by a gnawing suspicion that its pursuit of the quantitative dimension in economic development may have been overly zealous. More specifically, the question has been posed as to whether the resources so energetically mobilized were being used to optimum effect. For there is nowhere in sight the kind of superior economic return which had been expected to flow from the "more advanced" centrally guided social order of eastern Europe. Instead, the leadership has stumbled upon an important social lesson, namely that in modern industrial society there is an inescapable correlation between the level of efficiency in utilizing the factors of production (land, labor and capital) and an ever rising supply of products for personal consumption. On the evidence, there is willingness to accept the proposition that if Western standards of social welfare are to be matched, a more effective effort will have to be exerted to reach a comparable level of productivity per each unit of labor and capital employed in the economic enterprises of the state.

Beginning in the fall of 1962, the Soviet government initiated a wide public discussion of ways and means to improve efficiency in the existing method of economic planning and management. The specific purpose of this effort was to streamline the present system of communication between the central authorities and the managerial staffs of the industrial enterprises throughout the land. Under a less cumbersome system, it was hoped, local managers would have an opportunity to exercise greater initiative and authority over a given range of production decisions without at the same time diminishing the control powers of the economic planners at the summit.

The depressed status of the plant manager in the monolithic scheme of things was identified early in the discussion as the principal source of irrational decisions. The economy had grown vast and extremely complex since the existing mechanism of central planning was launched in 1928. The number of interconnection points in the production process had multiplied enormously by virtue of the explosive growth of the country's industrial base. In these circumstances, the activities of the large mass of enterprises could no longer be effectively directed in every detail from Moscow. It was necessary to redefine the rules of bureaucratic interplay between the center and the periphery and, specifically, to provide local management with meaningful criteria for resolving problems which would henceforth fall within its decision-making authority.

The yardstick finally agreed upon as the most important measure of economic effectiveness was profit. More precisely, it was the profitability rate, *i.e.,* the amount of gain expressed as a percentage of the capital (fixed as well as working) at the disposal of the given enterprise, rather than as a proportion of the gross value of output, as in the past. At the same time, the new quantitative indicator for measuring total performance at the factory level was to become the aggregate value of sales, instead of the former gross volume of output.

Unavoidably, the new importance assigned to such typically commercial categories as "sales" and "profits" has aroused some painful ideological dilemmas. Officials in high places were haunted by the dogma they had been professing for decades, that the essential difference between their own and Western economic systems could be reduced to the following simple proposition: under capitalism men produce what is profitable for the private owners of the means of production, whereas under socialism men produce what is beneficial for the whole of society.

While valiant attempts were being made to untie this ideological knot, the search for effective solutions to the practical problems of industrial management could not be delayed indefinitely. If economic stagnation was to be avoided, new techniques had to be devised, or borrowed from abroad. In short, if the political authorities were indeed serious about "unleashing" the plant manager to play a more activist role in production, they had no choice but to bring into play, and assign full importance to, such tested economic criteria as costs, profits, prices, bonuses, incentive pay, bank credits and interest charges.

At the official level, the critical attitude toward the traditional bureaucratic method of economic planning found expression in the now historic decision of the Central Committee of the Communist Party of the Soviet Union, dated September 29, 1965. This is the decision which, in fact, initiated the administrative phase of economic reform now underway in the U.S.S.R. and elsewhere in Eastern Europe:

> The Central Committee recognizes the advisability of eliminating excessive control over individual enterprises, reducing the number of planned targets which the enterprises are assigned from above, providing them with adequate means for the expansion and improvement of production, and making better use of such important economic stimuli as profit, prices, and credits, . . .[16]

Equally significant is the current drive to modify the environment in which daily business decisions are made. Its root lies in general disillusionment with the recent performance of the Eastern economies at the microeconomic level. It is not enough, the leadership has in effect admitted, to have a superior strategy for economic development, based on a more progressive social order and on the principle of public ownership of the means of production. Such an order is now recognized to be a factor of essentially institutional rather than operational significance. Social ownership seems to yield no visible payoff in the production process. Whether the working enterprises are owned privately or publicly, it still remains a matter of the utmost importance that the individual participant be motivated to show full regard for the known principles of effectiveness in production and for the needs of the particular class of consumers to whom it seeks to appeal.

Pockets of lingering bureaucratic resistance notwithstanding, by 1970 almost 75 percent of the U.S.S.R.'s enterprises were functioning under the new principles of economic management so audaciously proposed by Professor Evsei Liberman in 1962.[17] But the battle is far from being won. The results achieved to date have been admittedly disappointing.[18] A startlingly frank diagnosis of the prevailing situation has recently been offered by three eminent members of the Soviet academic establishment:[19]

> Comparing our economy to that of the United States we find that we are behind not only on the quantitative plane, but also—and this is much sadder—on the qualitative plane. The gulf between the United States and us is all the greater in the newest and most revolutionary sectors of the economy. We are ahead of America in coal extraction, but behind in oil, gas and electric energy; we are ten years behind in chemicals and infinitely behind in computer technology . . . We simply live in another era.

Having accepted the need for reform, the Soviet authorities have been too timid in securing its implementation. Faced with a sluggish economic record, they now seem to have nowhere to go except further and faster in the direction of decentralized, profit-oriented management.

The other eastern European countries have wasted less time in picking up the cue of the liberal Soviet economists. Except in Czechoslovakia, where an atmosphere of political and human demoralization has brought all progress to a virtual standstill, the region is forging ahead with a program of structural changes which would have been heresy a decade ago. At the center of this program is the admission that effective economic planning needs the mechanism of the market place.

Hungary has registered the most rapid pace of reform. Economic tools of management are taking preference over rigid administrative directives predetermined by central government agencies and imposed upon individual enterprises in the form of detailed targets. Manufacturing plants are no longer passive economic units, but rather entrepreneurial entities that draw up their own production and sales objectives. One of their chief interests lies in augmenting profit yields, part of which is distributed among the management and the work force.

Viewed in this light, we can see an organic link between the present active response to pressures for economic reform at home and the practical measures taken in recent years to enlarge and rationalize the participation of the Soviet and east European economies in the international division of labor. In both cases, the stress is on efficiency. And efficiency has come to be identified with greater reliance on economic, as against political, considerations in the organization of production and commodity exchange.

To a considerable extent, this has meant borrowing long-tested Western techniques and adapting them to the socialist system of planning and production. The adaptation has been frankly admitted and recommended on the highest authority—indeed, at the summit of the Soviet State Planning Committee itself.[20] However, to equate the quest for greater efficiency with outright endorsement of "creeping capitalism" would be, on the evidence, recklessly unwarranted.

2

COMMUNIST INTEREST IN FOREIGN COMMERCE

A. Present Outlooks on the Capitalist World

As it wore on, the postwar period brought to the Soviet Union, no less than to the United States, a more acute awareness of the complexities of international political life in a setting of rapidly changing economic conditions. Many of the traditional assumptions of Marxist doctrine failed to be validated by the actual record of business activity around the world. The capitalist countries of the West, in particular, came to demonstrate a surprising degree of sustained economic vigor. For reasons which the theory of historical determinism could not readily explain, they failed to repeat the pattern of economic regression, unemployment and stagnation that characterized their experience during the decades following the first World War.

Instead, the highly industrialized "bourgeois" societies, in which the conditions for a socialist transformation were presumed to ripen first, continued to improve their economic performance within the traditional framework of a market-oriented production system and a democratic political structure. Most of these countries, in fact, proceeded steadily to expand their aggregate output, as well as per capita income, while at the same time demonstrating a continuing capacity for adaptation to the accelerated tempo of technological change. Public interest in the once insistent proposals for nationalization of industry declined, in light of accumulating evidence that the Western economies were visibly enlarging the average wage earner's share in the annual product of the community and (by increasing his purchasing power) further expanding the capacity of the internal market to consume a growing volume of goods.

As long as the Stalinists dominated the climate of opinion, the prevalent Eastern contention was that economic trends in the two disjoined halves of the world, living separately under their respective capitalist and socialist institutions, were unfolding in accordance with the "scientifically based forecasts" of communist theory. The Western nations were supposed to be facing an immediate future in which "their control over world resources will contract, export conditions will deteriorate, and the number of idle enterprises will increase."[1]

For the post-Stalinist breed of Soviet leaders it became increasingly difficult to shut out the perceived realities of the international economy. Nor could they enjoy the psychic satisfaction of being able to uphold Marxist infallibility in predicting the proximate as well as the distant future. Although they remained loyal communists, those who took over the helm of state in the mid-fifties were not so strongly committed to the operational validity of party doctrine as to be willing to base their immediate practical policies on a political illusion. As men of action, they refused to ignore an outside world which could make a direct and useful contribution to the modernization of many branches of their own industry. To be sure, they had not ceased believing in the ultimate doom facing the West, as against the bright future awaiting countries that have taken the road to socialism. But they were simply no longer as intent upon anticipating the "final decision" of history on the issue of two coexisting, competing social systems. Suddenly there was no apparent reason why the future should be allowed to dominate the political present, why the long-term decline of capitalism could not occasionally be interrupted by extended periods of relative economic stability or even prosperity.

Eastern economists have long been thoroughly familiar with the findings of the United Nations' Economic Commission for Europe. While often critical of the staff's textual commentaries, they did not question the careful calculations embodied in the Commission's published findings. These findings disclosed a record of consistent growth for most of western Europe. Economic expansion proceeded at a fairly respectable tempo during the early fifties, although it tended, quite naturally, to vary from country to country. In the case of the United Kingdom, the annual growth rate of the total net national product was only 3.0 percent per annum between

1949 and 1955, whereas the corresponding rate was 3.4 percent for France, 4.0 percent for the Scandinavian countries, 5.6 percent for Italy, and 10.1 percent for West Germany.[2]

The emergence of a stable western Europe, without serious economic disarray or any credible threat of severe cyclical fluctuations, was most unexpected and perhaps ideologically unpalatable, but nonetheless a fact to be reckoned with. Nor was it necessarily inconsistent with a more flexible interpretation of the doctrine of dialectical materialism. With a little imagination, it could perfectly well be explained in terms of what Lenin liked to call "the zig-zags of history." In due course, western Europe's economic revival had become part of the new reality on which the Soviet Union, as well as its smaller allies, had to base their practical policies.

For the short term, at least, the steadily improving performance of the private enterprise economies has carried with it two implications in the policy sphere: one in the nature of a warning; the other in the form of an opportunity.

In the first instance, there is an important political lesson to be drawn from the fact that mature, and presumably decadent, capitalist societies can somehow manage to stabilize their economies and continue to raise real income over an extended period of time. The free enterprise mode of economic development therefore demands more careful appraisal as a viable method of organizing production in a modern society. No longer can it be so easily discredited with the younger generation at home or with representatives of newly independent nations. Above all, this means that for some time to come the capitalist countries of the West, along with their ways of structuring economic activity, must be regarded as serious competitors in the market place of ideas, as well as in the race for higher norms of economic productivity.

At the same time, the dynamic performance of the economies of western Europe, Japan and North America has undoubtedly confronted the East with a unique opportunity. To the extent that these countries continue to expand the scale and variety of their economic activity, they will inevitably be consuming more minerals, more farm products, more fuel, timber and industrial materials, including the kind of commodities that are normally exported by the Soviet Union and the other communist states.

What is more, a condition of sustained industrial expansion in the West is certain, over the long run, to be reflected in a great wave of technological innovation. This, too, could be a factor of palpable economic benefit to eastern Europe. New production ideas, generated and developed under the pressure of competition in market-oriented economies, could once again be profitably absorbed into the industries of the East, as they had been in the past.

As shown by the record, Soviet commodity exchanges with the industrial West have been marked since the mid-fifties by an unusually rapid tempo of growth. Between 1955 and 1960 the expansion proceeded at an average annual rate of 16 percent; in the subsequent five-year period the rate was some 8 percent. In 1969, out of a global turnover of $22 billion, $7.6 billion, or around 35 percent, accounted for trade with the noncommunist world.[3] Obviously, the simple economic dogmas inherited from the past had been allowed to wither away.

B. The Pull of the Outside Market

Another proposition which has gradually lost its authority in the official credo is that a large nation such as the U.S.S.R. ought to produce most if not all of its requirements at home. Any line of domestic manufacture, it is now generally admitted, can be either profitable or unprofitable. This is where the world market comes in. It has emerged as a permanent frame of reference against which a nation can check the scale, technology and, ultimately, the profitability of a given segment of its industrial activity.

In keeping with this recognition of the positive role of international trade, the Eastern policy-makers have recently laid down a new rule to be followed by economic planners. The fact that a material, or a finished article, can be physically produced within the boundaries of the nation is no longer conclusive. Instead, the cost of its production relative to the cost of importation should henceforth be used as a criterion. Under this approach, the whole structure of Eastern trade became subject to radical change. In the future, according to the "Directives" of the 23rd Congress of the Communist Party of the Soviet Union, the accredited trading agencies of the government should work toward "improving the import structure of Soviet foreign trade" by selecting for procurement "such types of raw materials, commodities and finished goods as involve higher current costs and capital investments when produced within the country."[4] On the export side, the Ministry of Foreign Trade was instructed to play a more active role in stimulating domestic producers to be more sensitive toward the changing needs of the world market.

Even with the best will in the world, such a transformation cannot be accomplished in one fell swoop, not even in an authoritarian society.

We are still dealing here with guidelines intended for the long term. It is important, however, to consider the level at which these guidelines were laid down. At this level, the arguments for and against continuing to pursue a policy of economic self-sufficiency, have certainly been heard in full. At last, the communist economies were to be reoriented toward a more active recognition of the principle of a world-wide international division of labor. In fact, the new attitudes have evolved to a point where it is openly denied that autarchy was ever an official communist doctrine.[5]

In a very real sense, Soviet trade officials now feel that their hands have been united. They read the official "Directives" to mean that the party will henceforth approve of a substantial increase in trade turnover with capitalist countries. Accordingly, they are ready to exert pressure upon local industry to show more initiative in seeking out opportunities for improved performance and increased profit by closer contact with the external market place.

In terms which curiously echo chronic Western balance of payments concerns, Soviet economists complain that "our officials in industry all too often continue to regard foreign trade as something quite secondary. This radically wrong view has to be changed." Industrial executives are expected to study foreign needs and to create or expand specialized lines of production in order to "increase the present range of the kind of export products that are in demand on the world market, in particular, machinery and equipment."[6]

The preoccupation with exports is understandable. Soviet demand for imports from the West, especially machinery, has always been far stronger than the capacity to earn enough convertible purchasing power. Shopping lists presented by local enterprises to the Ministry of Foreign Trade have had to be trimmed severely, and the necessary foreign exchange has had to be rationed carefully among high priority claimants. To expand the supply of available export earnings, industrial planners are now urged to uncover areas of production which offer a clear comparative advantage. For this purpose, the more outward-looking plants would, of course, have to bring their production process up to the optimum levels of existing technology.

Premier Kosygin has said explicitly that he would like to see an intermingling of new, indigenously developed industrial ideas with those of the more advanced economies. As a modern technocrat, he viewed such interaction as an essential stimulus to industrial innovation within the U.S.S.R. "In our time," he declared solemnly to the political elite of the nation assembled at the 23rd Party Congress, "it is becoming more and more evident that the scientific and technical revolution under way in the modern world calls for freer international contacts and creates conditions for broad economic exchanges between socialist and capitalist countries."[7]

Foreign trade on a global scale has thus been endorsed as an economic necessity. If it wants to develop as a major competitive world power, the Soviet Union can no longer afford the luxury of splendid isolation, whether behind a national or regional trade barrier. What has been proven by the economic experience of the recent decades is the indivisibility of technical progress. Men living apart on their own side of the ideological fence cannot possibly generate as ample and varied a range of goods as can be produced by the entire world pursuing innovation and freely exchanging its fruits. In this respect, the odds have been all along against the Eastern nations. Because they are late-comers to the feast of industrialization, they have found themselves preoccupied with the quantitative dimension, with the growth in size of their production plant. Two main objectives have stood out: to fill the numerous bare patches on their industrial horizon, and to catch up with the scale of output already achieved by the major economies of the West.

Except for some specially favored, or uniquely endowed sectors, most of the available resources have been funnelled into lines of production in which techniques were already fully tested and well-known either at home or abroad. The pressures to experiment, to test novel processes, to introduce new products or to establish advanced large-scale manufacturing facilities have not been strongly at work in the region. Perhaps this, more than anything else, helps to explain why the U.S.S.R. is so far behind the United States in most economic sectors, from agriculture to cybernetics, and particularly in the development and application of computer technology.

Be that as it may, the upshot has been an attempt at closer cooperation with the West, as a means to absorbing and diffusing the results of technical experimentation within a framework of rigorous economic calculation. If the gap in industrial development is to be narrowed, East–West intercourse must extend well beyond the mere exchange of physical goods. The domain of ideas, in both technology and management, must be given primary attention.

C. The Attraction of Western Technology

Even a cursory analysis shows that the main thrust of the East's recent commercial effort has been directed toward acquiring a better understanding of the whole economic process as it has evolved abroad. For the short term, attention is being focused on keeping in touch with new technological developments. This is reflected in the striking fact that almost half of all goods acquired by the U.S.S.R. from the West during the past decade falls under the heading of "machinery and equipment." For the East as a whole, the same category approaches one-third of total imports.

Time has gradually changed the image of Russia as a backward economy in search of the shortest possible route to industrialization. The late fifties witnessed the heady initial successes of Soviet science and technology in the exploration of space. Hence, it took courage to admit that the vast industrial landscape of the nation was still unevenly developed, and that many areas were virtually untouched by the winds of modernization. Yet this is precisely the message which Khrushchev conveyed to the world in March of 1959, when he climbed onto an improvised platform in the Soviet pavilion of the Leipzig Fair, introduced himself as "a representative of the business circles of the U.S.S.R.," and announced to the assembled Western executives that his country was again in the market as a buyer of new technology, with a special interest in complete plants, along with the patents, licenses and know-how needed to launch them into operation.

Actually, almost a year earlier, Khrushchev had chosen to emphasize in even more dramatic terms the severe lag which had developed in certain sectors of Soviet industry. Having decided to face the issue squarely, he adduced a wide variety of facts and figures to show that the whole wave of new processes and synthetic materials generated by modern applied chemistry had literally by-passed the East. This was the price of preoccupation with the safety of communism's economic frontiers. The chemical industry, he said, would have to be modernized by means of "crash" programs of foreign procurement, by adding a large enough number of advanced, market-tested manufacturing facilities to swamp outmoded lines of production. Such an approach, he argued, would lead directly to "the more rapid fulfillment of our program for the construction of new enterprises without having to waste time on the creation of designs and mastering the process of production of new types of equipment."[8]

Shortly thereafter, complete modern factories began to move Eastward to revitalize bottlenecked branches of industry. In the case of the U.S.S.R., the in-flow of machinery increased steadily from the mid-fifties. Imports of equipment from the noncommunist world in the chemical field alone picked up at a strong tempo, rising from $20 million in 1957 to $200 million in 1968. It did not take the other members of Comecon very long to absorb the lesson inherent in these developments. By the beginning of the last decade, they too had begun to perceive the practical utility of an import policy seeking to transplant into their industrial systems the latest achievements of foreign production technology.

Behind the dry statistical figures lies a truly dramatic story of the flow from West to East of integrated sets of equipment, designed to embody the most advanced findings of industrial research, ready to be assembled into complete factories on their chosen sites. By way of illustration, within the past several years Britain alone has provided the U.S.S.R. with packaged plant complexes and equipment, including patents and know-how, to produce triacetate fiber, viscose tire cord, acrylic fiber, acetate yarn, polyester fiber, acetic acid, paraxylene and copper tubes. Other leading Western industrial nations, most prominently West Germany, Italy, France, Sweden and Japan, have contributed a comparable range of supplies.

On the face of it, the recent practice of importing "turn-key" plants from the West, with all the necessary technical accessories, may be viewed as a mere resumption of a practice followed by the Soviet Union some forty years earlier. During the first two five-year plans (1928–1937) Western engineers, it will be recalled, were invited to Russia in large numbers to help install their equipment and train local personnel in the skills of industrial production. Upon closer examination, however, the present approach may be recognized as resting on more sophisticated economic assumptions. In the earlier phase, the Soviet leaders had persuaded themselves that the task of modernization could be achieved by working with a limited list of primary industrial projects, over a fixed time schedule. As soon as that list was exhausted, they naively proclaimed to the world that their erstwhile dependence on imports from abroad had come to an end; the process of scheduled industrialization had been completed. Official commentators made the bold forecast that "in the future we can fulfill our plans without the need for imports." [9]

No such illusions becloud the minds of the present generation of communist executives. They seem to accept the fact that the much smaller industrial plant of the Eastern orbit could not possibly reproduce, on the basis of its own resources, the whole spectrum of physical facilities and human innovations that have evolved within the frame of the industrial community at large. Cooperation with the outside world is viewed as a continuing necessity, an eminently desirable method of stimulating and sustaining economic and technological progress at home.[10]

D. Industrial Cooperation with the West

Trade in the traditional sense of a balanced, two-way exchange of physical goods is no longer considered by the East as a sufficient channel for economic intercourse with more advanced industrial nations. If urgently needed purchases of Western equipment and technology are to be adequately financed, the structure as well as the volume of exports, both visible and invisible, must be expanded.

At the present time, new methods of direct cooperation with foreign firms are being actively favored, particularly by the more inventive, smaller nations of eastern Europe. Such cooperation covers a broad scope of economic, industrial, scientific and technical arrangements, including complex, long-term agreements for the delivery of plants, mutual exchanges of patents and know-how, and various types of joint ventures in production, marketing and the service industries.

One important development has conditioned the new communist eagerness for closer involvement with foreign industrial firms, namely that over the years the East has managed to create an extensive, indigenous research base. This circumstance has given rise to a sense of accomplishment. A feeling is emerging on the part of communist enterprises that they can meet their Western counterparts on equal terms and appear in the competitive world market of technology not only as purchasers, but as vendors.

There are few reliable figures by which to gauge the extent of the Eastern investment in industrial research. We do, however, know the enormous strides made by Soviet science, particularly theoretical science, and the annual expenditure incurred in the process. In 1965 the total outlays amounted to $7.7 billion; for the year 1969, the budgeted appropriation was $10.0 billion.[11] The Soviet Union today is a major technological power, as evidenced by the sheer size of its scientific establishment. As of the end of 1968 it boasted 823,000 "scientific workers."[12] The annual cost of research has been estimated to consume 2.5 percent of the country's gross national product.[13]

A measure of the U.S.S.R.'s growing eagerness to exchange its technological innovations with the West is provided by the steady rise in the registration of Soviet patents abroad. According to the Chairman of the Chamber of Commerce of the Soviet Union, this accumulation augurs well for the future prospects of Soviet commerce with the West. At the very least, he states, it represents a body of factual data which "can serve as a basis for the development of trade in licenses and for the expansion of the export of machinery and equipment" from the U.S.S.R.[14] A 1967 survey of license transactions with capitalist countries has, in fact, brought to light the sale by the U.S.S.R., since 1962, of a large and growing number of patents to France (its biggest customer in this field), the United Kingdom, the United States and other Western countries.[15]

Official party opinion has, in recent years, firmly underwritten the endeavor of the U.S.S.R. and its neighbors to raise the level of their industrial sophistication by enlarging trade in patents and licenses with the West. In this connection, Premier Kosygin took it upon himself to usher in a promising era of cooperation:[16]

> Until recently we tended to under-estimate the importance of trading in patents and licenses. Such trade is playing an increasingly prominent role in the world today and is developing faster than commerce in industrial goods. Our scientific and technical personnel are able to create—and this can be proven in practice—up-to-date machines and equipment. We can and must, therefore, assume our due place in the world's license market. In some cases, we too could profit by purchasing licenses, rather than resolving the problems concerned ourselves. Purchase of patent rights will enable us to save hundreds of millions of rubles on scientific research during the coming five years.

For the foreseeable future at least, direct Western participation in the equity capital of Eastern state enterprises cannot be contemplated, although such enterprises have not shied away from joining private firms in the formation of mixed companies abroad. Thus far, only Yugoslavia has been able to reconcile its efforts to attract capitalist investments with the obvious ideological problems they pose.[17] The rest of the region is experimenting with pragmatic devices intended to offer the private foreign firm a semblance of comparable economic incentives.

In the main, the cooperation relates to the development of natural resources and the creation of industrial infrastructures in the East and, occasionally, in less developed countries. Invariably it entails enduring and elaborate contractual relationships, to which we will return in connection with East-West exchanges of technology. Examples of joint projects conceived on an exceptionally large scale are the long-term 1969 and 1970 Soviet agreements with West German, Italian and Austrian firms for the construction of pipelines and the delivery of natural gas, and 1968 agreements with Japanese firms for the exploitation of Russia's Far Eastern resources.[18]

The twenty-year pact with West German industry, one of the largest commercial transactions ever concluded by the U.S.S.R., calls for the supply of huge quantities of large diameter rolled steel and related equipment. For this purpose, a consortium of local banks has arranged some $350 million of long-term, low-interest export credits. As part of the Soviet Union's ambitious drive toward western Europe's hungry energy markets, a growing network of pipelines will furnish Germany, Austria, Italy and France with Siberian-origin natural gas delivered via Czechoslovakia.

Of foreign countries, Japan has played the principal role to date in Russia's plans for the development of its Asian areas. These plans call for the mass purchase of technology and assistance in the building of a modernized timber industry in Siberia and the eventual exploitation of the natural gas and oil resources in Sakhalin, the Amur valley and the sea of Okhotsk. The first basic contract, signed in Tokyo on July 29, 1968, envisioned the delivery of $133 million-worth of Japanese wood-processing machinery and materials on five-year credit terms and an additional $30 million-worth of related goods on an accelerated payment basis. In return the Russians undertook to supply, over a period of five years beginning in 1969, around 8 million cubic meters of timber at fixed 1968 international prices for the first two years and at adjusted formula prices for the next three years.

In a multitude of more current coproduction ventures, the Western side undertakes to supply technical know-how, capital goods, managerial skills and foreign sales outlets. The Eastern side, on the other hand, contributes labor, raw materials, basic plant facilities and other locally available elements. On this basis, the former is able to purchase finished goods at a price well below what would have been its own cost of manufacture. The latter, meanwhile, by paying for its acquired technology and equipment out of production, is able to conserve its meager foreign exchange. Moreover, it is assured in advance of markets which might otherwise be difficult to penetrate.

E. The Drive toward Emergent Economies

Eastern trade with the newly developing countries has witnessed a lively expansion within the past decade. The fermenting regions of Asia, the Middle East and Africa acquired too much significance to be ignored, either politically or economically. For the Soviet Union, as the nominal leader of the communist orbit, it became a matter of particular importance to keep these regions from falling under the economic tutelage of capitalism.

True, many of the newly emerged states continued to be commercially oriented toward the West, often by reason of former colonial associations. There was, furthermore, a well-established condition of economic complementarity between the Western industrial nations and the producers of primary materials in the underdeveloped areas of the world. Apart from its commercial value to the West, a trade pattern of this sort was fraught with political meaning. As economic determinists, the leaders of the East could not but view these relationships with apprehension.

By the mid-fifties it became quite evident that the casual treatment accorded to these vast and potentially important areas was short-sighted in every conceivable respect. The newly independent countries were beginning to demonstrate, with every passing year, that they were not, as Stalin had labeled them, "the backyard of the imperialist powers." In fact, they were proving themselves to be independent political entities, having a wide variety of real and enduring interests of their own, that could serve as a basis for future economic cooperation and, even more important, political influence.

From an economic point of view, the acceptance of the "third world" as a theater of active interest meant, in the first place, that the socialist states would have to adjust the structure of their foreign commerce in such a way as to allocate a sizable component of industrial commodities for the less developed countries. In the past, the Soviet Union found it rather difficult to generate enough exports to these areas. The results of commercial activity showed up largely on the import side of the ledger, in the form of occasional purchases of primary commodities such as rubber, cotton, cocoa, tea, jute and coffee. Even during the second half of the fifties, the U.S.S.R. still had little to sell. The trade balance did not, in fact, shift in its favor until the early sixties.

To appreciate the effort made by the Soviet Union toward stimulating exports to the less developed regions, it is helpful to note the relative tempo of increase in the two-way movement of this trade. Between 1962 and 1967, for example, Soviet imports increased by 32.7 percent, while exports expanded by as much as 35.6 percent (respectively 5.8 and 6.3 percent per annum). The countries of Eastern Europe as a group have shown also that they can supply a respectable quantity of machinery. Between 1962 and 1967, their exports increased by 60 percent, reaching some 8 percent ($980 million out of $12,910 million) of all the machinery absorbed in the latter year by this sector of the world market.[19]

This trend meant, furthermore, that if Eastern Europe in general and the U.S.S.R., East Germany and Czechoslovakia in particular wanted to play effectively the role of industrially advanced trade partners vis-à-vis the economically backward states, they were expected to provide, in addition, a substantial amount of development assistance. The available data reflect considerable effort along these lines in the direction of selected countries in Asia, Africa and the Middle East.

Briefly summarized, the Soviet program of economic development assistance has evolved a complex of features which are in part unique and in many respects congruous with the practices that have become standard in the foreign aid programs of the Western industrial nations. What is distinctive about the communist approach, and particularly attractive to the recipient countries, is that it tends to concentrate on industrial construction, with special emphasis on the heavy sectors of manufacturing: steel mills, coal mines, oil wells, electric power stations, cement factories and basic, heavy machinery plants. In this manner, the East is actually recommending its own strategy of economic development. First, it helps to promote the idea that the process must begin with the building of a broad domestic industrial base. A nation thus equipped is in a strong position to create its own diversified industrial plant, to mechanize agriculture and to introduce modern mass production techniques in the area of consumer goods and the building of transportation facilities. This mode of economic reasoning is clearly evoking a strong echo of approval from those for whose ears it is intended. It also carries obvious and potent political implications.

Another prominent feature of the foreign aid program is the stress it lays on geological prospecting. Most of the projects initiated by Soviet enterprises include provisions for the supply of qualified engineers and modern scientific equipment to explore and bring to the surface the presumed mineral riches of the client nation. These minerals can then be used for processing by its own domestic industry or for diversifying its export structure.

Training of technical personnel also often constitutes a major element in such a program. This type of assistance, which comes under the heading of "developing national technical cadres," can be offered on one of two levels. Groups of trainees from the recipient countries are regularly welcomed in the Soviet Union, where they undergo a production apprenticeship for the kind of skilled or semiskilled industrial labor they will be expected to perform at home, once the aided plant is launched into operation. At the academic level, the Soviet Union undertakes to build technical schools, both in the form of secondary and higher educational institutions.

The terms of loans extended by the U.S.S.R. and China in connection with aid are made as conspicuously attractive as possible. Interest charged is around 2.5 percent. The period of maturity runs from ten to twelve years and the indebtedness is usually liquidated by supplying the donor nation with traditional export commodities. This means of repayment is regularly cited as evidence of an earnest desire on the part of the U.S.S.R. to "help the recipient country to conserve its scarce resources of foreign exchange."[20]

For some unknown reason, possibly associated with its impact on the local public, the U.S.S.R. has not to date published a systematic account of its activity in the sphere of foreign aid. The global figure often repeated in published sources as representing all credit commitments under the aid program has remained for some time at the level of 4 billion rubles ($4.4 billion). Western estimates place the amount much higher. For the East as a whole, including China, the cumulative total between 1954 and 1968 is assumed to be in excess of $10 billion (although even this figure is minuscule compared with programs carried out by the West). Actual utilization is, of course, well below this level, perhaps one-third of total commitments.[21] The largest part of communist aid has been earmarked for countries in Asia, chiefly India, Afghanistan, Pakistan and, prior to 1966, Indonesia. Next in importance is the Middle East, which includes such major recipients as the U.A.R., Syria and Iraq and more recently, Iran and Turkey. As a newcomer in the field, Africa trails well behind, major recipients being Algeria, Ethiopia and Ghana.

There is, in addition, a form of financial involvement between the U.S.S.R. and a number of less developed countries, namely the systematic extension of military credits, which is diplomatically far more sensitive than economic aid, and therefore impossible to quantify on the basis of open sources. The 1967 armed violence in the Middle East has suggested that perhaps as much as $2 billion worth of Soviet supplied and financed military equipment had found its way to this particular region. The U.A.R. alone is assumed to have received more than half of this total prior to the Six-Day War. Substantial deliveries of new armaments have been made since, in order to reconstruct the battered Egyptian military machine.

A series of distinctive difficulties have confronted Eastern efforts in the developing world, aside from the problem of countering prior Western entrenchment in many of the areas involved. First, the communist countries have had to overcome a strong reluctance to engage large amounts of capital in long-range foreign projects. Second, they have been hard put to provide sound managerial advice and training for the operation of enterprises in underdeveloped but nevertheless market-oriented economies. Third, they have had to find a proper equilibrium between the net benefit of bilaterally balanced trade to their own closed-currency economies, and the increasing need to satisfy domestic demand for higher quality goods.

The issue of foreign aid has, in fact, generated considerable controversy in the East, although debate is much more muted than in the parliamentary appropriation committees of Western nations. The Chinese in particular have vocally wondered whether Eastern assistance, supplied separately or in cooperative ventures with Western interests, has not strengthened rather than weakened the local postfeudal structures. Sino-Soviet rivalry in specific areas of influence has further dramatized the difference of approach.

The logic of the Chinese query has not escaped the attention of policy-makers elsewhere. Insofar as communist aid contributes to the economic progress of uncommitted countries, the long-term interests of the West are thereby served as well. A consistent Marxist might indeed argue that effective aid to these countries gives them something more to lose than their chains, thus making the soil less fertile for revolution. Whether they think of themselves as revisionists or not, the Soviet and east European party theoreticians have brushed aside such obstacles of doctrine in their determined drive toward the emerging areas of the world. The value to these areas of the attention which is thus being showered upon them will be considered in the next chapter.

3

WORLD-WIDE INTEREST IN TRADE WITH THE EAST

A. Changing Directions of Communist Trade

In the main, western countries are attracted to the East as a market for their manufactured products. The communist states are markedly less important as a source of goods. The typical exports offered by the region are, with very few exceptions in the raw materials category, readily available elsewhere. The West is certainly not dependent upon communist supplies of critically required imports. During the peak years of the cold war, the members of the NATO alliance, the United States in particular, developed virtual autonomy with respect to Eastern origin supplies affecting defense production and other basic industrial needs.

The relative importance of trade with the East varies considerably among Western nations. But its current volume and dynamics are such that few countries, regardless of the maturity of their economic development or their political attitude, can afford to ignore its benefits. The fact that total turnover between the East and the industrialized outside world accounts for only 3 percent of international commerce (approximately $10 billion each way) does not diminish this proposition; on the contrary, it helps to spotlight East-West exchanges as a major trade frontier of the future.

The East's participation in world commerce has grown impressively in the recent past. In the important 1956–1965 decade following the end of the Stalin era, exports as well as imports made conspicuous gains. The flow of Eastern goods to all destinations increased from $9.4 to $21.7 billion. During the same period, imports too expanded from $8.9 to $21.1 billion. By any known measure, this is a respectable rate of progress, registering better than 8.5 percent per annum. A closer look at the record reveals several interesting developments. In the first place, there was a slowdown in growth of the total trade of the East during the second half of the decade, most pronounced among the communist countries themselves. By contrast, exchanges with the rest of the world continued to expand at a more active pace. Exports to the West grew at a rate of 10 percent; to the newly developing countries, at a spectacular rate of 18.8 percent. This experience was unique enough to suggest to policymakers in the East that they may have reached the limits of intraregional exchange. From that point on, new opportunities would have to be sought in markets lying outside the orbit of politically preferred partners. That the conclusion was correctly drawn and fully acted upon is evident from the subsequent broadening of this segment of commerce. The following figures eloquently describe the evolution of Soviet trade with the industrialized "capitalistic" countries (in millions of dollars FOB):[1]

SOVIET EXPORTS

1956	1957	1958	1959	1960	1961	1962
580	713	702	887	1014	1093	1136

1963	1964	1965	1966	1967	1968
1261	1311	1495	1755	1934	2096

SOVIET IMPORTS

1956	1957	1958	1959	1960	1961	1962
600	697	656	787	1115	1116	1305

1963	1964	1965	1966	1967	1968
1423	1763	1632	1777	1815	2183

For the near term, East-West trade is likely to continue its growth in pronouncedly asymmetrical patterns. While in the case of the smaller

East European nations—Poland, for example—it represents as much as 30 percent of the total, for Western states the level is seldom above 5 percent. This fact clearly suggests that the importance of current exchanges is much greater for the communist countries than for the market-oriented systems. In the latter, moreover, the primary impact is felt by a few dozen firms, rather than by the national economy as a whole. Hence, the East's far greater preoccupation with the bilateral equilibrium of exports and imports.

In the long run, the principal obstacle to expanded commerce is the precarious Eastern trade balance. Exports of raw materials and agricultural commodities are no longer adequate to pay for all the imports that can be absorbed by the East. The Western interest in increasing the present volume of sales, therefore, demands a lowering of some of the existing commercial barriers. Particularly, the Common Market countries have it in their power to open the doors more widely to the traditional exports of certain east European countries. There is also, in this respect, a need for greater diversification of Western purchases in general.

Fundamentally, the future growth of East-West trade depends on the ability of the East to provide, and the West to absorb, a much larger volume and variety of manufactured products. Movement in this essentially new direction is, in fact, already under way. But in the ultimate analysis, Western Europe can only accommodate a marginally and gradually increased inflow of Eastern goods. For the smaller communist countries a major impetus to further integration into the world economy can only come from a sizable opening in the markets of the United States.

American trade with the communist world has been a frozen river for almost a quarter century. The complex issues which enter into that particular segment of East-West intercourse, from economic interest to political reaction, are therefore discussed separately.

B. Patterns of Intra-European Commerce

The nations of Western Europe have been, historically, the most active traders in the world. Imports have traditionally constituted a high proportion of their aggregate national product, ranging from approximately 11 percent in the case of Italy to as much as 30 percent for the Netherlands. In ordering their own economic development, this group of nations long ago opted in favor of following the example set by England during the first half of the nineteenth century. Like her, they elected to become "the workshop to the world," pursuing their comparative advantage in the international market by specializing in the manufacture of a surplus of finished industrial goods and exchanging them with other countries for raw materials and agricultural produce.

Eastern Europe has played an important role in this global pattern of exchange. In contrast to the Western half of the continent, it was sparsely populated, with most of its forest areas still largely intact, and its rich and diverse mineral resources only partly exploited. By dint of its ability to earn purchasing power through Westbound exports the Eastern orbit was able to qualify as a natural trading partner.

Certain types of raw materials from the East are even today an object of considerable economic interest to the market economies of Europe. The Soviet Union alone exports yearly 65 million tons of primary commodities. This includes petroleum, coal, coke, iron ore, manganese ore, chrome ore, asbestos, apatite, potash and timber. In addition, the U.S.S.R. supplies some 20–25 percent of all platinum, 70–75 percent of all palladium and 60–70 percent of all the rhodium moving in world trade.[2]

Even more important from the viewpoint of the West is the economic complementarity of the Eastern region, which labor under the handicap of delayed industrial evolution. The new communist regimes have been moving aggressively to make up for lost time, to complete the industrialization of their economies and to provide a basis for the creation of a modern, technologically diversified society.

Although the socioeconomic structure which came to be established throughout the East has presented distinctive difficulties, the existence nearby of a large, rapidly developing and presumably noncyclical market, stretching toward the Urals and beyond to the Pacific Ocean, could not but whet the appetites of the surplus-producing Western manufacturers. The opportunity to establish itself firmly and rapidly in all of the communist markets has seemed particularly attractive to West European industry in light of the virtual absence of American competition. From the vantage point of industrial Japan, the same generalization applies to the markets of Communist China and the Soviet Far East.

The fact that the East still allocates a relatively small proportion of trade to markets outside its own sphere does not appear to be viewed with pessimism in Western Europe. The business communities of these countries consider this characteristic to be essentially a part of the inherited pattern of the region's economic past. As they see the situation, the Eastern areas are continuing to trade well below their economic potential. The presumption that there is ample room for growth is based on the fact that the Comecon countries account for some 30 percent of the world's industrial output and 20 percent of its agricultural production, while contributing only 11 percent to the global volume of international commerce. Increased experience in the techniques of trade, as well as an emerging sense of cost-consciousness, are also likely to demonstrate the wisdom of participation in a broader international division of labor.

Very nearly everything that has happened within the past decade in the sphere of East-West economic relations, both in quantitative and qualitative terms, seems to have borne out this optimistic assessment. In particular, large blocks of technology have been acquired by the East in the form of complete plant installations, covered by long-term arrangements for credit as well as for the protection of industrial property rights. And, as we have seen, new and more direct forms of business cooperation conceived for mutual profit have also begun to unfold on an ambitious scale. A pattern of foreign trade based on so diversified a foundation, as seen by Western Europe, is likely to be capable of developing its own further momentum.

C. The Continental Trading Blocs

Toward the end of the last decade, six countries accounted for the bulk of western European trade with the eastern half of the continent: West Germany, France, Italy, England, Austria and Sweden. Three of these are members of the European Economic Community; the Benelux group, taken together, ranks not far behind them in order of importance. Communist exchanges with the E.E.C. have developed more rapidly than those of any other bloc of nations, although, necessarily, more slowly than intracommunist trade. From 1958, the year in which the Treaty of Rome came into effect, to 1965, imports from eastern Europe grew by 132 percent, while exports rose by 126 percent.[3] There was continued, although slower, progress in the last few years, with the result that the trade of the E.E.C. with the East now exceeds $2 billion each way.

Combined imports of primary products from the East, including mainly foodstuffs and fuels, run at an annual rate of $1.5 billion. The Community currently absorbs close to 20 percent of all Comecon food exports, as compared with a share of 10 percent in 1955. Imports of manufactures have also been rising steadily. On the whole, the East at present accounts for slightly more than 5 percent of the global trade of the E.E.C. The evident strength of this exchange would appear to be firmly based on the traditional economic complementarity of the two regions, while the results of more effective industrial specialization are beginning to play a larger role in the exports of the East. Quite clearly, communist forebodings over the "exclusive" tendencies of the Six have not materialized.

Common Market and Comecon countries conduct their mutual trade on a strictly bilateral basis, in accordance with the latter's general practice. Some forty agreements, negotiated on a country-by-country basis without direct interference from the central authorities of the Community, are currently in force. Their duration ranges from three to five years.[4] As in the past, each accord stipulates conditions which reflect the economic interests and political attitudes of the immediate High Contracting Parties, with little deference to the positions of the respective trading blocs.

Neither the U.S.S.R. nor its allies have thus far seen fit to extend official recognition to the E.E.C. or, for that matter, to the European Free Trade Association. The smaller communist countries have been particularly alarmed by the implications of European integration. All have insisted, albeit with diminishing conviction, on dealing with each member state individually.[5] Since most of the Eastern countries remain outside the GATT, they are not bound under Article 24 of the General Agreement to recognize the established international customs unions (although the U.S.S.R. has, after years of reticence, officially acknowledged the existence of the Benelux Union). Today, semiofficial contacts with the Common Market are quite extensive and the progressive integration of the area is pragmatically accepted as an established fact. Nor have the Common Market countries been able, thus far, to agree upon an effective, uniform approach toward trade with the East. There has been extensive debate with a view to policy coordination by the 1970 deadline established under the Rome Treaty.[6] But apart from a full-scale commercial agreement with Yugoslavia (a precursor of similar pacts with other states of the region) only in isolated areas, notably in the agricultural sector and the sphere originally assigned to the Coal and Steel Community, have there been meaningful steps toward a combined position. This guarded action has mainly concerned the impact of quantitative import restrictions upon Eastern products, now enforced nationally, but in the future to follow Community guidelines.

Under the prodding of an agriculturally anxious France, the Brussels authorities make no secret of their intention to immunize a so-called "green

Europe" from aggressive outside competition. And the more rural economies of the East have already begun to feel the brunt of this exclusion. The future emphasis in economic relations between the two markets may therefore be placed on the availability and tariff status of Eastern industrial exports acceptable to the E.E.C. economies. The fact that there cannot be a significant expansion of Western sales to the East without conditions which open the way to counterpart imports seems to be well understood in Brussels. It is even more acutely appreciated by the chancelleries of the member states (notably Bonn), far more, in fact, in political than in economic terms.

Although the European Free Trade Association's exchanges with eastern Europe have also expanded quite rapidly, it enjoys a lesser share of East-West trade than does its Common Market rival. This applies equally to exports and imports. Moreover, the trend continues to run in favor of the E.E.C. Thus, for the Outer Seven (Austria, Denmark, Norway, Portugal, Sweden, Switzerland, the United Kingdom, and, on an associate basis, Finland) the importance of exploiting the potential of the Eastern markets looms large, particularly since the area has yet to reach the relative levels of trade with the East which it had enjoyed prior to World War II.

As in the case of the E.E.C., most of the commerce is conducted on the basis of bilateral trade and payments agreements negotiated by individual pairs of countries. Limited as is the harmonization of the E.E.C.'s commercial policy toward the East, that of the E.F.T.A. is hardly coordinated at all, in concept or practice.

In recent years, both the E.F.T.A.'s exports to and imports from the communist nations have grown more rapidly than has its world-wide trade. The largest segment of sales to Eastern Europe is manufactures. Within this category, machinery and transport equipment, followed by semimanufactures, chemicals and consumer goods, constitute the most rapidly growing groups. On the import side the largest categories are agricultural commodities and raw materials, although the share of manufactures has been steadily rising. All in all, eastern Europe accounts for approximately 5 percent of the E.F.T.A.'s foreign trade.

The member countries which have most noticeably increased their exports are England, Austria and Switzerland. It is significant, however, that Finland, despite its small economy, ranks immediately after the United Kingdom as the E.F.T.A.'s most important supplier to and purchaser from eastern Europe as a whole, and second in exchanges with the U.S.S.R. The unique position of Russia's northern neighbor can be traced back to the end of World War II, when it was required to pay heavy reparations as the ally of a defeated Germany. Several new industries had to be established to meet deliveries. These industries, among them shipbuilding and wood-processing machinery, work largely for the U.S.S.R. and account for the bulk of exports to that market. As a result, Finland has often found itself on an economic and political trapeze. For example, presented with the ominous choice of joining E.F.T.A. or facing stagnation, it opted for an intricate settlement which recognized the most favored nation clause of its 1947 bilateral trade agreement with the U.S.S.R. over the preferential commitments due to fellow E.F.T.A. members.

While Great Britain is the E.F.T.A.'s most important exporter to eastern Europe, these sales account for only 3 percent of her total trade. Moreover, in recent years the United Kingdom has been buying considerably more from the Comecon countries than it has been selling to them. Although this fact has been a source of friction in the framework of current bilateral agreements, the adverse balance has tended to be redressed by means of communist purchases in other parts of the sterling area, *e.g.*, rubber from Malaysia, wool from Australia and copper from Rhodesia.

With her sophisticated engineering know-how and large productive capacity, Britain has fared exceptionally well in the new and growing categories of business dealings with the East, namely the delivery of capital equipment and the construction of integrated industrial complexes. Aided by the virtual absence of American competition, firms like Imperial Chemical Industries, British Aircraft Corporation and Leyland Motors have been able to outbid other Western suppliers in contests for lucrative contracts, although none have matched in magnitude transactions concluded with the East by Italy's Fiat or France's Renault.[7]

In recent years, Britain has been more conspicuous than the other countries of the Free Trade Association in its promotion of sales to the East. The promise of a larger export market necessarily holds a strong appeal for a country afflicted with a persistently adverse balance of payments. Similarly, the fear of losing its traditional, if small, Eastern outlets is also great. It is, perhaps, for this reason that the United Kingdom has been more reluctant than other Western countries to view East-West trade in political colors. Both the government and the business community have, in fact, pursued a pragmatic course in economic relations with the communist world. Although they have participated in the framing of restrictions on the flow of strategic goods and long-term credits, implementation of such restrictions has not gone much beyond lip service to the national bonds with the United States and the rest of the Western alliance.

D. Japan and Canada

Two differently structured economies, Japan and Canada, display unusual features in terms of their opportunities for trade with the East. Both have benefited from geographic proximity to particular communist markets and from the comparative advantage they enjoy in certain sectors of industry and agriculture.

In Japanese-Soviet commerce, much stress has lately been placed on large-scale programs for the cooperative exploitation of the natural resources of Russia's Asiatic provinces.[8] The magnitude of these projects is a reflection of Japan's coming of age as an industrial and technological power of the first order. Since 1965, its traders have begun to express more and more interest in eastern Europe as well, with excellent initial results. Japan, a highly developed country with few natural resources of its own, has an especially large capacity for absorbing Eastern supplies and furnishing finished goods and know-how, a circumstance markedly conducive to expanded two-way trade. Accordingly, by 1967, exchanges with the communist orbit had reached $1.5 billion, or 7 percent of the nation's world commerce.

China, more than any other communist country, holds out to Japan the promises of an enormous sales outlet and a possible solution to its growing balance of payments difficulties. Already Japan has become the most important of China's trade partners, supplying her with industrial products, farm equipment and chemicals. China in turn ranks closely behind the U.S.A., Australia and Canada as a supplier of agricultural products and raw materials.[9]

Unlike the United States, Japan and Canada have followed the example of the major European trading nations in maintaining active commercial relations with the Peking-dominated territories. The commodity content of this trade has, for a variety of reasons, undergone drastic shifts in recent years. During the first decade of Maoist rule, the goods imported from outside the East consisted chiefly of raw materials, fertilizer and metal products, supplemented by certain types of machine tools, instruments and electronic equipment. In 1961, China found it necessary to alter this pattern by emerging as a large-scale grain importer. Domestic production had faltered as a result of persistent drought, accompanied by severe economic and political dislocation in the farm community. Faced with the need to procure sizable quantities of grain, mostly from Canada, Australia and France, the government was temporarily forced to curtail its imports of machinery and other investment goods.

Tokyo's trade policy toward Communist China has long been forced to navigate in politically rough waters. While domestic clamor for improved relations with the mainland was increasing, pressures applied by the United States, Japan's principal market and ally, to stay aloof from extensive economic involvement could not be easily ignored. Moreover, while Japan's exports to and imports from China reached high figures—for example, $315 million in 1968—trade with Formosa exceeded that amount by more than $200 million. In short, the country could not afford to expose itself lightly to the political complications which unchecked economic intercourse with its communist neighbor could entail. The dilemma is illustrated by the controversy surrounding the so-called "Yoshida letter." There is reported to be in existence a written message from the late Japanese Prime Minister, Shigeru Yoshida, to Generalissimo Chiang Kai-shek, pledging that public credits would not be used to finance capital exports to the mainland. Since it was apparently transmitted in a private capacity, a strong body of Japanese official and business opinion has repeatedly sought to repudiate its terms. While the letter cannot be viewed as a legally binding commitment, an unequivocal declaration made by a head of government, regardless of its form, carries unmistakable moral force. Accordingly, those who agree with the position taken insist that the national honor has been engaged.[10]

China's dispute with the Soviet-led camp of "revisionist" communism brought about a sharp reduction in its dependence on industrial imports from the U.S.S.R. and the rest of eastern Europe. Its "lean-to-one-side" commercial policy, dating since 1950, came to an abrupt end by the close of the decade. Between 1960 and 1968, Chinese imports of Soviet goods declined from $815 million to $36 million. This decline reflected the deliberate phasing out of Soviet deliveries of equipment for complete plant installations. As could be expected, Japan was among the main commercial beneficiaries of the Sino-Soviet rift. By 1965 it emerged as one of China's leading trade partners and as a principal supplier of industrial equipment, complete plants and other investment goods of importance to the industrialization of the country.

Historically, Canada's trade with the East has been negligible. Vis-a-vis the European portions of the communist bloc, geography has been a natural obstacle. As to the U.S.S.R., Canada's close neighbor across the Arctic Ocean, the modest levels of commerce are explainable by the essentially competitive character of the two economies; both are major producers of lumber, oil, aluminum and grain. Nonetheless, it is in the agricultural sphere that business between them has reached its highest levels. Poor harvests and the high cost of transportation from the surplus-producing Ukraine to Russia's Eastern territories have compelled the U.S.S.R. to purchase sporadically huge quantities of wheat from Canada's Western Provinces. China has also consistently looked to Canada as a major long-term source of wheat for its ever precarious grain balance. And the same is true of other communist countries.

The magnitude of the U.S.S.R.'s grain purchases in 1963 was entirely unprecedented. In that year it became a net importer of wheat and pushed up Canadian sales of that commodity to the communist countries at large to $847.5 million. In 1964, the total amounted to $575 million and in 1965 to $352 million. Based upon projected requirements and the production potential of the East by 1975, Canadian wheat sales to that area are likely to remain significant.[11]

While the leaders of post-Stalinist Russia have not hesitated to sell gold in order to protect their people against drought, Canada cannot count upon a steady communist need, or willingness, to commit major resources to grain purchases abroad. Future sales possibilities must therefore be expected to fluctuate in accordance with the success of communist agricultural planning, climatic conditions and Eastern exchange earning capacity. It is true that the U.S.S.R., Czechoslovakia and East Germany are major producers of industrial equipment and to this extent enjoy a degree of complementarity with Canada. However, they cannot be expected, even under the best of circumstances, to hold their own in competition with American and British manufacturers, and thus to balance huge grain trade accounts with exports of this type.

E. The Less Developed Countries

The initiative taken by the communist regimes of Europe to establish normal commercial ties with all nations, regardless of their political systems, evoked a particularly favorable response among the newly developing countries. On economic grounds alone, the advantages of access to a regional market which in the past practiced a pronounced commercial reserve with respect to the outside world were too tangible to be overlooked. The leaders of the emerging independent states were no strangers to these new facts of international life. They knew that eastern Europe was an area in which rapid industrialization ranked high on the economic agenda. In this environment, the demand for primary products such as natural rubber, cotton, wool, jute, et cetera, is likely to grow with the planned expansion of the processing industries, and provide a dynamic outlet for new trade.

It was equally apparent that with the growth of economic productivity in the East, the expectations and the standard of living of the population would also tend to rise. In terms of world commerce, a trend of this kind promised to enlarge the market for a wide range of primary commodities including tropical foodstuffs such as tea, cocoa, coffee, citrus and other types of exotic fruit. By any manner of economic forecast, these were fairly realistic expectations. As it turned out, Russia alone increased its natural rubber imports from 3,400 metric tons in 1955 to 183,000 tons in 1960 and to 311,000 tons in 1966. Cotton imports also bounded upward from 18,700 tons to 144,200 tons during the latter five-year period.

Of no less importance to the developing economies is the industrial potential of the communist world. They could hardly overlook the fact that the Eastern orbit includes the second largest industrial nation, along with such traditional producers of manufactured goods as East Germany and Czechoslovakia. From the Soviet Union alone, these countries were able to acquire a steadily increasing flow of industrial machinery, measured by a leap from $5 million in 1955 to $141 million in 1960 and to $426 million in 1966. Counting supplies from the other Comecon countries, the 1966 figure rises to $940 million, or 16 percent of all imports in a class of merchandise which makes a direct and important contribution to economic development, *e.g.*, machine tools, tractors, trucks, power generators, oil-drilling machinery and earth-moving equipment.[12]

Owing to this new qualitative element, trade between the East and the less developed parts of the world emerged as one of the most dynamic sectors of international commerce during the decade 1955–65: Exports to communist countries grew from $580 million in 1955 to $1,404 million in 1960, and $2,815 million in 1965. Imports expanded even more sharply: $630 million in 1955 to $1,444 million in 1960 and $3,282 million in 1965. As a market, the East increased its importance from 5 percent of world trade with the less developed countries in 1960 to 8 percent in 1965.

The Eastern governments have placed themselves on record, since 1955, with a pledge not only to trade with, but also to help promote the industrialization of a number of emergent nations. This undertaking, of necessity, has had to be expressed in formal, long-term bilateral agreements between a particular donor country and its client, specifying the kind of installations to be built, the value of the machinery and technical services to be supplied, the credit terms, as well as the schedules and means of repayment. The recipients of development loans, for the most part channeled toward industrial construction schemes, have been widely scattered, with the largest amounts going to Asia and the Middle East. India and the United Arab Republic, as the two principal showcases of this type of Eastern trade and assistance, deserve to be singled out for special comment.

Up to 1955–56, India's commerce with the communist East was negligible, hardly reaching one percent of exports and imports. By 1960, exports reached 7 percent and by 1965, 18 percent; imports 3.5 percent and 10 percent respectively. In terms of value, India's sales to the East grew to over $300 million within a decade, thus rivaling exports to her historically most important markets, the United Kingdom and the United States. The U.S.S.R., Czechoslovakia and Poland were, in that order, India's most important communist trading partners. The principal categories in her export mix to the East were jute manufactures, tea, tobacco, iron ore, cashew kernels and coffee, skins and hides, pepper and raw wool. On the import side, the commodity composition is also significant: machinery, base metals, apparatus and appliances, and so forth. By 1964, the communist countries accounted for more than 11 percent of India's total imports, the U.S.S.R. delivering between 1955 and that year 64 percent of all imported plants and installations.[13]

Trade between the U.A.R. and the communist world made comparable strides. This country ranks as the East's second client, after India, among the less developed economies and fifth largest world-wide. The U.S.S.R. is its principal communist trading partner, followed by Czechoslovakia and mainland China. During the period 1955–64, the U.A.R.'s exports to the region increased by 194 percent: imports by 250 percent. The East's relative position in total U.A.R. trade grew from 23 percent in 1956 to 33 percent in 1960 and 36 percent in 1965. During this decade, the East absorbed 46 percent of Egypt's total exports, mostly cotton, and supplied 23 percent of its total imports.

In a characteristic effort at reciprocal adaptation between an underdeveloped economy such as the U.A.R.'s, and those of individual Eastern countries—all subject to long-term development plans—the latter have begun to encourage a diversification in import practice, and to absorb manufactures and semimanufactures of cotton, processed foods, chemicals, gasoline, fuel oil, artificial fibers and yarn, essential oils, medicaments, footwear and other consumer goods. The East, principally the U.S.S.R., Czechoslovakia, East Germany, Poland and Hungary, has been supplying Egypt with increasing volumes of industrial goods, including vehicles, ships, instruments and apparatus, metals, chemicals, fuels, timber, coal and foodstuffs. Machinery and equipment account for about 70 percent of the East's exports to the U.A.R. and cover more than half of her total demand in this category. Most of the technologically sophisticated goods come in the form of aid to industrial construction and land reclamation schemes, notably, the Aswan High Dam.[14]

While the cases of India and Egypt are by no means representative, the advantages which communist patterns of trade and development assistance hold out for less developed countries have been widely recognized within the United Nations.[15] Above all, they help to support measured progress in certain basic economic sectors and to reduce dependence on the more competitive markets of the industrial West.

4

TRADE AS AN INSTRUMENT OF FOREIGN POLICY

A. Commerce in the Service of Political Detente

The major countries of western Europe are today inclined to view their trade with the East in the light of the economic and cultural indivisibility of the continent, rather than its ideological cleavage. All the same, political undercurrents, both negative and positive, are also manifestly at work.

Within the Atlantic Community as a whole, a certain polarization of views has been observable for some time. At one end, there is the recurrent preoccupation with allied security; the European members of NATO have grudgingly responded to the American emphasis on the need to limit the flow of strategic goods to states belonging to a hostile military bloc. At the other end, there is a strong urge to increase contacts with the East in the hope of furthering the political thaw, particularly with the smaller communist nations.

The latter approach, initiated in Europe, appears to be prevailing everywhere as the order of the day. With the passage of time, the progressively diffused atmosphere within the communist-dominated areas has proved this position to be the correct one. Whether the West's more positive attitude was the cause, the catalyst, or merely the consequence of the relaxing continental climate is still a matter of speculation. Meanwhile, intra-European trade is thriving. Its growth is being promoted on both sides of the political barrier, and international relations are fitfully improving along with it. The invasion of Czechoslovakia interrupted, but also in a sense confirmed, the efficacy of this trend. In the long run, it is likely to be viewed as having affected the pace rather than the course of economic cooperation.

As the West European countries vie with each other for a larger share of sales to the East, the NATO-engendered strategic export restrictions and credit limitations continue to erode. Attitudes on the two sides of the ocean are, however, still significantly different. While many Americans continue to look upon East-West trade in Manichean terms of good and evil, and heated controversy is a permanent feature of the debate, most Europeans consider the question as utterly devoid of moral content. Whether this view reflects acute perception born of a richer historical experience or expedient rationalization of material self-interest, has become a rather academic issue. More directly relevant is the fact that official attitudes on both continents currently advocate an expansion of economic relations with the East, despite the differing scope of trade restrictions still inscribed on the national statute books.

The complexion of communism around the world has indeed changed a great deal during the last decade. In the eyes of Western policy-makers, the East can no longer be expected to reorganize itself into a homogeneous political camp. The recent effervescence of Czechoslovakia and Rumania has helped to validate this view. Nor is it plausible to speak of a lasting Sino-Soviet understanding under almost any foreseeable circumstances, after the bloody border incidents at the Ussuri and Sinkiang and the vocal clashes all around. In communist Europe, new frontiers have been opened up; for the moment, at least, a way has been found to pass political power from one individual or group of Party leaders to another, without bloodshed. While the quest for civil and intellectual liberties still remains unfulfilled in the region as a whole, a manifestation of national identity and a hesitant assertion of national sovereignty is clearly in evidence. Indeed, the Gaullist notion of *"Europe des patries"* has touched a more responsive nerve in the Eastern than in the Western part of the continent.

One cannot assume, however, that the West European approach to trade with the East is identical for all nations. Each follows an independent policy and seeks opportunities closest to its heart or grasp. Some countries tend to combine business promotion with imperatives of foreign policy, or even a politically motivated crusade for peace. Others pursue specific national goals, with trade serving as a pathfinder.

For example, West Germany, the world's largest trader with the East as a whole and with most of the communist countries individually, has a rather special interest in economic relations with the area. In the post-Adenauer era, many of its leaders, and most recently and dramatically Chancellor Willy Brandt, have embraced the hope that friendly commercial and industrial cooperation with all of the socialist states in the context of a new *"Ostpolitik"* will dissipate the lingering postwar fears of a strong Reich and pave the way to ultimate reunification.[1] Toward this end, maximum trade contacts with East Germany have long been encouraged as a way of keeping alive the common identity and the national spirit. In addition, since 1963 Bonn has exchanged permanent trade and quasi-diplomatic consular missions with Poland, Bulgaria, Hungary and Czechoslovakia, and succeeded in obtaining official recognition from the Eastern maverick, Rumania.

From an economic point of view the effectiveness of this post-Hallstein "opening to the East" is already quite evident. From a political point of view the Kremlin's recent efforts to improve the atmosphere on its Western flank is also likely to bear fruit. A striking manifestation of the new trend, hailed by both sides as a positive influence on unfolding political negotiations, was the conclusion, on February 1, 1970, of a mammoth long-term agreement for the exchange of German steel pipe against Russian natural gas.

Italy, starting with the huge barters of pipe for Soviet oil, introduced in the fifties by the late Enrico Mattei of E.N.I., has followed a particularly activist approach toward trade with the East, notably in the provision of large, long-term export credits on highly favorable terms.[2] On the whole, the Italians have been among the least vocal, but most persistent of Europeans in advancing their business relations with the communist orbit. This helps to account for Fiat's success in concluding the celebrated Tagliatti automobile plant deal. The rationale was presented in both political and commercial terms. In due course, the transaction was expected to stimulate a more generous allocation of Soviet resources to the consumer sectors of the economy. As it turned out, the U.S.S.R. has indeed embarked upon an ambitious program of highway construction to be followed, no doubt, by the erection of gasoline stations, road restaurants and motels.

Although France, long the most vociferous and persistent champion of the importance of closer economic relations, had long been lagging behind West Germany, Great Britain and Italy in Eastbound trade, it has gradually moved to the forefront.[3] Paris has also been the first NATO-country capital to propound the argument that a wholly negative and defensive posture toward the East was no longer responsive to the dynamics of the international situation. Its movement toward *détente* has survived the events of Prague with surprising ease and continued along the hopeful course of the Gaullist notion of a closely knit Europe from the Atlantic to the Urals.

While the offer of freer access to the Common Market has been held out only ambiguously to the smaller East European countries, the goals for expanded trade and economic and scientific cooperation established by the Franco-Soviet "Grande Commission" approach the spectacular. From 1970 to 1974 the two countries have agreed to double their trade in comparison with the previous five-year period, thus hoping to exchange a billion dollars worth of goods by the middle of the current decade.[4] Concurrently, ambitious undertakings such as the Eastern region's adherence to the French SECAM color television system and projects involving the construction or modernization by Renault of automobile assembly plants in Poland, Rumania, the U.S.S.R., and other Comecon states have been jointly conceived on the drawing boards. The sale of one million tons of wheat to Communist China in late 1964 can also be viewed at once as a profitable economic transaction and a factor which paved the way toward French diplomatic recognition of the Maoist regime.

Benelux has followed the Italian rather than the French approach. Officials have been stressing the long-term advantages of Eastern trade largely in economic terms,[5] preferring to leave the broad foreign policy aspects of the matter in the hands of the more activist Quai d'Orsay.

Meanwhile, outside the E.E.C. the United Kingdom continues to follow a highly pragmatic course in its commercial dealings with communist economies. The basic rationale has been appealingly simple all along: trade is intrinsically good because it fosters cooperative attitudes among states; besides, it stimulates the East's will and capacity to create a consumer society. A population with access to an abundance of material possessions develops a vested interest in peace. The United States was left virtually alone to fret over the question whether up-to-date Western supplies help to build the economic, political and military muscles of the Eastern system. All in all, this is perhaps inevitable, considering that America carries the primary burden of leadership within a loosening alliance. Further expansion of U.S. trade relations with the East is not the matter of economic importance that it tends to be in the case of certain other, more export-oriented industrial nations.

All of the European countries, including the members of the E.E.C., have found it not only economically, but also politically expedient to deal with communist states individually and on a bilateral basis. The latter have also come to appreciate the political aptness of this method. In the upshot, the Common Market Commission's valiant efforts to shift commercial treaty negotiations to the multilateral level, as required by Article 113 of the Treaty of Rome, have been an uphill struggle. In connection with the Kennedy Round of tariff negotiations, the agreement of the Six to speak to outsiders with a single voice turned out to be a workable goal; here commerce was commerce. But in East-West relations commerce is deeply interwined with diplomacy, and as long as the hope of a politically coordinated community lags far behind economic integration, each country zealously guards its right to make independent arrangements with selected Eastern governments.

In effect, a subtle acrobatic dance has unfolded between the two groups of states. Stepping deftly so as not to provoke the U.S.S.R., the western European countries (and increasingly the United States) seek to wean their Eastern partner from economic and political dependence upon the Comecon complex. The latter, in turn, responds not only with a manifestation of commercial self-interest but also with a symbolic expression of national independence through the medium of growing business intercourse beyond the ideological reservation. The Soviet Union cannot easily deny the economic advantages which such bilateral exchanges hold for its smaller allies.[6] Consequently, it has shown a measure of tolerance toward these flirtations, even to the embraces which Mr. Nixon and Mr. Ceausescu have bestowed upon each other in August of 1969 before approving Bucharest crowds. But an imponderable condition governs all couples. The accompanying articulation of policy must not be so bold as to suggest a collusive pattern of economic bridge-building aimed at the eroding core of socialist cohesion.

B. Building Bridges to the East

In the United States, the case for an accommodation with eastern Europe, including a better climate for mutual trade, began to make headway in 1963, once the heightened tensions created by the Cuban missile confrontation began to recede. Political leaders became more acutely aware of the need for some new pattern along which to order future relations with the communist countries. In his now historic address "Strategy for Peace," delivered in June 1963, President John F. Kennedy called for an end to the state of permanent political belligerency between East and West and suggested specific steps by which a reconciliation could be effected between the prime antagonists.

In effect, the Kennedy gambit initiated a cautious shift in foreign policy toward east Europe, changing the emphasis from unrelieved hostility to an earnest search for areas of common interest. An objective of immediate relevance to both sides was to find a way to reduce the hazard of a general war. One significant opportunity to take a bold step in that direction soon presented itself in the form of a proposed international treaty to ban nuclear tests in the atmosphere. In expressing his own strong recommendation in favor of adherence, President Kennedy quoted an old Chinese proverb: "A journey of 1,000 miles begins by taking one step." The treaty was formally signed in Moscow on August 5, 1963, and subsequently approved by the United States Senate by a vote of 80 to 20.

Soon thereafter, it became known that owing to a bad domestic harvest, the Soviet government was negotiating with Canadian grain merchants for a large purchase of wheat. The quantity sought turned out to be well in excess of available export stocks. The development raised hopes among American exporters and farmers for a rare chance to sell wheat to Russia. Beyond this short-term expectation, agricultural experts welcomed the opportunity to reduce vast surplus stocks, which were not only devouring enormous storage fees, but also acting as a price-depressant on the world market. Although the issue was profoundly controversial, President Kennedy, on October 10, 1963, announced his approval of the proposed sale and of the Export-Import Bank guarantees for medium term credit that might eventually be required to match prevailing market terms. In the end the Russians opted to pay cash, and the sale, amounting to 65 million bushels valued at $140 million c.i.f., was consummated in mid-1964.

The endorsement of this huge transaction was a notable turning point in U.S. policy toward the non-Asian East. More than any other move of that period, it helped to underscore the proposition that trade with the European communist countries is a continuation of politics by other means. Business dealings began to recommend themselves as a new, constructive bilateral activity involving sustained bargaining and productive competition. While it remained perfectly clear that an improvement in commercial relations, by itself, cannot settle the larger problems at issue between the United States and the Soviet Union, it seemed reasonable to expect that the negotiation of specific deals could serve a useful role in maintaining an open dialogue on all questions of mutual interest.

The decision to approach trade as a medium for reducing animosities gradually became part of settled policy. In 1964, President Johnson gave it a ringing formulation when he expressed the wish "to build new bridges to eastern Europe—bridges of ideas, education, culture, trade, technical cooperation, and mutual understanding for world peace and prosperity." [7] The United States, he suggested, ought to use all readily available means, whenever an opportunity arises, to encourage the movement toward greater national independence in eastern Europe, as well as to provide concrete proof of America's belief in mutually beneficial peaceful relations. Two years later he put this policy into higher gear: "Our task is to achieve a reconciliation with the East—a shift from the narrow concept of coexistence to the broader vision of peaceful engagement." [8] In President Nixon's inaugural address the same basic theme received a new label: "after a period of confrontation, we are entering an era of negotiation." In sum, these initiatives represented no more than a modest alignment to policies which western Europe and particularly Gaullist France had been practicing for years in an effort to span the gulf between the two estranged segments of the continent.

This new emphasis on trade with the East is based not so much on an expected gain in direct economic terms, which will probably never be very large for the United States, as on broader considerations such as the fact that the day-to-day conduct of business involves contact among peoples, an interplay of ideas, tastes, customs, techniques, along with the turnover of goods and services. Quite apart from the actual volume of exchange that could be generated by a more permissive American climate, it began to make good political sense to remove some of the existing restrictions on trade as part of a broad re-evaluation of national policy toward the communist world as a whole, even mainland China.

Having emerged from an ideological dream world, the European communist states still continue to be conscious of the things that divide them from the West; but they have, in the process, gained ample awareness of the dangers of destruction that all of us face in common. Nor is the evidence on this score entirely a matter of conjecture. We need only note that since 1963 Russia and the United States managed to agree on a test ban treaty, a consular treaty, an air travel agreement, an agreement barring nuclear weapons in space, and more recently, on a highly controversial convention to bar the proliferation of nuclear weapons. Within such a reorientation of common aims, East-West commerce has a distinctive function to perform as an integral component of foreign policy.

As it continues to frame its programs for the nineteen-seventies, the Nixon administration will have to decide whether to hasten the search for solid links with eastern Europe, or to convert the Johnson design into mere drawbridges. Vis-à-vis post-Vietnam communist Asia, it will have a more tantalizing opportunity of choice: whether to build on the corroded foundations which have supported twenty years of American policy toward China, or to lead the Congress and the public toward new ground. The recent relaxation of the total embargo is indicative of movement along the latter course, one that leads to progressively expanded economic, commercial and cultural contacts and, eventually, to outright diplomatic recognition.

C. Strategic Implications of Trade

The primary objective of Western export controls is a negative one: to withhold from the East the kind of goods that may help in the build-up of military and political power. In practice, the pursuit of this objective involves the authorities in an organized effort to interfere with the flow of various tangible and intangible supplies. It is, of course, recognized that in the long run such restrictions cannot prevent the development of a modern arsenal of weapons. However, even a modest time advantage in the perfection of military capabilities is assumed to be highly significant in the event of an armed clash.

It is even now frightening to envisage what might have happened in World War II had the Axis Powers been first—if only by a few months—in developing the atomic bomb. The earlier possession of radar by the Allied forces was also a factor in the outcome of the contest with fascism. Many other examples could be cited where a small time advantage in the discovery of new or better weapons was critical in conditions of actual conflict. In an era when science and technology have made possible destruction on a scale never before envisaged, relatively minor disparities in technical competence take on great importance. Billions of dollars are spent annually on computer communications to afford early warning of attack, and on antiballistic missile systems designed to respond to such warning several minutes sooner. Important as these advances are under "hot" war conditions, they are equally significant in times of "cold war," if the potential enemy is convincingly made aware of their existence.

Most Western countries have confined their controls to a limited objective, grounded in considerations of military security. They have not sought to undermine the communist bloc's overall economic position. Only the

United States has gone beyond this aim. Legislation initially passed in 1949 and amended in 1962 prohibited shipments contributing not only to the East's military but also to its economic potential.[9] Toward China, other communist-dominated areas of Asia and Cuba, the U.S. has long pursued a solitary policy of political, diplomatic and economic excommunication.

Viewed in strategic terms, the economic expansion of the communist orbit has meant that increased power could be utilized to improve the military posture of the states which comprise it and to spread their influence among free and uncommitted nations. The rapid growth has been accomplished basically through a very high rate of capital investment directed toward heavy industry. While Western technology and productive equipment have contributed greatly to this growth in the Soviet Union, particularly in the twenties, procurement abroad no longer looms as a major factor in economic development. Some individual sectors of basic production are, however, noticeably benefited by selected imports used to correct imbalances in the industrial structure.

Although it is exceedingly difficult to gauge their impact, these benefits have become more tangible with the continuing relaxation of Western controls. For under such conditions the East may be expected to procure a substantial volume of sophisticated technology not otherwise available to it, *e.g.,* in the sphere of second- and third-generation computers. This would undoubtedly be used to alleviate domestic shortcomings which have developed as the result of uneven rates of progress between high-priority and low-priority segments of the economy.

To what extent recurrent, unhedged shortages affect overall economic momentum in the communist world is not clear. Reliance on imports has tended to be marginal, oriented toward relieving the burden on research facilities or saving development costs in relatively poor quality or remotely located natural resources. The short-term advantage of such supplies to specific areas of the economy is, however, significant. Thus, large-scale importations of copper, oil pipe, trawlers, ships and tankers have undoubtedly played a useful role. Imported rubber constitutes a principal material for the tire industry and fills an essential military and civilian need pending the expansion of local capacity (now being created in part with Western technology).

In the field of semifabricated and finished industrial products, advanced design machinery and equipment are in the principal categories of Eastern interest. Another class of goods which ranks high on the shopping lists is high-quality modern machine tools of west European origin. These supplies, particularly in the case of Communist China, represent a good deal of the basic equipment essential to the development of a modern military-industrial economy. In addition, procurement is actively proceeding in areas of lesser strategic relevance: synthetic fibers, food processing, refrigeration equipment, sugar refineries and other light industry plants and supplies.

Within these various groups the East is successfully acquiring the most advanced, high-productivity capital goods in the form of complete industrial installations and associated engineering services. Although there is no clear evidence that current imports are directed primarily toward the expansion of military facilities, they obviously provide a broadened base of productive capacities and human skills for any type of future mobilization.

In some instances, imports from the West do assist projects which have simultaneous strategic and economic applications. For example, the progressive extension of oil and natural gas distribution pipelines forms a pattern with obvious military implications. This pattern not only furthers industrial expansion, but also provides logistic support along the most probable routes available to Red Army troops in the event of land invasion. Concurrently, the lines offer a basis for continued expansion of exports to west European markets. Several countries are already heavily committed to take Soviet fuel. Among the consequences of this development is the danger of undue allied dependence on communist supplies; for it might prove difficult to adjust to their sudden loss in conditions of emergency.

Urgent plans to improve land transportation are at the basis of important Eastern orders for coordinated manufacturing facilities designed to overcome shortages of high-grade tires, for more efficient railway locomotives and advanced signaling systems. The resultant boost in capacity, and the general ability to switch road and railway traffic from civil to military use, needs no further emphasis.

At the very least, therefore, expanded trade with the West tends to ease the problem of meeting civilian development goals. Obviously, it could also permit a somewhat greater concentration of research and production resources on military hardware. To assume that the communist leaders can be induced, by pressure or temptation from the outside, to depart from their posture of maximum autonomy as regards alien supplies would, however, be naive. This is most emphatically true in the sphere of defense.

The strictly military sector of communist industry is governed by a fully integrated support pattern and is supplied almost entirely from indigenous sources. Enjoying the highest priority status in the economy, it commands available material, equipment, technology and scientific resources in preference to all other spheres. In certain instances, especially in connection with advanced design equipment such as precision machine tools and electronic devices, interest in foreign prototypes has appeared to be related to a current military production objective. In general, external resources are, however, a very marginal logistic factor.

Except for the United States, the industrial West possesses little in the way of military goods or know-how that the Soviet Union has not already achieved and surpassed. Nonetheless, if the NATO countries were to seek an expansion of trade through abolition of the remaining strategic controls, it is probable that selective procurement of useful military equipment would greatly expand. This expansion would not place the East in a position of dependency, but would tend to eliminate quality shortcomings and supply prototypes for effectiveness analysis. Miniaturized electronic communication and navigation systems are particularly obvious examples in this connection.

The compensating advantages to the West of expanding trade with the communist orbit are not significant from the strictly military point of view. Years of cold war tension have led to the development of autonomous or, in any event, non-Eastern sources of sensitive supplies, adequate to meet essential military and civilian production requirements. Even chromium, of which the Soviet Union is a principal producer could, in dire need, be obtained from boycotted Rhodesia. It would, of course, be unsafe to ignore the possibility of preclusive Eastern buying of strategic raw materials required by defense industries. For example, the Congo is a principal source of such rare commodities as cobalt, uranium and tantalum. And it is not impossible to imagine political circumstances in which the continued availability of such supplies might become threatened. However, at present there is no indication that communist countries are disposed or able to deploy disruptive tactics of this type.

D. The Two-Edged Weapon of Embargo

In light of the constant possibility that relations with certain segments of the East could, for one reason or another, once more become as unstable as they have been in the past, it is useful to consider two overrated questions regarding the future course of trade: (1) What degree of leverage could the West derive from a threat to cut off purchases and deliveries, with a view to discouraging renewed communist militancy? (2) What are the prospects for maintaining (and broadening, in times of greater tension) a measure of effectively coordinated multilateral limitations on the sale of strategic materials and technology?

In the current political climate, such terms as "NATO," "SEATO," "Alliance," and "embargo," have tended to acquire a certain staleness and remoteness of meaning much as have phrases such as "Eastern bloc," "socialist brotherhood of nations" and "ultimate victory of communism." Yet all of these symbols still convey a touch of reality to the minds of large segments of the population in both East and West; and, to that extent, a potential exists for the international atmosphere once more to reverberate to the sound of these verbal tocsins. Along with this, the prospect of suspended trade with certain communist areas could, at some point in the future, acquire immediate and practical relevance for individual Western firms—indeed, entire industries which are, or hope to be, constant suppliers to or purchasers from the East.[10] For this reason alone, if for no other, the issue of embargo merits brief scrutiny in a work concerned with obstacles to existent and expanded East-West commerce.

1. Impact on Communist Economies

Although Western statute books are still replete with provisions restricting Eastbound exports, the communist countries can, in fact, obtain most products, machines or materials of a nonmilitary character from European, Canadian or Japanese sources.[11] Even during the tensest diplomatic encounters, such as the Berlin crisis of 1961 or the Cuban missile confrontation of 1962, attempts at an effective allied alignment of strategic trade practice proved to be manifestly ineffectual. Nor is there any assurance that perfect execution of joint policies could have more than an ephemeral impact upon communist military and economic capability.

By now it has become amply clear that total embargoes are impossible to establish or maintain, and that limited embargoes cannot be made impervious to leakage. Indeed, the longer the restrictions last, the more they tend to defeat their own purposes. For the denial of essential supplies inevitably breeds intense efforts to open new and autonomous sources at home or abroad. This is no less true of America's experience with Cuba than of France's experience with Israel. An embargo can yield a degree of desired effect when it is imposed suddenly, just prior to the outbreak of military hostilities. For then the blockaded country is compelled to mobilize for and fight a war, while simultaneously seeking to replace with domestic production items which were formerly obtained elsewhere.[12]

In the military-industrial area—the target at which twenty years of Western restrictions have been most directly aimed—the consequence has been only to stimulate the natural Russian and Chinese autarchic reflex. They have certainly not hampered the development of an advanced arms and space technology. Nor have they induced economic stagnation or the erosion of official ideology. Reforms in the direction of administrative decentralization, the emergence of a communist polycentrism and the broadening of the Sino-Soviet cleavage are essentially a product of indigenous causes.

The economic leverage enjoyed by the United States itself is clearly insignificant. Unilateral severance of trade relations can, under present circumstances, have no seriously disruptive consequences for any of the Eastern economies. As regards mainland China and contiguous communist-dominated Asian areas, the embargo has been complete for many years. Vis-à-vis the U.S.S.R. and most of the other east European states, the long-term denial of most-favored-nation treatment, of export credits and of a broad range of materials considered to be strategic, have reduced dependence on the American market to a minimum.

For the East the United States has quite simply ceased to count as a source of unique and irreplaceable supplies. Nor is it likely that expanded American trade with the U.S.S.R. would release significant Soviet resources for military investment. That privileged sector has consistently enjoyed high immunity from outside influence. At the level of the Atlantic (and SEATO) alliance the picture is somewhat different. Communist trade with the outside world, particularly the industrial West, has expanded dramatically in recent years. Its economic and technological importance to the East has now reached a point which lends credence to the notion of leverage.

Although it is necessary to caution the reader that he is being invited to an excursion into the realm of conjecture, several conclusions seem warranted as to the likely impact of a uniform, total and sudden Western embargo, if such an embargo should ever prove desirable and feasible.

1. The Soviet economy would not suffer widespread dislocation as a result of complete cessation of trade with the West. Despite increased cultivation of world markets, the U.S.S.R. has not abandoned its traditional posture of rockbottom economic self-sufficiency.

2. The Soviet Union would, however, be hard pressed to fulfill certain

segments of its economic plan in the form in which it is currently conceived. Present schedules for selective industrial expansion are predicated on the continued availability of industrial supplies and prototypes of advanced technology from western Europe, and on continued opportunity to dispose of marketable goods abroad.

3. Ambitiously conceived schedules for modernizing retarded Soviet industries and the inspirational goal of overtaking the United States in total production would have to undergo considerable revision. This is particularly true of the sectors of transportation, petrochemicals, chemicals, electronics, plastics, man-made fibers, synthetic rubber and fertilizers. While Soviet industry and technology have developed sufficient momentum to achieve almost any high-priority tasks with an appropriate allocation of resources, the targets would take a longer time to attain, not to mention the additional research cost and development effort involved.

4. The military side of the Soviet economy would, of course, remain largely unaffected, owing to the long-established scale of Soviet priorities and the fact that many years of strategic embargo have produced virtual autonomy from Western suppliers in the defense sector.

5. For the smaller Warsaw Pact countries the consequences would be relatively more severe. The bulk of these nations' imports from the West consists of industrial raw materials and semimanufactured goods (various steel products, pipe, chemicals and chemical fertilizers) which are in short supply within the bloc; machinery, equipment and other finished industrial goods also represent a large share of imports. Economic planning would be subject to considerable disruption because of the unavailability of such Western imports as well as the loss of Western markets for the disposal of surpluses. In particular, export-oriented economies such as Czechoslovakia and East Germany would be markedly affected.

6. Frictions which are now apparent in the sensitive area of Comecon coordination of economic policies might be augmented. The forced pattern of trade with the U.S.S.R., in itself something of an aberration, would become even more distorted. It is useful to recall that eastern European countries have occasionally been compelled to pay the Soviet Union higher prices for comparable goods available in the outside world, to accept lower prices for goods which they could sell more advantageously in the West and to accumulate non-convertible and non-transferable balances derived from exports to the U.S.S.R.

7. China's need to rely once again upon Eastern sources would be seriously magnified. The impact of a denial of wheat from Canada, France

and Australia (if SEATO were to join in the embargo), and of other food products in conditions of threatened famine, is difficult to measure and can be easily exaggerated. However, Chinese imports from the NATO area are heavily concentrated in such categories as (a) chemicals, metals and metal manufactures which are not readily replaceable within the East, and (b) chemical fertilizers, almost all of which are supplied from the industrial West.

8. Finally, the cessation of imports, deliveries and export credits would tend to slow down the Eastern aid programs for underdeveloped countries. A total embargo would undoubtedly trigger a switch in priorities, making it more difficult and costly to fulfill at once commitments for long-term internal development, and for the provision of low-interest loans and of capital equipment to client nations.

2. *Impact on Western Economies*

Having examined the likely consequences of a Western embargo on communist economies, the obverse side of the coin is the extent of losses which would be incurred within the alliance should all commerce with the East be discontinued. This question, no less than the other one, goes to the heart of the problems of leverage, contingency planning and the plausibility of broader trade interdiction at any particular time.

In the first place, it should be reiterated that the political East does not today hold any significant position as a source of essential imports into allied countries. Such hardships as might arise must be looked for on the export side of the equation. There, the extent of dislocation would, of course, be determined by such factors as the level of economic activity within the trade curtailing country, the current balance of payments, the availability of alternative markets, the competitive position of major exports, and so on.

Orders placed by Eastern purchasing monopolies are often a matter of vital economic interest to individual firms in the West, even when the communist country itself is a trade partner of only marginal importance. Such a sale can make the difference between a middling and a good year even for a large company. In addition, entire industries, not necessarily the same from year to year, have come to look upon the East as one of their major export theaters. If this outlet were to be choked off at short notice, serious dislocations would assuredly make themselves felt before an adjustment could be made to alternative markets.

Countries like Turkey, Greece and Iceland, whose trade with the East has exceeded 10 percent of their respective totals, would be faced with relatively serious economic disruptions in the event of a stoppage of all business dealings. In absolute terms their trade with the East is, however, modest. The cost to the economically stronger members of the alliance of contracting the resultant loss to a tolerable level, by the provision of direct aid or alternative markets, cannot be ruled out as prohibitive. Some of the other NATO countries could expect to absorb, without unbearable economic repercussions, the damage caused by a self-imposed embargo. West Germany and Italy, for example, enjoy a balance-of-payments situation which would render adjustment quite tolerable. In the case of Denmark, Norway and the Benelux countries, the effects would be felt by several major industries, while for France and England the impact might be more national in scope.

In considering the adjusted cost to the alliance, and the availability of needed alternatives to compensate for a renunciation of commerce with an aggressive segment of the East, one should bear in mind that the actual imposition of embargo is seldom a primary aim. Cards of this type are stronger when held than when played. But in order to achieve any convincing leverage at all, a way must first be found to impress upon intractable adversaries that a realistic balance has been drawn of the likely damage to both the embargoed and the embargoing economies, and that in the face of intolerable provocation this loss will be unhesitatingly underwritten.

This is, however, the theoretical shape of the problem; on the practical plane its outlines are quite different. To put it bluntly, as the experience of the last two decades has unfolded the West has shown itself less and less capable of maintaining a cohesive and credible position on this issue, even in circumstances of dire crisis.

The extent to which allied economies would be harmed by stopping their exchanges with the East is also the measure of the East's economic leverage upon the West. A market economy is not as well placed as a command system to absorb and diffuse the shock of withheld trade, sustained in pursuit of political objectives. Nor is it as well placed to deliver the shock. A communist economy may implement trade boycotts or discriminations with quasi-military discipline, yet without public disclosure or debate.

Essentially, embargo is a totalitarian device. Except under wartime conditions, market oriented nations cannot expect to employ it effectively. The practical calculus in any long-term trade blockade yields a result which is not only different from but actually opposite to that yielded by the theoretical calculus. In pondering this fact, we need not stop at the evidence offered by the East-West situation. If a colony such as Rhodesia, with the great weight of the world seemingly against her, could not be brought to heel by means of this type, how futile is it to attempt to subdue the Soviet Union or mainland China? American policy is at long last beginning to stir toward this conclusion.

5

AMERICAN DILEMMAS IN TRADE WITH THE EAST

A. Economic Potential

The United States is not nearly as complementary a trade partner to the East as is western Europe. On the basis of industrial capacity alone it could easily play the part of a major supplier of modern machinery to the region. What it lacks is the other basic prerequisite for an effective commercial partnership, a level of demand for the exports of east European countries sufficient to support a sizable flow of industrial imports. This, together with the highly political United States approach to the issue of East-West trade, explains why the volume of recent exchanges has been so small and business interest in its growth so limited.

While overall East-West commerce exceeds an annual value of $20 billion, the United States remains a relatively declining factor in this trade, with a share of less than one percent. Its share is somewhat greater if we take into account the sale of licensed technology, shipments abroad which are reexported to the East and trade by overseas subsidiaries of American companies which benefit from proximity to the region, less stringent export controls and credit insurance made available by local governments.

Historically, a high rate of commerce between the United States and eastern Europe has been an exception rather than the rule. Exports to the U.S.S.R. have reached significant levels only on special and limited occasions: from 1930 to 1932, when foreign investments were freely admitted, between 1934 and 1938, when Germany was discredited on political grounds as a trade partner in the eyes of the Soviet government; from 1942 through 1945 when exports under the lend-lease program ran at the rate of several billion dollars annually; during the first two years after the War, when noncommercial exports, including relief and deferred-payment shipments, dominated bilateral exchanges between the two countries; and in 1964, the year of a huge nonrecurrent sale of wheat.

During the period just prior to World War II, the United States became briefly a leading supplier of goods to the U.S.S.R. Judging by the large industrial orders which the Soviet Union has placed abroad during the last few years, a considerable potential market for American sales still exists. Continental Europe, Great Britain and Japan have, however, been much quicker to supply it. While East-West trade as a whole has more than doubled in the last decade, American sales to eastern Europe have hardly attained their 1938 level.

Paradoxically, a large proportion of U.S. exports in recent years has been composed of agricultural commodities, notably hides, tallow, soya beans grain, sorghum and other foodstuffs. Yet the primary interest of the Eastern countries today is in acquiring advanced industrial technology. Within this category, the United States maintains a considerable competitive edge, particularly in computers, chemical equipment, petroleum installations, synthetic rubber, food processing machinery, metallurgy, pharmaceuticals and automobile engineering. In many sophisticated sectors of industry sizable numbers of manufacturers abroad operate under American patents and licenses. Despite what would seem to be a natural opportunity for high-technology companies, the value of transactions entered into by U.S. manufacturers has been negligible. The explanations are many. Stringent export restrictions cover the sale (and resale by foreign purchasers) to the East of technical data as well as physical products. U.S. firms fear that profits derived from dealings with a communist country will be more than offset by losses resulting from consumer boycotts at home. The East's inability to make substantial cash payments in convertible currency, and lingering doubts concerning the adequacy of industrial property protection under Eastern law and practice, also operate to limit U.S. business interest.

The future composition of America's Eastbound trade points to dealings in packages of technology and sophisticated equipment, rather than in a broad range of physical goods. Exports in the latter category can, with few exceptions (and much less difficulty from a political, regulatory and transportation point of view), be obtained from other industrial countries of the West. Yet the fact remains that the United States has much to offer the East not only in its quest for rapid industrialization, but also in its search for means of production to satisfy the long-neglected needs of private consumers. With a population of 350 million, eastern Europe bears a singular resemblance in its absorption potential to the denuded and insatiable markets which American factory and farm production found in western European countries following World War II.

One of the main obstacles to a substantial expansion of trade is the fact that typical Eastern exports have rather limited appeal for American importers. Another is the fact that the bureaucratic foreign trade apparatus of the Soviet-type economy is not well adapted to the painstaking job of responding, in volume, variety and quality, to the demand patterns of highly competitive North American markets. These are obstacles which cannot be removed merely by improving the political climate or by repealing legislative trade restrictions. It must therefore be assumed that if trade were to grow the flow of U.S. exports to the East would exceed imports for some time to come.

Clearly, increased American trade with the Eastern region can only proceed along a two-way street. If it desired to expand business contacts, the U.S. government would need to show not only a stronger willingness to facilitate exports of goods sought by the East, but also a considerably greater leniency toward imports. Extension of negotiated nondiscriminatory tariff treatment would go a long way toward increasing the scope of the United States market for goods of Eastern origin. Poland is a case in point. Following her exemption from the onerous Smoot-Hawley tariff rates, under which most communist goods are priced out of competition, that country's exports to the United States rose, in round figures, from $40 million in 1960 to $65 million in 1965 and almost $100 million in 1969.[1]

If its exports to the East are to reach volumes comparable to those of western Europe, the United States will have to make a conscious effort to become, both commercially and politically, a much more inviting outlet. The import product mix will have to go well beyond such minor staples as Polish canned ham and Russian caviar, vodka and furs. A great deal of market development would have to be undertaken by both sides. Even if Eastern industry were to perceive a lasting advantage in allocating scarce resources to the manufacture of specialty goods for export to the United States, the economic fruits born of such efforts would be long in ripening.

In the short and medium term, balance-of-payments considerations on the communist side would tend to inhibit Eastern purchases and, consequently, the growth of United States imports from the East. Inasmuch as the U.S.S.R and its smaller neighbors are neither ready nor able to divert significant quantities of gold, to take advantage of the International Monetary Fund's special drawing rights, to employ hard currencies earned elsewhere, or to sustain persistent bilateral trade deficits, expanded business relations in this area would require sizable American export credits. But to date there has been no willingness, at least not within the U.S. legislative branch, to allow either the Export-Import Bank or private financial institutions to support business on this basis.

The longer a normalization of commerce is put off, the harder it will be to alter the patterns of exchange which the East has established with other market economies. In the event of an abrupt change of diplomatic winds drawing Russia and America closer together, the ever submissive state-trading monopolies could probably manage to divert a large segment of their procurement from western Europe and Japan. At this time it would not, however, be realistic to envision the prospects of American trade with the East in vastly enlarged figures. If political tension were lessened, active promotional efforts undertaken and artificial barriers abolished, the likely annual volume of U.S. exports to the Eastern region in the early seventies might reach $500 million.[2] While this projection represents a steep rise above current levels (around $200 million), it is not quite so impressive when compared to the total United States export figure of approximately $40 billion.

The reopening of trade with communist Asia and Cuba, now completely off-limits to American firms, would, of course, considerably augment these estimates. This possibility is not as remote as may appear from the current international situation. During 1969 the U.S. government made several small but politically significant changes in the flat ban on commerce with mainland China which had prevailed since the communist takeover. In July the prohibition on tourist purchases of Chinese goods was lifted, and individual travelers were permitted to bring home up to $100 worth of goods for personal use. In December this $100 ceiling was removed. More significantly, overseas subsidiaries of American firms were authorized to trade in, finance, ship and insure Chinese goods. Although direct commerce between the United States and Peking-controlled areas is still forbidden, the cautious process of liberalization may be expected to go on. And in this connection it should be noted that the absence of outright diplomatic recognition has not always been a barrier even to direct trade. The United States was able to conduct extensive commerce with the U.S.S.R. prior to 1933, the year the Soviet government was accorded recognition.

In an economy such as the United States', which enjoys a gross national product of around one trillion dollars and contributes over 25 percent of all merchandise going to the world market from the industrially developed countries, sales of the magnitude projected here are, of course, barely significant. However, to individual industries—manufacturing enterprises, farmers and institutions offering services in connection with export and import of goods—the prospects of additional commerce cannot help but be immediately attractive. It is not surprising, therefore, that large segments of the American business community have shown impatience with repeated losses of lucrative orders to west European and Japanese firms. To the extent that political considerations permit, American companies (both domestic and offshore) will henceforth tap the increasingly inviting markets of the East much more eagerly and systematically, seeking to carve out for themselves a meaningful position against their entrenched Western competitors.

B. The Emotional Issue

For more than two decades the United States has been locked in a struggle with the Soviet Union, involving America's fundamental interests and requiring a significant portion of its material resources and political energies. Many U.S. citizens have died in armed conflicts linked in one way or another to the clash of Washington and Moscow's foreign policies. The very survival of the United States has been solemnly pledged as security against the threat of Soviet attack on certain other Western states. Even where the military interests of the two blocs have not been counterpoised the struggle has frequently been continued by other means—diplomatic, ideological and economic.

Understandably enough, the grim scenario of East-West relations, which began to unfold in the early forties and late fifties, affected the political psyche of Americans at all levels. Tensions rose continuously over such issues as the attempted Soviet takeover of northern Iran, the Czechoslovak coup d'état, the Berlin blockade, the Greek civil war and the invasion of South Korea. The American public reacted with extreme apprehension to this seemingly endless procession of crises, and braced itself for an imminent military confrontation. The whole complex of legislative and executive restrictions on trade with the East which entered the statute books between 1948 and 1951 must, therefore, be viewed in the perspective of the belief, widespread at that time, that conflict with Russia was inevitable.

Public memory, faulty as it is, holds on tenaciously to the emotional residuum left by each critical national experience. That a large segment of the U.S. economy depends on the making (and selling to the government) of military goods to help meet the communist threat is also not devoid of impact. When an $80 billion industry has been built upon the foundation of such a threat, the fears engendered are very hard to assuage. With few exceptions, the entire political spectrum of the country, from liberal to conservative, has long been strongly anticommunist. There have been important differences, to be sure, in the extent to which individual politicians have founded their foreign policy views upon opposition to communism. Moreover, a widening gulf has opened up between those who continue to place anticommunism at the center of their domestic political views and the increasingly influential younger groups who dismiss it as largely irrelevant. But even the strongest proponents of détente do not question the premise that the juxtaposition of the two superpowers makes a long-term economic and political struggle inevitable. They merely hope to move the contest out of the shadow of annihilation and into the arena of peaceful coexistence and competition.

This underlying attitude has caused Americans to look at East-West trade from a highly political point of view. Arguments about it are rarely conducted in economic terms. Advocates usually stress the concept of "building bridges," with the idea of normalizing diplomatic relations between the two blocs. Opponents are concerned lest trade subvert the security of the United States by adding to the military and economic power of the Soviet Union, Communist China and their respective satellites.

The constant flow of communist rhetoric is not calculated to ease the minds of a people who have come to regard the U.S.S.R. and its allies as implacable foes of "the American way of life." Although emanating from a distant and militant past, Lenin's boast that the capitalists will compete to sell the rope for their own hanging still carries a jarring echo. By any measure, Nikita Khrushchev's blunt dictum that his system would "bury" ours was hardly more reassuring. Today, against the background of costly Soviet support for Hanoi's and Havana's attempts to subdue or subvert their neighbors, Party Chief Leonid Brezhnev's reminders about the coming of the "world victory of communism" reinforce the image of the Soviet Union as a relentless enemy. It is not just the words but also the acts of communist leaders that periodically confirm and deepen American suspicions. Every time the long, slow, laborious process of repairing East-West relations seems to be bearing fruit, a setback is precipitated by some calculated or clumsy Soviet move, such as renewed threats to Berlin, construction of missile bases in Cuba, military occupation of Czechoslovakia, or injection of Russian combat pilots into Egypt. Given almost a quarter century of this kind of experience, it should not be surprising that many Americans regard trade with the East either as immoral or as a weak reed upon which to hang hopes for a radical reversal of communist policy.

In a free society leaders ignore these popular feelings at their peril. Quite naturally, they are on guard against being defeated in a federal or local election by virtue of a rival's ability to exploit a recurrent crisis with the Soviet Union or to discredit them as "too naive about the true nature of communism." The emotional overtones which color the American debate on East-West trade, erroneous as they may be in regard to the nation's economic and political interest, cannot, therefore, be discounted in a coldly rational manner. They must, regrettably, even today be reckoned with as significant and recurrent forces in the shaping of public opinion and business and government attitudes.

In Europe, close cooperation between government and business in promoting exports, regardless of destination, is a time-honored tradition. The mercantile community is more readily guided by official attitudes than in the United States. In England (and the major continental countries) the commercial policy of the nation, in all its aspects, is forged in the privacy of the Board of Trade's oak-paneled conference rooms rather than in the heat of partisan parliamentary debate or in emotion-tinged public discussion.

Such is not the case on the opposite side of the Atlantic. In the highly charged atmosphere in which the issues of East-West trade are contested, the more fanatic opponents of commercial traffic with communism have occasionally, and with some success, sought to penalize offending companies. Boycotts have been organized against products imported from Eastern countries. Letter-writing campaigns have been conducted against firms willing to export to the communist bloc, often combined with a threat to sabotage their sales in the home market.

In many parts of the United States random individuals and organized groups have often taken it upon themselves to obstruct all forms of economic intercourse with communist countries, in ways which prompted one highly placed Washington official to suggest that "their patriotism exceeds their understanding."[3] A wide range of spontaneously blossoming techniques has been adopted. The picketing of stores and supermarkets handling goods of Eastern origin has been a favorite form of protest. In certain towns permanent "Committees to Warn of the Arrival of Communist Merchandise on the Local Scene" have sprung up. Under the auspices of such organizations, political warning notices have frequently been attached to hams imported from Poland, vases from Czechoslovakia, baskets from Yugoslavia, and so forth. Moreover, in response to local pressure groups, state laws and municipal ordinances of doubtful constitutional validity have been promulgated with a view to restraining the sale of communist merchandise. Typically these ordinances require shops to tag goods imported from the East and to obtain special licenses authorizing their sale.[4]

Such activities have more than once caused the cancelation of transactions which were on the verge of being completed. In an unknowable number of instances they have inhibited companies from entering into negotiations with Eastern trade representatives for fear of the political consequences. A number of major U.S. corporations have actively considered trade possiblities and have decided, in the end, that potential economic gains are outweighed by the possibility of adverse effects on their public relations. This is why the bulk of American involvement in East-West trade is carried on by companies that do not market consumer-oriented goods and are, therefore, relatively less vulnerable to pressure from right-wing elements.

The rash of initiatives by well-meaning but overzealous citizens to enforce a home-brewed "patriotic" attitude in the conduct of U.S. foreign affairs has at times reached a point where it became necessary for the administration to take determined counteraction. George W. Ball, Under-Secretary of State in the Johnson Administration, stated the problem in these terms:

> It is absolutely unacceptable that right wing or left wing or any other kind of groups should by intimidation or by threat of boycott try to subvert or to undermine the foreign policy of the United States, which has to be conducted by the President and Congress under the American Constitution.[5]

The same issue surfaced in another guise, in connection with the Vietnam Moratorium and the Dow Chemical Company's production of napalm bombs under contract with the Pentagon. In any democratic society, where the right of dissent is constitutionally sanctified, those in authority cannot avoid facing the music from whatever political direction it may come, once public emotion flows over into the streets. Even within communism's own bosom, the maintenance of normal business traffic with the most conspicuous "enemies of the working class movement" has occasionally taken on moral and emotional overtones. A bitter polemic was sparked at the 19th Congress of the French Communist Party, held in February 1970, over deliveries of Polish coal to Spain while the Asturian miners were on strike and of a Soviet electric power station to the "fascist government of Greece." But the tortuous processes of dialectical materialism never fail to provide an exit from ideological dilemma.[6]

In the United States, Cabinet level officials, the Secretaries of State, Defense and Commerce, have gone so far as to issue, in 1965, a joint public statement denouncing the idea of privately inspired boycotts and supporting the right of business firms to engage in the legal importation of goods from Eastern countries. Clearly, this was an unusual action, taken after due deliberation and based on the valid assumption that patriotism is an emotional force of unpredictable impact when it bursts into the essentially rational sphere of private business calculation and public policy-making.

In much the same vein, the Department of State found it necessary in 1966 to release a pamphlet which spelled out in popular language the case against the obstruction of foreign policy and the harassment of private merchants acting entirely within their rights and in accordance with the laws and regulations governing the nation's commerce. In one passage the pamphlet, entitled "Private Boycotts versus the National Interest," makes the following points:

> Any citizen may properly exercise his constitutional right to speak freely. But any organization, however patriotic in intention, that undertakes to boycott, blacklist, or otherwise penalize or attack any American business for engaging in peaceful trade with eastern European countries or the Soviet Union is acting against the interest of the United States.[7]

Nevertheless, the issue has not been laid to rest. In the wake of every recurrent political crisis involving Russia or China, popular feeling wells to the surface and spills over into some act of overt indignation. This has included a general call for economic ostracism of the Warsaw Pact powers that participated in the military occupation of Czechoslovakia, a refusal on the part of longshoremen to unload goods of communist origin and pressure by seamen, motivated by self-interest rather than a sense of public duty, to enforce the use of domestic tonnage in the delivery of American cargo to Russia. It will be recalled that in connection with the highly controversial 1963–1964 wheat deal President Kennedy felt compelled, in the face of such tactics, to announce that American bottoms would transport at least 50 percent of the quantities shipped. The considerably higher costs were partly absorbed by the taxpayer through federal subsidies.[8]

The Janus-faced compromise reached by Congress in December 1969 on the extension of the Export Control Act, a piece of legislation of early cold war vintage, suggests that some U.S. politicians are now willing to chance the consequences of being tagged as supporters of increased trade with the East. Whether they are right in their assessment of the public mood and whether efforts to boycott communist goods are destined to fade as a meaningful weapon are questions likely to be answered in the early 1970's.

C. The Stigma of "Trading with the Enemy"

Given this background of intense, widespread public feeling on the issue of trade with the communist world, individual business firms have had to act with great caution. The ramifications of the Vietnam conflict have clearly militated against the open consummation of many major transactions. One of the most instructive examples of this was the 1965 controversy surrounding the importation of tobacco grown in Yugoslavia. A virulent campaign emerged against the blending of such tobacco (1 percent of the total) into American cigarettes. All the major cigarette manufacturers, those who used the ingredient and those who did not, joined to reject the threat of boycott.[9] The principal factor which made this refusal effective was industry-wide solidarity.

Yet, in another instance which raised a similar challenge to an entire industry, such solidarity was conspicuously absent; leading competitors could not resist the temptation to make hay out of the public relations predicament of one of their peers. This involved what was probably the most ambitious and effective case of harassment directed at a single firm: the campaign of the "Young Americans for Freedom," a group with a strong anticommunist bias, against the Firestone Rubber Company. In late November 1964 it became known that the company was about to proceed with a $50 million contract to build a synthetic rubber plant in Rumania. Firestone's action was taken partly under prodding from the Department of State, which earlier that year had signed a bilateral agreement with the mellowing Bucharest government in anticipation of a substantial increase in two-way trade. At this point the Young Americans began to picket the company's headquarters in Akron, Ohio, with placards bearing the legend: "Firestone is building the future war machine of Communism." Nor did their zeal stop there. The next step was to urge various dealers who sold Firestone products at retail to cancel all contractual arrangements with the company. Two or three of the dealers succumbed to these pressure tactics. The company took alarm, decided not to sign its contract with Rumania, and the much-publicized deal collapsed.

This incident points up the vulnerability of large firms in the East-West arena. A revealing contrast is provided by the outcome of a comparable situation. At about the same time as Firestone, the Universal Oil Products Company of Des Plaines, Illinois, had reached an agreement with the Rumanian government to build a petroleum cracking plant near the Ploesti oil fields. This firm was able to execute its contract without pressure from vigilante groups for the simple reason that its products are generally sold to industry and not to the public at large. Hence, it did not have to worry about safeguarding its precious trademark against unfavorable publicity. In due time, a substantial Export-Import Bank guarantee was secured and the project proceeded to successful completion.

Few American companies, large or small, can afford to close their eyes to the risk of harassment. Even firms which serve corporate clients, and not the man in the street, will pause before offending stockholders, employees, customers or suppliers who sincerely believe that business dealings with a communist enterprise constitute a disservice to the United States. Moreover, harmful action may be stimulated by interested competitors under the guise of publicly manifested concern. In one instance the lobby of a heavily protected industry was able to work its will against an importer of Soviet school supplies in the form of an amendment to the National Defense Education Act which prohibited the purchase by the government of any teaching equipment in the field of science, mathematics or modern languages, "originating in or having been exported from a communist country."

Wholly foreign firms too, particularly those substantially involved in the U.S. market, have been known to decline or camouflage legitimate transactions with the East for fear of displeasing their American clients. Occasionally such firms have been victims of attitudes adopted by their governments. This was demonstrated by the angry American reactions to Sweden's persistent harboring of deserters from the Vietnam war and the announcement, in October 1969, of a proposed $40 million aid grant to Hanoi. Prices fell on the Stockholm stock exchange, especially those of large and vulnerable companies such as Volvo (automobiles) and Stora Kopparberg (mining). The latter was reported to have lost 33.6 million dollars in instantly canceled orders.[10]

Even when offered the possibility of lucrative, government-approved transactions with communist enterprises, many United States companies weigh with extreme caution the extent to which they may be endangering sales in their permanent domestic market. As a rule, they prefer to shield such transactions under the veil of an off-shore subsidiary, usually one incorporated in Europe. Activities in this area are entrusted to foreign-based executives versed in the subtle art of minimizing political hazards. The subsidiary may be established abroad for the purposes of a specific project, with a corporate name other than that of the parent company. Alternatively, the contemplated transaction may be structured in such a way as to furnish supplies, know-how, or services through a foreign-owned firm, an extraterritorial licensee, a joint venture, or a consortium including western European or Japanese groups, with the non-American parties taking the ostensible leadership in contract negotiation.

A measure of safety may also be found in official administrative endorsements. The much maligned export licensing system performs a welcome function in this respect. To the extent that it places upon the Federal government responsibility for judgments concerning the security of the United States, a considerable burden is removed from the shoulders of the willing exporter. During the Johnson Administration explicit written endorsements were occasionally sought from the Department of State or even the White House before an East-West transaction was concluded. These documents were intended for release to the press at the time a major agreement with a communist enterprise was signed, or later on, in the event public controversy arose. Endorsements of this type amounted to either a general policy statement, or an expression of approval addressed to a particular company or industry (*e.g.,* the letter of the Secretaries of State, Defense and Commerce to the major cigarette manufacturers in connection with the threatened Yugoslav tobacco boycott).[11] An example of the former was a declaration issued by Secretary of State Dean Rusk in 1966:

> All American citizens should know that any American businessman who chooses to engage in peaceful trade with the Soviet Union or Eastern European countries . . . is acting within his rights and is following the policy of his Government.[12]

It remains to be seen whether outright support for firms engaged in East-West trade will also be available under the Nixon Presidency. Thus far the

American trading community has not been given clearly to understand that the Administration whole-heartedly approves of expanded exchange with the East. Accordingly, business efforts in that direction are still plagued by self-doubt and timidity. Until such time as the government takes forthright steps to enlighten and reassure the public on the complex ramifications of this effervescent issue, many would-be traders will either shy away from dealing in the area or seek protection against its inherent political risks.

D. Policies in Flux

After the legislative and administrative inhibitions which dominated the nineteen-fifties, the Kennedy and Johnson Administrations cautiously began to lead congressional and public opinion toward acceptance of the more sanguine view that under present world conditions it is important for political as well as security reasons to develop trade and other constructive relations with communist Europe. The principal arguments offered in support of this view—some of them echoing long-standing attitudes of other Western governments—were as follows:

1. Increased contacts with the East would help to counteract or reduce the suspicions, tensions and frictions that arise from time to time in various parts of the world and bring violence in their wake. It is precisely the presence of grave differences that require the exploration of possible points of agreement.

2. The "iron curtain" erected by Stalin was one of the most serious threats to international understanding and peace. Consequently, whatever could be done to encourage contacts—through tourism, trade, consular relations, joint scientific research—would help foster acceptance of the value of Western experience to Eastern economic development. This, in turn, would lead to an atmosphere of mutual tolerance and the emergence of more open societies within the communist orbit.

3. America's close relations with its own allies in western Europe would continue to suffer, and the United States would become steadily more isolated and less relevant to the European situation, if it persisted in striking an inflexibly negative attitude toward peaceful trade relations with the Eastern half of the continent. The degree of economic interdependence that had gradually evolved within the West, moreover, made it quite urgent for common responses to commercial problems all around the world to be based on a shared appreciation of the economic realities of contemporary international life.

4. Concessions facilitating expanded trade, cultural exchanges and other contacts with eastern Europe would strengthen the hands of those in the communist countries who favored a peaceful solution of foreign policy differences. More specifically, this posture would cast weight on the scales of international politics against the virulent brand of communism practiced and advocated by the present leaders of mainland China, who were preaching the doctrine of inevitable conflict between the socialist and the capitalist world.

5. Since the smaller economies of eastern Europe are heavily dependent upon foreign trade, broader opportunities for the exchange of goods and know-how with the West would reduce their economic and political dependence upon the Soviet Union.

In general, the opponents of liberalization make the following major arguments:

1. Attempts to increase trade with the Eastern countries, even in such peaceful goods as farm products, are in conflict with the professed objective of reducing communist influence in the world: "We cannot feed and fight communism at the same time."

2. Any expansion in trade with the Soviet Union and eastern Europe helps to reinforce the potential enemy's strategic power: goods imported from the outside help to free local resources for work on advanced weapon systems.

3. To assume that by helping to create an affluent society in eastern Europe the United States can make the leaders of these countries less belligerent toward the outside world is a thesis not validated by history. Germany, under Nazi rule, launched an all-out war not because it lacked industrial sophistication, but because such a war was justified by the official ideology.

4. Mutual confidence between America and the Soviet Union will not be a by-product of increased trade. To argue differently is to put the cart before the horse. If the other side demonstrated its goodwill in helping to make the world more secure, the necessary climate for better trade relations could then be easily created.

5. Advocacy of increased commercial shipments to Russia to help develop its industrial complex contradicts efforts to bring the Vietnam war to an early and successful end, since the Soviet Union ships modern weapons for use against America's own armed forces.

6. Before entering into any undertaking to relax restrictions on com-

merce, the ground must first be prepared. Precise demands should be made upon those countries of the East which want and need American exports and the credits necessary to support them. If such political objectives were not achieved in advance, the communists alone would gain from a relaxation of trade controls.

Under the influence of the more benign policy approach, the actual movement of goods to and from eastern Europe registered modest gains. In its efforts to further the trend, however, the government found itself repeatedly caught in crossfire. On one side it was vulnerable to attack from segments of the population who continued to resist expansion of East-West trade under any circumstances, as a matter of basic political conviction. On the other it was severely criticized by those among the public and the business community who were of a more pragmatic bent of mind—that is to say, those who favored ampler contacts across the ideological barrier and freer access to the rapidly opening markets of the East.

Differences among departments responsible for the promotion of sales abroad and those charged with foreign policy and national defense have also come to the surface, particularly in arriving at a definition of proscribed strategic exports. At the heart of these differences is the gnawing question of whether the United States should sell that which the East most desires—packages of high technology. Yet herein resides a fundamental paradox. The universally acknowledged American lead in applied scientific know-how over communist (indeed, all other industrial) countries, the notorious technology gap, should probably be narrowed rather than widened. Is it not axiomatic that he who sells the most advanced technology sells obsolescence? By definition, the vendor country is bound to remain ahead of the vendee. It is sufficient, even preferable, that the distance between the two be small, perhaps five to ten percent. Once it becomes much larger, the market shrinks accordingly, since that much less can then be productively absorbed by the potential buyer.

Be that as it may, the Executive branch, within the laws which it administers, enjoys a substantial amount of flexibility. When President Johnson announced on October 7, 1966, that he was reducing export controls on "hundreds of nonstrategic items," that he had "signed a determination" allowing extension of commercial credit guarantees to Poland, Hungary, Bulgaria and Czechoslovakia and that his administration was negotiating a civil air agreement with the Soviet Union, he was exercising existing powers. Clearly, the President had significantly altered U.S. policy without feeling a need to appeal for legislative assent.

There is, however, a decided limit to what any administration can accomplish on its own initiative. Much more is required to eliminate the underlying political obstacles to East-West trade. The Departments of State and Commerce, and even the White House itself, have sporadically encouraged public protrade statements on the part of business and industry leaders whose patriotism, public service records and worldly realism are beyond question. While such initiatives may create a better political climate for administrative liberalization, the critical authority—to abolish discriminatory tariff walls, credit restrictions and various other impediments—can only come from the Congress. Nothing can be more effective in assuring the business community of the legitimacy of East-West trade than a positive act of law expressing the sense of the Senate and the House of Representatives that such trade should be increased.

In 1966, one year after a committee of distinguished citizens appointed by the White House had recommended liberalized trade, the Administration submitted its own proposal for legislative action in the form of a draft "East-West Trade Relations Act."[13] While the bill failed, its omnibus approach remains valid for the future. Congress delegates to the President the right to negotiate commercial agreements with individual countries of eastern Europe in order "to obtain concessions and benefits that will serve the national interest of our country in return for granting the same tariff arrangements already available to other countries."[14] The President is allowed to extend most-favored-nation treatment in return for balanced concessions of various kinds. The resultant nondiscriminatory basis of importation remains in effect for the duration of the particular agreement and only as long as the countercommitments are faithfully carried out. Bilateral negotiation affords the U.S. government an opportunity to deal with communist countries one by one and to review specific issues, whether related to trade or not, as they arise from time to time. The government-to-government arrangements only provide a legal framework for commerce (as in the case of the Soviet-United States commercial agreement of 1937); specific business dealings are left to the discretion of individual firms.

The Congressional attitude toward any East-West trade measure is as difficult to assess as the prevailing Executive position. Both houses include inchoate blocs of supporters as well as opponents of expanded economic contacts with the East, and occasionally the issue is turned into a political football irrelevant to proper legislative behavior.

The Vietnam war, in which European and Asian communist nations ostentatiously supported the enemy forces opposing the U.S., had temporarily strengthened Congressional opinion against a more liberal trade and credit policy, just as Soviet actions did in the 1948–1952 period. A highly revealing Senate vote came on August 10, 1967, with regard to the extension of the lending authority of the Export-Import Bank. Even though the President's position on foreign policy issues carries more weight in the Senate than in the House, opponents of East-West trade used the Vietnam situation as their vehicle to push through an amendment barring a credit guarantee by the Bank for $50 million-worth of American machine tools sought by Italy's Fiat for use in building a Soviet automobile plant.[15] This vote, 56 to 25, was an impressive victory for the restrictive forces.

Against this background of long-standing hostility, it is quite apparent why several attempts, by both the Executive branch and individual members of the Congress, have failed to produce any fundamental modification in the legislative and administrative framework of East-West economic relations. During the rest of his term, President Johnson did not even resubmit his own 1966 proposal. Decidedly, the odds seemed too heavily weighted against any conspicuous shift in policy toward the communist world, as long as the Vietnam conflict remained unresolved.

By January 1969, when the Democrats left office, little had been accomplished beyond opening the subject of East-West trade for public debate. Yet this was no small accomplishment. Until the 1963–1964 sale of wheat to the U.S.S.R., office holders and corporate executives were rarely willing to risk the political or economic sanctions that seemed likely to be visited on those foolhardy enough to advocate expanded commerce with the East. Although the positive achievements on this issue were relatively modest under the Kennedy and Johnson Administrations, they must be credited with changing the psychological climate, making it respectable for businessmen to think actively about commerce with eastern Europe and encouraging some members of Congress to talk openly about mitigating the trade control system erected at the height of tensions with Russia.

In this new climate a number of U.S. companies began cautiously to explore trade prospects. Some were even prepared to question publicly the logic behind the strict supervision imposed by the United States on the sale of "strategic" goods. When the incoming Nixon Administration requested an extension without change of the Export Control Act of 1949, hearings before the Senate Banking Committee brought an impressive outpouring of testimony from executives of leading high technology companies, calling for freer exchange of goods.[16] This new boldness in the business community abetted the determination of key Senate members to amend the statute. Their efforts were resisted by the White House, which contended that relaxation of trade restrictions should await a broader East-West accommodation. The House of Representatives supported the latter position, though there also the proponents of change seemed stronger than in the past. The outcome, reflected in the Trade Administration Act of 1969, was something of a stalemate. Much of the cold war rhetoric was eliminated from the legislation, together with certain licensing criteria that encouraged refusals. But the final compromise preserved the President's fundamental authority to control all transactions which might impair the national security. Although Congress directed the freeing of most of the items now available to the East from other Western sources, and by implication established a propitious setting for other liberalizations, supporters and opponents alike acknowledge that practical results will depend on the nature of the Act's day-to-day administration.

The United States government's present attitude toward East-West trade can only be described as ambivalent. It is too early to say whether President Johnson's request for broad enabling legislation on the subject will be revived by the Nixon Administration. Certainly, the almost unreserved hostility toward wider contacts with the communist orbit, which characterized the late 1940s and early 1950s, is no longer present. Given the Administration's current hopes for a negotiated settlement of an entire spectrum of unresolved political issues, it would seem essential that the President should have authority to normalize economic relations as well, and to use the prospect of increased trade as a chip in the overall bargaining equation.

At this writing, therefore, it would be unsafe to conclude that the United States has passed a turning point in its commercial relations with the Soviet Union and eastern Europe. American misgivings about a stepped-up exchange of goods remain strong and widespread. Even those favorably disposed to it accept the need for strategic commodity controls. Only future developments can determine whether 1969 was a true dawn for East-West trade. For instance, although the initiative of leadership on the issue has passed to Congress, oncoming elections could make it impossible for Senate sponsors of the new legislation to pressure the bureaucracy into a liberal pattern of administration. Yet the attraction of the eastern European markets, long submerged by cold war antagonisms, has unmistakably begun to surface. A great many companies are eager to indulge their impulse to trade and are only awaiting the government's nod of approval.

Finally, the issue of trade so far has not suggested a clear American response to the important policy conflict between the U.S.S.R. and China, over the propriety of war as an instrument to resolve international political disputes. In spite of the Administration's recent gestures of symbolic liberalization, any ambitious effort to adopt, via the Congress, a more permissive overall posture, with meaningful impact beyond the European communist countries, must await a healing of wounds opened by the war in Southeast Asia and by the use of Red armies to stifle democratic aspirations in neighboring states. These are the horns of the American dilemma at the beginning of a new decade.

6

WESTERN REGULATION OF EAST-WEST TRANSACTIONS

A. The Scope of National Restrictions

The West's economic relations with communist countries are covered by a maze of national and international restrictions on exports, imports, credits and other activities auxiliary to trade. The result stops short of a *lex specialis* for dealings with Eastern enterprises, comparable to the separate legal framework which the East has developed for relations with capitalist firms. Basically, all market economies allow their general commercial regimes to govern East-West transactions. But particularized provisions, with their source in parliamentary legislation, governmental regulation and inter-state agreements, have been sporadically engrafted onto norms of universal application.

Despite the recent perceptible relaxation of American controls and western Europe's determination to go its own way, the highlights of national and international practice in this field retain more than historical relevance. For we must not lose sight of the condition of political flux which is perennially built into the East-West situation. Successive periods of armed truce, local hot-war skirmishes, trends toward peaceful coexistence and unexpected return to the cold war have all left an imprint on the manner in which governments implemented their long-standing statutory measures on commerce with the East as a whole or with any of its regional components. Few Western countries, even in periods of prolonged diplomatic thaw, have shown eagerness to dismantle their control schemes entirely. Only criteria of administrative interpretation and enforcement have been eased here and there.

American policy has long followed a graduated approach toward East-West trade. Three distinct degrees of severity were consistently reflected in national law and practice: total embargo on business dealings with Communist China, North Korea, North Vietnam and Cuba; selective restriction on trade with the U.S.S.R. and its more orthodox Warsaw Pact allies; a more permissive and even promotional attitude in regard to the rest of the region.

Because the United States has had to carry the primary burden not only of its own defense, but also of that of the free world as a whole, its overall controls on economic dealings with the Sino-Soviet orbit have, unavoidably, been more sweeping than those of other Western nations. A mélange of special legislation, specific riders to laws of general application, broad interpretation of permanent "emergency" statutes (such as the Trading with the Enemy Act) and discretionary use of government authority has closed the doors of the American economy to enterprises of Eastern origin almost to the same degree as the communist markets have been placed beyond the spontaneous reach of Western firms.

In the upshot, the American business community's ability to compete freely with firms of other Western nations has been regulated away. A measure of parity in the contest for Eastern orders has been achieved by means of subsidiaries or joint ventures based in western Europe, Canada or Japan. Opportunities for escaping the highly controlled domestic environment are, however, still very limited.

At home, on pain of criminal prosecution, those who act on behalf of any government are required, under the Foreign Agents Registration Act, to file with the Attorney General information revealing the nature of their relationships, activities and other data, such as income earned and disbursements made in the process. The law exempts persons active in connection with their principals' private commerce, but registration may, nonetheless, be required if the activities are deemed to be political in nature, *e.g.,* lobbyists, public relations firms, purchasing agents, sales representatives, investment offices and other government-sponsored functions.

Since commerce in the East is a sovereign function performed exclusively by the state, the line of demarcation between what is private and non-private in the activities of an American business representative cannot help being a hazy one. This fact, and the stigma which may attach in the

American political climate to the technical words "foreign agent" (particularly when the principal is a communist state instrumentality), are serious deterrents to the creation of an effective Eastern marketing organization.

The resultant difficulties are more acute than would appear at first sight. Unlike other Western countries, the United States has never admitted official, diplomatically immune Eastern trade delegations to engage in commerce as permanently resident organizations. The possibility of dealing through the incorporated, and therefore, nonofficial Eastern export-import enterprises offers a poor substitute for full access to the United States market. Such enterprises have turned out to be ineffective business promotion tools even in far more receptive markets. Nor is the Soviet-staffed Amtorg Trading Corporation of New York more than an instrument of limited utility, owing to its administrative and equity links with the Soviet Foreign Trade Ministry and the high degree of United States scrutiny to which it is consequently subject. The Foreign Agents Registration Act's application to Amtorg is only one instance of this surveillance.

Entry, sojourn and circulation within the United States of communist trade officials is closely circumscribed by Federal regulation. Under the Immigration and Nationality Act, aliens with current or past Communist Party affiliations are excluded, unless they are duly accredited by a recognized foreign government and formally accepted by the Secretary of State. The Secretary has wide discretion to rule on the admissibility of Eastern trade representatives seeking to purchase or sell goods in the American market. As a rule, visas are granted if a legitimate business purpose is involved.

Once admitted, the representative does not automatically enjoy the same freedom of movement as visitors from other countries. In 1952, special restrictions on travel to designated areas were imposed upon Soviet citizens (other than members of the United Nations Secretariat) present within the United States, as retaliation for comparable restrictions practiced by the U.S.S.R. against American citizens. Waivers for visiting business officials may be, and usually are, granted, if there is a proper reason for entry into a restricted area.

U.S. administrative authority is exercised over American businessmen as well, in connection with travel to potentially lucrative Eastern markets. In particular, Communist China, North Korea, North Vietnam and Cuba[1] have been placed off limits and infringement is considered a ground for passport revocation.

Other discriminatory provisions affect communist enterprises less obviously. For instance, United States guarantees of private investments in less developed countries do not extend to economically backward areas of the communist East.[2] The effect of this limitation is to withhold incentives from such investments as may become feasible in these areas.

Similarly (and understandably enough, because the U.S. sees no reason to assume any special responsibility for their advancement), the less developed countries within the Sino-Soviet orbit are expressly excluded from the exceptions established in favor of lagging economies under the Interest Equalization Act of 1963 and the Foreign Direct Investment Regulations of 1968. The former imposes a tax on American purchases of foreign stocks or debt obligations. The latter forbids the outflow of funds for direct investment abroad (in excess of amounts determined by formula) without Department of Commerce authorization. Only Yugoslavia among the east European countries has been granted dispensation along with "other less developed countries."[3]

Beyond this assortment of restraints which directly or indirectly affect economic relations with the East, American regulations extend, with both domestic and extraterritorial impact, to export and shipment controls, import discriminations, specific product prohibitions, credit limitations and other provisions of a trade inhibiting nature. In addition, the United States has arrogated to itself the right, based on its role as a donor of foreign aid, to legislate and even impose sanctions, with a view to discouraging friendly foreign countries from selling strategic goods to the East.

The American restrictions extend far beyond the limited sphere of commerce with communist countries. To ensure effective execution of its legislative mandate, the Administration has evolved systematic procedures for the supervision and punishment of Western buyers in connection with the unauthorized transshipment of strategic goods and know-how of U.S. origin. Similarly, it regulates the Eastern trade activities of foreign companies controlled from within the United States. In this manner, America's world-wide commerce, the activities of wholly alien firms which import from the United States and of foreign-based business ventures in which American groups participate are all affected by U.S. security measures, and the psychological environment in which they are implemented.

At the multilateral level, Western controls have their source in treaties, inter-state coordination procedures and arrangements for mutual assistance in matters of enforcement. Regionally, the European Common Market offers an example of national and emerging supranational measures governing the admission of Eastern goods. Even broader geographic cooperation is required by the so-called Berne Union, in connection with the provision of suppliers' credit. In more global terms, COCOM, an offshoot of the NATO alliance, has been the vehicle for maintaining a strategic list of internationally embargoed commodities. Their shipment to the East is subject to screening by fifteen participating powers: the United States, the United Kingdom, France, Italy, the Netherlands, Belgium, Luxembourg, Norway, Denmark, Canada, West Germany, Portugal, Greece, Turkey as well as Japan.

B. Import Restraints

1. United States

The Trade Agreements Extension Act of 1951 was the basic legislative enactment under which the United States withdrew most-favored-nation treatment from Eastern-origin goods. As a result, imports from communist-dominated areas lost their automatic entitlement to conditions of entry comparable with those accorded products of other nations. Yugoslavia, having demonstrated its independent aspirations in the 1948 Tito-Stalin rupture, was the only east European state to escape this restriction. Poland was restored to most-favored-nation standing in 1960, on the basis of a Presidential determination that it was not "subject to domination or control by a foreign government or organization controlling the world communist movement."

Currently, the status of imports from the East rests upon Section 231 of the Trade Expansion Act of 1962. Under this measure most-favored-nation privileges may not be granted to any communist state. However, a 1963 amendment enabled the President to determine that extension of non-discriminatory treatment to Yugoslavia and Poland was important to the United States' national interest and would promote the independence of these two countries from "domination or control by international communism."[4]

The net result is that imports from all other communist countries labor under an onerous competitive disadvantage. Specifically, they face custom levies established under the Smoot-Hawley Tariff Act of 1930, at rates materially higher than those which affect goods from friendly nations. In other words, the far-reaching tariff concessions which the United States has extended over the years under bilateral and multilateral agreements concluded from 1934 to the Kennedy Round of 1967 are not available to most of the Eastern countries. By the same token, American importers must often buy elsewhere at higher prices goods which might otherwise have been acquired more cheaply in the East.

In addition, the entry of goods originating in Communist China, North Korea, North Vietnam and Cuba is foreclosed altogether under the Foreign Assets Control Regulations and the Cuban Assets Control Regulations, issued pursuant to the Trading with the Enemy Act of 1917.[5] Purchases from these areas (with symbolic exceptions recently established in favor of non-commercial Chinese and Chinese-type imports) can be introduced into the United States only on the basis of a license issued by the Treasury's Office of Foreign Assets Control. Such licenses are rarely granted.

Moreover, the prohibitions affect not only commercial entities, or individuals who are nationals or residents of the United States, but also foreign firms, corporations and business associations controlled by Americans. Except for Chinese articles, liberalized in this respect as of the beginning of 1970, such foreign entities cannot even acquire goods of proscribed Chinese origin for utilization or consumption abroad. The continuing embargo encompasses commodities originating in the designated areas, as well as products made therefrom, regardless of where the manufacturing takes place. For example, Bolivian cigars containing Cuban tobacco would fall within the scope of the blockade.

Implementation of the embargo poses considerable product identification difficulties. Doubts as to the actual origin of goods traditionally supplied by the quarantined regions are resolved in favor of exclusion. The resultant interference with admittedly legal trade is deemed to be outweighed by the desire to maintain an effective bar against imports from this part of the communist world. The buckshot approach to exclusion is mitigated to the extent that certificates of origin are available from the exporting country under procedures approved by the U.S. government. Virtually all exports from Hong Kong or Macao are presumed by the Treasury to be communist-Asian goods, unless otherwise certified.

The same applies to certain Japanese articles. Indeed, one of the legislative criteria which render goods susceptible to Japanese export control is whether a certificate of origin is required. This verification process was instituted mainly to placate the United States and to help in the implementation of its regulations affecting imports from adjacent communist areas.[6]

The erratic impact of the Treasury's policy was vividly demonstrated by an incident which involved the entry of foreign-made wigs. In November 1965, the Office of Foreign Assets Control, having learned that Communist China had become a major supplier of human hair, decided to embargo all hairpieces containing such strands. However, in face of the utterly insuperable identification difficulties, a ruling was issued excluding products made from human hair of any Asiatic origin unless accompanied by an acceptable certificate.[7] Shortly thereafter, the Treasury took the further step of excluding *all* uncertified human hair products shipped from the United Kingdom, France, Belgium, West Germany and Italy. No approved system of certification as to origin was then in effect in these countries. The embargo threatened to put out of business most European makers of wigs, eyelashes, moustaches, beards and related items, whose aggregate sales to the American market exceeded $10 million per year. That some of the affected exporters had been supplying the United States for generations and were willing to guarantee the European content in their products did not mollify the Treasury.

A scurry of diplomatic activity ensued on both sides of the Atlantic and endless embarrassments were averted by the rapid establishment of bilateral certification procedures with each of the supplier countries.

Inevitably, in this hair-conscious era, the incident prompted irreverent references to bureaucratic hair-splitting.[8] For it is, in fact, difficult to ponder with solemnity the difference between Caucasian and Mongolian tresses; let alone distinguish a Korean hair plucked North of the 38th Parallel from a lock raped in the noncommunist South. The perfectly serious aspect of the issue should not, however, be overlooked. The United States had succeeded in imposing upon its allies elaborate administrative control procedures for the purpose of implementing a uniquely American policy. Moreover, as a concomitant of this policy, Washington had shown itself ready to disrupt the legitimate trade of European merchants in noncommunist goods.

Apart from this general scheme of import controls, selected products are subject to special regulation, occasionally inspired by domestic competitors who have been able to exploit the anticommunist sentiments of Congress. Thus the tariff legislation currently in force reproduces Section II of the Trade Agreements Extension Act of 1951, which embargoed the importation of furs and fur skins of mainland Chinese as well as Soviet origin, specifically ermine, fox, kolinsky, marten, mink, muskrat and weasel. The purchase of bamboo pipestems from communist Asia is also expressly prohibited. In addition, government funds appropriated for educational purposes cannot be used to purchase Eastern school laboratory equipment, unless unavailable elsewhere.[9]

Another prohibition with strong political overtones is the Tariff Act's exclusion of goods produced with convict or forced labor. In the past, this provision had been invoked against the entry of Soviet crabmeat. Imports of certain Siberian commodities, timber, for example, have also been vulnerable to attack on the ground that they were produced by political prisoners exiled to corrective labor camps.[10]

There is nothing abnormal about the fact that authority over the importation (and exportation) of highly sensitive goods from all origins may indirectly affect Eastern products. For instance, under various legislative enactments the State Department regulates the purchase of arms, ammunition and implements of war along with related technology; the Atomic Energy Commission exercises parallel jurisdiction within its own sphere; and the entry of gold and narcotics is controlled by the Treasury. In the area of general legislation, communist origin goods are, however, exceptionally vulnerable to certain types of penalties imposed at the custom house.

Antidumping and countervailing duties are examples in point. The former may be imposed if the goods in question are introduced into the United States at an "unfair price" as compared with the selling price at which they are offered in *their* own country, or their known cost of production. The result sought is a form of equalization. The latter levy is intended to neutralize foreign export subsidies. Pricing, costing and currency exchange rates are, of course, notoriously arbitrary notions in the framework of a collective economy. Furthermore, such an economy can easily conceal the earmarks of export subsidization. Inasmuch as all of these elements elude precise measurement, Eastern origin imports may trigger administrative inquiry and, eventually, protective action more readily than imports from market economies.

Import discrimination may also manifest itself in the exercise of day-to-day administrative functions. Thus under the "Buy American" Act of 1933 United States agencies and companies acting in execution of government contracts are required to favor local goods, unless the cost is unreasonable or the public interest is adversely affected. An Executive Order has added national security considerations as an element in the procurement equation.[11] Hence it may be assumed that political considerations militate against communist origin goods with respect to purposes covered by the Act, when such goods compete for selection with materials from domestic or friendly foreign sources.

An interesting application of this approach was President Johnson's rejection (made on the recommendation of the Interior Department) of a Soviet bid to supply giant hydro-electric turbines and generators for the Grand Coulee Dam. The superiority of Russian technology in this area was widely acknowledged. Although the refusal was based on factors of national security which were sufficient to exclude suppliers from friendly countries as well, a statement attributed to an official of the Department of the Interior suggests that the motivation was more complex: "It wouldn't do to have these generators, the largest in the world, labeled with a hammer and sickle."[12]

2. *Western Europe*

Although less severely than the United States, most Western countries also discriminate against communist-origin goods. Such discriminations include tariff penalties, quantitative restrictions and outright prohibitions. Whether openly stated or veiled, the true intent has not always been purely economic. In enacting at the height of the Korean conflict its own 1951 law designed to penalize Eastern imports, the United States Congress made no mystery of its political motivation in denying the communist countries of Europe and Asia the dollar exchange which they so eagerly sought to earn. Allied nations were, at the time, similarly motivated, partly by reason of independent conviction and, to some extent, under the impact of American pressure. Today, political factors tend to work in favor of a relaxation of such trade barriers, particularly on the continent of Europe.

Beyond politics, it has gradually become clear to all market economies accustomed to dealing with one another on GATT principles that a classically conceived exchange of most-favored-nation treatment promises with total state-trading countries is, at best, a one-sided trade concession; at worst a palpably dangerous one.

In the first place, an undertaking by a collectivist country to relax quantitative restrictions or to reduce tariff rates does not necessarily result in better marketing opportunities for foreign exporters. The actual decision whether or not to purchase a particular line of goods from a given supplier is made by a government agency; and the collection of a larger or smaller customs levy by another department of the same government does not affect that decision one way or another. Secondly, a similar undertaking by a Western-type economy is not only real in the benefits it offers, but also quite risky in that it renders the local market vulnerable to underpriced communist goods.

In 1964 the Economic Commission for Europe reported that completely nondiscriminatory treatment of imports from the East was rare, if not nonexistent.[13] As a rule, Western governments offer most-favored-nation treatment in this area only in the framework of bilateral agreements. Typically, the broader scope thus afforded to the entry of Eastern products is intended to be compensated by undertakings to purchase a targeted volume of the Western country's exports.[14] In this manner, the quid pro quo is particularized, rather than left to the hazard of abstract and conventional formulations of reciprocity. The disruptions which may accompany an unchecked inflow of cheaply produced or subsidized goods are also conveniently avoided in the context of bilateral quantification of exchanges.

European trade is, of course, deeply affected by the internal preferences operative within the Economic Community and the Free Trade Association. Both customs blocs have been bitterly opposed by communist governments in the East and by communist parties in the West as unacceptable discriminatory grouping.[15] Generally speaking the injustice complained of affects the East not very differently from other outsiders, the United States, for instance. The impact on the Eastern region tends to be more concentrated, however, insofar as western Europe is its traditional outlet for raw materials and agricultural produce.

Particularly disquieting to the East are the quantitative import restrictions practiced against it by individual member states, and the Community's proclaimed search for a common policy umbrella covering the transfer of these restrictions from the national to the Common Market level. Although the immediate effect is in the agricultural sector, probable future discriminations in the categories of manufactured and semimanufactured goods are no less disturbing to the planned Eastern economies. For they cannot look forward to developing secure markets for products which are repeatedly subject to quota negotiations; or to competing effectively with other outsiders who can supply the Common Market without the handicap of import licensing.

Thus far, the Community has failed to speak in unison on the question of commercial relations with the East. In regard to primary commodities, attempts at coordination have progressed somewhat further than in the industrial sector or in the area of export credit practice. But the repeated proposals of the Brussels Commission for the establishment of a fully concerted position have not fared well in the deliberations of the E.E.C.'s Council of Ministers, a forum where the intrusion of political and diplomatic factors is far more pronounced.

More progress has been registered under the auspices of the European Coal and Steel Community. During the years 1962–1963, fluctuations in the price of steel and coal products resulted in a sharp rise in purchases from communist Europe, to the detriment of both Community and outside suppliers. In an attempt to stabilize prices and quantities of imports, the member countries managed to agree on generally operative quotas and consultation procedures affecting Eastern origin steel, certain types of ferrous alloys and (in more casual fashion) coal.[16]

With a view to achieving a unified commercial policy by the end of the transitional period, as required under Article 113 of the Treaty of Rome, the several bodies of the E.E.C. have developed a plan looking toward the transposition of nationally created quotas to the level of the Community as a whole. Uniform lists, established and negotiated at that level with individual Eastern countries falling outside the GATT, were envisioned as the future order of the day.

A highly significant proposal, elevated to the status of a Commission ruling, is Regulation 3-63. Under its terms, each member country is required to submit estimates of its agricultural purchases from state trading nations. Imports in excess of the average 1960–61 level become subject to E.E.C. scrutiny. When the excess is more than 20 percent, the Commission may intervene. The measure is in terms preventive rather than restrictive, and the Commission has proposed to eliminate its openly discriminatory feature by means of substitute formulations cast in terms of "sensitive" products regardless of origin. Be that as it may, and even if Regulation 3-63 is never invoked, its impact upon west European import patterns promises to be salutary.[17]

On the surface, the challenge which the Common Market poses to the Comecon region appears to be a generalized one. True, as the vestiges of the internal tariff disappear and the common external tariff begins to approximate the arithmetical average of those formerly maintained by the member states, goods imported from the East become disadvantaged in comparison with intra-Community sales. But the implicit discrimination against Czechoslovak Skoda automobiles is not different from that affecting U.S. manufactured products of General Motors Corporation, when both compete against the customs free sales of Mercedes cars to Holland, for example. Similarly, tariff barriers against the entry of Bulgarian tobacco are not more discriminatory than those affecting American frozen chickens.

Upon further reflection, we find, however, that in certain respects the burden placed upon Bulgarian tobacco growers (and other Eastern exporters in their position) is heavier indeed. Being traditional suppliers of this commodity to the region, they face not only the obstacle of an E.E.C. policy designed to assist the development of local tobacco production, but also the fact that Greek and Turkish suppliers enjoy a competitive edge because of the privileged associate-member status with which these two countries have been accredited in Brussels.[18] Similar disparities apply to Polish pork which, as of 1968, faces a uniform Common Market price, and to the beef, fruit and vegetable exports of all east European states.

Over the years the Common Market has been able to evolve a series of rules affecting the importation of basic agricultural products such as grains, beef, pork, milk, eggs and poultry. With respect to these traditional exports, the East must overcome a levy imposed on all outside suppliers, as well as the barrier of nationally established quotas. Under a number of special exemptions, the Community has granted occasional relief (*e.g.,* from a supplementary tax in the case of Polish eggs and from the full tariff rate in the case of Russian caviar, crab meat and vodka.)[19] But the broad range of Eastern commodities must surmount a serious export handicap.

At the national level, a pronounced movement toward relaxation of import quotas against Eastern goods has been in evidence for some time, both in the E.F.T.A. and the E.E.C.

As early as 1964, the United Kingdom decided to abolish its severe quota system in favor of a more flexible trade-inducing policy of "autonomous liberation." Quantitative controls on virtually all goods of Polish, Czech, Rumanian, Hungarian and Bulgarian origin were lifted under so-called "open general license" in return for assurances by the countries concerned that prices would be aligned to world levels. Although a surveillance system exists with respect to products considered to be particularly sensitive, the criteria governing remaining country quotas have been considerably expanded. For example, in May 1967, the Board of Trade doubled and in some cases tripled the volume of importable Soviet consumer goods.[20]

Within the Common Market one of the first gestures toward relaxed import quotas was made by France in the context of her agressive policy of East-West political détente. In 1964, around 90 percent of the goods imported from the East were subject to quantitative restrictions, certain raw materials being the sole exception. By 1966, over half of the 1100 restricted items had been freed. As of 1968, only some 200 articles remained affected. The liberalization was a unilateral undertaking and the right of revocation was cautiously retained.[21]

Italy, which has been progressively reducing its import quotas for several years, took a major leap forward in May 1967. The restrictions on over 900 items which were removed at that time represented more than 80 percent of the country's overall purchases from the East. This move does not apply with respect to East German goods; nor does it extend to Eastern agricultural products, the import of which is now largely controlled at the Community level. In announcing the new relaxation, the Italian foreign trade minister warned that "if political or dumping prices are practiced, the liberalization for the imported products will be suspended."[22]

The Benelux countries have likewise freed many categories of Eastern goods from quantitative limitations. However, by and large, they have chosen to do this in the context of negotiated arrangements with individual Eastern states, rather than through unilateral concession. Thus, in 1967, about 70–80 percent of imports from Hungary and Poland were released from quotas under bilateral commercial agreement.

West Germany was the last of the Common Market countries to begin reducing the rigors of its import control system. In 1966, the Federal Republic instituted a quasi-liberalization under which a long-term permit may be issued for the entry of certain items without limit as to quantity. This new policy was immediately applied to imports from Poland, Hungary, Bulgaria and Rumania, and thereafter to Czechoslovakia in a pattern intended to become the rule for the region as a whole.

All in all, the West European countries have now liberalized their imports from the Comecon countries to a point beyond which they cannot easily go without stepping on the toes of other suppliers. In particular, considerable trade diversion from its Common Market partners would ensue if any of the member states made substantial further concessions on a unilateral basis. In the future, it would seem, major progress can only come within the framework of multilateral E.E.C. agreement.

This need, and the desire to bring the two halves of the continent closer together, may be expected to give a new impetus to the adoption of a Community-based policy on East-West trade. If the member countries lack economic incentive, the political pressures at work are sufficiently potent to propel movement in that direction. For their part, most of the Eastern countries have clearly begun to reconcile themselves to the existence of the E.E.C. as a trading unit, and to express interest in closer liaison.

C. Credit Limitations

The policies which gave birth to Western export controls, import limitations and other restraints, quite consistently led to the restriction of financial facilities as well. The extension to Eastern borrowers of direct government loans, government guaranteed credits and funds from entirely private sources has been kept within specific confines throughout the West. Since the mid-sixties, however, the exchange-starved communist import enterprises have been treated with increasing flexibility by Western financial institutions, both private and state operated.

No doubt, the provision of credit, particularly of the medium- and long-term variety, constitutes a form of external assistance to the recipient communist economy. However, once it is decided that the sale of nonstrategic goods is proper (and this decision has been made by all Western governments), it becomes difficult to treat a request for suppliers' credit as anything more than a logical corollary of such a sale. The use of credits is, in fact, customary in most export transactions, and quite standard in the case of major capital equipment. Whenever a Western country denies such facilities, it in effect requires the Eastern purchaser either to divert to the desired procurement a large portion of its chronically scarce hard currencies, or to turn to other, more accommodating sources of supply. The United States has been a victim of this fundamental fact of international economic life.

1. United States

American credit restrictions are exceptionally severe. The principal item of governing legislation is the Johnson Debt Default Act of 1934. In terms, the Act prohibits loans to (or the purchase or sale of securities of) a foreign government which is in default of debts owing to the United States. Only member countries of the International Bank for Reconstruction and Development and of the International Monetary Fund are exempt, pursuant to a 1945 amendment.

In practice, the measure was interpreted as affecting all private credits other than normal, short-term commercial facilities and usual acceptances and drafts. Violations by any individuals, partnerships, corporations or associations, entail criminal punishment.

Although the Johnson Act is not aimed at communist countries as such, only Bulgaria and Albania are considered not to be in default of payments to the United States, and only Yugoslavia is a member of both the World Bank and the I.M.F. Credit transactions with all Eastern states except these two are therefore within the ambit of control.

Except in the case of Russia, the defaults of the affected states are largely technical. But the President is required to treat all proscribed countries indiscriminately, with obvious loss of the foreign policy leverage which selectivity in denial or approval of credit entitlement might otherwise afford. As to the U.S.S.R. itself, the U.S. Treasury has quantified the amounts outstanding, mainly from World War I obligations and World War II Lend-Lease indebtedness, at more than a half billion dollars. Repeated attempts to negotiate a settlement have yielded no practical results.

The term "loans" in the meaning of the Act has been construed almost from the outset not to apply to commercial credits of up to 180 days. Since most sales of commodities entail financing not exceeding six months, current export-import is little affected. However, in transactions involving the supply of goods for industrial installations, a category in which the East is today particularly interested, far longer credit terms have become the rule. For such installations involve an extended period of construction and therefore long delays in the repayment of original investments. The initial interpretation thus constituted a major obstacle to expanded sales.

A significant change came about in connection with the 1963 sale of wheat to the U.S.S.R., which was to be based on a deferred payment plan. In an opinion issued on October 9, 1963, Attorney-General Robert F. Kennedy sanctioned the financial aspects of the proposed transaction (eighteen month terms) on the ground that the Act did not preclude credits "within the range of those commonly encountered in commercial sales of a comparable character."[23] At the same time, evasive devises, such as credits in the nature of financial assistance, or of inordinately long duration (generally viewed as extending beyond five years), were ruled to be within the legislative reach and intent. In effect, the opinion opened the way for private medium-term financing, thereby enabling not only the sale of primary commodities, but also of certain classes of capital goods.

In the same spirit, Attorney-General Ramsey Clark's opinion of May 9, 1967, responding to questions raised by acting Secretary of State Nicholas deB. Katzenbach, further clarified the meaning of a "loan" under the Act. Lines of credit, barter arrangements and deferrals of payment pending development of earnings are now deemed permissible. As a rule, transactions tied to specific exports are likewise unaffected, to the extent that they are based upon bona fide business considerations and do not involve a public distribution of securities.

It is important to note that the Johnson Act does not extend to foreign subsidiaries or offshore licensees of American corporations, if the transactions subject to financing are wholly effectuated outside the United States. In consequence, subsidiary companies formed or licensed in western Europe, Japan or elsewhere have generally been free to supply goods on credit, often underwritten by local state export insurance instrumentalities, under criteria described hereafter. To the extent that such arrangements displace exports of U.S. origin, the American balance of payments suffers in the process.[24]

Outside the domain of purely private credits, the Johnson Act has no application. Government-controlled institutions, such as the Export-Import Bank or the Commodity Credit Corporation, are specifically exempted from its restrictions although they, in turn, fall under special enactments.[25]

In considering the degree of permissible official involvement in credits to the East, we must bear in mind two distinct sources of financing: publicly guaranteed private funds, and funds furnished directly by public entities. The first method is the more important one for our purposes. Export incentives in the form of state provided credit insurance are extensively available in the West. Whenever a sale qualifies for coverage of this type, financing can be obtained at a preferential rate of interest.

In the United States, credit insurance is offered to exporters by the Export-Import Bank and by the privately sponsored Federal Credit Insurance Association. As a rule, the former assumes political risks, and both share equally client credit risks in a coordinated scheme of operations which is administered by the F.C.I.A. as agent for its member insurance companies and for the Bank.

Under a statute passed in 1964, the Export-Import Bank is foreclosed from using its funds to guarantee, insure or otherwise participate in the extension of credits to any communist state, except in cases where such participation would be in the national interest. The President has used his authority to make determinations enabling medium-term guarantees, *i.e.*

six months to five years for sales to Bulgaria, Czechoslovakia, Hungary, Poland and Rumania; long-term guarantees, *i.e.* more than five years for sales to Yugoslavia; and medium-term guarantees for sales of agricultural commodities to the U.S.S.R.[26] An interesting, if rare, example of Export-Import Bank liberality was the provision, in 1965, of a guarantee in support of Universal Oil Products' construction in Rumania of a catalytic cracking plant. The term of the underlying credit was five years from delivery. Taking cognizance of the fact that the contract specified delivery within two and a half years, the result was a debt maturity of seven and a half years.[27]

Having created the Bank in the first instance, Congress stands guard over it like a watchdog, and limits quite stringently its participation in the financing of exports to the communist world. A dramatic illustration of this was the denial of guarantees for the sale of American machine tools to Italy's FIAT required to fulfill its huge automobile plant construction contract with the U.S.S.R. Despite the presence of surplus production capacity, a strong economic interest on the part of the American firms concerned, an adverse balance of payments and favorable testimony from the Joint Chiefs of Staff and several Cabinet officers, the approximately $50 millions-worth of sales at stake were relinquished to bidding by foreign competitors. Firms that were able to fill the orders found themselves compelled to seek private, uninsured financing.

A 1968 amendment to the Export-Import Bank Act of 1945 specifically prevents the Bank from participating in the extension of credit "in connection with the purchase or lease of any product by any (non-Communist) foreign country, if the product to be purchased or leased is, to the knowledge of the Bank, for use in or sale or lease to, a Communist country."[28] While this particular provision can be waived pursuant to a Presidential determination of national interest, a further interdiction (provoked by Eastern aid to North Vietnam) cannot be—namely, participation in credits covering sales to any country which furnishes by direct governmental action "goods, supplies, military assistance or advisers" to a nation with which United States armed forces are engaged in a declared or undeclared military conflict. It is under this Congressional directive that reprisals were threatened against Sweden following that country's offer of $40 million in aid to North Vietnam in the fall of 1969. In concrete terms, the threat included a proposed denial of more than $200 million in Ex-Im Bank credits for the purchase of American Boeing-747 aircraft by SAS (an airline which Sweden, Norway and Denmark own in common).

Two additional areas of restriction should also be mentioned. The first arises under the Agricultural Trade Development and Assistance Act of 1954, better known as Public Law 480. Under its terms, agricultural commodities may not normally be sold on credit to any country dominated by international communism. Yugoslavia was deemed not to be such a country and, following a 1956 determination, Poland as well. Under a 1964 amendment, the permissible duration of credits to Poland had been limited to five years, compared with the normal twenty-year term applicable to friendly countries. Moreover, as to both countries, the same amendment prohibits sales of agricultural commodities for local currency.[29]

In conclusion, an entire area of restrictions to which allusion must be made in the present context relates, of course, to the general United States embargo on dealings with Communist China, North Korea, North Vietnam and Cuba. No U.S. citizen or corporation may extend credit or transfer payment in connection with any commercial transaction whatsoever involving these countries.

2. *Berne Union Members*

The credit policies applied to Eastbound trade by other Western governments stand in sharp contrast to those of the United States. Even NATO countries have sought to expand their economic relations with the communist orbit on the basis of a willingness to permit long-term financing and to provide the customary government guarantees. In the process they have competed with one another in a manner approaching a credit war. And the U.S.S.R., as well as its allies has known how to fan this rivalry to its own advantage.

International efforts to align export credit practice date back to the establishment in 1934 of the *Union d'Assureurs des Credits Internationaux* in Berne, Switzerland. The "Berne Union" at present consists of some twenty-three governmental and private credit insurance organizations from eighteen countries, including nations of Western Europe, North America, the British Commonwealth, South Africa and Israel. It was conceived as a forum to promote the rational development and co-ordination of international credit insurance.

The rules of the association amount to no more than a loosely drawn gentleman's understanding, without binding legal force. Represented countries may deviate from the jointly approved practices by unilateral decision. Moreover, the rules have no application in the area of outright state loans; they relate only to government guarantees and insurance policies with respect to privately extended supplier credits.

As of 1958, it was agreed that commercial credits to the East should be limited to five years and be subject to an initial cash down-payment of at least 20 percent of the purchase price. The rationale behind these limitations was not just to ward off unfair competition in a scramble for export markets. Part of the intention was to prevent government supported credit from becoming a virtual extension of financial aid, enabling communist countries to divert more of their own resources to investment in military and other strategically significant areas.

In Europe, the "five-year rule," instituted largely at Washington's urging, has never achieved the general legislative underpinning that the Johnson Act of 1934 supplies in the United States. To the extent it is considered "generally accepted practice" at all, it is honored more in the breach than the observance. Violations date back almost to its inception; in large part they were stimulated by a need to counter competition from nonmember insurers. Not being a participant in the activities of the Berne group, Japan in particular began, in the late 1950's, to extend credits to the East for more than five years. Italian state-owned institutions followed suit.

Acting almost contemporaneously, Great Britain, Germany and France, among others, began to close the competitive gap opened outside and inside the Berne Union, with a view to covering the East's placement of industrial orders.

In October 1960, the Export Credits Guarantee Department (ECGD), a governmental body attached to the British Board of Trade, introduced a "matching policy." In effect, it declared itself prepared to meet financing terms beyond five years' duration granted by any foreign competitor with respect to a specific order, provided that "normal commercial considerations warranted and that the foreign credit concerned did not constitute aid." [30] A further step in the same direction was taken in April 1961 with the implementation of a "financial guarantees" scheme, designed to provide long-term insurance for major projects, such as plant and machinery installations.

Under defined circumstances, the ECGD insures against the political risks that are inherent in East-West commerce: nonpayment as a result of war, denial of Eastern import licenses, cancellation of a contract by the purchaser's government, unilateral or multilateral imposition of new Western trade restrictions, etc. Certain private risks, notably the insolvency of the buyer, are also insured, although purely commercial coverage is generally available from private English concerns. London banks, it may be noted, regularly finance major long-term transactions with the East on condition that they are covered by an ECGD policy. By way of illustration, we need only refer to the U.K. government's 1964 approval of an offer of fifteen years' credit, in an amount of some $300 million, to facilitate local procurement of complete factories. The offer was made to the U.S.S.R.'s Vneshtorgbank by a consortium comprising Midland Bank, Lloyd's Bank and Barclay's Bank.

West Germany maintains a comparable financial system, administered by Hermes Kreditversicherungs AG, a company which, in addition to performing the English-type governmental role, operates also as a credit insurer for its own account. Guarantees for eight-year periods were first provided by the Federal Republic in 1966, in connection with the sale of a diesel engine plant to Hungary and of various types of petrochemical equipment to Rumania; considerably longer terms have been specified in subsequent transactions.

France's supplier credit instrumentality—*Compagnie Française d'Assurance du Commerce Extérieur* (COFACE)—has been no less liberal. It provides coverage against the risks of nonpayment in most export transactions including sales to communist countries. With regard to political and exchange risks, the government stands behind the COFACE guarantee. With respect to commercial risks, COFACE functions as a private guarantor and only its own funds and reserves support the policies it writes. In trade with the East, the French government began officially to authorize and insure long-term credit around 1964. Indeed, the Franco-Soviet Commercial Agreement of October 30, 1964, envisioned that Russian orders of machinery would be financed half by credits of seven years from the completion of delivery or the commencement of factory operation, whichever is stipulated by contract, and the other half (without cash payments) by five-year credits. Later that year, the government approved arrangements by a consortium, including such state-owned banks as Crédit Lyonnais and Société Générale and such private banks as Banque de Paris et des Pays Bas and Union Européenne Industrielle et Financière, to extend to Vneshtorgbank credits of ten years' duration in an amount exceeding $300 million.

Italy, too, has been extending long term credits in major transactions with the East through the *Instituto Mobiliare Italiano,* the government export credit organization. Undoubtedly, the most spectacular illustration of its policy is the highly publicized FIAT project, which has entailed an IMI credit of more than $350 million, extending as long as eight and a half years from the completion of the Togliatti automobile plant in the U.S.S.R., *i.e.,* a possible fourteen years in all.

Examples illustrating the international trend can be easily multiplied. The tenor of current policy and practice in the sphere of credit is, however, clear. Long-term private funds accompanied by government guarantees extended in connection with sales to the communist East have become increasingly common features on the European commercial landscape. Competition in the area of export credit is too brisk to allow meaningful multilateral coordination. Even the six Common Market countries have shown themselves unable to respond to their Commission's 1962 consultation proposals aiming at a uniform policy. The five-year standard established more than a decade ago within the framework of the Berne Union, having proved incompatible with present-day commercial and political realities, has been allowed to fade into retirement.

7

STRATEGIC EXPORT RESTRICTIONS

A. An Overview of Western Legislation

Historically, governments everywhere have restricted deliveries abroad of various classes of goods and services in time of war, and have limited the export of certain categories of products (*e.g.*, military implements, materials in short supply) at all times.

States organized according to a communist pattern have no need of a regulatory scheme to control strategic exports. Within their collectivist social structures, government agencies and officials not only implement the public policy of the nation, but also make the basic decisions as to what should or should not (for commercial, security or other reasons) be made available for shipment abroad. If the U.S.S.R wishes to block the sale of certain strategic goods to a Western buyer (or a wayward "fraternal" country such as Czechoslovakia or Rumania, whose military establishments can no longer be trusted to defer to Moscow in all foreseeable circumstances) this is an easy matter to accomplish, without any of the open controversies which accompany the enforcement of controls in a market-oriented economy.

What distinguishes modern United States export control legislation (the Export Control Act of 1949, as well as its replacement, the Export Administration Act of 1969) from similar measures of the past is that it renders possible, in time of relative peace and on a permanent basis (albeit with periodic Congressional renewal), the maintenance of a highly complex network of controls over exports, regardless of destination. Although more narrow in reach, the enabling legislation of most other Western countries can also be regarded as fairly permanent.[1]

Three specific purposes are within the American legislative aim: to safeguard the national security, to promote foreign policy objectives, and to prevent excessive drain of materials in domestic short supply. Originally, the declared national security object of the law was to stop the flow to communist countries of goods having military or strategic significance. In 1962 its scope was extended to encompass exports which might significantly enhance the economic potential of such countries to the detriment of United States security and welfare.[2] Over the years the controls have been extended beyond the ambit of Eastbound exports. For special foreign policy reasons, prohibitions upon shipments to South Africa and Rhodesia have been promulgated in deference to United Nations Security Council resolutions. A 1965 antiboycott amendment sought to frustrate restrictive trade practices against Israel, fostered among American firms by the Boycott Committee of the Arab League. With regard to goods in short supply, controls have been imposed on the outflow of copper and nickel to any foreign destination.

The current U.S. Export Administration Act, passed in December, 1969, after profound disagreements among the White House, the Senate and the House of Representatives, represents a cautious but unmistakable shift of Congressional sentiment toward more liberal policy positions. While the new legislation reaffirms the President's authority to control all export transactions for reasons of national security, foreign policy and domestic short supply, it calls for a reexamination of any existing restricted commodity list "with a view to making promptly such changes and revisions in such list as may be necessary or desirable in furtherance of the policy, purposes and provisions of this Act."[3]

Although the central objectives of national export controls elsewhere in the West are basically similar, the scope of regulatory formulation and enforcement differs from that of the United States. Whether stated expressly or inferred from underlying legislative intent, all controls (with the apparent exception of Japan's) extend not only to physical goods, but also to such intangibles as strategically valuable technical data. Each legislature places the administrative responsibilities involved in the hands of a designated agency, usually the ministry concerned with foreign commerce. Specialized government departments are occasionally given jurisdiction over particular classes of goods, *e.g.*, military ordnance.

U.S. policy has long reflected a comparatively broad conception of what should be withheld from the East for strategic or political reasons. Allied countries proscribe exports much more selectively, as a rule under the narrower limitations agreed upon within the so-called coordinating committee (COCOM). While West Germany's lists and, more marginally, Japan's, are considerably longer than COCOM's, the excess does not account for strategic or even industrial products; both countries seek, as well, to control the quality of exports, to prevent local shortages and to satisfy international commitments. The British and Canadian export lists, on the other hand, are virtually identical with that of COCOM.

Like its American counterpart, Japan's law on the subject has been in effect since 1949.[4] Its objectives are stated more euphemistically, however, and in economic rather than foreign policy terms: to develop foreign trade, to safeguard the balance of payments and the stability of the currency, and to ensure the most economic use of foreign exchange. Moreover, the law expressly looks forward to the minimization and eventual abolition of restrictions. Canada's 1954 legislation, on the other hand, is closer to the United States' pattern. If its aims also derive from foreign policy notions, they are, nonetheless, limited by specific national security considerations.[5]

The law promulgated in 1961 by West Germany emulates the Japanese approach in its emphasis on both the economic aim and the temporary nature of the legislation.[6] Excluded from its purview is trade with East Germany, which is not recognized as an independent sovereign state. For obvious political reasons, sales to that destination are therefore not regarded as exports, and the necessary controls are enforced by agencies of the Federal Republic under regulations of allied power origin.

The United Kingdom, pursuant to legislation enacted in 1939, vests discretionary export control authority in the Board of Trade. The Board exercised this power in 1959 and 1960 to establish a licensing system, substantially less ambitious and severe than that of the United States, for limited classes of goods going to general destinations, and for strategic goods going to communist destinations.[7] Domestic short supply and foreign policy export restrictions (*e.g.*, on shipments to Rhodesia) are a current feature of the system.

France's export licensing system is based on a series of decrees, the latest of which dates from November 30, 1944. Additions to and deletions from the list of controlled commodities are published periodically in the government's official journal. General licensing jurisdiction is in the hands of the Ministry of Finance and Economic Affairs. Permit applications involving strategic and foreign policy questions are scrutinized by the Ministry of

Defense and the Ministry of Foreign Affairs under a complex procedure which was laid bare by the celebrated 1969 removal of five Israeli gunboats from the port of Cherbourg.

Italian legislation, peculiarly, forbids all export and import by local residents or firms. Derogations are granted pursuant to general or particular authorization. In practice, however, the position is reversed, trade in most goods being today completely open with many countries and extensively liberalized with all others. Licenses, issuable by the Department of Export-Import of the Ministry of Foreign Commerce, are required only for items listed in the Export Table.[8]

In most countries the regulatory export control authority of the executive branch is more precisely circumscribed than in the United States. West German law, for example, promulgates the general principle that all exportation is free; the power to restrict is considered to be exceptional, and proposed restrictions are placed before Parliament for review. By contrast, in America very broad powers have long been vested in the President, and in theory all exports are subject to administrative control. The restrictions apply to U.S. citizens and residents, and to companies, partnerships and business associations, both local and foreign. In addition, American law is applied to control the reexportation of U.S.-origin goods and technical data, and to conscript foreign nations into implementing its own policy objectives in this area.

Greater and more realistic self-restraint is reflected in the laws and governmental practices of other states which subscribe to the defensive aims of the alliance. In Canada, for instance, the reach of export control is limited to acts done within its borders. The Japanese regulations are basically confined to sales from Japan, and West Germany defines applicability not much more broadly, by reference to residents and activities within the German economic territory. To the extent that they exist, national differences in attempted legislative reach occasionally lead to abrasive conflicts of policy and law.

B. American Controls on Eastbound Trade

1. *Licensing Administration and Procedure*

For purposes of administration, the President's authority under the Export Control Act of 1949 has been delegated to the Secretary of Commerce.

The successor Export Administration Act of 1969 left the preexisting scheme of delegation undisturbed. Direct administrative responsibility continues to be exercised by the Office of Export Control of the Bureau of International Commerce, through four main divisions specialized by product category and licensing function.

The Office, which issues regulations, considers license applications, supervises the movement of goods, investigates violations and so forth, is guided by information and advice from several government departments and agencies, while the established channel for policy advice runs through several inter-departmental committees. At the apex of the hierarchy is the Export Control Review Board, consisting of the Secretaries of Commerce, State and Defense.

Other agencies exercise specialized licensing jurisdiction which bears on East-West economic relations along with general commerce. Thus the Department of State regulates the export of arms and related technical data; the Atomic Energy Commission controls sales of nuclear materials; the Department of Agriculture, the Maritime Administration and the Federal Power Commission issue export authorizations in their own respective spheres of responsibility and the Treasury Department supervises the sale abroad of gold and narcotics.

In certain areas of Treasury competence, the export licensing authority of its Office of Foreign Assets Control tends to overlap the more generalized functions of the Commerce Department's Office of Export Control. An important group of controls is allocated to the former, pursuant to the Trading with the Enemy Act of 1917, the Foreign Assistance Act of 1961 and related legislation with regard to designated areas. Thus, the Foreign Assets Control Regulations of December 17, 1950, prohibit persons subject to U.S. jurisdiction from dealing with communist China (liberalized slightly in July and December, 1969), North Korea and, as of May 5, 1964, North Vietnam. The Cuban Assets Control Regulations of July 8, 1963, impose similar controls vis-à-vis Cuba.

Further, pursuant to the Transaction Control Regulations effective as of June 29, 1953, designated exports (presumed to coincide with internationally classified strategic items withheld from the East as a whole) by persons or companies falling within the jurisdiction of the United States, including American-controlled foreign corporations, are subject to Treasury control even if the goods in question are of alien origin. American-controlled firms located abroad may export to non-Asian communist destinations goods and technical data of non-U.S. origin which are proscribed by the United States unilaterally, assuming, of course, that the foreign-based firm's national law permits it.

The Export Administration Act of 1969 may be expected to change the twenty-year-old export control regime from a system of general application to one in which restrictions will be exceptional. Meanwhile, under the regulations now in force, the exportation of all goods and technical data from the United States to destinations other than dependent U.S. territories and possessions is subject to the licensing authority of the Department of Commerce. Only exports to Canada (excepting copper scrap and alloy ingots, commodities related to the development and testing of nuclear weapons, and certain technical data) require no license, so long as they are intended for domestic consumption. Other than this, affected shipments abroad can be made either under "general license" or "under validated license."

The general license (of which there are several variants) applies to goods released for shipment without prior specific authorization. Although no formal document of approval need be obtained, certain customs and clearance procedures are compulsory. Thus, the Customs Office at the point of exit must be presented with a "shipper's export declaration" listing the goods in question, the parties involved and the ultimate destination. An "anti-diversion notice" must be attached, including an acknowledgment that the goods may not be delivered to designated areas. A validated license, on the other hand, is an official document which permits individual shipments of specified commodities or technical data to stated consignees and destinations. It is issued only upon express application to the Office of Export Control. As an exception, validated blanket licenses are granted to cover multiple shipments in connection with continuous dealings or projects which call for repeated deliveries. The classes of goods subject to licensing are set forth in the Department's published Commodity Control List. Items requiring a validated license are designated by country groups. The absence of such designation signifies that the export may take place under general license.

The application for a validated license must state the identity of the foreign buyer, the nature of the export and its intended use as certified (for values exceeding $500) by the ultimate consignee. The Department refrains from giving hypothetical guidance rulings. The applicant is required to show that he has a firm order or that his dealings have proceeded far enough to establish a reasonable expectation of an order. Although the attendant delays and uncertainties are in some instances responsible for decisions to forego potential business, the Office of Export Control invites consultation on possible or pending transactions of magnitude, prior to the formal submission of a license application.

Among the groups of countries into which United States export regulations divide the world (Canada excluded), three consist of communist areas, treated with different degrees of severity: Poland and Rumania; other "Soviet bloc" countries; communist China, North Vietnam, North Korea and Cuba.

Virtually all goods of U.S. origin intended for the last mentioned group are subject to embargo. Theoretically they may be sold under validated license, but in practice such licenses are seldom issued. Exceptions have been made of certain foods and drugs exported to Cuba on humanitarian grounds, and items such as household appliances and motor cars sold to friendly foreign embassies in Peking. Validated licenses must also cover the bulk of shipments to the former two groups. Here, however, approval is much more liberally dispensed. Furthermore, certain goods which require a validated license to be shipped to other "Soviet bloc" nations may be sent to Poland and Rumania—the most leniently treated communist countries—under general license. Within the "Soviet bloc" category, East Germany is controlled with particular stringency. Yugoslavia is treated as a west European country for U.S. export control purposes.

Whether or not a validated license is needed depends upon the types of goods to be shipped and their ultimate destination. For the answer to this question the would-be exporter must turn to the Commodity Control List. Whether or not the license will be issued in any particular case depends on the determination of the Office of Export Control. In making its determinations, the Office enjoys wide discretion. This, together with the complexity and unpredictability of its processes, has proven as inhibiting to trade with the East as the export restrictions themselves.[9] On the other hand, it must be recognized that the licensing function is a difficult one to exercise, involving as it does the constant weighing of conflicting objectives in a highly volatile setting.

Caught between a mandate to promote world-wide trade in peaceful goods despite a precarious balance of payments, and an injunction from a politically sensitive and watchful Congress to make a paramount concern of the nation's security, the attitudes of responsible administrators are bound to be arbitrary, changeable and hesitant, at least in borderline cases, with error on the side of caution. Often one agency (usually the more "visible" Department of Commerce) ends up taking the blame for license denials voted intramurally by others. A frank insight into the overall process, still valid despite the subsequent change of policy emphasis reflected in the Export Administration Act of 1969, was publicly offered by a former Assistant Secretary of Commerce:

> For commodities not so clearly non-strategic, we look at each application to determine whether in that transaction and for that particular end use the commodity may be considered to be strategic. Entering into this decision are such considerations as (1) Is the commodity designed for, intended for, or could it be applied to a significant military use? (2) Does it contain unique or advanced technology that is extractable? (3) Would it promote the military industrial base of the country of destination? (4) Would it contribute to the economy of the Communist countries to the detriment of our own security? (5) Are there adequate suppliers or good substitutes available elsewhere that would make any control by us futile? (6) Are the quantities and types of equipment normal for the proposed use? (7) Is the equipment an integral part of a larger package and therefore unlikely to be used for other than the stated purpose?
>
> Our East-West trade policy and our administration of the Export Control Act present an administrative area in which men of good will admittedly can and sometimes do see things differently. We interpret the Act to call for denial of export licenses when such denial is found to be in furtherance of national security and foreign policy objectives, and for approval when those national interests would benefit thereby.[10]

To be sure, if a license is denied, the dissatisfied applicant may request a statement of reasons for the denial, or an administrative review, or have recourse to the Appeals Board of the Department of Commerce. But there again little more than relief from obvious abuses may be expected, given the inherent difficulty of information-gathering and the political, economic and strategic value judgments which have to be made.

The question of what constitutes strategic goods is often a difficult one. Certainly no catalogue can be definitive. The pace of technological process is becoming increasingly rapid, not only on the Western side, but also in the East. A multitude of items considered sensitive several years ago are no longer in that category, either because they have become obsolete, or because communist science and industry have unlocked their secrets through local invention or the copying of imports obtained from less stringently supervised Western sources. In addition, many products are capable of dual military and civilian use. The most advanced third generation American computers can be assigned interchangeably to the task of operating an automated plant which manufactures peaceful consumer goods, or a highly strategic atomic installation. In instances of this type, the licensor must form an opinion in the gray area of the importer's most likely intention.

Inevitably, under the 1969 Act no less than under its 1949 predecessor, prevailing public attitudes, the diplomatic climate abroad, the political climate at home and, above all, the personality of the Presidentially appointed official in charge, all exercise a profound influence on the nature of export control administration. For example, the list of items requiring validated licenses for shipment to European communist countries was trimmed drastically in October 1966 and May 1967, without special legislative mandate, against the background of improving relations. Moreover, the discrepancy between what the United States considered worthy of restriction and the markedly narrower definitions followed by other Western countries has also made its mark upon both the Office of Export Control and the Congress as larger numbers of American firms have sought licenses in response to the growing communist appetite for advanced technology. Under current law, goods which are available to sensitive communist destinations from alternate sources may be denied a license if their export is judged detrimental to U.S. national security. But if licenses are required on the ground that considerations of national security override considerations of foreign availability, the reasons are to be reported to the Congress, to the extent that national security and foreign policy permit.

No durable guide to administrative practice can, however, be offered. The interested exporter must seek advice based on the published daily list of approved licenses, on the pattern of previous determinations, on related products legitimately made available by competitors in other Western countries and on a sensitive assessment of the fluctuating international and domestic atmosphere within which East-West trade must be conducted.

An inquiry into the types of goods which were found to be eligible or ineligible for licenses in the past would not yield much valuable information regarding the product mix that qualifies for export to the East at any other particular time. Serious negotiations are initiated and followed up with formal applications in respect to items considered likely to qualify for a license, and most items in fact do. In many cases where there is a commercial interest to buy and sell, and in all cases involving Asian communist areas, firms simply assume that licenses will not be forthcoming. It is in the thin layer of doubtful situations that the real problems are encountered. Actually only some 2 percent of all filed applications are rejected by the Department.[11]

Obviously, sensitive American goods and know-how cannot effectively be withheld from the East without safeguards against unauthorized transshipment from free world destinations. Consequently the regulations prohibit reexportation to a communist area of U.S.-origin commodities and technical data initially sent to Western consignees, unless the ultimate destination falls within the scope of general authorization, or unless prior specific authorization is obtained. The same restriction applies to parts, components and materials of U.S. origin taken abroad for use in the manufacture of end-products whose exportation is restricted, as well as to certain products manufactured abroad with U.S.-origin technical data.

Written nondiversion promises from Western purchasers are required in certain instances to ensure compliance with U.S. controls. Supplementary procedures have been developed to cover proscribed goods sold to NATO countries, Japan, Hong Kong, Austria and certain other free destinations adjacent to communist areas. Under the so-called IC/DV arrangements, used by the United States and other COCOM governments, the foreign importer is required to obtain an "import certificate" from his own state for eventual submission to the Office of Export Control. This document constitutes a solemn commitment by the buyer that the goods will not be transshipped beyond the authorized destination, and an undertaking by the issuing state to control the disposition of the commodities. A further step in the procedure enables the Office, if it so desires, to obtain a "delivery verification," *i.e.*, a locally issued official confirmation that the goods have actually reached their proper consignee.

2. *Dissemination of Technical Know-how*

The export controls are not limited to the shipment abroad of physical goods. An additional, particularly sensitive area of regulation covers the outflow of various types of technical data. Controls here are very wide in scope, extending even to certain kinds of strategic goods manufactured abroad, with or from American data or technological processes.

Except for the State Department's and the Atomic Energy Commission's selected areas of supervision, the Office of Export Control exercises jurisdiction over the entire range of unpublished and unclassified industrial know-how sent abroad in tangible or intangible form. The movement of data (and goods) handled by foreign subsidiaries or firms which are controlled from America is supervised additionally by the Treasury Department's Office of Foreign Assets Control, within the scope of its own regulations.

Validated licensing requirements of the Department of Commerce cover the passing of all unpublished and unclassified data to destinations in communist China, North Korea, North Vietnam and Cuba, and most of such data to the rest of the communist world. Data of a particularly sensitive nature require a validated license even when circulated to the free world, in order to prevent unauthorized transmission (and the unauthorized transshipment of strategic products made therefrom abroad) to various communist destinations.

Licensing practice in the sphere of industrial know-how is of great practical importance, first, because of strong and growing Eastern demand for up-to-date Western technology and, second, because of the complex control mechanics injected into dealings between American firms and all of their foreign customers, regardless of location. The complexity stems in part from the sweeping terms in which "technical data" is defined:

> . . . information of any kind that can be used, or adapted for use, in the design, production, manufacture, utilization, or reconstruction of articles or materials. The data may take a tangible form, such as a model, prototype, blueprint, or an operating manual; or they may take an intangible form such as a technical service.[12]

This language clearly suggests that not only patentable industrial technology, but also nonpatentable know-how, as well as manufacturing experience which is not manifest in any physical or written form, are all within the ambit of control. Subject to certain conditions, export to any destination of data contained in an application for a foreign patent may be made under general license.

Educational and scientific data and technical information which exist in published, unclassified and generally available form are allowed to go to all destinations. Needless to say, even such information is not always devoid of strategic significance. We may surmise that very considerable industrial and military knowledge is derived through the systematic combing of American scientific and technical literature—a task specifically assigned to the Soviet All-Union Institute of Scientific and Technical Information. Nor can limited destination controls prevent leakage of unpublished materials. In an open economic system such as America's, infinite scope exists for observation of industrial processes and procedures, for personal, professional and business contact with technicians and engineers, and for other information-gathering methods. At best, only data which fall within the graduated classifications of secrecy from the standpoint of military security can be rendered reasonably immune from political and industrial espionage. Most unpublished or generally unavailable unclassified data is exportable to free world destinations under general license, but in some instances the ultimate consignee may be required to undertake not to pass it, or any strategic product built from it, into unauthorized hands. To be sent to a communist country, such data must, of course, be covered by validated licenses, or other prior, specific U.S. government authorization.

The problems of supervision are truly insurmountable. For example, release of information even to a fully controlled foreign corporation comes within the area of control. Beyond this, what degree of care in the handling of U.S.-origin data may realistically be expected of an American engineer visiting abroad, or working there for a branch or subsidiary of an American company? How can one distinguish invisible technology which may not freely circulate from that which may, when one is engaged in oral communications, correspondence and demonstrations, or in carrying blueprints, written specifications, chemical formulae or any other information existing in one's mind, in the course of travel abroad? In reality, the risk of unwitting violation is unavoidably present whenever a sales pitch is made to a foreign customer, plants are opened for visitors' inspection, technicians are trained in local or overseas facilities, or scientific study groups of mixed nationality meet at home or abroad.

Difficulties which challenge the imagination may arise for non-American firms or individuals who happen to be dealing contemporaneously in related types of technical data with an American and an Eastern firm. A suggestive example is afforded by recent litigation in the State of New York. Two subsidiaries of Italy's ENI complex were sued for $182 million in damages by an American company active in the construction of chemical plants. Defendants had received from plaintiff technical information under a production license to build a plastics factory in Sicily. It was alleged (and denied) that some of the information was subsequently used by defendants in the construction of similar installations in Poland and Czechoslovakia in violation of the licensing contract and of the United States Export Control Act. The civil damage suit was eventually settled out of court. But the Department of Commerce entered a consent order against one of the defendant companies, Snam Progetti S.p.A., resulting from charges that unpublished U.S.-origin data was utilized without proper clearance.[13]

Not only must foreign firms meet the problem of segregating their technical knowledge by source; they are also required to submit written assurances that know-how of American origin which has come to their attention will not pass into the hands of communist users, without prior authorization. Aside from the questions of supervision, American insistence upon guarantees of this type occasionally creates offense and controversy, particularly when large, state-owned European corporations are involved.

The manner in which the Department of Commerce interprets its regulations and enforces the law in the area of technical data exports and re-exports is illustrated by the 1962 case of Hydrocarbon Research, Inc., et al.[14] Hydrocarbon, an American company, represented to the Department that it had a contract to design and build a petrochemical plant in Rumania. Based on the assertion that no unpublished U.S. technical data would be used, but only technology generally available in published form and engineering know-how developed abroad, the Department responded that its permission was not needed. However, it transpired that Hydrocarbon had previously constructed a similar plant in France using the proprietary business restricted technology furnished it by a U.S. company in the form of blueprints, drawings, process controls, specifications, operating manuals and the like. Hydrocarbon's foreign engineers working abroad utilized these materials as substantial guidelines to design and put into operation the Rumanian plant.

In due course, Hydrocarbon and its associates were charged with reexporting unpublished technical data to a proscribed destination. The administrative compliance proceedings were concluded with an order, consented to by the parties, denying the company and its chief officials certain export privileges and otherwise putting them on probation. The order made it clear that when plans, specifications, or other documents are prepared by an American firm to construct and operate a particular plant, and these documents are not made generally available, then they constitute in every respect unpublished technical data. It stated further that the use of such technology for the purpose of redrawing, redesigning, or commingling with foreign or published technical data, does not deprive the original data of its unpublished U.S. origin. The transmission of the resulting data to Rumania required prior Department of Commerce approval. Such approval was not obtained. Nor, under the circumstances, did Hydrocarbon adequately describe what it had intended to do in its original talks with the Department.

Published figures of license applications made to (or approved by) the Department of Commerce or the Treasury must be considered with caution. They do not fully reflect the extent of either Western or Eastern interest in transactions involving American technology. Some firms which follow the restrictive lists and are familiar with current administrative attitudes may feel that the likelihood of a particular validated license's being granted is too small to be worth the trouble of applying. Only in "borderline" cases, where the odds of approval are promising but difficult to calculate, are applications actually filed. Such hesitancy is, of course, absent in clearly eligible situations, but the East's commercial interest in such situations is also relatively smaller.

3. *Surveillance and Enforcement*

The export control legislation affords a broad range of administrative means to allow detection of violations and expeditious enforcement on a worldwide basis. At home competent officials have the legal power to conduct investigations, undertake searches and inspections, serve subpoenas with respect to individuals and documents, call for testimony under oath and resort to other reasonable measures necessary to ensure compliance. Abroad, assistance is available occasionally from friendly governments and through officials at American embassies and consulates who make post-shipment checks at the licensed destination.

The Office of Export Control conducts more than five hundred investigations each year. About two hundred of these develop into full-fledged actions. Violations are subject to severe criminal and administrative penalties. Suffice it to say that first offenders may be imprisoned for a year and fined $10,000. Given a willful offense, with knowledge that the illegal export would benefit a communist-dominated nation, imprisonment for as long as five years with a fine of $20,000 or five times the value of the goods in question may be entailed.

Administrative sanctions range from a warning letter addressed to American or foreign firms, to the imposition of civil penalties up to $1,000 for each violation, to outright denial of export privileges. The latter type of interdiction may be attached to a specified class of commodities or to all goods and technical data for a certain time, or even indefinitely, depending on the seriousness of the offense. In milder cases it may take the form of a probation order, *i.e.*, the denial of export privileges is stayed on condition of good behavior.

Shipment or intended shipment in violation of export control regulations may lead to the seizure and forfeiture of the goods or technical data in question, along with the vessel, vehicle or aircraft employed in carriage.

Further sanctions of a criminal or administrative nature apply in respect to the violation of other laws or regulations governing unauthorized shipment of goods abroad, or participation in prohibited transactions.

Denial or abridgement of export privileges is subject to review by the Appeals Board on grounds of inadequate evidence, mistake of law, arbitrariness or abuse of discretion. However, no form of judicial review is expressly provided. In many cases, proceedings are disposed of by consent, *i.e.,* agreement between the respondent and the Office of Export Control as to the basis and scope of the sanction. With or without consent, the consequences of an export denial order can be very far-reaching. Indeed, it may put an offending local or foreign firm entirely out of business, if such firm is heavily dependent on the American export trade.

Each denial order appears in the Federal Register and is accompanied by a press release at the time of its issue. In addition, an extensive list, world-wide in scope, is maintained and regularly updated to facilitate identification of offenders.[15] The resultant publicity is not only harmful to the reputation of those immediately affected, but constitutes warning at home and abroad that no one may have dealings falling under the export regulations with the parties implicated in proven violations. As far as American offenders are concerned, the notice affects not only domestic companies, but also foreign subsidiaries, branches and affiliated distributors or dealers.

Two enforcement actions may be cited to convey an impression of the scope and nature of the possible sanctions. In the Hydrocarbon Research case previously referred to, the punishment for transmitting unauthorized know-how to Rumania included denial for five years of the right to participate in any commodity or technical data export dealings involving communist countries. In addition, the company was placed under extensive surveillance and the president and management were put on probation. The second case, that of Raytheon Manufacturing Co., decided in 1959, involved the exportation of television microwave link equipment to an English company and its transshipment in assembled form to an unauthorized communist destination. Raytheon, the American exporter, was placed on probation for one year and required to make periodic reports with regard to all its exports from the United States. The English transshippers were denied, also for one year, the possibility of participating in any validated license exports involving American goods.[16]

As previously noted, under certain circumstances the various United States restrictions, those of the Treasury Department in particular, purport to extend to alien firms and individuals and to foreign based companies in which American interests participate (even in regard to sensitive goods of non-U.S. origin). Serious legal and practical problems of enforcement often ensue.

It has long been realized that the extraterritorial application of American law cannot fully prevent or punish unauthorized diversion of goods from initially legitimate destinations. To cope with this difficulty, cooperative (IC/DV) procedures have been worked out with certain friendly Western governments. The willing assistance of these governments stems not only from a mutual interest in security, but also from a hard-headed desire to enable their own industry to acquire advanced American equipment and technology. It is feared that without cooperation in this sensitive area, the needed supplies might not be forthcoming.

Thus the "import certificate" which the foreign buyer is required to transmit to the Office of Export Control via the American exporter is, in effect, an undertaking toward his own government not to transship the strategic commodities or technical information to any unauthorized point. Noncompliance places such buyer not only in violation of American law, but also, and quite directly, of the legal system of his nation, residence, place of incorporation, place of business, the situs of the goods, etc. Similarly, the "delivery-verification" which the Office may require constitutes a confirmation from the buyer's own government that the goods have, in fact, reached their destination. Inability to furnish such a document upon request again amounts to a violation of the local law.

The foreign law may, and occasionally does, intervene independently, with its own criminal and administrative sanctions. A non-American firm, whether or not controlled by American interests, may be prohibited from shipping or transshipping commodities or technical data of either U.S. or non-U.S. origin, under the strategic export controls of the local government. Moreover, the particular goods may be covered by international arrangements to which the local government is a party, *e.g.,* COCOM. In all such instances enforcement will follow without the direct or indirect intrusion of American authority.

C. Multilateral Coordination Measures

With a view to supplementing their nationally operative export regulations, the key countries in the European recovery program reached agreement in late 1949 on a cooperative scheme of security controls. The organization established for that purpose, the Consultative Group Coordinating Committee (COCOM), began to meet in Paris in early 1950. The number of participating countries was gradually increased until membership reached fifteen: Japan and all of the NATO countries excepting Iceland.

COCOM is an informal and amorphous grouping, with no direct links to any of the principal military or economic compacts of the West. It has no charter and is based on no treaty. The arrangements concluded within its framework are moral obligations rather than commitments binding under international law. Its basic function is twofold: to maintain lists of strategic items subject to "embargo" and "watch"; and to secure agreement on enforcement measures designed to minimize unauthorized transshipment. The lists, classified as "secret," and a variety of ancillary controls have fluctuated over the years as a result of periodic review. Items which ceased to be strategic have been deleted and entries of new technological importance have been added.[17] Developments in the East-West political climate have also had a bearing on the content of the multilaterally recognized lists.

At the time of the Korean hostilities, an extensive embargo, with shipping and bunkering limitations, applied to communist China and North Korea. A special China Committee dealt with controls affecting that part of the Far East. This separate regional scheme came to an end in 1957, by way of merger with the COCOM system. Subsequent American attempts to include Cuba within the scope of COCOM have not succeeded. However, a multinational embargo on trade with that country was imposed in 1964 at the level of the Organization of American States, and maintained in the face of strong opposition, notably from Mexico and, more recently, Chile.

Despite the patchwork nature of its organization and the continuing erosion of its strategic list, COCOM continues to provide a modicum of cooperation among the principal Western allies. It offers the participating governments a common forum for considering security trade control matters and machinery to ensure, as nearly as possible, equal treatment of their respective business communities. The obvious exception in this respect is, of course, the American business community.

As the preponderant power in the alliance, the United States has had a special interest in developing adequate international export controls from the inception of the cold war: to prevent shipment to the East of strategic commodities of allied origin and to safeguard the particularly extensive American category of proscribed goods against transmission to communist consignees.

The organizational efforts which culminated in the COCOM arrangement were stimulated by a succession of legislative proposals in the United States, linked with foreign aid debates and looking toward the cessation of assistance to countries engaged in uninhibited trading with the Soviet bloc. The Economic Cooperation Act of 1948, in effect, required from countries receiving Marshall Aid assurances against the export to the East of items which the United States considered strategic. The Mutual Defense Assistance Control Act of 1951 (Battle Act), passed in the tense climate of the Korean War, is a more systematically spelled out measure.[18] It encompasses relations with America's direct allies as well as other friendly nations. Essentially, its provisions seek to maintain a cooperative embargo on the export of arms, implements of war, atomic energy materials and other strategic goods; and to withhold U.S. military, economic or financial assistance from countries which knowingly permit the shipment of such items to nations threatening the security of the United States. Moreover, pursuant to the Foreign Assistance Act of 1961 a prohibition has been imposed upon sales of American agricultural commodities under the Food for Peace Act to countries that trade with North Vietnam or sell to Cuba anything other than limited categories of medicines and foods. Similar restrictions have been incorporated into the Foreign Assistance and Related Agencies Appropriation Act of 1968.[19]

The Battle Act itself bans strategic goods which are on the broader, unilateral U.S. embargo lists. Such goods have been divided by the Act's administrator into Category A (arms, ammunitions, implements of war and atomic energy materials) and Category B (sensitive military-industrial products). In addition, "other materials," of lesser strategic importance are restricted on a classified basis. Although international export control negotiations partly proceed from this list, the COCOM members do not automatically accept its content for embargo. As of 1960, following successive adjustments, the two lists have been largely conformed.

Along with general export licensing, items proscribed pursuant to the Battle Act are, as a rule, policed by the Department of Commerce's Office of Export Control. But goods falling within Category A are within the licensing authority of the Atomic Energy Commission and of the Department of State's Office of Munitions Control.

The President has frequently used his discretion to allow the continuation of aid to offending countries, deeming its cessation detrimental to the overall security of the United States; and, in fact, the sanction of aid stoppage has never been exercised. The Battle Act does, however, represent a strong and durable expression of policy which has strengthened the hand of the executive branch in negotiations with other governments. With time, it has also become a hindrance. Neutral or uncommitted nations are sensitive about appearing to take sides between East and West to the extent their compliance with the United States embargo might imply. And communist propaganda has gotten considerable mileage out of the charge that Washington attaches "strings" to its aid. As far as the allied countries of western Europe are concerned, the Act's coercive value has largely vanished with the cessation of Marshall Plan Aid and most other forms of postwar recovery assistance.

D. The Limits of Allied Cooperation

While continuing to play the leading role in COCOM, the United States has shown a persistent reluctance to accept completely the consequences of a negotiated multilateral system of controls.

Since December 1950 there has been a complete American embargo on trade with communist China (relaxed in some minor respects in 1969) and North Korea. Thereafter, full-scale financial and shipping controls were extended to North Vietnam and Cuba. No other nation of any trading consequence follows a policy even remotely comparable. The foreign policy of the United States toward the communist countries of Asia, and toward Cuba, differs in many respects from those of other Western countries. It is natural for these differences to carry over into the area of trade control.

As for the communist countries of Europe, the United States controls a considerably wider range of items, and while the severity of the denial rule has fluctuated, it has consistently gone much deeper into the general industrial and economic area than any other COCOM or major non-COCOM country. It is customary for the ministerial meetings of NATO to reemphasize the unity of the Atlantic (and COCOM) countries on basic strategic matters. But disagreements exist with regard to matters of implementation. These disagreements become more pronounced during prolonged periods of East-West *détente*; they tend to subside under the impact of events which emphasize the security threat from the East. But for years there has persisted a dual thread in the trade control field: one, the continuation of a multilateral program and the other, the maintenance of an independent American position.

United States regulations as applied to eastern Europe and the Soviet Union aim at withholding strategic materials and technology which might significantly augment the Warsaw Pact countries' military-industrial potential. The control is thus by definition selective. It is based on the recognition that the East is so largely self-sufficient that it is vulnerable with respect to only a few categories of items which must come from the outside. A continuing source of difficulty is the fact that the effectiveness of any unilateral controls depends on the degree of parallel action which other possible supplier countries are prepared to adopt, and that certain classes of commodities, technology and transactions embargoed by the United States are left open by such other countries. While today there is a clearer American realization that policy divergence should be permitted only when unilateral denial is likely to have a recognizable impact, highly complex technical judgments are involved. The result is a double standard under which firms in Europe, Japan and elsewhere may engage in commerce forbidden to American companies. Moreover, attendant licensing procedures baffle some buyers and sellers to such an extent that orders often are not placed in the U.S.A. even for items which are legitimately exportable.

In addition, the comparative severity of the various segments of American regulation causes frictions with other supplying countries. These frictions may entail a clash of sovereign power and come to the surface in the form of embarrassing diplomatic differences of opinion. Outright conflicts of national law are also involved, whenever U.S. controls operate upon foreign firms through the withholding of goods, technology and components, or through the imposition of administrative and criminal sanctions.

The authority of the Office of Export Control affects "any person," that is to say any firm or individual within or without the United States, regardless of nationality. Not only shipments from the United States, but also reexportations from one foreign territory to another are covered. The Treasury's regulations extend beyond this, to exports and other transactions which do not necessarily originate in the United States, its territories or possessions. In addition, the Commerce Department controls the shipment of various types of goods on U.S. flagships and aircraft even in trade between third countries. The intrusion of American authority into other nations' commerce is carried further by the Maritime Administration, which keeps an elaborate check on foreign shipping as well, including a blacklist of vessels used in the transportation of commodities to Cuba and North Vietnam.

An examination of the record shows that in many cases it is the foreign rather than the American firm that stands in violation; and administrative sanctions in the form of denial orders are frequently addressed to them for acts committed outside United States territory. Moreover, there is nothing in the export control legislation or the regulations issued thereunder to preclude the imposition of criminal punishment upon foreign nationals, residents or firms for acts which are illegal under the U.S. law, but entirely legal under the law of the country where they are committed. While this type of extraterritorial jurisdiction has never been exercised, severe administrative punishment has on occasion been meted out to foreign firms and individuals. In the Raytheon case, for example, the English transshipper was subjected to onerous sanctions with respect to deliveries which were perfectly legitimate under British law.

Treasury regulations issued under the Trading with the Enemy Act, which in certain situations restrict the export of foreign-produced goods from one country to another, were initially cast as financial controls over persons subject to U.S. jurisdiction. This type of approach encompasses, with unusual breadth, nationals and residents (regardless of where they or their activities are located), nonresident aliens who happen to be within United States territory, American companies and even foreign business entities which are owned or controlled by Americans.

In net result, the several sets of regulations extend not only to alien individuals, but also to certain alien firms, even if incorporated under the law of a foreign country (or having their main or exclusive place of business there), and forbid them to engage in various classes of transactions with designated communist areas without prior clearance from the Commerce Department or the Treasury Department in Washington.

In relations with Canada, where American subsidiaries account for almost one-half of the economy's manufacturing sector, U.S. enforcement actions have furnished fertile soil for controversy. Two situations are illustrative of the basic problems involved. In 1957, the Treasury Department ordered the Ford Motor Company to require its Canadian subsidiary to repudiate a contract for the delivery of 1000 trucks to communist China. The dilemma entailed in this step was a serious one. On the one hand, the order could be viewed as an interference with Canadian policy on business dealings with the East, indeed as an indirect encroachment upon the sovereignty of a friendly foreign power.[20] On the other hand, failure to take such action might result in extensive evasion of United States law by means of real or dummy subsidiaries operated from neighboring Canadian bases.

In another situation the Treasury attempted to frustrate deliveries of Canadian wheat sold to communist China. Here the intention was to prevent ships under Chinese charter from utilizing suction grain loading equipment manufactured in Illinois and needed for the purpose of unloading the shipments at their destination. In the resultant diplomatic furor, President Kennedy revoked the stop-shipment order, thus waiving the purported application to the Trading with the Enemy Act.

On a more technical legal plane, a striking manifestation of the conflict of laws in this area was afforded by a 1965 case litigated in France. Here the operation of American law was simply over-ruled, insofar that it attempted (via the American corporate parent) to induce a French company to breach a contract with another French company despite the fact that the contract was valid and legal under the local law. Fruehauf-France S.A. was controlled by the Fruehauf Corporation of the United States. Acting under order of the U.S. Treasury, the American parent had sought to prevent performance of the subsidiary's contract with Automobile Berliet S.A. to deliver sixty vans for eventual shipment to mainland China. Berliet had refused to rescind the contract. The French minority shareholders of Fruehauf-France then successfully moved to place the company's administration under temporary, court-supervised receivership for the purpose of performing its contractual obligations, thereby circumventing the U.S. opposition.

The grounds of the decision were formulated with restraint, given the delicate issues in play: France's divergent policy toward China; its balance of payments needs; resistance to foreign interference with its export patterns and the fact that the national authority had expressly granted an export permit. Nor was the court impressed by the fact that as much as two-thirds of the French company's stock was held in the United States (although the U.S. Treasury purports to have jurisdiction even if a minority is in American hands, as long as effective control exists, *e.g.,* a fractional but controlling interest in a widely held foreign company). Quite reasonably, the stated legal grounds reflect concern with the company's fate and the minority's right under local law. All in all, the judgment is sufficiently embedded in basic principles to constitute a useful guide for the resolution of other conflicts of this type:

> The evidence demonstrates . . . not only the clear and present interest Fruehauf-France, S.A. has in the execution of a contract made with its principal customer, Berliet, S.A., which accounts for about 40 percent of its exports, but above all the catastrophic result which would

> have been produced, on the eve of the delivery date, and which would be felt even today, if the contract had been breached, because the buyer would be in a position to demand of the seller all commercial damage resulting therefrom, valued at more than five million francs, following upon the break-off of its dealings with China.
> These damages, which [the United States parent corporation] did not indicate any intention of assuming, would be of such an order as to ruin the financial equilibrium and the moral credit of Fruehauf-France, S.A. and provoke its disappearance and the unemployment of more than 600 workers;. . . the judge-referee must take into account the interests of the company rather than the personal interests of any shareholders even if they be the majority.[21]

No other Western country has ever contemplated, either legislatively or administratively, an extraterritorial reach for its laws as extensive as that claimed by the United States. That Washington's approach is singularly ambitious has already been stressed. But its problems are also quite unique. Elaborate powers of surveillance have had to be developed to cope with ingenious types of circumventive activities undertaken abroad.[22] In particular, the issue of foreign subsidiaries has posed, in rather practical terms, a peculiarly American problem, since no country maintains a scale of capital investment abroad comparable with that of the large multinational American corporations.

Today, there is widespread agreement among Western governments, including the United States, that the continuation and expansion of peaceful trade with the East is desirable, and that neither the communist economies, nor the military capacities which they support, could be critically affected by means of embargo. All export control administrations are moving in the direction of greater liberality and this trend is likely to continue, barring an abrupt deterioration in the international climate. However, as long as the United States maintains its elaborate arsenal of restrictive tools, a basic question remains unanswered: how to coordinate allied policy in this area so as to remove conflicts and to assure for the American companies a reasonable share in the evolving commodity trade with the East.

There would seem to be two possibilities: first, to make the COCOM list the operative standard for U.S. controls (subject to rare exceptions where unilateral denial would be desirable and effective, *e.g.,* in the case of innovations on the frontier of technology which other Western countries have not yet incorporated into their industries); second, to employ the bilateral, intergovernmental form of agreement for the purpose of clarifying on an annual basis what items the U.S. would agree to license to the particular communist country as orders are placed. On the assumptions postulated, either or both of these modifications would provide a more realistic method of operation than exists at present.

As to the Treasury regulations, or the export controls affecting the communist areas of Asia and Cuba, the policy cleavage between the United States and other Western countries is still too wide to enable an early approximation of practice. Nonetheless, there have been some signs of an American adjustment at the implementation level. In the aftermath of the Canadian and French experiences cited above and recent attempts to normalize relations with communist China, the zeal with which the Treasury has enforced its legislative mandate throughout the world has been considerably attenuated. Not only has self-restraint in matters of extraterritorial enforcement become the unofficial order of the day, but foreign companies (including American-controlled firms and banks) trading with communist China in peaceful goods of non-US origin and in non-dollar currencies have been exempted from legal prohibitions. In the case of Cuba, the Treasury has long relied on a program of voluntary compliance whereby American companies are "invited" to persuade their foreign subsidiaries to refrain from such trade. Experience to date bears out the practical and diplomatic superiority of this noncoercive method of international regulation.

BOOK ONE

SECOND PART

THE COMMERCIAL SETTING

8

THE ORGANIZATION OF TOTAL STATE TRADING

A. Commerce as a Public Function

1. Government Monopolies

Under a special decree promulgated by Lenin in April 1918, foreign trade was one of the first economic functions nationalized by the Soviet government. The principle of a state monopoly embracing all external commerce subsequently became enshrined in the 1936 constitution. With the advent of other communist regimes in Europe and Asia, the same principle was established throughout the affected areas.[1] In mainland China, the extensive private element in foreign trade was virtually eliminated by 1954.[2]

In matters of organizational and operational detail, considerable variation exists from one communist country to another. Moreover, some of the planned economies are currently experimenting with venturesome reforms. While a transitional phase is therefore in evidence and uniformity is not total, the fundamental characteristics of the state trading structure are nonetheless sufficiently similar to justify treatment as a distinct genus of which the Soviet system is the prototype.

State trading is not an invention of the Soviets. Its origins can be traced at least as far back as the city-states of medieval Italy.[3] Moreover, government-conducted foreign commerce exists today in the West as well. The contemporary capitalist world is far removed from the nineteenth-century concept of universal free trade, which prevailed in Great Britain during the period of her mercantile supremacy. Indeed, the United States may properly be regarded as one of the largest state traders outside the East. Its Commodity Credit Corporation alone, a government enterprise which buys surplus American farm produce and arranges for its disposal at home or abroad, has had annual turnovers of as much as $2.5 billion. A strong inclination toward state trading also manifested itself in western Europe during and immediately after the Second World War. Although on the decline in the past two decades, it is still today an extensively used technique. In the less developed countries, the phenomenon began to spread around 1950, and looms quite large at present in a number of basic commodity areas.

The fundamental distinction between Eastern and Western state trading is the existence of a prescribed government monopoly in the case of the former and of a preponderance of private commercial activity in the latter. In the East, the state alone decides what is to be bought, sold, bartered or "dumped" abroad. In the West, state trading is exceptional. It is conducted on the basis of commercial norms and on an equal footing with competing private enterprises.

The principle of public monopoly has far-reaching consequences, both theoretically and practically. It goes beyond the regulation, direction and control of a nation's foreign commerce. State instrumentalities alone, to the exclusion of all private entrepreneurs, have authority to transact with legal effect.

Taking the U.S.S.R. as our primary example, we find that the direction and performance of foreign trade activities is in the hands of a relatively small number of interlocking institutions: the Ministry of Foreign Trade, with its specialized departments at home and trade delegations abroad; the All-Union Chamber of Commerce with its subordinate facilities; some forty to fifty specialized export-import corporations; and various other domestic and foreign-based organizations.

At the apex of the bureaucratic pyramid is the Minister of Foreign Trade, the principal government agent to whom the monopoly power is delegated. As a rule, the Minister is a member of the Central Committee of the communist party. In the other communist countries, responsibility for foreign trade is concentrated in the hands of comparably placed officials and the departments over which they preside.

In terms of their functions, the ministries bear a superficial resemblance to the Foreign Trade Ministries of Western countries. They are concerned with administrative, regulatory and supervisory matters, rather than direct operational work. The substantive powers and responsibilities, and the hierarchical positions they occupy in relation to operating business entities are, however, quite distinctive. In fact, the Eastern ministries and their subordinate organs combine all the activities which market economies sharply segregate into sovereign and private hands.

The Soviet Ministry of Foreign Trade is divided into several geographic and functional administrations extensively staffed to attend to the entire range of the nation's business relations with the outside world: negotiation of commercial treaties with other countries, elaboration and administration of customs and tariff policies, issuance of export and import licenses, maintenance of quality controls over goods consigned abroad, preparation of periodic foreign trade plans, direction of official trade delegations and supervision of all corporate instrumentalities authorized to engage in international commerce.

Separate geographic divisions, covering relations with other communist countries and with the rest of the world, program, coordinate and supervise the export and import of goods. Other divisions, in addition to participating in the major functions just described, are also responsible for matters of financing, currency exchange, legal counseling, standardization, transport, research, protocol and personnel. The last function extends to hiring, firing and directing the individuals who comprise the country's principal foreign merchants and business executives.

At home, the Ministry operates a network of commissioners with permanent offices in highly industrialized regions, major ports and other locations of key importance to foreign trade. As the eyes and ears of the Ministry in their designated areas, the commissioners supervise the preparation and delivery of goods for export and afford liaison with the central administration in Moscow.[4] Abroad, the Ministry maintains numerous representatives who are assigned either to resident trade delegations or to temporary visiting missions. Other Ministry representatives serve as commercial counselors and attachés of Soviet embassies or as members detailed to specialized trade administrations or organizations.

Broadly, the responsibilities of the delegations are to represent the monopoly outside the U.S.S.R. to effectuate its policy in countries to which they are accredited and to facilitate and supervise the local business activities of Soviet enterprises. They issue import licenses, grant permits for the transit of goods through Russian territory, deliver certificates of origin, induce compliance with Soviet foreign trade regulations, study local economic conditions, report on sales possibilities and make available to local business firms information relating to market potential in the Soviet Union. At the transactional level, the delegations act as agents for Soviet buyers and sellers. In recent years their direct commercial activities have been substantially reduced in favor of corporate export-import enterprises, unprotected by sovereign immunity and diplomatic privilege. As a result, some of the abuses which were rife in the Soviet trade of the past are no longer major irritants.

By and large, the Soviet example in appointing permanent, quasi-diplomatic trade representations has been emulated. Thus, China has established a trade delegation in the U.A.R. and a purchasing mission in Berne. Poland has a large purchasing mission in London, East Germany maintains trade delegations in many locations of Asia and Africa, and numerous technical offices and after-sales servicing facilities in other parts of the world. In countries where a particular monopoly is not represented at all, because its trade there is minimal, or recognized diplomatic relations are absent, the commercial mission of some other communist country is relied upon.

The Ministry of Foreign Trade is not the only government department with responsibility for commercial relations beyond the nation's borders. Other ministries, acting through their own instrumentalities, have competence to deal abroad in a designated context. A most significant example for our purposes is the role played by the State Committee on Science and Technology, which exercises a policy-making and guiding function with regard to the acquisition of foreign patents and know-how, and the development of industrial cooperation with advanced Western economies.

A separate State Committee for Economic Relations (G.K.E.S.), with ministerial rank on a level equal to the Ministry of Foreign Trade, was created by the Soviet Council of Ministers in 1957 and endowed with broad responsibilities in the field of policy. Part of its assignment is the use of economic means for the purpose of bolstering political relations with selected groups of countries: to increase and strengthen economic cooperation with other communist states, to establish and expand relations with developing nations and to assure the fulfillment of obligations in the sphere of technical assistance.[5]

The Committee controls several foreign trade corporations with designated responsibilities: furnishing equipment and materials to industrial projects undertaken abroad, supplying technical help, assisting in the gathering of data, planning and aiding construction, and training the beneficiary state's national cadres for work in newly established industries. The presence of military men in high positions on the Committee raises the suspicion that certain aspects of military assistance also fall within its jurisdiction.[6]

A government body comparable to the G.K.E.S. has existed in China since January 1960 under the name of "Central Bureau for Foreign Economic Relations."[7] Similar departments have not, however, been identified in the other communist countries. Coordination of the policies and activities of east European nations in the field of foreign economic relations is one of the functions of the Council for Mutual Economic Assistance. The role played in Comecon by the G.K.E.S. seems to be no less significant than that of the Soviet Ministry of Foreign Trade.

2. *Chambers of Commerce*

Each of the Eastern countries maintains a national Chamber of Foreign Commerce. These institutions are, in fact, the most important of a number of auxiliary organizations with responsibility to promote and facilitate international trade. Although there are minor variations from country to country, the structure of the typical Eastern Chamber, the content of its by-laws and the nature of its activities show little divergence from corresponding French, American or English trade associations. Indeed, nowhere are the trappings of conformity to Western institutions more pronounced.

The specific functions of the Chambers include establishment of permanent relations with comparable foreign organizations, sponsorship of trade and industry fairs at home and abroad, provision of marketing information, issuance of certificates of origin on exported goods, certification of quality after expert examination of products, promotion of joint ventures between local and alien firms and maintenance of procedures for the resolution of commercial differences.

Some of the Chambers have responsibilities going beyond those of their Western counterparts. For example, the East German Chamber of Foreign Trade was assigned the delicate task of establishing trade relations with Western countries which do not recognize the G.D.R. politically and which must, consequently, refuse to deal with official representatives of the Pankow government. The Polish Chamber performs functions similar to those of the court-supervised *Registre de Commerce* in west European countries.[8] A trading enterprise is not deemed to have come into existence with the benefit of independent legal standing until it is inscribed in the Chamber's special Register. Similarly, the Soviet Chamber maintains a special section for the handling of foreign patent and trademark applications, a function which traditionally is performed by a government-operated Patent Office.

The All-Union Chamber of Commerce of the U.S.S.R. is a legally independent corporate person. While it is designated in its Charter as a "social," as distinct from a "state," organization, because its adherents participate on a voluntary basis, it is expressly placed under the supervision of the Ministry of Foreign Trade. Its operating revenue is derived from corporate capital, members' contributions, fees collected for services and government subsidies.

The membership of the Soviet Chamber consists of indigenous enterprises active in export-import, merchant shipping, insurance and banking. Also included among its more than 1000 participants are a number of industrial enterprises, institutes and other organizations without direct involvement in foreign trade. The Hungarian Chamber lists 250 members and the Czech, 500, most of them domestic industrial enterprises; foreign trade organizations, banks and research institutions account for only 10 percent of the membership.

The most important single function performed by the Chambers is the provision of specialized arbitration facilities for the settlement of international trade and maritime disputes. At an early date it was recognized that the regular people's courts did not offer a forum satisfactory to foreign litigants. On the other hand, the prospect of submission to the "class-biased" courts and arbitrators of the capitalist world evoked considerable aversion. In response to a manifest need, permanently functioning tribunals, with competence over foreign causes, were established under the auspices of Chambers of Commerce in the U.S.S.R. in the early nineteen-thirties and subsequently, as part of the postwar Sovietization of their institutions, in the other European and Asian communist countries.

Several joint Chambers of Commerce with permanent staffs of their own, have been established as a stimulant to closer trade relations between individual Eastern and Western nations. The oldest institution of this kind has existed in England since the end of the First World War. More recently, such Chambers have been organized in Finland, Italy, France and Belgium.[9]

The Franco-Soviet Chamber, by far the most dynamic, commenced activity in 1967. Its outstanding characteristics are the two permanent, mixed offices which it maintains in Paris and Moscow. The membership consists of more than thirty Soviet foreign trade organizations and a much larger number of French industrial and commercial firms, banking institutions and professional groups. The stated purpose of the Chamber is "to contribute to the development of economic and commercial relations and scientific and technical cooperation between the two countries."[10] Among the principal functions is to collect and disseminate information concerning economic trends, technological developments, commercial legislation, tariffs, transportation, insurance, tourism and other matters of mutual concern. It is also charged with organizing exhibitions and trade fairs in both countries, assisting in the exchange of commercial delegations and arranging conferences, colloquia and symposia on Franco-Soviet economic cooperation.

B. The Eastern Business Partner

1. Export-Import Corporations

The actual trading functions of the Eastern monopolies that follow the Soviet model most closely are still largely entrusted to a limited number of export-import corporations and to several related institutions such as shipping lines, rail and road transport organizations, insurance companies and foreign trade banks. In the U.S.S.R. the trading corporations are called *obiedinieniia* (combines) and are thus formally distinguished from *predpriatiia,* domestic producing entities. The distinction in terminology is not clearly drawn by the other communist countries. Poland and Hungary in particular have opted in favor of an accelerated mingling of responsibilities at the operational level and their example appears to be winning a measure of acceptance elsewhere in east Europe.

The Soviet-type trading corporations are legally autonomous entities with the exclusive right to deal abroad in defined groups of commodities or services—monopolies within monopolies, as it were. For example, Russia's Soiuzneftekspor is the sole national entity empowered to export and import oil and petroleum products; Stankoimport controls the purchase and sale of machine tools; Aviaeksport markets civil aircraft and helicopters; and Litsenzintorg negotiates the purchase and sale of patent licenses. This, and other manifestations of the principle of specialization run throughout the Eastern foreign trade apparatus with profound practical impediments and legal consequences to which we will return.

Several foreign trade corporations deal in a diversified range of products, but are confined to designated geographic regions. Within this category are the Soviet corporation Vostokintorg, which conducts business with certain Asian nations and the East German Gesellschaft Innerdeutschenhandel, which handles transactions between the two Germanies. Other enterprises hold a monopoly of functions rather than goods: Poland's Baltona, ship chandling to vessels of all flags; C. Hartwig Ltd., international forwarding; and AGPOL, advertising.

While most foreign trade enterprises are authorized to engage in both exportation and importation, some are specifically limited to one or the other. Instances of such functional delimitation exist throughout the East.

A fact of crucial significance is that the export-import enterprises are neither the manufacturers of the goods they sell, nor the users of the goods they purchase. Essentially they appear as intermediaries between domestic enterprises interested in buying or selling and foreign suppliers or customers. However, it would be an error to classify them as mere agents. In both communist and capitalist legal terms they have been appearing as full-fledged principals. Although the domestic consumer or supplier may assist in the negotiation and performance of a particular contract, he does not, without government dispensation, qualify as a party; nor does he execute agreements with foreign firms. In the future, domestic enterprises are likely to appear more and more as principals, and export-import enterprises as agents. This is suggested by the logic of current decentralization reforms and may already be an established fact in the case of Hungary.

Notwithstanding their administrative subordination to the Minister of Foreign Trade (who provides the working funds and appoints and dismisses the presidents and vice presidents) the export-import enterprises are held out, by their respective legal systems, as being separate and distinct from the states as well as from each other. In the U.S.S.R. their individual existence is decreed by the Council of Ministers, and their governing charters are issued by the responsible ministry. These charters cover the corporate name, object, powers, main place of business, amount of authorized capital, the authority of the principal officers, the method of contracting obligations, the fiscal year, provisions for the distribution of surplus and procedures for liquidation.

In the conduct of business, the foreign trade corporations act for their own account. They, and not the government Treasury, are responsible for their own debts, which are payable solely out of the corporate assets contributed by the state, or subsequently acquired as surplus. Moreover, they may independently acquire and hold title to property, sue and be sued in courts or arbitration tribunals at home and abroad and enter into binding commitments in connection with transactions which fall within the scope of their charters.

The degree of autonomy enjoyed by the export-import corporations varies slightly among the different communist countries, although the east European enterprises enjoy somewhat greater freedom of action than their Soviet counterparts. Even more independence exists in the case of Yugoslav enterprises, which are permitted to operate on a completely decentralized basis and to draft their own commercial plans in order to maximize profits, subject, of course, to the limits established by governmental trade and currency regulations.

Superficially, the Eastern trading entities do not differ from a public corporation in America (*e.g.,* the Commodities Credit Corporation) or a *société d'économie mixte* in France (*e.g.,* Sud Aviation). Characterizations by means of such analogies are, however, misleading. The concept of a communist corporation is *sui generis,* and quite distinct from the English limited liability company, the Italian *società per azioni,* or the German *Aktiengesellschaft,* whether privately or publicly held. Essentially, the Eastern enterprise is an integral organ of government administration, cast in corporate form and terminology.

2. *General Domestic Enterprises*

An extension of the principle that commercial operations with the outside world are in the hands of specialized export-import corporations, is the rule that all other entities are precluded from consummating transactions in this sphere. Exceptions, however, are increasingly encountered in the smaller east European countries. As the range of economic dealings with the outside world continues to expand, major industries are being given differential treatment appropriate to their particular production, servicing and marketing exigencies.

A number of Soviet enterprises which do not emanate from the Ministry of Foreign Trade, are authorized to contract transactions with foreign elements. Cooperative institutions, acting under the auspices of Centrosoiuz (the Union of Cooperatives) have considerable latitude in conducting commodity exchanges with corresponding organizations located abroad. Sovfrakht is active in international shipping under the auspices of the Soviet Merchant Marine; Soveksportfilm deals in motion picture production and distribution rights, cinematographic equipment and related products under the jurisdiction of the State Committee on Cinematography attached to the Council of Ministers; and Intourist handles visitors from abroad under the supervision of the Council of Ministers' Direction for Tourism. In the sphere of industrial cooperation with Western countries, Vneshtekhnika, an instrumentality of the State Committee on Science and Technology, performs an important function in connection with the acquisition of foreign patent licenses and know-how. All of these enterprises, as well as the foreign trade combines utilized by the State Committee for Economic Relations, are creatures of their respective ministries or government departments. But in connection with all international transactions in which they engage, they are subject to the regulation and supervision of the Ministry of Foreign Trade.

In East Germany, departures from the underlying principle have long existed even in connection with the exchange of physical goods. Although export-import transactions are, as a rule, conducted by the foreign trade enterprises, certain cooperative (volkseigene) associations with domestic manufacturing activities are permitted to maintain their own independent combines for centralized sale abroad. The same is true of certain major manufacturing concerns, notably Karl Zeiss (photographic equipment) and Chemianlagen (chemicals). Similarly, in Czechoslovakia, large industrial concerns (the Skoda complex, for example) that play a significant role in export production, have been given the right to deal directly with foreign firms, both in procurement and selling. A number of joint stock companies grouping several manufacturing enterprises are also used as export conduits.

In Poland, the external activities of the export-import combines are likewise supplemented by cooperatives and limited liability companies with competence to enter foreign markets. Several industrial concerns, notably H. Cigielski (power plants, marine engines and compressors), Rafamet (machine tools) and Befama (textile machinery), have been permitted, as of the beginning of 1968, to sell abroad without passing through the state's intermediary organizations. Bulgaria appears to have gone further in this direction than any of the other communist countries. Two-thirds of its exports are said to be channeled through domestic companies with the right of direct access to world markets.[11]

Until 1968, only eight Hungarian engineering concerns, Tungsram among the better known, enjoyed the right to engage in export and import operations. Recent reforms have extended this right to numerous other domestic firms and service organizations on a case-by-case basis, with the option of acting directly or through some twenty-five specialized foreign trade combines. Also, the Hungarian corporation Interag, a prewar privately owned agency representing locally a number of Western firms including Shell Oil, has lately been reactivated for the purpose of developing foreign trade and facilitating the establishment of extraterritorial business relations.[12] Domestically, Interag's primary function is to expand the now restricted network of Shell services for the convenience of Hungarian motorists and foreign tourists. Abroad, it will represent, as agent, those Hungarian enterprises authorized to export their own products. Some ten other agencies of this type are now available to render services to local and foreign business entities.

Comparable agencies are available to represent foreign companies in East Berlin (Transinter), Prague (Transacta), Sofia (Burpred) and Warsaw (Dynamo). To date, the U.S.S.R. has not seen fit to adopt the corporate agency concept. Since domestic enterprises generally lack experience in world market research, in negotiating extranational contracts and in selling their goods abroad, and since Western firms are severely limited in their access to communist economies, agency corporations of this type may be called upon to perform an important promotional role in the coming years. Counterpart Western corporations, with expertise in the peculiarities of East–West business, may also be expected to play a larger part.

Yugoslavia represents an extreme deviation from the general Eastern pattern. There, almost any sizable national manufacturing and distribution entity can, and usually does, have the capacity to engage in external commerce, provided it can persuade the Ministry of Foreign Trade that it possesses the necessary staff and qualifications.[13] In fact, several hundred firms are now eligible to operate in this sphere for their own account, occasionally in competition with one another.

In most communist countries, specific transactions not directly involving the purchase or sale of goods are, from time to time, entered into by entities with basically domestic responsibilities. This is particularly true in new spheres of joint activity between Eastern and Western enterprises, which extend to manufacturing, marketing and servicing. Thus the Czech national tourist company, CEDOK, has contracted with Western groups for the construction and operation of modern hotels. Similar agreements have been concluded in the name of the Rumanian National Travel Office General Board of Hotels and Restaurants and with the "Hungaria" Enterprise of International Hotels. Film Polski in Warsaw and Hungarofilm in Budapest regularly enter into agreements with Western firms for the production and distribution of motion picture and television films.

By and large, however, entities entrusted with internal economic responsibilities are excluded from the international sector and from direct participation in transactions involving foreign exchange. As a rule they have neither the qualified personnel, nor the capacity to muster the economic weight and bargaining power of a centralized trading combine. Manufacturing enterprises with licensed involvement in export-import still handle a limited portion of the overall trade of the Eastern countries. The bulk of commodity trade remains in the hands of the specialized corporations working within the framework of the state monopoly and under the supervision of the Ministry of Foreign Trade.

But the trend toward increased use of domestic enterprises is highly significant for the future. It is a logical extension of the economic reforms currently under way in most of the communist countries. More direct contact between Western and Eastern industries and the opportunities thus afforded to the latter to be privy to technological developments abroad are certain to add stimulus to the growth of patent licensing, joint ventures and general two-way trade.

3. *Communist-held Western Companies*

Aside from permanent trade delegations accredited abroad, the U.S.S.R. maintains or participates in a number of wholly and partly owned corporations established in foreign countries.

Because of past Soviet claims of sovereign immunity, the United States government has excluded the official delegations from engaging in business activities within its territory. Such activities have long been conducted by the Amtorg Trading Corporation, a company formed and having its principal place of business in the State of New York. Amtorg acts largely as agent on behalf of Soviet enterprises. Its shares are held in escrow for the Soviet Ministry of Foreign Trade, the State Bank and the Bank for Foreign Trade in Moscow.[14] Its officers are registered with the United States Attorney General as agents of a foreign government. They enjoy neither official nor diplomatic status and are subject, together with the corporation itself, to the normal operation of New York and federal law.

A similar company, Arcos Ltd., was set up in 1920 under the laws of England. Prior to the establishment of a Soviet trade delegation there, this company was the basic conduit for business relations between the two countries. More recently, it has served as a commercial division of the trade delegation. The U.S.S.R. also organized in England, as early as 1923, the Russian Wood Agency, a mixed brokerage firm trading in timber. Its members today include the Soviet foreign trade corporation, Eksportles, and a number of English brokerage houses.

The exigencies of world trade in oil and petroleum products have impelled the Soviets to establish institutionalized operating outlets in the West. Notable among these are Russian Oil Products (England), Derop (prewar Germany) and Erop (postwar Austria). In 1967 the U.S.S.R. acquired a majority interest in Nafta, a Belgian company based in Antwerp, in order to import, store in leased port facilities and distribute refined Soviet oil products.

In recent years companies with mixed management and equity have been established in numerous Western countries, particularly France, to facilitate the marketing of Soviet goods: in 1969 the foreign trade enterprise Soiuzkhimeksport joined French investors to form Sogo et Cie, S.A. (chemicals and pharmaceuticals); in 1968 Russe-Bois was organized with the participation of Eksportles (timber); and in 1966, Active-Auto, with Machineksport (tractors).[15] The U.S.S.R. also holds equity in such diverse, foreign-based sales organizations as a Brussels department store, Maison de la Russie, and two English firms, Technical and Optical Equipment Co., and Anglo-Russian Plant Hire Co. In 1969 the Japanese government approved the establishment of a new shipping and brokerage agency, Tokyo Kyodo Kaiun Kaisha, in which the Soviet Far Eastern Shipping Company holds 50 percent of the shares. The company will cater to transportation needs arising from the rapid expansion of Soviet-Japanese trade. In the less developed countries, mixed companies are also becoming an increasingly favored vehicle for joint operations. Thus, in Ethiopia, Soviet organizations participated in the formation of Ethso Trading Company; in Nigeria, Avtoeksport; in Morocco, Machineksport and so forth.[16] Ventures of this type are likely to become the wave of the future as Eastern industries attempt to break into world markets with finished and semifinished goods and a growing range of competitively priced services. The Eastern monopolies' long-term objective is to avoid selling through the intermediary of Western distributors and to get as close as possible to the lucrative foreign retail outlets.

The Soviet Union also controls an international network of banks based in western Europe and the Middle East. Banque Commerciale Pour l'Europe du Nord was founded in Paris in 1921 by White Russian émigrés and sold to the U.S.S.R. in 1925. It is presided over by a French national and a local board of directors. An even larger institution of this type is the Moscow Narodny Bank, Ltd., of London, incorporated in 1919, and now maintaining active branches elsewhere, *e.g.,* in Beirut. In 1966 the Wosschod Handelsbank was established as an *Aktiengesellschaft* under the laws of the Canton of Zurich in Switzerland. Another financial institution of some significance is the Russian-Iranian Bank of Teheran.

All of these banks enjoy excellent reputations for management, professional know-how and fair dealing. Although fully chartered deposit and credit institutions under the laws of their host countries, they transact most of their business in the sphere of East-West economic intercourse. Typical forms of financing are the discount of bills of sale drawn by Western exporters to the East and the acceptance of commercial paper issuing from Eastern enterprises. The banks have been known to make local loans as well and even to purchase Western government gilt-edged securities and municipal bonds. They are also quite active in the important sphere of Euro-dollar transactions.

In the insurance and reinsurance field the U.S.S.R. operates or participates in foreign-based institutions which cover risks both within and beyond East-West trade and shipping. Thus, Garant of Vienna is incorporated under Austrian law and writes policies which enter into the province of Western export credit insurers. A distinctive aspect of its business is coverage against shipping delays and damages. Its compensation patterns have been concentrated in the area of late payment rather than outright default. Similarly, the Black Sea and Baltic Insurance Company was incorporated in England in 1925. It operates as a member of the British Insurance Association and underwrites credit risks on exports to all East European countries, without relying on ultimate E.C.G.D. coverage.

While in no way communist-controlled, a number of Western-based firms act on behalf of Eastern organizations as specialized brokerage agencies, intermediaries and distributors. Functionally, such companies complement the Eastern trading establishment in finding outlets for exports, facilitating procurement, arranging barters and tapping sources of credit.

C. The Planning of Trade

The countries of eastern Europe are highly structured societies. All levers of power are in the hands of a small group of party and government leaders who have, over the years, devised an intricate apparatus for the organization and control of every activity deemed to be endowed with a public interest. In this environment, a strong disposition exists to reduce every aspect of national endeavor, external as well as internal, to a component "plan," as a way of encompassing its impact and fitting it into the prescribed order of priorities.

Central planning has long been one of the hallmarks of communist economic life. Production, distribution and exchange according to an authoritatively drawn up program is seen as a basic virtue, in contrast to the generally spontaneous, "aimless" character of market-oriented development. Yet with time the concept of total planning has shown itself to be a rather occult and inexact science. It is the complexity of the modern industrial economy and the unpredictability of the human element which most of all seem to interfere with the proper functioning of state-prescribed ground rules.

The Soviet planning mechanism is currently undergoing a cautious process of decentralization. This trend is even more pronounced in the eastern European countries, where a strong interest is emerging in the use of consumer conscious marketing techniques, operationally effective production costs and prices, and broader participation in the international division of labor.

While reforms are being instituted throughout eastern Europe, their nature and extent varies from country to country. All of the states of the region seem to be departing in one way or another from the principle of strict central management—the imposition upon individual enterprises from above of subjective, detailed instructions. By and large such enterprises are being transformed from units of mere execution to organs of decision and responsibility. In Poland, for example, the number of planning indicators, or authoritatively fixed targets, has been sharply reduced. At present, they are limited to the areas of employment, investment and foreign trade. Hungary, Rumania and Czechoslovakia are also strongly reform-minded in this respect.

Throughout, foreign trade remains, however, an integral part of the overall economic plan. On a medium-term basis, and with greater precision yearly, the range and quantities of goods desired from abroad to help meet essential domestic production and consumption targets, or for other pressing reasons, are calculated in advance under procedures laboriously worked out by a complex bureaucratic structure. In similar fashion, determinations are made as to the types and volumes of commodities which can most conveniently be set aside for export, in order to provide the means of payment for imports and other financial obligations abroad. In recent years, the trade plans have increasingly had to take account of exports required to fulfill foreign aid commitments. By the same token, the responsible ministries may be expected in the future to adjust their programs to the flow of receivables, for the most part in kind, under credits previously extended to newly developing countries. In these and other connections, the payment problem, especially the chronic shortage of hard currency, is a consideration that always looms large in preparing the commercial balance.

In the East, the export process does not start with a firm's desire to expand its sales and augment its profits. The impulse to sell abroad comes, or is supposed to come, from a loftier plane—a state command expressing the need of the economy as a whole. With regard to staple commodities, the problem of adjusting to world market conditions is found to be reasonably manageable. But in the case of special exports, the adjustment tends to be arbitrary and the nature of the goods and services required seems abstract to the enterprise which may eventually be called upon to fill the orders.

Export planning in the Soviet Union begins with general instructions from Gosplan (the State Planning Commission) to the Department of Planning and Economics of the Ministry of Foreign Trade and to other affected ministries (*e.g.,* the State Committee for Economic Development, the Merchant Marine) establishing broad annual goals. The Department then sets export-import targets, control procedures and foreign exchange guidelines to be observed by the appropriate trading entities.

Within this framework, operational directives are issued to the individual foreign trade enterprises in regard to the quantities of goods to be disposed of, their sales prices, the expenses to be incurred in the course of export, the countries to which sales are to be directed, the stocks to be retained in warehouses at home and abroad, the utilization of transport facilities and so forth. Pursuant to these guidelines, and under newly instituted procedures for consultation with domestic supplier enterprises, the export corporations draft detailed plans concerning their specific range of goods and submit them to the Foreign Trade Ministry, or other responsible government departments, for coordination with the overall annual economic plan and eventual approval by Gosplan and the Council of Ministers.[17]

Imports are planned along similar lines. Once again, the process begins at the top of the pyramid. Gosplan surveys the needs of the Soviet economy for foreign goods, particularly productive equipment and technology, in light of the applications sent in by domestic manufacturing and consumer enterprises, investigates existing levels of home production and prepares a balance sheet showing the estimated output and anticipated need for each major product. An attempt is also made to compare internal production costs with costs of importation on the basis of available foreign exchange. From this, a provisional import plan is drafted, by reference to which the Ministry of Foreign Trade prepares its own schedules, taking into account state obligations under bilateral trade agreements along with projected foreign exchange inflows from export and other earnings.

The final integrated procurement plan is prepared by the Ministry's import administration in collaboration with the operating trade enterprises, the state banks and similarly interested entities. It is then submitted to Gosplan and eventually to the Council of Ministers for review and ratification.

The coordinated, annual export-import plan sets forth with specificity the total values of commodities destined for various groups of countries (socialist, capitalist and less developed); the categories of goods to be purchased from or sold to individual countries, together with the form of payment; the volumes of designated goods to be exchanged with particular countries pursuant to bilateral commercial and payment agreements; schedules of deliveries for export, broken down by ministries whose subordinate enterprises are responsible for supply and schedules of deliveries to be made to the internal economy by the respective import monopolies.

Import requirements and the availability of saleable export goods dominate the overall planning of trade. Some scope is, however, left for the consummation of transactions outside the strict confines of the plan; and under the influence of current reforms, this scope is being constantly expanded. No matter who the Eastern trading partner may be, transactions of this type are, of course, subject to approval by the competent ministry. A typical precondition of approval is the submission of a scheme which promises not to deplete, and preferably to replenish, the sparse foreign currency reserves by means of export sales from imported industrial installations, long-term credits, barter deals and other exchange-saving arrangements.

D. Internal Arrangements for Export and Import

Within the framework of the plan, an export corporation acting under the authority of the Ministry of Foreign Trade or the State Committee of Foreign Relations, as the case may be, requests or, more precisely, requires the sales administration of the appropriate production ministry to arrange for the supply of goods from enterprises under its jurisdiction. Fulfillment of the requirement is made compulsory by means of an order (zakaz-nariad) of the relevant ministry. The resultant legal obligation imposed upon the individual producer, or the confident expectation that such an obligation will be created, enables the export entity to contract firm sales abroad.

Although the obligations established for all parties concerned in the execution of the plan, both in its export and import components, are quite imperative, formal contracts are nonetheless concluded. It is in domestically operative accords of this type that account is taken of such specific matters as quantity, quality, putative prices, available reserve stocks, timing and means of shipment. On the basis of related delivery orders the supplying enterprises proceed to establish quarterly production plans and monthly shipment schedules. Upon delivery of the goods, they are paid in national currency according to domestic wholesale prices.

On the import side, there is somewhat more room for contractual freedom than on the export side of an exchange. Again, the combine deals with the responsible unit of the consuming administration and with its subordinate end-user enterprise, in order to ascertain the precise goods desired, particularly if sophisticated equipment is involved, to establish the obligation to buy, the terms of purchase, the estimated price, quality and standards, the dates and conditions of delivery, commissions to be charged and so on. Failure to obtain execution does not expose the importing entity to any risk of loss. The authority of the plan and the Foreign Trade Ministry's import license create a binding obligation to accept and pay for the goods at prevailing domestic prices even in the absence of a formal agreement between the domestic parties to the transaction.

Even transactions falling within the ratified segments of the plan usually require specific export or import licenses and foreign exchange or payment permits from the Ministry of Foreign Trade. However, it is difficult to generalize about the procedures of individual communist governments in this area.

Communist China would appear to represent one extreme, with stringent and extensive licensing regulations. Every single transaction requires a separate permit, obtainable from the Foreign Trade Control Office, a department of the Foreign Trade Ministry, upon approval of the terms of the particular contract. Czechoslovakia, representing the other extreme, completely abolished its licensing requirements for foreign trade corporations as of 1957, although foreign exchange restrictions remain in force.[18]

Most of the Eastern states have, to varying extents, relaxed their licensing regimes in recent years insofar as specialized export-import enterprises are concerned. Standing authority is now usually granted to such enterprises limited, of course, to the lines of products in which they are empowered to deal and to the quantities and values envisaged by the national foreign trade and foreign exchange plans. Domestic enterprises which enjoy the special privilege of engaging in foreign trade activities usually are required to obtain licenses in connection with specific transactions.

The historic Twenty-Third Congress of the Communist Party of the Soviet Union, held in 1966, considered at some length the role of foreign trade in the U.S.S.R.'s economy. The need to expand its scope and improve its efficiency was given particular attention. The complex and artificial procedures interposed between the Soviet producer and consumer on the one hand, and the world market on the other, was probably uppermost in Premier Kosygin's mind when he solemnly called for a more flexible liaison between the individual enterprises of local industry and the export-import corporations.[19]

That a communist nation should seek to insulate itself from world market forces in order to shield its economic plan from disruptive influences is quite understandable in view of its governing philosophy. In the past, such insulation has been achieved through the use of monopolistic trading corporations as interposed broker entities which hermetically sealed off domestic and foreign buyers and sellers from one another. The absence of correlative costs and prices between internally produced goods and imported articles helped to increase this insular condition. The long-term economic loss, however, has been great in terms of manufacturing inefficiency, reduced stimulus to produce at minimum expense and lack of adequate and continuous contact with technological and economic progress abroad.

It is too early to judge the effectiveness of the recently introduced incentive programs to encourage production for sale abroad. The Soviet Union has put into operation a system of bonuses for both manufacturing enterprises and the trade organizations which market their goods. In addition, plants whose products find their way into the export stream receive foreign exchange allocations which may be spent on procurement of desired equipment outside the confines of the plan. Several eastern European countries, notably Hungary, Rumania, East Germany and Czechoslovakia, are moving even more conspicuously in this direction.

These incentives should help to overcome the persistent lethargy among enterprises that are expected to manufacture for the world market. As they take hold, unprecedented conflicts of interest may, however, arise between such export-oriented enterprises and the ponderous and remote trading combines. In anticipation of this problem, and with a view to achieving better coordination among managers with local and external responsibilities in foreign trade, special export councils were established in the U.S.S.R. in late 1967. Their functions are to ensure closer contact between state trading organizations and those ministries and departments whose enterprises supply goods for export and provide technical services for machinery, equipment and instruments delivered abroad.

The discernible overall design is to encourage participation by local producing entities in foreign trade operations. It is hoped that the direct links thus established with the outside market will, in due time, help to improve the quality of domestically manufactured goods and make them more competitive abroad. Better results and more efficient conditions of trading are also expected to follow if those who produce or consume take more direct responsibility for costs, prices, finishing, marketing, after-sale servicing and the ultimate economic value of the business transaction to which they are parties. It is unlikely, however, that the east European reforms will succeed in uprooting the deeply ingrained economic habits of the past. For this would entail a repudiation of many sacred Soviet legacies and taboos, a fundamental modification of the government monopoly concept and a relegation of the "directive" plan to the status of mere governmental guidelines no more authoritative than the French method of "indicative" economic programming. At the very least, if institutional reforms of so far-reaching a nature were pursued, the communist economies would have to submit to a measure of foreign competition with considerable risks for their less efficient manufacturers. They would also have to expose themselves to balance of payment vagaries and their managerial class to the potent and subtle influences of the international market place.

As far as can be surmised from the outside, pragmatic experimentation and adjustment rather than sweeping reconstruction seems to be the present course of Eastern economic policy. The political pressures for change within the Comecon region could conceivably lead to deeper reform, but there is little prospect that the fundamentals of communist centralism will be (or will be allowed to be) dethroned. This is obviously true of the U.S.S.R. Whether it is also true of the rest of eastern Europe depends upon incipient economic and political realignments on the continent and the extent to which the Soviets will practice their recently proclaimed doctrine of limited sovereignty.

9

COMMUNIST BILATERALISM VERSUS OPEN WORLD TRADE

A. The Eastern Preference for Bilateral Exchange

The bilateral agreement between states is very well suited to the purpose of enlisting external trade into the service of an overall national economic program. In theory, at least, the types and quantities of commodities included in a country's total register of trade agreements should provide the information needed to determine what abundant goods the domestic economy will have to mobilize for allocation abroad. Simultaneously, it should indicate what scarce goods the international economy will be able to contribute to help enrich the "product mix" of current domestic output and, in addition, provide new production ideas as a stimulant to technical progress. In the case of a wholly planned economy, the advantages of knowing in advance what will be available from foreign import sources and what must be provided for dispatch abroad are immediately apparent. Such arrangements are, in fact, an extension of the basic technique of domestic economic planning. In the drafting of a five-year development plan, it is convenient to have reference to previously established parallel treaty commitments for export and import, which stipulate an agreed volume of clearly designated goods that will have to be traded over a predetermined period of time. By contrast, open, unregulated trade could produce a strained, dislocating effect upon efforts to meet the targets and timing of the internal plan.

Actual practice in this case has not wandered far from theory. While market economies ideally prefer multilateral trade and payment patterns, command economies engaged in mutual commerce have, by contrast, tended to resort to strict bilateralism, or, at most, a quasi-multilateral approach using the limited facilities of Comecon's International Bank for Economic Cooperation. In trade with capitalist countries, the bilateral basis of exchange is also strongly favored, while in economic dealings with the less developed world, reciprocally ordered relations of various types have become standard procedure. Another basic reason underlying the Eastern bias in favor of bilateral exchanges is the chronic shortage of convertible funds. The intergovernmental agreement enables the Eastern High Contracting Party to balance its sales and purchases, thereby avoiding the reduction of already scarce reserves. This might not otherwise be possible since its manufactured products are generally less marketable in the West than are Western goods in the East.

A lasting solution to this problem is not likely to be found until definite long-term commitments are made to adjust the domestic-production system to manufacture for export and until the state-trading enterprises have learned more sophisticated techniques for marketing their goods in the intensely competitive environment of the hard-currency zones. The increasing inflow of revenue from foreign tourism and other invisible transactions may also be expected to yield a degree of liquidity.

Until recently, the ruble had been a purely domestic currency. Within the past few years, it has begun to play a role as the unit of account in settlements among communist countries. But even today it can have no significant function in world commerce, since it is not exchangeable for gold, has no international market value and may move neither into nor away from the U.S.S.R., owing to legal prohibition. This is no less true of the East German mark, the Polish zloty or the Rumanian lei.

Sporadically, the Soviet Union has been extending ruble credits to certain market-oriented economies in order to finance its own exports. Credits in respect of communist-operated development schemes have also been provided by the U.S.S.R., East Germany and Czechoslovakia to a number of underdeveloped countries. But trade with the noncommunist world as a rule is accounted for in convertible currencies, usually dollars, sterling and Swiss francs (or, where a bilateral account exists, in the national money of the trading partner) within the framework of carefully balanced arrangements.

From time to time, the U.S.S.R. has issued high-level policy statements to the effect that its currency was, in due course, to be elevated to fully convertible status. Indeed, the so-called revaluation, as of January 1961, which attributed to the ruble a higher gold content and an exchange rate more favorable to the Soviet Union, was presented in a propaganda context suggestive of a challenge to the dollar's top position in world-money markets. In actual effect, the event was partly a devaluation and partly a domestic-currency reform similar to the purely formal French change-over from old to new francs.

Because of the regimentation and isolation of the Soviet economy, the disparity between international and domestic prices (and costs), the refusal of the U.S.S.R. to reveal its gold holdings and the country's self-exclusion from International Monetary Fund arrangements, no realistic criteria for testing the value of its money are available. All in all, meaningful convertibility cannot be foreseen until the Soviet government acquires the objective economic strength and financial self-confidence enabling the exchange of rubles for gold or reserve currencies on the basis of a realistic coefficient.

Gold production in the communist East is restricted to the U.S.S.R. and Rumania. While the latter's extraction is minor, the Soviet Union is known to be one of the world's principal, if not most economical producers, ranking probably just after South Africa. In recent years, it has been able to sell hundreds of millions of dollars worth of gold to help bring its international payments in balance. During the Khrushchev era the sales were estimated at from $200 to $500 million annually, mostly in London and for sterling. The exact extent of gold reserves is a closely guarded state secret, but the Soviet Union's holdings certainly rank with those of the major world economies. Western estimates place the value at $3½ to $4 billion dollars.[1]

The International Bank for Economic Cooperation was established in Moscow in 1964 to function somewhat along the lines of the old European Payments Union, *i.e.*, to multilateralize and in general stimulate trade among member countries of Comecon. In mid-1966 the Bank announced that one-tenth of its capital was held in gold and convertible currencies. The balance is kept in so-called "transferable rubles," whose circulation is limited to member states.[2] The availability of the Bank's limited-gold and convertible-currency resources to facilitate purchases from non-Comecon countries has not been confirmed. Until either this happens or the eastern European states move individually toward a measure of free convertibility, escape from rigid bilateralism will not be likely.

Although the bilateral clearing approach at present serves as an ideal instrument in the hands of a planned economy with limited hard-currency supplies, the technique is in fact a borrowed one. The concept was pioneered during the great depression of the nineteen-thirties by Switzerland, a traditional champion of liberal economics.[3] It was refined by Nazi finance minister Hjalmar Schacht into a powerful economic and political lever to promote exports to weaker economies with Germany's considerable import capacity as bait.

B. The Nature of Intergovernmental Agreements

1. Economic Functions

The basic bilateral instrument in intra-East trade is of a formal type. In content it resembles a classical treaty of friendship, commerce and navigation. The exchange of goods which it comprehends is minutely regulated on a mandatory, rather than a merely indicative basis. Since no international economic planning takes place at the level of Comecon, a measure of coordination among the separate national plans is attained in this manner.

Trade agreements, generally for periods not exceeding five years, determine the value of the contemplated turnover in rubles and specify that commodity prices will be established by reference to prevalent world market quotations. Attached to the agreements are quota lists which indicate, either in quantity or in value terms, the broad categories of goods to be exchanged. The compartments thus created are not intended to be watertight; spillovers from one to another are admissible. Periodic, usually annual, renegotiations of targets take place in light of observed performance.

Within the limits stipulated by the High Contracting Parties, special contracts are negotiated and concluded by individual government enterprises with respect to particular transactions. It is at this level of private-law relations that quality, price, place and date of delivery and other essential terms are defined.

Arrangements with market economies are, for the most part, of the commercial agreement variety, in which many of the formal governmental undertakings are absent; otherwise, the content is similar. Invariably, the states solemnly declare their intention to expand two-way trade and set forth the general conditions under which such trade will be conducted.

Typically, the instrument is given a duration of from three to five years. More recently, automatic renewal has been stipulated, either for a fixed or an indeterminate time, unless one or the other of the governments rescinds at the end of the initial or extended period.

As a rule the trade accord is supplemented by a preexisting or concurrent payment and clearing agreement. Therein the parties provide for the evaluation of exchanged goods in internationally reputed and convertible currencies and for swing credit (overdraft) limits. They further provide for the opening of reciprocal accounts at the two central banks to which the respective exports and imports are credited or debited, as a rule in dollars or sterling. Some payment agreements, particularly those with European countries, specify the mode of trade financing by consortia of private banks.

Within this standard type of framework, the two sides proceed to hammer out the details of their commodity exchanges. These details are then spelled out in auxiliary annual protocols, which reflect realistic short-term requirements and possibilities. The goods to be traded are entered in two separate export lists, one for each country, showing specific annual quotas wherever appropriate. The total value of trade is also specified, in as evenly balanced terms as possible.

Based on actual experience, the proposed scope of the exchanges accepted by both sides is a goal rather than a binding obligation. Occasionally, it is stated that the indicated quantities should be viewed as minimum objectives and not as limits tending to restrict additional trade. By way of illustration, the 1967 Franco-East German trade agreement foresees an exchange of French industrial machines, tools and agricultural produce for East German mechanical equipment, optical instruments and chemical products.[4] All that is promised therein by the respective governments, however, is to license the exportation or importation of the specified goods. Exceptionally, under a 1966 protocol with Brazil, the Soviet Union has, in fact, committed itself to use 25 percent of actual receipts from the sale of machinery and equipment to that country, for the purchase of Brazilian manufactured and semi-manufactured goods.[5]

While a centrally planned economy has sufficient administrative control over its executive-trade instrumentalities to ensure compliance with specific undertakings, governments of market economies lack such influence. Despite the high degree of coordination which takes place between state authorities and business firms preparatory to the negotiation of a bilateral agreement, governments of market-oriented countries insist on leaving their private firms free to enter into such bargains for the export or import of goods as they themselves are willing to make. Although technically the state, a public corporation or a grouping of private traders could agree bindingly to make specified deliveries or purchases, this practice would represent far-reaching governmental interference with the market mechanism of a free enterprise economy. Few noncommunist governments, even those of less developed countries, where basic industries and large segments of the foreign trade function are often nationalized, have been willing to go to such lengths.

For these reasons, the nature of the obligations to buy or sell in predetermined patterns is left deliberately vague, hence not subject to legal action on the part of either side. However, this does not mean that the commodity listing is carried out entirely in the dark. The Eastern trade delegations or other representations established in the commercial centers of the Western trade partner maintain a close rapport with the local business community, and thus have a fairly good notion of what is likely to be bought or sold during a given twelve-month period.

As a matter of record, even the governments of planned economies have often failed to ensure fulfillment of treaty quotas, particularly on the purchasing side of the ledger. The Franco-Soviet experience in the early 1960s furnishes an illustration of chronic purchasing insufficiency on the part of the state-trading partner. Overselling is also an occasional occurrence. Such developments may arise from changing economic conditions which specifically affect the goods covered by an agreement or from fluctuations in world prices. The imbalances thus created may be covered by short-term credits to the debtor country, by decisions to limit further purchases and, as was strongly preferred by the French authorities, by settlement in gold, dollars or other hard currencies.

In an effort to expand business potential beyond the confines of a rigidly balanced exchange of goods, new forms of bilateral East-West arrangements have begun to appear on the scene, providing for economic, industrial, scientific and technical cooperation between the two contracting states. The Franco-Soviet agreement of June 30, 1966, is the most extensively utilized instrument of this type. Under its terms has been developed an original and ambitious institutional framework of collaboration at both the government-to-government, industry-to-industry and even enterprise-to-enterprise levels. Mixed working committees explore prospects for a pooling of know-how, joint production and common marketing efforts in such diverse areas as metallurgy, aeronautics, metrology, space and color television. In the sphere of science the cooperation seeks to take advantage of the complementarity which exists between Soviet progress in pure research and French advances in applied technology.[6]

Another innovation consists of specialized agreements between Eastern states on the one hand and private Western companies on the other. A precursor of this type of agreement was the U.S.S.R.'s arrangement with De Beers Consolidated of South Africa regarding the worldwide marketing of Soviet industrial diamonds. More recently, the Soviet Committee on Science and Technology has entered into broad agreements on industrial and technological cooperation with certain well-known European firms, notably J. R. Geigy AG of Basel, Switzerland.

Trade and other forms of economic relations between Eastern states and the less developed areas are increasingly conducted within a framework of long-term (typically five-year) bilateral agreements of various types. Usually, the agreements are concluded with a view to commercial exchange as well as financial aid. The Eastern nations favor such arrangements as part of their characteristic preference for bilateralism and also because they facilitate the structural adaptations which some of the wholly planned economies on the one hand, and less developed economies on the other, have lately undertaken. For example, East Germany is said to be specifically equipping textile mills for permanent processing of Egyptian cotton, while the assistance of Czechoslovak experts is helping to raise the standards of Indian tanning factories by enabling India to export to Czechoslovakia not only hides but tanned leather as well.[7]

Bilateral agreements with the emerging areas of the "third world," even more than with the capitalist West, currently extend beyond the sphere of export-import trade, to various specialty instruments covering broad areas of economic relations: the provision of long-term credits, the extension of aid in education and management training; and the furnishing of scientific and technical assistance. Industrial cooperation agreements deal with the supply of capital equipment, the exchange of technological ideas and know-how (one-sided as such exchanges may be), the two-way visits of scientists and experts, the organization of meetings and conferences, the training of workers, the admission of university students and the opening of research institutions to postgraduate scholars.

2. *Regulatory Functions*

Aside from being a convenient economic instrument, the bilateral treaty also performs a significant regulatory function in creating obligations both for the governments concerned and for the individual trading enterprises.

General provisions usually include reciprocal undertakings to promote and facilitate business dealings, to extend most-favored-nation treatment (absolutely, or in specifically defined contexts), to exempt from customs duties and excise taxes products imported for temporary purposes, to expedite railway, maritime and air traffic, to facilitate postal, telephonic and telegraphic communications, to allow entry and travel by individuals pursuing legitimate commercial activities, and so forth. Provisions which operate directly upon contracting firms require reciprocal recognition of the legal status of national business enterprises, offer unhampered recourse to local courts, allocate judicial and arbitral competence, prescribe the governing law and compel the recognition and enforcement of court decisions and arbitral submissions and awards. These privileges survive the treaty's expiration in their application to long-term transactions contracted while the intergovernmental arrangements were still in force.

For a trade monopoly, specific rules which over-ride contractually expressed party intent are tantamount to standardized terms. Only matters left moot remain for determination in individual agreements. The advantages thus afforded to state traders are similar to those derived by capitalist cartels, or unusually large concerns which require customers to accede to ready-made forms dictating specific legal solutions. Nationally owned trading entities, as appendages of governments, are well placed to leave such standardization to legislative action at home and, whenever possible, to treaty-made arrangements abroad.

The monolithic communist state is in a comparatively favorable bargaining position when it seeks special treaty arrangements with one country at a time. In the context of multilateral negotiations, this power is counteracted by market economies which gravitate toward the definition and assertion of a common interest. When the bilaterally concluded provisions fall short of the state trader's ideal requirements, advantageous contractual terms are, nevertheless, frequently attainable by virtue of the strong negotiating posture enjoyed by each export-import corporation, a posture attributable to its monopolistic character and sheer size as an economic enterprise. Viewed in this light, the Eastern reluctance to join regulatory conventions of universal application becomes readily apparent.

The Western preference for bilateralism at the law-making level is also quite evident. After all, it must be admitted that pending development of a better system, the two-party instrument affords the capitalist as well as the communist country the most expedient method of regulating their respective nationals in the conduct of mutual business relations. The rules incorporated into the treaty may not always be uniformly interpreted by the two High Contracting Parties, each being motivated by different national interests and legal traditions. But at the very least, they set forth solemn criteria for the guidance of the respective firms and limit the possibility of arbitrary and discriminatory practices on the part of the legislative, administrative and judicial organs of the participating states.

Among communist countries, the regulatory aspect of bilateral agreements has a supplementary objective. Here the function is not so much to afford protection in commercial relations between basically different and hostile systems, as to codify rules best suited to the economic cooperation of states with similar ideologies and trading techniques. Since all intra-East trade is conducted through state machinery, those who negotiate treaties and those who are required to comply with their provisions are, in essence, organically interconnected. The respective governments are therefore able to assume more detailed and firm obligations and to give direct assurances of their performance. Accordingly, protocols appended to the commercial agreements contain detailed and reciprocal government guarantees to secure the punctual and unhampered delivery of goods, to provide railway and shipping facilities, to furnish necessary credits, to ensure that specific types of goods will be made available in accordance with annexed schedules and to cause the performance of a variety of other matters. In this manner interstate undertakings substantially displace contracts between firms in the regulation of legal rights and duties. Only the most detailed terms, such as stipulations concerning quantity, quality, price and the time and place of delivery, are left to be determined by the individual trading enterprises.

Since trade in specific commodities is carried on by corresponding state entities on a specialized and permanent basis, controversies are usually ironed out in direct negotiation or, as a last resort, in arbitration. Court litigation, although theoretically possible, is nonexistent in practice. Treaty instruments, formerly bilateral but currently concluded on a Comecon-wide basis, apportion jurisdiction among the specialized foreign trade tribunals of the several communist countries in accordance with the domicile of the defendant enterpdise, establish the law of the seller's country as the governing law of the contract and guarantee the reciprocal enforcement of awards.

C. The Western Stake in Bilateralism

The concept of bilateral exchange has become accepted as a permanent feature of East–West trade primarily under the pressure of the Eastern side. In principle, at least, a multilateral approach to commerce is preferred in the West as providing a more congenial climate for the private firm and, in the long run, as capable of generating more trade. It would however be most difficult currently to persuade the governments of the Western nations to discard their bilateral arrangements in this area. A market economy finds that such arrangements offer the nearest thing to a substitute for most-favored-nation treatment; a planned economy has few, if any, concessions to make which would be more effective than a specific commitment to purchase. On the whole, recent experience has taught Western governments, perhaps to their own surprise, to appreciate the value of having at their disposal a written record of mutual undertakings.

Paradoxically, this particular development stems from the restoration of wide currency convertibility in the West. Under liberalized payment conditions, the Eastern country can make full use of the opportunity to sell a given quota of exports in the markets of its bilaterally tied Western-trading partner. This done, it feels free to use the earnings, which are generally convertible, to shop elsewhere for imports at the lowest possible prices. A number of Western countries have found it necessary, as a result, to invoke the agreements from time to time in order to call to the attention of the Eastern partner the deficit in their bilateral exchange and its undertaking to adhere to the principle of balanced trade.

Moreover, recent agreements with the U.S.S.R. have tended to list the Soviet export commodities in considerable detail, together with their specific quotas, while leaving unspecified the exact amounts of goods, especially machinery, to be imported by the Soviet Union. Some Western trade authorities fear that if this approach is suggested by the East as a first step toward multilateralization, there is danger that in practice it may also be the last step in that direction. For under such conditions the market economy would find itself severely handicapped. It would be only too happy to accept the invitation to trade on a multilateral basis, if the opportunities were equal on both sides. Unfortunately, private firms are not able to canvass communist markets with the freedom of Eastern representatives located in the West. There is no way, in short, to obtain a fair share of the market for their products unless the Foreign Trade Ministry of the wholly planned economy country lives up to its undertaking to make purchases roughly on the scale provided for in the bilateral agreement.

There are still other reasons why the Western side finds the bilateral device useful in the present East–West trade situation. In regard to East-bound exports, it can specify in advance the goods which are susceptible to clearance for shipment, thereby affording a method for government control over the flow of strategic materials. Beyond this, major European trading nations have found it necessary to place limits on the import of certain commodities from the East, generally in the interest of affording protection to less competitive industries. Under current practice, this objective is attained by specifying in the bilateral instrument the exact quantities in which these "sensitive" commodities are to be supplied by the Eastern side. Additional quantities can be imported only upon issuance of an appropriate import license. In this manner the threat of market disruption can be effectively controlled.

It is doubtful, therefore, that Western countries will, in the foreseeable future, consider it prudent to confront the national trade monopolies of the East without the benefit of certain mutual undertakings explicitly expressed in bilateral agreements. As long as the East continues to adhere to its system of authoritative economic planning and to conduct its trade through central government instrumentalities on the basis of criteria to which the outside world is not privy, the business community of an open economic system will need more than an exchange of formal pledges on the governmental level to assure itself of reciprocal, nondiscriminatory treatment.

The fact that communist countries reject the use of an open multilateral payments system, preferring to follow a more or less strict rule of balanced trade, need not be an insuperable obstacle to the further development of East–West commerce. In the final analysis, the multilateral approach has limitations of its own, arising from the practical need to achieve, as nearly as possible, an equilibrium in the exchange of goods and, above all, in payments. It does not appear, for instance, that the desire of the Eastern countries to balance all exchanges through bilateral agreements has seriously impaired the growth of their trade with the European Economic Community. In the decade from 1955 to 1965 the volume of this trade has virtually quadrupled in size with the trend continuing to be favorable. Nor have the Common Market countries rushed to place their commercial relations with Eastern states on a community basis. Despite the fact that the Treaty of Rome calls for the early creation of a united position toward outsiders, the bilateral mode of dealing with Comecon members has been preferred for economic as well as political reasons.

Currently, some forty bilateral agreements between E.E.C. and Comecon countries remain in force. Typically, they contain a classically worded most-favored-nation clause, in effect extending to the given Eastern-trading partner a standard of treatment equivalent to that accorded to the most favored nonmember of the E.E.C. In the absence of such a commitment, the Eastern party would not be entitled, for example, to the benefit of tariff reductions negotiated by Common Market countries with outsider nations in the course of the GATT's Kennedy Round. The E.E.C. countries do not, however, consider such a clause in their bilateral agreement with Eastern states as effective to establish a standard of treatment afforded to insider countries. To the extent that the latter accepts this position, they may be taken to have recognized by implication the discriminatory customs union feature. Accordingly, the U.S.S.R. has declined to take official notice of the common external tariff, even at the cost of foregoing duty reductions in respect of certain of its staple exports to that area.

Another interesting aspect of the E.E.C.'s Eastern trade entails a coupling of communist bilateralism and Common Market multilateralism. For political reasons which stem from the division of Germany, a special Protocol of March 25, 1957, concluded among the member countries, stipulates that exchanges between the area controlled by Bonn and that controlled by Pankow is considered as internal German commerce.[8] The consequences of this instrument have not become fully apparent. At best, the privileged entry of East German goods tends to affect the competitive position of the other members in the West German market. For the Eastern Zone is treated not as a third country but as an integral part of Germany. And it has sought to benefit from this status by exporting to the Federal Republic and under certain conditions to the other five members, through the mechanism of "interzonal trade".[9]

Special devices have been elaborated by the Brussels Commission, and endorsed by the Council of Ministers, to place at the end of the Common Market's transitional period, on a uniform, community-instituted footing the bilateral dealings hitherto conducted by member states individually. For instance, in 1960 the Council decided that all bilateral agreements must incorporate a so-called "E.E.C. clause," looking toward direct Community negotiation of adaptations which might be dictated by the evolving common commercial policy. Thus far, the member countries have consistently discarded this injunction, for fear of antagonizing their Eastern trading partners during a period of diplomatic détente and expanding trade.

Similarly, in 1961, the Council ruled that bilateral agreements must not exceed in their duration the Community's anticipated period of transition toward a wholly open internal market, and that accords which contain neither the E.E.C. clause nor a provision permitting termination upon one year's notice must be limited to a duration of one year.[10]

Germany has derogated from this policy in several agreements with east European countries. Neither an E.E.C. clause nor a year's termination was provided for in agreements of three years' duration, and the Common Market Commission has silently accepted this digression. In 1969, France concluded a five-year agreement with the U.S.S.R. This time, the Commission's approval was solicited and granted, but only *ex post facto*. Thereafter, it was vaguely agreed that subject to unspecified consultation procedures, bilateral agreements could be negotiated and continued in force until January 1, 1973. In this manner, the pre-existing freedom of the individual states has been largely reinstated. For the time being, the bilateral treaty instrument continues to serve certain members, Germany and France in particular, as a convenient device to forego the delegation of important powers in a sensitive political area to a supranational authority.

As a trading technique, bilateralism is primitive compared with multilateral exchange. Quite apart from its intrinsic rigidities, it tends to inhibit the spontaneous movement of goods and to restrict the benefits of competition. Inevitably, it narrows the choice of imports as well as of markets, encouraging the emergence of confined preference areas and of economic interdependence, particularly when one of the trading partners is a nation with limited resources. In the context of open trade, the exporting country can earn hard currencies which are good for conversion into purchases made in the optimum market. Credits resulting from sales within a bilateral scheme will not, as a rule, procure the most advantageous imports, insofar as the goods made available by the partner country are not likely to meet the best world standards of price and quality.

For certain less developed countries, bilateralism has opened an important means to dispose of surplus commodities in communist markets, often by bartering them against industrial products. Undeniably, this has yielded substantial short-term benefits. For great as the virtues of multilateralism appear to be in the abstract, it has become quite clear that the interplay of market forces does not adequately respond to the needs and aspirations of the backward economies. Surplus primary commodities cannot be easily disposed of in open trade. While desired capital goods are amply available from many sources, the convertible wherewithal needed for their acquisition is chronically short.

In light of these manifest facts, the Eastern boast that bilateralism, with the long-term stability and predictability which it introduces into commercial exchanges, performs a trade-generating, rather than a trade-diverting function, is not without substance.[11] Indeed, this line of argumentation is matched by a surprisingly faithful echo coming from a completely different direction, to wit, Pope Paul's 1967 encyclical *Populorum Progressio:*

> . . . Raw materials produced by underdeveloped countries are subject to wide and sudden fluctuations in price, a state of affairs far removed from the progressively increasing value of industrial products.
>
> As a result, nations whose industrialization is limited are faced with serious difficulties when they have to rely on their exports to balance their economy and to carry out their plans for development. The poor nations remain ever poor while the rich ones become still richer; in other words, the rule of free trade, taken by itself, is no longer able to govern international relations . . .[12]

Industrial cooperation agreements between individual Eastern and less developed countries, absent ulterior political motives, can also induce a degree of stability and growth and enable repayment of long-term credits with surplus commodities, or the manufactures of newly established enterprises. Bilateral arrangements have, however, opened the door to a large variety of problems for both purchasers in developing areas and their traditional suppliers. In a typical case, the less developed country selling to the East receives in exchange a credit entry in the bilateral clearing account. This credit is good only in the market of the given communist trade partner. It cannot, as a rule, be employed elsewhere. Its value, accordingly, will depend on the choice, quality and price of the merchandise the purchaser will be able to obtain from the state-trading country. Until that phase of the deal is reached, until the newly developing country finds out what products will be available and how competitive their prices will be, it is not really in a position to know at what price it has sold its own commodity. If the goods obtained from the East are of acceptable standard and competitively priced (or if the commodity exported originally was hard to dispose of in the world market), then the bilateral deal will have been satisfactory. On the record, the outcome has not always been favorable.

Producers of primary commodities with a degree of economic power in the world market have managed to disengage themselves from strict bilateralism. Argentina, for example, has gradually terminated all payment agreements with the East and has been conducting trade with these countries in hard currency since 1959.[13] Brazil has insisted on including in its bilateral agreement with the U.S.S.R. a provision for a triangular settlement of trade balances with the other countries of eastern Europe.

D. Communist Participation in Multilateral Arrangements

The proliferation of bilateral trade and payment agreements constitutes an increasing obstacle to the assimilation of communist commerce into the market-oriented world framework. This process is irreversible for the immediate future.

Sporadically, the value of progressively multilateralized trade has been recognized in the East. Thus, a trend in favor of convertible payment agreements and greater multi-clearing facilities is currently in evidence within and beyond the Comecon sphere. For instance, triangular payment arrangements have been practiced among Czechoslovakia, India and Pakistan and among the U.S.S.R., Burma and Czechoslovakia. Similarly, Canada's occasional surplus with the Comecon group of states may be compensated by the latter via surpluses which one of its members has accumulated in other Western countries in a particular year, Britain, for example.

Several Eastern countries have recently sought, and some have gained, admission to multilateral arrangements outside the Comecon orbit. The most significant moves have been toward the GATT. But successful attempts have also been made to force the portals of certain specialized "club," *e.g.*, the U.S.S.R.'s 1969 entry into shipping conferences covering the lucrative transportation of wool from Australia and New Zealand to Western Europe.

It is quite clear, however, that existing institutions, such as the GATT, the IMF, the International Chamber of Commerce, world-wide trade associations and commodity exchanges and various regulatory conventions, cannot easily cope with the peculiar phenomenon of totalitarian trading. Either communist countries refuse to join established international "gentlemen's agreements" or, if they do join, special waivers and dispensations are often a condition of the bargain. Thus, even though the U.S.S.R. and Cuba participate in the International Sugar Agreement of 1968, their trade in that commodity with fellow socialist countries is not subject to the limitations that govern other adherents.

Even where Eastern countries unqualifiedly subscribe to multilateral instruments of universal application, their obligations become distorted in the context of a state operated system. For such a system lacks the internal machinery needed to comply with the requirements of organizations and treaties conceived for the predominantly private patterns of world trade. In regard to permanently functioning organizations, this is best illustrated by the East's attitude toward GATT, and vice versa.

In the early postwar period the main trading nations of the West made a concerted effort, at a conference held in Havana in 1947, to formulate a world-wide arrangement as a basis for a projected international trade organization. The Havana Charter, including its section on "State Trading and Related Matters,"[14] turned out to be somewhat too ambitious and rather ahead of its time. But the principles discussed during the conference finally materialized as the General Agreement on Tariffs and Trade. This instrument today represents the main body of rules and the basis of the only permanent multilateral forum for dealing with problems of world commerce.

A number of the fundamental propositions enshrined in the GATT are relevant to our inquiry, particularly those which touch upon competition between private firms and state-trading organizations. For in addition to prescribing trade principles designed to place member countries on a footing of equality, the General Agreement also restricts undue protection of domestic producers, promotion of exports by means of government subsidies and other practices which encourage discrimination, dumping and related forms of unfair competition. Can the totally planned economies be fitted into the framework which GATT has established for the vast, noncommunist trading system in general? Can the narrowly circumscribed, bilateral circuits of East–West trade be opened to the potential of greater competition on the basis of transferable currencies? These are questions which have long baffled Western economists and to which some answers are beginning to emerge.[15]

The relationship between GATT and the various state-trading countries has had an interesting history. The Soviet Union, as the principal practitioner of the art, did not take part in the work of the Havana Conference. Yet the General Agreement included provisions expressly designed to deal with the practice of state-trading. As one would expect, the relevant norms are of a rather vague and hortative nature. In broad terms, they stipulate that if a Contracting Party endows a state enterprise with exclusive or special privileges in the field of foreign trade, such enterprise must act in a manner consistent with the general principles of nondiscrimination prescribed in the Agreement for private traders. In defining "nondiscrimination" for this purpose, the same article specifies that such enterprises are required to make purchases or sales "solely in accordance with commercial considerations, including price, quality, availability, marketability, transportation and other conditions of purchase or sale, and shall afford the enterprises of the other contracting parties adequate opportunity, in accordance with customary business practices, to compete for participation in such purchases or sales."[16] This language, and the subsequently introduced procedure for compulsory notification of particular discriminations or restrictions in effect in a member country, suggest that the rules in question were originally conceived not so much for total state-trading nations as for market economies which for one reason or another find it necessary on occasion to resort to government-conducted commerce.

Until quite recently the issue of total state-trading countries' adherence to GATT remained dormant. The only exception was a formal request by the United States in 1951 that it be relieved of its obligations toward Czechoslovakia, a founding member of the organization, in order to be free to comply with newly passed domestic legislation calling for the denial of most-favored-nation treatment to goods imported from the countries of eastern Europe.

Yugoslavia became the first centrally planned economy to request, in 1958, admission as a member of GATT in good standing. From the deliberations of the special working party established to study the application, Yugoslavia emerged as something of a special case. It was able to adduce evidence to the effect that its economy had adjusted itself to market considerations. In the formal presentation of his country's case, a government representative was able to describe the situation as follows: "The functioning of the market, economic relations among enterprises, price formation and the cost structure are technically along the same lines as in other economies," adding that "we do not have monopolistic enterprises, and State trading is a very rare exception."[17] To facilitate the process of accession, the government undertook to speed up the preparation of a national tariff schedule in order that negotiations with other Contracting Parties could begin and full membership could be established by the end of 1965.

The experience of Yugoslavia's admission is highly instructive. First, it reflects the very real interest of the existing Contracting Parties in finding a way to assimilate the communist economies into the Western trading system. Second, it demonstrates that when the foreign trade enterprises of a collectivist system enjoy operational autonomy and conform to market principles, their accommodation within the General Agreement becomes feasible. For they are then able to make tariff concessions which trade partners in market economies consider meaningful.

As a practical matter, however, the precedent was not too helpful for the purpose of dealing with the other, more orthodox communist economies. Poland, which followed suit in asking for full membership in 1959, in lieu of the observer status which it had enjoyed since 1957, could not make the claim that its economy operated on a basis comparable to that of a market-oriented system. Moreover, the complete absence of a tariff structure made for a strange situation indeed, in an international setting in which custom house concessions are the most effective medium for affording nondiscriminatory, most-favored-nation treatment. Although Poland offered to introduce a tariff schedule, the organization's membership tended to view this as a rather pointless formality in the case of an economic system where prices were not determined by the interplay of supply and demand and foreign transactions were determined by administrative decision rather than by consideration of domestic needs and costs. In due time, however, Poland succeeded in obtaining special standing, on the basis of which it was allowed to take part in the Kennedy Round of negotiations. But it persisted in the effort to gain full membership and thereby, among other things, to secure nondiscriminatory treatment for its traditional agricultural exports. To achieve this aim, it made a number of proposals to the other Contracting Parties which were practical in content and highly significant in principle. Most notable among them was a readiness to adjust its economic development plans to ensure a specific rate of expansion in the internal market for goods from other GATT members.

The Polish government, in effect, showed itself prepared to give assurances that increased export earnings realized through its trade partners' tariff concessions would be used to increase purchases from them. Specifically, it was willing to draw up legally binding agreements, based on five-year estimates, to increase by a predetermined percentage imports from countries that stood ready to grant appropriate tariff cuts. Among the most significant terms which conditioned Poland's final admission to full GATT status, as of October 18, 1967, was a commitment in the Protocol of Accession to increase by 7 percent annually over a period of three years the value of imports from other members of the General Agreement.[18]

Since the Polish version of a centrally planned economy is far closer, as compared with Yugoslavia's, to that of the other collectivist countries, this development opens the highly interesting possibility of more GATT accessions to come. Indeed, Rumania's and Hungary's applications for membership are under active consideration, and Bulgaria is also known to have expressed an interest in a relationship going beyond mere observer status. Despite the Warsaw Pact protectorate to which she is currently subject, Czechoslovakia may also be expected to seek activation of her long-dormant membership by conforming to specially negotiated conditions. The essential fact to bear in mind is that insofar as any of these countries are willing to undertake commitments along the lines of Poland, there are no manifest technical grounds for excluding them.

The great imponderable is, of course, the future action of the Soviet Union. It would not be safe, at this stage of the economic evolution which is taking place within the East, to venture a prediction which way the Soviet decision will fall. The economic bargaining power of the U.S.S.R. in the world market is strong enough to permit her to derive continued benefits from the present regime of East–West bilateralism. Furthermore, as the leader of the Eastern group of states, she is motivated to see to it that a certain political distance is maintained between the socialist countries and the largely capitalist world market for which GATT prescribes its rules. Yet, there are strong economic forces at work, not only in the smaller countries, but even in the Soviet Union itself, that are visibly pulling in quite the opposite direction.

International trade has recently undergone serious reevaluation throughout the East. It has come to be held in higher esteem than ever in the past, primarily as a link with the mainstream of world technology. In this setting, the government of the U.S.S.R. might well conclude, after due deliberation, that an opportunity to obtain equal treatment in the world market for its traditional and projected export products is well worth the risk of a multilateral undertaking to exchange goods on the basis of effective nondiscrimination. Nor is it impossible that some of the Eastern countries will move for the extension to nonmembers of the limited multi-clearing facilities of Comecon's International Bank for Economic Cooperation, or knock on the doors of the International Monetary Fund and the World Bank. The trade expansion possibilities afforded by the IMF's special drawing rights, or "paper gold," are bound to be as attractive to the Eastern economies, as the attendant financial disclosure and convertibility guidelines are likely to be repellent.

10

BUSINESS IN A MONOLITHIC ENVIRONMENT

A. The Intrusion of Political Considerations

Although the markets of the East present many attractive commercial opportunities, they are often unpredictable. For reasons of either foreign policy or economic strategy, a particular offer of a Western firm may be overruled in favor of one which is less advantageous to the communist buyer or seller. We may assume that the state then derives dividends of a noncommercial kind.

Communist negotiators are not at all times compelled to purchase in the cheapest market or to sell in the most highly priced one. Even if it has confidently submitted an attractive commercial bid for consideration by the state monopoly, a private company may be disqualified by an unexplained veto based on unknown national policy considerations. The concentration in the hands of a monolithic sovereign of all levers of economic and political control is one of the basic features of the commercial landscape of the East. State export-import entities and the Foreign Trade Ministries which supervise them have it within their power to deny domestic market access to firms of any country that has fallen out of favor. Similarly, firms from a nation being wooed for political reasons may suddenly find doors opening before the gentlest touch.

An important element in this setting is the unusual condition that in the centrally planned economies the executives concerned with practical conduct of commerce and the officials responsible for implementation of foreign economic policy are housed under the same roof. To be sure, this centralization of authority does not influence each individual transaction. Moreover, the businessmen and the politicians operate within different professional horizons and may even have conflicting views of their day-to-day responsibilities. Those who run a commercial enterprise are by nature primarily interested in making purchases and sales, and in earning their bonuses. To them, international politics are a secondary and abstract consideration. Nonetheless, the system does provide a built-in mechanism for latent discrimination that can, and sometimes does, cancel out any combination of attractive economic terms offered by a foreign trader, if for one reason or another his country has given political offense.

Even at the operational level, the trading entities are expected to fulfill a double role: besides selling mechandise on behalf of the domestic producer and buying foreign goods for the end-user, they are also required to help implement the commercial policy of their state. At the governmental level, there is all the more reason to keep trade and politics from drifting too far apart. Thus, a drastic shift in diplomatic relations with a given foreign government could be directly and expeditiously supported by means of an equally prompt change in commercial treatment. In such a monolithic environment, trade is considered as just another instrument for orchestrating a political overture toward a particular country or group of countries at any given time.

Soviet purchasing missions have often followed the flag in shifting the focus of their interest from one country to another. Frequently, they have been ready to offer their custom as bait for friendship. There are instances without number where the acceptance of a bid to construct an industrial plant was announced with great fanfare to a manufacturer in a country which was about to be visited by an important dignitary of the East.

While under normal conditions, the decisive factors are preponderantly commercial, revolving around price, quality, credit and delivery terms, the U.S.S.R. has been known to depart from the norm on occasions of particular political significance. Juicy purchase orders have been dangled before the eyes of hopeful manufacturers, now in England, now in Italy, with a view to driving in a political wedge or to tipping the scale in favor of some economic action advantageous to the Soviet Union.

When the U.S.S.R. sought to cultivate the political favor of General de Gaulle in the mid-sixties, its commercial agencies began to single out France as the special object of their attention. French business circles were invited to establish a joint Chamber of Commerce office in Moscow. A series of agreements on industrial and scientific cooperation followed in rapid succession. Soviet commitments to buy capital equipment were given wide public notice, among them a sizable contract ($50 million) with the Renault automobile company to expand and modernize the Moscow plant manufacturing the Moskvich passenger car. Another high level decision, made in support of this demonstrative rapprochement, was the Soviet's commitment to adopt the SECAM-3 French color television technology for their own domestic use. This decision naturally offered a high degree of assurance that the other east European countries would follow suit. Again, during General de Gaulle's battle to save the franc from devaluation in late 1968, the U.S.S.R. came forward with well-publicized offers to step up orders for French goods.[1]

Specific commercial undertakings have at times been breached by Eastern state authorities in patently political situations. Such was the case of the cancellation of firm orders for the delivery of fuel oil to Israel after the Sinai campaign of 1956. The retaliatory termination of wool purchases from Australia, following the celebrated Petrov asylum incident, is likewise a case in point. Even more far-reaching was the Soviet withdrawal of credit lines from Yugoslavia to demonstrate political displeasure with Marshal Tito's deviationist stance. Nor have Eastern countries hesitated to fish on occasion in troubled political waters. A recent example of this was afforded by Soviet flirtations with the government of Peru, following its 1968 expropriation of American-owned oil fields and refineries.

Generally speaking, United States firms are known to receive cooler receptions from communist buyers than do west European firms, at least when non-American goods of comparable specifications are available. This has to be viewed both as an expression of disapproval of Washington's restrictive trade policy and as an attempt to reverse it. In all such cases the private Western firm finds itself penalized for reasons which are in fact commercially irrelevant.

On the whole, the highly industrialized economies of the West and the large companies within these economies have not been vulnerable to political pressure. Given their strong competitive position and diversified commercial relations, they cannot be made to regard the threat of a sudden trade rupture with the East as a serious disaster. This is not the case, however, with regard to some of the smaller economies. A dramatic example is Finland. That country, in particular, has developed a high degree of dependence upon the markets of eastern Europe, largely as a result of the reparation obligations imposed upon it by the U.S.S.R. at the end of World War II. These obligations required Finland to establish new industries for which it had no outlet in the world market; its level of exports to communist countries has, therefore, been quite large, often well above 20 percent. In the fall of 1958, on the occasion of the formation of a new cabinet in Helsinki, the Soviet Union proceeded to exploit this vulnerability by recalling its ambassador and raising the threat of nonrenewal of the bilateral trade agreement between the two countries unless the composition of the successor government was in accord with Soviet wishes.[2] The mere possibility of boycott was sufficient to produce the results desired by Finland's big neighbor, following a political crisis which lasted forty days.

In the underdeveloped regions of the world, furthermore, the state trading institutions have also stood the Soviet Union in good stead for the purpose of developing another kind of politically profitable patron-client relationship. A classic example is the case of Egypt, which began such a relationship with the happy discovery that it did not, after all, require hard cash to obtain large quantities of Soviet arms. All that was needed was to pledge the bulk of its future cotton crop as a means of deferred payment. During the past ten years, as a result, about half of all exports from the U.A.R. have been committed in advance to the trading agencies of the East.

A number of other specific instances can be cited in which the Eastern bloc has made singularly large-scale purchases in countries where it sought to establish a diplomatic foothold (*e.g.,* Sudanese cotton, Ghanaian cocoa, Greek tobacco, Colombian coffee, Burmese rice, Ceylonese rubber, Icelandic fish, Cypriot citrus fruits). The extent of such market intervention need not be very great to have an impact, particularly where problems of periodic glut exist. Countries having close economic relations with the East, as well as those that would like to be able to turn to it in case of necessity, are induced to stay on the right side of the political fence. Nor does it seem to matter greatly, in cases of this sort, that in the past several countries have had reason to regret the extent of their economic dependence upon the East either as an outlet or as a source of supply.

Any review of operational problems encountered in East–West trade would be misleading if it conveyed the impression that every commercial transaction is tainted with some kind of willful interference by a meddling communist political authority; or that the behavior of Western governments is always lily-white in the international economic arena. The purpose of dwelling at some length on the noncommercial considerations which occasionally intrude into the normal course of business is to underscore for the benefit of interested but inexperienced private businessmen the less familiar characteristics of Eastern markets and to enable them to avoid pitfalls that may otherwise result in early frustration. Some of the political tactics just described are, happily, a thing of the past. Nonetheless, the essential point to bear in mind is that the unique economic power of a state monopoly in its relations with vulnerable trade partners, or in competition with private firms, remains as great as ever, and that the temptation to use this power politically may prove irresistible from time to time.

B. Methods of Price Formation

It is axiomatic in world commerce that business enterprises offer merchandise of desired quality at the lowest possible price. This essential criterion determines the willingness of buyers to accept and the ability of sellers to compete for a given order. As a rule, the quoted price is assumed to cover the cost of production plus a minimum acceptable margin of profit. A system which is largely unresponsive to normal market forces does not provide the foreigner with any reliable basis for gauging business potential. An understanding of cost and price determination methods in a communist economy is therefore of importance not only to firms which deal directly with the East, but also to those that are exposed to world-wide communist competition, both fair and unfair.

Where a Soviet-type economy is involved, calculations cannot be based on comparisons of domestic costs and prices, inasmuch as both tend to be artificial and arbitrary. These defects, characterized in the past by the absence of any real concern over the misinformation and waste inherent in faulty cost measurement, are beginning to be recognized throughout the East. But the major tone is still supplied by the necessarily unreliable accounting principles which prevail in a wholly planned system. Items not considered crucial within the framework of established bureaucratic computation procedures are simply not included in the cost structure and thus not given appropriate weight in the course of selling abroad. For example, in the exploitation of natural resources, only the direct costs of production figure in the calculus, while the scarcity value and the rate of depletion are ignored.

Another cause of distortion is that capital employed in the production process does not always, at least not fully, reflect an interest charge. Similarly, insurance premiums are calculated in a manner which cannot be considered meaningful by a Western observer. Availability of cheap export credits, absence of excise taxes on capital goods, along with the frequently uncompensated exploitation of foreign patents and designs, are added factors tending to distort cost and price formulations. Nor can estimates of the real cost of labor be made with any degree of precision. That it is cheap may be readily assumed. China, for example, has been known to quote the same price for piece goods and for the fully sewn garment. This would seem to suggest a readiness, rather original for professed disciples of Marx, to export at prices which altogether leave the cost of labor out of consideration.[3] Inland transportation costs are also an important unknown quantity. Price quotations on goods from Western Russia have often been the same, whether delivered to Japan or non-Communist Europe. The huge shipment differential is presumably absorbed either by the state-owned railways or by the trading monopoly.

In setting internal prices, similar arbitrariness prevails. A television set costs not much more than a pair of high quality shoes. Since the Soviet government assigns a high priority to electronics for reasons of defense and space research, and because television receivers are essential instruments for the formation of public opinion, they are made available to the consumer at a price which bears no relevance to their exchange value in terms of other consumer goods. Nor do local and world prices bear a meaningful relationship to each other. In the domestic sphere, prices are merely units of account reflecting the values of established social policy, with little or no reference to the full cost of production or the level of effective demand. When demand sharply outdistances supply, while consumer prices remain fixed by decree, the adjustments tend to be made either by means of a long waiting list or through a thriving black market.

It may well be that certain costs in a planned economic setting are in fact relatively low. The resultant competitive edge in world markets may therefore constitute a legitimate advantage for communist exporters and foreign importers alike. In reality, however, it is when these low or unknown costs bring in their wake the market distortions described hereafter that we approach the vague borderline between healthy competition and injurious dumping.

While Eastern trade officials seek to drive hard bargains, their awareness of world prices seems to be, at best, uneven. Fluctuations are not likely to come to their attention with the same rapidity as in the case of the experienced Western broker. Once the information does become available, inordinately long and precious time periods may elapse before it becomes translated into specific price adjustments. The Western firm which remains keenly attuned to market developments, particularly in the sphere of basic commodities, may discern a price trend weeks in advance of its communist counterpart. While the tendency may be toward increased prices, a state trading agency will frequently purchase forward at values which fail to reflect the impending change. If developments are suggestive of falling prices, the Eastern seller will often cling to the bureaucratically established higher quotations and thereby miss opportunities for cutting its loss.

As a rule, communist sales quotations abroad are still established by reference to prevailing terms and conditions in a given foreign market. For external purposes, the internal cost, profit and price structure are usually ignored. Goods may be, and often are, sold at prices considerably lower or higher than at home. Likewise, they are purchased on a basis which has no relationship to internal price formation. The Skoda 1000 MB automobile has been selling at the equivalent of $1,200 in West Germany, while in Czechoslovakia its list price was in excess of $3,000, in domestic currency, with a three-year waiting period and an initial down payment of $1,300. The Soviet Moskvich has sold recently in Finland and Belgium for about $1,800, while domestic buyers, when their turn came at last, had to pay in cash three times that amount. These outlandish discrepancies are explained by the need to make the models saleable in the highly competitive compact car market of western Europe.

Turning to intra-Comecon commercial relations, we find that the Eastern countries have also been unable to cope effectively with the problem of pricing among themselves. In the absence of a "socialist" price schedule, they have been compelled, to their own palpable distaste, to continue to use "world," *i.e.,* "capitalist," prices in the exchange of goods within the region. There is an apocryphal story about a prominent communist trade official who once while in a philosophical mood ventured the opinion that even after the universal triumph of the revolution it will be necessary to preserve one capitalist country, preferably a small one, to calculate prices at which the socialist countries will trade with each other. The arbitrariness which pervades the calculation of costs, profit margins and exchange rates helps to explain why communist economies are compelled artificially to adjust sales prices to levels generally prevalent in world commerce. Adjustments are also made, from time to time, by administrative fiat, in accordance with the dictates of trade policies or tactics of the moment. Thus, if goods are to be disposed of because an unexpected surplus has been created, or because foreign exchange is needed for the acquisition of essential Western products, quotations well below prevailing market prices may be offered to foreign buyers.

Sales made in this manner must be suspected of containing hidden state subsidization. To be sure, the phenomenon is not entirely without its parallels in the West. The disposal of American farm surpluses abroad may be cited as an example. The use of such devices is, however, exceptional and openly acknowledged to be offensive, to wit, the action required by the anti-subsidy provisions of Article 92 of the Treaty of Rome. In the case of a communist economy, subsidies of this kind are much less visible. At least in the abstract, they must be assumed to form part of the normal course of business. A United Nations inquiry dealing with this problem in fact disclosed the existence of enormous export subsidies in the foreign trade practices of two Eastern countries in particular, Hungary and East Germany.[4]

A good part of the subsidization is quite patent. In the Soviet Union, for example, the manufacturer of goods for sale abroad receives a credit based on local wholesale prices. The export enterprise retains an allowable margin of profit for itself and transfers the balance, if any, to the state treasury. In the event the proceeds fall short of the domestic price to the manufacturer, the deficit is made good out of funds supplied by the Treasury. The Ministry of Foreign Trade obtains annual subsidies from the national budget to cover eventual imbalances in its overall operations.

In the case of imports, the price paid by the local user to the foreign trade enterprise is also correlated to that of similar domestic goods. If such goods are not in circulation in the home market the price is fixed by the Ministry of Foreign Trade. In countries that have no tariff system of their own, the profit margin reserved for the intermediary organization includes a commission which is tantamount to an undisclosed customs duty or excise tax.

Because of the lack of articulation between domestic and foreign prices and the rudimentary nature of economic measurement tools, neither the planners nor the individual manufacturing enterprises have been in a position to determine whether their trade with the outside world has been economically profitable. Often, plants made higher profits with much less effort by selling at home, or within the socialist foreign market, rather than to the world at large. It is this range of basic and baffling problems that has recently attracted the concentrated attention of east European reformers. Hungary, Poland and Bulgaria in particular, have adopted, as of 1968, a mechanism designed to foster cost-consciousness by enabling enterprises to accumulate and use their own funds. A principal objective is the establishment of progressively closer links between production decisions and prices prevalent at home and abroad. Aside from officially prescribed regulations reflecting state policy, prices are also conceived as a function of reasonable allocation of resources, production costs and the interplay of supply and demand. For example, in Hungary, where economic reforms have gone furthest, trading enterprises are expected to resell imported goods at world prices converted into local currency by means of a specially prescribed multiplier. Similarly, in the purchase of domestic goods for export, real value, in terms of convertible currency and a weighted coefficient of conversion, is to be the dominant price criterion.

C. The Closed Economy

Historically, the Soviet Union, as the first communist country, proceeded to plan its development in such a way as to render the nation economically independent of the rest of the world. With that objective in mind, it was expedient to create a self-sufficient system of production and to place the economic gates to the outside world under the direct control of a government department. In effect, the management of foreign trade was so centralized as to make it more responsive to the changing political interests of the state than to the basic needs of individual production enterprises. Evidently, if there was a price to be paid for maintaining an elaborate administrative barrier between the domestic production system and the world economy, the political leadership of Russia was willing to pay it, in the interest of greater protection against her industrially stronger neighbors. Even after the Soviet Union was joined by more than a dozen other communist-ruled states, the inherent bias against trading freely with the world market persisted. During this period, the underlying reasons were primarily ideological. As the acknowledged progenitor and leader of a newly born "world system of socialist states," the U.S.S.R. was in no mood to offer the surplus-producing capitalist nations free access to the markets which had newly entered its orbit.

All the same, it would be somewhat simplistic to blame the autarchy syndrome on entirely theoretical factors. In large measure it has become a facet of ingrained methodology. As an approach, the notion of economic self-sufficiency makes the planner's task much easier, his forecasts much more controllable. Bureaucratic conservatism renders him reluctant to submit to the imponderables of a less regimented environment of exchanges, particularly in the area of resource allocation. Instead of attempting to bend official doctrine to the practical needs of the economy, his instincts impel him to use it as a shield against exposure to the variable, the uncertain, the adventurous.

Nor can a collectivist economy reproduce for outside firms the open and competitive conditions prevalent in a Western market. Since all imports and exports are predetermined by governmental agencies, state corporations purchase merchandise abroad in a manner suggestive of quantitative restrictions; indeed, the foreign trade plan itself functions as an overall supply and admission quota. On the export side, the main objective is to dispose of the planned volume of sales, along with some unforeseen surpluses that may become available. On the import side, the principal aim is neither to promote more trade *per se* nor to generate additional profits, but rather to procure a given schedule of goods required under the terms of the annual trade program or as a result of unforeseen shortfalls in the domestic economy.

The market stability afforded to foreign sellers within the scope of the established foreign trade plan is an undeniably welcome aspect of the system. But it hardly compensates for its trade-inhibiting features. The Western exporter has learned from experience that he cannot count on the traditional factors that enter into the determination of consumer choice, (price, quality, utility) in order to secure the share of the market to which he feels entitled by reason of the efficiency of his production and the comparative value of his product. No matter how much more reasonably priced, or more suitable his product may be to the needs of the eastern European consumer than similar goods available locally, a sale will not be consummated unless the decision to buy fits prescribed government objectives.

As a practical matter, the Western countries have thus far not found a way to achieve a clear definition of the conditions to be met in the conduct of their trade with the centrally planned economies. The record has amply demonstrated that in dealings with a state-trading economy formally restrictive devices are largely absent from the picture. At the same time, however, there are other instruments of policy that effectively limit entry into the markets of the East.

The Eastern economies need not, for example, resort to tariffs, quotas, excise taxes, exchange controls or any of the other unpopular devices that serve to inhibit the flow of imports. The closed nature of their system permits, much more efficaciously than meets the eye, the implementation of ultraprotectionist commercial policies by means of simple administrative directives. Since it is the state alone that decides what is to be bought or sold, exclusion of outside competitors is easily practiced as a general principle, while admission of foreign goods becomes no more than a rare exception. No economy can, therefore, be considered more protectionist than a totally planned economy functioning within the monolithic scheme of communist state authority.

The protectionism is, moreover, by its very nature invisible; it is built-in as an integral part of the process of commercial decision-making. The type of publicly aired, irritating economic restrictions which often strain relations among Western countries are entirely absent. The Russians, whose import duties are exhibited to the world as innocuous, minimal accounting tools, are, on the other hand, able to point in self-righteous indignation to tariff walls and other devices limiting trade access to the United States, the Common Market and various customs arrangements emerging in other parts of the world.

In theory, one would expect the task of forecasting business potential in a planned economy to be a relatively easy one for Western firms. The need for foreign goods and the availability of exportable products are, after all, known to be established well in advance. In practice, however, the national import-export plans are kept secret. Disclosure of many types of commercial information which in an open market economy are regarded as essential to the conduct of normal business may be considered in the East as divulgence of state secrets and be subject to criminal prosecution. Therefore, the interested foreign firm, unless it has stumbled upon an unusual source of information, cannot effectively gauge the likely levels of supply and demand, let alone take the necessary steps to influence them.

The novice Western trader soon becomes aware that the state entities with which he is dealing are remarkably well informed about market conditions in his own country, while he is completely in the dark as to current commercial possibilities in the country of his trading partner. As a rule, he finds that the state-trading country in question maintains, in the capital of his own nation, a large commercial establishment including many commodity and engineering experts. These experts are free to travel about, to inspect industrial plants and to compare notes with their colleagues stationed in other countries in the West, who are also regularly inspecting production facilities of competing manufacturers. Needless to say, their calculations and final commercial decisions are thus based on a solid accumulation of relevant data. By comparison, the Western seller or buyer must remain quite passive in tapping business potential in the East, and work from a very inadequate informational base. His own government is not in a position to collect and supply him with detailed commercial information. He himself cannot freely move about the state-trading country in order to make observations and interview the competent authorities on a given commodity area. Nor are the officials of the East in the habit of publishing a wide variety of statistical information on their own economies. This kind of data tends to be considered as a matter of executive privilege. There is an underlying assumption that no great need for public knowledge exists in such an economic setting, inasmuch as the duly authorized persons have at their disposal all the facts required to make the decisions that would be of most benefit to the state.

Even where a Western supplier succeeds in making repeated sales over a period of time, he cannot ascertain by way of direct market research what local production facilities are being built to supplant export lines. Demand for his product in the Eastern country may stop abruptly, precisely when aggregate demand appears to be at a peak. Similar problems may arise with regard to the continuity of supply from sources in the East at any time after purchases by a Western firm have fallen into a regular pattern. The predictability problem is likely to assume an even more complex character in the future, in regard to the export of Eastern equipment requiring a regular supply of spare parts and improved know-how.

It is, moreover, in the nature of an administratively planned and operated economic system that the foreign trader cannot be privy to the criteria by which imports are chosen from among alternate suppliers. He does not know, for instance, whether his goods are of a kind that can freely compete with those of manufacturers from other communist countries or from a third country with which the state-trading nation in question has a special payment problem. He cannot, therefore, be blamed if he perceives the various preoccupations of government officials as latent, discriminatory barriers which hamper his access to the particular Eastern market. In practice, the fusion of sovereign control over state trading and state policy serves to conceal all evidence of discrimination. It makes it wholly unnecessary, for example, to post regulations governing economic relations with a given Western country. The treatment of all trade partners can, in effect, remain "fluid" at all times, subject to the judgment of the Ministry of Foreign Trade and to the prevailing political and diplomatic winds.

D. The Merchant Civil Service

One of the most frequent criticisms leveled at the communist trading system is its interposition of a centrally controlled bureaucracy between the foreign firm and the ultimate customer. The frustrations which this can engender are well known to those who have had occasion to deal with representatives of nationalized industries in the West. In a wholly planned and government-operated economy, Kafka's universe, Parkinson's law and Peter's Principle take on their full dimension. The man-hours which underpaid business officials devote to the negotiation of transactions or the discussion of specific problems are much less precious than those of their profit-oriented Western interlocutors. Selling to the East is, for these reasons, extremely costly, particularly in a firm's early stages of entry into that market.

The Soviet trade apparatus is of necessity thoroughly bureaucratic, and distinguished for its elaborate and ponderous negotiation of commercial transactions. Being controlled from a single center, the trading corporations are left with little scope for prompt decision-making. Positions taken by working level trade officers in the precontractual stage may be subject to sudden and unexplained reversals, often traceable to noncommercial considerations. Moreover, those who explore and negotiate a transaction are generally separate, both from an institutional and personnel standpoint, from those concerned with its performance and ultimate economic effect.

The inefficiencies inherent in so elaborate a system of trading have long been understood and are now being given increasing attention in the East. Patterns of direct contact between producing and consuming enterprises and their foreign customers and suppliers have slowly begun to evolve. Basically, however, the bureaucratic institutions and the methods which they typify must remain an essential part of the market setting as long as the economies continue to be state-owned and operated. Hence, criticisms leveled from the standpoint of Western economic experience can only be marginally constructive.

To some extent, the problems will be mitigated as the new breed of "socialist businessmen" master the techniques of world trade through increased immersion. The Russians, in particular, have made noticeable progress in this direction. True, they still lack the sophisticated know-how of the Hungarian bankers or the Czechoslovakian salesmen. The smaller eastern European countries have retained many of the traditions and methods of prewar trade, including cadres who were, in fact, active in the same kind of endeavors on behalf of private interests. But the Russians make up for their deficiencies by greater economic strength, tougher bargaining methods and superior technical knowledge.

It has been often observed that the Russians operate at two levels, one completely theoretical, the other wholly functional. This phenomenon is not confined to foreign trade alone. It permeates all sectors of public life in the communist ruled states from China to Rumania. Lip service is ardently paid to the declared directives of the national government and the communist party. In practice, however, decisions are made by operating realists who have to pursue specific objectives and assigned tasks. Here, pragmatic hardheadedness is a frequent intruder, ideology notwithstanding. Having found it impossible to market its industrial diamonds in the outside world without the cooperation of De Beers Consolidated of South Africa, the responsible Soviet officials thought nothing of striking a bargain with a concern which is capitalistic and monopolistic par excellence.

This ambivalence is probably inevitable in a system which, on the one hand, enunciates economic doctrine with the reverence due to religious dogma, and, on the other, aspires to maximum efficiency of effort in each specific situation. Seeing through the semantic camouflage can be an art which the skillful Western businessman must learn to use to his own honest advantage. For example, planning mistakes occasionally create production bottlenecks which can be alleviated only by way of importation on an urgent basis. Western firms with the ability to discern and fill such needs have frequently concluded highly profitable supply contracts. Similarly, the performance of export-import corporations is judged by reference to the fulfillment of established plans. Bonuses are awarded to successful management at the end of each quarter. As a result, there is greater susceptibility to concluding transactions toward a quarter's end in order to adjust to the plan, and price then becomes a secondary consideration.

In dealings other than the sale of goods, the processes of bureaucracy can be even more frustrating. Whenever a transaction departs from the recurrent pattern, special governmental clearance must be obtained at every step of the way. Such clearance is often difficult to come by, and the communist negotiators may find themselves engaged in a major lobbying effort within their own administration. Again, once approval is obtained the transaction cannot easily be amended, even if adjustments are in the interest of both sides. In such cases, the reluctance to go back to the government with the argument that unanticipated or overlooked factors call for a change in previously approved terms is more pronounced than in the case of capitalist management facing a Board of Directors.

For related reasons, middle level officials cannot take the kind of liberties during the precontractual or contractual stage which a private businessman might chance in order to improve his position. Any risk taken invariably involves the state's sacred socialist property and this fact breeds inordinate conservatism. No matter how dedicated the motives, if the tactic should misfire the civil servant might be called severely to account for unauthorized initiatives. His safety lies in following the black letter of the executed agreement or the instructions which he is called upon to apply.

E. Distortions of Mutuality and Reciprocity

The history of trade relations with Eastern countries has revealed certain inadequacies in established regulatory institutions and procedures. These inadequacies affect Western governments no less than their respective business communities.

In their overtures for expanded trade with the West, communist planners display considerable skill in blurring a crucially important issue: under a conventional legal and commercial regime they are able to draw maximum advantage from the open and competitive marketing conditions prevailing abroad, without affording reciprocal entry to their own closed, state-operated economies. This inherent lack of equivalence runs like a thin red line through the entire range of East–West relations. Its cause lies in the innate difference between a stringently guided communist society and the pluralistic social order in existence in the outside world.

Thus, in the sphere of mass communication, official communist ideas obtain relatively easy access to the minds of Western populations via the public press, television and radio media. Communist literature enters most countries of the West virtually unhampered, through the regular mails. Western governments, on the other hand, have little scope for presenting their points of view to the citizens of Eastern states, except to the extent considered innocuous by the local political leadership.

The entire concept of mutuality is in a sense absent in dealings involving a centrally planned economy of the Soviet type. In the United States, for example, the Soviet Union is permitted to conduct export-import activities through the Amtorg Trading Corporation of New York. Soviet foreign trade corporations dealing in lumber, furs, chemicals or machinery can accredit a representative to Amtorg and be thus supplied with many kinds of commercial and industrial data covering, more often than not, all sides of the issue under negotiation. Amtorg can also freely deploy a team of salesmen with direct access to consumers, along with interpreters, secretaries, bookkeepers, technical advisers and so forth. Similar facilities, whether in the form of Soviet-controlled corporations or permanent trade delegations are afforded by other market economies in their main commercial centers. The Western trader must be satisfied with much less. Generally, he can enter into a transaction only if approached by a local communist commercial representation or by an export-import corporation based in an Eastern capital. A solicitation entity comparable to Amtorg cannot, as a rule, be established in the East. Even if it could, a good part of its commercial purpose would be frustrated, since it is the government that determines all demand for outside goods and designates all the channels through which they should be procured. Consequently, a right of market entry, extended on the same basis of formal reciprocity as that used in commercial relations among free enterprise countries, would be a gesture of little practical meaning.

When an instrumentality like Aeroflot (the Soviet state airline) opens an office in, say, Amsterdam, it acquires space on the street floor of a leading commercial thoroughfare, with direct access to the traveling public. By contrast, K.L.M., while enjoying adequate operational facilities, has not been free to rent space of a size, location and quality of its own choosing. Instead, it had to be content with accommodation in a crowded hotel suite on the almost-dark second floor of the Hotel Metropol in Moscow, out of sight, out of mind of the potential passenger. Similarly, the U.S.S.R. operates a fully owned, appropriately housed banking subsidiary in France, free to conduct its business on a basis of virtual parity with wholly indigenous banks. The Banque de Paris et des Pays Bas, on the other hand, was allowed, as a matter of exceptional favor, to operate no more than a quasi-clandestine Moscow office out of a hotel room, an office which lacks any right to appeal to a local clientele.

Most-favored-nation treatment promises—whether exchanged under national legislation, bilateral treaties of friendship, commerce and navigation, or multilateral arrangements such as the GATT—acquire a rather distorted meaning in relations with centrally planned economies.[5] Traditionally, the significance of an MFN commitment is expressed in the fact that one state accords to another terms of trade no less favorable than those accorded in similar situations to nationals and companies of third countries. If, in addition, a national treatment standard is promised, the conditions accorded foreigners must be no less favorable than those available to local nationals.

In the case of market economies where trade is in private hands and governments act as impartial regulators, commitments of this type generally yield the results for which they were intended, although unconditional MFN clauses are often supplemented by a matrix of ancillary rules. In the area of transportation, for example, they guarantee nondiscrimination to merchant vessels in their right to pick up, carry and discharge cargo. The standard must be one of equality with flag vessels of third countries. Coupled with a national treatment clause, the standard must, in addition, be no less favorable than that affecting vessels of the host country.[6]

Even when a private enterprise country imposes upon a segment of its economy an extensive degree of state trading, problems of accommodation arise in regard to third country privileges. The existence of government tobacco monopolies in Italy and France has resulted in discriminatory exclusion of foreign tobacco, regardless of price, quality, or tariffs. To counteract this, a standard has been framed, requiring the monopolies to operate "solely in accordance with commercial considerations," or to undertake specific purchasing commitments. Unsupervised cartel arrangements, it might be added, tending under purely private auspices to fix prices or to divide markets, can produce similar distortions. The problems under discussion are not, therefore, entirely peculiar to East–West relations. But it is there that they appear in their most aggravated form.

In a totally planned economy, where the trading party and the regulating body are organic parts of the same whole, neither a most-favored-nation nor a national treatment undertaking can amount to more than a theoretical assurance for firms and citizens of the market economy which has granted a reciprocal counter concession. Yet hundreds of bilateral commercial agreements currently in force between the Eastern countries on the one hand and the industrialized or less developed nations of the outside world on the other, typically stipulate formalistic obligations of this character.[7]

By the same token, the results of tariff negotiations also tend to be one-sided. We have already alluded to the fact that communist countries do not use custom duties for the purpose of aligning foreign and domestic price levels. While the types of mutual concessions which are normally extended in a negotiation such as the Kennedy Round would operate to increase exports from communist countries, no corresponding *quid pro quo* would accrue to the exporters of the signatory market economies. In the case of a collectivist trade system, tariff reductions do not automatically expand the volume of imports, just as increased duties do not automatically reduce it. In fact, none of the conventionally used devices need be employed by such a system to channel the flow of trade. Purchases and sales can be manipulated at will by covert administrative means, without overt infringement of treaty obligations.

The customs duty levied at the border of a centrally planned economy amounts, in effect, to no more than a transfer payment from one government pocket to another. If the duty is collected, the state treasury obtains a sum which the state-owned importing enterprise disburses. The same result can be achieved by varying the import enterprise's mark-up on the invoice for foreign goods addressed to the end user. Whether the levy is expressed as a customs charge or a profit is a mere formality. Thus, we find that Poland has been able to get along for a considerable time without any tariff system at all.[8] Similarly, in promulgating its new Tariff Code in 1961, the U.S.S.R. characterized it as "an instrument of commercial policy in defense of the most-favored-nation principle," rather than as a means of protecting domestic producers. In effect, the code, with its two-column duty schedule was designed essentially as a punitive measure "to counteract discrimination against its foreign trade in those countries which disregard the principles of equality and reciprocal advantage in their relations with the Soviet Union."[9]

Not without justification, the U.S.S.R. attributes Western denials of most-favored-nation treatment to Eastern origin goods to basically political motives. It is quite true that such motives have not always been absent. Western policy has, however, also been influenced by the fact that in arrangements with planned economies it is impossible to obtain truly reciprocal commercial treatment, or to protect the domestic economy from disruptively underpriced Eastern sales, by means of a conventional most-favored-nation clause.

In promulgating domestic regulations pertaining to foreign trade, and in negotiating international treaties, certain Western governments find themselves at a disadvantage vis-à-vis the communist state. In the case of the latter, the total identity of commercial and political interests is expressed in policies, laws and treaty negotiations without any of the conflicting pressures which legislatures and administrations in capitalist countries must constantly accommodate. The trading entities benefit from the full weight of automatically coordinated sovereign power. Were General Motors invariably backed up by the treaty-making power of the United States, it could not be better served. Nowhere is the maxim "what is good for General Motors is good for the country" more apt. The corollary holds equally true.

11

DEALING WITH COMMUNIST MONOPOLIES

Within the West, business both foreign and domestic is conducted against a background of private ownership and freedom of contract. Government intervention, either as a direct trader or by means of regulation, and the modicum of planning occasionally encountered do not change the fundamental climate. Profit is the *sine qua non* of commercial activity, while management remains at all times accountable to the suppliers of capital with respect to the earnings to be produced by dint of its efforts. In dealing with the East, capitalist firms find themselves in a drastically different environment. Apart from being seemingly hostile, this environment is peppered with intricate peculiarities. While a movement of deliberate reform is now in progress, it may be assumed that the distinctive institutional structures and methods of doing business, first evolved by the Soviet Union, will, at least in their basic aspects, remain in force throughout the communist orbit. The degree of acceptance which both the structures and the methods ultimately obtain around the world will depend upon the economic influence of the communist states beyond their own frontiers.

The anomalies which Western firms encounter in transacting business with Eastern enterprises are quite real. Too often, the latter are, however, indiscriminately blamed for factors which are at bottom political. Not enough attention is paid to obstacles of a technical nature. While abstract criticism of communist trading methods has turned many of the operational problems into banal clichés, we find that on the concrete level of day-to-day business adequate arrangements are nonetheless feasible. It is self-evident that those who venture regularly into East-West commerce draw tangible economic benefit; otherwise they would turn to less enigmatic markets. The balance of hardships against advantages weighs in favor of the latter, at least from the viewpoint of Western firms and countries which have an abiding and pressing economic need for foreign trade.

In some measure, the obstacles here encountered are inherent in external commerce everywhere. Widespread exchange control and the absence of currency convertibility are one clear example. Certain difficulties, to be sure, stem from novel communist trading techniques; to that extent, they may be susceptible to abatement without undue institutional dislocation. Others, in contrast, are rooted in the very structure of a wholly planned economy; while minor adjustments need not be ruled out in these cases, any expectation to reorganize the total state-trading apparatus would be tantamount to wishing away the communist social order itself.

In weighing the inconveniences, it is equally important not to overlook the positive side of the balance sheet. That the Western trader can generally look forward to dealing with a solvent, government-backed enterprise, that once his product is accepted he may become the supplier to a whole nation, and that in recent years the commercial, contractual and payment record of the communist countries has been virtually beyond reproach are advantages not to be ignored.

A. Access To Eastern Markets

Conventionally, three principal methods are available for gaining access to a foreign market: (a) licensing of patents and know-how; (b) direct investment in a business enterprise within the client country; and (c) exportation of goods.

The Western firm which contemplates the granting of a license to a manufacturing enterprise in the East cannot easily ignore communist attitudes toward industrial property rights. Businessmen who have patentable products or valuable trademarks can arrange for registration of these rights under the laws of Eastern countries. They are, however, understandably apprehensive about the extent of protection such registration affords, in view of the collectivist approach to the concept of private ownership. In the long run, moreover, there lurks the danger of building up an informed and economically powerful state competitor who might on his own initiative become commercially active, upon the expiration of the term of his license, both in his home territory and in the world market as a whole. In subsequent chapters, closer examination of this subject will lead us to conclude that these apprehensions are exaggerated and that the licensing of technology to the East is a promising new field.

Among the peculiarities of East-West economic relations is the fact that capital and labor must play a passive part. For the most part it involves the exchange of goods and services. Direct investment in the equity of companies chartered to do business in communist countries is not at present feasible. Yugoslavia has become a limited exception. Current reforms and evolving patterns of East-West industrial cooperation suggest that in the future modified forms of capital participation in local enterprises will not be excluded from consideration. However, for the time being there is no evidence that communist governments are contemplating an ambitious "New Economic Policy" comparable to that which Lenin initiated in Soviet Russia in the early nineteen-twenties.

Opportunities for normal commercial promotion with a view to obtaining sales in competition with foreign, much less domestic, producers are nonexistent or, at best, rigidly circumscribed. As a practical matter, the Western firm cannot reach the local industrial consumer by means of mail-circulated canvassing. It cannot effectively explore the market, supervise the aftersales service of its product, provide customer training or advice, ensure verifiable protection for its know-how, ascertain the level of resale prices charged for its goods, finance sales or leases with its equipment as collateral and the right of foreclosure upon default, or use tested merchandising techniques to influence demand.

Nor do foreign businesses enjoy many of the other facilities which have come to be looked upon as normal in relations among commercially active countries. Except at officially sponsored trade fairs or exhibitions, Western firms cannot conveniently display their products to potential users. By the same token they cannot, as a rule, avail themselves of local warehousing facilities, appoint Eastern individuals or organizations as trusted and fully authorized agents, offer services auxiliary to sales, perform normal banking operations, enjoy unhampered access to shipping and transshipping utilities, hire office space, or engage local technical and secretarial personnel.

A trend toward liberalization is unmistakably in evidence. It is particularly striking in the area of local advertising. Most of the Eastern countries, including the Soviet Union itself, have begun to welcome the placement of foreign advertisements in scientific, technical and trade publications, newspapers and certain other national media. The social value of such advertising has now been recognized in trademark legislation as a means not only of identifying the manufacturers of a local product, but also of popularizing it among consumers, and costs appear to be eminently reasonable compared with Western charges. Thus far, however, most of the copy has been designed to influence a particular segment of the official trading community, specifically buyers of capital equipment rather than the ultimate individual consumer. Under present law, the latter cannot, in any event, use his purchasing power to buy foreign goods, except to the extent that they have been introduced into the market by way of official conduits pursuant to the government's annual import program.

Foreign companies are generally sealed off from direct contact with domestic producers or distributors. In the Soviet-type economy, sales or purchases must be largely channeled through intermediary state agencies. An administrative barrier is thus placed in the way of business communication. This barrier has proved frustrating to the communist customer as well as to the foreign supplier.

The Western firm finds it difficult to ascertain and meet in full the real needs of those who will use its product. The Eastern end-user, in turn, has at his disposal only incomplete knowledge of the variety of available capital goods or of the special engineering which the foreign manufacturer can provide in order to satisfy particular requirements. The interposed purchasing combine often lacks the specialized knowledge needed to make complex technical decisions. As a rule, it deals with a broad range of products which fall within the ambit of its monopoly. By the time a plant manager's order for a foreign item passes through the maze of bureaucratic procedure, havoc may have been played with his original specifications.

Moreover, the trade combine is as much, if not more, concerned with the immediate questions of price and the national balance of payments than with the technical refinements drawn up by its local customer. The final decision with respect to a given transaction is, therefore, likely to be affected by the level of foreign exchange reserves of the State Bank rather than by the purely industrial merits of the situation. That these Byzantine procedures tend to inhibit the flow and diminish the benefits of trade is self-evident.

In recent years, however, end-users of Western goods have increasingly made their appearance during some phase in the negotiations between foreign suppliers and the import monopolies of the East. Furthermore, several eastern European countries have allowed some of the major production enterprises to move directly into foreign markets. How far this trend, now followed by Russia herself, will go is still not clear, but the signs are quite favorable.

B. The Right of Local Establishment

One distinct characteristic of the communist market is the foreigner's lack of a right to maintain a business presence. There is, of course, no possibility of organizing or acquiring equity in a local corporation. A few Western firms still show on their balance sheets shareholdings in currently operating eastern European companies of precommunist vintage. But this ownership, although never formally nationalized, remains entirely dormant.

To set up a form of commercial representation is also impossible, except in the rarest of circumstances. An example would be a contract calling for long-term presence by a foreign firm in connection with the construction of a factory or the operation of an airline office. A number of foreign nationals providing sales antennas for Western firms are allowed to reside more or less continuously in communist capitals. Their presence is, however, based on administrative tolerance rather than legally protected rights.

The commercial status of foreign individuals and firms admitted to business activities in the territory of a communist state is governed by domestic legislation. Occasionally, variations are provided by treaty. Depending on the nature of the endeavor, the applicable regulations tend to be quite liberal if only a temporary presence is desired for the purpose of performing specific transactions. In Hungary, for instance, the foreigner need only qualify as a "merchant"—a classification which is determined by reference to the law of his own country. Foreign companies are also permitted to negotiate and conclude isolated contracts on Hungarian soil without first submitting to any qualifying procedures.[1]

Similarly, in the Soviet Union no specific authorization, or registration is required before a foreign firm can validly enter into commercial, financial or insurance transactions with competent local enterprises. Originally, blanket permission was provided by a special Decree promulgated in 1931. It has now been reasserted in the 1961 Basic Principles of Civil Legislation.[2] The surprising degree of leniency is consistent with the Soviet desire to shift homeward a maximum of international trade activities. The state-trading monopoly welcomes negotiations, the signing of contracts and the settling of accounts by visiting foreign business representatives.

Rumania, in contrast to most other Eastern states, requires alien firms to obtain authorization from the Ministry of Foreign Trade as a prerequisite to negotiation and conclusion of foreign trade transactions in its territory.[3] This requirement is, however, more formal than real. In practice, business arrangements can be explored without a preliminary license, the willingness of the local entity to pursue such contacts serving as evidence of the government's implicit approval. Along the same lines, China's Provisional Norms on Supervision of Foreign Trade of 1950 declare: "All foreign dealers and agents of foreign trade organizations who carry out foreign trade in China . . . must . . . apply for registration in the local administration for supervision over foreign trade."[4] It is unclear to what extent, if any, this requirement is relaxed in day-to-day practice.

All the communist countries require special state authorization for the local presence of a foreign firm or merchant to conduct business on a permanent or long-term basis. The application must be directed to the Ministry of Foreign Trade, although the exchange control authorities also have a right of approval.

The Soviet Ministry operates a special Protocol Service for the purpose of admission to do business. The file submitted on behalf of a foreign firm must contain: (1) its name, address and date of formation; (2) a description of its activity and directive organs, and the names of persons empowered to represent it; (3) the date and place of registration of its corporate charter; (4) its authorized capital; (5) the name of the Soviet foreign trade organization with which it has reached a current agreement, the object and value of the agreement and its duration; and (6) the names of other Soviet organizations with which it had concluded contracts in the past. The first four items must be supported by appropriate documents, notarized and legalized according to the procedures followed by Soviet consulates abroad.[5]

The admission license defines the authorized scope of transactions to be locally conducted and the duration of the proposed activity. Once admitted to perform business operations in Soviet territory, the foreign firm is deemed subject to the local laws, administrative instructions and decisions. Standing regulations require the filing of quarterly reports with respect to all significant activities, commercial contacts established with Soviet organizations, export-import agreements concluded with foreign trade enterprises and so forth. In addition, the resident manager must inform the Protocol Service of arrivals and departures of other representatives of the firm and give notice if he is replaced by another manager. Violation of any of these requirements may result in termination of representative status. Termination may also follow unilateral notification by the Ministry that the activity of the foreign firm no longer corresponds to the interests of the U.S.S.R.

While the Ministry of Foreign Trade has complete discretion to grant, deny, prolong or revoke an admission license, the State Committee on Science and Technology also enjoys a segment of authority in this area. In connection with activities falling under the terms of bilateral agreements on industrial, scientific and technical cooperation, it may secure the admission of appropriate foreign personnel to continuous presence and activities.

Although the legal basis of admission is not always clear, a number of Western companies are known to be permanently established in the East. Aside from airlines, certain business and banking firms have for some time openly maintained makeshift premises in Moscow. Among them are American Express, Banque de Paris et des Pays-Bas, Krupp of Essen and Novasider S.P.A. of Turin (acting in the U.S.S.R. for such Italian firms as Edison, Fiat and Pirelli). At present, the Soviet Ministry of Foreign Trade appears to be ready to allow approved foreign firms to operate from independent offices with recognized commercial standing rather than from hotel room facilities on a tolerated quasi-tourist basis. The first accreditation permits under this policy were granted to several well-known Japanese companies: C. Itoh & Co., Tokyo Boeki, Mitsui and Ataka. The Régie Renault of France was also allowed to regularize a situation which had existed *de facto* since October 1966, by officially establishing a permanent Moscow office.[6]

Foreign individuals authorized to reside and engage in approved activities are by law subject to the "national treatment standard," unless an operative treaty establishes an alternative criterion. This approach has been recently affirmed in Article 122 of the Soviet Basic Principles of Civil Legislation. The alien is granted civil status equivalent to that of local nationals. Accordingly, when he enters into valid contracts, he acquires rights and obligations as would citizens of the host state; he has equal access to the courts to sue in case of breach, and exposes himself to suits in turn for his own defaults.[7] He may not exercise rights which surpass those possessed by citizens of the communist country, if such rights are violative of the "socialist rule of law." Thus, he may not own land, operate a shop or manufacturing enterprise or, absent special authorization, validly conclude contracts in respect of which local nationals lack capacity.

National treatment is invariably conditioned upon reciprocity. If the state of the foreign individual does not afford comparable facilities to citizens of the communist state, the latter may respond with discrimination of its own. In the Soviet Union such reprisals must, however, have the prior approval of the Council of Ministers.

While in principle the national's and foreigner's rights are coextensive, it must be remembered that various statutes restrict or exclude activity on the part of aliens in specific fields, such as fishing, sealing and mining. Moreover, the liberal professions are, as a rule, also closed to outsiders, although foreign lawyers are occasionally admitted to perform services in specified situations, *e.g.,* to negotiate agreements and litigate disputes before arbitration tribunals and even People's Courts.

It is worth reiterating that the legal status of foreign individuals and firms may be affected by international agreements which displace or vary domestic legislation. A number of commercial treaties with capitalist countries require reciprocal recognition of trading entities and define the conditions on which they may enter into business transactions within the territories of the states concerned. Although on occasion such provisions prescribe treatment equal to that of citizens, as in the case of the Soviet-Norwegian treaty affecting ships in distress, typically they are phrased in terms of a most-favored-nation standard. Thus, the treaty between the U.S.S.R. and Denmark of August 17, 1946, provides that legal conditions no less favorable than those extended to nationals and corporations of the most-favored-state while conducting economic operations in Soviet territory will be extended to Danish nationals and corporations. Soviet nationals and corporations are vested with similar rights in Danish territory.

The benefits which could accrue to Danish traders by virtue of this provision are difficult to imagine. In Denmark, as in most other market economies, foreign firms are admitted to do business in accordance with conditions solemnly prescribed by law. Authorization is automatic once these conditions are fulfilled. In the Soviet Union the conditions are largely a matter for the discretion of the Ministry of Foreign Trade; permission is in fact granted only if the proposed activities are considered advantageous to the state.

The application of such a policy by the U.S.S.R. or by any other Eastern country for that matter does not violate treaties of this type since the governing standard only requires a High Contracting Party to treat all foreigners equally. Even, as we might well suspect, if enterprises of "fraternal" communist countries are given better treatment than Western firms, the discrimination takes place invisibly on the administrative level, where it cannot be proved, at least in the absence of a systematic pattern of favoritism. A refinement on this theme arises from the Soviet insistence that most-favored-nation clauses "do not apply to the rights and advantages that the contracting parties have granted or will grant in the future to neighboring States in order to facilitate border relations with them." [8] This would appear to be an attempt to place the other countries of the socialist camp in a preferred category on the basis of an allegedly objective standard of geographic proximity.

C. Initiation of Business Relationships

Making contact with communist enterprises through the correct agency and at the proper level with a view to promoting a business transaction, is one of the most difficult problems in East-West trade. An unusually large number of deals are initiated more or less as a result of coincidence. Viewed in broad perspective, the approach to the Eastern market appears simple enough. Commodities are purchased and sold by a limited number of trading corporations and other specifically authorized enterprises. These entities are readily identifiable and duly qualified to receive inquiries and offers either directly at home, or through official representations abroad.

Possibilities for entering into direct relations with local producers and end-users are, however, still limited. And the obstacle is a serious one. Negotiations with interested customers are always more productive than those with an interposed trading entity. In the former case, the essentials of quality and suitability of the product receive the weight they deserve; in the latter, extraneous economic and political considerations are prone to enter the picture, and responsibility is splintered by line of product or geographical area. An Eastern user of, say, a Western elevator system for a hotel may have to deal with several import combines, one to procure the mechanical parts, another the electric cables and fixtures, a third the ornate internal woodwork.

Random business contacts made abroad rarely lead to concrete results. Eastern commercial missions which exercise broad functions in the country of the hopeful Western trader lack qualifications to appraise the feasibility of a locally initiated business proposal. Usually they act at the instance and upon the detailed instructions of home-based trading corporations. There are exceptions, to be sure. Soviet trade delegations located in such major Western capitals as London or Paris have both competent technical personnel and considerable commercial autonomy. But even there, it is only when particular commodities must be bought or sold under the terms of the foreign trade plan that the representations proceed to seek out appropriate Western suppliers or purchasers. Large orders can, as a rule, be concluded only in the capitals of the east European countries. Business can also be initiated via the several Eastern Chambers of Foreign Trade or the commercial attaché offices accredited by Western countries. The latter are often staffed by competent and well-informed consular officials, as is notably the case with the British, French and Italian embassies in Moscow and other communist cities. Promotional activities undertaken in this manner are, however, necessarily general in nature and seldom lead to concrete deals.

Fairs and exhibitions are important for business initiation, the most notable the annual 800-year-old Leipzig Fair in East Germany (the West's principal "display window" in the communist world), the Poznan Fair in Poland, the Budapest Fair in Hungary and the Brno Fair in Czechoslovakia. Attended by purchasing representatives from every communist country, these fairs provide a convenient way of entering and maintaining a position in the Eastern market through the regular exhibition of products available for sale. In particular, trade fairs provide smaller companies in the West with an opportunity to show and sell their wares directly. Often a sale will be made in order to avoid return shipment of the goods, a situation which communist buyers have learned to exploit by driving hard bargains.

Special purpose exhibitions, lectures and demonstrations to interested Eastern technicians of the latest in available technology, either at home in the Western country or in the cities of the prospective customers, have also resulted in substantial orders. Such methods have, of late, come to be recognized as being among the most effective ways of reaching end-users in the East. In recent years, it has also become possible to exercise a modest degree of influence on communist industrial executives through advertising and the active circulation of technical materials and information catalogues. A firm whose descriptive literature is at a potential buyer's elbow is more likely to obtain a sale when a procurement occasion arises.

Repeated visits to Eastern capitals in an attempt to establish direct contact with prospective buyers can be an efficacious way of breaking into a given market. Such visits are not likely, however, to yield results unless they are painstakingly prepared with a definite goal in mind. In the first place, it is necessary to reach an authority competent to decide on the expenditure of foreign exchange. Then one must ascertain whether the product to be sold is included in the current purchasing plan, for otherwise it is not salable regardless of its merits. On occasion it is possible to cause the product's inclusion in a future plan, or its upgrading in the present scale of priorities, if its superior qualities and competitive price are convincingly demonstrated on the spot to an interested industrial consumer of stature. Beyond these hurdles are others: the Western firm must make certain that its admittedly superior offer will not be undercut by a more favored Comecon competitor, by a supplier who can be paid in bartered goods or soft currency, or by one whose country is tied to the particular Eastern market by means of a bilateral commercial agreement.

Promotional trips can only be successful if undertaken with the active sponsorship of an appropriate organization in the East. Random visits by Western buyers or sellers are generally futile, in addition to being difficult to arrange in terms of visa requirements. Because of artificially established currency exchange rates, such trips are also relatively expensive. When a legitimate business transaction is in view, communist hospitality can be lavish indeed. Otherwise, businessmen have been known to sit around Moscow hotels for weeks without being able to secure an appointment with responsible officials or even to ascertain their telephone numbers.

Those who ultimately succeed in gaining their interlocutors' attention and confidence are likely to reap considerable rewards. Given the climate of suspicion which prevails in East-West relations, there is, understandably, a premium on long-standing relationships based on direct experience with an established Western supplier. Indeed, to ensure reliability and continuity, Soviet enterprises have been known to work through their own Western "man of confidence" as a conduit for dealings of a particular type. In a communist economy, perhaps more than elsewhere, personal decisions by powerful executives play an important part and can be beneficially influenced by sustained contact, a constant supply of relevant commercial information and an attitude which inspires individual trust.

D. The Negotiation Process

Business negotiations with communist concerns are lengthy, complex and arduous. The normal practice of state-trading officials is to engage first in a prolonged period of "shopping" designed to yield several competing offers, and thereafter in a bout of hard bargaining before deciding to place any major order. Once a transaction is deemed feasible, the determination of its specific terms requires much patience and perseverance. In effect, the Western merchant must function throughout as a businessman-diplomat.

The persons in obvious authority on the Eastern negotiating team are, as a rule, the head or the duly appointed representatives of the export-import corporation. They, in turn, are often assisted by engineers and technicians assigned by the local producer or end-user, by representatives of the Foreign Trade Bank, by corporate house counsel and, in the event difficult legal issues arise, by officials from the Ministry of Justice. Seemingly passive, but alertly observant political chaperons have also been known to audit negotiations of special importance.

It is easy to see that the monolithic character of the communist trading partner invests him with inordinate bargaining power. This power stems from the sheer size of the state monopoly and the fact that each export-import enterprise handles virtually all of its country's trade in particular product lines and brings upon the horizon one-shot deals of great magnitude. It also derives from the enterprise's ability to rely on other component departments of its own government to exercise subtle pressures on the foreign businessman or his government, from denial of visa and travel privileges to delay in the signing of a new bilateral trade agreement. While practices of this type are used only as a last resort, they do, nonetheless, present an unpredictable and unusual obstacle course.

The impact of the bargaining disparity is felt most acutely by smaller firms, especially when dealing with the U.S.S.R. The larger company, which is the most frequent venturer into the area, is far better able to resist the problems of size, certainly when it is negotiating with the small east European countries. Large or small, the Western trader must recognize at the outset that his choice is either to deal with a specially empowered government instrumentality, usually one having exclusive competence over the product in which he is interested, or not to deal at all. Strong as he may be economically, he will find himself jostled by other intensely competitive Western sellers or buyers in search of communist business. Eastern trade officials have not hesitated to play off one firm against another, generally for commercial, but occasionally also for political reasons.

The ability to stimulate and exploit such rivalry needs to be recognized as one of the basic attributes of the communist trading system. It is obvious that when a number of Western firms seek to sell to or buy from a monopolistic state corporation, the terms must be less advantageous than those which would be forthcoming in a normally competitive context. The result would be similar if bids made within a Western market were rigged in total disregard of the most basic rules of fair competition. On the other hand, an attempt at cooperation among competing private traders, even if feasible, might invite the application of their national antitrust conspiracy laws. It is important to bear in mind, in addition, that a state monopoly's tendency to introduce into its dealings a measure of invisible discrimination has significance not only at the trader-to-trader level, but also at the level of intergovernmental relations. The dividends (and the price) can be economic as well as political. Offers may come with the attached conditions that Soviet purchases or sales be delivered in Soviet ships, insured by Soviet insurers and cleared through Soviet banks. In the interest of proper perspective, however, it should be mentioned that such unwarranted requirements can also be posed by the Western side, to wit, the notorious shipping conditions attached by the United States in connection with the large sale of wheat to the U.S.S.R. in 1963.

Even as a purely commercial proposition, the typically large, discontinuous transactions, when offered by Eastern monopolies, often assume the character of a special "concession" which calls for a *quid pro quo* from the Western trade partner. If, for example, a sizable purchase is involved, the state buyer may succeed in extracting certain counterconcessions. These can take the form of a demand for a specially generous price discount, on the ground that such a show of "good will" is appropriate in dealing with an unusually large customer. Alternatively, they can take the form of a request that the seller agree to make a compensatory purchase of local goods.

Western firms which express misgivings about conditions of an extraordinary nature, such as referral to communist sponsored arbitration, frequently have their resistance dissipated with special benefits, *e.g.*, more attractive price terms. The state-trading enterprise, as we know, is in a position to make such offers since profit margins are not always the overriding consideration.

Past experience in business negotiations with the strongest Eastern entities, mostly with the U.S.S.R., has shown, moreover, that if the bargaining position of a Western firm is considered inflexible, such a reputation may lead not only to the frustration of a particular transaction, but also to *de facto* exclusion from the national market as a whole; for if the given state agency is seriously displeased, there is no one else to whom the company can turn for trade. The same applies in the course of a contract's performance. If the foreign party's interpretation of terms, or denial of special requests is considered as excessively technical, its future business prospects with the enterprise or country in question may dwindle. These risks are subtly emphasized whenever an impasse is reached in the negotiation or renegotiation of an important point.

Despite a certain measure of known cooperation among Eastern governments, usually through Comecon, there is no evidence that a Western company may, on that account, be informally black-listed in the communist region generally. By the same token, neither has international coordination among communist purchasing and selling monopolies been established as a fact. If anything, they have at times been observed to act in competition with one another in their dealings with the West.

E. Credit and Payment Techniques

Since it became a substantial buyer of industrial equipment, the East has been pressing Western sellers for broadened supplier credits in its favor. Individual firms as well as governments were tempted into this direction by the prospect of stepped-up communist procurement. As we have shown earlier, the United States has remained virtually alone in respecting the multilateral credit limitations established within the Berne Union.[9]

Private European banks, separately and in syndicates, are currently extending credit facilities in respect of Eastern purchases of capital goods for periods of ten to fifteen years. In medium term situations, usually up to five years, bills of exchange accepted by Eastern buyers are easily discountable without recourse to the Western seller, if he is insured by an export credit agency operated or sponsored by his government. In the case of small contracts, credit is occasionally provided by the seller from his own resources. While Eastbound trade financing is readily available in the West, straight bank loans are exceptional and state-to-state credits are even rarer. But this method of financing may also come into its own, should west European governments consider it expedient to stimulate the political *détente* through higher levels of transcontinental exchange.

Conventional financing and banking techniques are widely used in East-West trade; however, the potential inherent in such techniques is limited. For reasons of their own, communist states abhor the historical examples of such countries as Japan, Australia or even the United States, whose road to economic development was paved with foreign equity capital and long-term debt. Their desire to borrow is tempered by concern over the trade balance and the ability to meet payment obligations at maturity. To the extent that these preoccupations are sincere, they can only be reassuring to Western creditor nations and lending institutions. But because the Eastern need is far greater than the possibilities available under standard financing methods, ingenuity in the elaboration of various compensatory arrangements is, and will long remain, the key to consummating East-West transactions.

Credits and payments are usually channeled through the Eastern countries' specialized Foreign Trade Banks, entities which are legally independent but operationally subordinate to the respective central banks. An important and growing role for eastern European trade as a whole is exercised by a chain of Soviet-controlled banks incorporated abroad, notably the Moscow Narodny Bank of London, the Banque Commerciale pour l'Europe du Nord of Paris and the Wosschod Handelsbank of Zurich. The Foreign Trade Banks of the smaller socialist countries are also beginning to take equity participations in Western banks and finance companies, particularly in Vienna. The home-based institutions stand ready to guarantee trade notes issued by east European purchasing entities; the foreign-based institutions, while engaging in a wide variety of financial operations, discount without recourse to the Western seller commercial paper issued by state-trading enterprises and bearing the signature of their Foreign Trade Bank or National Bank.

The typical Foreign Trade Bank of a socialist country resembles Western banking institutions, except that it specializes and enjoys national exclusivity in transactions involving the international exchange of goods and services. For example, Poland's Bank Handlowy, founded a century ago and adapted to the needs of the present regime, acts in such conventional areas as discount of commercial paper, confirmation of letters of credit, endorsement of bills of exchange, payment against shipping documents, issuance and acceptance of guarantees, arbitrage, switch operations, purchase and sale of foreign currencies, precious metals, coins, securities and the like. In addition, it performs important advisory functions in guiding state companies with regard to the financial and other basic terms they may be negotiating for inclusion into contracts with international elements.

Each of the Eastern Foreign Trade Banks maintains an extensive network of stable correspondent relationships throughout the world. It is also noteworthy that their day-to-day operating procedures are quite orthodox and that they adhere to the Uniform Rules and Usages for Documentary Credits (1962) of the International Chamber of Commerce. Over the years Western firms have found that orders issued in their favor have been faithfully executed by these banks in accordance with the time, place, currency and manner of payment required by the underlying contract.

Misgivings as to the general reliability of communist commitments and memories of past abuses die hard. The private businessman who has had no exposure to this sphere of commerce is therefore often surprised to learn that the Eastern banks enjoy an excellent credit rating in world trading and financial circles. In fact, their undertakings, whether direct or by way of guarantee, have been judged reliable by the most conservative Western banking establishments. Even government-operated insurance agencies such as the Export Credit Guarantee Department of England, Hermes of West Germany and Coface of France, which cover collection risks of up to 90 percent of invoiced amounts, consider Eastern paper as being among the best available.

While some firms will only deliver to an Eastern country on the basis of shipping documents against a letter of credit confirmed by an acceptable Western bank, most exporters (and the financial houses which back them) are fully content with the obligation either of the National Bank or the Foreign Trade Bank. Others have shipped without incident on an open account basis. The buyer, it should be noted, no less than the banks, is government-owned; and in the ultimate analysis a state stands behind both, morally if not in a strictly legal sense. As a result the commercial credit risk which so preoccupies exporters to the world at large is virtually nil in this area; only the political risk may give some concern.

In connection with the financed procurement of Western plants, east European buyers prefer to execute "paperless contracts," *i.e.,* without negotiable instruments; such contracts are, nonetheless, often independently bankable. The Foreign Trade Banks are in turn reluctant to endorse promissory notes, to the extent that such notes are issued by corporate state buyers. This is not because of lack of power to endorse, or concern with the credit risk. The reluctance stems from a desire to prevent the uncontrolled circulation and negotiation of such paper in the world's capital markets. An irrevocable and unconditional bank guarantee, freeing the Western creditor of the preliminary obligation to sue the primary communist obligor is more readily obtainable. In special circumstances, a substitution clause is also possible to obtain, permitting the holder to assign the debt, together with the bank's own guarantee, to an unrelated third party, although not to negotiate it at will. Regardless of the form of the instrument, or of the financing arrangements made by the direct parties and their respective banks, the Western seller usually receives payment in cash, without risk of recourse, against delivery of clean shipping documents.

At the nation-to-nation level, trade settlement within Comecon is effected through the International Bank for Economic Cooperation. In the case of countries dealing in hard currency, payments are made openly or pursuant to bilateral intergovernmental agreements. Balances are usually settled in convertible funds, often at the point of renewal of such agreements. Technically, state monopolies can apply a balance accumulated in their favor to buy elsewhere and occasionally they sell the credit at a discount to another Eastern country. In general practice, however, they employ the balance to increase purchases from the other party to the bilateral agreement upon the latter's insistence.

In nonconvertible currency trade, typically under bilateral agreements and complementing payment protocols concluded with less developed countries, balances are cleared through accounts kept by the central banks of the two trading nations. No actual transfer of funds takes place, but debits and credits are required to cover each other over the lifetime of the agreement. Ultimately, imbalances must be settled by transfers of hard currency, or gold, although since the early sixties technical "swing" credits have become common practice.[10]

Since individuals and entities other than those empowered by the state monopoly are excluded from commercial operations beyond the national border, since travel abroad is held to a minimum, and since nontrade transactions are marginal, the flow of funds is easily controlled by the Eastern authorities. Consequently the elaborate exchange control regulations which frequently encumber business and banking operations in western Europe (*e.g.,* under the stringent rules of the Office des Changes in France or the Bank of England in Great Britain) are not required. All in all, the Eastern payment procedures are characterized by great simplicity. Issuance of an import license by the Ministry of Foreign Trade in respect of a particular transaction operates as automatic approval of the concommitant financial provisions of the contract.

F. Compensatory Financing Arrangements

Chronic shortages of hard currency and the rigors of bilateralism have caused the East to favor various unconventional methods of financing the international exchange of goods, including direct and triangular barter, switch transactions, linked export-import arrangements, compensation deals and other types of tied and parallel trading. Primitive as these forms of commerce may be in comparison with open, multilateral trade, their ultimate disappearance is not now in sight. Were they to be dispensed with, East-West trade would simply dry up to a trickle, since for the time being there is little in the way of viable substitutes. Experienced European firms have long realized that unless they adopt an attitude of flexibility on this score many lucrative transactions with Eastern enterprises will not be accessible to them. American companies and their European-based subsidiaries have shown themselves to be far more rigid, although in March 1970 the McDonnell Douglas corporation established a significant precedent with its sale of DC9 aircraft against part payment in Yugoslav export products.

Barter, a mode of exchange which dates back to antiquity, has become a standard device in East-West trade. In its strictest sense it involves a swap of two commodities, without their values being rendered in terms of money. As a rule this technique is encountered in trade between soft currency countries. At both the nation-to-nation and firm-to-firm levels, the Eastern countries have often resorted to barter arrangements in dealings with exchange-starved economies. Such economies welcome interlocking transactions, either in hope of making additional sales or for fear of losing established outlets. Thus, Czechoslovak tractors and Polish freighters have been extensively bartered against Brazilian coffee. Soviet crude oil has been exchanged for Greek tobacco and Italian steel pipe.

The United Arab Republic has received industrial equipment and large quantities of military goods in return for cotton. In the case of other less developed countries, sizable credits expendable only in communist countries have occasionally been amassed, in a manner reminiscent of the

Schachtian "blocked balances" used by Hitler's Germany, to exert systematic pressure upon vulnerable economies. In the process favorable quotas for communist origin goods are often opened, to the detriment of exports from Western countries.

A more complex variant is the triangular barter deal, where the communist goods obtained by a Western firm are in turn traded for goods in a third country. While not always unprofitable, such transactions are avoided by merchants in the industrially advanced countries, since they represent a form of forced exchange. As in the case of direct barter, the goods offered in return are often of little interest and must be disposed of through middlemen at considerable effort and cost.

In recent years, complex switch transactions have begun to thrive on the periphery of deliberately balanced trade between Eastern and Western countries. Akin to, but not identical with triangular barter, "switch" entails payment for goods by means of clearing currency—a unit of account arising from dealings under bilateral treaties. In effect, the device operates as an essential regulator of bilateralism, eliminating some of its inherent rigidities.

A would-be Eastern buyer who happens to have a surplus bilateral trade account with a country other than that of the seller may offer to settle in clearing currency. If the seller accepts, and the necessary approvals are obtained from the government concerned, he either may use the resulting funds to purchase the third country's goods for his own needs or for resale, or he may discount them for a currency of his preference. Often the seller will make stand-by arrangements to negotiate the currency and only then consummate his sale to a point of irrevocability.

The complexity of the operation calls for a graphic example. Let us assume that within a given period Brazil's sales to Hungary exceed its purchases. This situation can yield Brazilian-Hungarian clearing dollars. Let us further assume that Brazil seeks to purchase wheat from France without, however, wishing to use up its hard currency reserves. A switch banker will enable the sale to be effected on the basis of the available clearing dollars. The French vendor will ultimately be paid in fully convertible funds, absorbing the banker's fees and commissions. In one way or another, these discounting costs will be passed on to or shared with the Brazilian purchases.[11]

Although "switch" is a method which can assume many guises, in its standard form it is most frequently encountered in dealings with the exchange-starved Eastern nations. When cash or deferred payment in convertible funds is not feasible and a barter arrangement is also precluded, payment in "coffee dollars," "citrus sterling" or "onion francs" may, as a device of last resort, allow the transaction to take place anyway.

Some enterprising Western firms have made a specialty of switch dealings and barter transactions. Their practical knowledge of which country's clearing funds happen to be most accessible or what demand exists for a particular range of goods in a given market can be of considerable assistance in arranging for additional sales or securing advantageous purchases in the East. Less experienced Western companies, particularly manufacturing concerns, have benefitted extensively from a standing relationship with selected switch-trading and barter houses.

A Western firm with interest in commercial opportunities of this type and expertise in the underlying methodology will often seek to include in a contract the condition that its purchase of goods be tied to a countersale to the state trader. The resultant arrangements can take several forms, of which the following is quite typical. The foreign firm may be negotiating for the procurement in bulk of some commodity from the Soviet export entity, Prodintorg. A separate agreement is negotiated and the consideration expressed in dollars, sterling or other convertible currency. On the surface the transaction and the written contract appear to be complete. In fact, the finality of the deal is more formal than real. For it is contingent upon a parallel commitment to be made by the same, or some other, Soviet export-import entity.

Let us assume that Raznoimport is concurrently in the world market to purchase some category of manufactured goods. In order to induce completion of the commodity sale, if the Western buyer has the bargaining power to exact conditions, arrangements will be made to purchase the manufactures from or through him. Once again an independent contract is drawn, with a price fictitiously expressed in convertible currency. The funds may even be remitted by both parties pursuant to the usual letters of credit, but the balanced end result will, in fact, have been secured well in advance.

The mechanics of such a composite transaction are not only instructive in themselves, but also interesting as a comment on the issue of corporate inter-dependence which we encounter in the legal and business setting of the East. Ostensibly, both Prodintorg and Raznoimport, in our example, negotiate and conclude their bargains separately. In practice, however, neither transaction is in force without the other. The coordinating function is performed by the Ministry of Foreign Trade, which in effect dictates the terms of the compensating agreements to the Eastern parties. Often, too, the authorized signatories of one of the two participating state entities will countersign the contract between the other entity and the Western firm.

Among the devices most frequently employed by the Eastern monopolies is the all-too-familiar condition that the Western seller "show his good will" by accepting in part payment a quantity of merchandise designated by the state-trading entity. Attempts to attach such counter-purchase obligations come to the fore as large orders for manufactured goods are about to be placed, or whenever the relative bargaining position of the parties permits. In its most objectionable form, the demand requires the seller to create an artificial market for unneeded Eastern products either in his own country or elsewhere. More often than not, the goods thus "unloaded" on him are in the form of raw materials. They can just as easily be fruits, vegetables, jewelry, canned goods, watch cases or even finished machine tools. It goes without saying that staple or desirable commodities can be sold by the Eastern monopolies directly. What they are usually tempted to dispose of through the unwilling intermediary of their Western supplier is the "junk."

The Eastern side feels impelled to employ this tactic not only to save foreign exchange, but also because of lack of marketing experience, or inadequate selling facilities abroad. In effect, the hopeful Western vendor is pressured into becoming the foreign selling agent of the state export monopoly to the extent that he stands ready to accept the counter-purchase condition. Whether or not he succumbs will, of course, depend on his competitive position, the importance which he attaches to the order and, conversely, the extent to which his goods are adjudged unique or desirable by the communist purchaser. Many firms have declined such composite packages altogether. Others have reluctantly acceded, despite their lack of experience in handling the proferred products.

A long bout of negotiations is practically unavoidable in arrangements of this type. The central terms in contention include the price at which the compensatory goods are to be purchased, the areas within which they can be freely marketed and, above all, their proportion to the value of the proposed sale. The ratio may approach 100 percent, even more, but as a rule it can be bargained down very considerably, often to as little as 10 percent. Be that as it may, the experienced Western seller, knowing what awaits him, will add an adequate margin to his initial price quotation.

Forced sales constitute much more of a problem for the industrial firm which seeks to sell its manufactures to the East than for the commercial firm. As a rule, the former only operates an export department, while the latter engages in two-way trade and is therefore better placed to dispose of the unwanted goods, particularly if they fall into a category in which it has experience.

Nonetheless, certain Western manufacturers have consistently agreed to accept Eastern commodities which could be incorporated without intolerable inconvenience either into their production processes or, in the case of finished goods, into their distribution outlets. For example, an American manufacturer of agricultural equipment has found it expedient to take in compensation Eastern raw materials for processing at its west European plants.[12] More often, steps will be taken to enlist the services of an intermediary trading organization specialized in the types of transactions or products in question. Such an organization may be invited to enter the picture not only after the underlying East-West deal has been concluded but also, and more appropriately, at the time of the overall negotiations, to ensure the feasibility and terms of final disposal.

In recent years compensatory financing arrangements have taken on many guises. Patent licenses have expressed royalties in terms of the delivery of products manufactured under their authority. Agreements for the construction of turn-key plants have provided for the retirement of credits from the plants' export proceeds. Hotels have been built on the basis of loans to be partly paid off by means of hard currency income from advance tourist bookings.[13]

To the extent that Eastern enterprises insist on the Western side taking manufactured products by way of compensatory sale, they are in fact exchanging a short-term gain for a long-term harm. The products in question may be of variable quality or unknown design. They may change hands several times and ultimately be dumped with a minimum of selling effort, at distress prices. The Eastern manufacturer's trade name cannot help being depreciated in the process. Moreover, this mode of improvisation can hardly imbue him with incentive to search aggressively for new selling outlets, or to style goods so as to make them competitive in Western markets. To overcome the problem, interest has recently arisen in forming mixed and jointly managed companies for the distribution of Eastern products abroad. This method is strongly in evidence in Franco-Soviet relations and promises to become commonplace for East-West trade generally.

In time, the anomalies of doing business in the closed, bilaterally-oriented markets of the East will be marginally alleviated; this is evident from the course of current reforms which are being implemented in all of the socialist countries. Many distinctive commercial conditions are, however, here to stay, along with the irreducible ingredients of the collectivist economic structure. By and large, the Western merchant must learn to accommodate himself to this strange environment and to reap whatever benefits he can.

12

COMPETING WITH COMMUNIST MONOPOLIES

A. The Global Impact of Eastern Trade and Aid

The "socialist market" has manifestly fallen short of the self-contained, fully diversified and broadly innovative economic universe originally envisaged by the political planners of the region. Nonetheless, a number of important objectives have been attained with the creation in eastern Europe of a sizable commercial zone, experienced in the techniques of total state trading and deploying considerable economic power abroad. Beyond the socialist orbit itself, the merchant community, governments and international organizations responsible for regulating foreign trade, must take into account the growing impact of world-wide communist competition. In time to come this competition, even in the area of sophisticated manufactured products, may emerge as a serious challenge to Western industries. Eastern governments have already begun to place heavy stress on the export of indigenous equipment along with the needed know-how for production under patent licenses. Occasionally products embodying technology "borrowed" from the West have also been found to circulate outside the markets of the centrally planned economies.

Certainly, the threat is not immediate. Although the flow of Westward trade has sharply expanded in the last decade, the East still accounts for less than 5 percent of the commerce of the noncommunist world. The day is far distant when the Eastern industrial establishments (even China's, were it to manage a "leap forward" in imitation of Japan) will be in a position to dump an avalanche of raw materials, consumer durables, cameras, transistors and vacuum cleaners, in disregard of the needs and clamors of their own neglected populations. Yet, it is equally obvious that the countries of the East have come to exercise an economic influence in the rest of the world which is considerably more potent than might be suggested by the dollar value of their exports and imports. We have previously discussed the pull which Eastern nations exert as large-scale purchasers. Their exports likewise exert a considerable influence. Far from being limited to an inexhaustible supply of vodka and caviar, they include such products as petroleum, coal, asbestos, timber, pulp, flex, manganese, titanium, chrome, furs, fertilizer and, more sporadically, aluminum, tea and diamonds. We are also beginning to witness aggressive selling of civil aircraft, notably the supersonic Tupolev 144, in competition with the Franco-British Concorde and the American Boeing SST; and of various other products ranging from up-to-date watch movements to giant hydroelectric generators of the type for which the U.S.S.R. attempted to bid in connection with the Grand Coulee Dam in the state of Washington. And who can be sure that Russia will not once again emerge as a major exporter of wheat, in competition with the United States, Canada, Australia and France? For the markets of the less developed nations the constant exports in direct sale or barter already extend to machine tools, metallurgical equipment, oil field machinery, power generating plants, rolling stock, ships, trucks, tractors and farm implements.

In the service industries commercial rivalry also promises to be lively. Aeroflot of the U.S.S.R., Tarom of Rumania and Lot of Poland have been operating major international air routes for some time. More recently the U.S.S.R. has become active in the field of maritime transportation and insurance, even when the movement of goods neither originates nor terminates in communist ports. For example, Sovfrakht, the shipping agency, has attempted to capture a portion of the ocean traffic between western Europe and Australia at concession rates of as much as 25 percent. Likewise, Inostrakh and other Soviet-controlled underwriting concerns operated from domestic or foreign bases have been seeking insurance and reinsurance business which goes well beyond East-West trade.[1]

An inkling of the scope of future competition may be gleaned from Premier Kosygin's announcement to the 1968 United Nations Conference on Exploration and Peaceful Uses of Outer Space that the U.S.S.R. and other socialist countries are establishing their own satellite communications network to rival the American-sponsored INTELSAT. The services of the Soviet INTERSPUTNIK network, with two-way telephone channels and television program monitoring, will be offered to less developed countries and others willing to join.[2]

Since the early days of the Soviet state, Russian officials have been aware of their monopoly's ability to further national objectives and to influence Western action by manipulating purchases, engaging in wholesale dumping or simply by holding out the lure of profitable business with one of the world's greatest potential markets. There has not, however, been any cohesive evidence of a deliberate and sustained attempt to upset international trading patterns. Even if they could find a way to act in mischievous concert, the still-limited resources of the Eastern economies would prevent them from becoming a major unsettling factor for a long time to come. Nonetheless, an undeniable proclivity does exist for disrupting normal trade flows and for exploiting the economic vulnerability of individual countries. This incipient threat will become more formidable as the larger communist nations acquire an ability to divert more resources to international economic activity. Sweeping offers of trade from a group of states which are growing rapidly in economic power cannot help but appear attractive even to the most advanced industrial nation, particularly when they are put forward in periods of recession and unemployment.

The West, with its diffused political and economic structures, has no comparable framework for waging commercial diplomacy. Indeed, the world which faces such economic power as communist countries may bring to bear is one divided into competitive blocs and preferential areas with notoriously unstable prices of primary products.

While the communist motivation in dealings with the industrialized West is predominantly economic, in relations with the less developed countries, political and diplomatic motives frequently tend to intrude. The commercial activities of the state-trading nations which have expanded spectacularly since 1953 in certain target countries of the Middle East, Asia, Africa and Latin America, appear to be part of a long-range strategy.[3] Among the factors which attract the two contending leaders of the communist orbit, the U.S.S.R. and China, to the developing regions is an awareness that the political elite are searching for ideas most likely to meet their local conditions. In an attempt to influence the critical choices which will necessarily be made within the foreseeable future in these vast and unsettled areas, they are using all means at their disposal, including well-planned bilateral trade programs, to encourage economic trends fashioned in their own image.

If the Soviet government considers it expedient to demonstrate the alleged superiority of its economic system by building a model steel plant in India, a gigantic dam in Egypt or a large refinery in Morocco, in a propaganda contest for the minds of nations in search of institutions to imitate, the necessary appropriation of funds follows automatically. State enterprises proceed to do the job regardless of profit or loss. The material cost is underwritten in expectation of a political dividend. In the West, constitutional appropriation procedures and the need to rely on profit-oriented private companies are much less conducive to politically inspired competition. Although its material and management resources may be superior, a country with a liberal business structure is not organized to pursue intrinsically noncommercial objectives.

At the institutional level, the Soviet (and much more modestly and selectively, the Chinese) authorities are using such trade and aid leverage as they can muster to decrease the recipient countries' participation in multilateral trade, to liberate them from their former "colonial masters," to pre-empt private foreign investment, to promote the nationalization of Western firms and to encourage the growth of the state sector in the client economy. Thus, the techniques of Eastern trade have impelled India and Ceylon to establish a monopolistic government conduit for the exchange of goods with communist countries. Developments of this type tend to integrate entire segments of less developed economies into the East's institutional structures and economic development plans.

More modest gains are also acceptable. For example, by establishing an economic presence, Eastern policy-makers hope to be in a better position to nibble away at the roots of capitalist influence and to encourage leaders of less developed countries to adopt attitudes hostile to the West. The leaders are assured in advance that any economic sanction which they may incur as a result could be offset by direct aid or by the East's role as a buyer of last resort. Should the sanctions lead to balance of payment difficulties this in turn can push the country toward closer economic intimacy with the East and greater detachment from its traditional Western suppliers.

These optimal goals of communist policy are, however, frustratingly elusive. And Western, notably American, politicians tend to exaggerate and overreact to the problem. It must be kept in mind that the threat is still highly contingent and long-term. Given the economic difficulties, competitive inefficacies and centrifugal forces manifest within the communist empire, the potential political power wielded by the Eastern trading apparatus looks much more formidable on paper than it has proved in the flesh. Furthermore, the East's economic involvement in the world's backward areas, Afghanistan, for example, has begun to assume new and objectively beneficial forms, including neutralized cooperative ventures with private Western firms. No less significant are the unmistakable openings which Eastern markets are beginning to offer to commercial and industrial activity from the outside. Czechoslovak, East German and even Russian manufacturers cannot feel entirely comfortable in the knowledge that Western competitors, if given the chance, are likely to flood their less developed Comecon neighbors with superior and more attractively priced capital goods.

B. The State as Competitor

The communist trading system operates internationally from positions of weakness as well as strength. Because of long experience, bulk commodities are sold in the West with relative efficiency. But conspicuously poor results have been obtained in the marketing of manufactured goods. The causes of this well-known inadequacy are varied. Entanglement in red tape has made it difficult to determine the cost and profitability of production for export. Eastern manufacturers have not thus far been able to adapt their commercial apparatus to supply and service purchasers of equipment who operate under different climatic conditions. High maintenance costs, unfamiliar safety standards and great distances from some of the markets in question have also constituted obstacles to normal export activity. The fundamental problem can be traced to the bureaucrat's perennial inability to respond to the needs and desires of the consumer. This defect is pronounced enough in the domestic market. But the effort to meet the Western consumer's increasingly sophisticated requirements for variety, quality and packaging has proved to be even more frustrating.

Communist planners are now aware of these shortcomings. Their self-criticism has come to us on the authority of Premier Kosygin:

> It is doubly insufferable that our first class equipment—the fruit of the creative thought and skill of our wonderful engineers and workers—does not reach foreign markets just because due attention is not paid to its proper finishing and technical documentation, due to a lack of servicing and the absence of advertising.[4]

Of late, firm steps have been taken to decentralize the decision-making processes in production and to place greater reliance on the mechanism of the market. Trade officials no longer content themselves with the mere circulation to prospective buyers of lists of available commodities. Instead, attention is being paid to the proper selection of exportable products in terms of their quality and price, as well as to market research, to advertising and to merchandizing techniques. Moreover, the state monopolies have shown increased willingness to participate with capitalist groups in the equity of jointly organized companies for the purpose of distributing Eastern goods in Western countries.

How far the attempted adjustment to international competition standards will go, and how much time will expire before results become apparent, is not easy to predict. An export-conscious economy such as Czechoslovakia may be expected to improve its marketing techniques more quickly and effectively than China or the U.S.S.R. Meanwhile, the lack of sensitivity in responding to the needs of the foreign customer must remain a severe limitation upon communist sales to the West, except in a few tested, traditional product lines.

There is, of course, another side to the picture. For example, the power which a country like Russia exercises in a particular commodity market does not necessarily depend on the levels of its productivity. The Soviet coal industry is known to be highly inefficient: output per worker has been authoritatively reported at 15 percent of the United States level.[5] Moreover, the domestic price of the product is quite high. Yet the U.S.S.R. has no difficulty in selling annually more than 20 million tons of coal, of which over one-third finds its way to the markets of the West. Similarly, the rapid expansion of Soviet crude oil exports from 9 million metric tons in 1958, to 18 million in 1960 and to 43 million in 1965, was not due either to any remarkable rise in the productivity of its wells or to any dramatic growth in world demand.

The fact is, rather, that the state-operated system enables the Soviet Union to break into any commodity market as a large-scale exporter, regardless of the interaction between national costs and international values. All that is needed is an administrative decision to sell, taken at the apex of the trade monopoly, and the flow of particular goods is pumped out of the economy up to the levels dictated by domestic considerations. There have been enough instances of this to suggest that state-trading institutions can be used with major economic impact as sellers either of standard export products in new markets or of new commodity lines in old markets.

To be quite fair, one must allow that there is nothing startlingly novel in the method which communist enterprises have employed to further their international sales. It is not unusual for any trader wishing to find a new outlet for his product to offer it on preferential terms. What makes the situation essentially different is the monolithic nature and gigantic size of a state trader like the U.S.S.R. Whenever such a trader chooses to resort to commercial gate-crashing tactics, the economic effect is qualitatively different to the extent that first, its arbitrary domestic price system obscures the magnitude of the loss sustained and, second, the loss is absorbed by the public treasury and ultimately by the national economy rather than by a single firm.

At the microeconomic level, the Western competitor encounters a series of unique problems. The state-trading unit may be acting as the sole seller (or buyer) for its entire national market. This fact alone introduces an element of substantive inequality between the two. Unrestrained by normal commercial imperatives or antitrust rules, the combine confronts, in most cases, sellers or buyers who compete fiercely among themselves. Similarly, in bidding for an Eastern project, the private firm must contend not only with its normal Western competitors, but also with East German and Czech industrial establishments, which enjoy more ready access and more favorable terms in the "fraternal" communist markets.

Even the large multinational corporations of the West are not always able to blunt the monopolistic power wielded by a trading agency of the Soviet type. The very magnitude of the transactions which it brings upon the commercial horizon helps to sustain widespread interest throughout the business community and to raise the competition to a high pitch. This interest may even extend to the political authorities of the Western country, especially if a depressed industry or region would stand to benefit from a given order.

A major factor which bolsters the competitive position of a state enterprise, as compared with that of private firms, is its ability to tie in normal business activity with various forms of government aid. The enterprise is in a position to undertake an industrial development project in a client country not only with subsidized means, but also with quasi-conscripted technical personnel at salaries which are a fraction of those paid by private Western firms. In the world market at large, it is true, communist trading monopolies use their state's bargaining power with restraint, except where an overriding economic or political objective may be involved. However, in dealing with less developed areas they can, and occasionally do introduce the kind of side-pledges which the government of a market economy, lacking as it does direct control over the nation's business interests, cannot.

It is a stale exaggeration to assert that political factors consistently dominate the East's behavior in world markets. Comparative economic advantage remains the crucial criterion in most commercial exchanges. However, it is well to bear in mind that important decisions are always government decisions, dictated at least in part by considerations of national interest and public policy. Except in cases where they benefit from some form of organized action or public assistance, private competitors may find it difficult to muster the necessary countervailing power.

C. Propensities toward Market Dislocation

The case alleging a concerted communist effort to disrupt world markets is moot indeed. To the extent that such a goal may have been postulated, it is more likely to exist in the realm of political theory than in commercial practice. No doubt, the state-trading entities of the East are tough competitors. But the only clear charge justified by experience is that prices have at times been deliberately manipulated in otherwise stable or administered world commodity markets. Even within the West this is not an unheard-of technique. The price war in the sale of wheat, which erupted among the United States, Canada, Australia and France in the fall of 1969, is an example which comes readily to mind.

To date, the impact of sharp trading by the East has been only marginal. However, the rapidly growing economies of the communist orbit, helped by labor costs comparable to, or even lower than, those of Japan, could one day turn a latent propensity into a clear and present danger. The normal interplay of supply and demand, or the gentlemen's agreements in effect among traditional suppliers, have provided no foolproof deterrent to the occasional market disorientations we have witnessed in the past.

Some isolated incidents of alleged dumping, as reported by competitors in the country of import and by traditional third country suppliers, deserve separate scrutiny. Disruptions of a related but less common nature are, however, equally significant. For example, Eastern monopolies have been known to reexport an imported commodity (or to export a similar domestic commodity to make room for the import) at a price lower than that prevailing abroad. The result may be a glut, or threat of glut, in the established markets of the original supplier.

In 1963, Poland paid 587 foreign exchange zlotys per ton of raw sugar to Cuba, while exporting the refined product to West Germany at 572 zlotys. Other recorded cases have involved the movement of coal from

Poland to the U.S.S.R. at 14.26 rubles per ton and from thence to Sweden at no more than 4.18 rubles per ton.[6] Tin has moved from China to Russia at high prices, plus heavy transport costs, only to be resold in western Europe at a substantial discount. The much publicized resales by eastern Europe of Egyptian cotton, originally acquired in barter for arms, had their own depressing effect on dealings in this commodity.

Procurements of unusual scope are the obverse side of the coin. As conducted by Eastern monopolies, they can be unsettling both to competing Western purchasers and to stable channels of supply. Again, the motivation may stem from a need to compensate for unanticipated shortages, from planning errors, or from subsidized preemption.

Preclusive buying can be particularly disturbing if there is a suspicion of stockpiling for the future. In the past, fears have been expressed in connection with sudden and large increases in Soviet purchasing of such commodities as Malayan crude rubber and Argentine hides.[7] Even under the most generous hypothesis, a propensity to dislocate supply and demand arises from the state buyer's habit of procuring in great bulk, for an extended period and through centralized means.

By the same token, the monopolies are in a position to shift their concentrated purchases from one market to another. Such a change of pace and pattern can cause disquieting imbalances in vulnerable raw material and agricultural commodity exchanges. The aim may be simply to secure a better commercial bargain. Whatever the reason, it is far-fetched to impute a deliberate and malicious intent to upset outside markets. In times of economic recession and political tension, scope for such mischief may indeed be assumed to exist. But the danger is largely theoretical. Thus far, neither Russia nor China, much less the smaller communist countries, has shown any desire to misallocate its scarce resources in such an adventurous manner. For many years to come the competitive edge is clearly with the West.

One consequence of the fact that the East had, until recently, regarded the world market as a residual source of supply (or selling outlet) has been a tendency toward discontinuity in demand for outside goods. Western firms have reported frequent instances of "one-shot" orders due, more than anything else, to a malfunction in the overworked communist planning mechanism, with its highly centralized system of decision-making. The causes of this irregularity are often attributable to shortfalls in production on the part of major Eastern suppliers to the other centrally planned economies and to delays in established schedules for construction of new industrial plants within the Comecon region. Once the newly built plant goes into production, demand for the previously imported supplies dries up abruptly.

Equally unsettling in this context is the fact that programs for the construction of new plants, which are routinely reported elsewhere, do not normally become public knowledge in an Eastern country. The lack of such information is due to a strong penchant for secrecy in general and a particular unwillingness to share information with Western nations on an open and regular basis. The resultant uncertainty and the lack of continuous commercial communication with Eastern end-users make the Western firm understandably reluctant to expand plant capacity in expectation of repeat orders. Of course, changes in the domestic supply situation relative to foreign sources can and do take place in a market economy as well. But they are never quite as precipitous.

On the supply side, uncertainty is also a factor to be reckoned with. Western chemical and electronic firms, for example, have found it extremely difficult to assure themselves of regular deliveries of platinum from Soviet sources. The supply of certain industrial chemicals and nonmetallic minerals is also known to have been suddenly cut off in the past. The explanation of the mystery is quite banal. Outside the sphere of traditional exports there are a number of commodities and manufactured goods that enter the Westward flow at irregular and unpredictable intervals, but are not produced in sufficient quantity to be continuously responsive to world demand. Absence of the cushion effect of "warehouse trading" along with inept marketing methods abroad no doubt contribute to the unsettling phenomenon of discontinuity in supply.

The shifting terms of trade which Eastern agencies have freely practiced in the past work undeniable hardships on competitors. Pricing patterns are sometimes slanted in favor of Comecon countries (frequently to the prejudice of Western suppliers). But they may just as readily be tilted against them, as has been seen in the case of petroleum products. Often, too, the discrimination may take place against one Western country and in favor of another.

The possibilities afforded by strict bilateralism are occasionally utilized by Eastern monopolies—as a rule in dealings with a newly developing country—in order to export goods at artificially low prices. In such cases, the state trader offers its exports at a substantial rebate, on condition that import prices be set correspondingly low. For the buyer country, the terms will in the end remain the same as those obtainable in the world market.

But the export price charged by the Eastern combine will be so low as to undersell the nearest Western competitor.

More generally, uneven pricing as between one market and another, coupled with the fact that all trading units are state-operated, creates fertile soil for barter arrangements, clearing procedures, counterpurchases and other forms of linked transactions, all of which are intrinsically distortive of the process of free competition.

D. The Issue of Dumping

The General Agreement on Tariffs and Trade, by which the majority of the world's trading nations are bound, provides:

> The contracting parties recognize that dumping, by which products of one country are introduced into the commerce of another country at less than the normal value of the products, is to be condemned if it causes or threatens material injury to an established industry in the territory of a contracting party or materially retards the establishment of a domestic industry.[8]

The question of whether exports from the East violate this international standard, or the varying standards of domestic legislation, raises a thorny and perennial problem.

Trade agreements with Eastern nations usually include language to the effect that goods are to be sold at "reasonable prices," so as not to cause "material injury." These formulas are meant to protect domestic producers who feel that they are exposed to unfair competition when they encounter Eastern goods in their own markets. Although Western business firms seldom possess the information needed to prove unfairness, they are instinctively aware of a problem: that they are competing against a state-owned enterprise under instructions to meet planned targets but not necessarily subject to penalties if a profit is not made on every transaction. If there are losses, as there often are, it will not go broke: the national treasury will bail it out—on the assumption that public gain derived from the execution of the economic plan is a benefit of the highest possible order.

It is quite plain, on the whole, that such losses as are incurred in the process can be more easily borne by units of a state-trading system than by a profit-sustained private firm. In the first place, the former can justify exportation at "catch as catch can" prices on the basis of macroeconomic considerations. Sales of this kind, after all, provide foreign exchange to pay for imported machinery and thus contribute directly to the implementation of the social and economic policy of the state.

Secondly, the agencies of a state-trading system do not work under the normal compulsion of the market place. True, they are generally instructed to maintain a profitable operation, *i.e.*, to seek the highest prices on exports and the best discounts on imports. In practice, however, they are left free to accommodate themselves to the exigencies of each particular situation.

This peculiar environment gives birth to persistent complaints against alleged dumping. Not infrequently, justified protests are attended by palpable exaggerations, and by local competitors' self-righteous appeals to patriotic emotion. Some years ago a furor was caused in Boston when an American company dared to import from the U.S.S.R. a consignment of scientific apparatus for school laboratories. Despite tariffs ranging from 20 to 75 percent the equipment could be marketed domestically at one-third the price of that produced by local competitors. Aside from the charge of presumed state subsidization, the case against this import, which reverberated as far as the United States Congress and resulted in restrictive legislation, alleged the use of cost-free Soviet slave labor and politically inspired propaganda to win the minds and hearts of American school children. That the line between wholesome competition and extraneously motivated dumping is not always easy to trace can be clearly seen from the record of this particular Congressional debate.[9]

More recently the U.S. Treasury has inquired into Soviet sales of the Moskvich passenger car at a price which, owing to the discrepancy of the known domestic price in the U.S.S.R. ($6,250) and the export market price ($1,560), was alleged to be unfair and injurious. Similarly, the U.S. Tariff Commission has investigated and cleared Czechoslovakian exports of sheet glass, East German exports of muriate of potash and Rumanian exports of petroleum products. Instances of selling below cost have been found on a number of occasions, but determinations of injury to domestic industries have been few and far between, *e.g.,* 1968 rulings relative to the importation of Soviet pig iron.[10] An agency of the United Nations has reported that during the period 1960–1963, seventeen alleged cases of Czechoslovakian underselling were investigated in Western countries. Only three were condemned as dumping by the competent national authorities.[11]

The problem of dumping in East-West trade cannot be approached without a sense of perspective appropriate to the occasion. What constitutes exporting below "normal" value and how to determine whether an "injury" to an industry in the importing country is "material" have never been firmly defined to the satisfaction of all concerned. It needs to be borne in mind, furthermore, that the nations of the West are not entirely without their defenses on this score.

One corrective influence is the fact that the countries of the East are at present perceptibly sensitive to criticism of their trading practices which might come from the commercial community at large. Beyond that, they understand the danger of having some of their products blacklisted in outside markets, or of inviting legislation especially directed against their major export commodities. Communist trade negotiators are prone to point out, in addition, that bilateral trade agreements tend to eliminate the threat of dumping injury insofar as the quotas of goods moving each way can be set at mutually acceptable levels.

Needless to say, Western nations have at their disposal elaborate legislation designed to protect domestic industries against dumping practices on the part of foreign suppliers. It can be demonstrated, however, that classical laws are not always adequate to cope with the methods of total state trading. Thus some time ago an enterprising Soviet export organization found a legitimate way to circumvent the higher 1930 duty rates to which its sales in the American market were subject (as well as mark of origin requirements) by introducing low-priced Russian watch parts through the Virgin Islands. The legal loophole arose from the eligibility of the goods for duty free entry as long as they sold for twice the value of the parts imported into the islands, a U.S. possession. The facts being consistent with the law, the Department of Commerce declared itself unable to interfere.[12]

A centrally planned economy, by its very nature, need not bother with legislative safeguards against dumping. Were the markets of Russia or China to be thrown wide open to the influx of foreign goods, they would enjoy iron-clad and automatic protection against underpriced disposal, by virtue of the government-run commercial structure. If the goods are required under the import plan, the low price will be welcomed. If they are not deemed essential, they cannot penetrate the market at all, let alone injure or threaten a local industry.

Practically speaking, offensive underselling exists when an item is disposed of at a price below cost of production plus a reasonable margin of profit. Under American legislation, for instance, the concept of "fair market value" does not lend itself to meaningful determination in the case of communist-origin products. "Foreign market value," the amount for which the product is sold within the exporting country, is a useless criterion insofar as there is no free home market. "Constructed value," usually established by reference to the cost of production, also fails to offer a reliable guide in traditional Western terms. Nor can direct investigations be easily and reliably conducted within the communist country in question.

The fundamental objection against dumping is that it constitutes a form of unfair competition. In the case of communist sales, each complaint must be judged by reference to circumstantial evidence. "Fair value" distilled from prevailing world market prices contains the germs of a promising criterion from the standpoint of control and supervision. Whether the underpricing falls into a consistent pattern, whether sales in different markets show substantial price differentials, whether quotations abroad are lower than at home when converted at the official rate of exchange, and other considerations of this type are all meaningful tests in making a determination relative to communist exports toward free economies.

E. Underselling Third Country Suppliers

When a new or irregular supplier sells a sizable quantity of goods, the impact is frequently felt beyond the borders of the importing country.

A state trader seeking to break into a new market enjoys distinct advantages, especially under conditions of excess supply. Above all, because of its cavalier attitude to profit, it can offer substantial price discounts to buyers who otherwise may be reluctant to attach themselves to unfamiliar sources of goods. Selling tactics of this type are generally not covered by the antidumping legislation of the importing country, as long as local manufacturers suffer no direct injury. Primarily, the damage is caused to third country suppliers who thus become embroiled in an unequal competitive contest with free-wheeling state enterprises.

No case of deliberate and consistent underselling has thus far been made out against the Eastern monopolies. Prevailing norms of competition have, as a rule, been respected in regard to both the pricing and nonpricing aspects of transactions. When a communist monopoly is the seller it has no interest, under normal conditions, in upsetting the market and thereby depressing its own earnings. But conditions have not always been normal. Intermittent instances of deep price undercutting have occurred in the past, particularly in the sale of certain basic commodities. An impression of the chaos which state-trading agencies can sow in markets customarily served by private commerce was afforded by 1957–1958 Soviet forays into the British aluminum market and the world tin trade. Starting in 1959, Soviet exportation of crude oil has also caused concern in the West.

After a period of normal competition, Soviet aluminum began to appear in Britain, as of mid-1957, at a substantial discount from the quotations of other suppliers. Unusual sales arrangements included automatic de-escalator clauses in the event the general market price dropped, and traditional suppliers, mostly Canadian producers, were undercut by 4 to 12 percent. The price war resulted in a portion of the market being preempted by Soviet aluminum. Following vigorous Canadian complaints and the likelihood of British antidumping measures, the U.S.S.R. voluntarily limited the volume of its shipments.

Its extremely erratic behavior contradicts the theory that the U.S.S.R. was moved by a desire to become a regular aluminum supplier. From January 1956 to May 1957, Soviet aluminum was completely absent from the British market. After observing the effect of its "hit-and-run" tactics, the monopoly withdrew once again in mid-1958. This pattern is hardly consistent with an effort to become a stable, dependable source of export to a permanent market expected to yield maximum economic advantage. More persuasive is the hypothesis of a one-shot directive to dispose of an unplanned, sizable surplus of aluminum metal after a decision was made by the leadership to shift a segment of defense production from aircraft to missiles. However, since Soviet aluminum production and consumption statistics are not disclosed, traditional Western producers cannot feel entirely reassured as to the future.

Another example which does not augur well for the long haul is the Soviet excursion into the world tin market. In 1957 and 1958 Soviet sales, mostly in England and Holland, rose to more than 18,000 tons annually, compared with some 2,000 and 3,000 tons respectively in the preceding two years. Previously, the U.S.S.R. had been importing the metal from China, at the rate of some 17,000 tons in 1955 and 16,000 tons in 1956. In the upshot, the International Tin Council was rendered insolvent by dint of its buffer-building purchases in an effort to support a "floor price." The resultant collapse of the tin stabilization agreement led to a price drop of more than 15 percent.

This time the consequences were damaging to the Bolivian and Malayan economies. The balance of payments of Indonesia and Thailand were also deeply affected. Complaints of injury were taken as far as the United Nations. An invitation to the Soviet Union to join the Tin Council was flatly rejected. The issue was ultimately resolved when the U.S.S.R. agreed to accept a 13,500 ton quota for its 1959 and 1960 shipments to the West. Actual shipments turned out to be well below this level.[13]

The most controversial area of threatened dislocation has been labeled as "the Soviet oil offensive." Here, the competitive factor was coupled with ramifications of a strategic and political nature: Can NATO countries afford to become dependent on Soviet and Rumanian fuel? Is it consistent with the spirit of the Common Market and its declared policy on energy sources for Italy and West Germany to exchange steel pipelines for Russian crude oil and natural gas, to the detriment of their French and Dutch partners? Can the Arab countries ignore the long-term danger of Soviet inroads into their most lucrative markets? How vulnerable are the markets of developing countries to hard currency-saving barters of communist oil against surplus commodities?

Our primary concern is with the essentially commercial rather than foreign policy aspects of communist competition. In this perspective, it should be recalled that while Soviet sales of oil began to increase sharply in the late fifties, Russia had been a substantial exporter to western Europe some three decades earlier. During the period 1925 to 1935, its share of Western markets was approximately 15 percent. It was therefore not unnatural for Soiuznefteksport, the oil export combine, to seek to recapture a part of its prewar position. Its task was facilitated by western Europe's geographic proximity, by expanding demand and by the construction of pipelines with outlets to Black Sea and Baltic ports. Above all, the Soviet return to these markets was aided by competition based on price. As a cause of market dislocation, Soviet price cutting has greatly outweighed the relative importance of Russian oil measured by reference to the total volume of production and trade in this important commodity.

There is no serious proof that the U.S.S.R. has dumped its oil to disrupt world markets. A certain softening in prices as a result of Soviet sales, particularly during the period of overproduction caused by the opening of Sahara fields, was fairly inevitable. That the Soviet Union will have to be reckoned with as a major oil supplier for years to come is a fact. Yet there is increasing evidence to suggest that it is likely to become a net importer by the late seventies.

Be that as it may, thus far, price reductions have been used largely to obtain a required level of sales. To be sure, discounts are much more easily absorbed by a state-operated monopoly owing to relatively low costs of extraction, the absence of fixed royalty payments to producing countries, disregard of land and depletion factors, avoidance of high prospecting and distribution expenses abroad, shorter distances and, presumably, cheaper transportation. But in the long run Soiuznefteksport may be expected to be as anxious as anyone else to secure optimum world prices.

That price discrimination is practiced in the exportation of Soviet oil follows from the fact that Comecon allies such as Poland and Czechoslovakia have been required to pay considerably more per ton than many noncommunist countries, Sweden, for example. Prices to Latin American, African and Asian buyers have been lower still. In 1963, crude oil was sold to Italy and West Germany at some 33 to 37 percent below the average Soviet export prices. To all destinations, Soviet prices FOB Black Sea ports have been well below quotations at the Persian Gulf or on the Algerian or Tunisian coast.[14]

While Soviet competition has at times been uncommonly aggressive, and Western condemnation outspokenly self-righteous, the petroleum market appears to have taken the consequences in its stride. The giant international oil trusts have certainly had little difficulty in making the appropriate adjustments. Apprehensions as to the future are nevertheless quite understandable, particularly in light of the recent discovery of mammoth oil and gas deposits in western Siberia. Should the Soviet monopoly embark upon a deliberate policy of massive disposal with concentration on selected outlets, the results might prove disruptive even for the majors in the first place for Royal Dutch Shell and Standard Oil of New Jersey, the companies most deeply involved in the opening of the Groningen gas fields in northern Holland.

The dangers of underselling are not limited to basic commodities. The U.S.S.R. has been promoting the sale of its civil aircraft at prices and financing terms substantially more favorable than those practiced in the West. For example, the Aerospace Industries Association of America reported that the ANTONOV-24 had been offered in competition to its Fairchild Hiller counterpart at approximately one-half the price of similar United States, British and Japanese planes, with credit supplied at 3.5 percent.[15] Western firms have also had to cope with severe and reportedly unfair competition caused by the sale of Polish and Hungarian railroad equipment in such widely dispersed markets as the Middle East, Asia and Latin America. These developments can no longer be attributed to miscalculated overproduction. It is more likely that the smaller countries of east Europe are involved in an effort to develop alternative sources of raw materials for their domestic processing industries. In the background is the realization that the Soviet Union has lost interest in assuming a larger burden than it is already carrying as a supplier of fuels, minerals and metals to its Comecon trade partners.

While the countries and products affected by Eastern underselling may be different, the inherent issues remain basically the same. Thus, China was reported to be selling sugar in the Sudan in 1964 at 60 percent below prices charged by established suppliers, the United Arab Republic among them. The U.S.S.R. was accused of selling center lathes in Britain at 12 percent below the price of the cheapest imported article and 30 percent lower than the domestically manufactured product of comparable quality. An attempt was also made by some state-trading nations to break into the Singapore cotton goods market in price cutting competition with comparable Japanese fabrics. Other dumped products have included platinum, diamonds, cellulose, rubber and pharmaceuticals by the U.S.S.R.; bicycles, builders' hardware and haberdashery by Czechoslovakia, Poland and Hungary; rice, vegetables, newsprint, porcelain and footwear by China.[16]

In all such instances of disruptive underselling, the motives are not easy to discern; nor are they really relevant. That no willful mischief was intended, or that a sound economic aim was being pursued is an inadequate defense. What matters is the extent of market disorganization.[17]

Any search for constructive solutions to the problems discussed above must reconcile the need to avoid injury for local manufacturers and third country suppliers with the acceptance of legitimate competition. An approach seeking to test allegations of dumping by reference to fair value in a market economy with production costs similar to those of the communist country of origin would seem to point in a promising direction. Thus, the Australian Tariff Board has equated Chinese production costs with those of Japan to determine the fair value of cotton piece goods and with those of France to determine the fair value of allegedly dumped chemicals. In liberalizing its quantitative restrictions against Eastern goods, Great Britain has established a safeguard procedure under its bilateral agreements to measure the reasonableness of prices by reference to third country practice.[18] More recently, the U.S. Treasury has begun to make similar comparisons. In connection with imported Russian pig iron and titanium sponge, Italian and English costs were taken as the point of departure, a practice to which Soviet trade representatives take strong exception.[19]

BOOK TWO

FIRST PART

THE LEGAL FRAMEWORK

13

EASTERN REGULATION OF INTERNATIONAL TRANSACTIONS

A. The Emergence of New Institutions

Although internal economic stability had been achieved by the mid-thirties, Soviet foreign commerce remained disorganized for many years thereafter. Institutions were new and untested; trade officials were inexperienced and uninformed; and the bargaining position of state enterprises was weak. They were compelled to transact much of their external trade from alien locations, to use foreign banks, foreign ships and foreign insurance facilities. London more than Moscow was in fact the center of the monopoly's international business operations. Because of this, Soviet law and Soviet courts were relatively unimportant to those who dealt with the U.S.S.R. Today this is no longer true.

Increased economic power has enabled a shift to Russian soil of the center of gravity of commercial operations. Negotiations are now largely conducted at home. Western firms usually deliver their goods to consumer enterprises at Soviet destinations. Soviet exporters sell mostly by c.i.f. and f.o.b. contracts, on the basis of samples and descriptions, rather than from warehouses located abroad. Foreign and Russian ships are chartered within the U.S.S.R. Accounts with alien firms are settled through domestic state banks. Specialized arbitration facilities are available in Moscow to resolve commercial disputes. In general, the progressive domestication of foreign business has produced a more rational and efficient trade apparatus, operated by a more competent bureaucracy.

While the evolution of communist China's foreign trade system has been similar, the countries of eastern Europe have followed a different course. They had no need to operate from capitalist bases. Nor was the change-over to communist regimes accompanied by the same violent wave of nationalization and isolationism which marked the early years of Soviet revolutionary power. The prewar utilitarian orientation toward foreign commerce remained, and many individuals and institutions which had been privately active were drafted into the service of the state monopolies. This more moderate approach facilitated the alignment of the new bureaucratic trading organizations with the traditional business context of the West.

Within the Soviet Union and, to a lesser extent, within the rest of communist Europe, the environment is sharply different from that in which international trade is typically conducted. Official doctrine condemns the aims and methods of private business and holds it to be a legalized form of theft. Constant surveillance by the communist party assures that local institutions, the underlying legal system and prevalent economic practices give expression or, at any rate, pay adequate lip service to this article of faith. An atmosphere so alien and ostensibly hostile makes it difficult for the capitalist trader to respond with confidence to tendered business opportunities.

If the U.S.S.R. was to live up to the image of a major commercial and maritime power, and to influence the foreign trade activities of other nations, like England in her heyday, a special regime divorced from local concepts would have to be established for transactions with the outside world. In due course Soviet policy came to adopt this analysis. The creation of such a regime could be accomplished with relative ease, because of the collectivist nature of economic organization. Central planning and monopolistic state control permit the domestic sector to operate within one frame of reference, while the limited foreign trade sector is left free to function within another completely different setting.

As the situs of transactions shifted eastward, business relations between state and private enterprises became increasingly dependent on communist law. Thus in litigation before Eastern tribunals the applicable rules are, more often than not, those of the local legal system. The application of traditional conflict of law criteria often requires even Western courts to turn to communist law, because it happens to be the law designated in the agreement, the law of the place of contracting, the law of the place of performance, the law of most intimate connection, the national law of one of the parties or the law of the flag. However interesting these developments may seem to students of economics and jurisprudence, as a practical matter they tend to unsettle, if not alarm, the private merchant. Increasingly, his rights and obligations may depend upon the internal law of a communist country, the advice of a communist lawyer or the decision of a communist court. He finds small comfort in the fact that special foreign trade regulations rather than rules of general application will govern certain aspects of his transaction. Nor can he dismiss with total equanimity the prospect that communist laws will be applied to his situation by a Western court, perhaps even the court of his own country.

Those who trade or compete with the state monopolies are not the only ones to be affected by the intrusion of Eastern institutions onto the world scene. A Western judge or arbitrator may, in the normal course of adjudication, be faced with the problem of analyzing a novel communist concept under his own local law or under the applicable legal system of some foreign country, Eastern or Western. He may be called upon to rule on whether a communist regulation prescribing special contractual formalities is entitled to extraterritorial recognition, whether a state-trading instrumentality is entitled to plead sovereign immunity, whether a judgment pronounced by a communist forum should be accorded recognition, whether the public policy of his jurisdiction should be allowed to defeat an otherwise applicable communist rule.

A Western legislature may be confronted with questions as to the adequacy of its long-existing enactments, antidumping laws for example, in regulating the economic behavior of communist enterprises in its own market. Similarly, administrative officials may be called upon to decide whether an Eastern government department or court has violated the standard of treatment to which a foreign firm is entitled under principles of comity, reciprocity or international law. Negotiators of bilateral treaties or multilateral conventions, and world bodies concerned with trade, *e.g.*, the GATT, may have to inquire beyond the superficiality of orthodox nomenclature to determine whether communist laws and procedures effectively execute state-to-state undertakings.

The foregoing suggests that attorneys trained in Eastern law or admitted to practice in Eastern jurisdictions are needed to assist in the negotiation of agreements and the litigation of disputes. Obviously, the average lawyer who practices domestic law in Warsaw, Sofia or Peking is neither ideologically nor professionally qualified to represent a foreign firm in connection with international transactions involving his country. To be sure, specialists in the field, with the requisite knowledge of languages, are available at the bars of communist capitals, and their advice can be helpful, occasionally even indispensable. However, experience shows that in negotiations or litigations with state enterprises, private firms have been reluctant to turn over their files to such lawyers. As a rule they have done so only in conjunction with qualified and trusted Western counsel.

The bar of the Soviet Union comprises some 100,000 members. In addition, law-trained notaries are available to draft contracts, wills and other documents. The legal profession is divided into self-governing bodies. A potential client may ask to be represented by a particular attorney whose qualifications are known to him. A number of consultation offices in Moscow, Leningrad and other major cities with involvement in foreign trade and shipping have on their rolls not only experts in the legal aspects of international transactions, but also specialists in arbitration, patents, trademark protection, maritime law and the like. Fees are paid to the consultation office rather than to the lawyer who renders the professional services. The latter is paid in turn by his collegium.

B. Communist Law and the Capitalist Merchant

In the communist scheme of things, a nation's legal system is viewed as an instrument of party policy and state power, not as a normative body of impartially conceived rules. The distinction between private and public law is blurred or nonexistent. Almost exclusively, commercial relations fall into the latter domain. Directly or indirectly, the state is involved in all economic transactions. Virtually nothing may be settled or compromised without its consent, even in business arrangements which Western societies would consider purely private. Administrative regulation is all-pervasive and classical civil law relations are often enforced by criminal sanctions. Dogma professes that, while all law is temporary, communist law is of higher moral content than "bourgeois" law. Capitalist legal systems and those who administer them are viewed with suspicion. In theory at least, special contempt is reserved for the law of merchants.

While descriptions of this nature must appear somewhat simplistic to the experienced Western practitioner, the content of communist laws, whether "good" or "bad" in an abstract ideological sense, cannot but be viewed with some malaise. Thus, the 1964 Civil Code of the R.S.F.S.R. (the constituent Russian republic) and the 1962 Principles of Civil Legislation upon which it is based declare that "Civil rights are protected by law, with the exception of cases in which they are exercised in conflict with the purpose of these rights in socialist society in the period of the building of communism."[1] Similarly, Section 56 of the 1964 Code of Civil Procedure requires a Soviet court to "weigh evidence according to its own inner conviction . . . being guided by the law and its socialist legal conscience." Does a foreign merchant engaged in business for private gain contradict the purposes or offend the conscience of the communist order? Western legal systems know comparable concepts of abuse of rights and public policy. But in the East these concepts are much more loaded. In their operation upon acts, stipulations or rules born of contradictory social attitudes, they raise entirely legitimate concerns.

The prudent foreign company must also consider the effect upon trade contracts of an infringement of certain uniquely severe provisions of communist law. For example, under the former Soviet Civil Code, transactions made for a purpose prejudicial to the state were invalid and unenforceable. More strikingly, in cases of willful violation, all consideration derived from the illicit relationship was collected for the benefit of the state. Only if a "mistake" was the cause of invalidity could the aggrieved party obtain restitution on the ground of unjust enrichment.[2] Today, this policy finds expression in Section 49 of the new Code:

> If a transaction is consciously effected with an object opposed to the interests of the socialist State and public, then, if both parties intend this and both parties have performed their parts, everything received by them in pursuance of the transaction is forfeited to the State, but, if the transaction has been performed (only) on one side, then the State may claim everything received by the other party and everything due to the first party in return for it: but if only one of the parties had such an intention, everything received by him under the transaction must be returned to the other party, and everything received by the former or due to him in return for his performance is forfeited to the State.

A contrast is suggested by the Western rule whereby property which has passed pursuant to a contract rendered invalid by a mutual wrong of the parties is left in the hands of the possessor. Disapproval of the transaction is expressed by judicial reluctance to intervene. In Soviet law, the condemnation is much harsher—expropriation in favor of the state. Any attempt to extinguish their rights in this manner would be regarded by Western firms as punitive and wholly unacceptable. Accordingly, Soviet commentators have conceded that these provisions need not necessarily be applied to alien parties.[3] For the infringing Soviet party the possible consequences are more serious. Trade officials who attempt to evade the law, or who deal beyond the scope authorized in their enterprise's charter of incorporation, or who act in violation of the economic plan are liable to disciplinary action in administrative or criminal proceedings. Such action may follow regardless of whether the transgression is willful, or a consequence of mere negligence.

Enforcement of certain communist laws to the letter would obviously be detrimental to the foreign trade monopolies. Indeed, the resultant mistrust and insecurity could bring business to a standstill. Accordingly, norms with distinctive ideological coloration are expediently overlooked.

An interesting example of judicial revocation of local law for the benefit of foreign parties is provided by a 1964 decision of the Bulgarian Foreign Trade Arbitration Court. The case involved an amendment of the economic plan, reducing the quantity of goods available for export. The operation of a preexisting contract was thus affected to the prejudice of the alien buyer. The court found that the transaction was governed by the Bulgarian Code of Obligations and Contracts as the law of the seller's country. Yet, after citing a long line of contradictory decisions, it refused to subject the foreign firm to the consequences stipulated by the legislature:

> . . . It would, however, not be correct to assert that Article 6 of the mentioned law is applicable, since the text extends to organizations and according to the case law of the court one must understand by this term the internal organizations and not foreign contracting parties. The latter are not treated in their relations as Bulgarian organizations and the dispositions of Articles 5, 6 and 7 do not apply to them. Thus, even though Bulgarian law is applicable, the dispositions of Article 6, Paragraph 2 are not. Consequently the modifications in the plan do not entail a modification of the contract. . . .[4]

In effect, what we have here is an inverse application of the concept of public policy as it is known in the sphere of private international law. Instead of nullifying a foreign rule judged to contravene the forum's local order, it is the admittedly applicable domestic rule which abates, to the extent that it offends the basic standards of the international merchant community. An "outside" public policy, as it were, is invoked to cancel the impact of a local measure imbued with the extremes of indigenous philosophy.

The double standard is couched in hardheaded realism and has some theory behind it as well. It is frankly admitted that the writ of communist leadership does not as yet have global reach. Consequently a distinction must be made between legal relations confined to the national and intra-bloc level, and those extending beyond the socialist reservation. Any other approach would at once lack effectiveness and interfere with the current policy of peaceful coexistence and harmony among states. This rationale also justifies communist acceptance of public international law.

However comforting one finds the special treatment reserved for transactions with foreign countries, it should not be assumed that a state of lawless judicial informality prevails on the domestic plane. Legality in all walks of life has long ago come into its own throughout the East. After an initial burst of post-revolutionary nihilism sparked by Lenin's theory that law and the state itself are destined to wither away, the Soviet leadership realized that legal rules are indispensable to the orderly functioning of all human societies. During the years of the New Economic Policy (1921–1928), the pendulum began to swing back in the direction of tolerance and even recognition of the indispensable function of law. A renewed burst of juridical creativity was characterized by the promulgation of codes in the areas of family law, agriculture, civil law, civil procedure, criminal law and criminal procedure.[5]

While the communist and capitalist systems seem antithetical, they nonetheless reveal many practical parallels. Both types of societies are preoccupied with economic and social progress. Because of this, they often opt for similar solutions in pursuing specific goals. In the East, the eventual establishment of a principle of "socialist legality" was more dramatic in sound than in substance. All that the new terminology intended to convey was a feeling of respect for law and order in the process of socialist construction. The thesis that the legal system would disappear in a society which has evolved to the exalted level of pure communism was pragmatically shelved as a longer-range prophecy.

The lesson taught by the initial Soviet experience did not go unheeded in the other eastern European countries. Their respect for legal tradition has remained largely intact. Essentially, the basic laws of the prewar regimes of Hungary, Czechoslovakia, and Poland, with their roots in the great civil systems of continental Europe, notably those of Austria, France and Germany, were left unchanged. Only reforms considered necessary for the orderly development of communist society, occasionally no more than superficial adjustments to Marxist-Leninist phraseology, were injected by means of repeal, amendment and enactment.

The laws of the People's Democracies are, therefore, often different from Soviet laws. Moreover, they diverge frequently among themselves. For example, Albania, Bulgaria, and the Serbian parts of Yugoslavia show vestiges of the Byzantine legal order. This fact and the backward nature of their rural economies have made it easier than in the case of industrially more sophisticated states such as East Germany to adopt large segments of Soviet law, lock, stock and barrel. Theoretically, alignment with the Russian model is to be made as all these countries evolve further toward communism. Whether this pattern will in fact be followed and, indeed, whether the model itself will hold up in the meantime, remains to be seen.

Given the Eastern states' willingness to mitigate the operation of objectionable legislative provisions, a good part of the case against the applicability of communist law to foreign firms falls away. The main criticism which remains is that the mitigation has not been systematically solemnized. The Western party cannot always know in advance which rules of the domestic system will affect him in the event of a dispute. An invitation to assume that severely doctrinaire concepts will be waived by the grace of a communist tribunal must strike him as unfair. His safety lies in the applicability of clear-cut laws, not discretionary magnanimity.

In the prevailing circumstances, the prudent businessman must seek to immunize his transaction by means of tightly drafted contracts and deliberate choice of law provisions. We will see in the following chapters that this immunization can never be complete.

C. Special Regime for External Commerce

In fact if not in form, the deferential treatment of Western firms may be viewed as part of a separate regime for international commerce. The ad hoc abrogation of rules which reflect extreme tenets of communist ideology is one manifestation of this phenomenon. Another is the disqualification of the normal domestic courts from adjudication in foreign causes. Moreover, following the eclectic Soviet example, each communist country has passed a series of enactments, regulations and decrees specifically directed at the operations of its monopoly. Although these measures fall short of a consolidated foreign trade law, norms appropriate only within the domestic economy have been partly sifted out, and new principles designed to serve the needs of the state-trading apparatus have been specially elaborated.

To practitioners in the Anglo-American common-law system, the idea of a special law for international transactions seems more unusual than to their civil-law counterparts. On the continent, the separation of civil and commercial law is accepted as natural. France has known a *droit professionnel des commerçants* long before the Napoleonic codifications. West Germany's equivalent is the *Sonderrecht für Kaufleute*. Both systems apply to the subjects they regulate by virtue of their special merchant status. The communist nations have drawn upon this west European tradition. While in the Soviet Union commercial law does not appear as an independent branch, one can discern the existence of a domestic law of economic transactions applied by a judiciary (Gosarbitrazh) separate from that which is competent to settle controversies among private citizens (people's courts). The French division into *tribunaux de commerce* and *tribunaux civils* suggests an obvious analogy. Czechoslovakia has gone to the point of promulgating a special Economic Code for dealings among domestic enterprises. This instrument stands apart from the general Civil Code, which continues to apply to relations between physical persons, as well as between individuals and domestic enterprises. Here, the parallel with the French duality of *Code Commerical* and *Code Civil* is even closer.[6]

In the West, domestic and foreign business relations are characteristically governed by the same system of rules. On the other hand, the wholly planned economies tend to distinguish between the two. While the civil codes usually retain modified application, many rules affecting external dealings are legislatively (and on occasion judicially) detached from the overall legal structure. Once again, Czechoslovakia has been the innovator. It has formalized the cleavage by means of a specialty code for foreign trade.

Throughout the East, the originality of the special legal regime for commerce with the outside world is even more strikingly demonstrated by the divorce of jurisdictions. Disputes arising in the course of domestic economic activity are determined in one set of tribunals while controversies with foreign elements are heard in another. The governing rules of procedure are also fairly distinct. The reasons for the dichotomy will be apparent from previous discussions. In terms of their functions and capacity to act, state enterprises are categorized as either domestic or international. Each genus is recognized as having its own peculiar problems; the legal solutions must therefore be tailor-fitted accordingly.

Yet another regulatory regime exists for trade among wholly planned economies. Comecon countries maintain a distinct treaty-made commercial law, reserved solely for mutual intercourse. Its content differs not only from the rules prescribed for dealings with the noncommunist world, but also and quite significantly, from those which govern contracts between two purely domestic business entities.

Traditionally, commercial relations fall in the sphere of private law. The incursion of all governments into the foreign trade segments of their economies with an ever-growing ambit of administrative regulations does not change this basic classification. By contrast, communist commercial law, at least in its practical effect, belongs within the compass of public law, since all, or nearly all, economic activity is a state function. Nonetheless, the foreign trade monopolies purport to operate at a private-law level.

Substantively, the regime which governs relations between communist-trading entities and their Western business partners conforms, with few exceptions, to universal principles of commercial law. Occasionally, bilateral and multilateral treaties are also in play, as adopted parts of the Eastern legal systems in question. In short, the content of the *lex specialis* for trade with the West is drawn, to a large extent, from established world-wide practice, although its authority derives from the communist sovereign and not from any international source entitled to application of its own record.

The Eastern law of foreign trade cannot, therefore, be described as communist, just as the law which governs commerce in the West need not be called capitalist save in a historical sense. Both are means to the same end. Except where politics or diplomacy intrude, they are designed to provide an efficient framework for the international exchange of goods and services. At a 1962 colloquium of East–West jurists the issue was framed in these terms:

> In the field of international commerce, (the) purposes and needs change as does a growing child. They are adjusted under the impact of political or economic theories. They are conditioned in part by the various groupings of states. But constantly they are dominated by the basic concern of commerce for its own existence, its survival and its progress; by the demand of merchants for quick and effective methods of reaching results, and by the somewhat idealized ambition for simplicity in transactions.[7]

Two factors explain the far-going communist alignment with established concepts in this particular area. First, the Western approach, although of capitalist origin, was a tried and proven one. Interestingly enough, it was deemed suitable not only for commerce at large, but also for trade within the communist "commonwealth." In essence, the Comecon General Conditions of Delivery of 1958, as amended in 1968, bear much similarity to various Western systems of law unification.[8] Second, any attempt to revolutionize the terms of trade would have aroused harmful fears and reactions among those in the West with whom business was to be conducted. Surprising as the degree of communist conformity may seem, no heavy sacrifices were thereby entailed for the monopolies. Moreover, in real terms, the adaptation has been more limited than appearances suggest. Total state traders can often draw effects from commercial transactions which are unknown in a private-business context. This fact is occasionally obscured by the utilization of familiar institutional trappings and by the wholesale adoption of conventional Western terminology.

D. Sources of Foreign Trade Law

In the foreign trade sector of a centrally planned economy, where state activity is omnipresent, one might expect to find a complex maze of regulatory laws. That such complexity is absent obviously is not due to governmental self-restraint. On the contrary, the surprising simplicity in scheme and content stems from public intervention to the point of total ownership and control. The existence of only a limited number of trading entities allows for facile administrative manipulation. In addition, the export-import plan, foreign exchange plan and the transportation plan constitute a tight framework of mandatory economic rules for all those involved in commerce. This peculiar method of regulation and supervision supplements the more classically conceived segment of law: general and specific legislation, commercial treaties and conventions, adopted international custom and usage and the growing body of decisions handed down by the specially constituted foreign trade tribunals.

1. Local Legislation

Internally, the Eastern countries have not, to date, unified their laws of international sales. Relevant domestic rules must therefore be sought in the general civil codes and in miscellaneous regulations of a specific character.

Czechoslovakia alone has taken the initiative to enact a separate code for trade with foreign parties. The Law on Legal Relations in the Sphere of External Commerce, which came into force in April 1964, was inspired largely by Western law, including the 1956 Draft of the Hague Uniform Law on International Sales, the Uniform Commercial Code of the United States and the Swiss Law of Obligations.[9] It governs transactions between local and foreign enterprises whenever such transactions are deemed to be subject to the substantive domestic law.

As a pioneering document of great future significance, the outline of this Code, with its five chapters and more than 700 articles, is well worth noting. The first chapter defines the purpose, content and legal nature of the legislation. The second presents principles of general application to persons, things, rights, events, transactions, and so forth. The third chapter elaborates the rules of contract formation, the notion of legal obligation, the ways in which it may be secured and discharged and the nature and consequences of its breach. Chapter four deals with specific types of obligations, notably the respective duties of buyer and seller in international contracts of sale; while the final chapter concerns noncontractual obligations, such as unjust enrichment.

The particular advantage of such an enactment is that it insulates international transactions from the peculiarities of the local socioeconomic climate. In the words of a Czechoslovakian commentator, the Code was meant to be "a law of a socialist state which should, however, regulate the legal aspects of commercial relations mainly with contracting parties from the capitalist world and should be such as to induce them to subject themselves to it freely and without fears."[10] Whether the fears in fact can be totally dissipated will be shown by experience. That their existence is openly acknowledged demonstrates the persistence of the problem in the other communist countries which have not as yet chosen to follow the Czechoslovakian example.

In the Soviet Union, many substantive rules pertinent to foreign trade have found their way into the Basic Principles of Civil Legislation and Principles of Civil Procedure which became effective on May 1, 1962. In broad terms, both summarize prior legislation, legal commentary and, to some extent, case law derived from judicial and arbitral practice. The Principles have been implemented, supplemented and elaborated by Civil Codes in each of the federal republics. That of the Russian Republic came into force on October 1, 1964. In light of the leading role played by that Republic, and the fact that most trade organizations are headquartered in Moscow, it is the R.S.F.S.R. Code which is normally applicable in the sphere of Soviet foreign commerce.[11] In any event, the divergence among the various Codes is minimal, conformity to the Principles being constitutionally prescribed.

Unlike Czechoslovakia, the Soviet legislature has neither attempted a consolidation of foreign trade law, nor an insulation of Western firms from locally operative rules. The Civil Codes apply equally to international and domestic, commercial and noncommercial dealings. Article 3 of the Principles declares that "relations in foreign trade are determined by specific U.S.S.R. legislation regulating foreign trade and by the general civil legislation of the U.S.S.R. and the Union Republics."

This perpetuates a patchwork approach. The Western merchant is obliged to keep track (not without great difficulty) of various particularized enactments, such as the Consular Laws (1926 and 1927), the Mining Law (1927), the Law on Inventions (1959), the Air Code (1961) and the Shipping Code (1968). Moreover, he must also bear in mind that important matters are occasionally regulated by government decision or ministerial decree, *e.g.*, the Resolution of the Council of People's Commissars of November 26, 1937, regarding the disposition of real property belonging to nonresident aliens, and the Resolution of February 2, 1936, on the taxation status of foreign firms engaged in trade activities upon Soviet territory.

Other Eastern states likewise derive their substantive rules of foreign trade law from civil codes of general application and isolated legislative and administrative provisions. Thus, in Rumania, the Civil Code of 1864 is still in force for both foreign and domestic relations, but a 1949 Act extends to export and import transactions, a 1954 Decree governs the status of foreign trade enterprises and a 1957 measure regulates the local residence of foreigners. Several of the socialist countries have elaborately codified their international choice of law rules on an independent basis. These enactments open the door to foreign law.

Legislative consolidation of dispersed provisions pertinent to international commerce would be highly desirable throughout the East. As for the U.S.S.R. itself, it is unlikely that the Supreme Soviet will soon pursue the course pointed out by Czechoslovakia. The new Republican Codes and the Basic Principles on which they are founded culminate the first major legislative effort since the now-repealed 1922 Civil Code, and seem to represent the totality of contemplated codification.[12]

2. *Treaties*

Bilateral agreements and multilateral conventions perform a major law-making function in the Eastern countries' international trade. Often they direct specific substantive and procedural solutions for dealings among the enterprises in question. In the event of conflict between such intergovernmental instruments and the domestic laws of the communist states, the former take precedence.

The most significant international source of rules regulating commerce within communist Europe is found in the Comecon General Conditions of Delivery, last amended in 1968. As of 1958, the conditions were adopted into the legal systems of member countries pursuant to instructions of the respective ministers of foreign trade. In 1962, they were supplemented by the General Conditions of Installation Contracts for Machinery and Factory Equipment.[13] These two instruments replaced the Unified Conditions of Delivery recommended by the Secretariat of Comecon in 1951 for incorporation into bilateral state-to-state agreements.

The previous, bilaterally operative system was unclear in its legal impact. In 1957 the Sofia arbitration court held that the conditions agreed to between Bulgaria and East Germany were effective to displace the domestic law of the forum. A year later the same tribunal held that the conditions in force with Czechoslovakia were facultative and could therefore be excluded by party stipulation.[14] This judicial treatment of bilaterally adopted rules is still relevant in regard to Eastern trade with and among such non-Comecon states as communist China, North Korea, North Vietnam and Cuba.

Within Comecon the multilaterally established terms are integral provisions of all sales. They govern without express contractual mention and, presumably, even in the face of an explicit exclusion. The preamble attenuates this mandatory effect for contracts in which, "because of the specific nature of the goods and/or special characteristics of their delivery a departure from particular provisions is required." But the case law is not uniform on the issue of excludability. A 1963 decision of the Moscow Foreign Trade Arbitration Commission over-ruled a party-attempted variation of the prescribed period of limitations.[15] The same approach is followed in East German and Polish practice.[16] On the other hand, the Sofia tribunal refused to take a clear-cut position in a judgment rendered in 1964. In the Prague arbitration court the parties' election of jurisdiction prevailed, although Article 65 of the General Conditions pointed to Berlin as the domiciliary forum of the East German litigant.[17]

In the Comecon sphere, the General Conditions constitute a virtually self-sufficient substitute for domestic law. They prescribe rules of contract formation, define the requirements of delivery, regulate the passage of risk, establish procedures and remedies for breach and set forth an imperative criterion for choice of law. The accomplishment is quite unique and remarkable. For what we find here is a fully unified system of rules for the mutual commerce of countries with great social and political affinities, with similarly structured economies and with common attitudes toward ownership, contract and business enterprise—in scope, a veritable communist *lex mercatoria.*

With the capitalist world, the Eastern states have been reluctant to enter into multilateral legal conventions. This reluctance must not be judged too severely. A state trading system can hardly be expected to submit indiscriminately to rules primarily designed for private firms. The relative uniformity in law and practice which is attainable by countries utilizing similar institutions and benefiting from close governmental coordination is also lacking. Even so, communist states do participate in several multilateral conventions of universal application. East European adherence is often a survival of prewar ratification. Examples are: the Geneva Protocol on Arbitration Clauses of 1923, ratified by Poland, Germany, Czechoslovakia, Rumania, Albania and Yugoslavia; the Geneva Convention on the Recognition and Enforcement of Foreign Arbitral Awards of 1927, ratified by Germany, Czechoslovakia, Rumania and Yugoslavia; the comprehensive Brussels agreements on maritime transportation, in effect since 1910; the Warsaw Convention on International Carriage by Air of 1929; and the complex of conventions on the protection of industrial property, all widely accepted in the East. Equally important, the Geneva Convention on Bills of Exchange and Promissory Notes of June 7, 1930, was operative in Czechoslovakia, Hungary, Poland, Germany, Rumania and Yugoslavia, and the related instruments on Checks of March 19, 1931, were adopted by the same countries, with the exception of Rumania and Hungary.

In the case of East Germany, the legal continuity of adherence poses special problems by virtue of political partition and the fact that the Democratic Republic is not recognized by many Western signatories. These considerations notwithstanding, the Pankow regime views itself as a successor to the German Reich, bound by preexisting conventions, at least vis-à-vis those states which have granted it official recognition.

Under communist power, accessions have also taken place. Thus, in 1936 the Soviet Union ratified the Geneva Convention on Bills of Exchange and Promissory Notes. The New York Convention on the Recognition and Enforcement of Foreign Arbitral Awards of 1958 was ratified by the U.S.S.R., Poland, Rumania, Czechoslovakia and Bulgaria; the

1961 European Convention on International Arbitration prepared by the Economic Commission for Europe was accepted by the same countries as well as Hungary and Yugoslavia. In a move indicative of its changing attitudes, the U.S.S.R. acceded, in 1965, to the International Convention for the Protection of Industrial Property of 1883. A number of other multilateral arrangements have attracted certain east European states, among them the Universal Copyright Convention and the General Agreement on Tariffs and Trade.

The East has shown far greater preference for law-creating treaties of the bilateral variety. As we have seen, while such treaties are primarily concerned with commercial matters, they often prescribe detailed rules to govern relations with nationals and enterprises of the two countries in question. The long superseded treaty between the U.S.S.R. and Germany of October 12, 1925, was an exemplary document of this type, reflecting a high degree of early awareness that many orthodox clauses were ill-suited for East-West trade and should be replaced with particularized stipulations.[18] Its detailed provisions covered the legal status of trading entities, matters of insurance, shipping, patents, trademarks, court jurisdiction, arbitration, applicable law and a variety of related subjects. The U.S.S.R.'s increased political and economic bargaining power has made such treaty terms more difficult to obtain.

3. *Mercantile Custom*

Certain practices are so common that merchants expect their observance in all business relations. In effect, they have the status of binding rules, and make up an important source of law in the domain of foreign trade.[19]

Several segments of commercial custom have been consolidated by international institutions: the International Law Association's Warsaw-Oxford Rules for c.i.f. Contracts of 1932, the International Chamber of Commerce's Incoterms of 1953 and Uniform Customs and Practices for Commercial Documentary Credits of 1962. All these have come to enjoy wide acceptance in East and West.[20]

Standard contracts have also been developed by various trade associations with respect to their particular areas of interest: the London Corn Trade Association forms, the Gencon Charter of the Documentary Council of the Baltic and White Sea Conferences and the c.i.f. contract known as "Russian 1952," operative between the Soviet combine Eksportles and the British Timber Trade Federation. On a broader scale, the Economic Commission for Europe has developed general conditions and forms for the purchase and sale of specified commodities. Such standardization achievements reflect acceptable or accepted mercantile usage, although they cannot be said to enjoy the status of legally binding custom.

What is the communist position on commercial custom? Under what circumstances will Eastern tribunals apply custom in determining disputed contractual rights and obligations?

Eastern doctrine does not consider foreign trade and maritime practice obligatory unless it is domestically adopted as law in some unequivocal manner. The mode of proof is closer to that of continental rather than British courts. The latter, as is well known, insist upon a burden of proof which is practically impossible to discharge.

Over the years, a substantial body of rules inspired by widespread usage has, in fact, found its way directly into communist legislation. Striking instances are to be found in the Soviet Maritime Code. Universally followed rules have also obtained recognition in intergovernmental instruments. The Soviet-Swedish Arbitration Agreement of 1940 provided in Article 12 that courts of arbitration may apply "customs generally accepted in international trade."

Custom finds no application whatsoever within the confines of a wholly planned economy. Even in trade relations among such economies its role is, at best, only marginal. On the other hand, there is nothing in Eastern legislation which flatly prohibits the application of commercial custom in business dealings between local and foreign enterprises. On the contrary, according to an eminent Soviet authority, it is established "beyond any doubt that in appropriate cases" evidence of custom will be admitted; this may be inferred from the Rules of the Moscow Foreign Trade Arbitration Commission and of the other Eastern tribunals, which expressly authorize arbitrators to seek the opinion of experts with regard to trade usage. The Polish Chamber of Foreign Commerce goes so far as to maintain a special panel of experts for the purpose of determining which practices have acquired the status of binding rules.[21] Certainly, in order to prevail, the alleged custom must not contravene any mandatory provisions of national law. Where the parties in their contract, or the national legislature itself have failed to regulate the particular issue in controversy, and as a result a gap is found to exist, custom would be clearly eligible for application.

F.o.b. and c.i.f. terms, long employed by capitalist merchants, are commonly encountered today in contracts between Eastern and Western parties. Interpretative questions with respect to the legal incidence of these notions have repeatedly arisen in the practice of all the communist arbitration tribunals; their decisions have been relatively consistent with the uniform construction followed by courts elsewhere.[22] For instance, Polish foreign trade enterprises readily invoke Incoterms (1953), since the content of that instrument corresponds with the locally promulgated conceptions of f.o.b. and c.i.f. clauses, a fact confirmed by the Warsaw Chamber's Commission of Commercial Usages.[23]

The Eastern foreign trade tribunals have also been called upon to interpret international commercial usage in connection with agency contracts, the legal effect of insurance receipts, claims arising from disputes over the quality of goods, the effect of sharply fluctuating market conditions on the performance of obligations, and so on. With respect to these matters, communist arbitrators have frequently turned for assistance to the works of well-known English, French and German commentators on maritime and commercial law. Direct testimony and written opinions of highly regarded foreign experts have also been taken into consideration.[24]

This rather liberal acceptance of foreign trade custom by the communist tribunals in effect extends binding force to rules of international standing, without the formal sanction of written law. Once incorporated into the stream of Eastern adjudication, such rules serve as a guide to the solution of future controversies.[25]

4. *Case Law*

Perhaps the most interesting and, from the standpoint of day-to-day commerce, the most important source of communist foreign trade norms is the case law of the specialized Eastern arbitration tribunals. Foremost among them are the Moscow Foreign Trade and Maritime Commissions, but all of the other countries, from Czechoslovakia to communist China, boast similar institutions, shaped along the lines of their Soviet predecessors.

Although communist jurisprudence, following the civilist tradition, does not recognize the doctrine of binding precedents, the judgments of these tribunals constitute a significant and dynamic body of legal rules for the guidance of trading entities, both Eastern and Western. It is here that international custom, operative treaties, foreign legislation and alien court practice are considered along with applicable rules of domestic law. That many of the precedents of the Eastern tribunals have now been woven into the fabric of local civil legislation is a fact of particular interest.

It would not be too far-fetched to suggest that in the East–West trade area communist law formation has followed the Anglo-American method of judge-made law. By and large, the legislator has played a part subsidiary to that of the arbitrator. Moreover, on occasion, the more static written law has taken a direction pointed out by the adjudicators.

The accumulated decisions of the foreign trade tribunals, although not systematically and officially published, will in all likelihood remain a major source of guidelines for the future behavior of Eastern and Western enterprises dealing with one another, and for the continued elaboration of communist international commercial law. Accordingly, the institutional nature and *modus operandi* of these tribunals will be subjected to close scrutiny in chapters dealing with the settlement of disputes.

14

THE STATUS OF BUSINESS INSTRUMENTALITIES

A. The Autonomy of Eastern Enterprises

We have pointed out in our description of the East's major trading enterprises that the communist corporation is circumscribed by strict rules of restricted authority, limited liability, independent accounting and other signs of institutional separateness. But how real is this autonomy? The question is important practically and theoretically.

If the concept of corporate personality is a legal fiction, it is a double fiction within the framework of a monolithic economic system. Apart from Yugoslavia, where enterprises can compete with one another and be made bankrupt in the event of inability to meet their debts, Eastern corporations are administratively and organically interwoven with the state and with one another. To reason from Western analogies would be unsafe in this area. The underlying differences between communist enterprises and public instrumentalities of the West are more significant than the similarities.

It would be parochial and sterile for Western courts to characterize communist institutions, be they trade delegations, export-import organizations, domestic enterprises or the state itself, by exclusive reference to the forum's local law, with the terminological and conceptual limitations which traditional norms import. If the results are to be constructive and uniform, there must be some degree of deference to the economic imperatives prevalent at the institution's place of birth. Above all, the admittedly transparent corporate fiction cannot be lightly dispelled, for it is essential to the proper functioning of a state monopoly.

1. Scope of Authority

The operating business organizations of the East are subject to their government-approved charters of incorporation, the civil codes of their country of origin and the regulations which are sporadically prescribed for the state-trading apparatus as a whole. Transactions concluded in violation of these provisions are tainted with illegality and are precarious from the standpoint of foreign parties. This is as true under the more traditionalist approach of the East German legal system as under recent Soviet legislation.[1] Verification of the trading partner's authority to enter into a particular commitment is therefore essential, just as it is considered prudent to examine the articles of association and the powers of management of a Western company, filed in the Commercial Register or some other public depositary.

In view of the high degree of administrative supervision and the disciplinary measures available to punish infringement, transactions contracted beyond the corporate power are few and far between. For the same reason, instruments executed in disregard of prescribed signature and formality requirements are also rarely encountered. However, the possibility of an invalid contract resulting from such acts or omissions cannot be foreclosed.

As a rule, only foreign trade organizations and exceptionally empowered domestic enterprises can deal beyond the national border. International transactions entered into without a standing or special state license, or violating the principle of specialization, whereunder licensed entities can only deal in certain goods and services or in designated geographic regions, are void. The Western merchant must carefully heed this fundamental rule: unless the Eastern enterprise acts under an express grant of power issuing from its Ministry of Foreign Trade, he has before him a fatally incapacitated trading partner.

The consequences of restricted and specialized capacity and the practical problems which they entail, are suggested by a leading decision of the Sofia Arbitration Court rendered in 1964.[2] A Bulgarian firm contracted to manufacture and deliver to an East German enterprise a quantity of pipe. A portion of the needed raw materials was to be supplied by the purchaser. Export and import trading was outside the corporate object of both parties. Each therefore enlisted the services of a competent foreign trade organization. However, the Bulgarian manufacturer was unable to make timely delivery. Was the East German buyer entitled to damages for the resultant breach of contract? The court recognized the contractants' inability to export or import the raw materials in question as a basic limitation flowing from their corporate charters and national laws of origin. Further, it found a mutual intention to substitute competent entities for the portions of the transaction which the parties themselves were not authorized to execute. This, in the court's view, implied legal responsibility for the substitute enterprise's failure to perform. Accordingly, judgment was awarded against the Bulgarian manufacturer.

In a subsequent decision, the same tribunal refused to push the rule of corporate specialization to its logical limit. Presumably it saw the danger of locking communist enterprises into watertight compartments. A defaulting Bulgarian buyer of machines alleged that it had corporate authority to import complete installations, but lacked power to purchase the individual units. The court, nonetheless, upheld the contract in favor of the German seller. In the process it appears to have reinvented the universal principle of incidental capacity necessary to fulfill a company's main object:

> The contention of T (Bulgarian defendant) is without foundation. It was in fact published in the official journal that "the importation of complete installations and of boats" formed the object of T's activities. This signifies that T can, without any restriction, purchase the isolated machinery destined to equip enterprises or boats. The representative of T himself declares that under the term "complete installation" must be understood all that which, not being manufactured in the country, must necessarily be purchased abroad. One does not import machines or tools which are constructed in the country (sic!). It becomes evident, therefore, that T may purchase the machines separately to equip a factory, while the motors to complete them will be purchased at home, since they are manufactured here. T is therefore invested with capacity validly to enter into the contract.[3]

It will be noted that both cases involved disputes between Eastern enterprises. However, the reasoning extends to contractual relations in the East–West context as well. In similar factual situations, the decision would have gone against private Western plaintiffs, had the court found a lack of requisite power in the state defendants.

Whatever conclusions may prevail in an Eastern forum with regard to the capacity of an enterprise to contract a given type of transaction, or the authority of certain individuals to commit such an enterprise, it does not follow that a Western court would adopt the same view, despite the insistence of communist jurists that it should. For example, in the West, a court might invoke the notion of apparent authority, under which a binding agreement may be found to exist if the representative appeared to have power even though he may have lacked it in actuality, as long as the other party was not, or had no duty to be aware of the fact. But no matter where litigation may take place, East–West transactions concluded without proper authority on the state trading side are manifestly vulnerable from a legal point of view.

2. *Reality of Separatism*

Under Sections 23–40 of the Russian Civil Code, which constitutes a skeletal corporation law controlling the status, powers and functions of juridical persons, an enterprise is answerable for its own obligations only to the extent of the property it holds; it is not liable for the debts of the state or of other operating entities. Hungarian law also provides that foreign trade enterprises are not liable for their obligations beyond the assets with which they have been entrusted. Comparable provisions are found in the legislation of other Eastern countries.[4]

The question of limited liability is typically determined by the corporate law of origin, either that of the place of incorporation (the preponderant common law rule) or that of the *siège social* (the preponderant civil law rule). This and other consequences of the doctrine of corporate personality have acquired great significance for the Eastern trade monopolies. By adopting a well-established choice of law criterion which invariably points to the legal system of the corporation's origin, the socialist countries were able to extend the operation of their domestic laws over the worldwide activities of the state trading organizations; and conversely, to circumscribe the application of foreign law.

Eastern law does not confine the grant of juridical personality to the export-import combines which represent the state in foreign markets. Internal business units and industrial organizations enjoy a similar legal status. Every enterprise is required to operate on a basis of independent economic accountability and to produce periodic profit-and-loss statements. But the concept of separateness performs here a much different function from that which it is meant to have in "bourgeois" legal systems. Domestically, enterprises do not engage in business for the purpose of deriving profit from investments. The property in their control is allocated only for operational purposes. Ultimately, it belongs to the state and can at any stage be withdrawn or transferred to other entities. Moreover, the enterprises can be dissolved by their guardian-ministries whenever the ventures in which they are engaged become non-essential.[5]

Internally, the notion of juridical separateness and independent accounting is, therefore, largely a tool of management, helpful in fixing responsibility and measuring performance. It enables the state to own and operate all the means of production, distribution and exchange and, at the same time, to foster operational effectiveness by the threat of disciplinary action or the promise of personal reward.

Externally, the veil which separates an enterprise from the state itself and from other state instrumentalities serves an additional purpose. As we will see in the following pages, the unincorporated foreign trade delegations have found it increasingly difficult to invoke the defense of sovereign immunity in foreign courts. In practice, no such immunity is today claimed for the corporations. A compensatory result is, however, achieved under the shield of their personal laws. The state currently performs its commercial functions in world markets through interposed, suable enterprises. At the same time, its treasury at home and public property abroad are extensively protected from legal claims founded on diverse and occasionally hostile foreign laws, the absence of sovereign immunity notwithstanding.

Such adaptations need not be regarded as abusive. The commerce of collectivized economies would be unmanageable if all state organizations and departments were jointly and severally liable for obligations incurred by each. The purposes of independent bookkeeping and accountability would be largely nullified. Public assets held in foreign countries, bank accounts for example, would be subject to indiscriminate attachment at the instance of any party with an alleged grievance against an Eastern trading partner, for the purpose of obtaining jurisdiction and execution.

While it is true that assets allotted to corporate enterprises are limited, the danger that they might go bankrupt or become incapable of discharging properly incurred obligations is relatively small. Yet it exists. One can easily conceive of a judgment against them, entered by a Western or Eastern court in excess of their net worth, which is seldom more than $5 million. Should the state be allowed to insulate its colossal treasury resources in situations of such judicially or voluntarily recognized liability to foreign firms, simply because at the domestic level bureaucratic management needs to be kept on a tight leash? Insofar as the attendant risk is shifted to him, the private trader would be well advised, in all sizable credit transactions or other contracts susceptible of creating substantial liability on the communist side, to seek an unlimited financial guarantee from the relevant communist Foreign Trade Bank. In this manner the imperatives of the state and the safety of those who deal with its instrumentalities would be simultaneously underwritten.

The principles of corporate separateness and limited liability are well illustrated by decisions of the communist foreign trade tribunals. In the very first case heard by the Moscow Maritime Arbitration Commission, the Soviet shipping organization Sovtorgflot sought compensation from English shipowners for assistance rendered to the "King Edgar." Defendants pleaded that the ship ran aground as a result of plaintiff's negligence, the buoys in Russian territorial waters having been misleadingly placed by the responsible Soviet maritime authorities. The Commission rejected this defense as irrelevant to the litigation between the parties directly before it:

> Sovtorgflot operates as an independent unit on the basis of separate economic accounting; that is, it constitutes an independent juridical person. The supervision of buoys is a function of the People's Commissariat for War and Maritime Affairs. . . . By virtue of Article 4 of its charter of incorporation Sovtorgflot is not responsible for the debts of the State and of other enterprises and organizations, nor is the State responsible for the debts of Sovtorgflot. Consequently, . . . no responsibility can be attributed to Sovtorgflot for any acts or omissions of other Soviet organizations.[6]

In a case before the sister tribunal—the Moscow Foreign Trade Arbitration Commission—a similar view prevailed as to the relationship between an export combine and a foreign trade delegation. The Dutch plaintiff brought a quantity of apricots which were to be shipped c.i.f. to a French destination. France raised the customs duty on Russian apricots, but allowed a reduced rate upon the presentation of a special certificate from the resident Soviet trade delegation. The plaintiff's claim, based upon failure of the defendant combine, Eksportkhleb, to deliver the appropriate certificate, was dismissed on the ground that in the contemplation of Soviet law, the combine was a separate legal person and as such could not be held accountable for the decisions of the trade delegation.[7] Soviet doctrine would have required the same result even if the litigation had taken place in a French court.

There is no need to quarrel with this position or the fact that it has obtained recognition in the West, both in court decisions and intergovernmental agreements. Article 4 of the Annex to the Soviet-Danish Treaty of

Commerce and Navigation of August 17, 1946, states that contracts entered into by a trade organization which enjoys independent legal personality under Soviet law can be binding only upon such organization; and only its property can be subject to execution. Similar provisions are found in the commercial agreements of the U.S.S.R. with France of 1951 and Japan of 1958 and in the Czechoslovak-Swiss Commercial Treaty of 1953.

Eastern jurists react with vehemence to the argument that the notion of corporate personality, particularly in regard to financial liability limitations, has undergone fundamental transformation in the socialist scheme of things.[8] Their dissent is, however, founded on mere insistence that current communist practice follows traditional and universal conceptions. The occasionally abnormal consequences which these conceptions breed in a total state-trading context are ignored.

As is often the case in East-West legal relations, the relevant issues thus become obscured by parallels which derive from similarity of terminology rather than substance. In fact recognition of innate differences in the function of legal personality within the two diverse economic environments would not necessarily shatter the corporate structure of communist institutions. On the contrary, a candid approach to the problem is likely to yield more constructive results for both sides.

B. The Anomalies of Sovereign Immunity

Sovereign immunity is a dormant, if not an altogether dead issue. Practically speaking, it no longer represents the source of aggravation which it once constituted for merchants venturing into trade with the Soviet Union. The legal considerations, however, continue to be ill-defined, and clarification is needed for the sake of certainty and predictability.

The status of the sovereign is inextricably linked with the phenomenon of state trading. Serious difficulties may arise both for a private trader seeking a judicial remedy against a public instrumentality and for the forum called upon to decide the issue. Three intertwined aspects of the problem must be kept in mind: (a) how to establish jurisdiction over a state entity; (b) how to obtain judgment; and (c) how to secure execution once judgment has been entered.

On a nonjudicial plane, the sovereign's exemption from foreign law raises further questions. Aside from the policy of the regulating government, there are also involved here the interests of private parties, to the extent that freedom from legal supervision and taxation tends to create for the state trader conditions of unfair competitive advantage.

1. In Domestic Practice

In the sphere of East-West trade, private petitioners may encounter the bar of sovereign immunity in the courts of their own or of a third Western country. An attempt to sue a communist trading entity in its own domestic courts may also raise the same disturbing specter.

Traditionally, the common law jurisdictions, drawing upon mediaeval concepts of the royal sovereign's personal supremacy, have been more rigid than the civil law systems in their respect for the doctrine. French, Italian and West German government instrumentalities with economic functions have long been relegated to the status of private firms for regulatory and taxation purposes. In continental Europe as a whole, the state itself is subject to judicial process on an equal footing with other litigants. The pioneering in this direction was done by France, with its original hierarchy of administrative tribunals headed by the *Conseil d'État*.

In the United States, partly because of the federal division of power, in England and in the other countries of the British Commonwealth, the privileged status of domestic and foreign government entities is much more pronounced. State consent to legal process, jurisdiction and execution has remained the predominant consideration. Such consent, at least in regard to local courts, has come forth grudgingly, by sporadic legislation or administrative waiver. Given this background, the common denominator against which communist attitudes can be measured becomes rather elusive.

Eastern states make a sharp distinction between immunity at home and abroad. Domestically, they do not, and logically cannot, admit any such notion. Since all significant economic functions are exercised either by the state itself or by its organic components, there is no need to assert sovereign privilege. If the Soviet People's Courts lack competence to hear disputes between industrial enterprises it is not because such enterprises are considered to be imbued with supreme attributes, but rather because a separate and more effective system of adjudication, called "Arbitrazh," has been established for that purpose. As a matter of law, private citizens may take the domestic public entities to court, although in practice this seldom happens. Complaints are directed, in the first instance, to the higher echelons of the offending administration or to the office of the *Prokuror,* a Public Prosecutor whose functions include attributes of a Scandinavian Ombudsman and who deploys elaborate procedures in enforcing corrective action.

Foreign companies licensed to do business in the U.S.S.R. and foreign citizens legitimately resident there may sue in the People's Courts in the same manner as Soviet parties. They may implead the state instrumentalities without fear that governmental immunity will be interposed. Foreign companies not so licensed and nonresident aliens may also bring lawsuits without such apprehensions, provided their own courts offer comity to Soviet plaintiffs.[9] Strict reciprocity is, presumably, not required in this connection. That a Soviet enterprise could sue the Crown in Britain only on the same restricted basis as a local party would not be taken as a reason to deny the standing of an English firm petitioning the courts of the U.S.S.R.

Consistent with this approach is the application to government entities of administrative regulations and taxation levies. Both are, and must be, operative since virtually all of the nation's income is produced by such entities. With a few exceptions, the revenue of local government and municipal authorities is raised through taxes on property in the hands of public enterprises; the federal division of power poses no obstacle to these levies. The Union government taxes the income and the sales of such enterprises. Indeed, all surplus funds not allocated to the particular operating economic unit or its personnel is surrendered to the state in a manner which is no less suggestive of taxation than of a distribution of dividends.

2. *In Foreign Practice*

Enlightened as communist practice may seem at home, its aims and results abroad have been less than satisfactory. Initially, the Soviet trade monopoly sought to take full advantage of governmental immunities as recognized in international law and applied in Western courts. Its attitude gave no credence to the fact that such privileges were never intended for and could not cope with sovereigns whose economic function was all-pervasive. Theoretically, this attitude was not devoid of foundation. Encouraged by the absence of consistency in world practice, the U.S.S.R. in effect attempted to perpetuate the relatively generous British and American positions on sovereign immunity.

It is difficult to conceive of a more disturbing cloud over business relations than the exemption from suit and law of a government that monopolizes all of its nation's commercial activity. Nevertheless, this was the early Soviet posture. Originally, full immunity was claimed from the host country in respect of the officially accredited foreign trade delegations. In the Soviet view such delegations were integral arms of the state, charged with special functions in the sphere of international commerce, much as its embassies were charged with political functions abroad.

Growing government intrusion into economic life everywhere and the emergence of a bloc of countries practicing total state commerce provoked a strong reaction against the concept of sovereign immunity. For what can be more inhibiting to the development of trade relations than a basic inequality before the law which renders doubtful one party's redress against another for breach of contract or related abuses. In fact, the reaction came in various ways from business quarters, from courts and from administrative authorities. The most effective form of pressure arose from the natural reluctance of private firms to deal at all as long as this air of uncertainty persisted. Certain governments, notably the United States, simply refused to admit the purportedly sovereign trade delegation into their territories. Under a series of bilateral commercial treaties, the U.S.S.R. was required to waive, in respect of all economic activities, the entitlement to immunity which was allegedly afforded by customary international law.[10]

In varying degrees, national courts had long ago begun to qualify the exemption of foreign states from jurisdiction and, to a lesser extent, from execution of judgments upon their property. This trend originated in continental courts, notably in Belgium and Italy, toward the end of the nineteenth century. It was hastened by the nationalization of certain segments of economic activity in a number of European countries.

In 1952, the United States government took an important step toward aligning its absolutist view of immunity with these more restrictive notions. In a celebrated letter from its Acting Legal Adviser, the Department of State made it clear that in the future it would invite American courts to recognize the immunity of a foreign state in respect of *jure imperii* (governmental acts) but to deny it in respect of *jure gestionis* (private acts). A similar view began to gain support in England.[11]

There can be no doubt that the restrictive approach is more just and reasonable in the contemporary commercial setting—indeed, essential to eliminate the remnants of the immunity problem in business dealings with state traders of all origins. It remains to be seen, however, whether practical criteria can be articulated by the courts to distinguish between governmental and proprietary functions. Success to date has not been conspicuous.[12]

At the present time, the doctrine of sovereign immunity cannot be said to constitute a major obstacle to East-West trade. The initial communist position has mellowed with time. In practice, the alleged immunity of trade delegations is frequently waived by intergovernmental agreement, contractual stipulation or unilateral submission. Moreover, today the delegations appear as agents rather than principals. The bulk of foreign trade is conducted by corporate entities which are held out as being juridically autonomous from the state.

At the level of theory, Eastern jurists do not concede that state entities, corporate or otherwise, are precluded from pleading their exempt sovereign status.[13] Moreover, the new Soviet Maritime Code of 1968 reasserts this position into positive law. Since merchant vessels entrusted into the possession of the U.S.S.R.'s incorporated shipping lines technically belong to the state, Article 20 declares them to be immune from arrest or execution without the consent of the Council of Ministers.

As a matter of usage, no immunity is claimed on behalf of the East's corporate instrumentalities. The current pattern of submission to foreign process is explained on the basis of waiver, either made explicitly, or implied from such factors as the sue-and-be-sued clause which is usually included in their charters.[14]

Even more significant is the fact that the communist monopolies, whether acting through trade delegations, export-import organizations or domestic enterprises, readily agree to the settlement of disputes by arbitration. Such submission implies an undertaking, carefully observed in fact, that the Westerner's remedy will not be defeated by reliance on public status and that an award in his favor will be honored without fail.[15]

Quiescent as the problem of immunity may appear to be at the present time, Western firms would be well advised to seek an express contractual waiver from the communist state instrumentality with which they happen to be dealing. Such a waiver should be entitled to full effect in the forum which may subsequently become seized of a dispute. Courts, and the foreign ministries which occasionally guide them on this issue, would not be responding to the needs of the times if they continued to interpose historically inherited technicalities in the way of such a solution.

C. Act of State and Act of God

Nothing touches more profoundly on the reality of corporate separateness in a centrally planned economy than the principle of act of God or *force majeure* (a more apt designation in a system where the divine power is stripped of all authority). This defense, if correctly raised, may enable a state party to a contract to disregard a stipulated period of performance, to plead cancellation of an agreement or to escape the risk of loss.

Force majeure is universally deemed to cover all circumstances which occur independently of the will of man and which it is not within his means to control. In the standard contracts and general conditions of sale elaborated by the Economic Commission for Europe, the typical clause on the subject reads:

> The following shall be considered as cases of relief if they intervene after the formation of the contract and impede its performance: industrial disputes and any other circumstances (*e.g.*, fire, mobilization, requisition, embargo, currency restrictions, insurrection, shortage of transport, general shortage of materials and restrictions in the use of power) when such other circumstances are beyond the control of the parties.[16]

This comprehensive definition covers many of the practical difficulties encountered in East-West trade. For instance, communist negotiators are generally reluctant to recognize as a *force majeure* workers' strikes at the Westerner's plant, preferring a right to refuse deliveries retarded by events of this nature and to recover consequential damages and penalties. This reluctance is even more pronounced in regard to industrial unrest on a national scale. Shortage of materials, a circumstance which does not involve class solidarity, is also rejected as an excuse for untimely delivery.[17]

Western contractors, sellers, purchasers and others must, however, be urged to go considerably beyond the E.C.E. recommendation and to provide with care for a category of complex ramifications which are inadequately covered therein. Conventional analyses of the problem of *force majeure* tend to overlook risks which come into play as a result of a state trading monopoly's peculiar status. In consequence, the unwary firm is often left unprotected.

1. Responsibility for Government Action

Two examples, drawn from current contractual relationships, may be cited to spotlight the difficulties which arise in East-West business dealings as a result of the persistent confusion between *force majeure* and the consequences of governmental acts.

A Western group has agreed to participate in the financing, construction and operation of luxury hotels in several eastern European capitals. Its investment and remuneration are recoverable over a period of years following commencement of business. How would the parties be affected by a decision of the local government, taken after the Western group had commenced performance and provided all or part of the funds, to cancel the project altogether, or to convert the hotel into a hospital or government office? Would the government be liable for consequential damages and loss of profits? Would the contracting communist enterprises and guaranteeing state banks be absolved from such liability?

Western companies are increasingly entering into agreements to produce motion pictures in communist countries. Characteristically, such agreements require the Eastern side to provide studio facilities, equipment, orchestras, extra performers, access to sites and the like. Budgets of feature films usually run into millions of dollars and contractual commitments to stars, directors, composers, camera crews and other participants are made in advance of commencement of photography. How should an Italian producer or a Swiss financier calculate the risk of suspension of production or denial of the promised elements by the Eastern host government? Such administrative action may be prompted by a deterioration in the international climate, objections to an essential member of the cast (*e.g.,* because of previous appearance in a politically objectionable film such as *Dr. Zhivago*), or ideological exception to the film's scenario.

The notorious Soviet-Israeli oil arbitration, by far the most important case ever decided by a communist tribunal from the point of view of the amount at stake and the complexity of the issues involved, turned on the *force majeure* implications of an act of state.[18] Unfortunately, the political factors surrounding the dispute tended to obscure the legal principles inherent in the decision. The proceedings before the Moscow foreign trade tribunal, and the resultant award in favor of the Soviet party have been amply dissected and commented upon.[19] Soiuznefteksport, the defendant Soviet oil combine, stood in contractual relationship with the plaintiff, Jordan Investment Ltd. of Israel and another Israeli purchaser, relative to the delivery of fuel oil f.o.b. Black Sea ports. Following Israel's invasion of the Sinai Peninsula in October of 1956, defendant informed plaintiff that the Soviet Ministry of Foreign Trade had canceled all export licenses and would refuse to permit future deliveries. It may be fairly assumed that the action was diplomatically calculated to produce a favorable impact upon Arab opinion. Defendant's notification went on to say that "in accordance with the provisions of the contract concerning *force majeure,* paragraph 7, the said contracts are being canceled." The paragraph in question relieved the parties from liability if nonperformance was due to a cause beyond their control.

It was not disputed that Soviet law applied as the law of the place of contracting. Plaintiff argued that in the absence of a contrary indication in the contract, the obligation to obtain export licenses and the risk of their cancellation were upon the Soviet seller. It is on this point that issue was joined. Whether the governmental action was justified is not relevant in strictly legal terms. Similarly, we can put aside the fully debated question of whether the prohibition had created an objective impossibility of performance; the award found that the combine was, in fact, prevented from shipping Russian oil or oil which might have been procured elsewhere.

Article 118 of the R.S.F.S.R. Civil Code then in force (of which paragraph 7 of the operative contract was largely declaratory) absolved from liability a party who failed to perform owing to a cause beyond his control:

> Unless otherwise provided by law or contract, the debtor shall be relieved from liability for non-performance, if he proves that impossibility of performance resulted from circumstances which he could not prevent, or that it came about owing to unilateral design or negligence of the creditor.[20]

Nonetheless, it is a striking fact that Soiuznefteksport meekly accepted the Ministry's injunction without appeal, protest or any other effort to reverse or modify the decision. The fundamental duty of a contracting party to do all in its power to save an agreement was certainly not exercised in the best tradition of "contractual discipline," a doctrine which communist legal systems so forcefully extol.

At its crux, the case turned on whether or not a state monopoly should be permitted to assert the unilateral act of its own government as a justifiable excuse for nonperformance. On one side of the scale was the contention that a *force majeure* plea cannot obtain recognition in a system where the obligated entity and the responsible Ministry are, in effect, arms of the same administration. Plaintiff argued that the act of one is the act of the other and that there can be no conflict of will between the two such as is necessary to call into play the concept of insuperable force. On the other side was the forceful position of communist legislation, recognized in treaties and court decisions in the West, that the foreign trade enterprises are juristic entities in the nature of corporations and, as such, separate and distinct from the state.

From the judgment must be drawn a proposition which, if it were to stand, would augur ill for East-West trade: a state enterprise, by invoking an act of its own government, may evade with impunity all contractual obligations toward a damaged party. Without suggesting that this is what happened in fact, or that such conspiracies are current within a communist administration, one may wonder whether the president of a combine is not being invited to request the Minister by whom he is appointed and to whom he is hierarchically subordinate, to do away with a contract which is no longer interesting; indeed, whether the Minister is not being tempted to take the initiative unilaterally.

To be sure, international practice is far from uniform on the question of whether a denial of export licenses, import licenses or transit licenses warrants a release from liability for nonperformance under general notions of *force majeure*. One approach holds that in the absence of party agreement to the contrary, the duty to obtain a license and the risk of nonperformance occasioned by government denial or cancelation is on the seller. Another approach places the risk on the buyer. Neither of these rules, it is submitted, are suitable in the case of state-owned and operated monopolies, Western or Eastern, which are prevented from performing contracts by political acts of their governments.

Certainly, no one can quarrel with a 1967 decision of the Prague arbitration tribunal which places upon the private party to an East-West transaction the risk of its government's interdictions. There, the Spanish defendant pleaded inability to deliver ordered goods owing to export license denial. In their contract the parties had chosen to be governed by Czechoslovak law. Applying Article 334 of the 1963 Code on Foreign

Trade, the court ruled that the duty to obtain all necessary export licenses was the seller's. Damages were accordingly awarded to the local import enterprise.[21]

The Soviet-Israeli case helps to demonstrate one of the central theses of this book: time-honored legal concepts, such as the rule that a company is distinct and separate from its shareholders, break down entirely when the government itself, acting through an interposed corporate instrumentality, is the real party at interest in all national and international transactions. To persist in the application of conventional principles in this particular context is to enthrone the postetative condition whereunder the state-trading side unilaterally determines whether a contract to which it is a party is still in force, while the private party remains fully bound in the meantime. A Western court faced with issues of this type should be expected to disavow the Moscow Commission's approach regardless of the current requirements of communist law or traditionally interpreted Western law.

One may venture the opinion that the Soviet state, its oil monopoly and the Moscow tribunal itself would have benefited in the long run from a different line of reasoning than that which was expounded by the arbitrators. That an opposite result would have better served the cause of commercial relations can hardly be controverted. Fortunately, a more enlightened attitude on the various manifestations of *force majeure* appears to be prevailing in other communist tribunals.

2. *Change of Economic Plan*

In dealing with collectivist systems, it is of utmost importance to understand the legal impact upon existing contracts of a change in the national export or import plan. Does the amendatory decree of planning which alters previously established contingencies create for communist selling enterprises an objective impossibility of performance? Does the damaged Western party have a remedy for breach of contract? Does the supervening government act establish state liability under principles of public international law? These questions have been answered in Eastern case law in a contradictory manner. The vagaries of a Bulgarian line of cases are particularly revealing.

Disagreement on the issue within the Sofia court began to appear in 1956. In a case decided at that time a dissenting opinion put forward the enlightened view that treaty-adopted general conditions of trade must not be interpreted so as to characterize an act of planning as a *force majeure.*[22] *This* view did not prevail in subsequent case law. Nor was it accepted that the basis of *force majeure* must be an insurmountable natural cause, rather than a legal cause such as "sovereign act." However, by the end of 1964, the tribunal saw its way clear to declare:

> The act of planning . . . produces effects in regard to Bulgarian enterprises, but it does not free the Bulgarian enterprise from executing the contracts which it has concluded, nor from the consequences of its non-performance, vis-à-vis foreign parties. . . .[23]

In a 1957 case the Bulgarian defendant pleaded *force majeure* on the basis of a government ruling which unforeseeably restricted the quantities of agricultural produce available for export. Plaintiff responded that the reduction in the export plan, even if it created a real impossibility of complete delivery, entailed the seller's responsibility for consequential damages, the cause emanating from the Bulgarian government. Referring to Article 81 of the Bulgarian Code of Obligations and Contracts which relieves a debtor of responsibility if the obstacle to performance derives from a cause not imputed to his fault, the court rejected this line of argumentation:

> This conception rests upon a total identification of the State enterprise and the State. It is, however, in full contradiction with the fundamental principles which govern the structure of Bulgarian State enterprises. They are distinct subjects of law. It is not their province to direct foreign commerce. They must submit to the administrative dispositions of the authorities invested with this power, and, above all, to the dispositions of the council of ministers. The acts of these authorities are, of course, obligatory upon the enterprises. But they cannot impose upon the enterprises a responsibility with regard to third parties. The damages which third parties have incurred cannot be placed on the account of the enterprises. The problem is examined here only from the standpoint of the responsibility of the enterprise and the rights of its partner. The court abstains from analysing the hypothesis from the standpoint of the State's responsibility on the international plane by virtue of international treaties which it has signed. . . .[24]

The report fails to indicate whether the damaged plaintiff was another Comecon enterprise or a private Western firm. If the former, it may be assumed that the two governments have found, through their standing treaty machinery, a way to offset the sustained loss at a state-to-state level. In the event a Western firm was involved, the result of the decision is manifestly unsatisfactory. The last sentence of the above-quoted passage suggests that the tribunal's own conscience was not at ease.

In subsequent decisions the Sofia court overruled itself as to the extra-territorial consequences of governmental acts. One 1957 dispute arose from a 25 percent reduction in the local producer's plan; the export enterprise's plan was correspondingly reduced. The award states:

> It is necessary to establish that an internal act cannot modify nor abrogate an international agreement. But this does not mean that such internal act is devoid of obligatory force in regard to citizens and organs of the State from which the act emanates. . . . A legislative or administrative act obliges them to conform, be it even in contradiction with the terms of the international agreement. . . .[25]

It is to be hoped that the other eastern European legal systems will take their cue from the Bulgarian tribunal, or from the Czechoslovak Code on Foreign Trade under which the default of an official authorization necessary for the accomplishment of the duty of the obligee is specifically excluded from the realm of *force majeure*.[26] While the denial or cancellation of an export license would undoubtedly result in an impossibility of performance for the exporting state enterprise and would thus terminate its obligation to perform, it would not release it from reparation for damages caused. These provisions are indicative of the pragmatic quality of the Czechoslovak legislation. In juxtaposition, the Moscow tribunal's decision in the Soviet-Israeli oil dispute deserves to be dismissed as a political aberration.

3. *An Approach to Force Majeure*

In East-West trade, the eventualities which are ambiguously grouped under the label of *force majeure* are full of nuance. It is necessary to distinguish between various types of sovereign acts; for some are more objectionable than others in their aim and impact. The Soviet denial of export licenses to Israel is strongly suggestive of foreign policy maneuvering at the expense of the Western party. But one can also imagine a cancellation prompted by mere economic reasons. The latter, if damaging and uncompensated, are almost equally abhorrent. State variation of export planning is fundamentally not too different from an attempted cancellation of contracts by General Motors on the ground that market conditions have changed. It is small consolation for the Western party that a state is less likely to seek narrow advantage from an agreement invalidated in this manner—less likely because a segment of the domestic economy would also be affected by the deliberate change in the plan.

The problem with which we are here concerned is too complex to be presented in contrasting black and white. One need not automatically deny to all changes of plan the legal consequences of an excusable *force majeure*. For example, a decreed reduction in agricultural export quotas following severe drought may be justifiably, if indirectly, attributable to an insuperable natural cause. Nor is motivation an irrelevant factor. But how is it to be ascertained in the setting of a collectivist economic structure?

The sufficiency of the excuse for failure to perform may also deserve evaluation. In the Soviet-Israeli case, the application of an evidentiary rule requiring Soiuznefteksport to submit proof that it had tried, albeit without success, to obtain government permission to perform, would have made the decision somewhat more palatable. For the communist societies appear to have evolved to a point where the possibility of corporate management making an impact on government policy can no longer be dismissed as unrealistic.

To argue that the state must, in all situations, waive the right to act in contravention of a commercial contract would be futile. No government, and certainly no communist government, can seriously be expected to limit its sovereign power to this extent. Placing the risk and consequences of such action upon the shoulders of the state's corporate enterprises would entail some conceptual difficulties; the enterprise would simply declare its readiness to be judged on the basis of orthodox capitalist-made law, the long-established Western attitude, predicated on the premise that no firm can influence the political acts of its government. But an appeal to orthodoxy is not necessarily consistent with legal morality. In this instance, the long-established standard is deflected by the novel economic context.

True, U.S. Steel is not without influence in Washington, nor Fiat in Rome and Usines Marcel Dassault at the Quai d'Orsay of Paris. But the institutional incest with the government is at least absent. Only state-owned Western enterprises such as the British Overseas Airways Corporation approach the communist degree of organic interrelationship. Such enterprises should no more be released from obligations as a result of their government's directives than Soiuznefteksport, traditional law in the East or the West notwithstanding.

The price which a wholly planned economy may justifiably be invited to pay for its reserved freedom to annul or modify established contractual relations is liability to the consequentially damaged foreign party. Whether the liability should be that of the state itself, under principles of public international law—a possibility hinted at by the Bulgarian foreign trade tribunal—or that of the state's formally independent contracting enterprise is of secondary importance to the Western trader. Of the two approaches, the latter would seem to be the simpler legal solution. The ultimate burden would, in any event, be borne by the author of the damaging act—the omnipresent state.

In most instances, Eastern parties have refused to assume responsibility for possible acts of their state. On the contrary, they usually seek and obtain broad contractual *force majeure* definitions which include such events as "fire, acts of the elements, war, military operations of any character, blockade, *prohibitions of export or import,* or any other contingencies beyond the parties' control." A Western firm occupying a sufficiently strong bargaining position may get away with a clause which omits specific mention of acts of state. Occasionally, one comes across stipulations that government clearances are to be obtained by the state trader, or warranties that all requisite authorizations to perform the particular contract have been obtained in advance. At best, such euphemistic undertakings offer a way of avoiding a drafting stalemate and of building a basis for the contention that the communist entity should be held responsible for damages in the event of its state's denial or revocation of permission to perform.

In the absence of clear precedent, one can do no more than hope that an arbitration panel faced with the issue would, in fact, draw this inference from the admittedly ambiguous language. However, the words of Professor Genkin, one of the Soviet arbitrators in the Israeli oil dispute, do not inspire great optimism: "In conditions of State monopoly of foreign trade, economic organizations cannot assume absolute responsibility for obtaining licenses. . . . It must not be allowed for economic organizations to take upon themselves obligations which may conflict with acts of organs of authority which exercise control over foreign trade, and in connection with this incur corresponding monetary responsibility." [27] For the sake of safety, this position must be taken seriously by the Western negotiator; he should not overvalue cleverly phrased clauses in terms of the corresponding concessions he is asked to make.

Eastern state banks have frequently shown themselves willing to guarantee the unconditional performance of all obligations undertaken by local instrumentalities toward private foreign parties. However, such guarantees usually import the terms of the underlying contract and unless the consequences of a state-created *force majeure* are appropriately defined, their effectiveness becomes dependent upon a court's or arbitrator's eventual appraisal.

While in principle the risk of state cancellation or modification of a transaction is insurable, to date, such insurance does not seem to be available in the West. However, private firms have occasionally accepted counter-guarantees from Western banks and substantial companies which stand in continuous business relationships with the East, assuring that contracts will be performed according to their terms and that injured parties will be made whole. The language of such assurances is usually broader than that which is acceptable to Eastern enterprises and therefore more prone to mitigate the consequences of an eventual act of state.

Evidentiary criteria to determine state motivation, or party effort to reverse government interference with performance, implied contractual suggestions to an eventual adjudicator, insurance coverage, sporadically available counter-guarantees or other improvisations by the parties do not offer permanent solutions to the fundamental problem of *force majeure*. Nothing can be more satisfactory than a provision which deals with the question directly and in specific detail. Ideally, it should obtain universal application pursuant to treaty stipulations, legislation and adoption by the courts. Meanwhile, the optimum goal to which the Western firm can aspire is a clause in all East–West agreements to which it is a party to the effect that the risk of state action should lie on the state corporation whose government is at cause. Soviet law would seem to allow such a solution under Sections 222 and 235 of the Civil Code of 1964, which recognizes the board defense of *force majeure* as a dispositive provision subject to limitation and variation by the parties.

Paradoxically, the result needed in the sphere of East–West commerce is, in fact, to be found in the law which governs economic activity within the U.S.S.R. itself. Internally, a selling enterprise may not invoke the excuse that its own superior administration prevented delivery to a domestic purchasing enterprise falling under the control of another administration. In the absence of such a rule, the seller could procure a prohibition from its higher echelons and thereby evade a contractual obligation with impunity. Internationally, both the problem and the need are substantially analogous.[28]

15

THE ROLE OF CONTRACT

A. The Sanctity of Assumed Obligations

> I can inform you officially that among Soviet foreign trade organizations there has never been a case of non-performance of their obligations. Foreigners often say to me in conversation: "your merchants, it is true, often dispute prior to signing a contract, sometimes even on trifling matters. But once they sign an agreement, they perform it with accuracy."

These proud words, uttered by Anastas Mikoyan, long a prominent Soviet leader and foreign trade expert, are not without foundation.[1] They aptly describe not only the contractual behavior of Soviet trade organizations, but also that of their counterparts in other communist countries, including China. Inevitably, a claim of this type brings to memory impressions that militate the other way. What about the defaulted First World War Russian bonds, the uncompensated postrevolutionary expropriation of foreign property and the failure to repay United States Lend-Lease obligations? And if the moral responsibility entailed in these matters has been obscured by special historical and political considerations, what about the wholesale piracy of Western copyrights and the past, unauthorized exploitation of foreign patents? That no technical infringements of law or contract have taken place is hardly an adequate answer.

The present discussion is not concerned with the broad question of whether the Soviet, Chinese or other communist governments are trustworthy interlocutors or reliable treaty-partners. Nor are we at the moment reviewing the total communist business record; in a sense, that is a subject to which the bulk of this work is devoted. As background to an investigation of Eastern contract law and practice, our attention is here concentrated on the more limited issue of whether the foreign merchant may safely give credence to contractual undertakings solemnly assumed by his state-trading partner. For what is the use of painstaking negotiation and drafting if there is apprehension that the promises may not be worth the paper they are written on?

Experience accumulated in recent years prompts a reassuring reply to this question. To be sure, the history of communist economic and commercial behavior on the international scene is far from perfect if it is to be assessed from the inception of the Soviet regime. There is, however, an ample basis for asserting that in contemporary terms Russian and other Eastern state enterprises have, as a rule, scrupulously adhered to their contractual commitments. Indeed the standard of their behavior has often exceeded that of certain Western firms involved in East–West trade.

Something more than normal business morality is involved. Despite the strong Marxist-Leninist contempt for capitalist aims and methods, the pragmatists whose task it is to operate a collectivist economy have long ago realized that international business will for an indefinite time have to be conducted within a capitalist frame of reference. This fundamental truth builds defenses against the abuse of prevalent commercial ethics. Were communist trade officials to be guided by hostile dogma in their day-to-day dealings with private entrepreneurs, they would quite promptly land in a spontaneously enforced quarantine. Such are the inexorable guarantees of international business life.

A series of more specific factors shape Eastern motivation in the observance of strict contractual discipline and what we have previously described as "socialist legality." They stem from the very nature of a centrally commanded economy, although innate honesty is also an element which cannot be lightly discounted.

If a private Western firm engages in willful and systematic evasion of undertakings, its defaults will not fail to come to the attention, through Dun & Bradstreet reports or other means, of persons with whom it is dealing, and those whose future custom it seeks. Sooner or later, ostracism and perhaps even bankruptcy will follow.

In the case of a communist enterprise, this phenomenon takes on an additional dimension. The foreign party can look forward to a high quality of performance on the Eastern side if only because a government invariably stands in the background. Certainly, the business of Litsenzintorg, the Soviet patent licensing agency, must suffer if it fails to honor the terms of an agreement. But the opprobrium engendered by this loss of reputation would also be dangerously contagious for the entire Soviet foreign trade apparatus. For under the surface of such legalistic refinements as corporate separability, there is the fundamental fact that Russia's Litsenzintorg, and even its New York incorporated Amtorg, Czechoslovakia's Skoda and Poland's Dynamo, are all part of a single, monolithic state structure. The transgressions of one instrumentality will not be regarded in isolation, as if it were the only black sheep in a shining flock. The stigma automatically and conspicuously attaches to the entire government-operated monopoly and to all of its formally autonomous branches. Would-be business partners are guided accordingly.

Another reassuring circumstance arises from the nature of bureaucratic mentality. A private merchant may be tempted to play an occasional game of poker in the realm of contractual compliance, or to waive generously some term of his transaction in the hope of winning goodwill. An official's safety lies in the black letters of his agreement. He will take infinite pains and try his opponent's patience during the negotiation and drafting process. He may seek to exploit an ambiguity of language or a technicality of law in the course of performance, for example, by questioning the validity of a contract which has been executed by someone other than the signatory formally designated by his Ministry of Foreign Trade. But what he will not do is negate a clear commitment which is ultimately the state's. Nor will he be prone to release the foreign firm from expressly undertaken commitments. Were such a stratagem to misfire the consequences could be most unpleasant. In the first place, he may find himself called to account by a higher authority, in civil, administrative or even criminal proceedings, for a breach of the discipline which is so essential to the functioning of a gigantic state monopoly operated by a diffused civil service. In addition, he may become dangerously embroiled in lingering controversy with the foreign supplier whose counter-refusal to perform could have dislocating consequences for that segment of the national economic plan which is dependent upon the timely delivery of the products in question.

For the same reason, those who run a public enterprise will not lightly take to juggling its books. There may be truth in the anecdote that European businessmen tend to maintain several balance sheets: one for their tax collector, one for their partner and one for themselves. In the case of a communist corporation there is not only a lack of incentive to embark upon such a course, but also inordinately great peril. For the books are always government books and the notion of fraud is intimately linked with such concepts as theft of sacred socialist property, sabotage and worse. The liability is never merely civil. Consequently, when a Western firm establishes by agreement an entitlement to compensation based on volume of production or value of sales, it has reason to feel relatively secure that the accounting submitted to it will be accurate. The presumption of regularity stems not only from the contractual rights enjoyed by the outside firm but also from the unrelated internal needs of the planned economy.

All of this gives sufficient theoretical foundation for an optimistic hypothesis. At the level of firm-to-firm contracts, the principle *pacta sunt servanda* retains both validity and efficacy. This hypothesis is, in fact, verified by actual experience. That communist bureaucrat-businessmen are exacting negotiators who seek to drive the hardest possible bargains under all circumstances has by now become common knowledge. But once an agreement is reduced to writing and executed with all the due formalities required by law, no malevolent refusal to comply with its terms need be anticipated.

This does not mean that performance is always impeccable. Errors of commission or omission are encountered here no less than elsewhere. Perhaps more than elsewhere, manufactured goods shipped under an agreement of purchase and sale frequently fail to live up to precise quality specifications or packaging requirements. Only the buyer of staple commodities, such as timber or cotton, encounters a uniformly outstanding pattern of compliance, particularly if clear delivery dates and penalty clauses are written into his contract. However, the essential thing to bear in mind is that wherever fault is found, it is generally attributable to inefficiency of methods rather than to premeditated breach.

The willingness to discharge the agreement in a businesslike fashion in accordance with its terms is usually present. Only in situations complicated by political factors such as, for example, the Soviet cancelation of agreements for the delivery of crude oil to Israel following the Suez conflict of 1956, need one fear an outright refusal to perform; and even then a painstaking attempt is made to ground nonperformance on considerations deriving from applicable law or contractual content.[2]

Further, we find that the communist payment record is unimpeachable in the eyes of Western creditors. Both in Europe and increasingly in the United States (to the extent permitted by federal law) bankers readily accept bills of exchange drawn by Eastern business entities and endorsed by their national or foreign trade banks. Invariably, they find that payment is punctual and accurate.

In their attitude toward business disputes, the Eastern traders have also accumulated a satisfactory record. In the first place, a strong preference exists for amicable adjustment of claims. There is a marked reluctance to allow a dispute to go to a court or an arbitrator, even if the adjudication is to take place in the enterprise's own, locally sponsored foreign trade tribunal. Once an arbitral award is rendered against the Eastern party, settlement is prompt and complete, regardless of whether the forum whose jurisdiction has been contractually recognized is Eastern, Western or neutral.

B. Contract in a Planned Economy

Although communist enterprises employ the terminology of Western contract in domestic as well as foreign commerce, the conventional concepts are superimposed upon a fundamentally different economic structure. It is imprudent for the private trader to approach the negotiating table with the belief that the Eastern party possesses a business orientation and a view of consensual relationships similar to his own. This will prove increasingly true as more and more local producing and consuming enterprises enter the world market directly. For the communist negotiator, like his capitalist counterpart, cannot easily cast aside the notions which he employs in a domestic context, and which reassert themselves from force of habit in international transactions.

A grasp of the role and significance of contract in dealings within and among communist economies as well as in East-West trade is therefore essential to enable private firms to understand the attitude and psychology of their communist business partners. Such insight may help the foreign concern not only to protect itself against unusual pitfalls, but also to draw advantage from the peculiar conditions prevalent in a planned economy, just as the informed state trader is often able to exploit, through the free play of contractual arrangements, the opportunities afforded by the open markets of the West.

If commercial contracts between state enterprises mirror classical conceptions, the reflection is one of form rather than substance. In the West, an agreement is negotiated, concluded and enforced according to the private interests of the signatories, with minimal governmental interference. The Eastern contract, on the other hand, is imposed upon the parties by the specific commands of the national economic plans and subplans, and by the centrally prescribed allocation of materials. The state is in effect a third party to all agreements, lack of privity notwithstanding. The main substance of every transaction and even the contractors themselves are predetermined from above with a view to achieving public objectives. Indeed, the implementation of the economic plan is the *raison d'être* of both the contract and the entities which conclude it.

Theoretically, one could conceive of collectivist economic activity being conducted by means of administrative directive, without the need of corporate entities, or a meeting of the minds among them. Yet, these institutions play an important, probably indispensable role in the communist industrial state. Above all, they inculcate a form of bureaucratic discipline which aids in the accomplishment of assigned tasks. Bonuses for the fulfillment or overfulfillment of production goals are an incentive to execute contractual obligations, to seek specific performance or, in case of default, to recover penalties on a predetermined scale. Similarly, failure to perform or even to enter into certain types of contract is a wrongful breach of civil obligation as well as a punishable violation of state interests.

Bulgarian law is illustrative. It provides that "the organs required to execute the national economic plan, being invested with this power by law or by an act based on law, can impose an obligation to give or do something or to conclude a contract."[3] The act of economic planning creates at once, a public law obligation on the part of two affected enterprises to comply with the directive of a competent government department and a civil-law obligation to enter into an appropriate contract with one another. Both obligations are legally enforceable. A refusal to observe the former entails sanctions of an administrative nature. Failure to comply with the latter may be tried and corrected in precontractual adjudication proceedings leading to the compulsory creation of a definite agreement.

Such is the strange world of communist contract. It is no less effective for being strange, given the logic and needs of a wholly planned economy. What is confusing and surprising is the Eastern persistence in employing the classical nomenclature of contract.

The Soviet Basic Principles of Civil Legislation shed further light on the communist conception of agreement. They distinguish between contracts of sale and contracts of delivery. The former are used primarily in retail trade and in transactions of minor importance consummated outside the economic plan. The great bulk of exchanges takes place under contracts of delivery, pursuant to a mandatory act of state planning.[4]

The characterization of the compulsory contract as one for delivery rather than sale emphasizes the fact that physical transfer is the primary legal event. Logically, it is this undertaking which is most essential to the public interest. The seller's right to payment is accorded secondary consideration. All basic terms and conditions are administratively prescribed. Only matters of an auxiliary character are subject to interparty negotiation. In contrast to Western preoccupations, passage of ownership is basically irrelevant in domestic contracts of delivery, since "title" at all times rests in the state; the enterprises are merely entrusted with managerial possession of the property in question.

Numerous articles of the Russian Civil Code demonstrate the predominance of the public interest in the sphere of contract. For example, an obligation arising from compulsory contract may not be discharged by mutual consent. In delivery contracts, the buying enterprise is not entitled to waive the minimum quality requirements set by the state, although it may waive requirements which exceed these standards.[5] Inordinately short periods of limitation are designed to encourage the prompt settlement of disputes in order to avoid disruptive delays in the implementation of the plan. These periods, generally one year or six months depending on the particular cause of action, may not be extended by agreement of the parties. What is more, they will be applied by the court spontaneously, even if not raised as a defense.[6]

That it is the state's benefit which is primarily in play, not the interests of the immediate parties, is even more acutely shown in cases where both sides fail properly to perform. If substandard goods are shipped and accepted without proper inspection, or if the goods are neither shipped nor received at the time specified, and no complaint is lodged, the state may levy penalties against both parties. Similarly, if a nonbreaching enterprise fails to bring a timely action for default, it may itself be subject to a punitive levy.[7]

The principal remedy for breach of contract is specific performance, although money damages may be awarded in addition as a penalty for delay. This approach is a natural one in a collectivist setting. The plan creates a chain of economic obligations. Any broken link may produce disruptive repercussions all along the line. Since domestically available resources are centrally allocated and world markets are still generally inaccessible to a local enterprise, monetary compensation would not enable an affected party easily to procure equivalent goods or services elsewhere.

The reformist trend toward decentralization may, to some extent, alter the role of contract as described above. It is likely to lead to greater freedom in the selection of co-contractors and in the determination of terms and conditions. A proposal emanating from the foremost Soviet reform economist, Professor Evsei Liberman, seeks greater relaxation of state control over the allocation of resources.[8] Assuming it is effectively implemented, such a step could profoundly change internal attitudes toward breach of contract and the remedies available to the aggrieved party. The availability of alternative sources of supply would likely reduce the emphasis upon specific performance. However, regardless of what course the current economic movement may follow, the state's interest and indirect participation may be expected to remain dominant in all contractual relations.

C. Contract in Foreign Trade

1. Within the East

Contract practice in commerce among the several collectivist countries must be clearly distinguished from that prevalent in trade with the West. As in purely domestic exchanges, the central objective of consensual dealings between two Comecon countries is to facilitate the implementation of their respective economic programs. Foreign trade enterprises are required, pursuant to each nation's plan, to enter into appropriate arrangements with corresponding communist enterprises abroad.

Ideally, commerce among the state-trading economies, just as within them, should fall into a well-defined pattern. There is, however, no central, multilateral planning authority. In practice, only limited coordination is achieved, and this by means of a network of bilateral treaties and protocols concluded at the level of governments.

To an unprecedented degree, the long-term interstate agreements encroach upon the traditional domain of interparty contracts. They often go so far as to specify the types and quantities of goods to be traded, the enterprises to be linked by direct commitments, the delivery schedules, the methods of payment, the manner of extinguishing debts which may arise from the contemplated exchanges and sometimes even the price of the merchandise.[9] In effect, both High Contracting Parties guarantee that their domestic entities will conclude appropriate accords. National enforcement procedures are, of course, available if the management of the organization concerned fails to obey its sovereign's command to contract.

Once the mutual promises become binding between enterprises of the states in question, the resultant rights and obligations are assertable on the plane of private law. Each party is expected, in accordance with the strictly policed principle of independent accountability to deal with the other at arm's length and in an economically adversary fashion. As a last resort, one enterprise may institute litigation against another in the permanently functioning foreign trade tribunals.

As we shall see hereafter, party autonomy is a recognized principle of Eastern contract law. Its ambit is, however, almost as limited in commercial relations among collective states as within them. Thus, foreign trade enterprises may not undertake to purchase or sell goods in excess of the treaty-made quotas, except with the special permission of their Ministry of Foreign Trade.[10] As in the domestic setting, they cannot decline purchases or sales within the governmentally established obligations. In short, no substantive terms deriving either from the bilateral trade agreement or from the coordinated national plans may be altered by party stipulation.

The enterprises' residual function of negotiating and defining the detailed conditions of their relationship is also narrowed down considerably, since it is in large part preempted by government-to-government arrangements of yet another kind. Within the orbit of Comecon, the General Conditions of Delivery, which carry the force of a multilateral treaty, prescribe in minute fashion the norms of applicable substantive law. The content of this instrument is, in effect, part of all commercial contracts for the exchange of goods between enterprises of member states. The bulk of the provisions may not be varied by the parties, except where deviation is deemed justifiable by special circumstances. In this manner, the legal aspects of all transactions are, for the most part, prescribed on a uniform basis. The scope of negotiated contractual terms is reduced accordingly.

Despite the underlying affinity between contract practice in trade within and among planned economies, the legal effects are not the same. Thus far, no supranational machinery has been created to give an act of bilateral state planning automatically binding force on the level of domestic law. Contracts between individual enterprises are certainly affected by the creation or modification of treaties dealing with the contractual subject matter. As we have seen in our discussion of the *force majeure* consequences of an act of state, they may even be affected by the unilateral act of internal planning of one of the signatory governments. But the precise effects of an intergovernmental agreement on preexisting contracts between corporations of the two countries concerned is as yet unclear in communist law and practice.

The dilemma is understandable. Two enterprises may either bind themselves freely or have a contract dictated to them by a higher organ of state. This organ operates within each government under the authority of national law. It is constitutionally delegated to impose legal obligations only within the confines of the nation's borders.

A treaty, or other form of interstate agreement, operates internationally; its force does not derive from any centralized planning authority. Should such an instrument be given self-executing force within the territory of each High Contracting Party? Should it be allowed to alter existing contracts and to operate retroactively upon previously created, vested rights? Or should it be limited to the establishment of obligations for the states alone, leaving to each state the responsibility in turn to impose corresponding legal duties pursuant to its internal constitutional authority?

However difficult the answers to these questions may be in treaty relations among countries with market economies, within the communist orbit they are even more elusive. Above all, the legal separation of the state from its operating enterprises bars the conclusion that commercial undertakings on the part of a socialist government are *ipso facto* binding upon its domestic corporations.

Issues arising from the interplay between a treaty instrument signed by two Comecon governments and a contract entered into by two of their operating enterprises have caused conceptual difficulties in several of the Eastern foreign trade tribunals. Available case reports shed light on both the nature of communist contract and the extent of governmental interference in civil-law relations.

In 1957, a Czechoslovakian buyer sued a Bulgarian seller for contractually stipulated penalties attributable to a failure to deliver required quantities of tobacco by end-1955. After mutual review of their commercial balances, the two governments had agreed, by special protocol signed in May 1956, that deliveries which fell short in 1955 were to be completed in the current year, within a time schedule to be agreed to by the trading enterprises of the two countries. The two disputants then contracted accordingly. The Sofia court rejected the Bulgarian defendant's argument that the extension of delivery periods eliminated the buyer's initial right to a penalty. It found that the intergovernmental protocol (and the second contract executed in virtue thereof) established, by means of a bilateral act of planning, new delivery terms as of January 1, 1956. To that point, the treaty of May 1956 was retroactive. But anterior delays were subject to the compensatory penalty clause contained in the original contract.[11]

Hungarian practice seems to go much further. The Budapest arbitration tribunal has ruled that if the nondelivered quantities are not added to the treaty quotas of the current year, no indemnities are due. This applied, moreover, to both short delivery and nondelivery. The contract is simply to be considered as retroactively canceled by subsequent intergovernmental agreement.[12]

A reading of the inconsistent maze of arbitration awards on this subject brings to mind the intellectual gymnastics practiced by precedent-bound common law judges in distinguishing one case from another. Thus, in 1959 and 1962 decisions, the Sofia court ruled that an intergovernmental agreement could not operate as a novation of an existing contract or as a prolongation of contractually agreed delivery periods. In the absence of a contrary provision in the contract, the state-to-state action relieved the defendant enterprise neither of the obligation to deliver on time, nor of responsibility for delay.[13]

This approach is now shared by the Budapest and Warsaw tribunals.[14] The latter has had a chance to express itself at the instance of an East German plaintiff, in a claim arising from nondelivery of a machine. The award confirmed the Polish defendant's liability for nonperformance despite the fact that the machine had not appeared in the list of goods to be exchanged under a protocol signed by the two governments.

The Soviet Foreign Trade Arbitration Commission faced the issue in a 1957 case. Essentially, it took the view that an intergovernmental agreement which canceled all future contractual relations between the national enterprises was dispositive of the plaintiff's claim. The then-existing contracts had been concluded pursuant to a previous intergovernmental agreement. As of the date of the new agreement, but not retroactively, all penalty clauses were suspended.[15]

2. *Between East and West*

Contractual arrangements take on an entirely different significance in trade between communist and noncommunist enterprises. Since Western governments will not compel a private firm to assume obligations against its will, Eastern states cannot hope to establish with them the rigid system of intergovernmental trade agreements which characterize relations within the socialist world. By necessity, communist enterprises are compelled to enter the international market place; to search for and select co-contractors; to negotiate terms and conditions; in short, to behave like private companies in the pursuit of individual transactions. As a consequence, the state-trading entities have more freedom to bargain over arrangements with Western firms than could ever be imagined in a wholly collectivist environment. The execution of trade planning goals is also more permissive than in other areas.

Within this context, contracts are more truly consensual and discretionary than in internal and intra-Comecon commerce. The content of bilateral trade agreements is also quite different. They do not attempt to establish a detailed blueprint for contractual relations, much less dictate the conditions of individual transactions. Usually, the quantities of goods to be traded are not strictly fixed. Quota guidelines and broad commodity lists are incorporated to indicate, but not to make obligatory, the level of desired exchanges.

The High Contracting Parties rarely, if ever, undertake to guarantee performance on the part of their domestic enterprises. Such an obligation would present little difficulty for the Eastern state, for it controls all local economic activity. In a capitalist system, an undertaking of this type, which might entail government coercion of individual firms, would be resisted as an intolerable interference with the most fundamental principles of private enterprise. Nor can the notion of compulsory contract and the far-reaching impact of treaties upon pre-existing contractual relations find the same application in this sphere. One may speculate as to whether market economies will some day adopt compulsory contract concepts for their government-owned instrumentalities. But in the case of private firms, it is clear that both Western law and treaty practice will respect the principle of party autonomy as basically inviolable.

Albeit reluctantly, the socialist states have learned to live with this fact of international business life. Bilateral commercial agreements with Western countries are no more than loose frameworks for the achievement of flexibly defined goals. Within the structure of these agreements, business entities are permitted to negotiate with one another freely and to contract more or less as they please.

The Comecon General Conditions have no application to East–West trade. Nor is there any multilateral substitute of binding norms. The communist states participate in several specialty conventions; they are also parties to a network of bilateral commercial agreements which contain an assortment of provisions affecting individuals and institutions engaged in trade. For the most part, however, the terms and conditions of contracts are hammered out in a process of hard bargaining.

Whether an agreement can be concluded or not depends to a large extent upon the willingness and ability of each side to understand the peculiar considerations which may influence the options of the other. Sharp differences in commercial, administrative and legal practice make it difficult to determine the terms of transactions which go beyond elementary purchase and sale. Because of the stronger economic position of communist trade monopolies, or simply lack of perception, unconventional terms and conventional terms with distorted impact are often accepted by private firms without protest.

Beginning in 1950, the Economic Commission for Europe began to develop contracts designed to eliminate the diversity of terms sought by vendors, particularly in the sale of plant and machinery. Item No. 188 in the Commission's series, which appeared in 1953 as "General Conditions for the Supply of Plant and Machinery for Export" did not, however, make allowance for the peculiarities of East–West trade. The special difficulties which enter into the drawing up of contracts between socialist and capitalist enterprises were referred to a Working Party on Contract Practices composed of experts from both systems. Item 574, produced in 1955, stipulated revised general conditions for the sale of plant and machinery in East–West trade. In addition, a series of standard forms applicable to various categories of goods were published by the Commission with a view to making available to traders, on an optional basis, a uniform set of contract rules and practices.

A comparison of Item 188, designed for trade in general, and Item 574, specifically directed at East–West trade, reveals few significant differences. The clauses defining *force majeure* and providing for the arbitration of disputes diverge considerably. But beyond these two areas (and to some extent even within them), the Commission either unwittingly or deliberately glossed over the broad range of problems which arise in commerce between states with fundamentally dissimilar economic and commercial structures.

The E.C.E. conditions have obtained little acceptance in East–West trade. In the absence of effective international regulation, each party prefers its own standard form of contract. Soviet enterprises dealing in capital goods use at least two different texts. If they are sellers, the clauses providing for inspection are meager. If they are buyers, the inspection provisions are far more specific.

The more powerful Western firms likewise attempt to hold on to the uniform pattern of their own agreements. Even if they succeed, such attempts are often misguided. Contractual forms adapted to the Western environment cannot be expected to operate satisfactorily within the alien economic and legal climate of Eastern commerce. American firms, whose standard contracts are markedly parochial and inordinately detailed, have experienced particular difficulty in having them accepted.

On the Eastern side we find a marked preference for exhaustively drawn agreements. Considering the divergence between the legal systems of the parties to an East–West contract, amplitude of drafting should be considered a welcome technique. The more explicit and self-regulatory the terms, the more limited are the chances of an unacceptable construction by adjudicators required to defer to the law of one or the other country in question. While the affinity in this area is greater with common law practice than with the more skeletal continental approach, its causes are quite different. If draftsmen of the Anglo-American tradition and of the communist countries both seek to anticipate a maximum of foreseeable contingencies, it is because the former are breach-oriented, whereas the latter are performance-oriented. Representatives of Eastern trade organizations expect literal compliance with the terms of the documents they execute. When the fulfillment of a prescribed plan is at stake, flexibility in performance cannot be a virtue. The contract is construed and applied in a strict manner, often in disregard of whether the immediate result favors the state enterprise or the foreign firm.

Under the influence of a planned economic environment, certain provisions are sought by the Eastern party as a matter of need and habit. Thus, planning entails a high degree of predictability as to the co-contractors' performance. Above all, shipments must be delivered in accordance with exact specifications and time schedules. Clauses providing for inspection of specially manufactured capital goods at the place and in the course of production are therefore a usual feature of Soviet orders. Smaller east European buyers who do not maintain permanent technical staffs in the major industrial countries of the West content themselves with the usual contractual warranties.

Since prompt delivery is a prime consideration, Eastern purchasers typically favor hefty penalties for delays. The effect sought is deterrence rather than liquidated damages, which may indeed be incalculable if untimely shipment impedes performance of an integrated segment of the national economic plan. Penalties usually take the form of a price rebate in proportion to the length of the delay, assuming a recognized *force majeure* has not intervened. Another form of inducement to prompt delivery is provision for the premature opening of letters of credit made payable upon the condition of delivery within a designated period.

Of special importance in the framing of East–West contracts are *force majeure* definitions, arbitration submissions and choice-of-law elections.

As we have seen, *force majeure* clauses conceived and interpreted in traditional terms are inadequate, for they tend to excuse nonperformance under orders of the government with which the operating enterprise is organically and administratively linked. While the willingness of Eastern state instrumentalities to waive their sovereign status is highly reassuring, the permanent arbitration tribunals of communist countries reveal structural flaws which overshadow their adjudication processes. Furthermore, the selection of noncommunist law, although permitted, is narrowly circumscribed by overriding rules of the Eastern forum. All of these anomalies require specific rectification at the point of negotiation and drafting.

D. The Limits of Contractual Freedom

The latitude communist negotiators enjoy in framing transactions with Western parties is highly surprising to the observer of authoritarian societies. This does not, however, mean that state enterprises are absolutely exempt from local law in opting for particular terms. Certain provisions of domestic legislation imperatively apply to all foreign trade dealings, whether intra-East or East–West, and cannot be displaced by an autonomous exercise of will. Any attempt to vary such provisions, whether by a contractual choice of foreign law or by an attempt to create a totally self-regulating agreement, may turn out to be fatal in subsequent adjudication, regardless of the forum which hears the dispute. The controlling question is whether the selected law or inserted terms must give way to an undisplaceable rule which emanates from the national legal system of the state trading party.

In the internal economic life of a socialist country, party autonomy is severely restricted by the dictates of the national plan; both the parties and the basic contractual terms may be determined from above. If freedom of will is given ample play in external commerce, it is nonetheless also circumscribed by provisions which the state monopolies consider essential to the regulation of their activities. The law-making character of the export-import plan, the capacity of operating corporations, the authority of foreign trade representatives and the formalities governing the execution of contracts are all territory upon which contracting parties, foreign law, international custom and treaty instruments are forbidden to encroach. Allegedly this prohibition extends to litigation at home as well as abroad. Widespread communist adherence to standard contracts prepared by international trade associations, to unified law systems and to conventions cannot be expected unless such provisions are somehow specifically accommodated.

Beyond this ambit, the parties are, at least ostensibly, as independent of domestic law as in the West. Both the state trader and the private merchant are left free to establish the regime they desire for their bargain. The Bulgarian Code of Obligations and Contracts contains an example of this legislatively established freedom.[16] It is paralleled by comparable dispositions in most of the other countries of eastern Europe as well as in the U.S.S.R. itself.

Totalitarian sovereigns are said to frown upon party autonomy in contractual relations. Although accurately descriptive of Soviet jurisprudence in the militant postrevolutionary era (and of the legal systems of fascist Italy and Germany), this commonly held view is no longer valid in reference to communist contract law. Invisible, extralegal methods of controlling business activity are more readily available within the absolutist structure of a wholly planned economy. Today, freedom in the choice of contract terms can be held out as a fundamental principle of commercial intercourse.[17]

In trade with the capitalist world, Eastern parties are allowed even greater freedom. They enjoy virtually unlimited discretion not only to stipulate the terms of their transaction but also to select the forum in which controversies will be litigated and the system of law under which they will be resolved. Although highly significant from a legal point of view, this unexpected display of sovereign liberality must not be taken at face value. In fact, there is little renunciation of authority, and the appearance of laissez-faire procures considerable advantages for the state.

On closer analysis we discover that contractual autonomy affords maximum scope of expression for the state monopoly's strong bargaining power in commercial dealings with individual, generally less powerful foreign firms. The "planned will of socialist society" has ways and means of invading East–West contractual relations through a variety of administrative channels peculiarly available to a collectivist government.

The benefits flowing from the superior negotiating position of state enterprises must not be overstated. Similar inequalities arise in transactions between two capitalist concerns, one of which is economically more potent and able to dictate terms. An important point of difference, however, is that an Eastern state entity enjoys total immunity from internal competition. Soiuznefteksport, although superficially comparable to Standard Oil of New Jersey, is distinctive in that it does *all* of Russia's international petroleum business, is not subject to any antitrust law, and can automatically (and without special lobbying) rely on the full backing and resources of its government. Given these attributes it can more readily make submission to Soviet law and arbitration a condition precedent to contracting. A foreign firm's rejection of such proferred terms may lead to a rupture of negotiations and to its consequent exclusion from the national market. Soiuznefteksport's bargaining posture is further enhanced by the legislative and treaty-making power of the state, which constantly seeks to provide the most favorable conditions for the exercise of its trading functions with the outside world.

Like all business concerns, a state enterprise should not, of course, be denied the privilege of opting for a forum, a law or a term it considers suitable for its purposes. The danger resides in the fact that the doctrine of party autonomy may become a vehicle for near-constraint when applied as part of organized government policy.

On the operational level, the communist entity probably enjoys much less latitude of choice than its Western trading partner. The relative freedom reflected in the law is more apparent than real. What is given by the state with one hand is, as it were, taken away with the other. Effective supervision over contractual content is exercised at the point the trading entity's business intentions are created. The unitary nature of the commercial structure affords the Ministry of Foreign Trade ample opportunity to require its licensed trading instrumentalities to forego submissions to alien forums, alien laws and other "unapproved" clauses. The party's formal autonomy to express contractual intentions is thus largely negated by the lack of a will independent of the state's.

While these underlying considerations must be constantly borne in mind, it is worth while to reiterate that party autonomy exists as a broad legal principle in pertinent legislation, treaty provisions and judicial decisions. Once properly concluded, the contract is recognized as the primary source of the parties' rights and duties. It is not the sole source, however. An attempt at total self-regulation is deemed null and void. Those who are privy to a transaction cannot create for themselves a binding relationship which is to operate in a vacuum insulated from all national law. Each contract must derive its validity from, and be subject to, some legal system, whether local or foreign. As a matter of strict law, the limits of contractual freedom are circumscribed by those rules of communist domestic law which are considered imperative and which are analyzed in greater detail hereafter.

16

CREATION AND PERFORMANCE OF AGREEMENTS

The elements of contract formation and the rules governing purchase and sale play a comparable role wherever and however commerce is conducted. The relevant provisions of Eastern law examined in the following pages reveal nothing which need alarm merchants accustomed to operating under the familiar conditions of a market system. But a preliminary caveat is in order: entirely novel considerations and differences of emphasis intrude into the picture here and there, owing to the divergence of economic conceptions. The incongruous incidents of property and ownership are an example in point. All goods which enter the stream of commerce belong to the state. They can be alienated only in accordance with strictly prescribed government plans and procedures.

Among the most important aspects of contract in any legal system are the prerequisites of formality, offer and acceptance, passage of title, location of risk, relief from the consequences of default and foreclosure of claims due to prescription. To place in proper perspective the characteristic communist treatment of these questions, we must bear in mind that significant discrepancies exist among the major legal systems of the West as well. Our approach must therefore be broadly comparative.

A. Requirements of Form and Execution

Agreements concluded by handshake or telephone, or which are confirmed by telex or cable, are always risky. In dealings with communist enterprises they are in danger of being declared unenforceable, even invalid.

If the parties intend to reduce their contract to writing but fail to do so, the bargain they have struck will not be legally binding; this is a fairly universal rule. Certain legal systems, Eastern and Western, go so far as to require a signed instrument regardless of party intent. In the U.S.S.R., for example, absence of an integrated writing, and failure to comply with other statutory procedures for execution, will render a contract entirely void. In this respect, Soviet law exceeds in severity even the old English Statute of Frauds, which retains modified application in the sale of goods.

United States jurisdictions likewise have always maintained extensive contractual formality requirements. With the widespread adoption of the Uniform Commercial Code, these requirements have been simplified and standardized. Under Article 2-201, a contract for the sale of goods priced at $500 or more must be evidenced by a document featuring the signature of the party to be charged.

The markedly strict American and Soviet positions may be contrasted with the more liberal views of continental Europe, where sales contracts generally need not be in writing. France, for example, will enforce oral agreements between professional merchants. As between nonmerchants, "a commencement of proof in writing" must be tendered to the court in the case of obligations exceeding 50 francs, before other evidence of the oral contract will be admitted.[1]

Eastern practice is not entirely uniform. In 1961 an East German law prescribed a written form for contracts involving the sale of goods or services. Rumanian and Bulgarian laws set forth similar provisions for foreign trade agreements. On the other hand, the Czechoslovakian Law on Economic Relations Between Socialist Organizations, as well as the special Law on Foreign Commerce, and the Hungarian Civil Code of 1959 do not prescribe any particular form. While it is difficult to discern the precise Chinese rule, it seems that in practice the state enterprises do not always insist on written contracts. Italian experience suggests that where deliveries are made on a regular basis for a number of years, orders may be safely placed by telephone; occasionally such orders are filled even before a sales confirmation has been dispatched to the Italian buyer.[2]

Looking at the minutiae of Soviet law, we find that observance of formalities in domestic contractual relations is a fundamental rule. The provisions of earlier republican codes were, in fact, so elaborate and rigid that the courts found it necessary to moderate their effect.[3] The present codes have not significantly deviated from these statutory standards. With few exceptions, domestic transactions among public organizations or private citizens involving more than 100 rubles must be reduced to writing and signed by the parties. Failure to comply with this requirement destroys the right to furnish oral evidence of the agreement, with the frequent consequence that the parties are obligated to return everything received under the purported understanding.[4]

Since the policy behind these rules is to enable the state to supervise contractual arrangements, particularly private ones, noncompliance may induce a Soviet court to vitiate the contract even if invalidity is not argued by either of the parties. In America, by comparison, the purpose underlying the statute of frauds requirement of the Uniform Commercial Code is to facilitate in evidentiary terms the determination of whether a contract exists. If a party admits the existence of a contract in his pleadings or testimony, if he has signed any writing which refers to its existence or if he has agreed in advance to waive the defense of the statute of frauds, enforcement may be obtained against him even though the required document was never executed.

In their application to international agreements, Soviet formality rules are even more stringent. A special statute passed in 1930 has compulsorily prescribed a form and manner of signing contracts to which a foreign firm or individual is a party. It is, furthermore, specifically declared in the current Russian Civil Code that avoidance of this procedure invalidates the transaction.[5]

The monopoly's policy to have all foreign trade contracts properly recorded has led the Moscow tribunal, in a case involving a French corporation and a Soviet export-import entity, to the unusual view that Soviet formality requirement apply even if the transaction is governed by the law of another country. This view has now been codified: "The form of foreign trade transactions carried out by Soviet organizations and the procedure for signing them, regardless of the place where these transactions are carried out, are determined by the U.S.S.R. legislation."[6] Moreover, according to Soviet writers and to several intergovernmental commercial agreements, the prescribed formality rules are entitled to overriding effect in foreign no less than local courts whenever a Soviet party is involved. Some of the other communist countries, Poland for example, do not go to the same lengths, as will be seen from the detailed discussion of this subject in a conflict-of-law context.[7]

The special Soviet "statute of frauds" requires international agreements to be signed by two persons. Contracts, bills of exchange, all types of monetary obligations and powers of attorney made by trade delegations must be signed by the chief trade representative, his deputy, or the head of a division. In addition, they must be signed by a trade delegation member whose name appears on a special list approved by the Ministry of Foreign Trade and submitted to the Council of Ministers of the U.S.S.R. This list is transmitted to the host government and published in the appropriate legal gazette. Successive amendments have authorized trade representatives alone to sign contracts involving not more than 40,000 rubles. A single signature committing in excess of this amount requires the special approval of the Ministry of Foreign Trade.

International contracts entered into by export-import corporations in Moscow require the signature of two persons, one of whom must be the president or his deputy and the other an individual acting under the president's power of attorney. Bills of exchange and other financial obligations issued in Moscow must bear the signature of the president or his deputy, as well as that of the chief accountant. Outside Moscow, whether in the U.S.S.R. or abroad, the personal signature of the president is indispensable. The names of all authorized signatories, and those whose authorization has been revoked, are published in *Vneshniaia Torgovlia,* the official monthly periodical of the Ministry of Foreign Trade.

The Soviet foreign trade tribunal has applied these provisions to block the proof of orally settled terms. Thus, a French firm sued for transportation costs in excess of those stipulated in the original contract, relying upon an oral promise of the defendant combine's representative in France.[8] The promise to reimburse the costs, which were incurred as a result of the devaluation of the franc, was held not to be binding for lack of compliance with the statutory signature requirements. It should be added that the statute caught only the alleged *modification,* not the properly executed underlying contract.

In a case brought by a Dutch firm, the tribunal rejected the Soviet party's argument that a duly signed contract should be read in the light of unrecorded negotiations which took place prior to signature.[9] The documents were held, on their face, to constitute the complete transaction. This rationale in effect adopts the English "parole evidence rule," which excludes antecedent or contemporaneous evidence tendered to supplement, vary or contradict the content of a signed contract.

Chinese foreign trade enterprises are reported to stipulate that all prior correspondence, agreements and other documents "shall be null and void from the date of the present contract entering into force." It is not uncommon, however, to find in addition a reference to pre-execution discussions, as follows: "This contract is concluded on the basis of the negotiations held between both parties at the Canton fair (August 1966)." [10] Since the judgments of the Chinese Foreign Trade Arbitration Committee are not published, one cannot know what effect, if any, is given to such a provision. While extracontractual proof may be admitted to explain an ambiguity in written terms, it will not, in all likelihood, be allowed to modify an explicit stipulation in China any more than in the U.S.S.R.

Although the Soviet arbitral jurisdiction refuses to recognize oral agreements in foreign trade, it gives effect to written contracts which have not been reduced to a single document. On a number of occasions the applicable statutes have been held to be satisfied if offer and acceptance were expedited by letter or even cable. A 1940 decision upheld a Dutch claimant's contention that a properly signed exchange of letters was sufficient.[11] In another case, there had been only an exchange of telegrams. The telegraph agent, in transmitting the French party's offer to buy, had erroneously indicated a greater quantity of goods. The Soviet combine's telegraphic acceptance did not reiterate the terms of the offer. A binding contract was nonetheless found to exist. The risk of distortion in the cabled offer was held to be that of the sender.[12]

Current law, expressed in Section 161 of the 1964 Russian Code, provides that the requirement of a writing may be satisfied "either by drawing up a single document signed by the parties, or by way of an exchange of letters, telegrams, telephoned telegrams, etc., signed by the party sending the same." The Comecon Conditions parallel Soviet law and practice in their requirement of writing. Article 1 provides:

> The order and the offer as well as confirmation of the order or acceptance of the offer shall be valid on condition that they are in written form. Written form shall be understood to include telegrams and communications by teletype. Offers, additions to and changes in the contract shall be accomplished by the same procedure.

By contrast, major multilateral instruments developed in the West reject strict formalism as a burden upon international dealings. Thus, the Hague

Draft of a Uniform Law on Formation of Contracts for the International Sale of Goods of 1964 states in Article 3 that an offer or acceptance need not be evidenced in writing or in any other form and that oral testimony by witnesses is an admissible element of proof. The same position is taken by the Rome Draft of the Uniform Law on Formation of Contracts of 1959.

Despite the increased flexibility which is today afforded by Eastern law, it is unsafe to assume that a binding contract is in existence unless an appropriate writing has been duly executed. Both the original agreement and the subsequent variation of its terms should be fully documented. If changes, made face to face or by telephone, result in additional costs for the Western firm, there is likely to be no recovery in the absence of subsequent confirmation by amendatory protocol, letter, telex or cable. Most important, an oral agreement to arbitrate contractual disputes will likewise prove to be inoperative, leaving the private firm to seek its remedy in a communist People's Court. By the same token, an award entered in a Western country pursuant to an unrecorded arbitral submission may be denied enforcement in the country of the unsuccessful state trader.

B. Elements of a Binding Commitment

Observance of statutory formalities may be the *sine qua non* of enforceability, but the signed writing must also manifest a meeting of the minds on relevant points before a contract can be deemed to exist at all. The basic principles of contract formation are relatively uniform and fairly conventional throughout the East: A bargain becomes binding when agreement is reached by the parties on all essential terms and consent is inferred from offer and acceptance. To be effective, the acceptance of the offer must be unconditional and timely. Within this classical framework, factual complications have arisen in all legal systems, and they have been resolved in a variety of ways. The most noteworthy problems have revolved around the revocability of an offer and the requisite language and communication of acceptance. Since a private Western firm may see its contract tested under rules prescribed by the national law of the Eastern trading partner, it is useful to compare these rules with general international practice.

It has long been the law in Anglo-American jurisdictions that a gratuitous offer may be revoked at any time before acceptance by merely communicating the revocation to the offeree. Moreover, a promise to keep the offer open for a specific time does not prevent effective prior revocation as long as no value was received in return for the promise. This follows from the common law doctrine of consideration. An exception introduced in the United States by the Uniform Commercial Code (U.C.C.) provides that where a merchant promises to hold his written offer open, that offer is nonrevocable for the period stated or, if no time is stated, for a reasonable period (Sec. 2-205). To that extent the requirement of consideration on the part of the offeree has been discarded.

Civil law goes much further. In France, for example, an offer has always been treated as firm, even in the absence of an explicit assurance by the offeror; before it may be withdrawn he is required to give reasonable notice of his intention to do so. For an offer to be revocable without prior warning, the right has to be expressly reserved. A promise to keep the offer open for a stated period remains effective for the duration of that period.[13]

Modern continental thought stands squarely on this civil law tradition. The so-called 1958 Rome Draft provides that an offer which has arrived may not be revoked unless the offeror has reserved to himself the right of revocation. In 1964 the Hague Convention retreated somewhat from this position by stating that an offer "can be revoked unless the revocation is not made in good faith or in conformity with fair dealing or unless the offer states a fixed time for acceptance or otherwise indicates that it is firm or irrevocable."[14] As in the U.C.C., revocability is presumed, unless irrevocability is clearly indicated. But the exercise of the right of revocation is conditional upon highly subjective tests of "good faith" and "fair dealing," in the spirit of the civilist approach.

In substance, the communist position runs parallel to the Rome Draft. Soviet civil law follows the notion of the "firm offer." There can be no revocation during the period allowed for acceptance. A written offer which indicates a deadline may be accepted prior to its expiration; otherwise it may be accepted within the "normally necessary time limit." Only in the case of an oral offer not specifying a time factor must acceptance be immediate. The Comecon Conditions, although mute as to revocability, allow 30 days for the receipt of an acceptance, after which the offer may be withdrawn. Beyond this, reference must be made to the national law of the seller's country.[15]

Most legal systems require that an acceptance be unconditional and avoid injecting new or different terms into the offer. A conditional acceptance is typically regarded as a rejection of the original offer and, at the same time, as a new proposal to contract. The point is succinctly formulated in Article 6 of the Rome Draft: "Any acceptance containing additions, limitations or other modifications shall be considered as a rejection of the offer and a new offer." The Hague instrument takes the same traditional position on the central issue. But it goes on, in terms reminiscent of the U.C.C., to provide that "a reply to an offer which purports to be an acceptance but which contains additional or different terms which do not materially alter the terms of the offer shall constitute an acceptance unless the offeror promptly objects to the discrepancy; if he does not so object, the terms of the contract shall be the terms of the offer with the modifications contained in the acceptance."[16]

Soviet law once again follows the Rome formula: "An answer agreeing to make a contract on different terms from those proposed in the offer is treated as a refusal of the offer and at the same time as constituting a counter-offer." [17] Similar provisions may be found in the codes of other Eastern countries.

While there is general agreement that acceptance must be timely, the definition of timeliness differs from one legal system to another. A classical example is the case where an acceptance and a revocation cross in the mails. If the former is effective, the latter can no longer be operative; contractual rights and obligations immediately spring into being. The common law countries have selected the moment of dispatch as the test for effective acceptance. According to this so-called "mailbox" theory, the contract is formed at the moment the unconditional, timely acceptance leaves the control of the offeree. For the most part, French law adopts the same approach under its "expedition theory."

The "reception theory" dominates in West Germany, Austria, Norway, Sweden and Denmark and works on the principle that acceptance is effective upon its receipt by the offeror, even though it may not have come to his attention. A variation, known as the "knowledge" or "information" theory, which is common in Italy, Spain, Portugal and Belgium, goes one step further. The offeror must not only receive the acceptance but must also have actual knowledge of it before an effective contract will be deemed to exist.

The 1964 Hague Draft favors "reception." Acceptance "consists of a declaration communicated . . . to the offeror," that is to say, "delivered at the address of the person to whom the communication is directed." However, in partial alleviation of the offeree's burden, a late communication is deemed effective if in the normal course of the selected mode of transmission it would have been received in due time. The offeror may avoid the acceptance in such a case only by giving notice that he regards his offer as lapsed.[18]

Eastern law prefers the Hague "reception" approach. A case decided by the Moscow foreign trade tribunal in 1956 involved a Soviet offer by correspondence to purchase equipment from a Hungarian export entity. The reply contained alterations to which the Soviet party agreed. Finding that the Hungarian acceptance was, in effect, a counteroffer, the arbitrators held that the contract came into being upon receipt of the subsequent Soviet acceptance at the office of the export enterprise in Budapest.[19] None of the communist states follows the common law "dispatch" rule. Bulgaria and Rumania have, on occasion, been found to require actual knowledge by the offeror that his offer has been accepted. This is, however, no more than a variant of the basic reception doctrine.

In addition to ascertaining when an agreement is concluded, the theories of acceptance are often used to determine where it is concluded. Under sections 162 and 163 of the Soviet Code, a contract is deemed made at the place where the acceptance is received. The same rule applies in East Germany, consistent with traditional local practice.

The *locus* of a contract is of great importance because under many legal systems it determines the national law under which the rights and obligations will be defined. Thus, pursuant to the reception theory, if a Soviet enterprise accepts by mail the offer of an American-based firm, the transaction is deemed concluded in the United States. Any subsequent dispute referred to a Soviet forum would be resolved in accordance with the law of the particular American state. This very analysis has led to the application of Hungarian law as the proper law of the contract in the case just described.

All things considered, the Soviet and other Eastern positions with regard to contractual offer and acceptance are strikingly orthodox. They certainly do not appear to depart from the common denominator of world practice more than one Western position diverges from another.

C. Risk of Loss and Damage

The subject of responsibility for accidental loss, destruction or deterioration of goods, which inheres in every sales contract, is treated as extensively in Eastern as in Western legislation. At the outset, it is useful to point out that communist tribunals take a highly practical, somewhat Solomonic approach to the allocation of risk, fault and consequential liability. This is illustrated by two cases, one decided in 1964 by the Moscow Maritime Arbitration Commission, the other in 1967 by the Prague Arbitration Court. The Czechoslovak case involved an Italian supplier of frozen fish and a local import organization. The contract provided for inspection at the port of Hamburg. The tribunal held, *inter alia,* that the buyer could only claim damages in respect of damage which was notified to the seller promptly upon examination of the goods. In addition, the buyer was under a legal duty to minimize the seller's losses. Because a portion of the shipment was transported as far as East Moravia and Slovakia in inadequately refrigerated railway cars instead of being treated closer to the point of origin, Bohemia, for example, damage entitlement was reduced by 30 percent.

In the Soviet case the baby was cut in two. Rice belonging to a Czech shipper was damaged on board a vessel of the Black Sea Shipping Line. The Commission held that since the loss could have been caused by the carrier's negligence or by an independent cause or by both contributorily, and since it was impossible to ascertain the precise origin or degrees of fault, liability should be borne equally by both parties.[20] It is interesting to note that in order to establish an actionable breach, Article 222 of the Russian Civil Code requires not only a failure to perform, but also proof of fault, grounded either in wilfullness or in negligence.

In France, risk in the strictly legal sense passes with the transfer of ownership. As a general rule, the operative event is the formation of the contract, notwithstanding the fact that delivery is to take place later. This is the rule *res perit domino*. It applies only where the goods have been ascertained, the price agreed upon and the parties have not otherwise provided.

The common law, as codified in the English Sale of Goods Act, is in basic accord with French law. Unless the contrary is stipulated, risk follows title. A different solution has been adopted by the Uniform Commercial Code. Under Section 2–509 risk passes with delivery. The concepts of title and property, which produced troublesome anomalies under prior law, have been discarded. German, Austrian and Scandinavian rules likewise relate risk to delivery. In the international sphere, the Hague Draft conspicuously omits reference to transfer of ownership in provisions dealing with risk. Article 970 states quite simply that "risk shall pass to the buyer when delivery of the goods is effected in accordance with the provisions of the contract and the present law."

The Comecon Conditions, which cannot be varied by the parties, contain interesting innovations. Detailed provisions determine such questions as the point of time at which ownership is transferred, responsibility for loss or damage and costs for which vendors or purchasers are responsible. All of these factors are coupled with effective possession or control. The decisive test is delivery and, more specifically, the means by which delivery is accomplished. If a railway or motor carrier is chosen (except when the goods are shipped by the buyer's means of transportation), title and risk pass with the crossing of the state boundary. In cases of delivery by water, the rules vary in accordance with whether the contract of sale is of the f.o.b., c.i.f. or c. & f. variety; as a rule, the crucial moment is when the goods cross the ship's rail at the port of loading. Where delivery is by air, the elements of title and risk shift contemporaneously with the placement of the goods in the hands of the air carrier in the seller's country. Finally, if the goods are to be sent by mail, receipt by the post office of the seller's country is determinative.

Soviet domestic law also links the transfer of risk to the transfer of ownership. Both pass with delivery. The parties are, however, left free to stipulate alternative arrangements. A concept of fault is introduced in the event of delay, the responsibility being the seller's if he delayed the delivery, the buyer's if he delayed receipt of delivery. The Russian Code defines delivery in a more or less conventional manner as the handing over of the goods to the buyer, a carrier or the mails.[21] Delivery of shipping documents is tantamount to delivery of the goods themselves.

The Eastern method of allocating risk in the purchase and sale of goods, although basically traditionalist, is nonetheless influenced by distinctive factors. These factors emanate in large measure from the different economic conditions which prevail in West and East. In a free enterprise system, the ever-present possibility of a buyer going bankrupt impels the seller to withhold title as a means of security pending full payment of the purchase price. For the same reason, it is clearly in the seller's interest to transfer the risk of loss at the earliest practicable moment. To satisfy both aims, passage of risk and passage of title have historically been treated in most places as two separate and distinct matters.

In a collectivist economic system, bankruptcy risks are minimal, perhaps nonexistent. The problem of securing collateral is therefore also largely theoretical, at least in strictly domestic trade or in commerce among socialist countries. Settlement of the purchase price is morally if not legally guaranteed by the buyer's state. For these reasons, the contemporaneous transfer of risk and ownership has been found to be both the simplest and most suitable solution.

D. Breach of Contract

The most striking contrasts between traditional and communist conceptions in the law of sales are found in the area of breaches and remedies.

Characteristically, Western law permits the buyer to reject tendered goods if they fail materially to conform to the requirements of the contract, either owing to delayed delivery or to qualitative or quantitative shortcomings. In a planned economic setting far more often than in a market environment, the state-operated buyer is prone to accept late or nonconforming deliveries, if the merchandise can be utilized in its existing condition or if the defect can be removed. An abatement in price or a grant of special compensation is a frequent by-product of such compromise. The fundamental approach to breaches of this type, in practice as well as in law, is preventive rather than remedial. The right to rescind the contract is exceptionally provided and sparingly employed.

Specific performance is emphasized as the basic remedy in the relevant Comecon Conditions. The rationale behind this departure from universal practice becomes apparent when one recalls that in a collectivist economy it is not the individual situations of the contractants which are primarily at stake, but rather the overriding national interests of the two trading states. Communist enterprises interacting with one another are not supposed to elevate profits above all else in the conclusion and execution of contracts. Their primordial function is to help insure the planned development of the economy as a whole. Failure to accept merchandise because of technical but remediable shortcomings is looked upon as an abusive and harmful exercise of rights. Its consequences tend to disrupt government-programmed production and distribution all along the line. Under Article 70 of the General Conditions of 1968, contract cancellation due to the defective quality of goods sold is envisioned only in the narrow case of a term agreement, where the seller has failed, within the stipulated period of delivery, to remove the defect or to replace the merchandise.

Rejection and damages are therefore relegated to secondary status as extraordinary forms of relief. They are reserved for cases where delay in delivery is "excessive" (four months for most goods) or where it defeats the underlying object of the contract, *e.g.*, the supply of seeds after the planting season. In these situations damages are allowed, since no purpose would be served by requiring specific performance after the need for the merchandise has passed.

Closely related reasons of public policy explain the frequency and importance of contractually stipulated penalties. While Western legal systems consistently frown upon all punitive forms of compensation, the Comecon Conditions and the national laws of the several communist countries both uphold and prescribe them. It is again the state's and not the individual parties' interest which is to be served by such inducements to prompt and complete delivery. Even in contracts with private Western firms, state enterprises seek to stipulate for ample penalties and, eventually, to collect them. It is noteworthy that the resultant proceeds go into the treasury of the enterprise and may affect the year-end bonuses awarded to its management.

Penalty clauses designed to prevent or compensate the imperfect supply of goods and services (in terms of time, quality, or quantity), or unscheduled delays in construction projects, are strictly enforced by Eastern courts and arbitration tribunals. Disputes on this issue between communist enterprises have most frequently arisen in connection with contracts which are to be executed in stages. That such clauses go beyond what might properly be regarded as liquidated damages, indeed openly describe the liability as a "fine," evokes no concern whatsoever either among adjudicators or among negotiators.[22] In sharp contrast to conventional practice, Eastern foreign trade tribunals lean over backwards to save such punitive provisions from invalidity. For example, section 64 of the 1958 Comecon Conditions required arbitral penalty claims to be preceded by an explicit request for payment made within three months after the penalties had ceased to run. In a series of litigations initiated in 1965, the Rumanian tribunal ruled that failure to make a timely request did not destroy the right to collect as long as the arbitral claim was filed within the prescribed three-month period.[23]

Whether Western courts could be persuaded to emulate this break with tradition remains to be seen. In our opinion such a shift in attitude would be justified, given the uncommonly serious problems which delayed performance may entail on the Eastern side. For the time being, a precondition to enforcement is a contractual term unambiguously formulated and governed by the favorably disposed domestic law of the state-trading party.

E. Periods of Limitation

In communist legal systems, statutes of limitation are treated as falling within the realm of substantive rather than procedural law. Consequently, the forum's limitation provisions apply to claims upon a foreign trade transaction only if the contract is governed by local law. This is borne out by the practice of the Eastern arbitration tribunals.

In a 1950 decision, the Moscow Commission applied the Soviet statute of limitations to a contract executed locally, rejecting the Swiss defendant's plea that the action was banned by Swiss prescriptions. The corollary to this rule also holds; foreign limitations have been applied to contracts concluded abroad. The same tribunal has in the past deferred to the East German, Bulgarian and Hungarian statutes on this express ground.[24] Similarly, the Warsaw tribunal has applied the Yugoslav period of limitation where the contract was concluded on Yugoslav territory. This principle is confirmed by legislation. The Polish Code on Private International Law provides that limitation periods are ascertained by reference to the proper law of the contract.[25] Soviet maritime law had long ago stipulated that the issue is governed by the same legal system as the substance of the disputed contractual relationship.[26]

Eastern prescription periods are unusually short by Western standards. The Russian Code allows three years for the commencement of civil actions. This is shortened to one year for disputes between local economic organizations, and to a mere six months in suits involving liquidated damage claims, defective goods, incomplete delivery or defective quality. An eminent Soviet jurist offers assurances that the full three-year period would be applied as the more appropriate term in international disputes, the six-month period extending to foreign parties only in respect of claims predicated on defective goods.[27]

Promptness in the enforcement of economic obligations is considered essential for the effective operation of the planned economy and the vindication of the underlying state interest in all commercial transaction, local and foreign. The importance of short limitation provisions is underlined by the fact that, where Soviet law governs as the proper law of the contract, the prescribed periods are considered to be mandatory and unalterable. Judicial and arbitral tribunals are required to apply them *ex officio,* and regardless of any party stipulation or plea to the contrary.[28]

Because of the overriding policy reasons involved, a foreign statute exceeding, or at least exceeding substantially, the three-year period, will be inoperative, even though it may be part of the proper law of the contract. This is illustrated by a decision of the Supreme Court of the Republic of Azerbaidzhan. The foreign plaintiff sued in the People's Court of the city of Baku upon a contract concluded with representatives of a workers' cooperative of Azerbaidzhan. The contract was made in Turkey and Turkish law was held to govern its substance by virtue of Article 7 of the Code of Civil Procedure then in force. The Supreme Court upheld the first instance, ruling that the local three-year statute had barred the claim and that the Turkish ten-year period was inapplicable. The grounds given by the lower court throw light on the entire communist approach to issues of limitations:

> It is impossible to draw the conclusion that the question of limitations is a question of the Civil Code. Public interests are inherent in the question of limitations. For their protection, the short three-year period has been decreed. This short period is due to the special conditions of the U.S.S.R.'s economy with its fast rate of development and the constantly changing marketing conditions. If legal enforcement were to take place many years after a given right came into existence, the application of a longer period of limitations could result in the right not being realized in conformity with its social and economic purpose —a result which would contradict Article 1 of the Civil Code.[29]

The subsequent fate of Article 1 in Soviet domestic interpretation has now deprived this decision of some of its force. Originally viewed "as a commanding height, as a rule which defines the character of Soviet civil law," it had gradually fallen into disuse. A part of its substance has nonetheless been carried forward in Article 5 of the 1964 Code.

The majority of decisions by the two Soviet Arbitration Commissions on the issue of limitations concerned contracts concluded in Russia; hence they did not touch upon choice of law aspects.[30] The Soviet period was applied as part of the over-all governing law. Since in principle limitation questions are referable to the proper law, where the discrepancy between two competing periods is not very great, the Commissions can be expected to recognize the applicable alien statute. There is, of course, nothing to dictate rejection of a non-Soviet limitation period shorter than that established by the Russian Civil Code.[31]

In intra-Comecon relations the periods of limitation are relatively short. Currently, the basic limit for the commencement of proceedings is two years from the time the cause of action accrues. But claims arising from disputes as to quality, quantity and the payment of penalties must be brought to arbitration within one year and the demand for redress from the party at fault is required to be made within an even shorter interval.[32] These provisions, like the limitations established by national law, carry mandatory force.

It should be noted that the periods imposed by the Comecon Conditions cover only those situations in which the buyer is the aggrieved party. No consideration has been given to the aggrieved seller. For communist countries, it is the delivery of goods in the manner agreed upon, rather than payment of the purchase price, that has paramount importance, since it is there that the greatest danger of economic disruption exists.

At present, the limitation provisions operative in East–West trade are almost as diverse as the legal systems in play. The conflict of prescriptive rules has only been resolved in the sphere of international contracts linking two Comecon enterprises. Notwithstanding the Eastern preference for inordinately brief periods of foreclosure, the variety of provisions still in force at the national level indicates that there is room for compromise.[33]

17

INDUSTRIAL PROPERTY RIGHTS

A. The New Communist Rationale

The initial communist approach to industrial property protection had been markedly negative. Patents were viewed as characteristically capitalist devices by means of which strong and aggressive corporations could assure themselves of monopolistic profits either by preventing others from undertaking the manufacture of a particular product or by charging royalties for the use of their private know-how.[1] A communist society would presumably have no need for such artful contrivances and no reason to tolerate them. In the Eastern ideology, patents, know-how, trademarks, copyrights and the like are regarded as the common heritage of society, a form of property which yields to the primacy of the community's interest.

As long as this attitude prevailed in practice, there was little regard for the rights of the foreign patent-holder. Typically, a Soviet trade organization would buy one or two samples of a given machine in the West for the express purpose of copying. It has been a rather common experience for a Western manufacturer visiting a Soviet factory to recognize equipment of his original design, based on the single specimen he recalled having sold. This type of abuse is now a thing of the past.

Two reasons help to account for the new policy. In the first place, the industrial managers of the East, particularly Russia, are becoming increasingly sophisticated in matters of industrial innovation. They have long realized that to reinvent what already exists in the West is wasteful and time-consuming. More recently, they have discovered that the practice of copying is self-defeating, given the tempo and complexity of modern technological progress. Indeed, past practice had helped to build obsolescense into Eastern industry. By the time the newly imported machine could be disassembled, passed through the pilot-plant stage and launched into full production, it was likely to be neither adequate to sustain an efficient production line at home nor competitive enough for the export trade.

Today, most of the Eastern countries are eager to acquire for installation in their new plants only the last word in available productive machinery. They are naturally reluctant to launch a new enterprise on the basis of designs known to be outdated at the time of installation. The widely held concern over uncompensated imitation is therefore exaggerated.

The second reason why the East is now willing to acquire and pay for Western patents and know-how is that in recent years the developed communist countries have become aware of the wealth inherent in the industrial property rights of their own economies. As a result, Eastern industry has acquired a strong interest in protecting the inventions that are beginning to flow from its advanced research laboratories. This has provided a strong incentive to avoid copying and to extend a higher standard of treatment to foreign inventors. Russia, Czechoslovakia and East Germany in particular have made it known that they would like to develop a systematic export trade in production licenses, hoping some day to reach a scale that would not only provide earnings with which to pay for licenses imported from abroad but also yield a favorable balance of payments in convertible currency. The desire to become active licensors may be expected to inculcate a greater sense of responsibility and fairness in the patent and licensing practices of Eastern countries.

The communist position on trademarks and trade names is also evolving at a rapid pace. Initially, these concepts were only used to establish a link between a product and its responsible manufacturer. Current legislative and administrative policy has begun to take into account the further objectives of consumer product identification at home and promotional advertising in the highly competitive sales markets abroad.

In brief, this is the background against which we must view the historic Soviet decision, effective as of July 1, 1965, to ratify the Paris Convention for the Protection of Industrial Property. With the exception of Albania, all other eastern European countries had adhered long ago, and their membership has survived into the communized postwar order. Only East Germany constitutes an unresolved problem in this connection, at least in regard to such Western governments as refuse to recognize its political regime. Beyond Europe, neither nationalist nor communist China has ever deposited instruments of ratification.

B. Eastern Legislation in an International Context

Despite the existence of elaborate international machinery, the protection of industrial property rights remains fundamentally a matter for national law. However, a far-reaching unity of principle underlies the various legal systems in their individual regulation of this sphere. As between East and West, divergence in the treatment of patented property rights is found more often at the level of economic theory than in the specifics of legislation.

The most striking feature which national systems have in common is the territorial limitation of protection. A patent granted in one country has no *ipso facto* validity in another, except to the limited extent allowed by treaty. Only by means of repeated registration can the inventor protect and exploit abroad the fruits of his intelligence.

Protection is limited in point of time: Italy allows fifteen years, England sixteen years, the United States and Sweden seventeen and Belgium twenty. The varying Eastern limitation periods fall well within this range.[2]

As a rule only inventions of commercial utility are patentable. Furthermore, they must be "new" inventions, although there are differences as to what constitutes novelty. Many valuable Soviet patents have become unprotectable abroad owing to premature publication of descriptive data in ignorance of this aspect of foreign law.

Modes of patent issuance diverge considerably. In some European countries registration follows almost automatically upon compliance with the prescribed formalities of filing. If challenged, the validity and scope of the patent is decided by the courts. In the U.S.A. and West Germany, the grant is made only after a preliminary inquiry into patentability and novelty. The Soviet position falls into the second category.

Everywhere the rights are perpetuated by payment of renewal fees. This is no less true of the Eastern system of maintenance. Many countries add the requirement that a patent must be "worked" within a certain time from issuance or else be subject to revocation or compulsory licensing.

Thus Bulgaria and Poland require utilization within three years of grant, Rumania four and Hungary two. East German law provides no specified period, while Czechoslovakia has no provision at all in this regard.[3]

The power of a state to expropriate, utilize or compel the grant of a license to third parties is by no means limited to the East. But there considerations of national interest which condition this power tend to assume much broader scope and to raise distinctive questions of compensation.

Internationally, the principal source of rules is the Union Convention of Paris for the Protection of Industrial Property of 1883, adhered to by some 75 countries, including all of industrialized Europe, East and West, as well as the U.S.S.R. and the United States. The Convention mitigates to some extent the rigors of the territoriality principle by establishing the national-treatment standard for locally registered foreign patents and certain other forms of industrial property. Each member country owes the individuals and companies of other signatories the same degree of protection as it provides for its own. It should be noted that Soviet domestic law had reflected this position, subject to reciprocity, even prior to ratification of the Convention.[4]

"Know-how" is not dealt with by the Paris Convention. Nor is it the subject of any separate system of international protection. The term itself is of popular rather than legal origin, and the substance it denotes is generally viewed as something less than industrial property in the strict legal sense. Within the East, however, know-how receives unusually broad recognition both nationally and regionally, and generates valuable rights in the hands of the innovator.

The second basic feature of the Convention is its scheme of priorities. A patent application filed in one signatory country constitutes notice to all others that a similar application may be filed in their territories within a one-year period. As a result, any action by competitors which would otherwise prejudice the original applicant's rights is deprived of legal effect. In other respects, the local law of each country governs.

The rapid development of technology and trade has revealed serious shortcomings in an international regime devised in another century. The costs and delays inherent in fragmented procedures of application under differing requirements of law and language have created strong interest in a unified, multinational method of protection. The creation of an international patent is still a distant goal. But a treaty with a single filing, clearance and processing system has been envisaged by the United International Bureau for the Protection of Intellectual Property (B.I.R.P.I.), the institutional administrator of the Paris Convention, in whose deliberations the U.S.S.R. and other Eastern countries consistently participate.

Even the most advanced communist societies do not consign the fruits of intellectual invention to the public domain. Pressure for accelerated industrial development has necessitated the creation (or preservation) of old-fashioned material incentives for all inventors, at least until communist society has found a way to fashion the new, altruistically motivated "socialist" man. By and large patent rights continue to be recognized. Moreover, the scope and variety of protectable innovations has been significantly broadened by the introduction of supplementary concepts. All of the Eastern countries currently provide for the protection of trademarks and trade names as well.

Since the October Revolution, the Soviet Union has been tortuously shaping a distinct system of industrial property. In 1919, the Bolshevik government began by abolishing the then-existing tsarist mode of protection. All intellectual property rights were nationalized, but individual inventors became eligible for modest pecuniary benefits. The next change took place in 1924, at the height of the New Economic Policy. In order to attract foreign investments, a special law restored elementary patent principles, along with the protection of private proprietary rights. Virgin soil was broken in 1931 with the introduction of the "certificate of authorship." This novel device came close to supplanting the patent by virtue of legislation passed a decade later. In 1947, a right to discoveries was introduced and in 1959 a comprehensive statute reinforced both the classical vestiges of patent protection and the pioneering legislative efforts.[5] New Soviet laws on trademarks and industrial designs have been the most recent addition.[6]

Here as in other spheres, Soviet law has served as a pacesetter for the emergent legislation of the communist orbit. However, while many of its innovations have been transplanted into other Eastern legal systems, it would be misleading to speak unqualifiedly of a "socialist law of industrial property." True, the underlying imperatives of doctrine and the juridical vocabulary is strikingly identical. But the similarity is often more apparent than real. Underindustrialized states such as Albania, Bulgaria, Hungary and (before it began to go its own way) Yugoslavia, have tended to embrace the Soviet system wholesale. The technologically more developed economies, Czechoslovakia and East Germany in particular, have preferred to maintain their own national traditions and to impose a minimum of "socialist" adaptations upon their established patent laws.

Nor is the current trend in the direction of uniformity. Emulation of the Soviet "certificate of authorship" was initially evident in Czechoslovak, Hungarian and Bulgarian legislation passed in 1957, 1959 and 1961 respectively. The corresponding Rumanian legislation dates back to 1950.[7] China's law too was originally modeled upon the Soviet system of co-existing certificates and patents. In 1963, however, the latter concept was abolished there altogether. This break from the Eastern mainstream was more than a local aberration; Hungary in 1957 and Yugoslavia in 1960 discontinued the certificate. Czechoslovak and Rumanian reforms are also pointing in the direction of more traditional, patent-based methods of protection.

Within all of the communist nations the sphere of industrial property is centrally administered. In the Soviet Union the function is performed by the State Committee for Inventions and Discoveries, a self-styled "independent agency" responsible directly to the Council of Ministers. The other states, East Germany for example, have assigned comparable responsibilities to their prewar Patent Offices.[8] However, the nature of these institutions has undergone considerable change. Far from being classically conceived centers of authentication and registration, they also execute important economic tasks in evaluating and selecting inventions which are most appropriate for development, in coordinating their integration into the national economic plan, in supervising their exploitation and in assisting with the protection and exchange of patents abroad.

Intra-East traffic in patents and know-how is based on the several national laws, a multilateral treaty on technical assistance and a network of bilateral cooperation agreements which stand apart from the world-wide system of protection. Attempts at outright law unification have not made any significant headway, but the exchange of industrial experience has often proceeded on an essentially gratuitous basis.[9]

C. Enjoyment of Patent Benefits in the East

Patent rights properly so-called can be acquired and protected under the laws of each of the East European states. Foreign as well as local nationals and firms can register for protection. Somehow a way has been found to reconcile the underlying principles of socialist morality with legislation of a basically capitalist flavor. Article 48 of the Soviet Law of 1959 provides, in terms substantially similar to—let us say—Article 1 of the French Law on Patents, that "no one may utilize an invention without the consent of the owner of the patent."

One major difference between the West's individualist and the East's collectivist approach to protection stands out above all others. The former accords an effective monopoly of ownership and control, a right to restrain use by third parties and to grant a license to those prepared to pay the highest price. The latter stops short of exclusivity. To the extent that a formal right to restrain others exists, it is illusory. The only possible users and bidders are entities of the state. Realistically speaking, these entities cannot be prevented from exploiting a patent as long as compensation is paid to the inventor, for the latter has no meaningful alternative.

In fact if not in law, Eastern legislative policy elevates the concept of eminent domain to a general rule; for practical intents and purposes, all valuable domestic patents are taken over by the state. The owner is entitled to no more than a limited recompense. This finds a parallel in the pre-emption prerogative enjoyed by Western governments, even that of the United States (subject to payment of fair compensation as determined by the Court of Claims). Outside the communist orbit such practices are, however, most rare.

The power of formal expropriation is known in the East as well, whenever an overriding public interest comes into play. Nor is there a lack of procedures to ensure due process to those whose rights are pre-empted. In the Soviet Union an inventor cannot be divested without a decision of the Council of Ministers. In Czechoslovakia the acquisition is made under the authority of the national Patent Office. Ultimately, the amount of compensation is determined by the courts. But why should the state go to the trouble of expropriating, as long as it alone controls all access to production and marketing? Are not all privately held patents in effect expropriated from the start for the very same reason?

Insofar as the patentee has no alternative means of exploitation, it is difficult to grasp the reality of his bargaining power in any negotiation for recompense, either in the event of outright pre-emption or normal state use. Yet a Czechoslovak commentator reports that in many cases where inventors have appealed to the courts, their remuneration has been doubled or tripled upon submission of proof that the invention was of greater importance than the enterprise had pretended. Be that as it may, the foreign patent-holder can derive definite comfort from the fact that outright divestment is uncommon.[10]

Certain radical features of the Eastern system turn out, upon closer examination, to be superficial. Even in the West, the age of individually owned patents is largely past. Increasingly, industrial property rights belong to big business. An originator of a new process is more likely to develop his discovery in the course of employment at Imperial Chemical Industries, Saint Gobain or Du Pont de Nemours than while working for his own account. In the East, self-employment is virtually nonexistent. All would-be inventors, even those who putter about in a backyard garage, are salaried employees of the state. The fruits of their intellectual genius are the property of the institution for which they work and therefore fall within the scope of the state's "socialist" ownership. Nor would broader rights to own and enjoy patents constitute a meaningful benefit to the individual citizen. As we have indicated, only the state and its corporate nominees may engage in manufacturing and distribution activities. At best, the private inventor's rights are confined to utilization for immediate personal purposes. Moreover, patents, no matter how valuable, may not be worked at all, even by a state-operated enterprise, unless their exploitation is called for by the national economic plan.

While the business climate into which he ventures may be quite alien to him, the prospective Western registrant must bear in mind that national patent legislation within the East is as similar and as divergent as legislation within the West. Nothing startlingly unique is encountered in the procedures of application or in such basic matters as what may be made the subject of a patent, what criteria must be satisfied to qualify for protection, what constitutes novelty, what is the effective period of protection and so forth.

For present purposes, we need only recall that in the U.S.S.R. protection is accorded for a period of fifteen years from the date of filing. The same period is prescribed under Bulgarian, Czechoslovak, Polish and Rumanian law. East Germany preserves rights for eighteen years, Hungary for twenty. Patents of addition are generally protected for the unexpired term of the main patent, but Rumania appears to allow a further fifteen-year period.[11] The validity of a patent can be disputed throughout its life. Industrial property rights may be both licensed and assigned, but to be enforceable the grant must be recorded. In the case of the U.S.S.R., recordation is with the State Committee on Inventions and Discoveries.

Despite this conventionality and simplicity of regulation, the Western patentee is faced, as we shall see, with considerable practical difficulties.

D. Certificates of Industrial Authorship

One of the most interesting Soviet contributions to the field of intellectual property protection is the "certificate of authorship." Consistent with the requirements of the new socio-economic order, this concept seeks to reconcile the state's monopoly over all industrial life with the fundamental need to encourage technological innovation and progress.

The certificate is issued to a qualified inventor in his personal capacity, but ownership of the inherent rights vests automatically in the state. The individual holder is entitled to recognition as the inventor and, if his discovery is accepted for use, to compensation on a predetermined scale based upon resultant savings and benefits. The importance of attendant status symbols should also not be underestimated. Aside from the pecuniary aspect and various material benefits such as a privileged tax position, better living accommodations and preferred access to holiday resorts, there are significant moral rewards in the form of distinctions, medals and honors attesting to the enjoyment of high social prestige.

In this manner Soviet law has managed to create a system of effective incentives toward expanded, state-controlled productivity. It has also exercised an inspirational influence upon other countries within its orbit. Albania, Bulgaria, Rumania and, initially, Hungary, have adopted the certificate of authorship outright. Poland has gone part of the way, issuing certificates together with, rather than in lieu of, patents. In East Germany, so-called "economic" patents have been introduced, and in Hungary, as of 1957, "service" patents. In both countries and in Czechoslovakia patents are in effect divided into two categories, one conventional and the other fulfilling the function of the Soviet-type certificate. The latter category, although not conferring any exclusive rights upon the inventor, requires interested state users to enter into a contract providing for the inventor's compensation and role in the development or improvement of production.[12]

As used in the U.S.S.R., the certificate of industrial authorship is an optional alternative to patents in their purest form:

> The inventor may, at his discretion, request either mere recognition of his invention or also recognition of his exclusive right to the invention. In the first instance a certificate of authorship is issued for the invention, in the second instance, a patent.[13]

A certificate is available not only for inventions, but also in respect of certain nonpatentable discoveries referred to in Soviet terminology as technological innovations and industrial rationalization proposals—know-how, to use the more colloquial Western term. These new areas of protection have been opened uniformly in all east European systems of industrial property.

Moreover, for certain classes of inventions which are freely patentable in the West, certification is the only substitute. Pharmaceuticals, alimentary products manufactured in a nonchemical manner and new medical processes are in this category, under the theory that public health should not depend upon the private interests of a patentee. Persons employed or subsidized by a scientific research institution or other state enterprise (*i.e.*, the majority of inventors in a government-operated economy) are eligible for certification only.

Filing procedures are substantially simpler than in the case of patents. A short form application may be submitted by the inventor, his heirs or an assignee institution to the State Committee on Inventions and Discoveries, which then conducts a thorough examination into the industrial character, the novelty and the utility of the invention. Novelty in this context is tested in accordance with relative rather than absolute principles. It is sufficient if the discovery or proposal is new for the particular segment of industry or even a particular enterprise. The criterion of utility is a stricter one. In the U.S.S.R. and Bulgaria, direct usefulness to the economy must be shown. In Poland, Hungary or Czechoslovakia, the mere possibility of practical use is considered sufficient. Moreover, the test of economic usefulness, both in the case of patents and certificates, seems only to apply to inventions of local origin; foreign applicants are apparently exempt.[14]

While a patent may be converted into a certificate of authorship prior to its being licensed, the reverse is not true.[15] Further, an initial flaw in patentability renders a patent vulnerable throughout the term of its validity. Certificates, on the other hand, are only subject to challenge within one year of their issuance. Finally, patents attract both original registration and annual maintenance fees; certificates issue without charge. Even more important is the difference in the mode of remuneration. First, a patentee is compensated only if the invention is in fact exploited, while a certificate holder is entitled to his fee regardless of exploitation. Second, payments in respect of a patent license or assignment, while subject to agreement, are generally computed by reference to economies resulting to the state from the invention's exploitation; in the U.S.S.R. a range of decreasing percentages from 25 to 2 percent of actual savings is established by law. The current ceiling on compensation payable in respect of an inventor's certificate is 20,000 rubles; for certified discoveries and rationalizations it is only 5000 rubles.

Elsewhere in eastern Europe compensation patterns vary from country to country, both as to method and amount. The scales are no more generous than in Russia. Hungary, where the patent is generally granted to the enterprise by which the individual is employed rather than to him personally, places no limit on the allowable premium. The amount is established by means of a negotiated contract between the two parties. Alternative computation guidelines are established by law: a single fixed payment; a variable sum based on cost of production; or a proportional amount calculated on savings. In the event of failure to reach agreement, remuneration is determined by the courts.[16]

All disputes arising in connection with an invention (except for the question of entitlement to registration, which is resolved by administrative procedures) are subject to judicial determination.[17] Such disputes may involve the right to compensation, the method of computation, inconsistent claims of authorship, alleged contributions of third parties and so forth. Actions of infringement in the Western sense are practically nonexistent. Certificate-holders by definition lack a right of exclusivity, while patent-holders of local origin, who theoretically enjoy this right, are few and far between. Realistically speaking, only a foreign patentee may have occasion to petition the local courts in cases of violation.

We have already alluded to the inventor's lack of real bargaining power in a country where the public sector of industry, distribution and exchange is coextensive with the economy as a whole. Being unable to utilize his invention for commercial purposes, he has no option but to accede to the terms tendered by one possible client, the state. Only the presence of an authority which can balance the two interests with fairness can afford him a measure of meaningful protection. Eastern courts seem to exercise their jurisdiction in this sphere in a manner designed to encourage a quest for innovation and to preserve the incentives which give it momentum.

From a decision of the East German Supreme Court, rendered in 1960, one would assume that communist judges are reluctant to abandon local inventors to the mercy of the state monopolies. In its contract with the plaintiff, the defendant-enterprise agreed to pay compensation only if his invention was developed and applied. It did not bind itself to proceed to exploitation, and in fact failed to do so. Deprived of all pecuniary advantage, the patentee sued to recover a reasonable sum for efforts devoted to the discovery in question. The Supreme Court upheld the claim on the ground of the "socialist principle of performance and counter-performance" (mutuality of obligation, in more orthodox terms). A contrary result, it was feared, would enable state enterprises to take over inventors' intellectual achievements without responsibility for putting them to practical use.[18]

From here it was only a short step to the imposition of civil liabilities and even administrative sanctions upon enterprises which fail to implement useful innovations or to share newly acquired knowledge with other state instrumentalities. This step has been taken in the East.

Although available to local inventors as a matter of law, patents have in fact been supplanted in domestic use by the alternative of the author's certificate. It is reported that, in 1964, out of 100,000 Soviet applicants all but two requested the latter form of protection. Foreign inventors, on the other hand, are more attracted to patent registration. The year 1964 saw twice as many non-Soviet parties apply for patents as for certificates of authorship. By 1967, the U.S.S.R. had issued 250 patents to foreign inventors,[19] and since then the rates of application and issuance have both been on the increase.

The certificate of authorship is readily accessible to foreign inventors. Yet it is largely applicants from other communist countries who opt for the advantages afforded by this right. Most Western individuals and firms consider the scale of pecuniary remuneration too limited to warrant the effort of application. The moral rewards, although locally meaningful, hold even less interest. Inventors from such diverse origins as Great Britain, France, West Germany, the United States, Sweden, Israel, Canada, Australia, Austria and Finland have, as a rule, preferred patents.

E. Trademarks and Trade Names

One would not expect to encounter in a communist economy a mature system of trademark and trade-name protection. Both are essentially tools of competition. They cannot therefore play a significant role except in a setting of free enterprise. Such was indeed the initial postrevolutionary Soviet rationale.

Not until 1936 did the U.S.S.R. legislatively recognize the trademark as a device of significant utility. Two modes of product identification were provided for: a trademark properly so called, subject to voluntary registration on the basis of fairly conventional criteria, and a production mark mandatory for all manufacturers and requiring conspicuous exposure of their identity on the product in question. Of the two, the latter was far more important. By establishing a fixed point of responsibility it gave the diffuse government-operated industrial structure a way of imposing appropriate standards of uniformity and quality.

Several East European countries recently enacted new trademark legislation in an effort to align their systems with international methods of protection. The motivation was twofold: (a) given the new, post-Stalinist emphasis upon consumer expectations, it became desirable to introduce competitive sales procedures and to create a basis for product identification; (b) in order to facilitate renewed activity in export markets, the utilization of advertising devices became a competitive necessity.

The content of current Eastern law is surprisingly similar to that which several of the planned economies have preserved from the prewar era, indeed, to the French and Austro-German systems which have exercised such a strong influence upon that region.[20] In addition, most of the communist states adhere to the Paris Convention of 1883, which offers a six-month priority for the registration of trademarks in other signatory countries as well as a guarantee of national treatment.

Another relevant component of the world trademark regime in which there has been some Eastern participation is the Madrid Convention of 1891. A trademark registered in a member country and filed with the so-called Berne Office is deemed to be duly registered in all other member countries for a period of twenty years, with the possibility of prolongation. At present only Rumania, Czechoslovakia, Hungary and East Germany among the communist states hold membership. Nor has this instrument achieved great importance in the West; such major economies as the United States, Great Britain and the Scandinavian countries fall outside its purview.

The latest changes in domestic law, while not going so far as to stimulate artificial "brand buying," encourage keen marketing rivalry among state enterprises. In this context, one must bear in mind two underlying developments: the planners' belated interest in satisfying some of the vast local consumer demand and the desire of management to fulfill and overfulfill assigned production and sales tasks in order to qualify for pecuniary bonuses.

Internationally, the intense competition encountered by Eastern industries in the sale of finished products has emphasized the value of established trade names and trademarks. In recent years, vigorous attempts have been made by communist state enterprises to recapture world exclusivity in nationalized trademarks developed by once-private businesses. The most dramatic series of cases actively litigated in many countries, most notably and unsuccessfully in the United States, involved conflicting West German and East German claims to the world-wide optical and precision-instrument trademarks of the old Carl Zeiss firm of Jena.[21] This extraordinary example of communist attachment to capitalist devices is a fascinating triumph of practicality over the dictates of Marxist doctrine.

The Soviet law of 1962 (amended in 1965 upon adherence to the Paris Union, and again in 1967) added a new dimension to domestic trademark practice.[22] Manufacturing units which fail to employ trademarks must still exhibit factory signs for purposes of identification and eventual responsibility. They are, however, encouraged to develop and protect exclusive marks of diverse types and in this manner to emphasize the uniqueness of their goods and services.

Protection derives from a system of compulsory filing with the State Committee for Inventions and Discoveries. As to the methods of determining registrable trademarks and the composition of categories which are nonregistrable, nothing startingly unconventional can be singled out. Only one perennial exception bears specific mention: the denial of protection to "representations conflicting with the public interest or the requirements of socialist morality."[23]

The treatment of applications by the Prague Patent and Invention Office demonstrates some of the typical Eastern criteria of registrability. Marks which consist of mere letters or numbers have been found to be too indistinguishable. On this ground the symbols SPTK and VRT were rejected. *Spitzenmeister* (Top Master) and *Bellezza* (Beauty) were denied protection because they refer to the quality of the named goods.

Trade names may not be overly descriptive of the properties of the product or too similar to terms of common usage. On the first basis, the name *Ferrolite* was refused registration; on a combination of the two, *Lasso* was rejected as the mark for a binding substance. Similarly, *Direktaprint* was held to be a combination of ordinary words which did not qualify as a name for a reproduction process. The Patent Office rejected the applicant's contention that *ekta* was the root of the name, and that other names based on the same root, *e.g., Ektachrome* and *Ektacolor,* have been widely accepted for registration.

On the other hand, names such as *Compakte* and VOLKSWAGEN (People's Car) have been accepted in Czechoslovakia on the basis of long prior use, registration in the country of origin and widespread reputation. By way of additional justification it was noted that VOLKSWAGEN is always written in capital letters and hence is not likely to be taken as a merely descriptive, common word.[24]

Registration procedures are also fairly conformist. In the U.S.S.R., an examination into registrability may be requested as a prelude to formal application. Denial of recognition to a chosen trade or service mark after application may be challenged only before a higher instance of the State Committee on Inventions and Discoveries. No appeal lies to any judicial authority. Proof of prior use is not a condition precedent to registration, and indeed disputes over conflicting applications are determined under a priority system favoring the first to file over the first to use. The Bulgarian rule is similar to the Russian. In Rumania, on the other hand, only the actual user can obtain protection. Trade names cannot be registered on an abstract, stand-by basis.

Qualified trademarks are registrable in the U.S.S.R. for any requested period up to ten years from the date of filing. Neither the initial time of protection nor subsequent renewals can exceed this life span. The application must fall within a tightly designated classification which parallels the classification systems used by most countries belonging to the Paris Union. Although separate applications may be filed within several classes of goods, the protection afforded through registration is operative only within the class applied for and approved.

Registrants of trademarks may grant a license or assignment, both subject to recordation in the State Register of Trademarks. Quality maintenance provisions must be incorporated into the agreement. All significant entries in the Register are published in the Bulletin of Inventions, Trademarks and Designs, a periodical disseminated by the State Committee on Inventions and Discoveries. In the event of infringement, a registrant may seek compensation from the unlicensed local user with respect to both domestically manufactured and imported goods. A form of injunctive relief is also available. All litigation in this area falls within the jurisdiction of the People's Courts. In the rare instances where disputes go to trial, state enterprises are not involved. Apparently settlement is reached intramurally, within the competent administrative departments.

The elaborate provisions of Eastern law which govern protection, licensing and assignment of industrial property rights are largely dormant. It is difficult to imagine an actionable use by one local state enterprise of the trade or service mark of another in an economy where each industry functions under the centralized authority of a single government ministry. By mere directive, the ministry may require an enterprise to abstain from using its own certified trade name, to share the use with another enterprise, to introduce a new name or to adopt one controlled by a distinct manufacturing or distributing unit.

Litigation between two foreign firms or a local and a foreign firm based on the protection afforded by a particular Eastern law is, on the other hand, both conceivable and existent. In 1966 an appeal was carried as far as the Supreme Court of the U.S.S.R. in a dispute initiated by an East German enterprise against the Belgian firm Gevaert-Agfa, N.V.[25] The plaintiff had obtained registration of the long-established German name *Agfa* from the Soviet Committee on Inventions and Discoveries in 1955. Subsequently the Belgian firm used the name (to which it held a valid license from a Western source) in connection with a display of its products at a Moscow trade fair. The Supreme Court upheld the Moscow City Court's order requiring the Belgian company to desist from using the Agfa name in Soviet territory. It found additional support for the lower court's judgment in the provision of the Paris Convention which had been ratified while appeal was pending.

F. Protection of Western Inventions

In the case of patents, certificates of origin, trademarks and all other forms of industrial property, foreign citizens and corporations are eligible for the same protection in a communist country as local parties. The only condition is that the applicant's own country must extend reciprocity of treatment. This situation obtains in the Soviet Union and, as far as can be ascertained, elsewhere in the East under normal operation of domestic law.

Individuals and entities from signatory countries are entitled to "national treatment" under the terms of the Paris Convention as well. The major change brought about by the U.S.S.R's 1965 adherence to that instrument was recognition of the "right of priority"—a commitment to grant foreign patent applicants a one-year period from the date of first filing in another member country within which to deposit a corresponding local application. For trademarks the priority period is only six months.

All foreign applications to the State Committee on Inventions and Discoveries, be they for patents, authors' certificates or trademarks, must be channeled through the Patent Bureau of the All-Union Chamber of Commerce. Similarly, all foreign complaints and actions must be prosecuted through the Chamber, pursuant to an agency conferred upon it under a customary power of attorney. Clearly this system, which also obtains in Rumania and Bulgaria, simplifies the Westerner's chore. But it has the disadvantage of placing him in a wholly passive position and of curbing his opportunity to determine independently whether the given application or complaint has received adequate consideration. Czechoslovakia, East Germany, Hungary and Poland require the foreign applicant to use the services of local patent counsel, a profession which has thus far survived and which is likely to be resurrected in some of the other countries in the context of their current economic reforms.

While certificates of authorship and analogous devices have largely replaced the classic patent in domestic use, the latter is by far the more popular form of protection with foreign applicants. As already noted, the certificate is rarely sought, even in circumstances where a patent is not available. At first glance, this may seem surprising. For communist legislation provides an uncommonly generous area of protection by issuing certificates with respect to certain types of nonpatentable know-how, notably technical improvements and suggestions for the rationalization of manufacturing procedures. Western firms prefer to offer their know-how to the East on a purely contractual basis, hoping thus to obtain better remuneration than the limited sums awarded to locally certified "industrial authors." In many instances, contractual arrangements of this type have even been elected in lieu of registered patent protection.

Lately, Western firms have shown considerable interest in Eastern patent registration.[26] The growing list of applicants includes such well-known companies as Imperial Chemical Industries of Great Britain, Rhône Poulenc of France, Montecatini of Italy and Radio Corporation of America. This development needs to be examined in light of the handicaps which a communist economy places upon the normal enjoyment of industrial property rights: Soviet protection is comparatively costly to secure and maintain; the volume of an invention's use is difficult to ascertain; prices on which royalties can be computed are prescribed without realistic reference to market values; the Council of Ministers has power to foreclose rights at a fixed rate of compensation; and no alternative exists except to license a designated enterprise of the state. If the benefits are so theoretical, one is prompted to ask whether it is not a waste of time and money to apply for a patent at all.

In fact, however, registration does yield certain advantages. The mere circulation of a locally established patent gives useful exposure to the holder's know-how and products and therefore serves as an advertising device aimed at industrial managers. In addition, registration constitutes clear legal recognition, fully operative within the particular communist country, that the beneficiary is the proprietor of the rights and that he derives his title from local legislation, not merely from the unverified recitals contained in his contract. It is often overlooked that in the absence of registration, Eastern copying of Western technology does not constitute a violation of law regardless of the morality of such practices.

Psychologically no less than legally, the existence of a patent in an Eastern country gives the Western firm a tangible edge over unregistered Western competitors in negotiating for royalty entitlements. Moreover, its holder is better placed not only to license his process in a given communist territory but also to exclude therefrom the importation of foreign goods lawfully or unlawfully manufactured from his ideas at the place of origin. In particular, registration helps to prevent copying for domestic use or export to third markets of items the recognized Western patentee has exhibited locally or agreed to sell and deliver.[27] A special right of priority is granted to foreigners who show their inventions at Soviet exhibitions and trade fairs and thus expose themselves to the risk of lawful piracy. They are allowed six months from first display to file for a local patent.[28]

While compulsory acquisition of foreign-controlled rights in the East is extremely rare, one reported instance of pre-emption has actually turned out to be advantageous to the patentee. The Swiss pharmaceutical company, Sandoz, A.G., was granted a Hungarian patent but failed to work it within the three-year period prescribed by law as a condition of continued protection. Upon special application, the Municipal court of Budapest granted exploitation rights to Richter, a state-owned company, fixing a 1.5 percent royalty in favor of Sandoz. On appeal, the Hungarian Supreme Court increased the rate to 3 percent, with a substantial minimum guarantee. It is evident that without registration in Hungary the Swiss patentholder would not have been entitled to any benefit at all. As it turned out, he was able to reap compensation without exerting any manufacturing effort of his own.[29]

Eastern laws and the Paris Convention enable registration of foreign trade names and trademarks along with those of local origin. Here the interest in seeking protection is no less apparent than in the case of patents, although the incidence of filing is much less frequent. One observer has summarized the advantages in these terms:

> Although there is little experience on which to base any meaningful judgments regarding Soviet treatment of foreign trademark rights, it is apparent that an American registering his trademark in the U.S.S.R. will establish (1) a legal basis for enforcing it against imitations in that country, (2) a focal point around which to develop any market promotion for the subject products that may be possible, (3) an important identification for his imported products, and (4) a better basis for concluding licensing agreements where "package deals" which include patents and technical know-how as well as trademarks are the only types that can feasibly be negotiated.[30]

To date, registration has been motivated by hopeful anticipation of extensive markets in the East rather than by any immediate possibility of promoting voluminous sales. Given the closed nature of the Eastern economies and their shortage of convertible currency, the prospect of selling to local consumers by brand name is very limited. The opportunity of licensing trademarks to the East for income purposes is also virtually nonexistent. Yet in Bulgaria, Hungary and Poland the great bulk of all trademark registration stands in the name of foreign concerns.

More tangible benefits are likely to flow from expanding sales of machinery and equipment. In this category, trademark registration enables the supplier more effectively to guarantee, advertise and identify his goods. Furthermore, as the Soviet Supreme Court's judgment in the Gevaert-Agfa case has shown, a failure to register may result in total territorial foreclosure of the Western firm's position to a pirate, or one laboring under local color of right. By the same token, someone else's competing registration may cause world-wide complications for the legitimate trademark owner, *e.g.*, in the case of competing exports to destinations where his mark has not been filed or maintained.

18

TRANSACTIONS INVOLVING TECHNOLOGY

A. Trends in Industrial Cooperation

As East-West business expands in a better political climate, it tends to assume new forms. In addition to simple export-import transactions, we are beginning to encounter elaborate patent licenses, agreements for the supply of know-how and engineering services, arrangements for the delivery of plants and equipment on extended financial terms and various types of joint efforts in production and marketing. Transactions based on the sharing of patents and know-how have proved in practice the easiest to work out. But even this simple method of industrial cooperation involves prolonged negotiations, novel legal issues and unusually refined contractual terms.

Traffic in the granting of patent licenses has moved mainly in the direction of the East. In 1968 Czechoslovakia alone is reported to have acquired 65 licenses from the West (as compared with 42 in 1967, 66 in 1966, 25 in 1965, 12 in 1964 and 2 in 1963); the ratio of expenditure to income in the technological balance has been 5 to 1. The most frequent and ambitious licensors to the East have been west European and Japanese companies.[1] By far the largest parcel of rights, involving licenses, know-how, technical cooperation and the delivery of plants, was granted in conjunction with the celebrated 1966 deal between the U.S.S.R. and the Italian automobile manufacturer FIAT. American companies and their offshore subsidiaries have thus far played a comparatively limited role in the Eastern licensing markets—an incongruous phenomenon, obviously influenced by extraneous considerations, given the size of the United States' economy and the abundance of highly advanced technology available for export.

The reverse flow of technology is also acquiring momentum. An important new factor has influenced Eastern thinking in the course of increasingly flexible dealings with industrial firms of the West: The U.S.S.R has by now developed a research establishment with its own considerable capacity for technical innovation. The result has been a feeling of self-confidence on the part of Soviet negotiators that they can deal with their Western counterparts as equals. This presents a vivid contrast with the past, especially the late twenties, when the U.S.S.R. appeared in the market of industrial ideas exclusively in the role of borrower. It now acts extensively as both licensor and licensee. The smaller industrialized economies of Czechoslovakia and East Germany are also becoming increasingly active vendors of industrial property rights. In fact, all Eastern governments today energetically promote the exportation of technology to the West. There is a prestige value in such transactions to the extent that they imply the existence of superior Eastern industrial techniques and processes. Further, licenses help to earn the hard currency which is so essential to the expansion of trade with the outside world.

All eastward licenses of industrial property reflect pragmatic efforts on the part of private firms to adapt themselves to the conditions of the socialist market. The originality of the arrangements is explainable by the peculiarities of legal principle and the practical difficulties generally encountered in exchanges with the East. In the past, Western inventors have preferred to sell prototypes for a substantial lump sum rather than to embark upon the complex and uncertain course of securing patent protection, policing volume and quality of production, and collecting royalties. Today vendors still lean in favor of contracts for the use of know-how rather than formal patent licenses. Such contracts are frequently coupled with an undertaking to furnish an operating installation, specialized equipment, technical assistance and, on occasion, trademarks. A major example of this is the long-term contract between the U.S.S.R.'s Tekhmashinimport and the English Polyspinners consortium, which requires Imperial Chemical Industries to furnish its know-how in the production of plastics, synthetic fibers and petrochemicals. Another example is a contract recently concluded by three Japanese firms—C. Itoh & Co., Chisso Corporation and Chisso Engineering—with a Czechoslovakian enterprise. The Japanese have undertaken to deliver a $10-million polypropylene resin production plant with attendant patents and know-how supplied by Avisun, a company incorporated in the United States.[2] In this manner the Western parties seek to reap a pecuniary benefit without undue involvement in the problems and risks inherent in the communist system of industrial property protection.

A variety of arrangements much more elaborate than licensing has lately begun to emerge in commercial relations between capitalist and communist countries. In the East these arrangements tend to assume the form of cooperative undertakings in production; in the West they are, above all, joint marketing efforts of one type or another. Western firms have found such arrangements eminently rewarding. Often they have been able not only to sell a costly infrastructure but also to draw advantage from the plentiful supply of skilled, inexpensive Eastern manpower which can produce for outside markets in conditions of stability, free of labor unrest or strikes. Their communist co-venturer is attracted to dealing on this basis because it is able to acquire a largely self-supporting installation which generates with its own production the foreign currency needed to pay for the goods and ideas imported from abroad.

Although they are becoming increasingly significant from an economic point of view these evolving patterns of industrial cooperation must still be regarded as undertakings of an experimental character. Complex practical, ideological, financial and legal difficulties confront the co-venturers at both ends. They range from problems of cultural adaptation on the part of personnel transposed for extended periods from one environment to another, to questions of shared ownership, management and profits—elements which run counter to the basic socialist principle of state-operated production and distribution.

B. Western Patent Licensing to the East

1. Terms of Agreement

The Eastern environment is not conducive to conventionally styled licensing arrangements. State enterprises abhor the customary requirements of reporting and inspection necessary to protect compensation entitlements and to obtain evidence in support of infringement actions. Another potential complication is the communist principle of freely exchangeable experience and know-how. Far from imitating the secrecy and nondisclosure covenants which are invariably required by a Western licensor, Eastern industrial enterprises are governmentally encouraged, even legally required, to share with one another all significant improvements in the manufacturing process. This contrast in practice is a natural manifestation of the intense competition present among Western firms and its total absence within the national confines of a collectivist economy.

The Western owner of valuable rights will habitually and justifiably expect a licensee, or any other recipient of confidential data, to safeguard his secrets from circulation into unauthorized hands. The obvious conflict between such requirements and the positive duty of national enterprises dealing *inter se* to share, publicize and promptly utilize all valuable technological intelligence (without a right to hold back for reasons of competition or other economic advantage) tends to discourage classically conceived contract clauses.

If Eastern enterprises are reluctant to enter into secrecy covenants, Western firms in turn entertain few illusions as to their effectiveness. But recent experience suggests that such undertakings, once made, are scrupulously observed, both domestically and internationally. Universal Oil Products Company, which has supplied petroleum cracking plants and processing units to several Eastern countries, notably Rumania and Yugoslavia, reportedly has encountered no breach of confidence. Indeed, it has been recalled to Yugoslavia to construct new facilities identical to those previously erected, an indication that unauthorized data and know-how sharing has not been attempted.[3]

Although a nondisclosure covenant flies in the face of communist domestic practice, it is unlikely to be so repugnant to Eastern legal systems as to invalidate an international transaction on grounds of public policy. Breach of such a provision may therefore be expected to entitle the Western licensor to a claim for damages enforceable in the licensee's jurisdiction. Only the problem of obtaining proof may turn out to be insurmountable.

Since most licenses require the Western party to furnish newly developed related technology, the possibility of withholding information may provide a lever for inducing compliance with the secrecy condition. However, such threats may poison the atmosphere for the long term and invite counteraction, e.g., a refusal to pay installments or royalties as they fall due. In the circumstances, compliance is best assured by the Eastern desire to develop and maintain good relationships in the domain of technology. Breaches, more easily detectable as the planned economies continue their process of decentralization, would reflect on the entire state trading apparatus and destroy the reputation for reliability in business dealings it is so eager to cultivate.

In the East–West context, agreements involving the supply of technology must be drawn with uncommon care. A license is in many respects more than a simple contract. It deals with the transfer of proprietary rights and gives rise to a legal relationship which continues for years. State enterprises, such as Litsenzintorg of the U.S.S.R., Polytechna of Czechoslovakia, Polservice of Poland or Technoeksport of Bulgaria, seek to inject their standard forms as a basis for negotiation, particularly when they act as licensors. However, all are legally free to commit to whatever terms the Western party may insist upon; certainly terms which conform to prevalent international practice.[4] In the ultimate analysis, the content of patent and know-how contracts depends on the relative bargaining position of the parties.

The direct Eastern party is usually a state entity serving as a national conduit for the acquisition of licenses. The engineering personnel of the end-user participate in all technical phases of negotiation and a special clause is included to permit assignment to such user. In current practice licensing transactions are no longer exclusively funneled through a specialized foreign trade entity. Major manufacturing enterprises are permitted to sign their own names as licensees, although they may be assisted and represented by entities such as Limex GmbH of East Germany or Licensia of Hungary. In Hungary all enterprises active in foreign trade are now entitled to contract directly for licenses in areas which relate to their particular competence.

As a rule, government approval of licensing agreements is required throughout the East. In the U.S.S.R. decisions to acquire foreign patents are made at the level of the Council of Ministers. Specific acquisition proposals are subject to review by the Ministry of Foreign Trade and the State Committee on Science and Technology. Moreover, to be valid, assignments, licenses and sublicenses must be recorded with the State Committee on Inventions and Discoveries. The obligation to record must be observed not only to ensure a superior right against third parties but also to perfect the transaction as between the immediate signatories of the agreement.[5]

Since patent licenses are considered by Soviet law to be contracts in foreign trade, the submission of disputes to the Moscow arbitration tribunal is possible and indeed typically sought by Litsenzintorg. Conflict-of-law provisions also extend to licensing agreements in the same way as to commercial contracts. On the other hand, the standard licensing contract of East Germany prescribes judicial rather than arbitral settlement, jurisdiction being awarded to the country of the defendant.

Litsenzintorg has been known, however, to agree to alternative arrangements. A license contract with the Japanese firm Copal for the production of photographic shutters refers all disputes to the permanent arbitral body of the defendant's country, i.e., either the Association of Commercial Arbitration of Japan or the Moscow Foreign Trade Arbitration Commission. A contract with the Danish firm Durmeister & Wein for the production of naval diesel motors requires controversies to be decided by arbitrators designated by the Stockholm Chamber of Commerce.[6]

Production and sales exclusivity usually covers the whole of the licensee's country. In isolated instances the territorial definition has embraced the rest of eastern Europe as well, although such additional rights are concurrent rather than exclusive.[7] The licensee-enterprise, if it stands in a constant relationship with the Western firm and can be trusted faithfully to police and report for the common account, may thus become the agent or sublicensor for a large segment, perhaps even for the entirety of the communist orbit. Western firms have also been known to grant exclusive or concurrent exportation rights in respect of specified less-developed areas which are more susceptible to communist-market penetration. As a rule, extraterritorial exploitation is conditioned upon the licensee's willingness to guarantee quality and after-sales service of a standard set by the licensor. Moreover, the licensee obligates himself to impose upon foreign sublicensees or importers a commitment not to re-export the goods manufactured under the license. This limitation is designed to protect the exclusivity of the licensor in his remaining markets.

An undertaking to exchange improvements pertinent to initially licensed technology is automatically and strenuously insisted upon by Eastern negotiators. Such a provision is, of course, quite standard in Western practice. In licensing to the East it poses no special difficulties other than that of detecting useful developments at the plant of the communist user. A further problem is future know-how which might be covered by national or multinational restrictions on the delivery of strategic goods and technology. In other words, the particular innovation may clearly fall within the scope of the patent license yet be unexportable to the licensee's territories. It is consequently wise to make all such executory undertakings subject to continued government approval. In the West, state interdiction is beyond the control of the private licensor and therefore constitutes a true *force majeure*.

East European parties have on occasion, albeit reluctantly, given pledges not to re-export licensed technology to territories proscribed by the licensor's government. Such re-export prohibitions may be extended to the foreign customers of communist licensees as well. This issue is of considerable importance to American firms, as the United States practices control on the circulation of technical data at various levels of severity: comparative liberality toward much of eastern Europe, far-reaching selectivity toward the U.S.S.R., and outright prohibition in the case of mainland China, North Vietnam, North Korea and Cuba.

2. *Terms of Payment*

For reasons previously given, neither the licensor nor the communist licensee can be satisfied with standard royalties based on production and the manifold refinements which enter into their calculation. The U.S.S.R. and Poland simply refuse to negotiate royalties based on the volume of production or sale. Hungary and Czechoslovakia are not opposed to this form of payment as a matter of principle, but seek to avoid it in practice. Where compensation is proportional to the number of units produced or sold the right to examine corporate records is also granted, although actual verification by foreign auditing firms is rare if not nonexistent. Characteristically the Eastern side prefers to commit to a fixed sum, payable in installments. The Western firm, on the other hand, expects a range of royalties from 3 to 10 percent, with a substantial down payment and fixed annual minimums.

Of necessity, the level of desired consideration is estimated on an arbitrary basis. How is one to ascertain the reality of pricing and the volume of production or sale in an Eastern economy, particularly one of the magnitude, geographic scope and complexity of the U.S.S.R.? The Western firm must draw remuneration guidelines from free markets of comparable size and potential, and quantify expectations in terms of what licenses to such markets might yield. The result is often a highly oversimplified compensation formula, but one that at least has the merit of being immediately bankable.

Shortages of hard currency have led in many instances to payment in goods manufactured under the license. Such an arrangement, although fundamentally a barter sale of technology, has the appearance of a joint enterprise, the Western party profiting from the low cost of Eastern labor and acting as distributor in designated outside markets. Thus Czechoslovakia's Skoda produces machine tools under license from the Simmons Machine Tool Corporation of New York, making part payment in finished tools for exclusive North American distribution.[8] Now and then, raw materials are offered in compensation. Whether cash or kind, the *quid pro quo* is expressed in terms of convertible currency.

Since composite licensing transactions generally run for a term of years and involve substantial amounts of money, Eastern licensees must seek credit in order to make payment in convertible currency. Indeed, a favorable credit arrangement with the licensor or, more often, a third party, is often a precondition of the sale of technology. For example, the 1966 FIAT agreement, in an order of magnitude of $800 million, is supported by a separate financial protocol between the Istituto Mobiliare Italiano (the state export credit organization) and the Soviet Ministry of Foreign Trade; $320 million in credits cover the cost of patents, know-how, engineering services and imported machinery, 65 to 75 percent supplied by Italian companies. Repayment over a period of eight and a half years in seventeen semi-annual installments is not to commence until six months after scheduled completion of the auto plant. Interest accumulates at a rate of 6.5 percent. All payments are guaranteed by the Soviet Foreign Trade Bank. On a lesser scale, arrangements of this type are quite current in the eastward sale of equipment, technology and know-how, except as regards United States firms, which are required by law to limit themselves to shorter-term credit, generally not exceeding five years.

Contracts for the sale of plant and engineering products, with or without a licensing feature, present a series of special problems. The price of a machine is frequently geared to the levels of performance set forth in the user's specifications. Assuming that these specifications are appended to the contract of sale and that final payment is conditioned upon the passing of completion tests, as is commonly the case, the seller will be held responsible for production shortfalls. Failure to attain defined levels may result in a reduction of the purchase price or outright rejection of the installation, together with the concomitant technology.

It is worthwhile to reiterate that communist-state enterprises tend to interpret industrial contracts in a highly formalistic and literal manner. The Western seller should therefore establish in advance, and in the minutest detail, the terms and scope of guaranteed performance. The guarantee should moreover be tied to utilization of a specified quality of raw materials, a specified caliber of auxiliary services (i.e., electricity, hydraulic pressure, etc.) and a specified standard of operational skill and experience. Only production capability under optimal conditions can be safely underwritten. Moreover, it is prudent to provide for a price-adjustment schedule to cover quantitative variations in performance. Actual output at a rate of, say, 80 to 85 percent of plant capacity should be prescribed as constituting substantial fulfillment of the seller's obligation, and hence not a basis for calling the guarantee or rejecting the equipment.[9]

C. Eastern Patent Licensing to the West

1. Contractual Provisions

The number and variety of Soviet, Czechoslovak and East German patents licensed to the West are no longer negligible. Such licenses have been offered by the state monopolies either directly or through specially appointed Western agents experienced in the intricate procedures of protecting and selling industrial property rights. Westward licensing is not fraught with the same difficulties which face suppliers of industrial property to enterprises of a wholly planned economy. Eastern licensors benefit from normal eligibility for protection under local and international law and from the open commercial conditions prevalent in most Western markets. Accordingly, they are more content with agreements cast in conventional terms.

A 1965 contract between National Patent Development Corporation, an American company, and the Academy of Science and the Institute of Macromolecular Chemistry of Czechoslovakia is representative of the East-to-West sale of technology. National Patent acquired the right to produce, sell, distribute and sublicense in the Western Hemisphere a new plastic used in manufacturing soft contact lenses. The territory was subsequently extended to include Western Europe, South Africa, Israel and noncommunist Asia. The agreement called for mutual development of the new product's potential and extensive cooperation and exchange of experience. The Czechoslovak licensor was remunerated by way of royalties computed on the sale of all products using the plastic, subject to a minimum annual guarantee.[10]

In the negotiation of payment terms the Eastern licensor pursues the same variety of objectives as his capitalist counterpart: a lump price; a down payment followed by periodic installments; annual royalties with or without a fixed minimum; a paid-up sum against percentages based on production or sales, and so forth. A level of yield below which the agreement may be rescinded is also a standard feature. The East Germans prefer a contractually established price with an immediate down payment and fixed annual installments. Moreover, they require the foreign party to set up an irrevocable guarantee through a correspondent of the Deutsche Notenbank as a condition precedent to the license's entry into force.

To be acceptable, the Western licensee must be a concern able to produce in appropriate quantity and quality and to open up markets of adequate magnitude. Exclusivity is usually granted for a period of ten years. The right to inspect the licensee's production facilities and books of account is a standard condition; so is the obligation to exchange data concerning subsequent modifications and improvements.

One of the essential points to be verified prior to the consummation of any transaction in this area is the corporate capacity of the purported Eastern licensor (or licensee, for that matter). Does it have the faculty to enter into a limited or composite license covering patents, know-how, technical assistance, trade names and other elements which customarily enter into an East-West agreement involving technology? This determination is made by reference to the charter of incorporation and to special government permissions, as shown in our discussion of the legal status of state enterprises. Similarly, the authority of individual representatives to bind the licensor, be it a specialist-monopoly such as Russia's Litsenzintorg or Vneshtekhnika, or a general industrial enterprise such as Czechoslovakia's Skoda, should be ascertained with the care which normally enters into the acceptance of a power of attorney.

No less important is a requirement that both parties exhibit their government's approval of the particular licensing agreement. If the Western licensee's government does not practice exchange control and no special authorization is required, a legal opinion to this effect should suffice. Short of that, the absence of express authorization may result in the contract being void *ab initio*. Thus the standard East German licensing agreement stipulates that to be legally valid:

> It is necessary that the contract—signed by the parties—be approved by the competent authorities of the contracting patries. It comes into force at the date of the last given approval. The parties bind themselves to apply for this approval immediately.[11]

On the Eastern side, initial government authorization is a prerequisite to the validity of any foreign licensing contract. Beyond this, it may be queried whether the official stamp of approval, once obtained, constitutes an effective guarantee of noninterference with future performance. Will a change in economic plan permit the Eastern licensor to escape with impunity its unperformed obligations after having received an advance on royalties? Caution calls for a detailed definition of *force majeure* so as to exclude this disturbing eventuality. Such a definition is conspicuously absent from the standard East German license. Hopefully, the omission can be rectified in the course of negotiations.

A problem not peculiar to this area of intercourse, but which nonetheless plagues state-operated communist licensors, arises from the general absence of double-taxation treaties between Eastern and Western states. As a result, royalties, installments and other payments are often subjected to withholding taxes at the source, under the internal tax laws of the licensee's country. The same difficulty may, of course, present itself in connection with a license from West to East, whenever a communist government collects a levy upon income derived in its territory. In both cases, a clause providing that all compensation shall be paid net of taxes helps to forestall subsequent disputes. In addition, tax-planning possibilities may lead to the immunization of the affected income, usually by means of a third-country conduit which takes advantage of treaty arrangements with one side or the other. To date, communist enterprises have not made a practice of incorporating foreign tax-haven subsidiaries for this particular purpose.

An interesting arrangement, effective as of January 1, 1966, exists between the U.S.S.R. and France. An exchange of letters between the two governments, proclaiming a mutual desire to develop cooperation in the field of industrial property, reciprocally exonerates from income and turnover taxes all payments generated by the sale or licensing of patents, trademarks, trade names, service marks, designs and models. The waiver extends to remuneration for the use of manufacturing processes, of industrial and scientific equipment and of all related technical assistance.[12] Conceivably, this instrument could serve to advantage firms from countries which have no similar accords with the Soviet Union. Thus an American or British patent-holder seeking to enter the Soviet market might well be advised to utilize a French conduit subsidiary. Such a subsidiary would presumably benefit from the back-to-back application of the treaties which both countries have with France and the Franco-Soviet arrangement just mentioned. Likewise, one can imagine a Russian sale of technology to a French licensee for ultimate exploitation by an American or British sublicensee with a view to obtaining corresponding tax savings. Recent Soviet investments in newly formed Western corporations suggest that this *modus operandi* may already be a reality.

2. *Legal Protections*

Licensing typically implies that a registered patent is in force in the territory covered by the agreement. A Soviet estimate has it that 1800 Russian patents were filed abroad in 1965, and 2200 in 1966. The rate of Eastern applications as a whole has grown considerably in recent years, the major concentration being in western Europe.[13]

A communist inventor's interest in foreign protection must be viewed against the fact that certain Eastern countries, the Soviet Union for example, forbid the extraterritorial filing of patents without express permission from a central agency, such as the State Committee on Inventions and Discoveries. Nonetheless, in the future the socialist governments themselves may be trusted to indulge their recently aroused appetites for lucrative portfolios of patents and for the exportation of technological ideas to markets protected by registration.

Initial ignorance of how Western patent systems function in law and practice has proved costly for the U.S.S.R. Russian inventors, unaware of the rule that prior publication constitutes a statutory bar to patentability, have rushed to publish their discoveries in domestic journals. Valuable rights have been irrevocably lost in consequence. To guard against such defaults, special regulations now require research institutions and other bodies concerned with technological innovation promptly to inform the State Committee of an invention's economic potential. The Committee then becomes the exclusive channel for the preparation and filing of patent applications abroad.[14]

To date, the primary Eastern motivation behind the drive for patent registration in Western countries has been a desire to collect convertible revenue. In due course, a policy of shielding exports from patent-infringing unfair competition may also be expected to emerge. Under a series of joint-venture agreements, state enterprises are already selling manufactured goods into third markets protected by the foreign partner's patent rights, either directly or under special licensing arrangements.

The same is true of trade names and trademarks, which have lately come to be recognized as useful tools of competition in the international arena. This is demonstrated by the numerous lawsuits which state-controlled plaintiffs have seen fit to prosecute in French, German, Dutch, American, Japanese and Brazilian courts for the protection of new and long-established (but nationalized) rights. Among them are the well-known Soviet mark *Treugolnik,* the German mark *Zeiss-Ikon,* the Czechoslovak mark *Carborundum* and the Hungarian mark *Tungsram.*[15]

To Soviet state enterprises owning patents and trade names, the possibility of filing for protection abroad was available under normal operation of many Western domestic laws even prior to the U.S.S.R.'s adherence to the Paris Convention. American industrial property law, for example, does not condition eligibility either on the basis of national origin or of reciprocity. Under the Convention, applicants from all signatory communist countries are entitled to privileges which go beyond local law. Among these privileges are the valuable "right of priority" for a period of one year from filing at home or elsewhere in the case of patents, six months in the case of trade names; and the right in certain member countries, e.g. the United States, to obtain registration even though the particular patent or mark had not been put into use.

The extent to which Eastern countries can benefit from the provisions of the Convention has not been fully tested. As we have seen in the preceding chapter, local inventors seldom elect to apply for patents under their domestic laws; they prefer alternative forms of protection, which communist industrial-property legislation provides in abundant variety. Since entirely novel concepts have thus come into extensive use, difficult questions arise with regard to their recognition at the international level. Can Western countries be expected to offer reciprocity in the case of rationalizations, discoveries, general know-how and other rights which may be freely enjoyed in the East but which are alien to their own system of industrial property? More specifically, are Eastern-origin rights acquired under a mere certificate of authorship entitled to the same protection as rights acquired under patents? Can a Soviet enterprise-assignee of an invention acquired from the holder of a previously issued certificate of authorship claim in a country which requires a preliminary examination of novelty the priority right the Convention extends to patents?[16]

Such questions must await judicial determination in international forums interpreting the operation of the Convention, or in national courts or arbitration tribunals ruling upon the rights of individual parties. In terms of their basic nature and purpose, the benefits entailed in certificates made available by Eastern legal systems would seem to merit treatment analogous to that accorded conventional patent rights. This view has recently prevailed in Italy in connection with the issuance of a patent to the holder of a Bulgarian certificate of industrial authorship.

D. Partnerships in Production and Marketing

It is axiomatic of a communist economy that private capital, domestic or foreign, cannot be admitted to participate in local industry. The interdiction is not always as explicit as we find it to be in the U.S.S.R. In Hungary, for example, requisite approvals from the central bank need only be withheld to exclude outside investments, in the same way as such exclusion is practiced in England, France or other countries which maintain exchange control.

A noteworthy exception is Yugoslavia, where a law enabling foreigners to invest in domestic enterprises was promulgated in 1967. The law limits the outside investor's role to that of a minority shareholder; his participation can neither exceed nor equal that of the domestic partner. There are other restrictions, such as an obligation to reinvest a portion of the profits realized each year.[17] But the essential novelty of the law is the fact that the Western party's return from the investment is directly tied to the profitability of the joint enterprise. He is also permitted to negotiate for an effective voice in management and for representation on a board which supervises the enterprise's activities.

The foreigner is not deemed to hold equity in the strict sense of the word. His rights are contractual in nature, deriving from an investment agreement with the local entity. In this manner, the sanctity of socialist property is presumed intact, if only for the sake of appearances. While the terms of the common undertaking are, in the first instance, subject to autonomous party determination, any resultant agreement must be approved by the government as a precondition of validity. Ultimate state control is therefore carefully assured.

One of the first Western firms to make use of the new law was FIAT of Italy. For more than a decade its vehicles have been assembled and sold in Yugoslavia under license by a local enterprise, Crvena Zastava. This relationship has now been converted into a joint venture, with a capital of some $50,000,000. FIAT shares in the profits of the undertaking and participates in management through a mixed committee of experts. Another joint venture was concluded between the East German enterprise Lacke und Farben, and the Yugoslav chemical-metallurgical enterprise Cinkarna, for the production of titanium dioxide. The foreign partner is given an equal voice on a two-man board of directors, notwithstanding the fact that its investment is limited to 49 percent. A balanced committee of experts, named for a two-year period, implements the decisions of the board. Day-to-day operations are conducted by the managing director of Cinkarna under the board's supervision.[18]

Although the Yugoslav variety of international joint venture is still a solitary institution in the East, it may prove to be a precursor of comparable developments in adjacent countries. As East German, Czechoslovak, Hungarian and other enterprises in the region increasingly take advantage of similar opportunities, their appreciation of the potential and methodology of cooperative East–West production and marketing will undoubtedly grow, and with it the possibility of legislative innovation and liberalization. After all, Russia's New Economic Policy of the nineteen twenties constitutes a Leninist precedent for the mobilization of capitalist assistance for an industrial leap forward. The unknown quantity is, of course, the political climate within the communist camp and the extent to which the Soviet Union will allow its smaller neighbors to experiment with new economic tools.

Certainly, communist economic philosophy cannot tolerate a pattern of far-reaching exceptions to the central notion of state ownership and management. It is virtually inconceivable that a controlling vote in the decision-making process of domestic enterprises will be relinquished to aliens. At least, this is the prognosis for the foreseeable future. With the limited exception of Yugoslavia, business partnerships in the classical sense are even more difficult to envisage. Allowing private Western investors openly to draw profit from local industrial or commercial activity would be tantamount to introducing capitalist, or worse, foreign capitalist, exploitation into a socialist society.

Yet a variety of functional arrangements which give Western firms a stake in the Eastern economies have come into the realm of the feasible in the last few years. These arrangements are predicated upon an advantageous division of labor which extends to the sharing of technical know-how, production facilities, marketing outlets and management skills, occasionally in combination with other factors. The cooperation which they envisage, both in the manufacturing and service industries, is characterized by a marked degree of continuity and a solidarity dictated by the pursuit of common objectives.

Joint East–West undertakings are presently encountered at four levels:

government-to-government, government-to-enterprise, industry-to-industry and enterprise-to-enterprise.

An example of the first is the Franco-Soviet Agreement of June 30, 1966, which provides a broad insitutional framework for economic, industrial, scientific and technical cooperation between the two countries. Within this framework, major cooperative projects have been undertaken in the fields of television, atomic energy, automobile production, mining, oil and gas exploration, data processing, transportation and so forth. Examples of the second are agreements on industrial and technological cooperation concluded by the Soviet Committee on Science and Technology in 1968 and 1969 with J. R. Geigy A.G. of Switzerland in the area of pharmaceuticals, with Polimer Corporation of Canada in the area of synthetic rubber and with Nebiolo S.p.A. of Italy in the area of polygraphic materials. An example of the third is the Japan-U.S.S.R. Agreement for the Development of Soviet Forestry of July 29, 1968, which encompasses a large group of companies from both countries.[19]

Cooperative enterprise-to-enterprise arrangements based on private law relations are much more current and varied. A sufficient number of them has now emerged to enable their classification into several distinct categories.[20]

First, East–West licensing must be stressed again in this context, because of its unusually elaborate and long term features. The arrangement between French and Soviet enterprises to exploit the SECAM color television system is an illustration in point. All the underlying industrial property rights are shared, the Soviet party holding title to the U.S.S.R. territory and the French party to the rest of the world. The latter is to license the process on a global basis (including the East European countries) and to reserve for the former a share of the proceeds. Each side is to produce a determined segment of the required components.

More often than not, the grant of industrial property rights is combined with the sale of a complete plant or the lease of special equipment. In such situations, the foreign licensor frequently agrees to purchase a fixed portion of annual output or to distribute the manufactured items in designated territories. The relationship invariably extends for a number of years.

In several instances, Eastern enterprises have undertaken to produce goods for delivery to a Western firm, in accordance with the latter's specifications. Some or all of the export proceeds thus realized may be earmarked for the procurement of production equipment from the Western side. In this vein, a Hungarian enterprise, Gants, manufactures generators while its West German co-venturer produces boilers for integration into completed electric power stations.

Another variant is the device of sub-contract. The Eastern party agrees to furnish components which its Western partner integrates into finished products. The latter usually undertakes the task of merchandising and distribution. Thus, a Polish furniture enterprise supplies semi-finished elements to IKEA, a Swedish company, which in turn attends to finishing and marketing in designated Western areas.

Similarly, an Eastern and a Western enterprise may pool their technical expertise to produce a fully integrated line of products. The state entity takes charge of the segment of manufacture in which it is more specialized, in a pattern of far-reaching technical complementarity. This is illustrated by an agreement for the production of motorcycles concluded by Motokov of Czechoslovakia and Italjet of Italy. The former builds the engines, the latter the frames.

Joint marketing ventures are becoming increasingly popular. Production may take place at an Eastern plant, a Western plant or both concurrently. As a rule, the communist partner is allotted sales exclusivity in its own and in other Eastern markets, while the Western partner concentrates on the remaining territories. An example is an agreement under which the Simmons Machine Tools Company of Albany, New York, sells in the United States equipment manufactured by Czechoslovakia's Skoda.

A new class of contracts calls for one side to assist the other in markets (usually those of less developed countries) which happen to be more easily accessible to it for geographic, economic or political reasons. Hungary has helped to pioneer this particular method. Nikex, a foreign trade organization acting on behalf of a domestic enterprise, has contracted with the West German Rheinstahl group to co-produce semi-hydraulic mining equipment of a type which it has hitherto been importing. Manufacturing responsibility and local sales were assigned for five years to the Hungarian industrial enterprise. Nikex was given international distribution in Turkey and India (where bilateral treaties facilitate its access) and eventually in other foreign markets, when production outstrips demand. The West German firm has undertaken to supply all necessary technical aid, as well as special parts, castings and equipment.[21]

Joint efforts in the service industries offer exceptional latitude for foreign management and profit participation. A significant straw in the wind is the willingness of Russia's Intourist travel agency to rent automobiles under a royalty remunerated Hertz franchise. Avis is not too far behind in other East European regions.

In 1967, Intercontinental Hotels Corporation, a fully-owned subsidiary of Pan American Airways, in conjunction with Tower International, a company controlled by the Cyrus Eaton group of Cleveland, entered into agreements for the construction and operation of luxury hotels in Hungary, Rumania and Czechoslovakia. The Western firms are assisting with design, construction, personnel training, supervision, bookings and, above all, finance (interestingly enough obtained in part from the Soviet-owned Moscow Narodny Bank in London). An important aspect of the agreements is a license to use the Intercontinental name as a magnet for foreign tourists. Compensation is akin to, and in many respects better than a profit participation, namely, a percentage of the hotels' gross, hard currency receipts over a term of years, payable in convertible funds free of withholding taxes.[22]

The cooperative production of motion pictures and television films is a related form of activity to which Rumania, Hungary and Czechoslovakia have been particularly receptive. Here again, new ground was broken by Tower International with its unconditional guarantee of due performance by the Eastern side. Typically, the Western producer is offered low-priced studio facilities, secondary native actors, technicians, a variety of picturesque locations and various other facilities. Little or no legal restriction stands in the way. Personnel can be brought in from abroad without the opposition of local trade unions; nor are any tax or customs obstacles interposed. The consideration accruing to the Eastern party may include a cash payment in convertible currency, a participation in profits realized from the film's world-wide distribution and exclusive exploitation rights in local theaters or in other territories within the communist orbit. Outright co-productions between Eastern and Western companies and arrangements for the coupled distribution of Eastern films in the West are also quite current.

Although the socialist countries have been reluctant to allow split ownership in domestic co-ventures, they no longer demonstrate the same ideological aversion in the case of foreign-based activities; nor is it considered unpolitic to share the profits which such operations might yield. It is even becoming commonplace for capitalist firms and communist instrumentalities to register jointly owned patents and to establish jointly owned corporations under Western law, as vehicles for a continuing relationship. Of great potential importance are international marketing ventures conducted through mixed companies. Formed in jurisdictions which are hospitable from a legal and taxation point of view, the companies are conceived on the basis of divided equity, a balanced board of directors and jointly appointed management. We have noted earlier that such partnerships are becoming current as avenues for the more effective distribution of finished and semi-finished Eastern goods in foreign markets, and for the provision of various types of services, such as transportation and insurance. In due course, jointly owned firms, or consortia of communist and capitalist enterprises formed on an *ad hoc* basis, may be expected to bid for supply and construction contracts anywhere in the world, including the industrialized West.

Collaboration between Eastern and Western interests in development projects destined for backward economies is becoming too frequent to be dismissed as aberrational. Here, the Eastern role is increasingly that of supplier, or part-supplier, rather than mere recipient of technical know-how. Thus, Hungarian and Czechoslovak enterprises have ventured with Austrian firms in building thermal power stations for Lebanon, India, and Egypt; Czechoslovak and French companies have cooperated in the delivery of a textile plant to Iraq, and Morocco has received Austrian mining equipment built under Hungarian license.[23]

By now, sufficient evidence has accumulated to suggest that in the East-West context a significant movement is afoot from commodity trade to diverse forms of economic cooperation.[24] As the conventional exchange of physical goods reaches a ceiling imposed by hard currency shortages and the East's inability to market a broader range of exports, joint production, marketing and servicing ventures may become the most dynamic sector of commerce between planned and free economies.

The development of legal concepts necessary to sustain such a movement is still in an embryonic stage. But once again necessity is coming to the rescue as the mother of invention. A new range of pragmatic tools is being subtly hammered out by business executives and attorneys on both sides of the ideological barrier. To overcome the strictures of communist doctrine which preclude direct investment within the confines of a socialist economy, workable camouflage devices have been developed by imaginative draftsmen. The mutually desired economic results seem to be attainable nonetheless. Thus profits may be expressed in terms of royalties, service fees and interest, rather than dividends. The Western partner's yield is no less immediate or certain; in fact, his benefit is often greater. The substitute for outright ownership is a sale of capital goods on extended terms; transfer of title coupled with a lease-back arrangement can also perform this function. A posture approaching major equity control can be rendered politically palatable by means of a well conceived management contract.[25] Joint ventures based outside the borders of a communist country can be structured with even greater openness and facility.

In any event, the experience of the last decade suggests that when an objective is demonstrably and mutually advantageous, the communist partner will spare no effort to meet his capitalist partner halfway.

19

EAST-WEST COPYRIGHT RELATIONS

Although a highly specialized field which is not centrally within our frame of reference, copyright deserves separate attention in the context of intellectual property exchanges. For one thing, the degree of recognition, in law and practice, which communist countries accord to any class of foreign-created rights has a bearing upon the general climate of East–West legal and business relations. For another, the status of Western copyrights in the East and of Eastern copyrights in the West cuts across the entire range of cultural intercourse in literature, science and the arts, and carries significant commercial implications for the future. In one way or another, authors, playwrights, research scientists, composers, choreographers, performers, designers, artists generally, publishers, broadcasters, motion-picture and television producers, and even originators of taped industrial computer programs are all directly affected. Their concern is, moreover, not only with material considerations, such as uncompensated reproduction, but also with the basic problem of artistic distortion.

Since the Revolution, more than a billion copies of foreign works have been published in the U.S.S.R. alone. State publishing houses have reproduced, mostly in Russian translation, the writings of Western authors for domestic consumption and, occasionally, for export to less developed countries. Soviet statistics admit that in the years 1918 to 1960 there have been 182,290,000 copies printed of the works of 441 French authors; 103,290,000 copies of 324 British authors; 96,540,000 copies of 239 American authors; 69,340,000 copies of 324 German authors; 6,386,000 copies of 7 Canadian authors; and 4,480,000 copies of 11 Austrian authors. In 1959 it was alleged in a Moscow court that some five million copies of Sherlock Holmes had, over the years, been produced and sold in the U.S.S.R.[1] In the same year a 300,000-copy edition of the collected works of Ernest Hemingway was placed on the Russian market.

Through an extensive network of foreign agents, the U.S.S.R. procures annually thousands of book titles and learned periodicals in the field of science and technology for unauthorized and uncompensated reproduction under the auspices of the Soviet Institute of Scientific and Technical Information. The works of dramatists and composers have also been extensively performed. Soviet film organizations have been known to multicopy prints of foreign motion pictures and to release them with defective color and sound tracks. Popular songs by Western recording artists are also widely sold on Soviet discs without payment or offer of royalties to copyright holders.

Nor have foreign authors been able to prevent the unauthorized adaptation of their titles and story lines for films and television shows. In a particularly flagrant case, a Soviet production enterprise widely distributed at home and abroad a film based on Edgar Rice Burroughs' "Tarzan" without clearance from either the author's estate or the assignee of the motion picture rights. The French language version was entitled "Tarzan of the Seas" and referred to the hero by that name in the sub-titles. In an action instituted in 1965 on behalf of the American producer of the authorized film series, the Tribunal de Grande Instance de la Seine ordered the defendants, Soveksportfilm, a Soviet corporation, and Liberalfilm, a French corporation, to suppress all name references both in the film and in the related publicity.[2] The case illustrates the proposition that a foreign party may be able to vindicate his rights when the plagiarized work circulates in the West. He is, however, impotent within the confines of the U.S.S.R. itself.

Although the use of foreign works has gone largely uncompensated, some modest *ex-gratia* payments have been forthcoming from time to time. For example, Upton Sinclair, William Saroyan and Erskine Caldwell have received small dollar payments. André Gide, Romain Rolland and Françoise Sagan were compensated more generously, but in blocked rubles, expendable only within the Soviet Union. Somerset Maugham,

Graham Greene and Arthur Miller have also received occasional remuneration. Such payments, tendered without legal or contractual obligation, are neither accompanied by an accounting nor computed by reference to sales volume or to the royalty schedules applicable to local copyright holders. The vast majority of pirated authors receive nothing other than the personal satisfaction of seeing their works circulate within an important, albeit intellectually protected segment of humanity.

Of course, Russia has not been the only international delinquent in matters of foreigners' copyrights. One need only recall the long-lasting, insular approach of Anglo-American law in this area and the nineteenth-century wholesale United States pirating of English works, especially the novels of Charles Dickens. Such comparisons, however, cannot mitigate in contemporary, particularly Marxist terms, the uncompensated exploitation of the toil of foreign intellectuals.[3] To place the communist record in proper perspective, it is first necessary to consider the philosophy and nature of Eastern copyright law within its domestic confines.

A. Authors' Rights in a Communist Society

Private interests in any publicly marketable creation, be it an original writing or a patentable invention, seem basically irreconcilable with the principle of socialist property. Since communist society conditions the individual to feel that he owes his education and training to the state, his intellectual output should, it might be argued, rightfully belong to the community as a whole. Nonetheless, here as in other areas, the Eastern states have found it expedient to retain institutions of bourgeois origin. Their copyright laws are largely structured along conventional lines, with one pervasive difference: whereas Western policy seeks to protect the personal and proprietary interest of the creative individual, the Eastern aim is first and foremost to promote the declared values of a communist society. To that end, the law is conceived to stimulate the production of "socially wholesome" works, by means of pecuniary incentives, various intangible rewards and the recognition of limited authorship rights.

That the attributes of intellectual property are of only secondary importance is readily admitted by Eastern commentators.[4] Vivid demonstration of this fact can be found in legislative provisions which, in a number of instances, dispense with the requirement of consent to the use of an author's work and with the state organization's duty to compensate him for its exploitation. The extent to which acquired private rights may be enjoyed is, practically speaking, further circumscribed by the state's control over the individual's possibility to publish and, indeed, to express himself at all.

It is not only the whim of Russia's notorious official censorship but also the state's hand on every financial, industrial and commercial lever of the nation, publishing included, which ensure that "unpalatable" works will not see the light of day. This is true even if there has been no trespass beyond the decreed limits of political dissent. For example, in the past, Stalin's dogmatic preference for the now discredited genetics of Lysenko meant that proven scientific truths could obtain neither public nor academic exposure. Manuscripts containing invasions of privacy, libel, pornography—problems with which courts and law enforcement officers everywhere have wrestled for centuries—can never reach the potential reader, let alone become justiciable; the state simply denies funds for their publication and outlets for their circulation. Romantic love, religion, destiny, the riddle of existence, the infinite nuances of the human psyche are also themes which invite a bureaucratic frown, unless treated in a socially "desirable" context. This is particularly true in connection with works originating in the "decadent" West. The same strictures apply to abstract modernism in music, sculpture and painting. For years a wealth of French impressionist canvases was stored away in the attic of Leningrad's Hermitage Museum to make room for the perennial beauty of the tractor.

In a free economy, where publishing is largely governed by the profit motive, talent may also be denied expression. No doubt, many novels, musical compositions and film projects have at first been dismissed as non-commercial, regardless of their artistic merit. But the judgment is at least left to the hazards of public taste. In a society where the notion of "illegal" art stands as official credo, the judgment is a function of administrative caprice. One can only speculate on how many masterpieces have been lost to posterity as a result of arbitrary or incompetent decisions by a group of political hacks set up as a literary tribunal of last resort.

It is in the nature of the system that the broad public can have access to a work of science, literature, or music only through the channels of the government's publishing, broadcasting, television, motion picture or performance hall monopolies; and that such monopolies have a mandate to make acceptability judgments in terms of social harmlessness and usefulness. To hope for alternative channels is tantamount to wishing away the very basis of the communist economic system. The political partiality charges which are occasionally levelled at government-operated broadcasting and television instrumentalities of the West, the French O.R.T.F. or the B.B.C., for example, offer a small glimmer of the problem's true dimensions. In the East the state's monopoly is generalized to all media of public expression.

The author or artist whose works do not conform to the objectives of the politicians currently in power or, more specifically, the General Administration for the Protection of Military and Government Secrets in Printing (in the past known less euphemistically as the General Administration for Literary and Publishing Affairs) can derive little legal protection or material advantage from his copyright. Not only will he find it impossible to disseminate his work through legitimate outlets at home or abroad; worse, he will be under pressure from party, press and unions of his peers to toe the officially prescribed line. In this connection, we may allude to the chequered political fortunes of the composer Shostakovitch, the film director Eisenstein and the writer Ehrenburg during the dark Stalinist era, and of the poets Yevtushenko, Voznesensky and Okudzhava thereafter. Even more striking is the contrast in treatment of a Pasternak and a Sholokhov. The former was intimidated into renouncing the Nobel prize for literature; the latter, whose writings have always enjoyed party approval, was permitted to accept it with fanfare.

Against the background of public prosecutions directed against dissident intellectuals (to wit, the spectacular cases of Daniel, Litvinov and Siniavsky) it does not need a rabid anticommunist to stress that the Eastern societies have failed to provide their culturally creative elements with a constitutionally protected environment of free speech and expression, or that the exercise of author's rights is conditioned upon rigid observance of prescribed ideological norms. Censorship no less severe than Pushkin and Dostoievsky knew in the time of the Tsars hangs like an oppressive cloud over the entire cultural landscape. Its scope has been courageously described by Alexander Solzhenitzyn in an open letter circulated in Moscow in 1967:

> Many delegates to this congress know how they themselves have had to bow to the pressure of the censorship, to capitulate. They have rewritten chapters, pages, paragraphs, phrases; they have sweetened them only because they wanted to have them published; in so doing, they have damaged them irreparably. What is best in our literature is mutilated before it appears.[5]

An impression of the prevailing climate is provided by the experience of Solzhenitzyn himself, even prior to his recent expulsion from the Soviet

Writers' Union. Patronized by the leadership in 1962, he managed to publish *One Day in the Life of Ivan Denisovitch* in the liberal literary magazine *Novyi Mir*. After the fall of Khrushchev, he came under sharp attack from die-hard fellow-writers and politicians. His popularity, nonetheless, continued to grow as a result of two further novels, *Cancer Ward* and *In the First Circle*, which were widely passed from hand to hand through the clandestine "Samizdat" system of typescript and carbon copy reproduction. To date, the books have not been published in the U.S.S.R., thus sharing the fate of many other "illegal" works of literature, such as *Doctor Zhivago*.[6]

For a time, there appeared a trend toward more flexible publishing standards, under the Khrushchev regime in the U.S.S.R. and the Dubcek interlude in Czechoslovakia. Today, neo-Stalinist controls once again seem to govern authors in communist countries, regardless of whether they seek to circulate their "socially harmful" works surreptitiously or on a legitimately copyrightable basis. The controls apply with *a fortiori* force to Westerners who seek Eastern outlets for their creative ideas and artistic accomplishments.

Dissident or *avant-garde* authors who hope to have their works published abroad are confronted by a much more embarrassing situation. In fact, two courses are open to them. The timorous may proceed through the regular channels of the official publishing agency and accept the risk of having their plans vetoed or their manuscripts doctored by the censors. The more ardent may allow the unadulterated version of their book to be smuggled out of the country. Under the Soviet criminal code, wilful dissemination of slanders against the state and the social system is a severely punishable offense. And, of course, the government itself (with the perfunctory endorsement of the courts) decides when such slander has been committed. An ominous choice therefore arises: either to disavow the Western publisher in order to avoid prosecution and officially sponsored ostracism, or to defy the state, on the ground that punishment would contravene the freedom of expression purportedly guaranteed by the Soviet Constitution of 1936. The second alternative calls for the bravado of a kamikaze. Experience has shown that it leads to oblivion in a Siberian prison camp or insane asylum.

The Western author who wishes to be read in a communist country and the Western publisher who is interested in bringing the works of an Eastern writer to foreign markets, find that they must enter a strangely surrealistic world. But their view is blurred by a traditional outlook upon civil liberties, law and economic organization. In a system founded on wholly different social assumptions, be it Russia, South Africa or Spain, the absence of our cherished constitutional guarantees seems less disconcerting.

Nonetheless, returning to the more strictly legal plane of our discussion, it is well to reiterate that the concept of copyright enjoys recognition in all of the communist countries and that many privileges resembling the conventional are effectively granted and protected. As in other branches of law, Soviet legislation calls the tune for all of Eastern Europe, although a number of discordant variations are discernible from country to country, particularly in the treatment of foreign authors.

B. Soviet Principles of Copyright Protection

In the U.S.S.R., the basic provisions of copyright law were first promulgated in 1925 and more comprehensively in 1928 in a federal statute which remained in force until the 1960s. Its essential features were then incorporated, in somewhat modified form, into the Basic Principles of Civil Legislation and the Civil Codes of the several Soviet Republics. These provisions (supplemented by government-prescribed standard publishing and production contracts and fixed remuneration schedules) as interpreted over the years in a substantial body of judicial and administrative case law constitute the major sources of current copyright law.

Conceptually, Soviet law is closer to the continental notion of *droit d'auteur* than to American "copyright." Neither registration with a designated authority nor any other formality is required as a condition precedent to the enforcement of rights.[7] Protection stems from the creation of the work. It is sufficient that the subject matter exists in some presentable form: an unpublished manuscript, sketch, photograph, motion picture film, sound recording or the like, which would permit reproduction and dissemination. Otherwise the Soviet approach is closer to the more restrictive Anglo-American position, which views copyright as a privilege with limited monopoly benefits and a relatively short life span.

According to Article 96 of the Basic Principles, protection is broadly available for "any scientific, literary or artistic work, regardless of its form, purpose or value, or of the manner of its reproduction." Section 475 of the Russian Civil Code covers all oral matter such as speeches, lectures and reports, dramatic, dramatic-musical and purely musical works, translations, scenarios, theatrical and television films as well as radio and television broadcasts, tapes and gramophone records. The scope of copyright protection is thus virtually coextensive with that of most Western systems. A Soviet citizen enjoys its benefits irrespective of whether the eligible work is published at home, abroad or not at all.

Essentially, the author acquires two kinds of benefits: personal and proprietary. The former includes the right "to publish, reproduce and circulate the work by any legal means, under his own name, a pseudonym, or anonymously" and the right "to the integrity of his work." Within the latter category is the entitlement "to receive remuneration for the use of his work by other persons, except in the cases provided by law." Rates of remuneration are prescribed by legislation at the federal and republican levels.[8]

The benefits of copyright endure for the life of the author. At death, they pass (with certain limitations, including a 50 percent reduction in the rate of royalties) to his successors and subsist for a period of fifteen years. In the event that the holder is an institution, the rights endure in perpetuity. Upon reorganization or dissolution, title passes to the new entity or to the state.

A number of specific provisions significantly narrow the scope of these broadly declared advantages. Thus the right to publish is not considered in Soviet law as an exclusive one. The state reserves the power to purchase compulsorily from the author the right of publication, performance or other use. Moreover, the author's consent is not required for public performance of a published work, use of a published literary work in the creation of musical compositions with text and use of an artistic work of photography in connection with manufactured articles. In each of these instances payment of remuneration to the author is, however, guaranteed by law.[9]

In certain other legislatively defined situations, the right of both consent and remuneration are laid aside. For example, one may borrow from a published work in order to produce something new and creatively independent, or reproduce generous portions of its text in scientific, critical, educational and political publications as well as in newspapers and on screen, radio and television. In all of these cases it is sufficient merely to indicate the name of the author and the source.

The treatment of translations, a subject of special interest to foreign authors, offers one of the clearest illustrations of the supremacy of the public interest over private rights. To ensure prompt dissemination of creative works throughout the U.S.S.R. in the various languages of the republics, Soviet law goes so far as to permit translation without the author's prior consent. The author, however, must be notified, and the meaning and integrity of his work must be preserved. He is also entitled to a fee with respect to the published translation.

The right to preserve the integrity of a creative work is intended to prevent distortion or misuse. In French law this notion is enshrined as *droit moral.* Like all civilized countries, Russia affords the author meaningful protection on this score. To the extent that he has stayed within the limits of what is officially considered wholesome and permissible this safeguard is largely a matter of private interest. However, if the manuscript deviates from sanctioned guidelines as to form and content, the publishing organization may refuse to accept it (notwithstanding a prior contractual undertaking) unless appropriate modifications are made. In effect, the author is then compelled either to violate the integrity of his own work or to forego its publication altogether.

On this point we have the startling testimony of Anatoly Kuznetsov. In 1965 the Soviet author won a lawsuit in France against a publisher and translator for unauthorized and distorted publication of his novel *The Continuation of a Legend.* Following his defection to the West in August 1969, the author took the highly unusual step of petitioning the French Ministry of Justice to set aside a judgment which had been entered in his favor and affirmed on appeal. In a published confession of what was, in effect, contempt of court, he declared that the lawsuit had been instituted under compulsion from the Soviet authorities. The real literary distortion was allegedly perpetrated by the Soviet censors at the time of original publication; the altered French version "succeeded in catching the very essence of my novel."[10]

An author's position with regard to the use of his work, except in the instances already indicated, is further defined in his agreement with a particular state publishing house. The scope of contractual autonomy, however, is extremely narrow. Standard contracts, in most cases administratively decreed, operate with the force of law. Nor are the government-prescribed schedules of remuneration susceptible to any real bargaining.

The principal types of standard agreements are publishing contracts and production contracts. The former, newly promulgated by the Government Publishing Committee of the Council of Ministers on April 10, 1967, deal separately with works of literature and various other writings, *e.g.,* scientific and educational. Prescribed production contracts extend to the film industry as well, in the case of scriptwriters and composers. Directors, members of the cast, decorators and other creative personnel are deemed to be employees rendering services under labor contracts rather than authors, as

—

they are generally viewed in continental coypright systems, *e.g.* France. It is not the fact that such persons are salaried which disqualifies them from enjoyment of authorship rights. Soviet laws recognize that a creative work originated in the course of employment vests in the employee, not the employer organization—an interesting abatement of conventional labor law principles in a society where few persons are self-employed. The determining consideration is the nature of the function, not the status of the individual.

Despite its peculiarities, the author's contract is a two-party agreement which typically calls for the creation and delivery within a fixed time of the work described therein. The author undertakes to correct and modify his manuscript, if the state publishing or production organization should so request in writing. While the contract is in force, the author may not authorize the same mode of exploitation to any other organization without the express consent of the party with whom he stands in privity.

On its side, the production or publication organization agrees to receive and examine the work within a specified period and to inform the author regarding its acceptability. If the decision is affirmative, the organization assumes the responsibility of publishing, performing, or producing the work under the terms and conditions of the preexisting contract and to pay fees in accordance with predetermined schedules. Occasionally it agrees to pay advances against royalties on the strength of the contract alone. In the event of breach on the part of the author, such as late delivery or refusal to insert requested corrections, any payments so received must be returned. On the other hand, the liability of the state organization is clearly established in case of failure to make use of the approved work within the contractually specified period. Assuming the author was not contributorily responsible, he may demand full payment of the stipulated royalties, rescission of the contract and return of the work he has delivered.[11]

A rather paternalistic aspect of Soviet legislation is that it declares null and void an author's voluntary abridgment of rights which leaves him with something less than what is afforded by law and by the standard contract. Here again a parallel with West European, particularly French, law exists. In the continental scheme of copyright, defined limits are established beyond which an author lacks the capacity irrevocably to divest himself of advantages. In the U.S.S.R., the invalidation of contractual waivers extends to the administratively prescribed levels of remuneration as well.[12]

Royalty scales, although restated in publishing and production contracts, are generally determined not by a process of free negotiation but by reference to fixed schedules established by republican decree. From the standpoint of the Soviet author, this arrangement is probably not as disadvantageous as may seem at first glance. Since he must deal with the state publishing monopoly, his bargaining position is in any event very weak.

The compensation schedules divide copyrightable achievements into distinct categories: belles-lettres, non-fiction, dramatic and musical plays, pictorial and graphic items reproduced in printed form, works for television and the like. Within these classifications, further subdivisions are created. Belles-lettres, for example, are broken down into fiction, short stories, one-act plays and poetry. The principal criterion for calculating the royalty due on a given work is the size of the volume. In the socialist mentality, this should correspond to the quantity of labor attributable to its creation. The unit of measurement for prose is the "author's sheet" (40,000 letters); for poetry, the number of lines is determinative.

This assumed interrelation between expended effort (reflected by the physical dimension of the work) and ruble entitlement is not consistently respected. For certain classes of literature a distinction is drawn between mass editions (generally 25,000 copies or more) and regular editions, higher royalties being paid in the former case, notwithstanding the absence of any additional labor on the author's part.[13]

Recognition of an entitlement to additional fees for new editions of old works is also difficult to reconcile with the declared theory of compensation. Further, in the dramatic, musical and cinematographic fields, supplementary royalties have occasionally been awarded in respect of performances attended by a paying public. Here the computation has been by reference to a percentage of box office receipts. The posthumous continuation of royalties for the benefit of heirs, even though they have done nothing to earn them, is perhaps the clearest departure from theory. Controversy among Soviet jurists over such inconsistencies has led, in recent years, toward a compromise reduction of allowable rates of compensation in the special instances just mentioned.

Implicit in the sub-division of creative works for royalty purposes is a judgment as to their social value. Thus, not all items of the same size fetch comparable scales of remuneration. According to the schedules, technical treatises are worth more than fiction. The piano score of an opera is better remunerated than a symphony of the same length.[14] Operas earn the composer between 1200 and 3000 rubles for a printing of 5000 piano copies; symphony scores command between 800 and 1200 rubles and are printed in more limited editions. An ultimate consideration in all cases is, of course, the ideological quality of the particular work. A sliding scale for fiction permits remuneration to be set within a range of 250 to 400 rubles per author's sheet in the case of mass editions. The higher rate apparently rewards the author who has best epitomized the qualities of socialist realism.

Not to be underestimated is the importance of non-monetary rewards. Creators of exceptional merit or talent are stimulated by means of supplementary incentives which may be either lucrative or honorific in nature: Lenin prizes, medals, special housing priorities, income tax exemptions, grants and subsidies from various cultural funds. The prestige which accrues from such distinctions can bring considerable material benefit as well.

Paradoxically, writers, poets and playwrights constitute the most opulent class of the classless Soviet citizenry and the most successful among them enjoy considerable wealth. Chukovsky, long the dean of modern Russian authors, who died in October 1969 at the age of 87, is reported to have left an estate worth one million dollars in cash. The source of this fortune is a lifetime's accumulation of royalties from best-selling books of poetry, children's stories and popular translations of Western authors such as Oscar Wilde, O. Henry and Walt Whitman.

C. East European Variations

In their general outlines, the copyright systems of eastern Europe follow the model evolved by the U.S.S.R. With the exception of Hungary, which has professed to realign its pre-existing law, all the countries of the region have promulgated new legislation following the installation of their communist regimes.[15]

Despite an underlying similarity of principle, certain departures from Soviet concepts warrant special mention. Since some of the socialist states participate in international copyright arrangements, their internal laws have practical relevance for foreign parties. Thus, in contrast to the U.S.S.R., the continental preference for rather long periods of copyright protection has generally been preserved. Under current Czechoslovak, Hungarian and Yugoslav law, the duration is fifty years from the death of the author. Soviet law, on the other hand, has confined protection to fifteen years *post mortem auctoris*.

Bulgaria and Rumania have more complex rules, varying the time limit according to the author's family relationship with his heirs. In both countries, the surviving spouse may inherit the copyright for life or until remarriage. Likewise, the author's parents may take a life estate. Beyond this, Bulgarian law upholds a bequest to a minor until majority or completion of education (the limit being twenty-four years of age) and to incapacitated persons until the end of their incapacity. In Rumania, descendants of the author may enjoy the fruits of copyright for fifty years, but all other heirs are limited to fifteen years (or until majority or completion of education, but not beyond twenty-five years of age). Although precommunist Poland prescribed a fifty-year period, a 1952 law grants only twenty years from the death of the author for most works, and ten years from the date of first publication for photographic and cinematographic works and certain musical adaptations.

An interesting deviation covers juridical persons. While Soviet law, anxious to maximize the benefits of state-owned entities, grants them copyright in perpetuity, most of the other Eastern countries confine protection to narrower periods than in the case of individuals. Hungary, Rumania and Yugoslavia limit the duration to fifty years from the creation of the original work. Poland grants a life of twenty years to corporate copyrights, Bulgaria fifteen years and Czechoslovakia ten years.

The Soviet prototype is quite faithfully followed in the definition of circumstances under which the consent of the author for use of his copyrighted work and his right to remuneration may be dispensed with. Such divergence as exists in this particular area is not fundamental. One significant exception is the sphere of translations, where the U.S.S.R. seems to be largely alone in discarding the element of author's consent. If other Eastern countries follow suit, they do not do so expressly. Bulgaria goes part way, recognizing the author's right to permit but not to enjoin translations. Under Hungarian law and a 1961 decision of the Budapest City Court, on the other hand, the unauthorized reproduction, publication or dissemination of a translation into any language constitutes an infringement.[16] It is useful to note that with respect to nationals of Berne Union countries, this right to authorize translations is exclusive for a period of ten years from the date of original publication. In the case of authors from countries which are members of the Universal Copyright Convention, the exclusivity is limited to seven years.

Like the Soviet Union, the other Eastern countries maintain the institution of the prescribed publishing and production contract, with standard obligatory forms and fixed remuneration tables, generally computed in units of author's sheets. The sole exception is Yugoslavia, where this method of calculation has become optional: parties may establish the amount of fees either as a percentage of selling price and volume or as a lump sum. The former technique is reportedly still the most prevalent.[17] However, a 1968 Yugoslav law has broken away from communist tradition by recognizing the parties' right to fix appropriate remuneration independently of state control. The sales possibilities of the work and the material advantages which a contracting party could be expected to draw from its exploitation are stated to be relevant considerations.

A limited exception in favor of foreign authors exists under the 1965 Czechoslovak copyright law. In certain cases non-nationals are permitted to escape from the rigors of the predetermined royalty schedule. This and other innovations have undoubtedly been prompted by Czechoslovakia's adhesion, as of 1959, to the Universal Copyright Convention for the Protection of Performers, Producers of Phonograms and Broadcasting Organizations. Thus it has been specially provided that no radio or television presentation of the works of foreign authors can take place without consent.

Further, with a view to facilitating all types of international commercial transactions, a degree of decentralization has been injected into the method of licensing authors' rights abroad. Under a 1953 proclamation, dealings in Czechoslovak books, brochures, periodicals and similar works, as well as dramatic, dramatic-musical, choreographic and pantomime creations, were funneled exclusively through the Theatrical and Literary Agency with headquarters in Prague. Currently, other state organizations, such as music publishers, film companies, and radio and television instrumentalities, are permitted to negotiate independently in their respective areas of expertise. Individual authors cannot, however, circumvent the intermediary function of the state agency.

To the extent that the Czechoslovak legislation established a special regime with respect to foreigners' copyrights, it is an isolated phenomenon in the East. This approach may be considered an extension of that country's originality in the general treatment of economic relations with the capitalist world. Elsewhere, Western parties who may be entitled to locally available protection, either under contract or by virtue of an intergovernmental treaty, should expect to fall under the normal domestic regime. International conventions operative in the field of copyright have, generally, adopted a national standard as the basis of reciprocal treatment.

D. Communist Recognition of Western Copyrights

1. Under Local Law

Soviet copyright law, viewed from an international perspective, is a one-way street, affording protection solely to works or persons emanating from the U.S.S.R. Citizens and their heirs acquire domestic rights even if the work in question is first published abroad. A foreign author, on the other hand, obtains no local rights unless his work is first published in the U.S.S.R. or found there in material form prior to publication elsewhere. If the work had previously appeared outside Russian territory, access to Soviet copyright is entirely foreclosed and no legal basis exists for attacking plagiarized, uncompensated or distorted exploitation.

To arrange first publication of a foreign work in the Soviet Union is not a simple matter. The alien author must be prepared to run the gauntlet of public censors without any certainty of success. He must locate a state publishing house willing to print and disseminate. Even if he succeeds, all he can look forward to are the limited pecuniary benefits prescribed by local law. Soviet publishing organizations have little incentive to accept a foreign work for copyrightable first publication. If they are interested in having the book appear, they can simply reprint it after initial publication abroad, without any need for either consent or remuneration.

The residue of cases in which a foreigner might become vested with copyright under local law involves contributions to Soviet publications, films photographed in the U.S.S.R., recordings and tapes of music produced there, and so forth. Whether technical protection can be obtained by mere presentation of the foreigner's finished manuscript to a Soviet publisher prior to its publication elsewhere remains to be tested.

Even if the foreign work were copyrighted in the Soviet Union, it follows from our previous discussion of translators' rights that the author could not enjoin an unauthorized rendition into another language. Nor could he control or influence the selection of a qualified translator. At most, he would be entitled to notice of the proposed translation, preservation of his work's meaning and integrity and remuneration for use.

Non-Soviet authors (and their heirs and assigns) whose works are first published outside the U.S.S.R. can acquire no rights whatsoever under the operation of local law. The Basic Principles have perpetuated the long-standing Soviet position in Article 97: "Copyright in works first published or located in some presentable form on the territory of a foreign country shall be recognized as belonging to [non-Soviet citizens] . . . only on the grounds and within the limits of pertinent international agreements concluded by the U.S.S.R." Such agreements are few and far between even within the East. An isolated example is that concluded with Hungary for a three-year period as of January 1, 1968.[18]

In 1959, the executors of the estate of Sir Arthur Conan Doyle initiated litigation in the U.S.S.R. with a view to testing both Soviet law and Soviet intentions with regard to remuneration rights of foreign authors (or their successors) whose works had been reproduced in Russian translation. *The Adventures of Sherlock Holmes* has long been favorite reading in the Soviet Union and repeated editions had yielded to several state publishing houses an estimated revenue of 25,000,000 rubles (roughly $6,250,000 at the then prevailing rate of exchange).

The claim, heard at first instance in the Moscow City Court and on appeal in the Supreme Court of the R.S.F.S.R., conceded that under Soviet copyright law no relief was available in the absence of treaty provisions. Any attempt to argue otherwise would have been specious. Instead, the case was founded on a rather ingenious theory of unjust enrichment. Article 399 of the Civil Code of 1922, the substance of which had been taken from the German Civil Code, provided for restitution where one party became unjustly enriched at the expense of another. Plaintiff sought restoration to the author's estate of a portion of the profits realized by the defendant state publishing organizations. The Supreme Court, affirming the first-instance tribunal, rejected the claim on the ground that reliance upon unjust enrichment principles was an attempt to circumvent explicit and imperative provisions of Soviet copyright law.[19]

2. *Under International Law*

The international system of copyright protection is presently based on two major multilateral instruments: the Berne Union of 1886, administered (along with the 1883 Convention on Industrial Property) by the United International Bureaux for the Protection of Intellectual Property, and the Universal Copyright Convention of 1952, administered by the UNESCO Secretariat. In the evolving field of "neighboring rights," the UNESCO-sponsored 1961 Rome Convention for the Protection of Performers, Producers of Phonograms and Broadcasting Organizations is also becoming increasingly significant. On the bilateral plane, a number of agreements establish reciprocal copyright relations between individual pairs of countries.

The Berne instrument, which is essentially European in concept and scope of participation, counts among its adherents all of the continental communist countries except the U.S.S.R. and Albania. While the membership of this group of states antedates their present regimes, the rights and obligations of the Convention remain fully operative in international law. The basic criterion of protection is the national treatment standard: the literary, artistic and scientific works of citizens of other member states must be given a degree of protection at least equivalent to that accorded to local citizens. A work's copyright status in its country of origin is irrelevant.

The Convention also attempts to unify certain provisions of domestic legislation. Above all, it declares that the enjoyment and exercise of copyright shall not be made subject to any formality requirements. Further, it establishes a number of substantive rights, e.g., the author's exclusive power to authorize adaptations, arrangements, translations and other alterations of his literary, scientific or artistic work throughout the term of protection.

In 1948, the so-called Brussels revision of the Berne Convention prescribed, among other things, a standard term of protection measured by the life of the author plus fifty years. Only Yugoslavia among the member countries of eastern Europe has adhered to this revision. The others have limited their ratifications to an earlier revision, adopted at Rome in 1928, wherein shorter periods are tolerated. The Berne Convention underwent still another variation in Stockholm in July 1967. As an inducement to communist countries to accept the new text, members not bound by the Brussels draft were specifically exempted from compliance with the "life-plus-fifty" term. East Germany has been the only country to accede to the Stockholm version.

In contrast to the Berne Union, the Universal Copyright Convention is world-wide in scope, the United States also being a member. Among the communist countries, only Czechoslovakia, Yugoslavia and (pre-Castro) Cuba have adhered.[20] The governing principle is, likewise, the national treatment standard, but the minimum criteria of protection flowing from the instrument itself are more limited than in the case of the Berne Convention. The operation allotted to national law is correspondingly broader.

The U.C.C. extends protection to literary, scientific and artistic works of nationals of any contracting state, whether or not such works be published. It also protects authors of nonmember states who first publish within a member country. The minimum period of coverage, shorter than that allowed by the Berne Union, is twenty-five years *post mortem auctoris.* Moreover, the author's exclusive right to translate or authorize translation is limited to seven years from the date of first publication. Thereafter, under specified conditions, member states may permit unauthorized translations into the national language, but their domestic laws are required to protect the author's right to a rate of remuneration which is just and consistent with international standards, to allow the remittance of such remuneration and to afford legal remedies tending to ensure the correctness of the translation.

Several of the Eastern countries have long-standing bilateral copyright relations with Western nations. For example, a treaty between Italy and Hungary dates back to 1891. The United States has stood in agreement with Hungary since 1912. The continued effectiveness of this agreement following World War I and World War II was confirmed pursuant to the Treaty of Trianon (1920) and the Treaty of Peace (1948), respectively. A copyright agreement between the United States and Rumania which first came into force in 1928 was also revalidated in 1948. A similar arrangement between the United States and Poland has been in existence since 1927. Its effectiveness has been affirmed by the Polish delegate to UNESCO in 1962. Although a reciprocal copyright agreement has also existed, as of 1927, between the United States and Czechoslovakia, it was expressly abrogated by the latter in 1953.[21]

Typically, the several bilateral agreements call for mutual application of the national treatment standard and preserve the formalities prescribed by national norms. As in the case of multilateral conventions, the enjoyment and exercise of copyright is generally independent of the existence of protection in the country of the work's origin. The period of protection is freely determinable by the law of the country where protection is sought.

In passing, it should be mentioned that a 1924 Soviet agreement with Italy and a 1925 agreement with Norway vaguely stipulated that reciprocal most-favored-nation treatment in regard to industrial, literary and artistic property should be regulated by special convention. A 1924 agreement with the United Kingdom also provided for two-sided protection, but without making reference to the most-favored-nation standard. To date, however, no conventions have been concluded either with Italy or England. An instrument between the U.S.S.R. and Norway signed in 1928 left out all mention of copyright, limiting its application to industrial property matters only.

As for most of the East European countries, we may say in summary, protection comparable to that afforded local beneficiaries exists in favor of foreign parties, within the limits afforded by the Berne Union, the U.C.C. or isolated bilateral treaties. The U.S.S.R. and China, on the other hand, have chosen to continue their copyright isolation from any meaningful scheme of internationally established ground rules. Nor do their domestic laws offer any comfort to affected Western parties.

In fact, this isolation perpetuates a situation which is far less satisfactory than that which prevailed in connection with industrial property protection even prior to the U.S.S.R.'s 1965 adherence to the Paris Convention. For in the Soviet Union, as in other Eastern states, a foreign patent or trademark holder could, at all times, secure a measure of protection by registering in accordance with local law. In the copyright field, on the other hand, no provision at all is made for registration. Foreign authors are, therefore, wholly deprived of the benefits flowing from the normal operation of both domestic and international copyright law. Fundamentally, the same situation prevails in the case of Communist China. Nonetheless, since no protection whatever is provided either by treaty or by law, unauthorized or uncompensated publication does not constitute a violation of legal rights. Soviet and Chinese exploitation of foreign works may be condemned as ethically reprehensible, but it cannot be challenged on strictly juridical grounds.

3. *Prospects for Eastern Adaptation*

There is no realistic basis for predicting that the Soviet Union will follow up its 1965 ratification of the Paris Convention on Industrial Property with adherence to the U.C.C. A record exists of numerous intercessions over the years at the level of professional associations (notably the International Confederation of Authors' and Composers' Societies), governments and individual statesmen, such as President Roosevelt, Prime Minister Churchill and, in a private capacity, Governor Adlai Stevenson.[22] To date, such initiatives have yielded nothing but recurrent rumors of imminent Soviet adherence to an existing, or a specially conceived scheme of international copyright cooperation.

That the current trend is in the direction of greater Eastern compliance with world-wide arrangements in the field of commerce, may be considered a good omen by those who are interested in copyright. Solace can also be drawn from the fact that an increasing number of Western authors find themselves unexpectedly rewarded with Soviet royalty checks. That the amounts are modest and arbitrarily arrived at and the selection of beneficiaries sporadic and discriminatory can be explained on the ground of extreme Soviet reluctance to establish costly precedents. For the reproduction of foreign books has long proceeded on such a scale as to threaten considerable losses of convertible funds if their authors had to be compensated systematically and in determinable amounts. Presumably, it is for the same reason that formal adherence to an international pattern of protection is still considered inexpedient. Of course, a variety of other considerations are also in play. The Soviet analysis with regard to a future posture must necessarily weigh the inconveniences of membership in a copyright treaty against the advantages it would yield. Although the negative side has prevailed thus far, a sudden shift in the balance cannot be excluded.

What are the vital factors likely to determine the Soviet decision? First, there is the financial element. On the one hand, adherence to the U.C.C. would prevent the future pirating of published foreign works, aside from requiring the payment and remittance of compensation in conformity with international standards. On the other, the U.C.C. does not apply retroactively to works already in the public domain at the time of adherence. There would therefore be no massive liability for past exploitation by the state publishing monopolies.

Annual profits accruing from the translation of protected foreign works would be somewhat reduced by the need to pay royalties in accordance with domestically applicable schedules. More important, however, the conventional undertaking to observe international norms may well demand a special exemption from local remuneration ceilings in regard to foreigners, as is already the case in Czechoslovakia. Also, it is doubtful that the Soviets could satisfy the monetary "transmittal" requirements by merely setting up blocked ruble credits for the account of the foreign author. Consequently, a significant depletion of convertible currency supplies can be anticipated.

Further, a number of modifications, either general in scope or specifically intended for international purposes, would have to be introduced into local law. The U.C.C. precludes reservations to any of its terms. Soviet federal law would therefore have to guarantee foreigners a minimum twenty-five-year period of protection, in lieu of the present fifteen-year time limit. In regard to translations, Soviet law would have to acknowledge the foreign author's exclusive right to grant or withhold permission, at least during the first seven years following publication—a difficult concession for a country which has entirely abolished the element of consent.

Modifications to disqualify foreign parties from the enjoyment of privileges not available under prevailing world standards may also be indicated. Thus, unless the U.S.S.R. were ready to curtail the perpetual protection it grants its corporate copyright holders, the national treatment standard of the U.C.C. would require comparable benefits for Western publishing companies which hold direct copyright in a particular work.

On the side of the ledger which favors international compliance is the value of effective protection in the case of indigenous works published abroad in original or translation. Such protection would afford world-wide exposure to the U.S.S.R.'s considerable cultural achievements on the most lucrative basis.

To be sure, Russian authors are not wholly in the wilderness at the international level. Some of them have been known to receive their due on the basis of simple business morality or the anticipated impact of certain national laws. A striking illustration is the disposal of the multimillion-dollar revenue yielded by Western publication and adaptation of *Doctor Zhivago*, and other works of Boris Pasternak. During his lifetime the author granted foreign exploitation rights through all media to the Italian publishing house Giangiacomo Feltrinelli. By will he gave the bulk of his estate to two sons and his long-time companion, Olga Ivinskaya, all Soviet citizens and residents. Following years of controversy and negotiation, a settlement calling for the transfer of undisclosed sums to the legatees was reached in February, 1970.[23] Similarly, Alexander Solzhenitsyn has retained Western counsel with a view to prohibiting the unauthorized publication of his works abroad and to marshalling royalties due from extensive world-wide exploitation.

Western countries occasionally protect Soviet interests on a national treatment basis without insisting upon reciprocity. In a 1959 case which reached as high as the French Cour de Cassation, the rights of a Soviet composer whose musical work had been incorporated without consent into an American-produced film shown in France were found to be protected by local law. The seizure of the prints and proceeds was upheld as valid. A law was subsequently promulgated establishing reciprocity as a precondition to the protection of foreign copyrights in France.[24]

Existing loopholes in the international protection system might permit Russian authors to qualify for "side-door" benefits. Thus, a Soviet work could probably obtain copyright recognition in the U.S.A. or other U.C.C. countries by means of concurrent publication at home and in the territory of one of the Convention's adherents, France or Czechoslovakia, for example. Indeed, for many years preceding United States accession to the U.C.C., American authors took advantage of a similar loophole in the Berne Treaty to secure geographically widespread protection through quasi-contemporaneous publication in Canada. There is no evidence of communist resort to such devices. Nor would the resultant one-sided benefits be tolerated over the long term. The price for denying acceptable protection and recompense to Western parties is a renunciation of effective reciprocity for works of communist origin.

To the extent that Eastern rights are deprived of international protection, the loss in economic terms is not negligible. The extensively circulated works of Chairman Mao Tse-Tung himself, and the hard currency which might have been forthcoming to communist China's treasury from their protected exploitation, is an illustration in point, although a nonrepresentative one. Potentially, therefore, there is something tangible to be gained from formal participation in world-wide arrangements and from the consequent enjoyment of foreign copyrights on the basis of legal entitlement rather than by way of artful device or reliance upon discretionary goodwill.

Another plus, from the Soviet standpoint, would be the favorable impression created by participation in the U.C.C. While adherence would represent a significant and reassuring step forward, Western copyright beneficiaries could hardly reap extensive benefits. This is apparent from the experience of such communist countries as are now members of the Berne Union. In effect, membership means little more than an undertaking to equate the rights of foreigners with those of nationals. The outsider must still contend with the state publishing monopoly. Moreover, in material terms, he is limited to the extremely modest local royalty regime. Rewards provided extralegally, such as honors, prizes and medals, are neither accessible nor meaningful to him, with the exception of a Louis Aragon or a Howard Fast.

Authors of Eastern origin would, on the other hand, find themselves substantially advanced, since they would benefit from access to the open Western markets and to competitive royalty scales on the same basis as local copyright beneficiaries. This is a phenomenon which we encounter repeatedly in the sphere of East–West relations, once we discount the distorted operation of orthodox terms and concepts. National treatment within a communist system does amount to a concession of sorts. It cannot, however, approach the degree of reciprocity which is afforded by a Western convention member which practices market economics, legally protected freedom of expression and contractual autonomy. In short, a society which curtails its citizenry in a given field of activity offers much less than one which allows independent endeavor and broad enjoyment of private property rights.

Finally, the principle of state monopoly over all economic dealings with the outside world, and all publishing and distribution activities at home, ensures that only foreign works which are ideologically palatable will be imported or locally produced. Whether the particular book, essay, musical score, recording, film or artistic design might win an extensive public is basically irrelevant. Such spontaneity of demand as might exist is held in check by administrative fiat. The government reserves unto itself uncontrolled discretion to protect the local mind as well as the local market.

BOOK TWO

SECOND PART

THE SETTLEMENT OF DISPUTES*

* The author is grateful to the *Harvard Law Review* for permission to draw upon pre-1959 materials treated in his two articles "Soviet Conflict of Laws in International Commercial Transactions," 70 *Harv. L.R.* (1957), pp. 593–656, and "The Communist System of Foreign-Trade Adjudication," 72 *Harv. L.R.* (1959), pp. 1409–1481.

20

ARBITRATION VERSUS LITIGATION

An analysis of the principal methods of settling disputes must be at the heart of any inquiry into the law and practice of East–West trade. Nothing can be more important to the Western firm (and its legal adviser) than a thorough understanding of the nature and process of the court which will ultimately rule on its rights. In the final analysis, any bargain with an Eastern enterprise is worth no more than the decision which will resolve possible controversies.

In recent years, interests active in East–West trade have encountered a determined effort on the part of the state trading monopolies to domesticate litigation involving their executive enterprises. Permanently functioning adjudicatory institutions, styled as arbitration tribunals, with special jurisdiction over foreign trade (and maritime) causes, were established by legislation first in the U.S.S.R. and thereafter, as part of the postwar sovietization of their institutions, in Poland, Czechoslovakia, East Germany, Hungary, Rumania, Bulgaria, communist China and Yugoslavia.[1] These tribunals soon acquired a virtual monopoly of jurisdiction over international disputes between communist enterprises. What is even more surprising, they have achieved considerable success in displacing domestic and foreign courts in the resolution of controversies between socialist and capitalist concerns.

The projection into international business life of communist-administered justice presents difficulties from many perspectives: for merchants pressed by monopolistic state enterprises to recognize as exclusive the competence of Eastern tribunals; for Western lawyers faced with litigation before them; for foreign courts in determining the legal effect of submissions to and decisions of such tribunals; and for governments in negotiating legal and commercial aspects of international treaties. A dramatic illustration of these problems was provided in the late fifties by the widely heralded multimillion-dollar Soviet-Israeli oil dispute, which the parties were committed to litigate before the Soviet Foreign Trade Arbitration Commission in Moscow.[2]

In the eyes of capitalists, communist justice is highly suspect. When the rights and liabilities of private businessmen trading for profit are finally determinable by communist courts, and under their own legal and procedural standards, such justice calls for careful scrutiny. Two additional considerations lend particular interest to this aspect of our inquiry. First, the communist foreign trade adjudication system vividly demonstrates the thesis that conventional concepts and institutions become distorted in the framework of a state-operated economy. Second, in no area of commercial law have the Eastern countries made a more original and significant contribution.

A. The Role of the People's Courts

The exercise of adjudicative power in the various legal systems is not based on any single theory of jurisdiction. Eastern practice follows the continental rather than the common law pattern. The forum at the defendant's residence or place of business has power to hear a dispute, unless alternative dispositions are made by treaty or by a special agreement of the parties. A Soviet court, although technically competent, will not assume jurisdiction in a claim by a local enterprise against a foreign national who is not resident in the U.S.S.R., or against a foreign corporation which has no permanent status there; the plaintiff will be referred to the courts of the defendant's domicile.[3] This approach seeks to accommodate the conflicting interests of the parties and to eliminate the injustice frequently caused by the archaic common law "presence rule." Transient sojourn in a country at the time an action is started (and many foreign merchants do fleetingly appear in the U.S.S.R. to promote or negotiate business transactions) is too slight and fortuitous a basis for jurisdiction. Besides, the outsider may have to defend in a hostile environment and incur great expense in presenting his case far from home.

The fact that the alien defendant is protected from such undue burdens does not really hamper the state claimant. What incentive would the latter have to sue at home unless he could reasonably expect the resultant judgment to be satisfied? As a rule, he could not seek enforcement at home, since very few foreign nationals or corporations own property inside Eastern territory. Recognition of a People's Court judgment abroad, in non-communist countries at least, would be difficult to obtain in the absence of appropriate treaty provisions. The rule of jurisdiction by "defendant's domicile only" is therefore no more than a reflection of the conditions in which an Eastern claimant is likely to invoke the authority of his country's courts over alien merchants. In reality, the theory which underlies the communist approach to jurisdiction over outsiders is the pragmatic one of judicial effectiveness.

In certain circumstances, any court is empowered to hear suits against nonresident parties if it wishes to do so. Article 118 of the Russian Code of Civil Procedure specifically declares that "An action against a defendant having no place of residence in the U.S.S.R. may be brought where his property is situated." Although there is no known case in which a local plaintiff tried to invoke this option, an East German enterprise did in fact successfully bring to court a Belgian company, Gevaert-Agfa, which displayed samples at a Soviet trade fair. The plaintiff's claim of unfair competition, based on trade-name infringement, was heard and held meritorious by a first-instance court. The decision was affirmed on appeal to the Soviet Supreme Court on the basis of the Paris Convention on Industrial Property.[4] However, this could not have founded jurisdiction at the level of the People's Court, since the 1965 ratification of the Convention by the U.S.S.R. took place while the appeal was already pending. Although the precedent casts a shadow of doubt on the issue, enlightened self-interest may be expected to dissuade Soviet entities from judicially harassing foreigners who visit their country on business.

The U.S.S.R. allows contracting parties to accept as exclusive the jurisdiction of any tribunal, by mutual agreement concluded either before or after their dispute has arisen. This concept of submission, well recognized in continental law and on the rise in English and American courts, has long been confirmed in Soviet judicial practice and in treaty provisions. In 1932, the Supreme Court of the R.S.F.S.R. ruled:

> The Code of Civil Procedure does not prohibit a stipulation in a contract of territorial jurisdiction (venue) of disputes which may arise under the contract. Therefore the Plenary Session advises the courts . . . to take jurisdiction in disputes arising from such contracts in accordance with the contractual stipulations except where an exclusive jurisdiction is established by the law for a specified category of actions (*e.g.*, actions against railroads or the State Bank).[5]

This ruling was not confined to purely domestic contracts; its terms were equally applicable in the foreign trade area and illustrated the surprising extent to which Soviet courts were prepared to go in making concessions to the autonomy of party choice. The principle of contractually established jurisdiction has now been recognized in Section 120 of the Code of Civil Procedure.

Treaty provisions on the subject vary from instrument to instrument. For the most part jurisdiction is conferred upon the country where the contract was concluded; at least one treaty allows the choice of a Soviet court if the contract is to be performed within the U.S.S.R.; others permit the courts of either state to assume power under appropriate election clauses.[6] Where the possibility of choice is expressly provided by treaty, contractual submissions will be honored, provided they elect a forum which has some relation to the transaction in question. When a treaty is silent on the subject, Soviet courts will read into it an implied right of choice, not only because this jurisdictional basis is a general rule of domestic civil procedure but also in order to afford the trade monopoly an opportunity to claim the benefit of a similar interpretation in the courts of the other signatory country.

Foreign firms authorized to do business in the U.S.S.R. have access to local courts and enjoy procedural rights equal to those of Soviet citizens, irrespective of whether their claims arise inside or outside Soviet territory. Firms not so authorized may sue resident defendants upon all claims arising abroad on the condition that the courts of their country extend reciprocity to Soviet nationals.[7]

The freedom of aliens to sue state enterprises in the U.S.S.R. is virtually unrestricted, since it is the policy of the government to transfer into local tribunals as much foreign trade litigation as possible. Soviet judges will be reluctant to practice self-denial in proceedings voluntarily initiated before them by an outside firm, provided the disputes in question are not subject to contractually stipulated arbitration. Furthermore, free access to courts is often reciprocally guaranteed by the nations concerned on a most-favored basis.

In the last few decades, arbitration has emerged everywhere as a preferred method of settling international commercial disputes. In the East–West context, where mutual mistrust is rife at all levels of intercourse, the factors behind this trend are particularly compelling. The forms which arbitration may assume are quite diverse. Eastern state enterprises and private foreign firms have often agreed to submit to permanently functioning Western tribunals, to specialized tribunals of trade associations and commodity exchanges, or to mixed *ad hoc* panels contractually constituted for the determination of isolated disputes. A number of treaties make provision for balanced arbitration courts competent in connection with commercial disputes between nationals and organizations of the contracting states. Concurrently, the special system of communist tribunals is available to adjudicate controversies involving foreign parties, both Eastern and Western.

B. The Scope of Eastern Arbitration

The evolution of the Soviet arbitral process has followed a confused course. State monopoly over the administration of justice was established as a fundamental principle in Article 2 of the Civil Code of 1922, which provided that "waiver of the right to invoke the court is void." Such statutory zeal, designed to safeguard public jurisdiction against private encroachment, is by no means unique; onerous restraints on arbitration are not unknown in the West. Italy offers one of the most extreme examples; displacement of the local courts in favor of foreign arbitrators by agreement between Italian and foreign parties is invalid unless permitted by treaty.[8] This view has a nonstatutory echo in the common law itself; English and American courts have traditionally refused to recognize as irrevocable arbitral clauses designed to oust their jurisdiction.

What is remarkable is that despite the imperative injunction against it, the Eastern arbitral process has made more rapid and extensive inroads into the normal administration of justice than has the arbitral process in any common law or civil law country of the West. Indeed, although the national courts ostensibly retain jurisdiction over foreign trade causes, in practice their authority has become little more than fiction, having been largely displaced by a specialized system of arbitration.

In the Soviet Union, arbitration is not only tolerated by the state; it is actually state-instituted. The same is true of the other communist countries. Export-import corporations, authorized domestic enterprises and government departments such as the foreign-based trade delegations may, and regularly do, submit to arbitration at home and abroad. Even in militant communist China, while foreign trade disputes literally fall within the jurisdictional limits of the People's Courts, in practice they are regularly referred to arbitrators.[9]

The origin of general Soviet arbitration law may be traced back to a 1924 statute which authorized this manner of settling private disputes. Enacted in furtherance of the New Economic Policy, the statute marked a significant retreat from the principle of judicial centralism. It prescribed detailed rules for *ad hoc* arbitral settlements between private interests in internal as well as external commerce. Gradually its provisions have been reduced to a dead letter by the attrition of free enterprise. However, with the shift of economic activity into public hands, the scope of government-instituted arbitration assumed unprecedented dimensions. A unique hierarchy of permanent tribunals known as *Gosarbitrazh* (State arbitration) was established for litigation between domestically active government enterprises. These tribunals virtually evicted the jurisdiction of the People's Courts from adjudication of disagreements in industry, production, distribution and exchange.

The distinct *Arbitrazh* method of settling domestic economic disputes (extensively imitated in the other Eastern countries) has evolved far beyond arbitration in its classic sense. To be sure, the separation of the commercial from the civil judiciary is not unknown in the West. In continental Europe the division is standard. Just as the French *Tribunal de Commerce* stands apart from the general civil courts, so *Gosarbitrazh* functions in the manner of a separate and specialized judiciary. As a system of adjudication placed at the disposal of a new economic order it is, however, unrestrained by legal tradition and continuity. In fact, it combines those elements of informal arbitration and state jurisdiction which its founders have considered most appropriate to their new purposes.

Stripped to its essence, *Gosarbitrazh* appears as a method of settling disputes within the framework of one gigantic economic enterprise—the state. A controversy between domestic industrial or commercial concerns resolved by this form of adjudication may be likened to a dispute between two divisions of Ford decided intramurally by an offshoot of the Board of Directors. Nonetheless, it is also an elaborate system of national economic courts with expert, state-appointed adjudicators, exclusive and compulsory jurisdiction and automatically enforceable decisions. As a judicial arm of state administration it operates at three levels: Union, Republic and Province. Competence is apportioned in accordance with the importance of the disputed matter and the nature of the disputants. In effect, an American type of federal "diversity jurisdiction" is at work: an enterprise of one republic seeking redress against an enterprise of another republic must bring suit at the Union level.

Gosarbitrazh is neither suitable nor available for adjudication in foreign commerce. An analogous process, called *Vneshtorgarbitrazh,* or Foreign Trade Arbitration, has been created for that purpose. The term, deriving from the same root as *Gosarbitrazh,* establishes a semantic distinction between this form of arbitration and the prerevolutionary *treteiskii protsess,* which is currently used only in connection with the rare settlement of disputes between private parties.

The Soviet Maritime Arbitration Commission, established in 1930, and the Foreign Trade Arbitration Commission, established two years later, fall within the *Vneshtorgarbitrazh category*. Neither tribunal is based on a general law of arbitration; nor has such a law ever been promulgated in the U.S.S.R. The legality of the arbitral settlement of disputes between Soviet and foreign enterprises is derived from international treaties providing for or permitting arbitration [10] or from the constitutive statutes of the tribunals themselves, statutes which are, in fact, independent acts of legislative power. No other instrument authorizes submissions to foreign or mixed arbitration; such submissions are, however, tolerated and frequently encountered in practice.

The legal foundations of the current foreign trade arbitration system of Czechoslovakia, East Germany and Poland are to be found in laws of either prewar or post-war origin, enabling and regulating resort to this method of dispute settlement both at home and abroad. A more restrictive attitude prevails in Rumania, Bulgaria and Yugoslavia. Outside the framework of the national economic plan, the arbitral process has no legal status; submissions thereto are legally protected only if one of the parties is foreign. This qualification is sufficiently broad to cover all types of international commercial disputes.

Whenever a foreign party cannot be induced to submit to Eastern arbitration, the state enterprises have shown themselves to be legally and administratively free to accept arbitration elsewhere. Thus, Yugoslav enterprises have often submitted to such tribunals as the Arbitration Court of the International Chamber of Commerce in Paris, the Arbitration Court of the Trade Chamber of Zürich, and even the American Arbitration Association.[11] To a somewhat lesser degree, the same is true with respect to enterprises of other Eastern states, both in Europe and Asia. Italian sellers have been able to extract from communist Chinese buyers arbitral clauses stipulating a Swedish, Dutch, or Swiss venue. Often, the Chinese opt for arbitration in Burma or Ceylon.

Eastern countries have also shown an increasing willingness to apportion arbitral jurisdiction. In 1961, the Soviet Chamber of Commerce reached agreement with the Federation of Indian Chambers of Commerce and Industry to recommend to their respective national trade organizations a contractual clause calling for exclusive arbitration at the defendant's residence or principal place of business. The "recommendation" is undoubtedly followed by the Soviet combines, notwithstanding their strong negotiating position vis-á-vis Indian co-contractants. Between 1956 and 1961 the Japanese Commercial Arbitration Association concluded a network of similar agreements with the Chambers of Commerce of most of the East European countries.[12]

C. The Displacement of State Jurisdiction

The Soviet Union had long ago begun to feel the need for a universally appealing system of adjudication in order to attract aggrieved foreign traders and shippers to local forums. Economic weakness during the initial postrevolutionary period compelled the U.S.S.R. to litigate business disputes abroad. A Soviet claimant could only sue and obtain satisfaction of a judgment at his foreign opponent's place of residence, whereas the latter could seek a remedy in his own national courts, either by attempting to serve process on a resident commercial representation or by attaching locally found assets. Despite ingrained aversion to the arbitral settlement of disputes, treaty or contractual clauses provided wherever possible for mixed or neutral arbitration panels in lieu of state jurisdiction. Not until the foreign trade and shipping monopolies were in a position to assert their concentrated economic bargaining power in world markets did it become practicable to transfer the adjudication of disputes to Russian territory.

It is hazardous to attribute motives to the Soviet effort to domesticate commercial disputes with foreigners. Several concrete aims are nevertheless evident: to circumvent allegedly prejudiced "bourgeois" courts and arbitrators; to free public enterprises from unfavorable and sometimes genuinely unsuitable provisions of foreign law; to enforce compliance with certain peremptory provisions of domestic law deemed essential for the regulation of a government trading monopoly; and to compensate for the widespread denial of sovereign immunity to trading instrumentalities of the state. Related considerations dictated the creation of special foreign trade arbitration facilities elsewhere in the East.

In China, indigenous tradition also played a role. There, as in Japan, the preference for arbitration is at least partly attributable to the widely held social ethic that court litigation is a disgrace and a manifestation of the failure of sensible men to resolve their own differences. Arbitral settlement is considered to be more honorable, while negotiated compromise is preferred above all else. This attitude is dramatically reflected in the fact that as of 1960, all disputes heard by the Chinese foreign trade tribunal were disposed of before final award. Similarly, in the well-publicized case of the M/S *Varild,* the Chinese maritime tribunal is reported to have negotiated repeatedly with both parties in an effort to accommodate their disagreements on a fair, reasonable and practical basis.[13]

Eastern policymakers were well aware that a capitalist merchant would not contentedly submit to the jurisdiction of the regular People's Courts; nor were they equipped to render decisions in an area governed by social and economic notions alien to communist doctrine. Only a process substantially insulated from prevalent domestic conceptions and responsive to traditional standards could be expected to further the cause of localized foreign trade adjudication. The answer was found in arbitration.

An agreement to arbitrate amounts to a binding renunciation by the parties of the right to invoke any forum except the one designated. Awards rendered pursuant to such an agreement are widely recognized as final and conclusive and cannot be relitigated in national courts. The law of the territory in which the arbitration is held governs the constitution and procedure of the tribunal, and frequently the substance of the dispute as well. Since the arbitral process is consensual in nature, economic superiority is an added advantage for a state trading enterprise seeking to induce acceptance of a tribunal of its choice. Monopolies, public or private, are always in favor of arbitration.

A willingness on the part of communist legislatures to adapt their foreign trade adjudication systems to the precepts of Western arbitration explains, at least in part, the tribunals' effective intrusion on the world scene. The expanding volume and diversity of their decisions and the growing number of foreign judgments and treaties which carry them into effect bear witness to the surprising degree of acceptance they have come to enjoy at home and abroad. While no statistical proof is available, it may be assumed that thousands of East–West contracts contain clauses of submission to the Eastern party's foreign trade tribunal. The relationships which emerge on the surface in the form of full-blown, arbitrated disputes constitute only the upper part of this iceberg.

The rise of the tribunals cannot be wholly divorced from the universal trend toward arbitration as the most suitable method of settling international trade disputes. This trend is attributable to such factors as the expense, delays, formality, public character and adversary atmosphere of court litigation, the parochialism of national judges, and the unpredictability of judicial action in an area not covered by any single body of commercial law. In trade between politically and socially antithetical systems, the defects of court litigation, be they real or imaginary, appear to have even greater impact. Arbitration in a mutually acceptable forum thus becomes the natural alternative.

The campaign to secure merchants' acceptance was facilitated by the fact that a submission to the tribunals is not devoid of advantages for the private trader. Above all, it carries the assurance that a just remedy will not be barred by the state entity's reliance on sovereign status, and that a duly pronounced award will be performed without fail. The initially hostile reaction of Western trading and shipping circles to the U.S.S.R.'s attempt to shift jurisdiction homeward was countered with the argument that a power of Russia's stature had as much right to an indigenous arbitration process as England or Germany, and that in concept and practice the tribunals conformed to established international standards.

It is noteworthy that the circumstances surrounding the creation of foreign trade tribunals in other Comecon countries did not wholly coincide with those which prompted Soviet pioneering in the field. The desire to ensure such immunity from the reach of "bourgeois" courts and arbitrators as their considerably weaker economic position would permit was, of course, equally real. But no less important was the need for facilities to resolve differences arising in trade within the newly formed community of Eastern states. Indeed, with the emergence of a communist bloc of countries, the two prototype Moscow commissions themselves acquired an additional and perhaps paramount dimension not originally envisaged by their founders. In commerce between planned and market economies the tribunals were expected to overcome fundamental antagonisms and conceptual differences. In intra-East trade their primary function was to provide an effective system of adjudication for intercourse among friendly nations, operating on the basis of similar economic institutions and encountering commercial problems susceptible of uniform legal solution.

In this context, the displacement of state jurisdiction was a decidedly lesser task. In the first place, contractual disputes leading to court litigation are of comparatively rare occurrence in Comecon trade. Here the governments themselves are in a position to assume obligations which in privately conducted commerce would normally find their way into individual contracts of purchase and sale. Controversies arising from failure to honor such intergovernmental assurances are settled by the respective foreign trade ministries. The undertakings of individual trading entities are limited to such matters as the quality, purchase price, and time and place of delivery of merchandise. Moreover, the corresponding trade enterprises, being for the most part national monopolies, are compelled to deal with one another on a continuous basis. The consequent need for amicable relations provides an unusually strong incentive to iron out differences by negotiation, conciliation or arbitration, rather than by means of adversary proceedings in open court.

In the second place, within the narrow bounds in which litigation does arise, the Comecon General Conditions of Delivery have made short shrift of court jurisdiction. The permanent arbitration tribunal of the defendant's country is designated as the exclusively competent adjudicatory body for disputes between contracting enterprises of member states. Similar provisions are found in bilateral agreements between Comecon and non-Comecon nations of the East.[14]

D. Communist Foreign Trade Tribunals

1. Institutional Structure

The Moscow Foreign Trade Arbitration Commission consists of fifteen arbitrators appointed for a period of one year by the Presidium of the Soviet Chamber of Commerce from among representatives of commercial, industrial, transport and similar organizations and persons possessing special qualifications in the field of international commerce. Its competence extends to all kinds of disputes arising in foreign trade, particularly disputes between alien firms and Soviet trade combines, submitted either by advance stipulation in the parties' contract or by special agreement after the dispute has arisen.

The Maritime Arbitration Commission is organized along the same lines. It consists of twenty-five arbitrators chosen from among representatives of maritime, commercial, insurance and similar concerns and experts in the fields of navigation, maritime law and insurance. Its jurisdiction has been progressively extended. As of 1960, it has power to decide disputes arising from compensation claims for assistance rendered to ships, collision of ships, damage caused to harbor installations, contracts of salvage, charter parties, bills of lading, marine insurance policies and all other matters relating to the carriage of goods by sea. Damage caused to fishing vessels, fishnets and other fishing gear and claims arising from navigation of international rivers are also within its province.

Although the Moscow Commissions have served as models for the formation of the other Eastern tribunals, the institutional identity is not complete. For example, the panelists of the Prague arbitration court hold tenure for as long as five years. In the main, the Bulgarian and Rumanian institutions are closer imitations of the Soviet prototype than those of Poland, Czechoslovakia, Eastern Germany or Yugoslavia. With the exception of the Foreign Trade Arbitration Committee of the Chinese People's Republic which functions under the auspices of the China Committee for the Promotion of International Trade, all of the tribunals are attached to their respective national Chambers of Commerce.

In comparative terms, the tribunals are not easy to place within the international framework of arbitration. Western institutions fall into a number of more or less distinct categories.[15] The principal division is into *ad hoc* boards, variously constituted for the resolution of specific disputes and dissolved after their function has been accomplished, and tribunals available for arbitration on a permanent basis. In recent years, the latter have acquired greater popularity.

Institutionalized arbitration facilities are provided by bodies which function under either national or international auspices. The former may be open to the public at large, for the settlement of diverse disputes (e.g. the well-known London Court of Arbitration), or to a defined class of disputants engaged in the purchase and sale of specified commodities (e.g. the London Corn Trade Association, the *Bremen Baumwollbörse* and the *Union Lyonnaise des Marchands de Soie*). Both types of tribunals hear controversies arising in domestic or in foreign commerce.

Arbitral institutions functioning under international auspices are less common. They comprise bodies of generalized competence, free to hear any trade dispute and bodies restricted in function to special segments of commerce. An obvious illustration of the former is the Arbitration Court of the International Chamber of Commerce in Paris, whose services are available on a world-wide basis; the latter are exemplified by the *Bureau International de la Récupération* and the *Union Européenne du Commerce en Gros de Pommes de Terre.*

International tribunals are occasionally constituted on a bilateral or regional basis to determine commercial or maritime disputes between nationals of the countries concerned. Such tribunals may function under treaties, or under special agreements between private institutions. An example of the former is the tribunal provided for under the Convention on the Exchange of Goods and Payments concluded between the U.S.S.R. and Sweden on September 7, 1940. An example of the latter is the Cooperation Agreement of November 23, 1963, between the Associazione Italiana per l'Arbitro and the Polish Chamber of Foreign Trade, which provides for the establishment of a mixed panel of arbitrators whose decisions are in effect assimilated to Italian and Polish domestic awards for purposes of enforcement.[16]

In the communist world, institutional arbitration assumes a different aspect. Specialized panels, corresponding to those available within Western trade associations and commodity exchanges are exceptional. Only the arbitral facilities of the Gdynia Cotton Association set up in Poland in 1938 and preserved by the communist regime, and possibly the Moscow and Peking maritime tribunals, can be placed in this category. The International Arbitration Court for Maritime and Internal Navigation, created in Gdynia in 1959 under the authority of the Foreign Trade Chambers of Poland, East Germany and Czechoslovakia, should also be mentioned in this connection.[17]

The explanation for this must be sought in the patterns of Eastern economic organization. A public enterprise which enjoys a virtually exclusive license to deal in specified commodities, is essentially a nation-wide commodity exchange; were it to operate an arbitral tribunal it would, in effect, be acting as judge in its own cause.

In a sense, the adjudication dispensed by the communist tribunals themselves is strongly suggestive of closed trade-exchange arbitration. Since commerce is conducted by the state alone, the overall government monopoly resembles a huge trade association, except that the commodities dealt in are diverse. The export-import enterprises comprise the bulk of the membership of this "association," which promulgates standard contracts, standard arbitration clauses and so forth. An Eastern Chamber's arbitral facilities, in contrast to those of customary associations are, however, inaccessible to members disputing *inter se*. The only exception is the Moscow maritime tribunal, which occasionally hears disputes involving solely Soviet entities. All of the other institutions now under review are primarily intended for the resolution of disputes between "association" members and foreign nonmembers.

In recent years the tribunals have begun to intervene in disagreements between two foreign enterprises even where no domestic entity was in any way involved. Within Comecon, submissions to a neutral member state by entities of other member states is tolerated under the General Conditions of Delivery whenever a contractual election has been made. Thus, in 1961 a dispute between a Rumanian and an Albanian enterprise was presented to and decided by the Moscow tribunal.[18] While the General Conditions are declarative of such jurisdiction, they do not constitute its source; the Statutes and Rules of the tribunals themselves have been interpreted to extend to disputes between two foreign enterprises. For example, before the 1958 Conditions came into effect, the Czechoslovak tribunal had accepted a reference to itself in disregard of the forum of the defendant's country, East Germany.[19] Nor have the tribunals limited themselves to the hearing of disputes in intra-East or even East–West trade. In 1963, the Moscow Commission decided a dispute between two Western parties, stating that even if an exclusion of this power could be inferred from its Rules, in practice such controversies are dealt with.[20]

Another point of difference which emerges from a comparison of arbitral institutions in market and collectivist economies is the fusion of jurisdiction over domestic and foreign causes in the case of the former, and its separation in the latter. In the West, tribunals with exclusive competence over foreign causes are rare; the few that exist function strictly under international auspices. In communist countries such tribunals are nationally sponsored.

2. *Economic Courts of Mercantile Arbitration*

Far from representing a startling innovation, the two Soviet tribunals were in fact carefully fashioned in the image of well-known arbitral bodies long in existence in the principal trading nations of the capitalist world. Their organization and rules of procedure were inspired by such adjudicatory institutions as the London Court of Arbitration, the arbitration tribunal of the Liverpool Cotton Exchange, Lloyd's Maritime Arbitration Board and the German Maritime Arbitration Court of Hamburg.

The Soviet Commissions function under the auspices of a Chamber of Commerce as do many self-governing institutions in the West. They maintain panels of specialists from among whom the parties are free to select their arbitrators and umpires. Their jurisdiction is expressly conditioned upon voluntary and written submission, in conformity with orthodox Western notions.

Notwithstanding this conformity, the communist tribunals cannot be viewed as arbitral bodies pure and simple. Probing below outward appearances, we find them to be more akin to specialized courts cloaked in the wrappings of arbitration. As we will see below, both the Soviet Foreign Trade and Maritime Commissions and the sister institutions of the other socialist countries consider themselves competent to rule upon their own jurisdiction. They also reserve the freedom to hold that valid submissions in their favor exclude all other domestic and foreign tribunals. Although the Rules do not expressly require that the arbitrators be local citizens, in practice they invariably are. Moreover, they are a far more closely knit group than members of Western arbitration panels. For example, the arbitrators on the Hungarian list meet at least once every three months under the chairmanship of their President to discuss and settle questions of principle which have arisen in the course of adjudication.[21]

The Chamber of Commerce under the auspices of which the commissions function is itself an arm of the government, not a private organization in the conventional sense. Judgments and dissents are required to be fully stated in writing and to comply with the law in force. Proceedings must be conducted in open public session. Except where the tribunals' statutes provide otherwise, the governing rules of procedure and evidence are similar to those which obtain in general domestic tribunals.

Decisions of the Maritime Commission rendered in violation of the law may be overruled on appeal to the Supreme Court of the U.S.S.R. Although such appeals are rare and reversals even rarer, they are a significant aspect of the system. For example, in 1960 the defendant-appellant, the Hamburg–South American Steamship Company, successfully challenged a surcharge on reparations awarded to the Soviet plaintiff for damage caused to a port crane in Riga by the ship *Santa Inez.* In 1961, there were five appeals, all affirming the challenged awards; in 1962, there were four, one of which was reversed and remanded for a new hearing with respect to a question of fact. Apparently, the Supreme Court cannot impose its own decision; it may only cancel the Commission's award and return the case for new proceedings before different arbitrators.[22] But the power of review extends both to the merits of the dispute and to the fundamental issue of competence.[23]

No appeals procedure is provided in respect of the foreign trade tribunals of the Soviet Union and of the other Eastern states. Indeed, in 1964, the Sofia tribunal ruled that the submission of Lebanese and Bulgarian parties was vitiated by a contractual provision making any resultant award appealable to the arbitration court of the Gdynia Cotton Exchange. The decision held that to be effective, a submission cannot qualify the tribunal's competence as the court of first and last resort. Particularly objectionable was the contemplation of review by an institution of specialized jurisdiction (the cotton trade). The hearings proceeded to the merits after the parties had waived the appeal requirement.[24] One courtlike peculiarity of the Polish and Czechoslovak tribunals must be noted, although it can hardly be equated with an appeal procedure. The Presidiums of the two institutions, appointed by the respective Chambers of Commerce, may be asked by the arbitrators in the course of proceedings to give their opinion on questions of domestic, foreign or international law.[25]

No foreign trader can be compelled against his will to sue or defend in an Eastern tribunal; in the final analysis, he must express his unequivocal consent. This consensual basis of jurisdiction is inconsistent with the attributes of a normal court of law. In practice, the parties' autonomy is, however, abridged by considerations of an economic and administrative character. Insofar as it is expected to further the objective of domesticated adjudication, the state trader usually tenders a standard contractual form containing a reference to its national tribunal. Depending on his own bargaining position, and assuming that he is aware of the implication in the "fine print" clause, the foreigner may resist. Occasionally he succeeds in having it deleted.

In a large number, perhaps the majority, of East–West commercial contracts, Western parties accept Eastern arbitration, often after having received a price concession to compensate for the added risk. In the submission of existing disputes, as distinct from those anticipated at the time a transaction is negotiated, less scope for duress exists. Such submissions are nevertheless also common. Frequently they are sought by the alien party, since the People's Courts do not represent an acceptable alternative for a private firm seeking a remedy against a state enterprise without visible assets abroad. Nor is the state trading party itself immune from pressure to submit to its own national tribunal. In strict law it is not bound to do so; indeed, it is legally free, in the absence of contrary treaty provisions, to agree on any form of arbitration at home or abroad, notwithstanding the fact that it is a public body with sovereign ties. In practice, however, it cannot lightly ignore the monopoly's preference for litigation at home in the tribunals especially established for that purpose.

When transacting business with an enterprise of another communist country, an Eastern commercial entity's autonomy is illusory both in fact and in law. Submission to the tribunal of the defendant's country is generally directed in advance by means of intergovernmental agreements; the immediate parties have no real choice in the matter. Here the situation approaches the settlement of controversies between domestic enterprises under the system of *Gosarbitrazh,* in which the principle of voluntary submission is no longer even a pretense.

A large segment of the tribunals' work derives, therefore, not from party choice but from sovereign power. The major source of treaty-created jurisdiction is, of course, the Comecon General Conditions and a number of bilateral instruments between communist countries, one or both of which fall outside the Comecon scheme. Another important document is the convention relative to Danube shipping of December 31, 1955, concluded among Bulgaria, Hungary, Rumania, Czechoslovakia and the U.S.S.R. Article 55 provides that all disputes are finally and compulsorily referable to arbitration in the country of the defendant, to the total exclusion of other forums.

Treaty-created jurisdiction does not necessarily entail a waiver of the state's adjudicatory power. It is merely a transfer of functions from the regular national courts to specialized national tribunals. The institution vested with decision-making power may be local or foreign but, as we have seen, the power is equally apportioned under an objective criterion. It is true that the tribunals of Comecon countries do not form a unified hierarchy with a common superior court of errors. They are nonetheless subject to a single substantive law—the General Conditions—interpreted in a basically uniform manner. Moreover, their Presidents meet periodically to exchange views, compare experience and coordinate applicable legal principles.[26]

It is therefore fair to say, in regard to intra-Comecon adjudication at least, that the foreign trade tribunals cannot be equated with arbitration pure and simple. This poses the question of whether the East–West segment of their jurisdiction, where voluntary agreement remains a legal condition of competence, can be viewed differently. The answer which suggests itself is that the free reference of disputes involving Western parties resembles submissions to the jurisdiction of regular courts, in the same manner as a contract between a Belgian and French firm may contain a clause electing litigation before the *Tribunal de Commerce de Paris*.

The formal and psychological climate of arbitration as practiced in the communist domestic context has clearly influenced the process of the foreign trade tribunals in determining controversies between enterprises from two planned economies. In the settlement of disputes with Western firms, the conventional arbitration features and labels with which the tribunals are endowed obtain more convincing application. But here too, taken cumulatively, their economic setting, legislative origin, peculiar structure, concentrated (one institution per country) jurisdiction, indigenous composition, public proceedings and responsibilities in the elaboration of foreign trade law, all impart to the tribunals a *sui generis* character. Whatever the term of art under which they are presented, in substance they reveal hybrid features of state economic courts and classical arbitration boards.

Herein resides a highly original development. Going one step beyond the continental legal systems which maintain a separate jurisdiction for commercial matters generally, the East boasts a specialized jurisdiction for international transactions as such. This jurisdiction, cast in the mold of traditional arbitration is, in fact, a creature of sovereign action, a system of state courts for foreign causes. Merchants from countries which practice market economics and which are not tied in to the East's treaty-established pattern of compulsory adjudicative authority are beyond the reach of these courts. However, they have the right to recognize their jurisdiction by means of voluntary contractual stipulation.

21

EASTERN FOREIGN TRADE TRIBUNALS IN ACTION

The outwardly conventional features of the Eastern trade adjudication tribunals obscure certain anomalies of composition, structure and status within their respective state monopolies. Pleading such latent flaws, foreign litigants have frequently invoked public policy grounds in attempts to impeach the communist arbitration process in both Eastern and Western courts.

Offensive as they may be to the noncommunist legal mind, the defects are not part of a deliberate scheme to subvert the rights of foreign parties. For the most part, they emanate from the distorted operation of familiar institutions when one of the contracting parties is an enterprise of a country practicing total state trading. Furthermore, while the problems involved are quite real, safeguards tending to guarantee a measure of due process are also present.

A. The Election of Arbitrators

If an arbitral submission or award is to qualify for legal protection, the chosen adjudicator must be capable of performing, and must in fact perform, with the detachment and impartiality normally expected of one exercising a judicial function. At the center of this axiom is the proposition that the disputing parties must be treated on a footing of equality.

The rules or procedure under which the tribunals operate recognize the independence of the adjudicative function. The arbitrators are expressly required to act in a judicial capacity and not as mere advocates of the respective disputants. Each tribunal maintains a list of candidates from which the parties select their arbitrators and umpires in accordance with a specified procedure. Customary provision is made for challenge and substitution on grounds of prejudice or material interest in the outcome of the proceedings.[1]

That the panels of arbitrators are established by the governing bodies of the various Chambers of Commerce is not in itself a basic defect; this system has long been in universal use as a means of avoiding the frustrations of *ad hoc* appointment. Nor is the limitation of party choice to a closed number of candidates a justifiable ground for criticism.

A more serious objection derives from the identity of the arbitrators available for selection. That the list must comprise persons with specialized knowledge and experience in the various aspects of international trade is quite normal—indeed, essential. What is surprising is that these persons, required by definition to hear disputes with foreign parties, are invariably nationals and residents of the Eastern country in which the tribunal functions. This fact casts an immediate doubt on the freedom of choice seemingly offered the outsider.

Given the still-isolated nature of communist society, foreigners confronted with a list of local names to which their vote is restricted have no realistic basis for distinguishing one from another. Although the Rules of the Polish and Bulgarian Arbitration Courts require that detailed information on the arbitrators be publicly on file in their respective Chambers of Commerce, in the various branches of their Foreign Trade Ministries and with diplomatic and consular representatives abroad, the virtual absence of personal and professional contact makes the choice illusory. In practice, Western litigants tend to waive their right to selection altogether.[2]

The rules of the Polish, Yugoslav and Bulgarian tribunals exclude foreigners from their panels. Even where the rules are mute on this point, multi-national arbitration boards are precluded as a matter of fact. Only the Hungarian and Czechoslovakian tribunals expressly recognize a foreigner's right to nominate a national of his own or a third country, whose name is not inscribed in their registers. Although a wish to make such a nomination may be respected in the other tribunals as well, even this concession, whether afforded explicitly or informally, fails to solve the problem in substance. As a Swiss court pointed out in connection with a Prague award, Czech nationals would nevertheless constitute a majority of the Board.[3]

There is nothing inherently wrong about the resolution of disputes by adjudicators whose nationality coincides with that of one of the parties. This is invariably the case whenever a remedy is sought in a foreign court of law. However, international merchants tend to associate neutrality with mixed or third-party boards. It is a central aim of commercial arbitration to overcome widely held suspicions of patriotic preference by means of panels which are balanced accordingly. In the hypersensitive area of East–West trade, the argument in favor of neutralization is even more convincing. Yet the guarantee of diverse nationality is conspicuously absent from the communist system of arbitration.

The Eastern tribunals are not unique in this regard. The legal disqualification of foreigners from acting as arbitrators is occasionally encountered in the West as well. Objectionable as such parochialism may be, it is considerably less disturbing in tribunals of generalized competence than in those with jurisdiction limited to foreign causes. Outside the communist orbit, nationality restrictions in the few existing institutions of the latter variety are unknown. On the contrary, the participation of arbitrators of diverse origins is part of their *raison d'être*. It may therefore be suggested that the nationality restriction practiced by the communist tribunals amounts to a form of discrimination against the foreign disputant.

If diversity of citizenship is a useful safeguard against national preference, it has a special function to perform in an area susceptible to the intrusion of ideological preference. In commerce between similar social systems a person acting as arbitrator is normally a fellow trader devoted to the same economic and ethical precepts as the disputants before him. In East–West trade, his personal outlook (unless he is selected with this problem in mind) is prone to diverge fundamentally from that of one of the parties. Only eminent specialists qualify for appointment to the panels of the Eastern tribunals. One may safely assume that in communist societies persons who attain such rank are unequivocally committed to the basic conceptions of Marxist doctrine—conceptions which are in obvious conflict with the capitalist aspirations of a private businessman. This does not mean that philosophical conviction has an automatic bearing upon actual decision-making. But how many firms in the West would be content to entrust their differences with a labor union to final determination by an officer of the national labor movement?

A comparable problem arises whenever a communist enterprise is invited to submit to tribunals composed solely of arbitrators from free-enterprise countries. It is important to stress that this and the nationality consideration were historically at the basis of the Soviet hope to escape the reach of foreign, "bourgeois-minded" judges and arbitrators. Consequently, it is fair to say that "bourgeois" judges are now being replaced with communist judges; rather than corrected, the prior disequilibrium is merely reversed.

It is perfectly natural that the persons selected for arbitration service are active in law, commerce, industry, shipping, insurance and related fields. But this proposition is only unquestionable in commercial relations within or among countries of free economic structure; it acquires a somewhat different aspect in a framework of total state ownership and planning. There the engineer, banker, business executive, lawyer—in a sense even the academician—is of necessity an officer or appointee of some institution exclusively operated or controlled by the state. Ultimately, he must be regarded as a civil servant employed and paid by the government. It is the public interest (and in a more remote sense his own, as a beneficiary of the collectivist state) that is invariably involved whenever such a person, preappointed through another state medium, is invited to resolve a dispute between an alien firm and a native instrumentality.

Furthermore, a professionally incestuous relationship may be said to exist within a closed club of arbitrators comprising mostly officers of public enterprises engaged in foreign trade. When such officers act as judges in lawsuits instituted by or against sister enterprises, a natural solidarity, fostered by the realization that on future occasions the roles could be reversed, may be justifiably suspected. The validity of this line of criticism is conceded in Hungary and East Germany, where employees of foreign trade enterprises are in practice not considered eligible for service on their Chamber's panels of arbitrators.[4]

The exercise of adjudicative functions by public officials has an obvious parallel in the West, whenever state-appointed judges resolve disputes between private parties and branches of government (such as a Ministry of Defense) or government corporations (such as the Tennessee Valley Authority in the United States, the Régie Renault in France or ENI in Italy). But to arbitrate is not the same as to judge. Arbitration is an essentially voluntary, private, informal and consensual process, while the judicial function, as understood in the major legal systems of the West, is compulsory, discharged in open court and governed by a tradition and solemnity of its own. It is also subject to rigidly applicable substantive and procedural rules, with irregularities readily reviewable on appeal to higher tribunals. Moreover, the judiciary's independence from state authority is at least formally guaranteed by a judge's professional and public reputation and by lifelong or protracted tenure of office, with removal limited to the narrow ground of misbehavior.

Our analysis leads to the conclusion that the designated method of composition and the actual membership of the Eastern foreign trade tribunals result in invisible but nonetheless significant inequalities as between a private Western concern and a local state enterprise. These inequalities evoke doubts concerning their acceptability as impartial arbitral institutions. To make these criticisms is not to dabble in sophistry or to place in issue the personal or professional integrity of the individuals assigned to discharge adjudicative functions. This author is acquainted with Professor Henryk Trammer, President of the Polish Court of Arbitration, and is willing to accept at face value his assurance regarding the independence of the arbitral process:

> . . . I have presided for several years in Poland over such a tribunal which has had to decide disputes from almost every part of the world, and I must state in all good faith that we have never been witness to the slightest attempt to influence our decision, nor even to an attempt to engage us in a conversation on the subject in dispute.[5]

But even if we admit that impartiality exists in fact, it is not sufficient that justice be done; equally important is the requirement that justice appear to be done, in accordance with objective guarantees of due process.

B. Impartial Justice or Administrative Directive

The links between the communist arbitration facilities and the governmental trade monopolies suggest flaws no less serious and no more apparent than those arising from their composition. This is illustrated by the manner in which the tribunals are treated in Western courts, a subject we shall cover in connection with the enforcement abroad of submissions and awards.

The difficulty which troubles Western courts is a basic one: should not the arbitral institution be disqualified from acting as adjudicator in matters involving local and foreign enterprises on the ground that the tribunal and the local enterprise are, in effect, organic parts of the same whole—the administratively and economically omnipresent state?

At first glance, it is entirely appropriate for a Chamber of Commerce to encompass the national business enterprises in whose interest it was established. The furnishing of arbitration services to members and nonmembers is one of its proper responsibilities. However, the Chamber of a communist country is a creature of public legislation and an integral arm of a monolithic foreign trade apparatus. Its primary function is to further the interest of the state under the express supervision of the Ministry of Foreign Trade.[6] All public concerns empowered to act as parties in commercial transactions and disputes with the outside world are likewise controlled by government ministries. The tribunals and the local trading entities are, therefore, inextricably linked to a common principal, the state, and to one another, as functional and constitutive participants in the Chambers of Commerce.

Indirectly, the arbitrators, along with the procedural guidelines which govern them, are designated by an agency of the very state which is the foreigner's ultimate adversary in each disputed transaction. Moreover, this designation takes place through a process in which his immediate adversary (a member of the local Chamber) is an active participant. That the panel system employed by the Eastern tribunals conforms to general practice is not in itself conclusive of its propriety; a great deal depends on the nature, status and composition of the body charged with the establishment of the panel. True parity between the parties cannot exist unless both have an opportunity to cooperate equally and effectively in the appointment of their adjudicators. Even if foreign nationals were also eligible to serve, parity in this sense would not necessarily follow.

Aside from inquiring whether the parties have an equal choice in the formation of the adjudicative board, we must also ask whether they participate in the process by which the general panels of arbitrators are made up. The answer is less than reassuring. In the framework of a communist Chamber of Commerce, the foreigner's apparent freedom of choice is, in effect, largely invalidated by a process of preselection. He may prefer one name or another from among those which appear on the Chamber-established list, but he cannot go beyond it.

Further insights may be obtained by returning to the question of whether the communist tribunals do not correspond to arbitral facilities provided under the auspices of trade associations or commodity exchanges. In arbitrations before an Eastern Chamber of Commerce the relationship between the local party and the foreigner is indeed similar to that between a member and a nonmember of a closed cartel. But the distortion of the process is considerably more pronounced.

Capitalist trade associations are essentially private bodies whose object is to serve the convenience of their members, not of the state. Frequently, as in matters of taxation or tariff protection, these interests are in conflict with government policy. The reverse is true of a communist Chamber of Commerce. In a special sense it also exists for the benefit of its members. But neither the Chamber nor the members can be presumed to have an independent will except as it is tolerated by the state. Moreover, the members *inter se,* the Chamber, and the ultimate owner of all—the state—have a total unity of interest capable of being expressed not only in biased adjudication but also in legislative and administrative action designed to give the trade monopoly an ideal climate for world-wide operation. Such misgivings as may exist in respect of cartel arbitration are thus magnified in the case of the Eastern tribunals.

It may be argued that since the tribunals enjoy, under their domestic laws, the status of individual legal entities, communist arbitration must be considered autonomous; this is the Eastern position. The Soviet Maritime and Foreign Trade Arbitration Commissions and the Polish Arbitration Court have repeatedly held that the principle of juridical separateness embodied in their respective charters of incorporation holds good as against disputing domestic and nondomestic enterprises.[7]

In an economic order where the sole source of ownership and control is the state, the flimsy legal veil which divides the Eastern arbitration tribunals from the public trading instrumentalities before them can hardly guarantee the independence of the judicial funution. After all, it is a basic premise of communist doctrine that the political cadres of party and government have a right, indeed a duty, to guide every phase of national life. In theory at least, not even the judiciary is considered immune from such intrusion. Why, then, should the formality of the arbitration tribunal's corporate status be regarded as a meaningful safeguard?

The "intangible ties" between the Soviet Foreign Trade Arbitration Commission and Russia's Amtorg Trading Corporation of New York, which disturbed the Supreme Court of New York in a landmark case,[8] may be illustrated in not too far-fetched a manner by means of the following examples: (a) arbitration before the Moscow tribunal between a

Western firm and the unincorporated Soviet trade delegation in Turkey is comparable to an adjudication between a foreigner and a division of General Motors Corporation conducted before one of its wholly owned subsidiaries; (b) arbitration between a Western firm and an incorporated Soviet foreign trade enterprise corresponds to a settlement between a foreigner and a wholly owned subsidiary of General Motors Corporation meted out by a wholly owned sister subsidiary; (c) arbitration between the Moscow Narodny Bank in London and a private English firm is similar to the determination of a dispute between a wholly owned subsidiary of General Motors incorporated in France and a French contractor, before another wholly owned subsidiary of General Motors incorporated in the United States.

In 1939, a French defendant invoked French *ordre publique* to challenge the tribunal's capacity to rule upon a claim initiated by a Soviet concern. In 1957, an Austrian defendant sought to demonstrate a similar inconsistency with the public policy of Austria. In both cases the tribunal understandably refused to sign what would have amounted to its own death warrant as an adjudicatory body in foreign trade causes. In terms which subsequently found a strong echo in Western courts,[9] and without offering any apology or rationale for its peculiar institutional characteristics, the Commission rested its competence on the defendant's own pledge to arbitrate in Moscow.

In the first case, the decision was reached on the basis of Soviet domestic law—which, as the law of the place of arbitration, governed composition and procedure. The second case appears to contain an additional element; jurisdiction was assumed with an eye to Austrian law and policy as well: "The defendant's plea to the effect that the determination of the given case contradicted the public policy of the Austrian Republic is unfounded, since Austrian law allows for the possibility of concluding contracts for the arbitral determination of disputes arising from contractual transactions."[10]

That this is a question-begging formula (insofar as the defendant's plea was not directed against arbitration as such, but against the particular variety thereof dispensed by the Moscow Commission) is less significant than the fact that in 1937 the arbitrators ventured to invoke foreign law in partial defense of their fitness to judge. The added confidence was well-founded; they could now point to a Treaty of Commerce between Austria and the U.S.S.R. with provisions for the reciprocal enforcement of arbitral clauses and awards—a tacit, if not express, recognition by Austria of the

Commission's acceptability as an adjudicative institution. In the background were similar treaties with certain other noncommunist countries, as well as a number of favorable decisions delivered by foreign courts.[11]

The standing of the communist tribunals is today implicitly recognized by multilateral instruments such as the New York Convention on the Recognition and Enforcement of Foreign Arbitral Awards of 1958 and the Geneva Convention on Foreign Trade Arbitration of 1961.[12] Moreover, their acceptability has been explicitly acknowledged by a number of Western governments. For example, Article 8 of the Sino-Japanese Trade Agreement of 1958 allocates jurisdiction over disputes between enterprises of the two countries to the Chinese foreign trade arbitration tribunal and a special Japanese arbitration board in accordance with the domicile of the defendant.

Unpalatable as certain of the tribunals' features may seem, we must not confine ourselves to the yardstick of jurisprudential notions nurtured in the soil of free enterprise. For we are concerned here with legal concepts meant to operate in relations between economies organized along wholly different lines. It would be senseless to close our eyes to the fact that communist societies, being what they are, cannot recruit at home arbitrators of diverse philosophical outlook, leading a life independent from state employment and party influence. Nor are they in a position to provide commercial institutions that are organically severable from the state. To require them to do so would be to contemplate the mirage of a basically transformed social and economic order.

C. Guarantees of Due Process

Available data suggest no mechanical answer to what is perhaps the central question of our inquiry: is the foreign litigant's fundamental right to a fair and impartial determination respected in practice? That the answer is not automatic is reassuring in itself. Communist courts of law have acquired a reputation abroad (and even at home since Mr. Khrushchev's startling 1956 revelations on the condition of "socialist legality" under Stalin)[13] which casts a shadow on the quality of justice they dispense. In regard to the foreign trade tribunals, despite their structural shortcomings, it would be unwarranted to conclude that a private merchant cannot obtain a "fair deal" in an arbitration before them. No cogent evidence exists to support an inference that the arbitrators are in any way coerced or instructed to favor the local concern.

Normally one would turn to the record of decided cases in order to assess the tribunals' neutrality. Such a course would, however, be neither practical nor fully reliable. Complete and officially authorized reports of the case law do not and, since arbitrations are normally supposed to be private, perhaps cannot exist. Only awards of special interest are published, usually in abstract form. Moreover, there can be no guarantee that cases reported or publicly filed in the tribunals' archives are not edited or preselected to convey a certain impression, although this is unlikely since domestic concerns would be misled no less than foreign firms. Nor would a statistical correlation of the number of known matters decided in favor of foreigners and those decided against them afford a useful test; many judgments have been rendered either way and the proportions do not appear distorted.

More reliable guidance can be obtained from an inquiry into the extent to which the guarantees solemnly set forth in the tribunals' rules of procedure are respected in practice. At the outset, it may be stated that the decisions cited throughout the present work, and others studied by the author in original or summary form, disclose no evidence of bias shocking to the conscience. To be sure, Eastern arbitration awards are occasionally susceptible to criticism for the internal inconsistency of their reasoning or the interpretation they give to applicable law, just as honest differences of opinion may exist with regard to isolated pronouncements of such outstanding judicial bodies as the English High Court of Justice, the Court of Appeals of New York, or the Commercial Tribunal of Paris. But no manifest denial of justice has been detected or, so far as is known, reported abroad by any aggrieved party. Even the highly unsatisfactory result of the Soviet-Israeli oil case, which allows state enterprises to evade contractual obligations by pleading a political act of their own government, can be attributed to the abnormal operation of recognized legal concepts rather than to an unfairly conducted adjudication.

Those nominated by the various communist Chambers of Commerce to serve as arbitrators are in general persons of considerable achievement and high professional and social standing. One cannot lightly assume that such individuals are devoid of intuitive feelings for justice and fair play or that they will react with an inadequate sense of responsibility and objectivity to the trust disputants place in them. But let us pursue a more pessimistic hypothesis: that they are not free agents, that they are unwilling to mete out impersonal justice between a capitalist and a state-owned enterprise, that they are activated by national and ideological chauvinism. Even then, expedient self-interest would seem to dictate respect for the rights of those with whom one would have stable economic intercourse. This conclusion is supported by a series of elementary propositions.

The immutable forces of international business life provide their own safeguards against arbitrary and outrageous practice. No country can afford to ignore the advantages of foreign trade. By the same token, no country can persistently tamper with the conditions of mutual confidence such trade presupposes. Flagrant disregard of prevalent commercial ethics and customs would invite its own unmistakable sanctions. In self-protection the business community may resort to organized measures of retortion, boycott, insistence on self-enforcing contractual terms and other preventive or retaliatory devices. Communist systems are exceptionally vulnerable to such measures; their entire state trading apparatus becomes tainted as a result of inequities perpetrated against foreign business firms by any executive, administrative, legislative or judicial organ of government.

It is for pragmatic reasons of this kind that the Eastern trade monopolies have sought to align their practices with international standards. In the present context, it must be additionally borne in mind that the principal aim behind the creation of the tribunals was to localize the settlement of disputes in home territory. Since their jurisdiction is based on voluntary submission, this aim could hardly be achieved without inspiring confidence abroad in the quality of the proposed adjudication. From the vantage point of the arbitrators, the long-range national interest would therefore appear to be better served by meticulous observance of due process than by cynical disregard of law and fact in order to pervert the outcome of individual controversies.

Occasionally, as in the Soviet-Israeli oil case, where important political considerations are involved, a jarring distortion may creep in. But by and large, if communist arbitrators are at all instructed or influenced by the state their attitude is, at worst, likely to be one of "premeditated impartiality"—an objectivity no less real for stemming from factors of policy rather than from spontaneous instincts of judicial fairness. To dismiss the Soviet Foreign Trade or Maritime Arbitration Commissions as unfair because (as the cliché goes) "there is no justice in Russia" would be to underestimate the fundamental expediency of justice.[14] Soviet trade officials have been known to complain that the Moscow Commission is "very hard on us" and to prefer arbitration abroad. There is no reason to impugn the sincerity of this complaint. To foster contractual discipline at home and confidence abroad, the tribunals may indeed be leaning backward to be harsh with their own.[15]

Another potently reassuring element is the simple fact that in large measure the effectiveness of the Eastern trade adjudication system depends on the cooperation of foreign courts. At least where the alien party is the defendant, a claim cannot often be brought to fruition without invoking the processes of the jurisdiction in which he has his place of business. An arbitrator who has resolved a dispute in favor of the state-trading party by means of a gross denial of justice has handed it a Pyrrhic victory. The Western firm, which normally has no permanent activities or assets in communist territory, will refuse to perform; and a foreign court will deny compulsory execution if an infringement of the defendant's fundamental right to a fair and impartial determination is brought to its attention.

The same degree of protection is not available to a foreign plaintiff committed to seeking his remedy in the East. But there too the danger is minimized by the fact that an accumulation of unfair tactics would stigmaize the tribunals' standing in the eyes of Western businessmen called upon to accept their competence and Western courts called upon to recognize the legality of their awards. Precisely because they function within a permanent and not an ad hoc framework, the Eastern arbitrators lay their institutions' reputation on the line with every abusive action. The significance of this fact is well appreciated in the communist ministries of both foreign trade and justice.

Finally, it is worth noting that the tribunals' work carries considerable educational and discipline-forming significance for the international activities of a state-trading monopoly. One of their main functions is to mold, by means of a growing body of decisions, the experience acquired in the course of business dealings into an orderly branch of foreign trade law and practice for the future guidance of individual enterprises. This quasi-legislative task presupposes adjudication consistent with clearly enunciated principles whose application may sometimes favor the alien and sometimes the local party. The need to inculcate rationality into the day-to-day operations of a bureaucratic monopoly and to avoid the confusions and uncertainties which accompany arbitrary action holds considerable preventive force.

D. The Voluntary Basis of Adjudication

Nothing can afford more effective protection against the possible injustices of a particular method of adjudication than the liberty to accept or reject its authority in the first place. Although the foreigner's autonomy of will in this regard is somewhat negated by the economic superiority his state trading partner usually enjoys, in the final analysis no one can be compelled either to sue or to defend in an Eastern tribunal without prior agreement signified in writing. This raises the crucial question of how and by whom the existence or absence of jurisdiction is determined.

In practice, the tribunals themselves assume power to make the decision conclusively, either at the level of the specifically constituted arbitral board or, as in Poland and Czechoslovakia, at the level of the standing Presidium of the Court, appointed by the Chamber of Commerce.[16] Moreover, no judicial review is available on this issue (except in the case of the Moscow Maritime tribunal, whose judgments are appealable to the Soviet Supreme Court).[17] This practice is not outrageous; most legal systems uphold the exclusion of the courts if the parties expressly authorize arbitrators to settle the matter with finality. The International Chamber of Commerce stipulates as final a ruling by its arbitrators on their own power to hear a dispute.[18]

Eastern case law dealing with the issue of competence has been quite extensive; contestation of the tribunals' right to hear specific disputes has arisen for the most part out of evasive tactics of recalcitrant foreign defendants. No manifest abuse of the power has, however, been noted. The arbitrators can hardly be reproached for rejecting pleas against their very eligibility to adjudicate, based on public policies allegedly prevalent in the defendants' countries of origin; a contrary attitude would have been tantamount to self-dissolution. Similarly, they cannot be blamed for ruling that a submission in their favor excludes any alternative forum at home and abroad; an arbitration clause is universally considered to have this effect. On the other hand, the tribunals' view of what constitutes sufficient submission is strikingly liberal in accordance with the national policy of domesticating foreign trade adjudication to the maximum extent possible.

That an agreement to arbitrate must be reduced to writing and signed by authorized persons has remained a cardinal principle; but in contrast to the onerous formality requirements of Soviet law for contracts in general and foreign trade contracts in particular, no special form is insisted upon. Clearly, special agreements or specific contractual clauses are not deemed indispensable; a mere exchange of letters which refers to the terms of a previous transaction or to general conditions containing an arbitral submission have been accepted as sufficient. The last proposition is exemplified by a 1966 Bulgarian case involving a local enterprise and an Italian party. First, the tribunal postulated that the question of competence is resolved in accordance with Bulgarian rather than Italian law. Then it ruled that Article 9 of the Bulgarian Code of Civil Procedure, requiring submissions to be in writing, was satisfied by the fact that the reverse side of the contractual text showed a set of general conditions which included an arbitration provision.[19]

While no special form is imposed, the parties' intent to refer their disputes to the particular tribunal must be unequivocal. In an action by a Liechtenstein firm against a Rumanian enterprise brought in the Bucharest tribunal, the arbitrators refused to accord a hearing because the contract purported to bestow competence on another tribunal as well.[20] Thus, an attempt by the parties to create concurrent jurisdiction in two arbitral bodies runs the risk of being ineffective in both. The plaintiff may then have to seek anew, and under more trying circumstances, the defendant's consent to arbitrate in one or the other contemplated tribunal. Alternatively, he may find himself compelled to sue in a People's Court.

Under the rules of the East German, Polish and Bulgarian tribunals, it is important to note, an arbitral submission is deemed to exist when the responding party defends on the merits without objecting to a notice of claim served in the absence of an arbitration clause.[21] Nor have rulings as to competence always gone against the foreign party. In 1966, the Sofia tribunal agreed to hear a case filed by a Dutch plaintiff against a local insurance enterprise despite the absence of an arbitration clause. The decision was founded on the ground that the Bulgarian defendant not only failed to object to the action, but also went on to defend on the merits.[22]

The effectiveness of the arbitration clause is not inescapably tied to the fate of the underlying business agreement. In 1968, the Prague court declared itself competent to rule upon a related counterclaim for damages filed by an American defendant pursuant to an arbitration clause contained in an allegedly invalid contract of sale. The Warsaw court considered its jurisdiction well founded in respect of an agreement without an arbitration clause, on the ground that the agreement which it replaced and superseded contained one.[23] The Soviet and Rumanian tribunals, on the other hand, insist rather strictly on proof of a written arbitral submission, although they permit a duly evidenced manifestation of consent to be made just prior to the commencement of proceedings before them.[24] Nonetheless, there are cases in which the Moscow tribunal has declined jurisdiction over foreign firms on grounds of *res judicata;* cases in which it has refused to hear a counterclaim by a Soviet party against a foreign plaintiff on the ground that it was not covered by the arbitration agreement; and cases in which it has responded favorably to attempts to bring into court as co-defendants Soviet enterprises against whom Western firms have sought to assert their claims.[25]

In addition, as we have already pointed out, a large segment of the tribunals' jurisdiction is founded on intergovernmental treaty provisions, multilateral in the Comecon region and bilateral in relations with certain Western countries. In this sphere the absence of a submission directly agreed upon by the parties is no bar to the tribunals' authority to judge.

E. The Quality of Procedure

An indispensable element of exemplary judicial proceedings is the principle of "a day in court." At the very least this presupposes effective service of notice of proceedings, a full hearing in the presence of the parties or their representatives and an opportunity to adduce relevant oral and documentary evidence. The statutes of the communist foreign trade tribunals are largely uniform and generally adequate in the provisions they make in this regard. Ample time limits are laid down (and strictly defined in order to prevent evasive tactics) within which the parties must comply with successive stages of the procedure.

The secretariats of the arbitral institutions are responsible for promptly notifying the defendant of the suit brought against him and for supplying him with copies of the statement of claim and all relevant documents tendered in support thereof. The date of the hearing is usually fixed by the chairman of the institution in consultation with the umpire of the selected adjudication board. Due regard is paid to the location of the parties in order to afford them sufficient time to file detailed pleadings and to participate in the hearings. A prompt summons to trial must be addressed to the parties or their designated agents, but nonappearance has been held to constitute no bar to the continuation of an action.[26] An interpreter may be appointed in the event that a party, a representative or a witness is not familiar with the official language in which hearings are conducted.

It is the parties' responsibility to submit proof in substantiation of their pleadings, but the board may seek evidence on its own initiative, either from the disputants or from local or foreign experts invited to submit opinions on technical questions of fact, commercial custom and usage, the interpretation of foreign law and so on. Admissibility of evidence is governed by the arbitrators' view of relevance, and the method of presentation and evaluation is left to their discretion.

All means of proof are admissible and the probative method is closer to the liberal continental approach than to strict common law practice. Direct and circumstantial evidence in the form of documents, oral testimony, presumptions, experts' reports and the like have all been accepted by arbitral panels for appreciation. The degree of permissible latitude is exemplified by a 1962 Bulgarian decision. The issue was whether a clear-cut admission by the defendant should be admitted as binding. The rules of the tribunal being silent on this point, the arbitrators proceeded to seek the answer in Article 127 of the Bulgarian Code of Civil Procedure. Thereunder, they felt free to evaluate the probative value of the admission along with all other evidence.[27]

Full records of proceedings are required to be kept and signed by the umpire of each tribunal. If the parties agree to settle their differences amicably before the board is finally constituted, or before a decision is announced, they may request that the terms of settlement be reduced to a formal award with all the consequences habitually flowing therefrom.

In addition, the tribunal's rules of procedure extend certain guarantees which go well beyond the protections afforded even by the most respected Western arbitral institutions. These guarantees are a reflection of the self-consciousness of the communist administration of justice in the area of international trade and its tendency to be "holier than thou" in order to allay the natural misgivings of capitalist businessmen invited to submit to local arbitration.

Thus, hearings are required to be conducted in public session (unless the parties request otherwise) despite the fact that arbitration is traditionally a private, unpublicized proceeding, usually held *in camera* in order not to compromise the commercial interests of the parties. Here the advantages of privacy were felt to be outweighed by the added mistrust secret proceedings could evoke abroad. The degree of protection afforded by a publicly held trial may vary in accordance with the interest which a particular dispute holds for third parties; it is nevertheless significant that persons wishing to follow the proceedings are readily admitted. The reality of open-court hearings and its importance as a safeguard of due process were demonstrated in the Soviet-Israeli oil orbitration, which was widely attended by the foreign diplomatic corps, representatives of the international press, lawyers, scholars and law students.

Legal counsel are occasionally denied standing before Western arbitral tribunals on the theory that one of the aims of arbitration is to eliminate the intricate and obstructive technicalities injected into the process of dispute settlement by the juridically conditioned mind. In appearances before the communist tribunals, the alien party may not only be represented by counsel but is expressly empowered to appoint a foreign attorney as well.[28] Distance, language and unfamiliarity with local law and procedure may establish out-of-court disparities between the foreign and domestic disputant which are no less onerous than those directly connected with the litigation. These factors cannot be overcome by entrusting one's case wholly to a local lawyer, since the legal professions of communist countries are considered by many abroad as obedient servants of the very state against which they are called upon to defend their clients.

In the case of foreign representatives or witnesses, the visa and travel restrictions still maintained by certain communist countries could constitute obstacles to effective appearance. However, no onerous impediments have been complained of in practice. It is evidently recognized that facility of access is a necessary condition of proper adjudication. Enlightened state policy may be expected to avoid the interposition of arbitrary difficulties where they would be particularly conspicuous and harmful.

Another major and unusual protection against abuses is found in the requirement that awards, as well as dissenting opinions, must be reduced to writing and include a full statement of the reasons on which they are based. Elsewhere, and particularly in common law jurisdictions, motivated awards are seldom required; indeed, they are usually avoided, owing to a rule that patent inconsistencies of reasoning or mistakes of law may lead to a refusal of enforcement or an order to set aside.

Opinions delivered by the Moscow, Warsaw, Prague, Sofia and other Eastern tribunals are frequently comparable in their analysis of law and fact to judgments of authoritative Western courts of high instance. As a rule, they recite the names of the parties and the arbitrators, the relevant facts, the main arguments submitted, the governing legal norms (and, where applicable, international custom and usage), the reasons for the order made and the time limits within which the condemned party must comply with its terms.

Detailed firsthand reports by Western counsel on two cases tried in Moscow indicate that the applicable rules of procedure as well as general principles of fair play are scrupulously respected in practice. In the first case, a member of the West German bar successfully prosecuted a claim on behalf of a Hamburg firm against the Soviet timber combine, Eksportles.

In the second, Israeli attorneys failed in an action for damages against the Soviet oil combine Soiuznefteksport. In both cases counsel were satisfied with the open, competent, speedy, cordial and dignified conduct of the proceedings, the visa arrangements, the translation facilities and as well the professional acumen and cooperative attitude of Soviet lawyers retained to assist on questions of local law and practice.[29]

22

THE CONTROLLING LEGAL SYSTEM

A. Communist Arbitration and the Supremacy of Law

1. Questions of Substance

Eastern legislation does not always make clear whether substantive law automatically governs the foreign trade and maritime tribunals—a crucial matter for Western traders inasmuch as a vast number of disputes in which they are involved are today litigated in these tribunals. The Soviet Civil Code which was in force until 1964 came into existence long before the arbitration commissions. Whereas some of its provisions were expressly amended to take into account the existence of the two tribunals, the question of applicability of the general law was passed over in silence. Nevertheless, the nature and role of the commissions led to the conclusion that they were intended to be bound, like ordinary local courts, by pertinent rules of domestic and private international law.

In fact, the decisions of all of the Eastern tribunals demonstrate a pattern of attempted compliance with law. Indeed, without such compliance, their determinations are deprived of validity. The adjudicators are not viewed as *amiables compositeurs* free to be guided by considerations of fairness and good conscience in disregard of prescribed legal requirements. Nor can they be exempted from the observance of law by party agreement.

The desire of businessmen to avoid the rigors of the procedural and substantive rules which govern judicial proceedings is at the root of the growing popularity of arbitration in international commerce. However, nowhere is the arbitrator completely absolved from judicial supervision. The degree and method of such supervision is not uniform. In France, Belgium and Latin America, arbitrators must normally adjudicate in accordance with law and their performance is reviewable by the ordinary courts. The parties may suspend this duty and direct the arbitral panel to act instead under the principles of good faith, natural justice and commercial usage.

Germany, Austria and the United States (under federal legislation) afford no judicial remedy to enforce an arbitrator's compliance with law even when he is directed to do so by contract. Certain minimal standards must, however, be observed if the resultant award is to be unimpeachable. Evidence of bribery, corruption, fraud, or excess of authority may result in a court order setting the award aside.

In the British Commonwealth the supremacy of law over arbitration is particularly pronounced. Unless the parties have expressly provided to the contrary, the arbitrators must conform to legal requirements and can be compelled to do so. The courts may be petitioned to determine questions of law before arbitral proceedings are terminated. In England, for example, the arbitrator may, if he wishes, consult the courts on his own initiative, by way of a "special case stated." Alternatively, he can make his ultimate disposition conditional on the court's resolution of the legal question in issue. Whatever the governing legal regime, its infringement may endanger an award's eligibility for judicial recognition and enforcement at home and abroad.

In the East-West area, where freedom from the real or alleged biases of national legal systems would be particularly welcome, we find, surprisingly, that compliance with law is rigidly required. With the seeming exceptions of the Polish and Rumanian foreign trade courts, the Eastern tribunals are not allowed to dispense free arbitration. Whether required to do so under their statutes or not, in practice they apply substantive domestic law (occasionally with mitigated ideological impact) along with conflict rules, treaty law, established commercial usage and significant case precedents. The parties may not exempt the arbitrators from this duty, much less instruct them to disregard legal norms, although subject to certain peremptory rules of the forum, they may direct the application of a specific foreign law or fill their contract with explicit stipulations.

The scope of judicial supervision is strikingly limited, considering that the system requires arbitration in accordance with law. The explanation lies in the fact that the People's Courts are no more qualified to supervise the arbitrators' highly specialized work than to exercise original jurisdiction in the area of international commerce. Here arbitration enjoys a position of absolute supremacy. Its links with the internal administration of justice are largely token. Corrective functions are performed either by the tribunals' secretariats or, as in Czechoslovakia and Poland, by special committees or presidiums established within the constitutional framework of the Chamber of Commerce itself, much as in the case of the Arbitration Court of the International Chamber of Commerce. In addition, individual boards usually include arbitrators with legal backgrounds and, if necessary, consult outside legal experts.

Four main reasons may be advanced to explain why the communist tribunals are bound to strict observance of law: (1) to compel compliance with certain imperative domestic statutes which regulate the activities of foreign trade instrumentalities and officials; (2) to maintain a maximum of uniformity and discipline in the formation and performance of agreements; (3) to stimulate the development of a consistent body of case law for legal relations in the capitalist setting of international business life—a need occasioned by the breach with the "bourgeois" past on the level of national law and by the atrophy of normal court jurisdiction in relation to foreign causes; (4) to emphasize that submission to communist-interpreted law (domestic or foreign) is more palatable to private traders than submission to unfettered communist discretion and to Marxist-Leninist "equity" drawn from strongly anticapitalistic notions of social and economic justice.

2. *Questions of Procedure*

Arbitrators who function on Eastern soil are no more exempt from the observance of prescribed procedural norms than from substantive rules of law, regardless of whether they function on an *ad hoc* basis or within the framework of a permanent institution. The governing regime may derive from the general code of civil procedure in force at the place of hearing, the standing rules of a particular tribunal, the agreement of the parties or a combination of all three. In either event, the arbitrators' discretion in the matter is narrowly circumscribed.

The composition and procedure of the continuously functioning foreign trade arbitration tribunals are set forth in the rules of each institution. Generally, a contractual submission to their jurisdiction is coupled with express language of acceptance of the rules. But even in the absence of such language, the acceptance is deemed to be implicit. In addition, since the tribunals have the peculiarity of being creatures of a legislative enactment, their rules carry the force of law. Neither the litigants nor the arbitrators can contradict them except in regard to provisions which are clearly permissive.

This view, held by a high-ranking member of the Soviet Foreign Trade Arbitration Commission, is not uniformly followed in the East. In at least one dispute, a Swiss defendant was invited to appoint a foreign arbitrator on an *ad hoc* basis—a method of election not envisaged in the rules of the Prague tribunal then in force.[1] A Bulgarian authority states that the Sofia tribunal would recognize the right of the parties to alter or supplement the rules, so long as the contractually stipulated norms do not imperil the object of the arbitration, its regularity or the dignity of the institution. This position is consistent with the 1958 New York Convention on the Recognition and Enforcement of Foreign Arbitral Awards, ratified by Bulgaria in 1961, according to which the parties may "fix the rules of procedure to be followed by the arbitrators."[2]

The validity and interpretation of the procedural criteria established by a tribunal's statutes, or by the parties themselves in the case of *ad hoc* arbitration, are in turn governed by the domestic law of the country in which the hearings are held. This is confirmed by the Soviet Commission's repeated rejection of arguments that its composition violates the public policy of the foreign defendant's country. The application of Soviet law in these cases is in strict conformity with international practice, as codified in Article 2 of the Geneva Protocol on Arbitration Clauses of 1923: "The arbitral procedure, including the constitution of the arbitral tribunal, shall be governed by the will of the parties and by the law of the country in whose territory the arbitration takes place." Nor are the arbitrators entirely free where the territorial provisions are silent. Only the Prague rules expressly permit procedural stipulations on issues which are left uncovered. Otherwise, gaps in the tribunals' rules and in the parties' agreements are filled in by reference to the national codes of civil procedure. The Rumanian rules say so specifically; elsewhere, this position is established by inference.[3]

In an illustrative 1962 Bulgarian decision, the arbitrators could not find in their rules any guidance on the admissibility of a defendant's confession. The tribunal's formulation of the issue and its conclusion are worth noting:

> In the silence of the texts, it is convenient to apply subsidiarily, the provisions of the Code of Procedure of the Bulgarian People's Republic . . . Article 127, paragraph 2 of this Code . . . authorizes the Tri-

> bunal to determine independently the conformity of the plea with the reality of the facts. This right of the judge falls within his obligation not to decide until after a search for the objective truth—a principle which is to apply equally to the arbitral procedure.[4]

The Moscow Foreign Trade Arbitration Commission appears to be bound by the new Principles of Soviet Procedure to the extent that they are relevant to arbitration.[5] This situation prevails in Czechoslovakia and East Germany as well. In Hungary, the arbitration court usually refers to the local code of civil procedure, but such reference is not compulsory. Poland is at the other extreme. It would seem that the Warsaw tribunal is bound by the same rules which govern the civil administration of justice.[6]

If no legislative provision is made, and the tribunal's rules have not been validly varied by party agreement, the arbitrators may select their own procedural norms with a view to reaching an equitable decision. This principle is generally recognized in the East. For example, the statutes of the International Arbitration Court for Maritime and Inland Navigation established in Gdynia in 1959 by agreement among Poland, Czechoslovakia and East Germany provide that unregulated procedural questions are decided by each adjudicative board, taking into consideration the rules of civil procedure operative at the venue if such rules address themselves to the issue in question.[7]

It is difficult to believe that the Eastern legislatures have intended their arbitrators to be slavishly bound by the procedural regime which governs court proceedings in general. If they have, the situation is unsatisfactory and will hopefully be played down in practice, as in the case of various substantive laws which turned out to be unsuitable for the East–West context. A submission to arbitration carries with it a refusal of state jurisdiction; the refusal implies a rejection of the state's judicial process as well. This simple proposition is of the very essence of the adjudication system which the Eastern countries purported to tender to the merchant community of the West.

It is highly probable that overt infringement of a peremptory rule of civil procedure, such as the Soviet prohibition on the administration of oaths to witnesses, would jeopardize an award's local enforceability. This is, however, a theoretical problem. In practice, the basic national principles of adjudication are faithfully applied by the communist foreign trade tribunals. But a certain flexibility in the choice of procedural criteria is essential in the settlement of disputes involving Western parties. Certain extraordinary local devices, such as the right of the Procurator General of the U.S.S.R. to interplead in litigation pursuant to his supervisory authority over the national administration of justice, or the extensive power of Soviet judges to intervene in proceedings *ex officio,* regardless of whether or not the parties wish to assert their private rights, would be intolerable. Even the right of the tribunals' own secretariats to guide arbitrators on matters of procedure, compliance with precedents, application of law and so forth have met with criticism in a Swiss court (although the Czechoslovak award in question was recognized in the end).[8]

In certain specific respects the parties must be free, whether such freedom is conferred by law, by the rules of the tribunals or by mere judicial tolerance, to establish for their arbitrators special procedural guidelines. For example, the adjudication board or the tribunal's secretariat ought not to have unchecked freedom to appoint its own experts to decide questions of fact. Let us assume that a dispute arises over whether a plant constructed in the East by a Western firm is functioning properly; i.e., whether the quality and quantity of its production complies with contractual specifications. In such situations, the expert's decision on a narrow segment of precise and highly technical considerations will, in effect, dispose of the case. Consequently, it would seem appropriate to allow the parties to name such an expert directly at the time of the arbitral submission rather than through the intermediary of the panel or institution to which he must report.

While the foregoing is pertinent to the settlement of non-Comecon disputes, the procedural regime governing foreign trade controversies among East European enterprises derives, under the General Conditions of Delivery, from the rules of procedure in force where the matter is decided. This provision is obligatory and requires that in the absence of a disposition in a given tribunal's rules, the national procedural regime be applied; the parties may not stipulate to the contrary, as they would be contradicting an international agreement concluded among their governments.

B. Admission of Alien Rules

Having established that the communist foreign trade tribunals must adjudicate in accordance with law (substantive and procedural), we may proceed to examine the criteria which condition the selection of rules in specific circumstances. At the outset, it is well to state that the process of selection may embrace not only domestic but also foreign law, as well as rules derived from international treaties and custom.

The diversity of national practice makes it difficult to appraise the nature of conflict of laws in adjudications between Western merchants and Eastern enterprises. International usage has not established any universal jurisdiction, choice of law, or judgment-recognition standards the mere disregard of which by local courts could lead to "denial of justice" proceedings through diplomatic channels or before supranational tribunals.

It would be misleading to build our analysis around the question of whether communist tribunals recognize foreign law to the same degree as French, Japanese or American courts. More to the point would be an inquiry into the extent to which the East complies with the common denominator of international practice, the explanation for any significant departures and the justification for nonconformity in light of the special needs of monopolistic state trading.

The basic conceptions of commercial choice of law have evolved in an era dominated by ideas of economic and political liberalism. Today, the assumption of commercial functions by governments, domestically and internationally, is a universal phenomenon. In the U.S.S.R. and the People's Democracies this phenomenon has reached its most extreme form. In contacts between countries with different trading structures, divergent bases of ownership and many dissimilar civil and commercial laws, the problem of ascertaining the legal system which governs a transaction holds special importance.

Conflicts rules are part of national law. Despite their pluralistic source, many choice-of-law criteria have, however, acquired universal validity. This is largely due to the high degree of human, material and cultural contact among nations with more or less similar social and economic traditions. In relations between communist and noncommunist countries the climate is less conducive to a merger of legal concepts and to an attitude of liberality in the admission of foreign law.

Soviet legal doctrine as expounded by earlier writers has vehemently denied the existence of a sufficient juridical community between socialist and capitalist countries to allow the emergence of common principles of private international law.[9] This undercurrent of hostility, particularly militant during the formative stages of Soviet civil law, is reflected in the restrictive nature of its choice-of-law provisions. A corresponding attitude is apparent in Western legal systems, although there courts find themselves able to express their antagonism to communist laws in terms of exceptions to general conflicts rules, usually by invoking public policy.

Theories advanced from time to time to explain why courts in general sometimes apply foreign law (*e.g.,* that justice requires the protection of vested rights, that nations are entitled to comity, that harmony of applicable laws is desirable to prevent the outcome of litigation from being dependent upon the place where suit is brought) do not adequately describe communist judicial behavior. A more valid rationale is to be found in considerations of practicality. Needs similar to those which led Soviet jurisprudence to concede that legal rules do not easily "wither away" and that social and economic relations have to be enforced by law have compelled the U.S.S.R. to recognize certain norms as operative on the international level. The concept of private international law has thus found acceptance as part of the general framework governing relations with the outside world.

In Eastern Europe, legislation dating back to the prewar regimes—and even recent communist-conceived laws—permit a more traditional range of choice. In the Soviet Union, owing to a historical and doctrinal reluctance to apply "bourgeois" law in local courts, the scope of conflicts is much narrower. Territorial and national criteria predominate in the sense that legal relations which arise in the U.S.S.R., or in which Soviet enterprises take part abroad, are referable to local law. Moreover, reciprocity is a cardinal condition in order to exact corresponding concessions abroad for Soviet law and Soviet-created rights.

In the foreign trade area this pattern has been qualified to some extent by treaty provisions and case law—a pragmatic accommodation to factors of economic necessity. The choice-of-law rules which find application in the practice of the Eastern tribunals must be viewed as a manifestation of compromise between strong dislike of alien conceptions and a need for some measure of conformity to universal practice.

Although the undercurrents of opposition to the admissibility of foreign law have been subdued in recent years both by scholars and legislators, Eastern (and particularly Soviet) attitudes continue to be markedly parochial. The reasons are not difficult to divine. The administration of a gigantic monopoly is facilitated by a standardization of practice. This calls for the reference of certain issues to a single or a special law, preferably the familiar domestic one. Accordingly, aside from a general bias in favor of local rules whenever a choice is to be made by a communist tribunal, certain matters are imperatively referred to the *lex fori.* To an extent this is understandable. Government instrumentalities have requirements which Western rules cannot always meet. Greater play must be given to the public interest, which is invariably involved. By the same token, alien legal provisions primarily designed for private trade must occasionally be set aside.

C. Sources of Private International Law

In Eastern countries, the primary source of conflict rules is found in national legislation. A significant scheme of pertinent provisions also derives from bilateral commercial treaties and multilateral conventions. In addition, as indicated previously, mercantile and maritime custom has received acceptance in the determinations of the two Moscow Commissions and the corresponding foreign trade tribunals functioning elsewhere in the East.[10] A court may therefore have to look to all three areas in its search for applicable legal norms.

A series of fundamental idiosyncrasies pervade Eastern private international law as a whole. In the regular People's Courts or the special economic tribunals active on the domestic level, the choice of law function has atrophied to insignificance, at least in relation to commercial contracts. The key to communist practice is found in the growing body of case law which has emerged from arbitral tribunals competent to adjudicate foreign causes. This case law constitutes, in fact if not in law, a veritable source of conflict solutions.

Even if the domestic law of a communist state governs an East–West dispute, a question arises as to which rules drawn from this law determine the contractual relationship. In the Soviet Union this question has two prongs: what Republican code applies to the transaction as a whole, and which of its provisions can be properly extended to the foreign party?

In the U.S.S.R. (contrary to the approach favored by the American Federation), international conflict rules are built upon a foundation which has no relevance at the national level. Judicial choice between conflicting Republican enactments is governed by special rules codified in the Basic Principles of Legislation.[11]

By virtue of the substantial uniformity of present Republican codes, all of which necessarily conform to the Union-sponsored Basic Principles, the area of domestic conflicts is greatly reduced. Nonetheless, the possibility of collision exists and its impact may be significant in a foreign trade dispute. Let us imagine a claim for damages by a Western buyer against a Ukrainian seller brought before the Foreign Trade Arbitration Commission in Moscow (Russian Republic) pursuant to a contract made in Kiev (Ukrainian Republic). Does the Russian or Ukrainian statute of limitations apply?[12] The tribunal would conclude first, under Soviet international conflict rules (Article 126 of the Basic Principles) that the law of the U.S.S.R. governs as the *lex loci contractus* and then, under intra-Union selection rules, that Ukrainian law governs as the *lex loci actus* (Article 18 of the Basic Principles).[13] Thus, a two-tier determination may be needed before the applicable rule can be isolated, although the content of that rule is likely to be similar from Republic to Republic.

The second aspect of our question is the more fundamental one. Does the national law of the Eastern party apply to the dispute in question, or some rule of foreign, international or customary law? One additional complication must, however, be noted before we turn to this subject.

We have shown earlier that the communist legal system tolerates the application of a mitigated *lex specialis* for foreign causes. Local courts and laws with extreme "socialist" content are, in effect, considered unsuitable for the determination of differences with Western parties; they abate accordingly.[14] This unusual phenomenon brings to mind the legal system of ancient Rome. There, jurisdiction in disputes among foreign merchants was allocated to a special *praetor peregrinus*. The governing law was in the nature of a *jus gentium*. As in modern communist states, the regime applicable to Roman citizens dealing among themselves, the *jus civile,* was separate and distinct.

In commercial relations among communist countries the similarity of economic institutions has been conductive to a process of law unification. The scope of conflicts is thus reduced to a minimum. But the aversion to foreign law which is so pronounced in dealings with the capitalist West is also minimized in this area, owing to greater social and ideological affinities.

The Comecon General Conditions represent an exhaustive regional codification of substantive rules for transactions among the member states. Only lacunae left by the draftsmen are subject to a conflicts solution. A single catch-all choice of law provision simply imports the legal system of the seller's country.[15]

Eastern states dealing *inter se* have also relied heavily upon bilateral agreements as a means of elaborating guiding principles of substantive, procedural and private international law. A network of treaties regulates such matters as judicial assistance, consular procedures, dual nationality and so forth. A 1963 agreement between Poland and Bulgaria, for example, provides that contracts will be subject to the law under which they were formed, unless the parties provide otherwise. Beyond this, the extreme specificity of intergovernmental commerce and navigation arrangements and the narrow limits left for direct bargaining between state enterprises have resulted in an extensive unification of the very terms, conditions and practices of trade.

In relations with the capitalist world, the East European countries have been more reluctant to enter into legal conventions (although prewar adherence has largely retained its effect). The essential provisions of several international instruments have, however, been implemented by unilateral legislative action. Thus, despite the U.S.S.R.'s refusal to join the 1931 Geneva Convention on Checks, the conflicts provisions of its own 1929 statute on the subject are virtually the same. Moreover, they are cast in mandatory terms and all judicial discretion in the choice of law is effectively eliminated. A hypothetical case suggests the content and import of the provisions. A Soviet enterprise issues a check in London, payable in Moscow by Gosbank (the state bank). Questions relating to the adequacy of formal execution or to the substantive obligations assumed thereunder arise in a Soviet tribunal. Both questions would be determined in accordance with English law, as the law where the check was issued and where the obligation was assumed. If the check complies with U.S.S.R. formality requirements, its validity can be salvaged by an alternative reference to local law. This choice of foreign law would not be precluded even in litigation between purely domestic enterprises.

Another example of multilateral treaty adherence, this time direct and recent, is the East's widespread ratification of the 1961 Geneva Convention on Arbitration. This instrument grants the parties freedom to designate the law which their arbitrators will apply to the merits of the case before them. But, typically, the Eastern preference is for bilateral arrangements. Commercial agreements with Western and less developed countries frequently prescribe substantive solutions on selected issues, as well as choice of law, choice of jurisdiction and arbitral enforcement criteria. In the event of irreconcilable collision between binding intergovernmental instruments and communist domestic law, the former take precedence.[16]

D. The Legislative Basis of Choice

Some of the Eastern countries have continued their prewar codification tradition in the sphere of private international law. In 1965, Poland replaced its 1926 statutory system with an equally elaborate specialty law. Czechoslovakia's 1963 Act on Private International Law and Procedure replaced a 1948 statute. Section 10 of the new Act, for example, indicates the law applicable to a number of specified relationships: contracts of sale are referable to the law of the vendor's domicile; transportation, insurance and agency contracts, to the law of the principal place of business of the carrier, insurer or agent; contracts respecting real estate, to the law of the situs; contracts of barter, to the law which "best corresponds to the settlement of the mutual obligations."

Even in states with comprehensive consolidations of this type, isolated conflict rules affecting foreign trade may be found in miscellaneous legislative enactments.

Elsewhere, legislative choice of law provisions are widely dispersed. In Bulgaria, one must turn to the 1950 Act on Obligations and Contracts, the 1952 Code of Civil Procedure and the 1953 Decree on Commercial Judicial Procedure, among other enactments. In East Germany, the private international law of the prewar Civil Code has remained in force, along with the conflicts provisions of the 1933 Acts on Checks and Bills of Exchange. Supplementary decrees on foreign commerce (1958) and on the legal status of foreigners (1956) have also been promulgated. Hungarian private international law does not appear to have emerged from the drafting stage, despite ambitious attempts at codification in 1947, 1959 and 1963; while in Rumania, the cardinal conflicts principles are still those enunciated in Article 2 of the 1864 Civil Code, which is in turn founded upon the Napoleonic *Code Civil*. Of more recent vintage are 1949 and 1957 statutes regulating export-import transactions and the position of alien residents, respectively.

This catalogue brings us to the U.S.S.R. itself. Specific jurisdictional and choice-of-law provisions are found in the Civil Codes of the constituent Republics. However, Federal legislation also plays a major part; Article 14 of the U.S.S.R. Constitution, it should be noted, places foreign commerce under the control and direction of the Union.

Until the 1960s, the most far-reaching principle affecting international contractual obligations was contained in Article 7 of the R.S.F.S.R. Code of Civil Procedure (1948). This repealed provision, upon which a long line of foreign trade arbitration decisions has been founded, merits restatement:

> The court, in examining contracts and documents made abroad, shall take into consideration the laws effective at the place where the contract of the document was made, provided that said contracts or documents themselves were permitted by the laws of the RSFSR or agreements between the RSFSR and the country where they were made.

The subsequent recodification of civil law and procedure has modified the content of all previous legislation. Particularly noteworthy today are Articles 125 and 126 of the Basic Principles, which have been incorporated verbatim in Sections 565 and 566 of the 1964 Russian Civil Code. They provide, *inter alia:*

> The form of a contract made abroad is governed by the law of the place where it was made. However, a contract may not be held invalid for informality if the requirements of the legislation of the U.S.S.R. and this Code have been observed.
> The form of foreign trade contracts made by Soviet organizations, and the procedure for their signing, are determined by the legislation of the U.S.S.R., irrespective of the place where they were made.
> The rights and obligations of parties under foreign trade contracts are defined by the law of the place where they were made, unless the parties otherwise provide by their agreement.
> Soviet law determines in which place a contract is deemed made.

Current law has not had time to undergo much judicial interpretation. However, we may safely assume that it was not intended to depart too far from previously accepted notions. Indeed, the pertinent terms of the new Code strongly suggest that Soviet private international law was fashioned by case law and learned commentary (much as in the Anglo-American legal systems), rather than consolidated by statutory act. The Foreign Trade Arbitration Commission has played the principal role in this process. Its decisions, together with those of the Maritime Commission, constitute the main available guide to Soviet conflict-of-law principles in action.

The words "made abroad" (in Article 7) did more than simply incorporate the rule of *locus regit actum.* In context, they implied that foreign law could govern only when the documents in question were made abroad (those made in Russia were *ipso facto* referable to local law). This result has been curtailed in the course of adjudication, and the new Code takes into account the change of attitude.

If judicial rejection of Soviet law in the case of a contract made in the

U.S.S.R. may amount to reversible error, would refusal to apply that law to a contract made abroad have the same effect? Previously, the answer to this question depended on the meaning of "take into consideration," a phrase significant for its failure to indicate whether the reference to foreign law was mandatory or discretionary. Soviet authorities took the latter view.[17] Thus, transactions concluded abroad in disregard of formality requirements at the place of contracting would not be rendered inoperative, so long as Soviet requirements were satisfied. This view is now explicitly vindicated by the legislature.

The language "provided that said contracts or documents themselves were permitted by the laws of the RSFSR or agreements between the RSFSR and the country where they were made" established a condition precedent to enforceability: contracts valid at the foreign place of contracting must not contravene any mandatory provisions of Soviet law. Likewise, under the new Code noncompliance with formal requirements of Soviet law will be fatal, no matter where the contract is concluded.[18] We will see that the People's Democracies of eastern Europe are less insistent on compliance with domestic formality standards.

Several items of Soviet specialty legislation also contain extraordinarily detailed choice of law criteria, *e.g.,* the Statute on Checks of 1929 and the Statute on Bills of Exchange and Promissory Notes of 1937, which embodies the substance of the Geneva Uniform Law on Bills of Exchange and Promissory Notes of 1930.[19] Even more important is the Maritime Code of 1968, as well as its predecessor of 1929, whose elaborate conflict-of-law rules have served as the basis for many decisions rendered by the Maritime Arbitration Commission.

The maritime law of the U.S.S.R. is based on the principle of a state-operated shipping monopoly. However, its content reflects an awareness that Russia's position as a major trading and seafaring power calls for compliance with well-developed world practices. The scope of private international law rules in admiralty cases is greatly narrowed by the fact that disputes with foreign parties arising from the collision of ships or from assistance rendered in salvage operations are governed by the Brussels Convention of 1910, to which the Soviet Union became a party in 1926.[20] But even outside this area local law does not hold a complete monopoly over the determination of shipping disputes in Soviet courts.

Article 4 of the 1929 Code contained a list of detailed choice-of-law rules applicable in the presence of specified factors connecting a given situation with the U.S.S.R. These rules held great practical interest for foreign parties involved in the carriage of goods and passengers by sea to, from and through Soviet territorial waters. For the most part, they pointed to the application of local law. However, the Maritime Arbitration Commission has not hesitated to allot a modest range to the operation of non-Soviet law as well.

There is nothing intolerable in the fact that the local regime was and is imperatively applicable to the exclusion of the law of the *situs* in all matters relating to the ship itself (the right to carry the Soviet flag, the right to ownership and the mode of alienation and mortgage of vessels, which in the U.S.S.R. are *res extra commercium*), the discipline and organization of the crew, the limits of shipowners' liability and the priority of claims. The corollary is that similar issues involving foreign ships will be submitted to the laws of their respective flags. Anglo-American practice is virtually parallel.

The compass of the old Code was, however, much more ambitious. By virtue of the comprehensive provisions of Article 4, it governed carriage between Soviet ports (cabotage), from Soviet ports to foreign destinations, from foreign ports to Soviet destinations and between foreign ports if one or both of the parties were Soviet nationals or juridical entities. Further, it extended to all issues of special and general average if the voyage terminated in a Soviet port, and to contracts of marine insurance concluded in the U.S.S.R. Disputes which arose from contracts of towage, claims for damages caused by collision, and compensation claims for assistance rendered in salvage operations were subject to domestic law whenever litigation took place in a Soviet forum, provided the Brussels Convention was inapplicable. However, disputes between shipowners and crew, and among members of the crew arising from the apportionment of compensation for assistance rendered to ships, were referable to the law of the flag of the ship rendering the assistance.

In its merchant shipping aspects the new Code follows a far less parochial and much more simple approach. Its choice-of-law provisions match corresponding enactments of many important Western maritime nations in their tolerance of foreign law. Basically, they reflect an attempt at harmonization with the Basic Principles of Legislation promulgated in 1961. The concept of party autonomy in the choice of law (circumscribed by certain mandatory rules of domestic law and by the requirements of local public policy) has been carried forward. However, while the old legislation set forth particularized conflict solutions for enumerated situations, most of them pointing to the law of the Soviet forum, the new Code simply prescribes the law of the place of contracting.[21]

In all spheres of litigation and arbitration, alien law, or the existence of an international trade or maritime practice alleged to be binding, must be proven as a question of fact by the party relying upon it. This requirement is not an unusual one. But under the inquisitorial procedure of Soviet courts, judges may take the initiative in establishing the content of a foreign law or custom, either by gathering evidence themselves or by appointing experts.[22] Arbitrators functioning under the auspices of the Moscow Foreign Trade and Maritime Commissions may enlist the aid of the tribunals' permanent secretariats. The Presidiums of the Czechoslovak and Polish tribunals are expressly authorized to render advice to the adjudicative board on all questions of local, foreign and international law. Hopefully, when this procedure is employed, the foreign party is given an opportunity to establish that the Presidium's interpretation is erroneous.[23]

In cases of undue difficulty, Soviet courts may request the Ministry of Foreign Affairs to obtain an opinion from the government of the country in question. Similar *ex officio* powers are granted to the courts of other Eastern states.[24] The adjudicators are not bound by the information so transmitted, and may overrule it upon the submission of contradictory evidence by the parties. Nor are they bound by the report of an appointed expert, although the judgment must give reasons for their disagreement. If the foreign law cannot be conveniently ascertained, the court will presume it to be the same as that of the forum. This approach is quite universal.

Under Polish procedure, foreign law is characterized as "law" rather than "fact." Because of this, the court rather than the litigant is obliged to establish the content of the alleged alien rule. Although the role of the judge tends to be equally expansive, the technical distinction may determine the scope of review on appeal (broader in regard to law, narrower in regard to fact).

E. Public Policy Displacement of Western Law

The notion of *ordre publique* or public policy is recognized in all Eastern states. In a number of instances it has received statutory formulation. Until recently, the Maritime Code was the only Soviet legislative measure enabling escape from an applicable foreign law on this particular ground.

A generalized public policy provision now appears in the Basic Principles and in the new Russian Civil Code: "A foreign law shall not apply where its application contradicts the fundamental principles of the Soviet system." The "fundamental principles of the Soviet system" are defined by reference to the 1936 Constitution and include, inter alia, "the socialist system of economy and socialist ownership of the means of production, affirmed by the liquidation of the capitalist system of economy and the abolition of private ownership of the means of production. . . ."[25]

Similarly worded clauses have also been included in a number of bilateral trade agreements, usually in connection with the reciprocal enforcement of arbitral awards. Thus, Article 13 of the Soviet-Finnish Trade Agreement of 1947, provided that "if the arbitration decision contradicts the public policy of the country in which the execution of the decision is requested," such execution may be refused.

The same concept is encountered in even more classic form in the legal systems of other Eastern countries. Poland and Czechoslovakia have adopted formulae of general application in their special codes of private international law. Poland's 1926 law, which deprived of force foreign rules repugnant to public order and morality, was re-enacted by the communist-controlled legislature in substantially comparable terms. Article 6 of the 1965 law provides: "Foreign law cannot be applied if its application would produce effects contrary to the fundamental principles of the legal order of the Polish People's Republic." The new Czechoslovak Code, carrying forward the approach of that country's precommunist 1948 law, states in Article 36 that "the rules of law of a foreign State cannot be applied if the consequences of application would violate such principles of the social and political system of the Czechoslovakian Socialist Republic as have to be adhered to without reservation."

Hungary takes an altogether different approach; while the public policy exception has only been endorsed in isolated instances such as the Decree of 1952 concerning marriage and family law, it nevertheless exists as part of domestic court practice. Foreign law must be discarded if its application "would entail a grave violation of the fundamental social, political, legal and moral principles on which the legal order of Hungary relies."[26]

When will a communist tribunal reject an otherwise operative foreign law on the ground that it conflicts with domestic public policy? How can any policy of exclusion be delimited in a forum which functions in an ideological environment hostile to that from which the questionable law emanates?

The Marxist precept that private commerce is "legalized theft" offers little utility in this context. Were it to serve as the guide, Western laws would be excluded wholesale; indeed, the validity of certain communist laws would also become suspect. The fact is that where we have a clash of rules prescribed by two divergent societies, the conventional yardsticks of public policy become too overburdened to retain practical effect. Either each side excludes the rules of the other *en masse*, or the outer limits of admissibility of foreign law must be redefined. The view of an eminent Soviet authority on private international law is reassuring on this score. He argues that notwithstanding the fundamental cleavage between socialistand "bourgeois" legal regimes, where the latter is the law which should properly be chosen, it will be applied by the Eastern tribunal unless consequences "unallowable from the point of view of our legal conscience" would follow.[27]

Evidently, what Professor Lunts is groping for is still a public policy basis of exclusion, but one of very restricted impact. A rule of capitalist origin which is offensive to communist doctrine may nevertheless be tolerated, particularly in the area of international commerce. Something more deeply rooted must be infringed before the axe will fall; the result must be an outrage to socialist morality.

This accommodation is reminiscent of the duality of practice we have found in the Eastern tribunals' handling of their own domestic law. To the extent that the relevant local provision has an extreme ideological content incompatible with the standards of the predominantly capitalist scheme of world commerce, its operation upon the private firm is stayed. The upshot is a fascinating inversion of the public policy doctrine. The governing local rule gives way in the communist forum, because its application would violate the order of the Western merchant community.

It is interesting to note that the earliest treaties on commerce and navigation between communist countries also included public policy escape clauses, particularly in connection with the reciprocal enforcement of arbitration awards. From 1957 onward such clauses were deleted. Philosophically, the notion that one socialist society could deny the validity of legislative and judicial positions taken by another on the ground of public policy differences was considered an unacceptable affront.[28] Presumably the fact that two market economies can tolerate the exclusion of one another's laws must be dismissed as a typical manifestation of the endless contradictions of capitalism.

Communist commentators have frequently and piously prognosticated that even though it exists as a part of positive local law, the doctrine is rarely if ever resorted to by Eastern courts. Professor Knapp, a well-known Czechoslovak jurist and arbitrator, has remarked that in his experience on the Prague tribunal, he has not encountered any case in which it was applied to defeat foreign law. A Soviet arbitrator has made the same observation with respect to the Moscow commissions. This testimony appears to hold good for the remaining Eastern arbitration tribunals as well.[29] Lack of stress at home on apparent public policy limitations explains the self-righteous hostility to the concept which communist legal writers can afford to voice, and particularly their strong criticism of the scope given to it in Western courts in connection with postrevolutionary Soviet expropriation decrees.

Recent decisions of Western, even American, courts have confirmed that legal institutions of communist countries will, in fact, be recognized and not deemed violative of public policy, "although the Soviet system of law and government differs radically from our own." The convergence of this view with that which—according to Professor Lunts—has evolved in the U.S.S.R., is quite striking.[30]

Eastern jurisprudence attributes the small role played by public policy in the practice of the foreign trade tribunals to the ability of communist courts to overlook their innate dislike of "bourgeois" law in the interest of peaceful co-existence and cooperation between different social systems. An alternative explanation also suggests itself. The issue of exclusion can only arise after it has been determined that in principle foreign law governs the particular transaction. The threshold question, therefore, is what scope for an initial choice of foreign law exists under Eastern conflict rules as interpreted and applied in practice.

To the extent that mandatory provisions of domestic law (e.g., specific formality requirements) enter the equation, no choice of foreign law is possible at all. Essentially, such imperative rules are in themselves an inviolable manifestation of state policy. Beyond this, it is an empirically established fact that the powerful Eastern trading monopolies have managed to go quite far in localizing the formation of contracts on home territory and thus subjecting them to local law. Since the scope of operation allowed to "bourgeois" law is therefore extremely narrow in the first place, *i.e.,* at the point of choice, it is seldom if ever necessary to invoke an extraordinary rule to escape its application.

In effect, choice of foreign law may be said to be the exception and the public policy of the forum the very basis of the private international law as applied by communist courts and arbitration tribunals in disputes of a commercial nature. Eastern authorities have uniformly and vehemently disagreed with this rationale, first formulated in 1957.[31] It is respectfully submitted, however, that the polemic remains inconclusive. Further evidence from the future case law of the foreign trade and maritime tribunals is required before a definitive judgment can be made.

23

LAW SELECTION METHODS

The science of conflicts is noted for the complexity of problems entailed in determining what law governs the incidents of an international contract. Inconsistencies of approach can be found not only across national borders but also within the same jurisdiction—indeed, the same court. The absence of firm guidelines leads adjudicators to select, often indiscriminately, from among the law of the place of contracting, the law of the place of performance, the law intended by the parties, the law of most intimate connection, the law where the damage was caused, the law where the arbitration is to be held and even the law which upholds rights and obligations.

In international transactions of purchase and sale, the choice-of-law difficulties are necessarily more pronounced than in other types of business dealings, since multinational factors are invariably in play. Such questions as the essential validity of an agreement, formalities of execution, contractual capacity, passage of title, allocation of risk of damage or loss, incidents of performance and applicable periods of limitation are seldom governed by the same law; nor do courts of different countries rely on uniform criteria in seeking the law which governs any particular issue.

In the sphere of contract, communist tribunals operate within the limits of a "legitimate" approach to choice of law. However, the emphasis given to classic connecting factors differs from Western and especially Anglo-American practice. The appropriate legal system is chosen in accordance with the circumstances of each individual case, but with rigid deference to such domestic legislation as is deemed peremptorily applicable to foreign trade transactions.

This does not mean that the process of selection is dictated by a wish to manipulate the outcome of litigation. Many cases may be cited where the selection of foreign law by the Moscow, Prague or East Berlin tribunals has led to judgments against local parties, and where local law was applied to give appropriate remedies to foreigners. To the extent that chauvinism may be suspected, it takes the form of a desire to ensure for state enterprises as wide an area of immunity from alien law as minimum conformity to traditional conflicts practice would allow.

Eastern tribunals do not proceed from the premise that all elements of a contract must necessarily be governed by one legal system even if their own law of the forum controls the substance of the transaction. Issues relating to capacity, to those aspects of formal validity for which communist law is not imperative and to the performance of obligations are often treated separately from matters touching upon the validity of contracts and the interpretation of their specific terms.

A. Party Choice of Law

1. Contractual Expression of Intent

In varying degrees all legal systems recognize that the law governing contractual obligations should be selected in accordance with the parties' expectations. Intent, whether manifested expressly or tacitly, is usually allowed to control. This principle finds definite acceptance in the domestic laws of communist states. Bulgaria, for example, permits contractual designation of the controlling legal system "so long as it is not contrary to the law, to the economic plan, and to the rules of the socialist community." In Hungary, a Decree of the Minister of Foreign Trade authorizes state enterprises to waive stipulations of local law. The concept of party autonomy is also recognized in the Polish and Czechoslovakian Codes of Private International Law, where it has received rather distinctive treatment.[1]

In the application of their own Rules of Procedure and of specific and general legislative enactments, party choice of law finds viable expression in the practice of the Eastern foreign trade tribunals. To cite one illustration, in a 1956 decision the Bucharest Commission declared, with reference to a contract of sale, that "Rumanian private international law accepts the principle of the autonomy of the parties' will, according to which the contract, its effect and its consequences are governed by the law designated by the contracting parties. . . ."[2]

The same approach obtains in the case law of the Sofia tribunal. In a recent decision, the arbitrators went to great lengths in searching for the law tacitly intended by the Lebanese and Bulgarian parties. The tribunal weighed all the circumstances preceding, accompanying and following the formation of a contract for the sale of cotton, cataloguing various indices of connection with multiple legal systems, including the fact that a Bulgarian arbitration forum had been elected, and finding, in the end, that the parties were "oriented" toward Bulgarian law:

> The international elements of the contract focus on the following points: (1) the different nationalities and the different domiciles of the parties, (2) the formation of the contract at Sofia, (3) the consignment of the goods, to be arranged at Izmir (Turkey), (4) the payment of the purchase price by means of a letter of credit opened at Eurobank in Paris through the intermediary of its correspondent in Beirut, (5) the clause attributing competence to the arbitral court of Sofia to resolve disputes which might arise from the contract. The modification of the contract finally, which occurred on 6 October 1963, also at Sofia—in the course of a personal meeting between the parties—is no less important as an international connection.
>
> Considering these rather contradictory international elements, which connect the contract to different countries (Bulgaria, Turkey, Lebanon), the arbitral court considers that it will have taken into account the intent of the parties only if it attributes a preponderant role to certain of these indices, which are: (1) the place of the conclusion of the contract, (2) that of the destination of the merchandise, (3) that, finally, where it has been agreed that eventual litigation would be decided. The court draws upon these indices and the contract is consequently shown to be connected with Bulgarian substantive law. . . .[3]

In Soviet legislation, arbitral practice and legal literature, considerable support exists for party autonomy in regard to choice of law. Article 5 of the 1929 Maritime Code (carried forward by Article 15 of the new Code of 1968) was the first Soviet measure of its kind to confer upon parties the express right to adopt a law for their agreement. A condition was, however, attached: there must be no attempt to evade the provisions which the Code makes compulsory in specified factual situations. The Maritime Commission has respected this legislative mandate. In at least one reported case it applied the party-chosen French law to issues upon which the operation of Soviet law was not compulsory.[4]

The Foreign Trade Arbitration Commission has also considered itself bound by the principle of autonomy, although there are few reported cases in which the application of a non-Soviet law was required by a contractual clause. This is explainable by the fact that, generally, merchants who submit to arbitration in Moscow do so by signing a standard contractual form. Included therein is a clause submitting the transaction to local law as well as to the local forum.

Occasionally, the submission to Soviet arbitration is silent on the issue of the governing law. But the absence of a reference to some legal system does not necessarily signify an abdication of choice. The parties may be acting in anticipation that the settled conflict rules of the forum will be applied to controversies between them. Now and again communist enterprises depart from their habit of concluding agreements on home territory. Their representatives have been known to travel to Switzerland for the purpose of signing contracts on the assumption that the Swiss Code of Obligations will rule any subsequent dispute.

In cases where contracts contained clauses stipulating for Soviet law, that law was applied on the sole ground of party choice. In a series of early decisions, the Moscow Commission referred to the contractually chosen local law even though the result was adverse to the Soviet party.[5] Applying the Russian Civil Code then in force, it refused to award damages against an Egyptian defendant in addition to the penalty the latter had agreed to pay in case of breach, even though the amount was not sufficient to cover the losses sustained by the state enterprise.

Pushing autonomy to its logical limits, in a dispute between a Belgian firm and a Soviet combine, the Moscow tribunal permitted the parties to stipulate in favor of local law at the hearing itself, the contract having failed to make any provision.[6] The Gdynia Maritime Arbitration Commission took a similar approach in a case involving a Polish seller, a West German buyer and a Polish ship sailing from New York to Hamburg. The bill of lading elected the American Carriage of Goods by Sea Act of 1936. This choice of law was held to be invalid under the Polish Private International Law of 1926 on the ground of inadequate connection with the United States. Faced with this, the parties orally opted for American law, the Brussels Convention of 1924 and the law of Poland in effect at the time the transaction was entered into. The tribunal recognized this choice and interpreted the bill of lading in accordance with Polish law.[7]

Czechoslovakia has taken a sharply different view as to the appropriate time for exercising the prerogative of party choice. In a 1954 decision, the Prague tribunal stated: "The choice of proper law must be effected with the required precision at the moment when the parties enter into contractual relations. It is not conceivable that the parties should remain in doubt as to the proper law of contract until the commencement of proceedings."[8]

The principle of party autonomy collided with the requirement of Article 7 of the former Russian Code of Civil Procedure to apply foreign law only in the case of contracts concluded abroad. Presumably, foreign law was not compulsorily applicable if its provisions were expressly excluded by the parties. Contracts concluded abroad were, however, always capable of being governed by the law of intention. Under Article 566 of the Code presently in force, contractual rights and obligations which arise on Russian territory between Soviet enterprises and alien parties are also subject to autonomy of choice. An explicit election of foreign law under these circumstances will now be recognized.

Party choice of law is sometimes specifically allowed in bilateral treaties to which Eastern states are privy. The effect is to afford opportunities for discarding the law of the place of contracting which the treaties usually prescribe. For instance, Article 10 of the Agreement Between France and the U.S.S.R. concerning Mutual Commercial Relations of September 3, 1951, enables the choice of Soviet (or, apparently, any other law) for transactions between the two countries, even though the contract is concluded in French territory. Under a treaty which establishes the territoriality rule, but remains silent as to the right of parties to choose a law, the situation is somewhat more intricate. Soviet commentators elevate the notion of party autonomy to a universal principle of private international law from which neither a domestic nor a foreign court ought to depart. They argue that treaty provisions of this type are merely declaratory of orthodox practice.[9] It follows that in an area encompassed by a treaty containing conflict-of-law rules, but lacking provision for autonomous choice of law, Soviet courts will infer a right to choose.

2. *Conditions of Validity*

The boundaries within which contractual election of law is permitted are neither uniformly nor clearly defined in the East. Public policy considerations are universally viewed as a legitimate basis for rejecting an applicable foreign law, even one chosen or intended by the parties. There are other limitations. Although in practice effect is given to implicit manifestations of will, communist commentators are opposed to the notion of "hypothetical" or "presumed" intent where none in fact exists. The polemics as to the objectively and subjectively ascertainable proper law which have so preoccupied English courts and jurists are absent from this sphere. The Prague tribunal, for example, has flatly declined to search for the law the parties would have chosen if they had thought about the matter.[10]

In the U.S.S.R., the principle of party choice is theoretically circumscribed only by the forum's view of policy and integrity. But an election seeking to evade imperative foreign trade regulations will also be ineffective. Similarly, and in line with universal attitudes, a reference to a foreign law in the hope of establishing more favorable conditions for the formation of a contract (e.g., to avoid onerous formalities, to establish capacity where it is absent) will fail.

The Hungarian, Polish and Czechoslovak arbitration tribunals all admit a right of free choice, but impose conditions which go beyond those of the other communist states. Hungary requires an element of tangible connection between the contract and the chosen law—a requirement frequently encountered in the West.[11] In Poland, under the 1926 Private International Law, the parties were expressly limited to an election from among the law of nationality, the place of domicile, the place of performance, the place where the contract was made, or the *situs* of the contractual subject matter. Within this range, the chosen law has frequently found application in the Warsaw foreign trade tribunal. In a 1961 decision, a contractual stipulation resulted in a reference to the Yugoslav statute of limitations. In a case involving a West German firm, the elected Polish law was applied.[12] But the inflexible statutory coupling of party choice with catalogued connecting factors was inadequate to cover many practical situations. Article 30 of the new Private International Law of 1965 provides more simply that contractants may select any system of law "with which the transaction is connected."

The Polish and Hungarian requirement of connection gives rise to the usual problems of interpretation and application and is therefore not appreciated within the Comecon sphere. The Czechoslovak experience is pertinent in this context. The Private International Law of 1948 declared in Article 9 that "The parties are authorized to refer their legal relations to a specified law, provided that the relation shows a significant connection with the chosen law, and that the choice is not contrary to the mandatory rules of the law to which the legal relation is referred pursuant to the provisions of this section." The article was applied in a 1954 decision. The disputed transaction concerned a purchase of jute from Pakistan. The parties had used the standard form contract of the London Jute Association, which referred to English law. The Prague arbitrators held that the stipulation was invalid, since England had no connection with the transaction.[13] With the enactment of the Private International Law of 1963, the nemesis of connection has been removed: Article 9 (1) states that "The parties to an agreement are free to choose the law to be applied to their relationship of an economic character; they can do it also by tacit consent in such circumstances as would raise no doubts as to their real intentions." It is interesting to note that the new rule discards both prior limitations, significant connection as well as the imperative operation of certain domestic laws, leaving only public policy to demark the outer boundaries of party autonomy.

This approach is consistent with the tendency elsewhere in the East to reject or minimize restrictions on contractual freedom. Thus a Bulgarian authority observes that enterprises of his country, especially when a purchase and sale of cereals is involved, often accept a stipulation of English law, even though no relationship with England is apparent. Such a clause is considered valid in the adjudication of the Sofia tribunal.[14] Yugoslavia, in its Statute on Contracts for the Employment of Sea-Going Vessels, limits party autonomy only by the principles of fraudulent law evasion and public policy with respect to transport of persons and goods by sea. Judicial practice has adopted the same approach for international sales transactions. Contracts with Western enterprises often provide that the Swiss Code of Obligations will determine rights and duties. Notwithstanding the absence of any connection with Switzerland, the Belgrade tribunal has uniformly applied the stipulated Swiss law.[15]

The Soviet, Czechoslovak, Bulgarian and Yugoslav degree of permissiveness, regrettably absent in Poland and Hungary, is in fact essential in the East–West business environment. The law of a third country is often chosen solely in order to reach a neutral compromise. Rules and interpretations which foreclose such compromise can hardly be expected to serve the interest of expanded trade. In addition, many existing contracts with Polish and Hungarian enterprises which unwittingly provide for Swiss, Austrian or Swedish law would be deflected from the parties' original intent if the factor of connection were rigidly applied. In the absence of contractual guidance as to the law which is to govern the transaction, it becomes the duty of the court to designate the applicable legal system.

B. Criteria of Judicial Choice

Except where treaties otherwise provide, the Eastern tribunals determine the proper law of the contract by applying domestically prescribed criteria. In some states, these criteria are articulated in legislation; in others, they are outgrowths of judicial and arbitral decisions. At all levels, they reflect a marked effort to promote the application of domestic law, an effort often obscured by verbal resort to conventional indicators of choice.

The lack of consistency in the judicial practice of the various communist countries is no less noticeable than in the West. Consequently, where the parties have not clearly and validly opted for a particular national law, the fortuitous circumstance of litigation in one forum instead of another may dictate the choice and along with it the outcome of the dispute. It is important, therefore, to consider the different methods of selection followed by the various Eastern tribunals when the question is left unregulated in the text of the agreement.

1. The Place of Contracting

In the Soviet Union, the Basic Principles and the individual Republican codes declare that in the absence of party choice, contractual rights and obligations in foreign trade transactions are established by reference to the substantive law of the place where the contract was made. This approach has long been favored by the Moscow Commission. In one reported case, French plaintiffs were held to have forfeited an advance of funds because under Soviet law such advance amounted to a deposit not recoverable by a party refusing to accept purchased goods. In addition, they were held liable for damages resulting from their breach of contract. Soviet law was given automatic operation as the law of the place of contracting.[16]

In the last two decades, most foreign trade contracts with Soviet enterprises have been negotiated and concluded in Russian territory, usually in Moscow. Judicial references to the law of the place of contracting have therefore generally resulted in the application of local law. However, the Commission has found occasion to apply this principle in favor of foreign law as well, in both East–West and intra-East disputes. The English, Belgian, East German or Hungarian legal systems have repeatedly prevailed as the law of the place where the contract was made.[17] In a dispute between a Bulgarian and Czechoslovak enterprise, exceptionally submitted to the Moscow tribunal for third-country arbitration, Bulgarian law was applied as the law of the place of contracting.[18] Under the new Code, it is manifestly clear that the place of making is not only a sufficient connecting factor, but by far the predominant one in matters of contractual rights and obligations. In a recent dispute between a Swiss plaintiff and an Italian defendant, again exceptionally brought in Moscow, the tribunal chose Italian law on this solitary ground.[19]

Since foreign arbitration of disputes was invalid under Italian law, the Commission did not feel justified in considering the merits with finality. It is, however, interesting to note the scope given to the place of contracting: not only was it determinative of the proper law of the contract, but also of the forum's jurisdiction to hear the dispute. This would seem to go further than Soviet law requires. In all likelihood, it reflects a realistic assumption that any award against the Italian defendant would probably not have been enforceable, owing to the repugnance with which Italian law views arbitration abroad. Undoubtedly, the fact that no Soviet enterprise was involved also played a part.

A similar defense raised by an Italian party in a dispute with a Bulgarian enterprise, heard in Sofia, was disposed of quite differently. The arbitrators held that, although Italian law governed the substantive issues of the case, the jurisdictional question concerning the validity of the arbitral clause was a separate matter, referable to the law of the forum; such was presumed to be the intent of the parties.[20]

According to two arbitrators of the Bucharest Commission, Rumania, like the U.S.S.R., applies primarily the law of the place where the contract was made, but only when the parties have failed to make their own stipulation. Thus, in a dispute involving Rumanian and Belgian firms, the tribunal declared that "in the absence of a manifestation of the parties' will to the contrary, the parties are assumed to have submitted the contract and the relations derived therefrom to the law of the country where it was entered into." However, in another case decided in the same year, the fact that the contract between an Italian firm and a Rumanian enterprise was entered into in Italy was considered outweighed by the fact that Rumania was both the place of performance and the seat of arbitration. The tribunal applied local law, having inferred from these circumstances that such was the intention of the parties.[21]

On a third occasion, the Bucharest tribunal referred to the coinciding places of contracting and performance, in order to come out in favor of its own law:

> Once the contract has been entered into in Rumania and been performed there, these circumstances lead, each for itself and with more reason when they are present together, to the legal consequence that Rumanian law has to be applied to the contractual relations which form the basis of the dispute.[22]

Rumania has failed to enact a conflict rule comparable to that now found in Soviet, Polish and Czechoslovak legislation. As a result, the published decisions of her tribunal lack consistency, and uncertainty prevails as to what law will be applied in future cases.

Since the place of contracting exerts such a strong influence upon judicial choice of law throughout the East, it is of crucial importance to know how the tribunals fix the *locus* of an agreement.

International transactions of purchase and sale are often the result of protracted negotiations, usually conducted by correspondence rather than on a face-to-face basis. The national laws of the parties involved do not always coincide on the method of determining the point at which their agreement came into existence. Soviet tribunals, following classic Western methodology, have consistently resolved this question in accordance with the rules of domestic law, an approach which has now been statutorily adopted. Contracts by correspondence are deemed to have been made upon (and therefore at the place of) receipt of the acceptance by the offeror. The principles relevant to this approach, which find fairly uniform application in all of Eastern Europe, have been discussed in detail in the context of formation of East–West agreements.

2. *The Place of Arbitration*

There is much to be said for the view that if a dispute is to be heard at a specified location, the arbitrators should apply the law of the place where they sit; that is, after all, likely to be the law with which they are best acquainted. Thus, English courts follow the rule that a submission to arbitration within their jurisdiction implies a wish to have the adjudication conducted in accordance with local law. This in turn establishes an inference that the parties intended the contract itself also to be governed by English law.

Given the permanent, institutionalized nature of the Eastern foreign trade tribunals, it would be almost nonsensical to deduce from the mere fact of submission a choice of the substantive law of the forum; for this would be tantamount to applying the local law to all contracts except those stipulating foreign law. Presumably because they anticipated this line of reasoning, the Moscow Commissions have never invoked Soviet law on the independent ground of its being the law of the place of arbitration. They have only resorted to it cumulatively, to reinforce a choice made for other reasons. For example, in an action by the Soviet combine Raznoimport against two foreign firms, the Commission said:

> It is necessary to note at the outset that the relationship of the parties under a contract . . . concluded in the U.S.S.R. must be submitted to Soviet law, particularly since the parties to the contract have chosen the Foreign Trade Arbitration Commission as the organ to determine disputes which may arise between them.[23]

A dispute involving a Canadian concern and a contract concluded in Moscow attracted the application of Soviet law. This followed:

> . . . not only from the presence in the contract . . . of a term requiring the determination of disputes in Moscow by the Foreign Trade Arbitration Commission . . . which permits an inference that the parties intended to submit their contractual relationships to Soviet law, but also from the fact that the contract was concluded in Moscow, which is in itself sufficient to require the application of Soviet law as the law of the place of contracting.[24]

In another case, decided in 1937, notwithstanding submission to the Moscow tribunal, Turkish law was applied as the law of the place of contracting to deny the Soviet trade mission damages in excess of a penalty for breach quantified in the contract.[25] However, the *lex loci contractus* happened to be the criterion set forth in the Soviet–Turkish Treaty of Commerce and Navigation of March 16, 1936; only a clear contractual expression of intent that Soviet law should govern would have sufficed to displace the territorial provision.

Bulgaria, like the U.S.S.R., rejects the idea that the choice of a particular tribunal is of itself a sufficient ground for attributing to the parties an intent to submit to the substantive law of the forum. At least one arbitrator of the Sofia Court is of the opinion that such a rule would be violative of private international law.[26]

Other Eastern states have taken different views of the matter. Relying on Article 28 of its 1954 rules, which provided that "if facts bearing on the case do not indicate another method, the court shall apply the *lex fori,*" the East Berlin tribunal held a submission to its jurisdiction to be a submission to the substantive law of the German Democratic Republic. This position was subsequently assailed both at home and in other Comecon countries.[27] In 1957, new rules were enacted, providing in Article 27:

> The Arbitration Commission shall apply the law chosen by the parties inasmuch as the rules for the choice of law, the conflict rules of private international law of the German Democratic Republic, do not refer to another law. In the absence of a stipulation about the applicable law, the law to be applied shall be determined by the Court.

Since then, East German practice has favored the law of the seller rather than the law of the place of adjudication. However, there have been further instances of local law application on the basis of the principle of "he who elects the judge elects the law."[28]

Decisions of the Prague Arbitration Court have gone exceptionally far in treating arbitral submission as evidence of an intention to adopt Czechoslovak law. In an action by a West German buyer, the tribunal pointed out that the disputed c.i.f. contract was made in Frankfürt, that its place of execution was Hamburg, that the merchandise was situated in China when the bargain was concluded and that the seller's head office was in Czechoslovakia. Nevertheless, the tacit preference for local law was deduced from the choice of local arbitration. The report is as significant for the enunciated rule as for the cited western authorities:

> . . . the parties have, by reserving the matter for the Czechoslovak Arbitration Court, tacitly subjected their relations to Czechoslovak law. This signification of the arbitration clause should be clear even to the plaintiff, an experienced businessman, for similar clauses are interpreted in the same way both by international doctrine and legal decisions (see for example Wollf, *Private International Law,* Oxford, 1945, p. 444) and in particular by German doctrine and legal decisions (Nussbaum, *Deutsches Internationales Jahrbuch für Schiedgerichtswesen in Zivil und Handelssachen,* edited by A. Nussbaum, V.II, 1928, p. 271 *seq.*—Frankenstein, *Internationales Privatrecht,* V.II, 1929, p. 171 and legal decisions quoted therein).[29]

The Polish tribunal has also accorded weight to the place of arbitration as a choice-of-law index, but in a manner which is much more acceptable. In one case an Italian defendant pleaded lack of jurisdiction, basing himself on the fact that the arbitration clause had not been executed in accordance with the requirements of Italian law. The plea was rejected on the ground that an agreement to arbitrate is always governed by the law of the place of arbitration, regardless of the law which applies to the contract as a whole. The decision may be explained as a banal application of the forum's own law to a question which is fundamentally one of procedure rather than substance.[30]

3. *Miscellaneous Connecting Factors*

In a series of cases the Moscow tribunal has cited, along with the place of contracting, one or more additional points of reference. For example, in an action by an English firm against a Soviet combine for failure to deliver part of the merchandise sold, local law was applied on twin grounds—as the law of the place of contracting and of performance. The plaintiff was awarded compensation for actual losses as well as anticipated profits. The same approach was taken in a case involving a French firm.[31]

The fact that the disputed relations arose in Turkey and the contract was to be performed there led to an application of Turkish law in an award rendered in 1940. But a separate aspect involving the mode of payment was determined by Soviet law as the law of the place of performance. On the same ground, a 1952 award involving a Belgian enterprise also displaced the law of the place of contracting with the law of the place of performance in regard to the mode of payment. A 1947 decision applied Iranian law on the basis that the contract was made in Iran, was to be partly performed there, and the damages for which compensation was claimed were caused in Iranian territory.[32]

More singular complications arose from a 1951 dispute involving British and American plaintiffs. The Soviet enterprise argued that the contract under which the English party sought completion of delivery should be considered side by side with another contract concluded with the latter's parent company, the Anglo-American Fur Corporation of New York. Both contracts allegedly represented a single transaction, wholly negotiated by the American corporation and signed simultaneously in the form of two agreements only at its express request. The Commission applied Soviet law as the law of the place of contracting and of performance, to find that the agreements were separate and required independent performance. Accordingly, the local defendant was ordered to complete delivery.[33]

Bulgarian practice has likewise shown a strong bias in favor of the law of the place of performance as the primary criterion to determine contractual rights and obligations, where the parties have failed to exercise their autonomy of choice. A decision of the Sofia Court of Arbitration reported in 1967 and carrying forward a string of similar decisions, took the view that under Bulgarian private international law contractual obligations are localized at the place where the characteristic aspect of their performance takes place. In sales contracts, the characteristic obligation is considered to be that of the seller rather than the buyer; the latter's main duty is simply to pay the price. Therefore, the court concluded, the obligation should be referred to "the substantive law of the state in which the seller must perform his obligation of delivery," which in the instant case was the law of Bulgaria.[34]

Czechoslovak cases have also demonstrated a preference for the law of the seller's country. Statutory support for this position existed in Article 44 of the 1948 Czech Private International Law; Article 10 of the 1963 law leaves open the same avenue of approach. Current Polish and Hungarian practice points in the same direction, the former more so than the latter.

Under Article 27 of the Polish Private International Law of 1965, the applicable law of obligations in the sale of movables, where the parties have remained silent, is that of the domicile or residence of the seller at the date of the contract. If his domicile or residence cannot be ascertained, the place where the contract was made takes precedence. Although the principle is not codified, the prevalent view in Hungary likewise favors the law of the vendor's domicile. While no established judicial practice can as yet be traced, the Budapest arbitration tribunal has in recent years also supported the principle of the seller's law. However, in at least one decision, the arbitrators have weighed the place of contracting against the place of performance and resolved in favor of the latter.[35]

If discrepancies of attitude are apparent from the case law of the Eastern tribunals, they are largely confined to disputes with the West. In litigation within the East European region extensive uniformity prevails. Post-1958 disputes between enterprises of Comecon countries are necessarily referable to the law of the seller's country by virtue of the General Conditions of Delivery, which displace competing national choice of law criteria altogether. It was solely on this basis that the Soviet Commission applied East German law in a dispute between enterprises of the two countries heard in 1959.[36]

C. Law Governing Contractual Form and Execution

It is a basic principle of private international law that issues of formality are referable to the law of the place of contracting. But few countries have followed this principle rigidly. The Anglo-American rule vacillates between the law of the place of contracting and the law governing the transaction as a whole. The German and Italian civil codes allow a reference to either one of the two, while French law provides a further alternative: the national law of the parties. Such is the common denominator of international practice.

The new Basic Principles and Codes have clarified the Russian choice-of-law solutions concerning procedure for signing foreign trade agreements. The rule that the place of contracting determines issues of formality has been preserved, but an attempt has been made to eliminate the ambiguities which arose from the previous terminology. Present law clearly provides that while the formal validity of contracts concluded in the U.S.S.R. is always subject to Soviet law, the formal validity of contracts concluded elsewhere may, but need not, depend upon compliance with the law of the place of execution. As a rule, a contract concluded abroad in violation of the law of the place of contracting will be upheld if Soviet law is satisfied. A contract valid where made, but contrary to Soviet formality requirements will be declared null and void if one of the parties is a Soviet organization.

In short, for would-be Western traders with the U.S.S.R. it is critically important to bear in mind that the Soviet requirements of form and signature (described in the context of formation and performance of East–West contracts) are mandatory regardless of where the agreement happens to be concluded. Where no local enterprise is involved, a Soviet court or arbitral tribunal is free to make an alternative reference, either to the law of the place of contracting or to its own domestic law, in order to ignore an infringement of one of the two sets of formalities. However, the imperative operation of the Soviet requirements upon local enterprises is postulated as a cardinal principle of private international law, binding extraterritorially upon foreign courts as well as domestic tribunals.

The alleged justification for this unprecedented position is the public nature of the U.S.S.R.'s foreign trade activities. It is simply contended that "the judicial organs of foreign states, in deciding cases falling within their jurisdiction involving the issue of the validity of a contract concluded in the name of the U.S.S.R. trade delegation, or in the name of a Soviet foreign trade organization, should apply the provisions of Soviet law. A contrary view by a foreign court would amount to an infringement of the sovereign rights of the Soviet state."[37] One authoritative textbook puts the argument thus:

> These laws clearly define the limits of the powers of trade representatives and other Soviet agencies engaged in foreign trade. Since the foreign court cannot establish the limits of these powers itself, inas-

much as it may not in general define the functional jurisdiction and the procedure of a foreign government agency, it is self-evident that a foreign court must base its decisions on the validity of contracts in foreign trade on the provisions of the Soviet law.[38]

Aside from coupling the issue of form with questions of capacity, this rationale lacks consistency, at least in regard to contracts entered into by corporate trading enterprises. As we have seen in a number of connections, for some purposes these enterprises are billed as entities juridically separate from the state, doing business independently and at their own risk; for others, they are held out as governmental agencies performing a sovereign function which entitles them to special privileges at home and abroad. This is clearly an attempt to derive the best from all possible worlds.

If the Soviet position amounts to an injection of "new law," regardless of the camouflage in which it is presented, are there considerations which justify such a revolutionary inroad into traditional practice?

It must be conceded that special and very real needs of the communist state are indeed present. These needs are an expression of the ever-present problem of protecting the public interest in a system where commerce is carried on through a diffused bureaucracy. The supervision of a vast monopoly with numerous branches at home and abroad cannot easily be abandoned to the operation of diverse laws. A uniformly applicable system of rules is necessary to perform the centralizing and regulatory functions. Insistence upon compliance with Soviet formalities cannot be dismissed as a subterfuge to evade foreign law or foreign courts. It is rather a safeguard against negligent or dishonest acts of the state's trade representatives when making a sizable commitment abroad. The necessary check is imposed by requiring a written contract, prescribed countersignatures and special permissions from higher echelons.

What objections may be leveled at the East's (and if the Soviet view is to prevail, at the West's) abrogation of the widely followed principle of *locus regit actum?* Undoubtedly, there is harshness in a rule which places upon a merchant the burden of ascertaining the formality requirements of a law other than that under which he is doing business. However, in anticipation of this complaint, Soviet law takes mitigating steps by ordering the publication in widely circulated trade journals of the names of persons authorized to assume international business obligations. In addition, the rule, together with its publication requirements, has found recognition in many

East–West commercial treaties to which the U.S.S.R. is a party. In view of the special needs it serves and the safeguards it provides, the Soviet position would appear to qualify for universal endorsement.

The other states of eastern Europe take a more conventional view of the matter. Although their positions are not identical, none asserts its formality requirements as mandatory conditions of contractual validity; this liberality of approach is the same vis-à-vis local and foreign courts.

Under Rumanian law, the formal validity of a transaction will be upheld if the law of the place of contracting is respected. East German civil law refers the issue to the proper law of the contract, i.e., the law governing its essential validity; but compliance with the law of the place where the contract was made is considered sufficient. Substantially the same rule applies in Poland, with the usual exception that dealings in real property must respect the formalities of the *situs*. Under the Czechoslovak approach, if the law governing the substance of the contract establishes a written form as a condition of validity, that law is decisive; otherwise, compliance with the formalities of the place of contracting will suffice. The Hungarian position is less clear. Some authorities are of the opinion that the place of contracting controls substantive validity. Others believe that the law of the forum and the law chosen by the parties are no less decisive.[39]

The net effect is surprisingly conformist. The similarity with the major legal systems of the West extends to both the unsettled state of court practice and the variety of rules which find application. It remains to be seen whether the extreme, if understandable, approach of Soviet law will eventually take root in the domestic laws of the other countries of the East. In trade among them, the General Conditions of Comecon, in the style of Soviet law, mandatorily prescribe that contracts must be concluded in written form; to that extent the domestic legislation of the member states is superseded.

In trade with the West too it has become a well-established and widespread commercial practice to reduce agreements to writing. But the hazards of informal dealing by force of habit continue to trap the unwary. The prudent private merchant will not rely on an oral promise, for he may find himself stripped of expected rights not as a result of willful dishonesty but because of highly technical and little-known legal requirements which the Eastern partner cannot waive even with the best intentions in the world.

D. Law Governing Capacity to Contract

Since the foreign trade of the wholly planned economies is conducted only by public organizations, conflict-of-law problems involving the capacity of individual citizens to enter into commercial relations have not arisen. Nor are such problems likely to arise with frequency in the case of individual Western merchants, since most transactions with the East are conducted on behalf of corporate institutions.

In civil law countries, the capacity of individuals to assume binding obligations is generally governed by their personal law—that of nationality or domicile. In England the domiciliary law, the law of the place of contracting and the proper law of the contract are used. In the United States, the latter seems to have the upper hand. Autonomy of will has little usefulness, since the parties must not be allowed to vest themselves with requisite capacity at their own pleasure.

In an area particularly pertinent to foreign trade—capacity in the issuance of checks and bills of exchange—the Soviet position follows closely that established by the Geneva Convention on Checks and Bills of Exchange. This convention is operative in most of continental Europe, East and West, as a result of prewar adherence or direct absorption into local legislation. Capacity to assume an obligation by check or bill of exchange is thus governed by the law of nationality (including any law to which the national legal system refers—a Soviet recognition of the doctrine of *renvoi*). Persons incapable under their national law are nonetheless bound if the obligation is assumed in a country which confers capacity.

Outside this specialized sphere, the capacity of foreigners residing in the U.S.S.R. is governed by Soviet law; the capacity of Soviet nationals is governed by Soviet law irrespective of where they reside; foreign nationals transiently present in Russia are not subject to Soviet law; Soviet law will, however, displace any foreign law which imposes an unacceptable disability, such as the legal inequality of married women.[40]

This set of rules differs in one notable respect from those followed in the rest of eastern Europe. Most states of the region determine the capacity of resident aliens by reference to the law of nationality, an approach which is now clearly articulated in the new Czechoslovak and Polish codes on private international law. The U.S.S.R., on the other hand, insists on applying its own law to all residents, regardless of their nationality, even though it attaches Soviet law to Soviet nationals resident abroad—again an attempt to blow hot and cold in basic choice-of-law matters.

Of much greater practical importance are problems arising from the status and contractual capacity of corporate entities. Two distinct approaches to the solution of these problems have emerged in the West. Common law jurisdictions generally agree that a corporation's capacity to engage in specific business activities, and everything related to intracorporate affairs should derive from its charter and from the law to which it owes its existence. The limitations imposed by these sources are considered to have extraterritorial effect irrespective of the regime prevailing at the place where the activities are performed, although the latter may further narrow the scope of what is permissible under the law of the corporation's origin.

The other approach, traditionally followed by the civil law countries, maintains that a juridical entity is governed primarily by the law of the *siège social;* i.e., the seat of administration and the principal place of business. This rule would allow a court, in a case where a company has its headquarters and performs all or most of its activities in one country, but happens to be incorporated for tax or other reasons in another, to ignore the incidental place of incorporation. Recently a tendency has arisen to defer to the law of the *siège social statutaire,* the headquarters stipulated in the corporate charter, without regard to the actual seat of administration.[41] These are the intertwined themes of international practice within which Eastern variations must be spotted.

Communist jurists heartily endorse the validity of all of the rules, and state enterprises tend to invoke them indiscriminately, particularly in foreign courts, in accordance with their immediate purposes.

The U.S.S.R. favors the law of the place of incorporation, although this is not expressly provided by statute. The extraterritorial effect which such an approach could afford to national corporation law acquired great significance in Soviet private international law following repeated refusals by foreign courts to recognize the sovereign immunity of state instrumentalities.

Under conventional conflict rules, the relevant provisions of the Russian Civil Code would indeed govern Soviet foreign trade organizations, regardless of the place where their acts are performed. What contracts an enterprise may conclude, what liabilities it may assume, what rights it may acquire and matters related to intracompany affairs are all questions which are justifiably referable to the law of incorporation. This is certainly the analysis when the matter arises in a Soviet forum. In a 1960 decision, the Moscow Foreign Trade Arbitration Commission clearly ruled that Italian law governed the legal status of an Italian corporate defendant. The law of the place of incorporation is also the dominant rule in Hungary, with the proviso that foreign companies, in order to acquire legal capacity to transact business locally, have to certify in advance their corporate standing under the national law of origin.[42]

In most other East European states, the capacity of both domestic and foreign corporations is controlled by the law of the corporate seat. Poland and Bulgaria give statutory support for this position. Article 9 of the Polish Private International Law Code of 1965 states that the capacity of legal entities is determined according to the law of the place where they maintain their principal place of business. Article 132 of the Bulgarian Law on Persons and Family of 1949 provides that "juridical persons have their seat at the place where their administration is found." It was pursuant to this approach that the Sofia arbitral tribunal turned to Sudanese law to determine the capacity of a Sudanese partnership and the power of an individual to act as its binding representative. The arbitrators apparently failed to consider the question of whether the partnership was a juridical person under Sudanese law (which it was not), although the result would have been the same.[43]

Domestic law is subject to variation by intergovernmental agreement. For example, Poland's 1959 judicial assistance treaty with Hungary adopts the law-of-incorporation principle, although the local Polish rule favors the *siège social.* The Soviet-Polish judicial assistance treaty of 1957 prescribes the law of the *siège social,* notwithstanding the Soviet preference for the law of incorporation. The 1953 commercial agreement between Czechoslovakia and Switzerland stipulates both principles even though Czechoslovak law follows only the *siège social.*

Neither the variously operating domestic choice-of-law rules nor their treaty modifications are likely to affect the legal capacity of Eastern enterprises; they invariably maintain their headquarters and perform their principal activities within the territory of the state that has granted them corporate existence. Accordingly, in all cases, their capacity is determined by the same familiar domestic law.

A choice of the *siège social* over the place of incorporation may, however, have important repercussions for the capacity of a Western firm as determined by a communist tribunal. What law will be applied to United States-controlled Swiss corporations that are operated from New York? In Eastern states which favor the *siège social,* will the statutory or "real" headquarters be decisive? Where the place of incorporation prevails, will this *modus operandi* be regarded as a subterfuge which justifies a judicial piercing of the Swiss corporate veil? The reported practice of the arbitral tribunals does not to date provide any ready answers to these questions.

The rule that the capacity of corporations and the authority of their representatives are governed by the law of incorporation, of the location of headquarters or of the principal place of business (all of which coincide in the case of Eastern enterprises) may seem harsh in its operation upon a bona-fide Western trader unaware of the content of communist laws which might possibly apply on this basis. However, the problem is not limited to trade with Eastern organizations. It is universally recognized that a person dealing with a corporation must take the trouble to find out, or be deemed to know, the limits of capacity imposed by the law of its origin. Filing and publication requirements help relieve the rule of much of its sting. In the case of communist countries, the consequences are further attenuated by the fact that only a limited and well-defined number of corporate entities are permitted to conduct foreign commerce and that the scope of their authority is relatively easy to ascertain from official trade journals which circulate freely abroad.

Our discussion would be incomplete without alluding to a question which arises prior to the judicial choice of law. How is the character of a communist corporation to be ascertained? At this stage of the analysis, the adjudicator may find that he has before him an organ of state rather than a juridically independent entity. His choice of law may be different, depending on the classification he decides to make. Should he classify the institution in accordance with the law of its origin, the law which governs the transaction as a whole or the law of his own forum? The Western judge cannot help bringing to the determination the terminology and habits of mind appropriate to viewing a corporation which functions in the orthodox environment of a market economy. But the results of his decision would be unbalanced if he inflexibly applied his own law as well. The conceptual tools of the *lex fori* alone are likely to be unequal to the task. The classification should, it is submitted, be made under the rules which prevail at the institution's place of origin. Any conceivable distortions which may arise in consequence of characterization based on communist law can, as a last resort, be subjected to the control of the forum's public policy. The difficulties entailed in forcing novel institutional creatures of communist public law into the ancient molds of private Western law offer ample justification for this view.

24

ENFORCEMENT OF ARBITRATION CLAUSES AND AWARDS

Each communist legal system provides a basis for the recognition and enforcement of foreign judgments. Soviet law makes the right dependent upon the existence of enabling treaty arrangements. The corresponding Rumanian, Czechoslovak and Polish provisions establish entitlement on the basis of local law as well.[1] Reciprocity of treatment in the courts of the petitioner's own country is a characteristic Eastern condition of enforcement and the requirements which must be fulfilled are not dissimilar from those generally encountered in West European legislation.

Little practical purpose would be served by detailing the circumstances under which Western judgments may be enforced in the East and Eastern judgments in the West. The main category of cases susceptible to recurrent court litigation in communist countries involves the personal status of aliens. Contractual disputes are largely resolved by arbitration. The role of the normal judiciary, both Eastern and Western, is highly limited. This is even more true of trade relations within the East, where the courts have been entirely removed from the scene. Consequently, it is to the international enforcement of arbitral agreements and awards that we must principally direct our attention.

A voluntary reference to arbitration entails a binding promise by the parties to sue only in the tribunal named and to comply with any resultant decision. In practice, recalcitrance in both respects is not uncommon, particularly on the international level, where no uniform, all-embracing means of legal compulsion has as yet been developed.

On the communist side, obstruction of the arbitration process or evasion of the obligations it imposes is all but nonexistent. Since the local tribunals are officially sponsored creatures of domestic legislation, such institutional defects as they may have cannot be placed in issue by the state trading defendant; and ample extralegal and legal means to compel compliance with clauses and awards are available to foreign claimants. Abroad, evasion is rife. Successful Eastern parties frequently have no alternative but to take further judicial action in the country in which the Western debtor has his assets. Courts petitioned by state trading enterprises to stay proceedings instituted in defiance of an arbitration clause or to enforce an ensuing award are understandably concerned with the quality of justice their national may anticipate—or has in fact obtained—before the communist arbitral tribunal in question.

A. Extrajudicial Inducement

It is a striking fact that the Eastern party's compliance with arbitral submissions and awards is always voluntary and prompt; in no instance has a Western firm found it necessary to enlist judicial assistance. That this should be so in the course of dealings among "fraternal" communist countries is understandable. Yet it may come as a surprise to many that the same standard of behavior prevails on the communist side in East–West trade as well.

Without detracting from this commendable manifestation of commercial morality, we may suggest that more mundane business reasons are also at work. Looking beyond mere appearances, we discover that a refusal on the part of a state trader to abide by a decision of its country's tribunals is in fact inconceivable. Such a position would not only reflect on its own reliability as a business partner and that of the state monopoly as a whole; it would also undermine confidence abroad and impair the ability of the local arbitral institution to adjudicate disputes with foreign firms. An attempt at unjustified noncompliance, unfortunately so common in other areas of trade, could lead here to disciplinary action by superior organs of the Foreign Trade Ministry and to criminal prosecution of responsible officers on serious grounds of law evasion.

In reality, submissions to the Eastern tribunals and awards issued by them are as self-enforcing at home as judicial decisions. And in disputes involving two state trading monopolies, they possess the same self-enforcing quality even abroad. Some of the countries do not even provide for the possibility of court intervention. In Rumania, the awards are enforceable directly, under the authority of the Presidium of the Chamber of Commerce.

Whatever the underlying motives, the extraordinary degree of voluntary compliance evident on the communist side constitutes a major advantage of submission to Eastern arbitration. Once the foreigner has obtained a favorable award, he may assume that performance will follow automatically, without the additional delay, expense and uncertainty of compulsory enforcement proceedings. Today, the total state trading monopolies are sufficiently enlightened to avoid repetition of the damaging Soviet refusal to honor arbitration agreements in the nineteen-thirties.[2]

On the Western side, the record is less perfect. Yet a refusal to comply with submissions or awards on the ground of the Eastern tribunals' imperfections is clearly inconsistent with the voluntary acceptance of their jurisdiction. To argue in advance of the proceedings that the arbitrators will be unfair also cannot be convincing. An aggrieved foreign party will have a chance to demonstrate their malfeasance once the proceedings have run their course, and before compulsory action is taken against him by a court of his own country. While the case for legal enforcement is therefore strong in principle, certain extralegal factors tending to induce performance are also operative upon the Western firm.

In arbitrations under the auspices of a self-governing institution—a trade association or a commodity exchange—the threat of internal sanctions for noncompliance, e.g., expulsion, publicity within the trade, exclusion from further use of arbitral facilities and boycott can be highly effective. Vis-à-vis non-members, such means of persuasion carry less impact, although one association may establish meaningful methods of cooperation with another which include mutual assistance in matters of enforcement.

The statutes of the communist Chambers of Commerce and of their subsidiary tribunals contemplate sanctions of this nature. For example, the Czechoslovak government reported success in obtaining satisfaction of an award following a complaint to an association of which the evasive debtor was a member. The Pakistan Chamber of Commerce agreed to exert pressure on a local firm which had refused to honor an award rendered against it by the Prague Arbitration Court pursuant to a valid arbitral agreement.[3]

In addition to generally used measures of this type, a state monopoly may resort to highly effective devices of its own. A private Western firm trading in certain types of commodities is obliged to deal permanently with one or several government enterprises. An attempt to renege on an arbitral clause or award may therefore bring in its wake unusually serious consequences. The Eastern creditor is in a position to exclude such a firm from its nation's market; it may also, by approaching a sister monopoly or chamber of commerce, cause its exclusion from the markets of the other wholly planned economies.

In the last analysis, the effectiveness of communist adjudication facilities in East–West trade must depend on the willingness of foreign courts to recognize that a contractual acceptance of their authority excludes the jurisdiction of any alternative forum and that decisions issuing from their arbitral panels are entitled to compulsory enforcement. Only a realistic expectation on all sides that such judicial assistance will be forthcoming can serve as an effective "sword of Damocles" in the hands of a state trading monopoly to deter the evasion of voluntarily assumed obligations in the sphere of arbitration in particular and contracts in general.

B. Enforcement under Domestic Law

1. In the East

With varying degrees of enthusiasm, most countries allow submissions to arbitral tribunals. References to arbitration are more readily enforceable than references to foreign courts; the latter are occasionally nullified as invalid attempts to oust the competent domestic jurisdiction. Arbitral awards, with their source in contract, are also recognized less reluctantly than court judgments, which are viewed as commands of an alien sovereign.

The procedures of enforcement differ sharply under the various legal systems. Some provide for direct and summary *exequatur* of a foreign award, whereas others consider it merely as a new cause of action. Often, the award's reduction to a judgment in the courts of the country where the arbitration was held is a condition precedent to judicial assistance abroad.

Normally a court will not suspend its proceedings unless it is satisfied that the arbitration agreed upon will be conducted in a fair and equitable manner. Similarly, before issuing a writ of execution based on a foreign award, it will seek to satisfy itself that the debtor has not been the victim of a denial of justice. That the award must not violate the public policy of the enforcing forum is also a universal requirement.

Communist enterprises may agree to arbitration at home, in the country of its trading partner or in neutral territory. Such arbitration may take place either before a permanently functioning tribunal or one constituted in an *ad hoc* manner for each specific dispute. We have already stressed the fact that state trading parties do not obstruct the arbitral process of their country's own tribunal. It is therefore unnecessary to dwell on the methods of legal compulsion which Eastern countries make available to Western traders.

In the unlikely event that a state enterprise should seek to invoke a People's Court in the presence of a valid submission to arbitrate, the action will be readily suspended at the request of the foreign claimant. By the same token, attempts to stay the process of the arbitral tribunals themselves on the ground that proceedings are in progress in a domestic or foreign court have also come to nought on presentation in evidence of a duly executed arbitration clause. To cite one out of many examples, the Soviet Foreign Trade Arbitration Commissioner rejected as inconsistent with his prior agreement to arbitrate an Egyptian defendant's plea that proceedings on his motion were pending before the Mixed Court of Port Said and that the Moscow tribunal was therefore incompetent.[4]

The laws of civil procedure of most communist countries provide conventional means for the compulsory execution of arbitral awards rendered at home. Under Soviet legislation, a writ of execution will issue as a matter of course from the People's Court in whose district the arbitration was held. Forced performance may follow after the time for voluntary satisfaction has lapsed. In regard to the decisions of the foreign trade arbitration tribunals the legislatively prescribed procedures are, however, a dead letter and in the case of Rumania they are dispensed with altogether. Within the jurisdiction in which these tribunals operate, enforcement can only be sought where the condemned party is a national enterprise, and then it is seldom if ever necessary. Foreign concerns, on the other hand, have to be pursued abroad, since as a rule they have no local assets.

Soviet legislation provides for the enforcement of foreign arbitral decisions in exceptionally limited terms:

> The procedure for the enforcement in the RSFSR of the judgments of foreign courts and the awards of foreign arbitrations is determined by the corresponding conventions of the U.S.S.R. with foreign States or by international conventions to which the U.S.S.R. is a party. The foreign judgment or award may be presented for compulsory enforcement within three years from the moment of its acquiring legal effect.[5]

This provision is interesting for two reasons: first, it places foreign court judgments and arbitral awards on the same footing; second, it refers to treaties as the sole source of law requiring enforcement in Soviet territory.

The apparent narrowness of this approach is misleading. In fact, the prospect of enforcement is offered even in the absence of an operative treaty. The only condition is reciprocity in the treatment of Soviet arbitration awards in the courts of the country in which the award in question has originated. This inference can be drawn from the text of ratification of the 1958 New York Convention on the Recognition and Enforcement of Foreign Arbitral Awards which the Presidium of the Supreme Soviet promulgated on August 10, 1960:

> The Union of Soviet Socialist Republics will accept the provisions of the present convention in regard to arbitration decisions made in the territory of states which are not participants in the convention, only on the condition of reciprocity.[6]

In one important respect, the possibility of enforcement borders on the precarious. Exacting contractual formality requirements in many Eastern countries sometimes extend to arbitration clauses. A state enterprise which enters into an oral agreement to arbitrate, or into a written agreement executed by individuals who are not expressly authorized to do so, or which lacks corporate capacity to submit to arbitration, is not bound to comply, regardless of the legal system by which such an agreement is governed. It follows that a clause or award tendered for enforcement in such an Eastern country would be denied recognition, to the extent that it emanates from an underlying agreement afflicted with defects of this type.

Soviet law lacks detailed procedural norms for the enforcement of eligible awards. One eminent writer attempts to fill this gap by resurrecting a circular issued by the Ministry of Justice in connection with the Russo-German treaty of December 12, 1925. Under the principles there enunciated, enforcement is forthcoming only on the basis of a petition to a Soviet court supported by an authenticated copy of the foreign award. The People's Court having jurisdiction for this purpose is either the court stipulated in the parties' arbitral submission or, in the absence of stipulation, that which would have been competent to rule on the dispute in the absence of an agreement to arbitrate.[7]

2. *In the West*

Communist jurists concede that each country may prescribe its own enforcement rules. But once the general principle of compulsory execution under domestic law is admitted, a refusal to recognize the clauses and awards of the Eastern tribunals is said to constitute a discrimination contrary to international law and the comity of nations. This attitude reflects a desire to have the cake and eat it. While the U.S.S.R. reserves the right to deny enforcement in the absence of a treaty, it demands automatic recognition for its own awards under the domestic law of any country which recognizes foreign awards, regardless of international agreement.

In recent years a growing number of Western courts have accorded such recognition; and no significant cases have been found in which recognition was ultimately denied. Two decisions, one rendered in England and the other in Burma, constitute exceptions to this uniform pattern. The grounds given are, however, so narrow and specific as to deprive both judgments of any persuasive force in regard to the international treatment of communist arbitration.

Both practical and theoretical considerations prompt a detailed review of the Western case law on the subject. Although decisions concerned with the validity of arbitration submissions are treated separately from those dealing with the enforceability of awards, each case is relevant to both categories of problems.[8]

a. *Arbitral Submissions:* In one of the earliest decisions of its kind, an Egyptian court automatically declined jurisdiction in the face of a party agreement to arbitrate before the Soviet Foreign Trade Arbitration Commission, then four years old. Similar judicial positions were taken repeatedly thereafter in various parts of the world. For example, the Second Commercial Court of Istanbul, instructed by the Turkish Court of Appeal to examine the status of the Commission and its Chamber of Commerce, found both sufficiently independent to be capable of valid adjudication. The grounds given in substantiation of this decision, rendered in 1940, were partly nonjudicial: they were deduced from a certificate of the Ministry of Foreign Affairs, whose assistance the court had enlisted. In the same year an English court, without inquiring into the nature of the Commission's process, conceded that certain issues involved in a dispute subject to an arbitral agreement were within the sole jurisdiction of the Moscow tribunal.[9]

Far more authoritative and fully considered is a 1952 judgment of the New York Court of Appeals which gave full effect to an arbitration clause framed as follows: "Any dispute arising out of this agreement or in connection with it is to be settled between the buyer's and seller's representatives in New York. Failing agreement, the matter is to be referred to the U.S.S.R. Chamber of Commerce Foreign Trade Arbitration Commission in Moscow, U.S.S.R. The decision of the said Commission is to be final and binding upon both parties." Upholding the Appellate Division, which had reversed the first-instance ruling of the New York Supreme Court, the final judgment stayed an action for breach of contract by Camden Fibre Mills, a Pennsylvania corporation, against Amtorg (the Soviet-controlled trading corporation in the State of New York) until the Moscow proceedings had run their course. In overruling the appellant's contention that the Soviet tribunal should be disqualified from acting as arbitrator, the court spoke with striking detachment and simplicity:[10]

> Camden chose to do business with Amtorg and to accept, as one of the conditions imposed, arbitration in Russia; it may not now ask the courts to relieve it of the contractual obligation it assumed.

Although this opinion rests squarely on parties' consent to Moscow arbitration, the Court of Appeals did not wholly overlook the Commission's link with the Soviet governmental trade structure. Avoiding comment on the elaborate analysis which led the first-instance judge to an opposite result, it found that:

> Such commission is a public organization subject to the general supervision of the People's Commissariat for Foreign Trade. It is however a juridical person, having power to own property, make contracts, sue and be sued; it has its own income, funds and budget, and conducts its own elections.

Nor did the court venture to examine the real meaning of corporate personality under Soviet law. It was content to dismiss the question in the light of customary criteria employed in Western legal systems to determine whether given organizations possess the formal characteristics of legal separateness and independence.

In ruling that the arbitral submission barred Camden's court proceedings in New York, the Court of Appeals seems to have assumed without doubt that the Soviet tribunal was comparable to arbitral institutions functioning in the principal trading nations of the West. It did not pose the less apparent question of whether the conventional arbitration trappings masked a process which in the given economic and legal setting amounted to an exercise of state jurisdiction. This might have been relevant in that the parties whom the Moscow submission purported to bind were two

American corporations—a fact suggestive of an attempt to evade the jurisdiction of local courts in favor of foreign proceedings.[11]

It does not follow from the rather summary rejection of Camden's argument that the American firm was abandoned to the complete mercy of communist justice. On the contrary, the court went out of its way to state that the appellant could seek judicial relief after it had complied with its contractual obligation to arbitrate, if the Moscow proceedings were to deny it a "fair deal":

> It may be noted that the order of the Appellate Division does not preclude Camden from taking appropriate action should the arbitration in fact deprive it of its fundamental right to a fair and impartial determination. . . .
>
> If such an award were enforced by action, it would be a valid defense that the proceedings were not conducted in such a manner as to result in a fair and impartial determination.

The extent to which the Soviet proceedings might be scrutinized in such an eventuality is not clear. The hint of future defenses can certainly not be taken as an invitation to Camden to disregard the Commission's award. That the type of sweeping challenge which had prevailed at first instance would fail follows from the authorities cited by the court.[12] Meanwhile, by upholding the original undertaking to arbitrate, the court preserved the submission's full deterrent force against blatant violation of contractual obligations and unreasonable refusal to settle differences.

In net effect, the Soviet tribunal was tacitly approved as an institution capable of administering equal justice. Moreover, this result was reached on the basis of the ordinary operation of New York law and in the absence of any such treaty arrangements on arbitration as the U.S.S.R. now has with a number of Western countries. It follows that the arbitration tribunals of the other state-trading countries—all modeled on the Soviet pattern—would be accorded similar treatment in the courts of New York and presumably elsewhere in the American Union.

The convenience of the Soviet forum in a dispute between what were after all two local corporations (although one was controlled from Moscow) was not placed in issue. On this score, an interesting contrast is provided by a decision of the English Court of Appeals. The judge at first instance had refused to stay a suit brought by the holder of a bill of lading which required all disputes to be judged in the U.S.S.R. in accordance with the Soviet merchant shipping law. Without questioning the quality or integrity of Russian adjudication (no specific tribunal was named in the clause), or controverting the principle of party autonomy in the choice of arbitrators, the court affirmed that in the circumstances the most convenient forum was to be found in England.[13]

In 1958, the Queen's Bench Division of the English High Court of Justice refused to disqualify itself in face of an arbitration clause between an English and a Polish company. The specific ground given was the absence of a binding arbitration agreement between the plaintiff and the two impleaded Soviet foreign trade enterprises, both of which were deemed to be necessary parties to the proceedings. The judgment cannot therefore be taken as a statement of the court's position on the status of communist arbitration in English courts. A similar conclusion may be drawn from a judgment of the Supreme Court of Rangoon (affirmed by the Court of Final Appeal of Burma in 1962) which had likewise refused to defer to the Moscow Commission, for whose jurisdiction the parties had opted. The court objected neither to arbitral submissions as such nor to the character of the tribunal. It merely took umbrage at the parties' attempted exclusion of the regular courts of both Burma and the U.S.S.R. Presumably, the arbitration clause would have been recognized as effective had the parties avoided the superfluous language stipulating the exclusion of national jurisdiction.[14]

On the other hand, in 1961, the Supreme Court of Calcutta flatly declined to take jurisdiction at the instance of an Indian plaintiff in the presence of a submission to the Moscow arbitration tribunal. A similar result was reached by the Superior Court of the Canton of Zürich in 1963 and by the Amsterdam Municipal Court at approximately the same time. The Swiss court rejected a Lichtenstein firm's attempt to impeach the independence of the Warsaw arbitration tribunal on the grounds of public policy. The firm's central argument was based on the provisions of the Polish Rules of Procedure which allowed the Presidium and the secretary of the arbitration court to participate *ex officio* in the hearings and deliberations of individual adjudication panels. In the Dutch case, the legitimacy of the Prague tribunal was recognized by implication, the agreement to arbitrate before it having been found valid under the applicable Czechoslovak law.[15]

b. *Arbitral Awards:* The first decision of a Western court involving an arbitral award pronounced by an ad hoc tribunal sitting in communist territory appears to have been rendered by the State Court of Berlin as early as 1927. The defendant, a German company, argued against enforcement on the ground that an agreement to arbitrate future disputes was invalid under Soviet law. The court ruled that treaty-created arbitral provisions operative between the two countries implicitly overcame the invalidating effect of domestic law at the place of arbitration. In 1946, the Turkish Court of Cassation enforced an award of the Moscow Foreign Trade Arbitration Commission over the objection of the Turkish defendant that it was a state court and that its decrees therefore could not be enforced on the same basis as arbitral awards. Similarly, a Brussels court of first instance ruled in 1950 that local law required the execution of an award of the Moscow tribunal rendered against a Belgian firm.[16]

The fullest exposition to date of the legal considerations underlying the enforcement of communist awards is contained in a 1958 decision of the Supreme Federal Court of Switzerland. The Court reversed both the judgment of the first-instance court and its affirmation on intermediate appeal by the Superior Court of the Canton of Zürich. At issue was the fate of an award pronounced by the Czechoslovak Arbitration Court against a Swiss firm for breach of a contract with a Czech trading entity.

Pursuant to an arbitral provision contained in the general conditions of sale printed on the Czech seller's confirmation order, the claim was filed in Prague in early 1954. Following notification, the Swiss defendant challenged the validity of the submission and refused to enter an appearance. The tribunal nonetheless proceeded to render a preliminary judgment asserting its jurisdiction and requesting the defendant to choose an arbitrator. Faced with inaction, the president of the Arbitration Court made the choice. The arbitrator so appointed, together with another chosen by the Czech plaintiff, selected a third as referee. The defendant having again refused to appear, a default judgment was finally entered on March 11, 1955.

Enforcement proceedings failed both at first instance in the district court of Zürich and on appeal to the Superior Court of the Canton. Neither the Arbitration Court nor its three-man tribunal were deemed sufficiently independent from the standpoint of Swiss jurisprudence. Consequently both the interlocutory decision on the issue of jurisdiction and the final award on the merits of the case were deemed violative of the public policy of Switzerland. The case law adduced in support of this position related to arbitrations between members and nonmembers of domestic cartels and trade organizations, which Swiss courts have refused to enforce since 1932.

The Supreme Federal Court, reversing the lower courts, upheld the validity of the Czech judgment.[17] Specifically, it found a fundamental distinction between the arbitral facilities of local economic groupings and those of communist Chambers of Commerce. The primary aim of the former is to maintain a certain internal discipline in the group; participants are required to submit to its jurisdiction by virtue of their membership in the association, membership which is generally indispensable to the exercise of a profession. The latter "are created in the interest of commerce in general, as special tribunals composed of experts in the field, to resolve commercial disputes between merchants who can decide freely whether to confer jurisdiction by clauses or arbitral submissions or to take their grievances to the courts of the state." Moreover, it was recognized that the rather strict Swiss attitude toward domestically established institutions may well be out of place with respect to foreign organizations.

The court held further that the Czech tribunal was sufficiently independent to satisfy the requirements of Swiss public policy. That policy does not go so far as to require that foreign tribunals conform to Swiss procedure. Neither the use of a predetermined list of arbitrators named by the Chamber of Commerce nor the absence of foreign nationals or residents from that list, nor the selection procedure employed following the defendant's default, were found to differ fatally from prevalent international practice.

In 1959, the State Supreme Court of Frankfurt, West Germany, was urged by a local defendant to deny enforcement to an award of the Yugoslav Foreign Trade Arbitration Commission on a broad array of grounds, including the fact that its panel of arbitrators excluded foreigners. The plea failed. The court was of the opinion that in concluding the agreement to arbitrate the defendant could and should have known the specific nature of the arbitration to which he was submitting.[18]

The actual number of affirmative Western court decisions in this area is less impressive than their cumulative effect, and the cumulative effect of existing treaty provisions. All in all, a pattern is beginning to emerge, and from it a principle: the competence and adjudication of the foreign trade arbitration tribunals of communist countries are entitled to the same degree of protection abroad as conventionally constituted arbitral bodies functioning in the West.

While the results reached in the cases are by and large satisfactory, no consistent rationale of recognition and enforcement is evident. What may be considered a proper rationale, in light of our overall appraisal of the communist foreign trade adjudication system, will be formulated hereafter. First, however, the content of applicable treaties must be reviewed.

C. Enforcement under International Treaties

1. Bilateral Agreements

Provisions for mutual judicial assistance in matters of arbitration form part of a number of bilateral agreements concluded by the U.S.S.R. with countries of free economic structure. The content of these provisions has evolved over the years, the earliest examples dating back to the 1920s. The most detailed and elaborate stipulations were contained in the Agreement with Germany of October 12, 1925.[19] This treaty deals not only with the mutual recognition and enforcement of arbitration clauses and awards, but also with matters affecting the organization and functioning of tribunals.

While more contemporary intergovernmental arrangements do not conform to any uniform pattern, they may nevertheless be classified into three categories: (1) treaties of friendship, commerce and navigation requiring mutual recognition and enforcement of arbitral agreements and awards;[20] (2) trade agreements establishing detailed rules and procedures to be followed in the selection of arbitrators and the hearing of disputes;[21] (3) instruments regulating conflicts of jurisdiction and facilitating the reciprocal enforcement of judicial and arbitral decisions.[22]

The grounds on which enforcement of arbitral awards may be denied are narrowly delimited. Whether expressly stated or not, proof of the existence of a written arbitration agreement between the parties is, of course, always an essential condition. Other specific grounds justifying denial of enforcement under the treaties usually are: (a) the award has not acquired the force of a final decision under the law of its origin; (b) it requires the condemned party to take action prohibited under the law of the country where enforcement is sought; (c) it contravenes the public policy of the enforcing forum. One need hardly belabor the point that in rendering awards against nationals of countries with which the U.S.S.R. maintains treaty relations, Soviet arbitrators have the means to ensure that grounds *a* and *b* will not constitute a bar to enforcement.[23] Realistically speaking, only ground *c* may interpose an obstacle.

Traditionally, the right of enforcement is grounded in the territoriality principle; that is to say, the award in question must have been rendered within the jurisdiction of a High Contracting Party. Article 8 of the Agreement on Commerce and Navigation between the U.S.S.R. and West Germany of April 25, 1958, is an example of a recent treaty which does away with this requirement. It is sufficient if the dispute is between parties emanating from the two countries; the place of rendition is considered fortuitous and therefore nondeterminative.

When confronted with an operative arbitration treaty arrangement, bilateral or multilateral, inconsistent domestic law abates. This fairly obvious fact is worth stressing, because certain legal systems take an exceptionally narrow attitude toward arbitral settlements. Variously, agreements to exclude the jurisdiction of national courts, to arbitrate abroad or to submit to arbitration a controversy which may arise in the future, or agreements which fail to indicate the object of the dispute or to name the arbitrators, are rendered inoperative under the legislation of a number of countries.[24]

The communist tribunals have justifiably held such laws to be inapplicable, once a more generous enabling treaty was in effect. Thus, in a 1950 decision the Moscow Commission ruled that although under his own law the Swiss defendant was only suable in his canton or in an arbitral tribunal constituted in accordance with Swiss law, these restrictions did not reach arbitrations intended to be held abroad. In part the decision was based upon Article 11 of the Commercial Agreement between the U.S.S.R. and Switzerland. In a 1957 decision the Moscow tribunal correctly took jurisdiction even though the Soviet-Austrian Agreement on Commerce and Navigation of October 17, 1955, came into force after the parties had signed their arbitral submission. The arbitration provisions of the treaty did not affect previously executed submissions, which consequently remained operative under the domestic laws of both Russia and Austria.[25]

The eligibility for enforcement of awards rendered by the Soviet Foreign Trade and Maritime Arbitration Commissions is not dealt with expressly in any treaty. Occasionally, abstract mention is made of both *ad hoc* and permanently functioning arbitration. However, insofar as these tribunals are the principal, indeed, the only institutions determining foreign commerce and navigation disputes in U.S.S.R. territory, and since they have not been specifically excepted, it must be assumed that their decisions were intended to qualify for enforcement as ordinary arbitral awards. Otherwise, the obligations assumed by the respective states would be one-sided in practice, operating consistently against, but seldom or never in favor of, the Soviet side. This conclusion holds equally good for the bilateral treaties and foreign trade tribunals of the other communist countries. Moreover, it extends to the crucially important question of the survival of prewar treaty obligations in respect of the awards pronounced in these countries.

2. *Multilateral Conventions*

The treaty survival question arises also in connection with such major multilateral conventions as the Geneva Protocol on Arbitration Clauses of 1923 and the Convention on the Execution of Foreign Arbitral Awards of 1927 to which several of the present-day communist countries had acceded in prewar years. Italy adheres to both instruments. Consequently, she recognizes the validity of commercial arbitrations conducted in other signatory states. In a 1965 decision the Court of Appeals of Milan endorsed a Rumanian award on this basis, Rumania being a prewar signatory.[26]

The Supreme Federal Court of Switzerland in the Baumgartner case examined the issue much more extensively vis-à-vis Czechoslovakia, under both a bilateral instrument of 1926 and the Geneva Convention of 1927, to which both countries had long been parties. Disapproving the Zürich Superior Court, it ruled that invocation of the doctrine *clausula rebus sic stantibus* was a matter for the political organs of government, not the judiciary; for its own part, the court was prepared to assume that the treaty obligations survived despite the intervening change in Czechoslovakia's governmental system.[27]

The U.S.S.R. has joined neither the Geneva Protocol nor the Convention. However, in recent years, along with other communist countries, it has manifested considerable enthusiasm for multilateral arrangements on the international coordination of arbitral procedure and enforcement. Laudable as this cooperative attitude may seem, it must nevertheless be noted that in the context of generalized multilateral treatment the novel aspects of communist arbitration are obscured by the use of traditional treaty terminology. To substantiate this conclusion, we may point to the proceedings of the United Nations Conference on Arbitration and of the Working Group on Arbitration of the United Nations Economic Commission for Europe which led to the adoption respectively of the New York Convention on the Recognition and Enforcement of Foreign Arbitral Awards of 1958 and of the Geneva European Convention on International Commercial Arbitration of 1961. The former simplifies considerably the procedures of recognition for arbitration clauses and awards established by its Geneva predecessor. The latter facilitates regional European arbitration by substituting for national rules criteria and procedures established by the Convention itself or by party stipulation. The U.S.S.R. and each of the Eastern European countries are adherents to both instruments.[28]

In debates on whether the New York Convention's definition of awards should specifically refer to decisions of permanent arbitral institutions, the communist delegations seem to have succeeded in dispelling the ill-defined misgivings of various Western participants concerning the real nature of total state trading arbitration; the tactic was to emphasize its outwardly orthodox character.[29] It is unnecessary to suggest that the communist tribunals should have been expressly or implicitly excluded from the scope of the Convention. But if, as was presumably intended, they are in fact included, their effectiveness has received a powerful stimulus. What degree of universality it will ultimately acquire remains to be seen, but the New York Convention certainly replaces its more modest Geneva precursors as the principal international instrument on recognition and enforcement of arbitral clauses and awards.

It is well to recall that enforcement procedures under the New York Convention are characterized by great simplicity and practicality. Once the applicant produces an award and an arbitration agreement upon which it is based, the burden falls on the contesting party to substantiate one of the few possible defenses to enforcement. Despite a public policy escape clause, it would be difficult to deny in the courts of an adhering state that a refusal to apply the Convention's considerably improved and liberalized provisions in favor of communist arbitration constitutes a violation of assumed treaty obligations.

3. *Compliance within Comecon*

Compulsory enforcement provisions are also to be found in bilateral treaties on judicial assistance in civil and criminal matters, and in commercial and maritime agreements in force among the several communist countries. Some of these arrangements are prewar; others were concluded more recently, both before and after the economic and legal climate was subjected to radical transformation. It is noteworthy that arbitral arrangements hammered out over the bargaining table between governments of different and antagonistic systems were initially deemed adequate in relations between like-minded countries aspiring toward uniform institutions and techniques of regulation. A partial reason is that the early treaties were concluded before the permanent foreign trade tribunals had been put into effective operation in Eastern Europe, and while heterogeneous arbitral forms were still in use.

The explanation for the prolonged continuance of these arrangements is probably twofold. In the first place, the legal formulas for recognition and enforcement of arbitral awards, which the U.S.S.R. has been able to persuade a growing number of capitalist countries to accept bilaterally, were considered completely appropriate for the U.S.S.R.'s global objectives in the field of arbitration. Secondly, the formal regime of enforcement embodied in treaties with its closest allies is merely of symbolic significance; the record of voluntary performance is perfect, owing to the extraordinary discipline which can be brought to bear reciprocally through the medium of interlocking monopolies and ministries of foreign trade.

Close economic cooperation and the abstract needs of ideology have gradually led to differentiations in intra-Eastern treaty practice. While the earlier instruments contained traditional public policy escape clauses excusing enforcement, subsequent texts have dropped such provisions. Official doctrine could not long tolerate the pregnant implication that conflicts of this type were possible within the fraternal communist camp. The new fashion in intrablock treaty content came to the surface with the Soviet–East German Agreement on Commerce and Navigation of September 27, 1957.

Contemporary arbitration relations among the wholly planned economies are largely regulated by multinational provisions adopted under the auspices of Comecon. The General Conditions provide that all disputes arising in connection with contracts between entities of the member countries are subject to arbitration in the country of the defendant or in a third member country designated by the parties. Express submission is not required in order to invest the tribunal of the defendant's country with jurisdiction over the dispute. Other instruments, notably an agreement of December 31, 1955, among Bulgaria, Hungary, Rumania and the U.S.S.R. relative to the carriage of freight on the Danube, also vest compulsory jurisdiction in the arbitral tribunal of the defendant's country, to the total exclusion of the general courts. Awards rendered pursuant to this exercise of exclusive jurisdiction are legally binding and enforceable; in practice they are unfailingly complied with.

D. A Theory of Recognition and Enforcement

Two central factors are pertinent to the treatment of communist arbitration in Western courts: the right of differently organized societies to evolve such institutions as they consider necessary and the equally important right of world traders to receive fair and equitable treatment at the hands of such institutions. Granted that the flaws inherent in the communist system of foreign trade adjudication reflect the peculiarities of economic structure and that latent possibilities for abuse are balanced by tangible guarantees of due process, misgivings concerning its fitness to dispense justice to private firms cannot be wholly dispelled. Notwithstanding these misgivings, the Eastern tribunals have acquired considerable and growing acceptance from foreign merchants, foreign courts and foreign governments.

Few prudent Western practitioners possessing a clear understanding of the nature of communist arbitration would advise their clients to submit to its processes, except as part of a calculated risk balanced by other terms of the proposed transaction. However, once they have agreed to do so businessmen ought not to be absolved of their pledge. A contrary position would breed added uncertainty, suspicion and bad faith in an area of commerce already plagued by severe ideological and political complications. Moreover, it would be unjust toward state trading parties who are effectively compelled in their own countries to honor both arbitral agreements and resultant awards.

In the cases decided thus far, the temptation to invalidate submissions and decisions on the abstract ground of presumed partiality has been rightly rejected. However, no consistent judicial approach has as yet emerged. Although the legal consequences may be the same, the cases should not be interpreted as equating party election of a communist tribunal with election of a regular arbitral institution. The innate defects of the system should be neither expressly condoned nor completely ignored; the correct rationale may be found in the doctrine of waiver or estoppel.

It is a time-honored rule of arbitration law that proof of certain ties between a party and an arbitrator (such as blood relationship, marriage, partnership or pecuniary interest in the outcome of litigation) which tend to deprive the latter of the opportunity to act as a free agent (regardless of whether or not impartiality exists in fact) establishes an irrebuttable presumption of bias. The presumption alone justifies a disqualification of the proceedings. But submission to an arbitrator with prior notice of his ties to the opposing party amounts to a waiver of otherwise valid objections. A party wishing to institute proceedings inconsistent with such submission, or refusing to honor an award rendered in pursuance thereof, will be estopped from pleading defects which were known or reasonably ought to have been known at the time his bargain was concluded.

An invitation to a capitalist trader to subject his rights in a transaction to the ultimate determination of communist adjudicators is sufficiently unusual on its face to induce inquiry into the quality of justice he is likely to receive at the hands of the designated tribunal. Since he has a clear option in the matter, if he submits he may be taken to have had either actual or constructive knowledge of the status, composition and procedure of the suspected arbitral facility. In short, he must be presumed either to have accepted or knowingly disregarded, in the context of his overall bargain, the ascertainable flaws he subsequently seeks to invoke.

A court should not deny on the ground of public policy the customary legal effect to a reference to communist arbitration. In the absence of fraud, misrepresentation, or undue influence, the pledge to arbitrate as promised should be deemed to subsist. This view is supported by the widely accepted rule that the constitution and procedure of an arbitral authority are matters for party autonomy and the law of the country in whose territory the proceedings are held. Only such an approach can provide the necessary climate and incentive for honest performance of contractual obligations in East–West trade.

How are the legitimate rights of a foreign trader to be protected against abuse? Clearly, he will not volunteer to perform a decision made in consequence of a denial of justice. An opportunity to afford him redress will therefore arise when enforcement is sought at his place of residence, place of business, or place where his assets are located. Here again, pleas tending to impeach an award on grounds of public policy should be limited to concrete allegations, supported by factual proof of partiality or misconduct on the part of the arbitrators. The enforcing forum will be in a position to ascertain whether the debtor has obtained a fair and impartial determination in fact by admitting such defenses as invalidity of the underlying arbitral agreement; excess of arbitral authority; failure to give appropriate notice of proceedings; denial of a hearing or of adequate opportunity to be represented or to furnish written or oral evidence; patent disregard of relevant or undisputed testimony; unfairness apparent on the face of the award and so on.

At the same time, the enforcing forum should be free to evaluate for itself, and in accordance with its own criteria, whether the decision in question is to be characterized as an award of an arbitral tribunal qualifying for recognition under domestic or treaty procedures pertinent to arbitration, or as a decree of a contractually chosen alien court entitled to consideration under procedures applicable to foreign judicial decisions.

Petitions for enforcement under a treaty on arbitration, whether bilateral or multilateral, concluded with the communist country of the award's origin after the establishment of its permanent foreign trade tribunal offer less justification for characterizing the decree as judicial. The government of the enforcing jurisdiction must be taken to have known of the existence and equivocal nature of the tribunal in the same way as the individual trader. Having failed to except its decrees, it must be presumed to have acquiesced to their enforcement in accordance with the procedures prescribed in the treaty for normal arbitral awards.

This approach need not block the issue of characterization where enforcement is sought under prewar treaties to which Eastern European countries became parties while still practicing market economics and while arbitration in its traditional form was still dominant in their territories. Nor need it block the issue under the domestic laws of Western countries which were never privy to treaty arrangements on arbitration with socialist states.

25

CONCLUSION: A PROPOSED CODE OF FAIR PRACTICES

A. The Search for an Equitable Framework

If East–West trade is to realize its full potential in an improving political climate, the institutional framework within which it is currently conducted must be drastically modified. Constructive modification would not only help to establish a better climate for mutually advantageous relations between planned and market economies; in the long term the benefits would make themselves felt in international commerce as a whole.

From the viewpoint of all concerned, it would be futile and self-defeating to set our sights on an overly ambitious program of reform. The most that can be hoped for is a gradual amelioration of trading conditions. Practically speaking, the question is not what changes would be ideal, but what improvements can realistically be brought to fruition, and at what pace.

Various proposals have been advanced from time to time with a view to placing the conduct of East–West commerce on a more satisfactory footing. Some of these proposals merit serious attention, although none seem to hold out the promise of a complete solution.

One avenue of approach leads to the formation of specialized national instrumentalities for the exchange of goods with all collectivist economies. A state corporation of this type is currently functioning in India relative to that country's trade with the communist orbit. All of Ceylon's commerce with mainland China flows through government hands, and a large segment of the United Arab Republic's export-import activities has been nationalized in the course of extensive barter dealings with the East. Italy too has long transacted sizable business with that region through an oligarchy of gigantic state entities such as Ente Nazionale Idrocarburi and Istituto Mobiliare Italiano.

To create an exclusive national conduit, however, would be tantamount to emulating totalitarian trading practices and inviting serious, perhaps irreversible, inroads into a domain which market economies ordinarily leave in private hands. The Frankenstein features of such a government-operated commercial monster, effective though it might be as a vehicle for trade and competition with Eastern states, would be more alarming than comforting to those whom it was designed to protect.

A coordinated approach to the Eastern market is feasible, indeed desirable, in the case of smaller and medium-sized firms. While Fiat, Krupp and General Electric can care for themselves, many lesser firms find it difficult to deal with the nationwide communist monopolies on an equal basis. To overcome the disparity, one could envisage cooperative trading companies formed by industry-based associations of exporters and importers.

Loose business associations have in fact recently been sponsored in France. Although each member reserves the right to enter into transactions independently, it also can call on a variety of services provided to the group as a whole. In addition, under strong government pressure prompted by a politically motivated desire to expand two-way trade with the U.S.S.R. a number of large French firms have created a joint purchasing entity for the exchange of Soviet goods against combined orders of local consumer products.[1] While this voluntary form of centralization is more palatable, it is a palliative rather than an over-all remedy.

Business relationships between private firms and state monopolies can in principle be made the subject of a separate segment of national legislation. Western parliaments could condition all purchases and sales involving wholly planned economies upon compliance with statutorily approved terms. However, this mode of regulation would be likely to yield highly undesirable by-products. Entire branches of law would have to undergo piecemeal amendment in order to accommodate East–West transactions as such, with resultant disturbance to the consistency of the established legal order. Institutionalized arrangements, the GATT or the International Monetary Fund, and many specialized treaties and conventions would also require considerable modification if the peculiarities encountered in this area of trade were to be treated side by side with matters pertaining to privately conducted world commerce.

Under present conditions, bilateral treaties remain an unquestionably convenient vehicle for the regulation of trade between collectivist and market economies. Aside from dealing with matters of direct concern to governments, such treaties could also provide an umbrella of minimum protection for private parties who seek contractual relations with state-directed enterprises. Through comprehensive instruments of this type the requisite regulatory regime could be effectively installed without disturbing the logic and unity of general domestic law. In practice, however, the objective is more difficult to secure. Few governments acting in isolation enjoy sufficient bargaining power to obtain from a total state trading country, particularly a large one, an adequate set of operative rules.

Standardized enterprise-to-enterprise agreements with provisions which anticipate and resolve specific difficulties can help to insure a satisfactory East–West business relationship. Predetermined texts tend to equalize disparate bargaining power and thereby to limit the abuses which often accompany such disparity. But they can just as easily become instruments of pressure enabling the stronger to make the law for the weaker. In the ultimate analysis, whether the impact is beneficial or pernicious depends upon the auspices under which the standardization takes place.

Nor can standard contracts cover all the needs and contingencies of possible business arrangements. Even in the area of simple purchase and sale, particular types of goods require their own unique provisions. To conceive forms for the variety of transactions which may arise in the normal course of business is virtually impossible. At best, only isolated clauses can be recommended for situations of a nonrecurrent type.

Considerable attention has been given to the possibility of including communist countries within world-wide or regional programs for the unification of laws pertinent to foreign trade.[2] That such schemes are widely appreciated in the East follows from the notable results accomplished within the Comecon sphere. A direct attempt to absorb any segment of socialist law into a globally unified system would, however, be impractical. In the first place, the Eastern states cannot be expected to dismantle their own General Conditions of Delivery with a view to general international integration. Second, they are not likely to abrogate the peremptory rules of national legislation which regulate their trade monopolies.[3] Third, progress toward uniformity presupposes basic institutional affinities. In the absence of a common core of legal concepts, particularly in the sphere of contract and property law, the search for unanimity seems futile. Unless the East's emergent economic reforms go far beyond what is now foreseeable, unification may never be a feasible objective.

As a rule, the problems encountered in world trade tend to be similar everywhere; adopted solutions happen, therefore, to fall along familiar lines as well. The issues which arise in dealings between market-oriented and state-directed economies are, however, often unique. Consequently, the remedies they require cannot be situated within a regulatory system which serves commerce universally. This is one of the principal findings of our study.

My own opinion is that East–West trade problems can best be handled by an internationally sponsored but independent system of regulation: a code of fair practices mitigating the disabilities of Western and Eastern enterprises alike and operating to safeguard the general structure of world trade as it strains to accommodate the growing phenomenon of total state commerce.[4] Crucial to such a code, the elements of which are sketched in the next section of this chapter, is a negotiated exchange of concessions and assurances, with each side giving up something of value to gain something in return. Difficult though they might be to negotiate, the provisions would in major part be self-enforcing, the reciprocally granted benefits acting as an automatic deterrent to infringement, through the risk of suspension of a specific undertaking for the loss of a particular privilege.

This approach is superior for conceptual as well as practical reasons. It pursues the aims sought through the other approaches outlined above, without entailing any of their drawbacks—the fear of government-operated Western monopolies, the distortion of domestic legislation, the fragmentation inherent in bilaterally negotiated treaties, the rigidity of standard contracts and the impracticality of unified national laws. In addition, a negotiated scheme of regulation implemented in successive stages would seem to blend political feasibility with the prospect of a comprehensive solution.

To be sure, commerce with the communist world would continue without mutually devised standards of behavior, indeed, even if the methodology were (as it long has been) dictated by the East. Most Western firms would simply go on trading on a catch-as-catch-can basis. However, the present quest for normalized East–West relations clearly points to the need for a balanced and permanent framework of economic intercourse.

A code cannot resolve outstanding political issues or remove all of the irritants which intermittently unsettle the commercial climate. Its immediate function must be a highly pragmatic one: to deal with subject matter of a primarily mercantile nature and to neutralize the more intractable vestiges of national law, regulation and practice. In their individual operation and total effect, particularized norms addressed to East and West should encompass principles declaratory of acceptable existing usage, measures anticipating the trend of current reforms and provisions inventive of suitable new standards.

Initially, the proposed code could serve as a convenient point of reference at two levels: first and foremost, for firms which engage or are affected by developments in East–West trade; second, for diplomats in the negotiation of commercial treaties, government agencies in the enforcement of national law, legislatures in determining the focus of needed enactments, courts in analyzing unfamiliar legal concepts and international organizations in coping with the impact of novel techniques.

It would be illusory to expect Eastern and Western states to conclude forthwith a full-blown multilateral convention for the compulsory regulation of business transactions among them. As a first step, the preparation of an optional set of provisions without legally binding force would be more realistic. Western institutions concerned with the orderly conduct of world trade, both national and international, may be counted on to induce widespread adherence to appropriately drawn rules of trade. Similarly, communist institutions, domestically and at the Comecon level, could be invited to recommend such rules to their own state trading entities.

Only after a verdict tested by experience could the goal of a formally binding convention be placed on the international agenda. Meanwhile, the mere existence of a model code can exert a significant educational influence and discourage systematic abuses. Potential violators in East or West could not easily ignore the possibility of moral censure, even if passed on an entirely informal basis, and without the teeth of legal sanction. Such are the inexorable checks and balances which organized business life generates for its own protection.

The idea of forcing upon the planned economies a scheme of unilaterally conceived precepts as a condition *sine qua non* of trade cannot be seriously entertained; it would encounter insurmountable opposition in the West and undermine the chances of agreement with the East. An appropriate system of regulation can only be constructed on foundations of reasonable compromise and mutual tolerance of the ways in which each side chooses to transact its business.

No individual mind can chart the content of a complete code, much less conceive language which would meet the tests of clarity and efficacy. At best, one may hope to fix a point of departure for further endeavor toward a juridico-economic framework of enduring value. The proposals made hereafter, which address themselves overlappingly to policymakers, legislators, administrators, adjudicators and, above all, negotiating and contracting parties, are therefore cast in the form of general guidelines. In large measure, these guidelines emerge from the findings of the present work.

The warning of an eminent British jurist and commercialist, formulated long ago in another context, supplies an appropriate preface to any solitary effort in this area as well:

> A practical and working code cannot spring from the head of the draftsman, as Pallas Athene is fabled to have sprung, fully equipped, from the head of her father Zeus. In legislation, as in other sciences, the a priori road is a dangerous one to tread. The province of a code, I venture to think, is to set out in concise language and logical form those principles of the law which have already stood the test of time.[5]

My sense of personal humility is all the greater because I am attempting not only to summarize the generalized experience of the past, but also to posit provisions which are often venturesome, untested and, in a few instances, perhaps even wishful.

B. Ground Rules for East–West Trade

1. Normalization of Western Policies

1. *Public Attitudes.* East–West trade is intermittently hampered by various forms of organized and spontaneous public opposition. Western government and business leaders should adopt forthright attitudes and take effective steps to familiarize the public at large with the complex economic, political and psychological ramifications of this controversial issue.

2. *General Trading Conditions.* Market economies should be prepared, in exchange for specific counterconcessions such as those described below, to apply to Eastern enterprises the general legal, administrative and judicial regime which normally governs their international commerce. Only measures rendered essential by genuine considerations of national security should constitute exceptions to this regime.

3. *Strategic Export Controls.* Western governments should limit their legislative and administrative restrictions upon exports to nonbelligerent Eastern countries to goods and technology of direct military significance. The enforcement of all unilateral and multilateral controls should be co-

ordinated at the level of the alliance in order to avoid persistent conflicts of national policy and law.

4. *Import Quotas.* Prohibitions and quantitative restrictions upon the entry of Eastern origin goods should be confined to exceptional categories of sensitive products. Licensing should be subject to reinstatement only in the event that sharp increases in imports threaten the disruption of local or traditional third-country trade.

5. *Discriminatory Tariffs.* Penalizing tariff differentials currently in force against Eastern goods should be abolished. Extension of equal treatment should be predicated upon negotiated Eastern commitments to import specified quantities of Western goods and to refrain from disruptive export pricing and marketing.

6. *Credit Restrictions.* Western nations should align their credit policies toward the East in order to avoid harmful competition in the sphere of government-provided, government-guaranteed and private-source funds. Limitations on the volume and duration of financial and supplier credits should be removed to the extent that they impede the ordinary course of commerce.

7. *Government Procurement.* Outside the area of military defense, Eastern enterprises should be permitted to bid on a basis of parity with other third-country enterprises for direct purchases and public works contracts sponsored by Western governments. Competition should be safeguarded, however, against noncommercial pricing.

8. *Admission to Do Business.* Subject to the imperatives of national security and an agreed-upon *quid pro quo,* Western nations should afford to Eastern enterprises a degree of market access comparable to that enjoyed by foreign firms in general. Such access should include the privileges of entry, sojourn and movement for *bona-fide* commercial representatives, the right to organize and manage local companies, to repatriate capital and earnings, to acquire and lease property and to hire suitable personnel.

9. *Recognition of Eastern Institutions.* Collectivist economies have evolved novel institutions and procedures for the conduct of trade with differently structured socio-economic systems. Governmental, administrative and judicial bodies of Western countries should take cognizance of these innovations and accord them full effect to the extent that no abuses are involved. Specifically, Eastern enterprises duly incorporated under their domestic laws should be universally recognized as corporate entities legally distinct from one another and from their state. By contrast, foreign

trade delegations attached to Eastern embassies abroad should be viewed as integral organs of the accrediting state, committing that state to direct liability in the course of their commercial activities as principals.

10. *Sovereign Immunity.* Communist states, their official trade delegations and independent corporate enterprises should be deemed to have waived sovereign immunity abroad with respect to all matters arising in the normal conduct of commerce. Such waiver should be taken as a submission to both contractual and tortious liability, the service of legal process, the jurisdiction of otherwise competent courts and arbitral tribunals, the execution of judgments and awards, the applicability of regulatory provisions and the imposition of generally operative tax levies.

11. *Attachment of Property.* Without protection against indiscriminate attachment of their foreign-located property, the monolithically structured Eastern states would be vulnerable to intolerable harassment by Western litigants. Government bank accounts and other assets held abroad should be immune from seizure for the purpose of obtaining jurisdiction or execution in matters involving the liability of individual state enterprises. Nor should the foreign-held property of public enterprises be subject to seizure for debts contracted either by sister enterprises or by the state itself.

12. *Western Coordination.* Market economies should establish an intergovernmental committee for purposes of mutual consultation, cooperation and information on matters pertaining to the development and regularization of East–West trade. A group of this type could conveniently function under the auspices of the Organization for Economic Cooperation and Development.

13. *Private Trade Associations.* While it would be manifestly inopportune to channel a free economy's commerce with the East through governmentally or privately sponsored cartels, collective action—particularly among medium- and smaller-size firms—might prove reciprocally beneficial. Nonprofit-making national associations of traders with the East should be formed to render auxiliary services enabling member firms to approach Eastern state monopolies on a footing of greater confidence and equality.

2. *Adaptation of Eastern Practices*

14. *The Quest for Multilateralism.* The multilateralization of East–West economic relations remains a distant goal which can only be achieved with the integration of planned economies into international arrangements such

as GATT and the adoption of meaningful pricing, costing and convertibility procedures. Pending development of suitable conditions, bilaterally balanced export and import should be considered a legitimate method of exchange.

15. *Bilateral Patterns of Trade.* The rigors of strict bilateralism should be alleviated by means of such devices as clearing arrangements, the settlement of trade balances in convertible or transferable currencies and the general utilization of credits due from one Eastern country to another. The average duration of intergovernmental agreements providing the framework of bilateral exchange with industrialized Western nations should be shortened, preferably to three years, with the possibility of annual review to correct persistent imbalances.

16. *Currency Convertibility.* Planned economies should strive toward full currency convertibility among themselves and, eventually, with market economies. Multiple exchange rates for various classes of transactions should be eliminated and realistic conversion ratios progressively established to facilitate more reliable estimation of comparative economic advantage.

17. *Reciprocity.* In the sphere of East–West relations, strictly reciprocal undertakings tend to be largely meaningless or one-sided. Concessions affecting economic, commercial and legal matters should be framed to ensure equality in terms of practical results rather than formal promises. Countries practicing monopolistic state trading should therefore be expected to make fully particularized commitments in return for general commercial privileges customarily granted by open-market economies.

18. *Most-Favored-Nation Clauses.* In exchange for normal most-favored-nation treatment, Eastern states should obligate themselves to purchase defined quantities of goods over a fixed period of time. Devices employed in this connection might entail the inclusion of agreed import targets in national economic plans, or the expansion of purchases in proportion to the total growth of exports. Such undertakings can be made on a bilateral basis, or multilaterally, by means of a promise to spread increased procurement among all countries of GATT.

19. *National Treatment Standards.* A traditional promise by an Eastern country to extend to foreign firms and individuals treatment equal to that accorded to local parties is largely devoid of substance, since state enterprises preempt all national business activity and the participation of private citizens in economic life is severely restricted. The reality contained in a Western commitment of this type should be balanced by means of

specially negotiated and fully itemized counterconcessions on the part of the planned economy.

20. *Political Preference.* State monopolies should be invited to trade on the basis of strictly commercial considerations and to abstain from politically, diplomatically and ideologically motivated decision-making in the conduct of business. Export and import policies should be freed of preference by country of origin or destination, whether or not the country is within the Eastern orbit. In the case of sales abroad, the governing criteria should be price, quality, availability, marketability and transportation costs. In the case of purchases, foreign suppliers should be afforded the opportunity to compete on an equal footing.

21. *Tied Transactions.* Eastern enterprises should refrain from attaching unrelated counterpurchase commitments as a condition of placing their orders. Unwanted goods should be rejected by the Western trading partner, except where the compensatory payment in kind is in the form of staple commodities or products which can be conveniently integrated into its standard line of sales. Similarly, payment in blocked local funds should be resisted unless possibilities exist for switch into other usable currencies.

22. *Preclusive Buying.* Effective guidelines should be established within and without existing international commodity agreements to mitigate the dislocating impact of massive Eastern procurement. State enterprises should refrain from abrupt switching of orders and bulk buying for storage in disregard of available supply patterns.

23. *Dumping.* Eastern exporters should submit to a negotiated method of measuring their costs of production, profit margins and general pricing practices. Persistent disposal in quantities greater than the average of the preceding five years plus a specified percentage should establish a presumption of dumping. Any resultant quotas or countervailing levies should be lifted following submission of proof that the exports in question reflect normal business principles and do not benefit from invisible subsidies.

24. *Underselling Third-Country Suppliers.* Special protection should be afforded to traditional foreign suppliers who compete with presumptively dumped communist exports, even if no injury is caused to indigenous manufacturers. Prevalent world prices, or cost factors operative in comparable market economies, constitute appropriate criteria for judging allegations of unfair underselling.

25. *Re-Exportation.* Foreign goods or technology acquired by communist enterprises should not, without consent, be resold abroad below the price of original purchase. In the absence of such an undertaking at the

governmental level, an appropriate limitation should be included in the original contract of sale.

26. *Transshipment.* Western export controls affect various destinations with differing degrees of severity. Although Eastern states cannot be expected to assist in the execution of this policy, their enterprises should contractually undertake not to transship any imported goods in violation of the licensing requirements in force in the country of origin.

27. *Certification of Origin.* Certain Western countries prohibit the importation into their territories of goods emanating from communist areas deemed to be particularly belligerent. Unaffected Eastern governments should cooperate in the identification of goods which their enterprises offer for export by issuing certificates of origin in accordance with procedures set up jointly with the country of destination.

3. *Access to Eastern Markets*

28. *Measuring Demand.* The failure of Eastern states to publish full economic and industrial data makes it difficult to anticipate cyclical market fluctuations and the movement of supply and demand. Governmental agreements on categories and quotas of goods to be exchanged offer an unreliable basis for gauging business potential at the level of individual firms. The command economies should be invited to make systematic disclosure of their annual foreign trade plans, the procedures employed in stimulating production for export and in selecting goods for import, and the information needed by the international merchant community to estimate continuing business prospects.

29. *Sales Promotion.* In a wholly planned economy, the scope for business promotion from the outside is extremely narrow. Hitherto the principal methods of sales initiation have been approaches to communist purchasing missions abroad, personal visits to Eastern capitals and participation in trade fairs and exhibitions. Western firms should be allowed a broadened range of possibilities to familiarize local end-users with the nature and variety of their products, to introduce and display sample wares on a customs-free basis, to register identification trademarks and trade names, to engage in merchandising via the mails, to advertise in commercial publications and, eventually, in media reaching the individual consumer.

30. *Intermediary Monopolies.* Eastern governments should eliminate or limit the intervention of middlemen state-trading entities in the consum-

mation of East–West dealings. To the extent that effective elimination is not feasible, Eastern producers in the case of exports and end-users in the case of imports should be permitted to appear as primary parties in the negotiation, conclusion and performance of international transactions.

31. *Domestic Resale Practice.* Upon local resale of imported goods, levies imposed by means of tariffs, or mark-ups added by intermediary state entities to landed costs, should be systematically disclosed and formally delimited. All forms of discrimination against foreign goods should end at the custom house, to ensure parity of treatment with local products in distribution, sale and use.

32. *Right of Permanent Establishment.* Admission of foreign firms to engage in independent local production, distribution and exchange would be inconsistent with the concept of a wholly planned socialist economy. Classic establishment treaty provisions must therefore be discarded in this area. Eastern states should nonetheless permit the maintenance of accredited representative offices for the legitimate exploration of business opportunities, demonstration of technical know-how, installation of plants and provision of after-sale servicing. The standard of admission could be derived from treatment accorded in the East to enterprises of socialist countries.

33. *Utilization of Local Facilities.* Western firms, whether permanently established or transiently present in communist countries, should be offered minimum facilities needed for the convenient discharge of their commercial functions. Specifically, they should have the right to rent office space, employ auxiliary personnel such as typists, interpreters and accountants, enjoy access to banks, insurance companies, warehouses, transportation services and postal, telephone, cable and telex media.

34. *Shipping and Transit.* Accredited Western airline, railway and ship operators should have reasonable opportunities to use local ports and to bid for shipping business on an equal footing with competing foreign operators. There should be a guaranteed right of passage through the respective territories, of breaking bulk and of changing the mode of transportation in mid-journey.

35. *Status of Aliens.* Eastern governments should extend to all legitimate representatives of Western firms the privileges of entry and exit, of local sojourn and travel, of obtaining adequate living accommodations and of access to available places of worship. The exercise of such privileges should be free of interference and subject only to the controls dictated by requirements of national security.

36. *Status of Foreign Property.* Alien firms should enjoy the right to bring in, keep and remove—in accordance with stated purposes—all necessary equipment, demonstration models, blueprints, trade secrets, books of account and other business related items. Foreign property maintained on Eastern soil, both tangible and intangible (such as locally registered patents, trademarks and copyrights), should be assured against expropriation. In the event of a state exercise of the right of eminent domain for a pressing public purpose, prompt and just compensation should be paid in an amount determined pursuant to agreement or neutrally conducted arbitration.

4. *Protection of Legal Rights*

37. *Publication of Foreign Trade Regulations.* Eastern states should undertake to promulgate and publish in easily accessible form all laws, decrees, administrative directives and judicial decisions with bearing upon international commerce. No secret or undisclosed provisions should be considered appropriate for application to foreign firms.

38. *Unsuitable Communist Laws.* East–West transactions are often subject to the domestic legal system of an Eastern country. Insofar as certain provisions of communist legislation have an ideological content inappropriate for relations in the preponderantly capitalist framework of world trade, their operation should be suspended vis-à-vis the private foreign party. This result can be best accomplished by the enactment of special laws to regulate dealings between local and alien enterprises.

39. *Mandatory Rules of Law.* Certain norms regulating their trading monopolies are considered by Eastern legal systems to have a mandatory operation, regardless of party intention. Matters subject to compulsory regulation include the right of enterprises to engage in foreign trade, the contractual capacity of corporations, the designation of persons authorized to make commitments, formalities of contracting and statutes of limitations. Such rules, if kept to an essential minimum, should be recognized by courts and arbitrators everywhere.

40. *Party Autonomy.* The parties to an agreement should be permitted maximum scope to immunize their bargain from the operation of national laws. Subject to the above-mentioned mandatory rules, the bounds of contractual autonomy should extend to the choice of transactional terms, the legal system governing the parties' rights and obligations and the jurisdiction of arbitral tribunals which will resolve their disputes.

41. *Industrial Property.* Through continuation of precommunist membership or postwar accession, most Eastern countries currently participate in international arrangements for the protection of industrial property rights. Classically conceived "national treatment" provisions of multilateral and bilateral treaties should be amended to afford Western inventors benefits appropriate to foreigners rather than the limited tangible and honorific rewards locally available to their communist counterparts. Conversely, protection abroad should be extended not only to Eastern patentees but also to those who hold certificates of authorship in industrial rationalizations, scientific discoveries and technological know-how.

42. *Recognition of Patents, Trademarks and Trade Names.* Communist domestic law affords native and alien registrants of industrial property rights a modest but meaningful measure of protection. Innovators with concrete business prospects in a given Eastern country should be encouraged to file for such protection. In its application to foreigners Eastern law should be amended to free royalties from unusually restrictive domestic ceilings, to allow payment in convertible currency, to prevent the divulgence of industrial secrets and to permit neutrally arbitrated compensation in the event of compulsory state acquisition.

43. *Licensing Agreements.* Eastern industrial establishments cannot be realistically expected to offer foreign licensors means of verifying compliance with licensing contracts comparable to those available in an open economy. Western holders of patents, know-how and trademarks should seek substantial down payments, guaranteed annual royalties and whatever facilities can be obtained to inspect manufacturing volume, quality, sales and accounting records.

44. *Cooperative Production Ventures.* While the notion of a state-owned and -operated economy remains sanctified socialist dogma, exceptional types of business arrangements are becoming increasingly feasible. In connection with Eastern-based industrial projects, the Western firm should entertain royalties, interest and service fees as the practical equivalent of dividends; the supply of capital goods on extended terms as a form of ownership; and long-term management contracts as the nearest counterpart of corporate voting control.

45. *Copyright Relations.* Eastern states which are still outside any international system of copyright protection should be expected to join existing conventions or to enter into special bilateral arrangements covering the rights of foreign authors, composers, performers, motion-picture producers and others in that category. While the publication of locally

unprotected works need not be enjoined in face of a foreign copyright-holder's refusal to grant a license, appropriate compensation should become automatically payable, and the work should be safeguarded against artistic distortion.

46. *Compensation of Western Authors.* Eastern publishing monopolies should be required to observe international standards of compensation in rewarding foreign authors for their locally exploited works. To the extent that protection under communist law is available to an alien, criteria for royalty determination should be drawn from prevalent world practice, rather than from the comparatively limited rates applicable to local copyright holders.

47. *Legal Representation.* Communist legal systems should afford outside parties the right to engage counsel for the purpose of assisting in administrative, judicial or arbitral proceedings. The outsider should be privileged to deal with such counsel on a normal lawyer-client basis, with all the attributes entailed in a fiduciary and confidential relationship. Concurrently he should have the right to be represented by Western counsel while negotiating, contracting or disputing business arrangements.

5. *Formation and Performance of Contracts*

48. *The State Trading Partner.* Western firms may find themselves dealing with an Eastern state as such, with one of its official foreign trade delegations, with communist-controlled companies established in the West, with corporate export-import organizations or with ordinary domestic enterprises. As a general rule, the three latter types of institutions should be considered more appropriate parties to contract with, particularly the last, to the extent that they are vested with requisite power to deal abroad.

49. *Limited Liability.* While government subsidization insures their continued solvency, it is conceivable that transactions involving sizable credits may render the Eastern enterprise's capital insufficient to meet its obligations. Since it is not legally possible to satisfy a proven claim from state assets other than those specifically allocated to the corporation, it is appropriate to stipulate for unlimited guarantees of the National Bank or Foreign Trade Bank of the country in question.

50. *Corporate Capacity.* In the East, the concept of *ultra vires* is applied with utmost strictness to the point of rendering invalid any transaction which exceeds the contractual capacity of a particular corporation, no matter how reasonable the reliance of the foreign party. The power of a state enterprise to deal in foreign trade generally, and in certain goods,

services or geographic areas in particular, should be warranted in the contract by means of a direct and officially authenticated extract from its charter of incorporation.

51. *Authority to Bind.* Regulations in force in planned economies often provide that foreign trade commitments can only be made by specially designated signatories; no doctrine of apparent authority is available to justify deviations. Eastern officials purporting to enter into contractual undertakings should be required to submit evidence of their corporate or administrative standing and of the scope of their authority in the form of documents certified by the Ministry of Foreign Trade.

52. *Formalities of Contracting.* The frequently encountered Eastern rule that contractual rights and obligations must be expressed in writing and signed in accordance with prescribed requirements should be entitled to universal enforcement. Foreign firms should be cognizant of this peculiarity of communist law and take the precaution of strict compliance with its terms.

53. *Incorporation of Prevalent Trade Terms.* Contracting parties should be free to incorporate into their agreements, by reproduction or simple reference, widely used commercial terms such as Incoterms (1953) and Uniform Rules and Usages in Documentary Credits (1962). These terms should be universally recognized and interpreted in accordance with established international practice, national law (other than mandatorily applicable rules) notwithstanding.

54. *Integrated Agreements.* Within the limits permitted by applicable treaties and national law, foreign parties and their legal advisers should seek to conclude East–West contracts in the most formal, detailed and integrated manner. Exhaustively drafted documents elaborating all foreseeable contingencies are to be strongly recommended in order to obviate difficulties which arise from the existing divergence of concept, practice and law.

55. *Use of Model Documents.* State enterprises should refrain from abusing their monopolistic power in efforts to induce acceptance of unreasonable contractual texts. Foreign parties should strive to deal on the basis of model sale, shipping, insurance and payment documents specifically devised to remove the distortions inherent in commerce between private firms and government-operated enterprises.

56. *Government Approvals.* The Eastern party should be required to submit evidence that its government has specifically approved the performance of a negotiated transaction or, alternatively, that no approval is required. In connection with the purchase and sale of goods, the agreement should recite that the requisite export, import, or transit license has been

issued or that responsibility for obtaining such a license is upon the state trading party. On the other hand, the private Western firm should remain free to make the delivery of goods or technical data contingent upon its government's issuance of an export permit.

57. *Force Majeure.* Conventional concepts of *force majeure* or act of God require modification by legislation, treaty or contract to encompass contingencies such as industrial strikes and shortages of materials, which in Eastern practice do not uniformly excuse performance. More important, the consequences of state cancellation or modification of agreements, or of any other state-created impossibility of performance should be borne by the party whose government is at cause.

58. *Intervening Change of Economic Plan.* While Eastern governments must remain free to undertake such sovereign action as they see fit, modifications in their economic plans which interfere with pre-existing contracts should not release the state trading party from liability for consequential damages. Pending treaty-accepted exclusion of such acts from the defense of *force majeure,* the risk should be shifted by means of contractual stipulation.

59. *Remedies for Breach of Contract.* Parties to East–West contracts should be free to elect remedies for breach to suit the peculiar needs of their respective economic environments. The traditional relief of contractual rescission and pecuniary damages should be allotted a secondary position. Instead, orders of specific performance and stipulated penalties for late or imperfect delivery should be liberally recognized to help the Eastern side safeguard its formal economic programs.

60. *Statutes of Limitation.* Discrepancies between the inordinately short Eastern time limits within which lawsuits may be brought and the generally longer Western time limits should be harmonized by intergovernmental agreement. A uniform rule should establish relatively brief periods (six months) for actions involving the quality of goods, negotiable instruments and checks; intermediate periods (two years) for other contractual disputes; and somewhat longer periods (three years) for breaches of warranty or liability sounding in tort. Agreed party variations should be permissible within strictly defined boundaries.

6. *Settlement of Disputes*

61. *Litigation.* National courts are not suitable for the settlement of East–West business disputes, owing to mutual suspicions of prejudice and

sharply divergent conceptions of business and law. In the absence of a treaty-sponsored exclusion of regular courts from adjudication in this area, the parties should invariably seek to submit their differences to settlement by arbitration.

62. *Apportionment of Jurisdiction.* Regardless of whether disputes are to be settled by courts or arbitral bodies, the parties should be free to select a tribunal and trial location of their preference. A predetermined location, such as the defendant's country, does not overcome concern over national or ideological bias to the same extent as trial on neutral soil or under international auspices. However, it helps to diminish the markedly broad range of jurisdiction which Eastern tribunals have acquired in recent years.

63. *Eastern Foreign Trade Tribunals.* Each of the communist countries has established a specialized adjudicatory institution for the hearing of controversies with foreign firms. While in general these institutions have shown themselves to be capable of competent and fair determinations, and admirably suited for the resolution of disputes in intra-Eastern trade, they suffer from certain structural and procedural flaws. Rather than to submit to their jurisdiction, parties to East–West contracts should opt for alternative methods of dispute settlement.

64. *Neutrally Sponsored Arbitration.* Pending establishment of a special system of adjudication, arbitration tribunals functioning on a multilateral basis, e.g., those of the International Chamber of Commerce in Paris, or procedures available on a third-country basis, e.g., those of the Chambers of Commerce of Zürich and Stockholm, are particularly appropriate for the settlement of East–West disputes. In addition, balanced *ad hoc* panels for the resolution of specific controversies (although less satisfactory because the prestige of a permanent institution is not at stake) can be contractually constituted by the parties along tripartite or bilateral lines.

65. *Rules of Arbitral Procedure.* Submission by the parties to the jurisdiction of a permanently functioning arbitral body should be deemed an acceptance of the standing rules of procedure of that body. Submission to an *ad hoc* panel should be deemed an acceptance of the rules of procedure adopted by the arbitrators, unless the parties stipulate special procedural guidelines. The arbitrators should have discretion to resolve all unregulated procedural points or to apply the code of civil procedure in force at the place of hearing.

66. *Applicability of Substantive Law.* It would be neither feasible nor appropriate to allow arbitrators of East–West disputes to function as *ami-*

ables compositeurs, free to adjudicate under general principles of fairness and equity without reference to any law. All competent tribunals, both judicial and arbitral, should be required to settle the merits of a controversy in accordance with their domestic law, including conflict-of-law rules, recognized custom and usage and the provisions of operative treaties.

67. *Party Choice of Law.* Adjudicators should be required to rule upon the validity of disputed contracts and the rights and obligations which they establish by reference to the legal system selected by the parties. The limitation that contractual choice of law can only be effective if it points to the laws of a country with which the transaction is connected should be relaxed to permit election on the basis of third-country compromise.

68. *Judicial Choice of Law.* In the absence of a contractually indicated legal system, disputed issues should be resolved under the proper law as defined by the tribunal. Criteria applied to ascertaining that law should include the nationality of the parties, the place of contracting, the place of performance and the place of trial, provided that the public policy of the forum and all rules which mandatorily affect one or the other of the disputants must remain overriding. Automatic referral to either the place of contracting or the place of arbitration would generally result in the application of the communist party's legal system insofar as the majority of transactions are currently signed or arbitrated in Eastern capitals.

69. *Recognition of Arbitral Submissions.* References to arbitration, whether incorporated into an over-all contract with a view to future controversies or concluded separately with respect to an existing controversy, should be universally upheld as binding. Any attempt to invoke the jurisdiction of courts or alternate tribunals should be stayed until the specified arbitration has run its full course.

70. *Enforcement of Arbitral Awards.* The Eastern countries have widely adhered to regional and global conventions on the enforcement of arbitration clauses and awards. The few Western countries that do not consider themselves obligated to enforce duly rendered arbitral decisions should be required to do so under operating conventions, special bilateral undertakings or amended domestic laws.

7. *Intergovernmental Cooperation*

71. *Membership in International Organizations.* Planned economies should exert best efforts to join international organizations (both governmental, such as GATT, and nongovernmental, such as the International

Chamber of Commerce) responsible for the orderly conduct of world trade. The governments of market economies should welcome such efforts and participate in the negotiation of special procedures designed to render Eastern membership mutually advantageous.

72. *Adherence to Multilateral Conventions.* Eastern states should be encouraged to broaden their adherence to established international conventions dealing with commercial, legal and procedural matters. Communist domestic laws should be adapted to render possible and meaningful compliance with the letter and spirit of provisions originally designed for privately conducted business.

73. *Bilateral Treaties.* Neither the domestic legal systems of market economies nor globally operative conventions can be conveniently amended to accommodate the unique regulatory problems of East–West trade. Pending international adoption of an instrument expressly designed to cover this segment of trade, bilateral intergovernmental agreements offer the most appropriate method of regulation. The terms of such agreements should be as uniform as possible to counteract bargaining inequities between the signatory parties. Their interpretation by national authorities should likewise be uniform, with inconsistencies or abuses submitted to mixed arbitration tribunals.

74. *Taxation Agreements.* Eastern and Western governments should conclude bilateral arrangements exonerating each other's enterprises from unreasonable or duplicated taxation. The incidence of income, turnover and property taxes, as well as withholding levies upon patent and copyright royalties, service fees, interest and other compensation should be consistent with internationally prevailing levels.

75. *Standardization of Practice.* Local, regional and international groupings of East and West should cooperate in standardizing the conditions of trade between state enterprises and private firms. Such groupings should seek widespread adoption of a uniform nomenclature for the classification of goods and of jointly elaborated commercial terms, definitions, documents, contractual clauses and usages.

76. *General Conditions of Trade.* Over the long term it is possible to envisage the universal adoption of a compendious and self-sufficient code of provisions for the conduct of East–West commerce, immunizing all contractual relations from the national legal systems in question. Such a code could comprise not only a scheme of selected correctives to pressing problems but also other suitable solutions drawn from commercial law, custom and usage among merchants. A model as to scope and form, if not

content, is suggested by the Comecon General Conditions of Delivery and by the Uniform Commercial Code of the United States.

77. *Joint Chambers of Commerce.* To promote and facilitate the exchange of goods and services between them, the governments of market and planned economies should sponsor joint chambers of commerce consisting of enterprises from both countries. Such chambers should maintain permanent offices and mixed professional staffs in the respective capitals.

78. *Exchange of Information.* A central clearing house should be established under international auspices to collect, publish and circulate information on matters pertinent to East–West trade. Governments of Eastern and Western countries should be required to furnish various economic, commercial and statistical data, copies of bilateral agreements and protocols, the content of laws, decrees and regulations affecting business relationships, rules of procedure of competent arbitration tribunals and other relevant materials.

79. *International Consultation.* Institutionalized machinery for periodic consultation among representatives of planned and free economies should be jointly devised by Eastern and Western governments. In due course, such machinery could be converted into an international organization with a permanently functioning secretariat of its own. Its principal function would be to recommend to governments common and separate action designed to correct serious market imbalances, to broaden the volume and composition of commercial exchanges, to inquire into abuses, to disseminate information and in general to facilitate the development of East–West trade on a stable and mutually advantageous basis.

80. *Complaint Procedures.* The creation of a supranational forum with authority to rule upon malpractices alleged by planned and free economies against each other is even more remote a goal than the adoption of a binding code of fair practices. Government agencies, public institutions, trade associations and individual enterprises may, however, be invited to bring their grievances to the attention of existing national and international bodies: Chambers of Commerce, the Comecon Secretariat, the Common Market Commission, the U.N. Economic Commission for Europe and so forth. While such bodies cannot take punitive or corrective action, they might be expected to investigate, consider and, if necessary, publish findings after offering adequate opportunity for rebuttal.

ABBREVIATIONS

1. BASIC PRINCIPLES (LEGISLATION)—Basic Principles of Civil Legislation of the USSR (1962).
2. BASIC PRINCIPLES (PROCEDURE)—Basic Principles of Civil Procedure of the USSR (1962).
3. BIRPI SYMPOSIUM—United International Bureaux for the Protection of Intellectual Property: East-West Industrial Property Symposium, held in Budapest in 1966 (Geneva 1967).
4. COMECON—Council for Mutual Economic Assistance.
5. COMECON CONDITIONS—General Conditions of Delivery 1958, as amended in 1968.
6. KOJOUHAROFF—"Chronique de Jurisprudence de la Cour arbitral près de la Chambre de Commerce bulgare," Journal du droit international, Vol. 94, 1967, p. 152 *et seq.* (in French).
7. LUNTS—Mezhdunarodnoe Chastnoe Pravo (Private International Law), Moscow, 1949, 1959 and 1963 editions (in Russian).
8. P.W.H.Z.—Prawo w Handlu Zagranicznym (Law in Foreign Trade), Warsaw (in Polish).
9. RAMZAITSEV—Vneshnetorgovyi Arbitrazh v SSSR (Foreign Trade Arbitration in the USSR), Moscow, 1952 and 1957 editions (in Russian).
10. RULES—Uniform reference to the Statutes and Rules of Procedure of the several Eastern foreign trade and maritime arbitration tribunals.
11. RSFSR CIVIL CODE—Civil Code of the Russian Republic of the USSR (1964).
12. RSFSR CODE OF CIVIL PROCEDURE—Code of Civil Procedure of the Russian Republic of the USSR (1964).

13. S.I.M.—Sbornik informatsionnykh materialov: sektsiia prava vsesoiuznoi torgovoi palaty (Collection of informational materials: law section of the All-Union Chamber of Commerce), Moscow.
14. S.R.M.A.K.—Vsesoiuznaia Torgovaia Palata, Sbornik Reshenii Morskoi Arbitrazhnoi Komissii (All-Union Chamber of Commerce, Collection of Decisions of the Maritime Arbitration Commission), Moscow.
15. SCHMITTHOFF (SOURCES)—Schmitthoff (Ed.), The Sources of the Law of International Trade (1964).
16. TRIBUNAL—Common reference for the foreign trade and maritime arbitration bodies of all the communist countries, which are variously described in their constitutive statutes as Courts, Commissions, Committees, Panels, etc.
17. UNCTAD—United Nations Conference on Trade and Development.
18. ECE—United Nations Economic Commission for Europe, Geneva.
19. V.T.—Vneshniaia Torgovlia (Foreign Trade), Moscow.
20. V.T.P.V.A.—Vsesoiuznaia Torgovaia Palata, Vneshnetorgovyi Arbitrazh (All-Union Chamber of Commerce, Foreign Trade Arbitration), Moscow.

NOTES

INTRODUCTION: KEY ISSUES

1. From 1921 to 1928, when foreign investments were freely admitted.
2. See Berman, "The Legal Framework of Trade Between Planned and Free Economies," (Meeting of Jurists on Peaceful Cooperation) UNESCO, 55, *Coop. Inter. 1, Annex III,* p. 1, 1958.
3. Schmitthoff, "Modern Trends in English Commercial Law," *Tidskrift Utgiven av Juridiska Forenger i Finland,* Vol. 6, Helsinki 1957, p. 349, at 354.
4. See Piotrkowski, "'The Great Importance of Commercial Law for Peaceful Economic Collaboration of all Nations," *The New Yugoslav Law,* Vol. IX, July-Dec. 1958, p. 6, at 8; and Goldstajn, "Submission to Arbitration of Disputes with a Foreign Element," *Revija za Medunarodno Pravo,* Vol. 1, 1958, p. 118, at 123.
5. See Pisar, "A New Look at Trade Policy Toward the Communist Bloc: The Elements of a Common Strategy for the West," *Joint Economic Committee of Congress,* U.S. Government Printing Office (1961).
6. "Do Communist and Free Economies Show a Converging Pattern?," *Soviet Studies,* Vol. 12, 1966, p. 333.
7. Views expressed by the eminent Soviet scientists Andrei Sakharov in an essay on "Convergence" and Pyotr Kapitsa, in a speech to the U.S. National Academy of Sciences, reported by the *N.Y. Times* on July 22, 1968, and October 9, 1969, respectively. Compare the doctrinaire replication to Sakharov by A. Cheprakov in "Problems of the Last Third of the Century," *Izvestia,* Aug. 8, 1968 (in Russian).
8. With the exception of Yugoslavia.

CHAPTER 1

THE CONFINES OF THE EASTERN MARKET

1. *Spravochnik po vneshnei torgovle* (Moscow 1958), p. 117 (in Russian).
2. *Pravda,* Jan. 30, 1949 (in Russian).
3. See J. V. Stalin, *The Economic Problems of Socialism in the U.S.S.R.* (New York, 1952), p. 26.
4. D. F. Fokin (ed.) *Vneshniaia Torgovlia S.S.S.R.* (1946-63) (Moscow, 1964), p. 11, at 76 (in Russian).
5. *Politicheskaia Ekonomiia* (Moscow, 1954), p. 610 (in Russian).
6. *Zycie Warszawy,* Feb. 19-20, 1967 (in Polish).
7. *The Economist* (London), May 13, 1967, p. 703.
8. *Zycie Warszawy,* Dec. 18-19, 1966 (in Polish).
9. L. Ruschick, in *Neues Deutschland,* March 6, 1960 (in German). See also the low-key but highly revealing survey of the economic press of East Europe published in *Planovoe Khoziaistvo,* No. 8, 1961, pp. 87-92 (in Russian).
10. Bogomolov, in *Mirovaia ekonomika i mezdunarodnye otnosheniia,* No. 5, 1966, p. 19 (in Russian).
11. *Ibid.*
12. *Vneshniaia Torglovia S.S.S.R.* za 1968 god, Moscow, 1969, pp. 51 and 88 (in Russian).
13. *V.T.,* Dec. 1966, p. 12.
14. V. Sergeev, "On the Question of the Category of the World Market," in *V. T.,* April 1963, p. 17. The Stalin essay is his well-known *The Economic Problems of Socialism in the U.S.S.R., op. cit. supra* note 3.
15. See Report of N. Baibakov, Chairman of the State Planning Committee of the U.S.S.R., to the 25th Party Congress, in *Pravda,* April 7, 1966 (in Russian).
16. *Pravda,* Oct. 1, 1965 (in Russian).
17. "The Plan, Profits and Premiums," in *Pravda,* Sept. 9, 1962 (in Russian).
18. Report of Leonid Brezhnev to the Central Committee of the Soviet Communist Party on December 15, 1969. See *Pravda,* January 15, 1970 (in Russian).
19. Joint letter from nuclear scientist Sakharov, historian Medvedev and physicist Turtshin to Brezhnev, Kosygin and Podgorny, dated March 19, 1970. See *Le Monde* (Paris), April 11, 1970 (in French).
20. See N. Baibakov, address to the All-Union Conference on the Application of Economic Reform, held in Moscow, in May 1968, as reported in *Le Monde* (Paris), May 16, 1968 (in French).

CHAPTER 2
COMMUNIST INTEREST IN FOREIGN COMMERCE

1. J. V. Stalin, *The Economic Problems of Socialism in the U.S.S.R.* (New York, 1952), pp. 26-27.
2. ECE, *Economic Survey of Europe in 1956,* Chapter VII, p. 7.
3. Source: *Vneshniaia Torgovlia SSSR* za 1959-63 gody, Moscow 1965, pp. 10-11; *Vneshniaia Torgovlia SSSR* za 1965 god, Moscow 1966, p. 10; and *Ekonomicheskaia Gazeta* No. 17, April 1969, p. 19 (in Russian).
4. *Izvestia,* April 10, 1966 (in Russian).
5. See, *e.g.*, Aboltin, in *Voprosy stroitel'stva kommunizma v SSSR,* Academy of Sciences of the USSR, 1959, p. 345 (in Russian).
6. *V. T.,* May 1966, p. 4.
7. *Pravda,* April 6, 1966 (in Russian).
8. *Pravda,* May 7, 1958 (in Russian).
9. D. Mishustin, *Vneshniaia Torgovlia i Industrializatsiia SSSR* (Moscow 1938), p. 139 (in Russian).
10. See generally, *La Coopération Economique Industrielle Scientifique et Technique entre les Pays de l'Est et de l'Ouest de l'Europe, Ligue Européenne de Coopération Economique*, Publication No. 41, Brussels, 1967 (in French).
11. V. F. Garbuzov, Soviet Minister of Finance, in *Pravda,* Dec. 11, 1968 (in Russian).
12. *SSSR v Tsifrakh v 1967 godu,* Moscow, 1968, p. 130 (in Russian) and *Narodnoe Khoziaistvo v 1968 godu,* Moscow, 1969, pp. 698 and 776 (in Russian).
13. *Pravda,* Dec. 16, 1966, (in Russian). See also *OECD, The Research and Development Effort* (Paris, 1965), pp. 70-71.
14. *V. T.,* March 1967, p. 13.
15. *The Wall Street Journal,* May 31, 1967.
16. Report on the 1966-70 Economic Development Plan, April 6, 1966, published in the *Daily Review,* Vol. XII, No. 80 (3231), p. 55.
17. See B. H. Paselj, "Yugoslav Laws on Foreign Investments," *The International Lawyer,* Vol. 2, No. 3, 1968, p. 449.
18. See *Le Monde* (Paris) Dec. 12 and 13, 1969, and "Nihon Keizai Shimbun"—*Japan Economic Journal,* Aug. 6, 1968, pp. 1 and 9. See also *International Legal Materials, Current Documents,* Vol. III, Jan. 1969, p. 48.
19. Source: United Nations, *Monthly Bulletin of Statistics,* March 1969, Special Table E, p. xxviii.

20. Vaganov, in *V. T.*, No. 2, 1965, p. 4.
21. See generally, U.S. Congress, Joint Economic Committee, *"Soviet Economic Performance 1966-67*, p. 127, 1968; see also, "Review of Trade Relations Among Countries Having Different Economic and Social Systems Including Problems of East-West Trade," *Report by UNCTAD Secretariat, TD/18*, Nov. 3, 1967, p. 21.

CHAPTER 3
WORLD-WIDE INTEREST IN TRADE WITH THE EAST

1. Source: *Vneshniaia Torgovlia SSSR 1918-1966*, Moscow, 1968 (in Russian) and *Le Commerce Extérieur* Nos. 7, 8 and 9, Supplément Statistique, Moscow, 1969 (in French).
2. See Nikolayenko, in *Soviet Export*, No. 3, 1967, p. 39. See also *Vneshniaia Torgovlia SSSR*, 1968, Moscow, 1969 p. 10 (in Russian).
3. See J. Rey, "Les Echanges extérieurs de la Communauté Economique Européenne, aspects particuliers des relations avec les pays de l'Est," *Les Communautés Européennes et les relations Est–Ouest*, Colloque de 31 mars et 1er avril, 1966 (Brussels, 1967), p. 23 (in French).
4. See W. Ernst, "Le Relazioni Economiche con l'Est Europeo nella Prospettiva della Formulazione di una Politica Commerciale Comune della Comunità Economica Europea, in *Le Relazioni Economiche dell'Italia con i Paesi ad Economia di Stato nella Prospettiva della Politica Commerciale della* CEE (Atti del Convegno Nazionale dell' Istituto Affari Internazionali, June 23-24, 1966, Milan), p. 65, at 69 (in Italian).
5. See Brown, Ermarth and Salloch, "Eastern Europe and the Common Market," *Communist Affairs*, Vol. VI, 1968, p. 11.
6. See F. Dehousse, "Les Positions du Parlement Européen à l'Egard du Problème du Commerce avec les Pays de l'Est," in *op. cit. supra* note 3, pp. 15–21 (in French).
7. See *The American Review of East-West Trade*, Vol. 1, No. 2, Feb. 1968, pp. 79–80.
8. *Nihon Keizai Shimbun*—Japan Economic Journal, Nov. 7, 1967.
9. *Le Monde* (Paris), April 2, 1968, Supplément au numéro 7722 (in French).
10. *The Journal of Commerce*, International Edition, June 17, 1968.
11. See I. Moravcik, "Prospects for Soviet and East European Purchase of Canadian Wheat," *East-West Trade: A Symposium*, The Canadian Institute of International Affairs (Toronto 1966), pp. 135, at 138, 151 and 152.
12. U.N. Monthly Bulletin of Statistics, March, 1968, p. XXIX.
13. A Case Study prepared by UNCTAD Secretariat on Trade and Economic Relations between India and the Socialist Countries of Eastern Europe,

Problems Arising in Trade Relations between Countries Having Different Economic and Social Systems, *UNCTAD, TD/18/129,* July 21, 1967, pp. 9–11, 14.

14. A Case Study Prepared by UNCTAD Secretariat on Trade and Economic Relations Between the United Arab Republic and the Socialist Countries, Problems Arising in Trade Relations between Countries having Different Economic and Social Systems, *UNCTAD, TD/B/130,* July 28, 1967, pp. ii–iii and 6–10.

15. UNCTAD, Final Act and Report (Recommendation A. VI. 3, adopted at 1st Session of the 1964 Conference), *U.N. Publications,* Sales No. 64, II, B. 11, p. 63.

CHAPTER 4
TRADE AS AN INSTRUMENT OF FOREIGN POLICY

1. See H. Schmidt, "The Future of Germany in a Changing European Context," *Adelphi Papers,* No. 33, 1967, p. 43, at 48–49.

2. See W. Ernst, "Le Relazioni Economiche con l'Est Europeo nella Prospettiva della Formulazione di una Politica Commerciale Comune della Comunità Economica Europea," in *Le Relazioni Economiche dell'Italia con i Paesi ad Economia di Stato nella Prospettiva della Politica Commerciale della CEE* (Atti del Convegno Nazionale dell'Istituto Affari Internazionali, June 23–24, 1966, Milan), p. 65, at 71 (in Italian).

3. See declarations of Foreign Minister Michel Debré, as reported in *Le Monde* (Paris), Jan. 10, 1969 (in French).

4. See Final Communiqué, published in *Le Monde* (Paris), Jan. 10, 1969 (in French), and *The American Review of East-West Trade,* February 1969, p. 12.

5. See, *e.g.,* Monfils, "Les Leçons de l'Expérience Acquise dans les Relations Commerciales entre la Belgique et les Pays de l'Est" in *Les Communautés Européennes et les Relations Est-Ouest,* Colloque de 31 mars et 1er avril 1966 (Brussels, 1967), pp. 103–116 (in French).

6. See P. Abelin, "Les Relations Economiques entre la C.E.E. et l'Europe Orientale," *Politique Etrangère,* 1963, p. 467 *et seq.* (in French) and Nessler, *"Report on the Political Aspects of East-West Trade,"* Consultative Assembly, Council of Europe, Doc. No. 1961, Sept. 9, 1965, p. 11.

7. See *Department of State Bulletin,* Dec. 21, 1964, p. 876.

8. "Making Europe Whole: An Unfinished Task," *Department of State Bulletin,* Oct. 24, 1966, p. 622, at 624.

9. *Report to the President of the Special (Miller) Committee on U.S. Trade Relations with East European Countries and the Soviet Union,* Apr. 29, 1965, p. 3.

10. This question has most recently come to life in mid-1968 in relation to East Germany's imposition of visa requirements upon West Germans journeying to West Berlin and, much more forcefully, after the Soviet-led Warsaw Pact invasion of Czechoslovakia. See, *e.g.*, article favoring embargo of the East, in *Le Monde* (Paris), Aug. 23, 1968, p. 7 (in French). Similar reactions appeared in the *London Financial Times* and elsewhere, stressing the uncertain impact of East-West political relations upon economic intercourse.
11. Leon Herman, "East-West Trade: An Overview of Legislation, Policy Trends, and Issues Involved," *The Library of Congress Legislative Reference Service,* June 17, 1968, p. 15.
12. See testimony of Robert L. Allen in *Hearings before the Subcommittee on Foreign Economic Policy,* Joint Economic Committee, U.S. Congress, Dec. 4–14, 1961 (U.S.G.P.O., Washington, D.C., 1962), p. 200.

CHAPTER 5
AMERICAN DILEMMAS IN TRADE WITH THE EAST

1. Guz, Rocznik statystyczny, Warsaw, 1969, p. 365 (in Polish.)
2. *E.g.,* such was the estimate of Eugene M. Braderman, Deputy Assistant Secretary of State for Commercial and Business Activities, in remarks to the American Management Association at Briefing on East-West Trade in New York, March 10, 1969.
3. Under-Secretary of State Nicholas de B. Katzenbach, *Department of State Bulletin,* Jan. 2, 1967, p. 2.
4. See generally, "Ordinances Restricting the Sale of Communist Goods," Vol. 65, *Columbia Law Review,* 1965, p. 310.
5. "Face the Nation" (television program), Sept. 26, 1965.
6. "Les Etats socialistes doivent-ils rompre toutes relations avec les Etats capitalistes," *L'Humanité* (Paris), February 20, 1970 (in French).
7. Department of State Publication 8117, *Commercial Policy Series 203,* August 1966, p. 19.
8. See N. McKitterick, *East-West Trade:* "The Background of U.S. Policy," 1966, p. 40 *et seq.*; see also, Goldman and Conner, "Businessmen Appraise East-West Trade," *Harvard Business Review,* Vol. 44, Jan.–Feb. 1966, p. 6.
9. See Industry Statement reproduced in "Private Boycotts Versus the National Interest," in *op. cit. supra* note 7, p. 13 *et seq.*
10. See *Le Monde,* Paris, Oct. 12-13, 1969.
11. Letter of October 11, 1965, reproduced in *op. cit. supra* note 7, p. 15.
12. As quoted by Robert B. Wright, "East-West Trade—The Position of the State Department," *The American Review of East-West Trade,* Vol. 1, No. 5, May 1968, p. 21.

13. *Special (Miller) Committee on U.S. Trade Relations with East European Countries and the Soviet Union,* Report to the President, April 29, 1965. See also Giffen, *The Legal and Practical Aspects of Trade with the Soviet Union,* New York, 1969, p. 287.
14. Letter of Secretary Dean Rusk, May 11, 1966, accompanying the draft legislative proposal, *Department of State Bulletin,* May 30, 1966.
15. See *The New York Times,* August 11, 1967.
16. See Hearings Before the Subcommittee on Internal Finance of the Senate Committee on Banking and Currency, 90th Congress, 2nd Session on Senate Joint Resolution 169 Concerning East-West Trade, Volumes 1–3 (1968).

CHAPTER 6
WESTERN RESTRAINTS ON EAST-WEST TRANSACTIONS

1. See Public Notices 289–292, 33 *Fed. Reg.* 4695, March 19, 1968.
2. Foreign Assistance Act, 1961, secs. 221 and 620.
3. Sec. 4916(b), IRC(1954). See also Reg. 1000.319, Schedule A and Release of Office of Foreign Direct Investments, April 22, 1968.
4. Determination of March 26, 1964; see *Basic Documents on East-West Trade,* Sub-Committee on Europe, Committee on Foreign Affairs, U.S. House of Representatives, Aug. 1968, pp. 20–22.
5. 31 C.F.R. Secs. 500.101–.808.
6. See Baker & Bohlig, "The Control of Exports—A Comparison of the Laws of the United States, Canada, Japan and the Federal Republic of Germany," *The International Lawyer,* Vol. 1, 1967, p. 163, at 180.
7. See *Notices from the Dept. of Treasury,* Office of Foreign Assets Control, *Fed. Reg.,* Nov. 10, 1965 and Feb. 2, 1966.
8. See Art Buchwald, "China's Close Shave," *New York Herald Tribune* (Paris Edition), Sept. 17–18, 1966; see also, B. Nossiter, "Asian-Hair Accords Calm United States-European War Over Wigs," *New York Herald Tribune* (Paris Edition), March 19, 1966.
9. National Defense Education Act (1958).
10. The ban on crabmeat was lifted in 1961, on the basis of a new Treasury finding that no slave labor was then known to be used in its canning.
11. Order No. 10582, 19 *Fed. Reg.* 8723 (1954).
12. *New York Times,* April 5, 1967 and May 19, 1967. See also article by E. J. Michelson, in *U.S. Congressional Record,* April 6, 1967.
13. "Trade Problems Between Countries Having Different Social and Economic Systems," *UNECE,* March 9, 1964, p. 20.
14. See Agreements between the USSR and the United Kingdom of 1934 (149 *League of Nations Treaty Series* 446, 1934) and the USA of 1937 (50 Stat. 1619).

15. See generally Brown, Ermarth and Salloch, "Eastern Europe and the Common Market," *Communist Affairs,* Vol. VI, 1968, p. 11.

16. See Löhr, "Rapport fait au nom de la commission du commerce extérieur sur les questions de politique commerciale commune de la Communauté á l'égard des pays à commerce d'Etat," *Parlement Européen, Documents de Séance 1965–66,* March 22, 1965, pp. 5–7 (in French).

17. *Official Gazette* No. 14, Jan. 29, 1963, as prolonged by subsequent annual regulations. See also Hahn, "Rapport sur les problèmes des relations commerciales entre la Communauté et les pays à commerce d'Etat d'Europe orientale," *Parlement Européen,* Doc. No. 205, March 6, 1968 (in French).

18. See Kamenov, "Certains Problèmes des Relations Economiques de la République Populaire de Bulgarie avec les Pays Membres du Marché Commun," *Les Communautés Européennes et les Relations Est-Ouest,* Colloque, 31 Mars et 1er Avril, 1966 (Brussels 1967), p. 117, at 121 (in French).

19. See J. Rey, "Les Echanges extérieurs de la Communauté Economique Européenne, aspects particuliers des relations avec les pays de l'Est," in *ibid.,* p. 23, at 24 (in French).

20. See "Developments in East-West Trade Policy and Techniques," Oct. 1966-Oct. 1967, *UNECE, Trade/198,* Rev. 1, Jan. 15, 1968.

21. Ministère de l'Economie et des Finances, "Les Echanges Commerciaux entre la France et les Pay de l'Est depuis 1961," in *Problèmes Economiques,* Sept. 26, 1968, p. 6, at 7 (in French).

22. *The Journal of Commerce,* International Edition, May 22, 1967.

23. 42 Ops. Atty. Gen. No. 15 (1963).

24. See D. Petroni, "Doing Business in Eastern European Countries," *Proceedings of the Southwestern Legal Foundation, Private Investors Abroad, Structures and Safeguards,* 1966, p. 261, at 300.

25. See, *e.g.,* Export-Import Bank Act of 1945, as amended, Sec. 11.

26. P. L. 88-258, Title III (1964). See *Basic Documents on East-West Trade, op. cit. supra* note 4, p. 54; see also, Newburg, "Trading with Communist Countries," *Practising Law Institute Bulletin,* April 1968, p. 12, at 16–17.

27. See M. P. Venema, "The Finance and Structure of Major Economic Projects in Eastern Europe—The Rumanian Refinery," *The American Review of East-West Trade,* Vol. 1, No. 6, June, 1968, p. 52.

28. P. L. 90–267, March 13, 1968.

29. P. L. 88–638, Sec. 11 (1964); see also Berman & Garson, "Possible Effects of the Proposed East-West Trade Relations Act Upon U.S. Import, Export, and Credit Controls," *Vanderbilt Law Review,* Vol. 20, 1967, p. 279, at 296 and 283.

30. See *East-West Trade,* PEP, London, May 1965, pp. 147–51.

CHAPTER 7
STRATEGIC EXPORT RESTRICTIONS

1. For a critical description of American practice prior to passage of the Export Administration Act of 1969 see Berman and Garson, "United States Export Controls—Past, Present and Future," *Columbia Law Review,* vol. 67, 1967, pp. 791–890; see also Baker and Bohlig, "The Control of Exports—A Comparison of the Laws of the United States, Canada, Japan, and the Federal Republic of Germany," *The International Lawyer,* vol. 1, 1967, pp. 163–191, for a description of practice in other Western countries.
2. See Export Control Act of 1949 (as amended) Sections 2(1) and 3(a).
3. Public Law 91–184, 91st Congress, 1969, Section 4(a)(1).
4. Foreign Exchange and Foreign Trade Control Law, No. 228 of December 1, 1949.
5. Export and Import Permits Act, 2-3 Elizabeth II, Chap. 27, March 31, 1954.
6. Law of Foreign Trade and Payments, *Aussenwirtschaftsgesetz* (AWG), April 28, 1961.
7. Strategic Goods (Control) Order, 1959 and Export of Goods (Control) Order, 1960. See Schmitthoff, *The Export Trade* (London, 1962), pp. 379–388.
8. *Official Gazette* No. 14, Jan. 17, 1967; see also Dal Maso, *La Pratica del commercio con l'estero* (Milan, 1967), pp. 7–17 (in Italian).
9. See debates on export control legislation in *Congressional Record—Senate,* Oct. 22, 1969, pp. 13067 *et seq.*
10. Testimony of Lawrence C. McQuade, March 7, 1968, "East-West Trade," *Hearings before Subcommittee on Europe of the Committee of Foreign Affairs,* House of Representatives, 90th Cong., 2nd Sess., Jan.–March, 1968, p. 177.
11. See statement of Assistant Secretary of Commerce Kenneth N. Davis to the House Sub-Committee on International Trade of the Banking and Currency Committee, June 4, 1969.
12. Export Control Regulations 379.1(a).
13. Halcon International, Inc. *v.* Snam Progetti S.p A. and Anic S.p A., see *International Herald Tribune,* October 23, 1968. See also Department of Commerce News Release No. FC 70-7, Feb. 3, 1970.
14. 27 *Fed. Reg.* 12487 (1962).
15. Table of Denial and Probation Orders Currently in Effect, Suppl. No. 1, Part 382, Export Regulations.
16. 24 *Fed. Reg.* 2626 (1959).

17. See *Our Changing Partnership with Europe,* Committee on Foreign Affairs, U.S. House of Representatives, Feb. 20, 1967, pp. 41–2.
18. Other legislative interventions included succeeding riders to appropriation bills such as the Cannon Amendment of September, 1950 and the Kem Amendment of May, 1951.
19. See *Basic Documents on East-West Trade,* Committee on Foreign Affairs, U.S. House of Representatives, Aug. 1968, p. 6.
20. See Haight, "United States Controls Over Strategic Transactions," *Illinois Law Forum,* 1965, p. 337, at 353.
21. Fruehauf Corp. *v.* Massardy, Sem. Jur. II, 14274 (1965); *Gazette du Palais* II, 86 (1965). See also Craig, "Application of the Trading with the Enemy Act to Foreign Corporations Owned by Americans: Reflections on Fruehauf *v.* Massardy," *Harvard Law Review*, Vol. 83, 1970, p. 579.
22. See *e.g., The Wall Street Journal,* Dec. 9, 1968.

CHAPTER 8
THE ORGANIZATION OF TOTAL STATE TRADING

1. Soviet Constitution, Arts. 11 and 14; Polish Constitution, Art. 7(2); Hungarian Constitution, Art. 6; Rumanian Constitution, Art. 8; Czech Constitution, Art. 7(1). See, in general, H. Trammer, "L'Organization Juridique du Commerce Extérieur Polonais en Général, et l'Organization de ses Institutions Exécutives en Particulier," *Aspects Juridiques du Commerce Avec les Pays d'Economie Planifiée* (Paris 1961), p. 197 (in French).
2. See V. H. Li, "Legal Aspects of Trade with Communist China," *Columbia Journal of Transnational Law,* Vol. 3, 1964, p. 57.
3. See Hazard, "State Trading in History and Theory," *Law and Contemporary Problems,* Vol. 24, 1959, p. 243.
4. See H. S. Levine, "The Effect of Foreign Trade on Soviet Planning Practices," *International Trade and Central Planning,* 1968 (A. A. Brown and E. Neuberger, eds.), p. 255.
5. See K. Voronov, "Sovremennaia Organizatsiia Vneshnei Torgovli SSSR," *V.T.*, No. 8, 1966, p. 48, at 51.
6. The GKES's deputy chairman is a colonel-general in the Soviet Army. Its executive representative in China, a colonel, arranged in 1965 the trans-China flow of Soviet military assistance to North Vietnam.
7. See Jen-min Jih-pao, Jan. 16, 1966, translated in *Ost-Probleme,* April 22, 1966 (in German).
8. See Trammer, *op. cit. supra* note 1, p. 209.
9. See M. Nesterov, "Torgovaia palata v deistvii," *V.T.*, No. 3, 1967, p. 9. See also *V.T.*, No. 11, 1969, p. 35.

10. Statuts de la Chambre de Commerce Franco-Soviétique, Art. 2.
11. See G. Gertsovitsh and I. Tshamrai, "External Economic Aspects of Economic Reforms in the Comecon Countries," *Voprosy Ekonomiki,* No. 4, 1968, p. 58 (in Russian).
12. *Le Courrier des Pays de l'Est,* June 14, 1967, p. 5 (in French).
13. See, generally, S. Margold, "Yugoslavia's New Economic Reform," *American Journal of Economics and Sociology,* Vol. 26, Jan. 1967, p. 65.
14. Incorporated May 24, 1924; see Vol. 2375, Corporate Records Section, N.Y. Dept. of Commerce, Albany, N.Y.
15. See *Les Echos* (Paris), Nov. 20, 1968 and Chambre de Commerce Franco-Soviétique, Note d'Information No. 10, Feb. 1969, pp. 15–16 (in French).
16. See M. I. Goldman, "The East Reaches for Markets," *Foreign Affairs,* Vol. 47, No. 4, July 1969, p. 721 at 730.
17. See generally, H. S. Levine, *op. cit. supra,* note 4, pp. 262–65.
18. See V. H. Li, *op. cit. supra* note 2, pp. 58–9. See V. Knapp, "The Function, Organization and Activities of Foreign Trade Corporations in the Eastern Socialist Countries," in Schmitthoff (Sources) at p. 58.
19. Kosygin, "The Directives of the 23rd CPSU Congress for the Five Year Economic Development Plan of the USSR for 1966–1970," in *The New York Times,* April 6, 1966.

CHAPTER 9
COMMUNIST BILATERALISM VERSUS OPEN WORLD TRADE

1. See B. Eliascheff, in *Le Monde* (Paris), Feb. 4–5, 1968 (in French).
2. See G. Garvy, *Money, Banking, and Credit in Eastern Europe* (Fed. Reserve Bank of N. Y. 1966), pp. 103–107.
3. See B. Metelius, "Le contrôle des changes et les accords commerciaux," in *Aspects Juridiques du Commerce avec les Pays d' Economie Planifiée* (Paris 1961), p. 151, at 153 (in French).
4. See *Actualités Economiques,* Bulletin d'Information Bimestriel de la Représentation en France de la Chambre du Commerce Extérieur de la R.D.A., Jan.-Feb. 1967, No. 1, pp. 7–8 (in French).
5. See *Pravda,* March 5, 1967 (in Russian).
6. See J. P. Saltiel, "La Coexistence pacifique et le développement des relations économiques entre l'Est et l'Ouest," *Revue Tiers-Monde,* Vol. IX, Nos. 35–36, July-Dec., 1968, pp. 772–73 (in French).
7. See "The Use of Long-Term Agreements as an Instrument for Promoting Trade Between Socialist and Developing Countries," Study prepared by

the Hungarian Institute for Economic and Market Research, *UNCTAD, Doc. TD/18/Supp. 2,* Dec. 29, 1967, pp. 39–40.

8. Protocole relatif au commerce intérieur allemand et aux problèmes connexes, Traité Instituant la Communauté Economique Européenne et Documents Annexes, S. L. 1963, *Services des Publications des Communautés Européennes,* p. 237 (in French).
9. See Brown, Ermarth and Salloch, "Eastern Europe and the Common Market," *Communist Affairs,* Vol. VI, 1968, p. 11, at 13. See also Hahn, "Rapport sur les problèmes des relations commerciales entre la Communautés et les pays à commerce d'Etats d'Europe orientale," *Parlement Européen, Doc. No. 205,* March 6, 1968, p. 20 (in French).
10. Decisions of July 20, 1960, and Oct. 9, 1961. See also Löhr, Rapport fait au nom de la commission du commerce extérieur de la Communauté à l'égard des pays à commerce d'Etat, Löhr, *Parlement Européen, Docs. de Séances* 1965-1966, March 22, 1965 (in French).
11. See *op. cit. supra* note 7, p. 22 *et seq.*
12. Text reproduced in *International Herald Tribune,* March 29, 1967.
13. See *A Background Study in East-West Trade,* U.S. Senate, Committee on Foreign Relations, 1965, p. 58.
14. Final Act of the Havana Charter for an International Trade Organization, CMD. No. 7375, C.4, SD. Arts. 29–32 (1948).
15. See generally, Stacey May, U.S. Delegation, "A Proposal for Applying GATT Trading Principles to Communist Bloc Trade with the Free World," Atlantic Conference, *Committee E, Reference CO/E/6,* June 5–10, 1959, London.
16. Art. XVII "State Trading Enterprises" (1)(a) and (b).
17. Statement by N. Popovic of the Committee for Foreign Trade of Yugoslavia, *GATT Doc. L–879,* Oct. 31, 1958.
18. Protocol for the Accession of Poland to the General Agreement on Tariffs and Trade, *GATT Doc. L/2851,* Sept. 19, 1967, Annex B.

CHAPTER 10
BUSINESS IN A MONOLITHIC ENVIRONMENT

1. See *International Herald Tribune,* Dec. 7–8, 1968.
2. See *New York Times,* Dec. 5, 1958 and Jan. 14, 1959. See also address by Senator H. H. Humphrey, *Congressional Record,* Sept. 20, 1961, p. 19186.
3. See Wilczynski, "Dumping and Central Planning," *The Journal of Political Economy,* Vol. 74, 1966, pp. 250 and 256.
4. *Economic Survey of Europe,* 1957, Geneva 1958, VI, pp. 22–29.

5. See generally, Domke & Hazard, "La Clause de la nation la plus favorisée," in *Aspects Juridiques du Commerce avec les Pays d'Economie Planifiée* (Paris, 1961), p. 75 *et seq.* (in French).
6. See H. Walker, "The Effect of Existing or Proposed International Trade Treaties and Agreements Upon Foreign Trade Between the USSR and the USA," *The Law of US-USSR Trade,* Assn. of American Law Schools, June 1965, pp. 80–81.
7. For an exhaustive description of such obligations see *"Rights of Businessmen Abroad Under Trade Agreements and Commercial Treaties,"* U.S. Council of the International Chamber of Commerce, 1960, p. 18.
8. See J. L'Huillier, "Problems Relating to the Expansion of Trade with Collectivist Economies," *Doc. No. 10211,* International Chamber of Commerce, Jan. 25, 1960, para. 16.
9. See *V.T.*, No. 10, 1961, pp. 5–6.

CHAPTER 11
DEALING WITH COMMUNIST MONOPOLIES

1. See Mádl, Foreign Trade Monopoly: *Private International Law* (Budapest 1967), pp. 59–60, and Szászy, *Private International Law in the European People's Democracies* (Budapest 1964), p. 213.
2. Decree of March 11, 1931, Sec. 12, and Basic Principles (Legislation) Art. 124; see also, Walter Rzepka, "Die Rechtsstellung der Ausslaender in der UdSSR," *Recht in Ost und West,* No. 2, 1964, p. 49 (in German).
3. Decree No. 199, Secs. 1 and 2 (1949).
4. See Crespi-Reghizzi, "Legal Aspects of Trade with China: The Italian Experience," *Harvard International Law Journal,* Vol. 9, 1968, p. 85.
5. See Note d'Information, No. 3, March 4, 1968, *Chambre de Commerce Franco-Soviétique* (in French).
6. See *Les Echos* (Paris), Nov. 5, 1968 (in French).
7. Basic Principles (Procedure) Art. 59.
8. Boguslavsky and Rubanov, *The Legal Status of Foreigners in the U.S.S.R.* (Moscow, undated) p. 31.
9. American and European restrictions on credit to the East are described in Chapter 6 *supra.*
10. See "The Use of Long-Term Agreements as an Instrument for Promoting Trade Between Socialist and Developing Countries," Study prepared by the Hungarian Institute for Economic and Market Research, *UNCTAD, Doc. TD/18/Supp. 2,* Dec. 29, 1967, p. 30.
11. See generally Charles H. Baudoin, "The Use of Switch Financing to Facilitate East-West Trade and Investment," *The American Review of East-West Trade,* Vol. 1, No. 6, June 1968, p. 46.

12. See G. T. French, "Problems of Conducting East-West Trade—One Company's Experience," in *ibid.* p. 19.
13. See *The Economist,* April 14, 1969.

CHAPTER 12
COMPETING WITH COMMUNIST MONOPOLIES

1. See M. I. Goldman, "The East Reaches for Markets," in *Foreign Affairs,* Vol. 47, No. 4, July 1969 p. 721, at 732–33.
2. See *International Herald Tribune,* Aug. 15, 1968.
3. For an analysis of the patterns and compositions of this trade, see J. Royer, "Trade Between Planned Economies and the Developing World," *Journal of World Trade Law,* Vol. 1, No. 5, 1967, p. 489.
4. The Directives of the 23rd C.P.S.U. Congress for the Five Year Economic Development Plan of the U.S.S.R. for 1966–1970, in 12, *The Daily Review,* No. 80, p. 55.
5. See V. Tabelev, in *Voprosy Statistiki,* April 1966, p. 43 (in Russian).
6. See J. Wilczynski, "Dumping and Central Planning," *The Journal of Political Economy,* Vol. LXXIV, June 1966, p. 250, at 258.
7. See *Journal of Commerce,* Aug. 4, 1959.
8. Article VI.
9. See *U.S. Congressional Qtly.,* June 19, 1959, p. 835.
10. See A Background Study on East-West Trade, U.S. Senate, Committee on Foreign Relations, 1965, pp. 49–50 and remarks of V. N. Nitchkov, President of Amtorg Trading Corp., to the American Management Association on March 10, 1969.
11. "Trade Problems between Countries Having Different Economic and Social Systems," *UNCTAD, Doc. E/CONF.* 46/34, March 9, 1964, p. 37.
12. See *International Herald Tribune,* Feb. 22, 1968.
13. See *Journal of Commerce,* May 23, 1960.
14. See J. Wilczynski, *op. cit. supra* note 6, at p. 252.
15. See *International Herald Tribune,* May 23, 1968.
16. See J. Wilczynski, *op. cit. supra* note 6, at p. 252.
17. See also Stacey May, U.S. Delegation, "A Proposal for Applying GATT Trading Principles to Communist-Bloc Trade with the Free World," Atlantic Conference, *Committee E, Reference Co/E/6,* June 5–10, 1959, London, pp. 5–6.
18. J. Wilczynski, *op. cit. supra* note 6, at p. 262.
19. See V. N. Nitchkov, *op. cit. supra* note 10.

CHAPTER 13
EASTERN REGULATION OF INTERNATIONAL TRANSACTIONS

1. R.S.F.S.R. Civil Code Sec. 5; Basic Principles (Legislation) Art. 5.
2. R.S.F.S.R. Civil Code Secs. 147 and 151.
3. See Genkin, "Pravovoe polozhenie sovetskikh eksportnykh i importnykh ob"edinenii za granitsei," in Lunts (Ed.), *Problemy mezhdunarodnovo chastnovo prava* (1960), p. 12 (in Russian).
4. Decision No. 41/64, in Kojouharoff, pp. 178–179.
5. See David, *Les Grands Systèmes de Droit Contemporain* (Dalloz, 1964), pp. 175–176 (in French).
6. Stuna, "L'évolution de la législation économique dans la République socialiste tchécoslovaque et l'objet de la réglementation portée par le Code économique," *Bull. dr. tchéc.*, Vols. 1–2, 1965 (in French).
7. See Foreword by R. H. Graveson, in Schmitthoff (Sources), p. vi.
8. An English translation of the 1958 version appears in Berman, "Unification of Contract Clauses in Trade between Member Countries of the Council for Mutual Economic Aid," *International & Comparative Law Qtly.*, Vol. 7, 1958, pp. 650–90. The 1968 modifications are for the most part marginal. See generally Hoya, The Comecon General Conditions—a Socialist Unification of International Trade Law," *Columbia Law Review*, Vol. 70, 1970, p. 253.
9. For a general discussion, see Kalensky, "Les traits essentiels des nouvelles codifications tchécoslovaques du droit du commerce international et du droit international privé," *Revue internationale de droit comparé*, Vol. 3, 1964, p. 568 (in French).
10. Kopáç, "Le Code tchécoslovaque du commerce international," *Journal du droit international*, Vol. 94, 1967, p. 789 (in French).
11. For English translations of the Principles and Codes see Kiralfy in *Law in Eastern Europe*, Vols. 7 (1963) and 11 (1966) respectively.
12. Yoffe and Tolstoy, "The New Civil Code of the R.S.F.S.R.: A Soviet View," *The International & Comparative Law Qtly.*, Vol. 15, 1966, p. 1090, at 1091.
13. Morozov, "Mnogostoronnye soglasheniia—deistvennaia forma ekonomicheskovo sotrudnichestva sotsialisticheskikh stran," *Sovetskoe Gosudarstvo i Pravo*, Vol. 12, 1963, pp. 75–85 (in Russian). See also *V.T.*, No. 1, 1963, p. 46.
14. Decisions Nos. 12/57 and 2/58, in Kojouharoff, p. 166.
15. Decision No. 31/62, in Kojouharoff, p. 168.
16. H. Wiemann, "Fünf Jahre Schiedsgericht bei der Kammer für Aussenhandel der DDR," Recht im Aussenhandel, *Der Aussenhandel*, No. 18, 1959 (in German) and Jakubowski, "Legal Regulation of Foreign Com-

merce among Socialist States," *Panstwo i Prawo,* No. 10, 1961, p. 528 (in Polish).

17. Decisions Nos. 23/64 and 57/59 respectively, in Kojouharoff, pp. 167–169.

18. *League of Nations Treaty Series,* Vol. 58, 1926, p. 7.

19. See Pereterskii & Krylov, *Mezhdunarodnoe Chastnoe Pravo* (Moscow 1959), p. 35 (in Russian).

20. See Schmitthoff, "The Law of International Trade, Its Growth, Formulation and Operation," in Schmitthoff (Sources), p. 18.

21. Ramzaitsev, "Private International Law in Soviet Foreign Trade Practice," *The Journal of Business Law,* 1961, p. 343, at 350. See also, *e.g.,* Soviet Rules Art. 23; Polish Rules Art. 28; Bulgarian Rules Art. 47; East German Rules Art. 27; Chinese Rules Art. 27 and Jakubowski, *Umowa Sprzedazy w Handlu Miendzynarodowym* (Warsaw, 1966) p. 264 (in Polish).

22. See, *e.g.,* Ramzaitsev, "FOB and CIF in the Practice of the Soviet Foreign Trade Organizations," *The Journal of Business Law,* 1959, pp. 315–322.

23. See Trammer, "The Law of Foreign Trade in the Legal Systems of the Countries of Planned Economy," in Schmitthoff (Sources) p. 48.

24. *E.g.,* In re "Il'ich" (1932), S.R.M.A.K., 1934, p. 47. The maritime tribunal considered itself bound to rule in accordance with shipping practice as evidenced in Carver, *The Carriage of Goods by Sea* (7th ed., 1925), Sec. 393; Kennedy, *The Law of Civil Salvage* (2d ed., 1907), pp. 202–13; Lowndes, *General Average* (6th ed., 1922), p. 182; and Scrutton, *The Contract of Affreightment as Expressed in Charter Parties and Bills of Lading* (13th ed., 1931), pp. 338–39. In Société d'Avance Commercial v. Soiuzpromeksport (1940), the tribunal relied upon the testimony of agents from Lloyd's of London and from an Alexandrian firm; see Ramzaitsev (1952), p. 68.

25. Much of the U.S.S.R.'s commercial and maritime custom is collected, systematized and published as binding by the All-Union Chamber of Commerce. See Samoilovich, *Pravovoe Oformlenie Morskikh Perevozok Gruzov* (Moscow 1954), pp. 142–59 (in Russian); see also, *Mezhdunarodnye torgovye obychai* (Moscow 1958), p. 11 (in Russian).

CHAPTER 14
THE STATUS OF BUSINESS INSTRUMENTALITIES

1. *E.g.,* R.S.F.S.R. Civil Code Sec. 50 invalidates transactions beyond an enterprise's corporate purpose; see also Spitzner, *Wirtschaftsvertraege* (Berlin 1965), p. 310 (in German).

2. Decision No. 2/64, in Kojouharoff, pp. 160–1.

3. Decision No. 57/64, *ibid.,* pp. 161–2.

4. See R.S.F.S.R. Civil Code Sec. 32; Hungarian Civil Code Sec. 31 (1959); Polish Civil Code Art. 40 (1964); Czechoslovak Foreign Trade Law Art.

11 (1964); Bulgarian Law on Enterprises Art. 6 (1960). See also Wiemann, "Zivilrecht und Handelsfaehigkeit der Gemeinsamen Unternehmen Sozialistischer Staaten und Ihre Internationale Respektierung," *Staat und Recht,* No. 13, 1964, p. 141, at 144 (in German).

5. See Genkin, "Pravovoe Polozhenie Vsesoiuznykh Vneshnetorgovykh Ob"edinenii," in Genkin (Ed.), *Pravovye Voprosy Vneshnei Torgovli SSSR s Evropeiskimi Stranami Narodnoi Demokratsii* (Moscow 1955), pp. 61–2 (in Russian).

6. In re "King Edgar" (1932), in *S.R.M.A.K.*, 1934, p. 9, at 13.

7. Gebreders Kats v. Eksportkhleb (ca. 1936), in *V.T.P.V.A.*, 1941, p. 34.

8. See discussion in Kojouharoff, pp. 162–3; *cf.* Pisar "Le traitement de l'arbitrage communiste devant les cours occidentales," in *Aspects juridiques du commerce avec les pays d'économie planifiée* (Paris 1961), p. 163, at 169 (in French).

9. R.S.F.S.R. Code of Civil Procedure Sec. 433.

10. See, *e.g.*, Soviet-Danish Trade and Navigation Agreement, Aug. 17, 1946, Art. 6; see also Boguslavsky, *Immunitet Gosudarstva* (Moscow 1962), pp. 146–50 (in Russian).

11. Letter of Jack B. Tate, May 19, 1952, 26 Dept. State Bull. 984 (1952). It should be noted that as an interdepartmental memorandum, this letter was not considered binding by the Justice Department and was, consequently, ignored by it in suits against the U.S. government abroad. See also Lauterpacht, "The Problem of Jurisdictional Immunities of Foreign States," *British Yearbook of International Law,* Vol. 28, 1951, p. 220, at 226–32.

12. See Sucharitkul, *State Immunities and Trading Activities in International Law* (London 1959), for a survey of judicial decisions in some thirty countries; see also C. W. Jenks, *International Immunities* (1961), p. 151.

13. See Lunts (1963), p. 52; see also Grosz (Poland) and Knapp (Czechoslovakia) in Sarraute, "Les Travaux de la Commission de Droit International Privé au 6e Congrès de l'Association Internationale des Juristes Démocrates," *Journal du droit international,* No. 4, 1956, p. 886, at 893 (in French); and Florescu, "The Legal Status of Foreign Trade Enterprises—Their Juridical Personality—in the Socialist Republic of Rumania" in *Rechtsfragen der Kooperation Zwischen Unternehmen in Ost und West* (Munich 1967), p. 47, at 49.

14. Boguslavsky, *op. cit. supra* note 10, at pp. 180–184.

15. See Pisar, "The Communist System of Foreign Trade Adjudication," *Harvard Law Review,* Vol. 72, 1959, p. 1409, at 1416.

16. Since 1953, the E.C.E. has drafted, with the cooperation of Eastern and Western experts, standard contracts and general conditions of trade for a wide variety of goods; see S. Michida, "Possible Avenues to Preparation of Standard Contracts for International Trade on a Global Level," in

Honnold (Ed.), *Unification of the Law Governing International Sales of Goods* (Paris 1966), p. 251, at 256–7.

17. See *"Memorandum on Contracts for the Export of Engineering Products to the Soviet Union,"* The London Chamber of Commerce, March 1965, p. 12.
18. Jordan Investments, Ltd. v. Soiuznefteksport, award of the Moscow Foreign Trade Arbitration Commission of July 3, 1958, in *S.I.M.*, Vol. 11, 1961, p. 23; an English translation of the award appears in the *American Journal of International Law,* Vol. 53, 1959, p. 800. The amount of damages sought was (U.S.) $2,396,440.69.
19. See Berman, "Force Majeure and the Denial of an Export License under Soviet Law: A Comment on Jordan Investments Ltd. v. Soiuznefteksport," *Harvard Law Review,* Vol. 73, 1960, p. 1128; Domke, "The Israeli-Soviet Oil Arbitration," *The American Journal of International Law,* Vol. 53, 1959, p. 787; Sassoon, "The Soviet-Israel Oil Arbitration," *Journal of Business Law,* London 1959, pp. 116 and 132; *cf.* Robert, "Observations sur une sentence arbitrale internationale," *Revue de l'arbitrage,* July–Sept. 1960, p. 76 (in French).
20. The new legislation prescribes a similar rule; see R.S.F.S.R. Civil Code Secs. 222 and 235.
21. Koospol v. Rawinad (Madrid), Decision No. 16/66, reported by E. Kafajova "Chronique de jurisprudence tchécoslovaque," *Journal du droit international,* Vol. 96, No. 1, 1969, p. 176, at 180–81 (in French).
22. Decision No. 21/56, in Kojouharoff, p. 178.
23. Decision No. 9/64, *ibid.*
24. Decision No. 2/57, *ibid.,* p. 163.
25. Decision No. 17/57, *ibid.*
26. See Kopáç, "Le Code tchécoslovaque du commerce international," *Journal du droit international,* Vol. 94, 1967, p. 789, at 811–15 (in French).
27. Genkin, "Pravovoe Polozhenie Sovietskikh Eksportnykh i Importnykh Ob "edinenii za Granitsei," in Lunts (Ed.), *Problemy Mezhdunarodnovo Chastnovo Prava,* Moscow, 1960, p. 18 (in Russian).
28. See Berman, *op. cit. supra* note 19, p. 1143.

CHAPTER 15
THE ROLE OF CONTRACT

1. Speech to the National Association of Importers and Exporters, Mexico City, Nov. 28, 1959, as reported in *Pravda,* Nov. 30, 1959 (in Russian).
2. See Jordan Investments, Ltd. (Israel) v. Soiuznefteksport, reported in *American Journal of International Law,* Vol. 53, 1959, p. 800, and discussed in the preceding chapter.

3. Law on Obligations and Contracts Art. 5.
4. Basic Principles (Legislation) Arts. 39 and 44. See also Bratus *et al., Soviet Civil Legislation and Procedure* (Moscow, undated), pp. 28–30.
5. R.S.F.S.R. Civil Code Secs. 166, 233 and 261.
6. *Ibid.,* Secs. 78–82.
7. See Decree of Soviet Council of Ministers, 1962, No. 12, Sec. 94.
8. Liberman & Zhitnitskii, "Ekonomicheskie i administrativnye metody khoziaistvennovo rukovodstva," *Planovoe Khoziaistvo,* No. 1, 1968, p. 19 (in Russian).
9. See Mádl, *Foreign Trade Monopoly: Private International Law* (Budapest, 1967), p. 46.
10. B. S. Vaganov (ed.), *Organizatsiia i tekhnika vneshnei torgovli SSSR i drugikh sotsialisticheskikh stran* (Moscow, 1963), p. 87 (in Russian).
11. Decision No. 5/57, in Kojouharoff pp. 180–182.
12. See V. L. Farago, "Zu einigen Entscheidungen der ungarischen Handelskammer," Recht im Aussenhandel, *Der Aussenhandel,* No. 1, 1961 (in German).
13. Decisions Nos. 19/58 and 20/62 in Kojouharoff, p. 181.
14. Decisions of the Hungarian tribunal No. 1022, December 4, 1961, and of the Polish tribunal No. 91/60, November 8, 1961.
15. Metalimeks v. Rudmetal, Decision No. 5/57 in Ramzaitsev, "Deiatel'nost VTAK v 1957," *Sovetskii Ezhegodnik Mezhdunarodnovo Prava,* 1958, pp. 465–466 (in Russian). See also Lunts (1963), pp. 110–111.
16. The only limitation on contractual autonomy stipulated therein is that "the contents of the contract is not contrary to the law, to the national economic plan and to the rules of the socialist community." Art. 9(1), *cf.* Polish Code of Obligations Art. 55.
17. See Lunts (1963), p. 140. See also generally, Pisar, "Negotiating, Structuring and Disputing East-West Agreements," *Conference on East-West Trade,* Vienna, May 1969 (Pisar, ed.), Management Center Europe, Brussels 1970, p. 54.

CHAPTER 16
CREATION AND PERFORMANCE OF AGREEMENTS

1. Art. 1341, C. Com. 109.
2. See Crespi-Reghizzi, "Legal Aspects of Trade with China: The Italian Experience," *Harvard International Law Journal,* Vol. 9, 1968, p. 85, at 115.
3. See R.S.F.S.R. Sup. Ct., Civ. App. Div., Letter of Instruction No. 1 (1927), as quoted in 2 Gsovski, *Soviet Civil Law* (1948–49), p. 54, instructing

the courts to take a more lenient attitude with respect to contracts which are not illegal or are not to the obvious prejudice of the state.

4. R.S.F.S.R. Civil Code Secs. 44, 46 and 48.
5. Rules for Signing Contracts in Foreign Trade, USSR Laws c. 583 (1930), as amended, USSR Laws c. 119 (1932), USSR Laws c. 54 (1933), USSR Laws c. 178 (1934), USSR Laws c. 459 (1936); see also R.S.F.S.R. Civil Code Sec. 45.
6. Shenker & Co. v. Raznoimport (1937), in *V.T.P.V.A.*, 1941, p. 25, at 26.; see also Basic Principles (Legislation) Art. 125 and R.S.F.S.R. Civil Code sec. 565.
7. See Ramzaitsev (1952), p. 32 (in Russian) and Agreement Between France and the USSR Concerning Mutual Commercial Relations, Sept. 3, 1951, Art. 12, in *Journal du droit international,* Vol. 80, 1953, p. 508 (in French). See also Polish Private International Law of 1926, Art. 5, and Law of 1965, Art. 12, under both of which formal validity may be established by foreign law, as either the law governing the substance of the contract or the law of the place of contracting.
8. Shenker & Co. v. Raznoimport (1937), *op. cit. supra* note 6.
9. Kattenburg v. Tekhnoeksport (1937), in Ramzaitsev (1957), pp. 72–73.
10. See Crespi-Reghizzi, *op. cit. supra* note 2, pp. 104–105.
11. Fanto Petroleum Maatschappij v. Soiuzpromeksport (1940), in Ramzaitsev (1952), p. 33.
12. Jean Rival Fils v. Eksportles (1957), in Ramzaitsev, "Deiatel'nost Vneshnetorgovoi Arbitrazhnoi Komissii v Moskve v 1958 i 1959," *Sovetskii Ezhegodnik Mezhdunarodnovo Prava,* 1960, p. 346, at 348–349 (in Russian).
13. Civ. 1.6.1953, Bull. Cass. 1953. 1. 147; Civ. 24.10.1950, Bull. Civ. 1950.1.155 (in French).
14. See Rome Draft Art. 4(2); *cf.* Hague Draft Art. 5(2).
15. See R.S.F.S.R. Civil Code Secs. 162 and 163 and Comecon Conditions Art. 110.
16. See 1964 Draft of Hague Convention on the Law Applicable to International Sales of Goods (1955), Art. 7(1), (2), *cf.* UCC 2–207.
17. See R.S.F.S.R. Civil Code Sec. 165.
18. See Arts. 6(1), 12(1); *cf.* Art. 9.
19. Technopromimport v. Nikexport (1956), in Ramzaitsev, "The Law Applied by Arbitration Tribunals," in Schmitthoff (Sources), p. 138, at 148–49.
20. See respectively, Koospol v. Zenith Trade Company, S.A. (Milan), Case No. 62/66, decided on July 11, 1967, reported by E. Kafajova, "Chronique de jurisprudence tchécoslovaque," *Journal du droit international*, Vol. 96,

No. 1, 1969, p. 176, and Czechoslovak State Insurance Office v. Black Sea Shipping Line, reported in Quigley, "New Soviet Merchant Shipping Code," *The American Review of East–West Trade,* Feb., 1969, p. 50.

21. See R.S.F.S.R. Civil Code Secs. 138, 135 and 136.

22. See Motoimport v. Motokov, case No. 131/66 decided on April 17, 1967 and other awards rendered by the Czechoslovak arbitration court, as reported by E. Kafajova, *op. cit. supra* note 20, pp. 176–78; also, for example, the standard contract used by Metalexport of Poland, discussed by A. Harding Boulton, "Common Form Contracts in Planned Economies," *The American Review of East–West Trade,* February, 1969, p. 43.

23. E.g. Cases Nos. 257/1965 and 258/1965, reported by Nestor, "A Theoretical Survey of Arbitration Practice in Foreign Trade Issues," *Revue Roumaine des Sciences Sociales,* No. 4, 1967, pp. 258 and 267.

24. See Stankoimport v. Swisstool (1950), in Ramzaitsev (1957), p. 25. See also DIA-Bergbau (East Germany) v. Soiuzpromeksport (1956), in *ibid.,* p. 34; Metalimex v. Rudmetal (Bulgaria) (1956), in *ibid.,* p. 25; Technopromeksport v. Nikexport (Hungary) 1956, *op. cit. supra* note 19.

25. Award of June 6, 1960, cited in Jakubowski, "The Settlement of Foreign Trade Disputes in Poland," *International & Comparative Law Qtly.,* 1962, p. 813, at 814; see also discussion by Rajski, "Polish Private International Law," *International & Comparative Law Qtly.,* 1965, p. 464.

26. Maritime Code of 1929, Art. 4. A new Shipping Code became effective on October 1, 1968.

27. Secs. 78 and 79; see Genkin, "Sroki Iskovoi Davnosti Po Sovetskomu Grazhdanskomu Pravu Primeniaemye v Otnosheniiakh Po Vneshnei Torgovle," *S.I.M.,* Vol. XIX, Moscow 1965, pp. 43–44 (in Russian).

28. See R.S.F.S.R. Civil Code Secs. 80 and 82.

29. Decision of March 6, 1928, in *Zeitschrift für Ostrecht,* Vol. 4, 1930, p. 1007 (in German).

30. E.g., Eksportles v. Intercontinental de Bois Rufin P'erar (1950) in Ramzaitsev (1957), p. 27. The Moscow tribunal applied Section 44 of the Civil Code as part of the governing Soviet law and held that the Soviet plantiff's claim was not barred.

31. See, e.g., DIA-Bergbau v. Soiuzpromeksport (1956), *op. cit. supra* note 24.

32. See Art. 93.

33. See Trammer, "Time Limits for Claims and Actions in International Trade," in Honnold (ed.), *Unification of the Law Governing International Sales or Goods,* Paris, 1966, at p. 225 and, in particular, the Preliminary Draft of a Convention on the Uniform Effect of the Lapse of Time on International Sales of Tangible Movables, at pp. 228–233 (in French and English).

CHAPTER 17

INDUSTRIAL PROPERTY RIGHTS

1. See Y. Sergeev & I. Ivanov, "Patenty i Litsenzii v Mezhdunarodnoi Torgovle," *V.T.*, No. 1, 1960, p. 24.
2. See "The Protection of Patents and Technical Invention," UNECE Committee on the Development of Trade, *Trade/89,* August 5, 1959, p. 5.
3. See "Operating in Eastern Europe," *Business International, Roundtable,* Vienna 1967, pp. 22–23.
4. USSR Law on Inventions Art. 14 (1959).
5. Laws of June 30, 1919; Sept. 12, 1924; April 9, 1931, March 5, 1941; March 14, 1947 and April 24, 1959. (Many of the essential terms of the 1959 Law on Inventions and Rationalization Proposals were subsequently reproduced in Parts 5 and 6 [Arts. 107–116] of the Basic Principles [Legislation] and in the corresponding Parts [Secs. 517–526] of the 1964 R.S.F.S.R. Civil Code.)
6. Decree of Council of Ministers of May 15, 1962, Decree of the Committee for Inventions and Discoveries of June 23, 1962, superseding the Trademark Law of 1936, and Decree of Council of Ministers of July 9, 1965 on Industrial Designs. See *Revue de droit contemporain,* Vol. 14, No. 2, 1967, pp. 85–90 (in French and English).
7. Czech Law on Inventions, Discoveries and Rationalizations of July 5, 1957; Hungarian Decree of May 10, 1959; Bulgarian Law on Discoveries, Inventions and Proposals for Rationalizations of Feb. 2, 1961; Rumanian Decree of Sept. 7, 1950. For a systematic description of Soviet and East European law see Hiance and Plasseraud, *La Protection des Inventions en Union soviétique et dans les republiques populaires d'Europe,* Paris, 1969 (in French).
8. See H. Birklein, "Rolle und Aufgaben des Patentamtes der D.D.R.," *Neue Justiz,* No. 7, 1964, p. 212 (in German).
9. Sofia Convention (1949); see Katona, "Patents (Lizenzhandel)," *BIRPI Symposium,* p. 139 (in German). In the Soviet–Chinese Agreement of Oct. 12, 1954, the only conditions placed upon the recipient country are that it reimburse the donor's effective expenses and that it not export the know-how or derivative products without the donor's approval.
10. See Bystricky, "Patents (State of the Law)," *BIRPI Symposium,* p. 43, at 51.
11. See "Operating in Eastern Europe," *op. cit. supra* note 3.
12. See Boguslavsky, "Patents (Rechtszustand)," *BIRPI Symposium,* p. 31, at 36 (in German); see also Roditi, "Patent Protection in the USSR and Western Europe," *American Review of East–West Trade,* Vol. 1, Jan. 1968, p. 12, at 13. It should be noted that certificates of authorship formerly existed in Hungary but were abolished in 1957.

13. USSR Law on Discoveries, Inventions and Rationalizations of April 24, 1959, Art. 4(1); see also R.S.F.S.R. Civil Code Sec. 520.
14. See Boguslavsky, *op. cit. supra* note 12, at pp. 34–38. See also Hiance and Plasseraud, *op. cit. supra* note 7, at p. 18.
15. See "Propriété Industrielle," *Revue de droit contemporain,* Vol. 14, No. 2, 1967, p. 66, at 69 (in French).
16. A. Vida, "The Law of Industrial Property in the People's Democracies and the Soviet Union," *International & Comparative Law Qtly.,* Vol. 12, 1963, p. 898, at 906.
17. R.S.F.S.R. Civil Code Sec. 526.
18. Decision of August 16, 1960, in *Neue Justiz,* 1961, p. 109 (in German). A. Vida points out that the Office of the Procurator General of the German Democratic Republic endorsed the result of this case. See *op. cit. supra* note 16, p. 907.
19. See Boguslavsky, *op. cit. supra* note 12, at p. 34. See also *V.T.,* March 1967, p. 13.
20. See A. Vida, *op. cit. supra* note 16, pp. 909–10.
21. See R. C. Allison, "The Carl Zeiss Case," *The International Lawyer,* Vol. 3, April 1969, p. 525.
22. USSR Law of June 23, 1962 on Trademarks (as amended on March 1, 1967). For English translation, see Lightman, "Domestic and International Aspects of the U.S.S.R. Trademark System," *IDEA, The Patent, Trademark and Copyright Journal of Research and Education,* Vol. 12, 1968, pp. 791 *et seq.*
23. *Ibid.,* Art. 1 (2).
24. See Spunda, "Marken (Registrierung)," *BIRPI Symposium,* p. 231, at 238–9 (in German).
25. Film Fabrik Wolfen, V.E.B. v Gevaert-Agfa, N.V. (1966) in *Journal du droit international,* 1967 (in French); see also *Journal of Commerce,* April 29, 1966.
26. See H. Clesner, "Additional Aspects of Proprietary Rights and East–West Trade," *IDEA, The Patent, Trademark and Copyright Journal of Research and Education,* Vol. 9, No. 2, Summer 1965, at p. 196.
27. See *"Soviet Patent and Trademark Law,"* Report of a United Kingdom Delegation to the Soviet Union, London, 1960, p. 4.
28. The same privilege is provided in Hungary, Poland and East Germany. Czechoslovakia extends a right of filing within three months after the close of the exhibition. See Boguslavsky, *op. cit. supra* note 12, p. 33.
29. The case of Sandoz, A. G., *Gewerblicher Rechtsschutz und Urheberrecht,* No. 2, p. 70 (in German).
30. Lightman, "The U.S.S.R. Trademark System and East–West Trade," *IDEA, The Patent, Trademark and Copyright Journal of Research and Education,* Vol. 10, No. 1, 1966, pp. 11–12.

CHAPTER 18

TRANSACTIONS INVOLVING TECHNOLOGY

1. I. Skronek, Commercial Director of Polytechna, "Czechoslovak Licensing Practice," *Conference on East–West Trade,* Vienna, May 1969 (Pisar, ed.) Management Center Europe, Brussels, 1970, p. 75. See also Clesner, "Additional Aspects of Proprietary Rights and East–West Trade," *IDEA, The Patent, Trademark and Copyright Journal of Research and Education,* Vol. 9, No. 2, 1965, p. 183, at 198–99.
2. See *New Republic,* Feb. 18, 1967, and *Nihon Keizai Shimbun—Japan Economic Journal,* May 14, 1968, pp. 8–9.
3. See M. P. Venema, "The Finance and Structure of Major Economic Projects in Eastern Europe—The Rumanian Refinery Project," *American Review of East–West Trade,* Vol. 1, June 1968, p. 52.
4. See Katona, "Patents (Lizenzhandel)," *BIRPI Symposium,* p. 139, at 142 (in German). See also Winter, "The Licensing of Know-How to the Soviet Union," *The Journal of World Trade Law,* Vol. 1, No. 2, 1967, p. 162, at 169 *et seq.*
5. Instructions of the Committee on Inventions and Discoveries of February 16, 1968, as amended on April 29, 1968.
6. See Svyadosts, member of the Soviet Committee on Inventions and Discoveries, "Les droits du titulaire du Brevet et leur protection en U.R.S.S.," *BIRPI Symposium,* p. 159, at 167 (in French).
7. See, e.g., Arts. 3 and 4, Contract project between a French and a Rumanian enterprise for the manufacture and sale of French automobiles under license, in *Revue de droit contemporain,* Vol. 14, No. 2, 1967, p. 52, at 54 (in French).
8. See *Rynki Zagraniczne,* January, 1967 (in Polish).
9. See *Memorandum on Contracts for the Export of Engineering Products to the Soviet Union,* London Chamber of Commerce, March 1965, pp. 9–10.
10. See Kaye, "Case History in East–West Trade: National Patent Development Corporation," *American Review of East–West Trade,* Vol. 1, No. 1, 1968, pp. 36–9.
11. East German Standard Licensing Agreement, Art. 19.
12. Exchange of Letters of March 14, 1967 between ambassadors Hervé Alphand and Valerian Zorin published under Decree No. 68–251 of Feb. 29, 1968, in *Journal Officiel,* March 21, 1968 (in French).
13. See Nesterov, "Torgovaia Palata v Deistvii," *V.T.*, No. 3, 1967, p. 13.
14. Regulation of July 24, 1963.
15. See A. Vida, "The Law of Industrial Property in the People's Democracies and the Soviet Union," *International and Comparative Law Qtly.,* Vol. 12, 1963, p. 898, at 913.

16. See "The Protection of Patents and Technical Inventions," Note by the Secretariat of the UNECE, Committee for the Development of Trade, *Trade/89,* Aug. 5, 1959, pp. 21–22.

17. Law Amending and Supplementing the Law on Funds of Business Organizations, *Official Gazette* No. 31, July 10–11, 1967, in particular, Art. 64–0. See generally B. M. Paselj, "Yugoslav Laws on Foreign Investments," *The International Lawyer,* Vol. 2, No. 3, April 1968, pp. 499 *et seq.* See also Hanzekovic, "The Taxation of Foreign Enterprise in Yugoslavia," *Bulletin for International Fiscal Documentation,* Vol. XXII, Jan. 1968, pp. 3–9.

18. See *Business Europe,* June 21, 1968, p. 193.

19. International Legal Materials, Current Documents, Vol. VIII, January 1969, p. 48. See also "Accords de Coopération URSS–Pays Etrangères," *Note d'Information No. 12,* Chambre de Commerce Franco-Soviétique, May–June 1969, p. 29 (in French).

20. See generally *"La Coopération Economique, Industrielle, Scientifique et Technique Entre les Pays de l'Est et de l'Ouest de l'Europe,"* Ligue Européenne de Coopération Economique, Publication No. 41, Feb. 1967 in (French).

21. See Petroni, "Doing Business in Eastern European Countries," *Proceedings of the Southwestern Legal Foundation,* Private Investors Abroad, Structures and Safeguards, 1966, p. 261, at 286–7.

22. *The Sunday Times* (London), Dec. 3, 1967.

23. See Report by the UNCTAD Secretariat, *TD/18,* No. 3, 1967, p. 41.

24. See J. P. Saltiel, "Coopération économique Est–Ouest: problèmes et perspectives," *Projet, Civilisation, Travail, Economie,* No. 29, November, 1968, p. 1085, at 1089 (in French).

25. See Emil Benoit, "The Joint-venture Route to East–West Investment," *American Review of East–West Trade,* Vol. 1, June 1968, p. 39.

CHAPTER 19
EAST-WEST COPYRIGHT RELATIONS

1. See Levitsky, "Introduction to Soviet Copyright Law," in Szirmai (ed.), *Law in Eastern Europe,* Vol. 8, 1964, p. 240 and sources cited therein. See also Berman, "Sherlock Holmes in Moscow," *Harvard Law School Bulletin,* Feb. 1960, p. 3.

2. Banner Productions, Inc. v. Soveksportfilm *et al.,* Tribunal de Grande Instance de la Seine, July 16, 1965 (unpublished).

3. See Berman, "The Rights of Foreign Authors under Soviet Law," *Bulletin of the Copyright Society of the U.S.A.,* Vol. 7, No. 2, 1959, p. 67 *et seq.*

4. *See, e.g.*, Nesterov, "O sootnoshenii obshchestvennykh i lichnych interesov pri sotsializmie," *Uchenye Zapiski, Vysshaia Partiinaia Shkola pri TsK KPSS* (Moscow 1958), p. 80 (in Russian); see also Rudnicki, "Changes in Copyright Law and Practice in Poland after the Second World War," *Bulletin du Droit d'Auteur*, UNESCO, Vol. 14, No. 2, 1961, pp. 187–8.
5. Letter circulated privately among delegates to the Fourth Congress of Soviet Writers assembled in Moscow in May of 1967, as reported in *Time Magazine*, September 27, 1968, p. 27.
6. See *The Times* (London Edition) Aug. 20, 1968.
7. For a description of formalities applicable under American law, see generally *Nimmer on Copyright*, 1966, Chapter 7.
8. Basic Principles (Legislation) Art. 98.
9. Basic Principles (Legislation) Arts. 102–106.
10. See *The Daily Telegraph* (London), Aug. 6, 1969, and *Le Monde* (Paris) Aug. 8, 1969.
11. R.S.F.S.R. Civil Code, Secs. 511 and 512. See also Voksberg, "Publishing Agreements in the Soviet Union," *Revue Internationale du Droit d'Auteur*, Vol. LX, April, 1969 p. 3.
12. Basic Principles (Legislation) Art. 101.
13. See Spravochnik Normativnykh Materialov dlia Izdatel'skikh Rabotnikov, 1958, p. 40, and Sutulov, *Avtorskoe Pravo* (1966), pp. 61–66 (in Russian).
14. See Royalty Schedules reproduced in Levitsky, *op. cit. supra* note 1, at pp. 207–212.
15. Bulgarian Copyright Law of Nov. 16, 1951, amended by Decree of July 4, 1956; Czech law of March 25, 1965; Polish Law of July 10, 1952; Rumanian Decree of June 18, 1956, amended on July 24, 1957, Yugoslav Law of July 20, 1968 (which repealed and replaced the earlier Law of July 10, 1957); Hungarian Law of Dec. 29, 1921.
16. Hungarian Law of Dec. 29, 1921, Art. 7 and Decision No. 16 P. 211270–1961 (Budapest City Court).
17. See Stojanovic, "Du Contrat d'Edition," *Revue Internationale du Droit d'Auteur,* Vol. 52, 1967, p. 108 (in French).
18. Convention on the Reciprocal Protection of Copyright between Hungary and the Soviet Union, in *Copyright* (BIRPI), March 1968, p. 63.
19. The Sir Arthur Conan Doyle Estates v. Goslitizdat, Detgiz, Geografizdat *et al.*, Aug. 17, 1959 (Moscow); see Berman, *op. cit. supra* note 3.
20. Czechoslovakia's accession dates from Oct. 6, 1959; Yugoslavia ratified the Convention on Feb. 2, 1966. Czechoslovakia also acceded as of May 13, 1964, to the International Convention for the Protection of Performers.

21. See Rothenberg, *Copyright Law; Basic and Related Material* (N.Y. 1956), p. 486. See also *Lois et Traités sur le Droit d'Auteur,* UNESCO, 1964 Supplement, p. 312 (in French).
22. For a full discussion, see Levitsky, *op. cit. supra* note 1, pp. 243–248.
23. See *The Sunday Times* (London) March 1, 1970.
24. Société Fox, Europe v. Société Le Chant du Monde (as Licensees of Shostakovitch *et al.*), Cass. Civ. 22 December 1959, Bull. Cass. 1959.1.466, D.1960.93 J.C.P. 1960, 11580. See also Loi No. 64–689 Sur l'Application du Principe de Reciprocité en Matière de Protection du Droit d'Auteur (*J.O.,* 9 July, 1964) and Decret No. 67–181 (*J.O.,* 10 March 1967).

CHAPTER 20
ARBITRATION VERSUS LITIGATION

1. The Soviet Foreign Trade Arbitration Commission and Maritime Arbitration Commission were established in 1932 and 1930 respectively; the Court of Arbitration at the Polish Chamber of Foreign Trade in 1949; the Arbitration Court of the Chamber of Commerce of Czechoslovakia in 1952; the Arbitration Court of the Chamber of Foreign Trade of the German Democratic Republic in 1954; the Court of Arbitration Attached to the Hungarian Chamber of Commerce in 1949; the Arbitration Commission Attached to the Rumanian Chamber of Commerce in 1953; the Foreign Trade Arbitration Commission of the Bulgarian Chamber of Commerce in 1952; the Foreign Trade Arbitration Committee and the Maritime Arbitration Committee of the China Committee for the Promotion of International Trade in 1954 and 1958 respectively; the Court of Foreign Arbitration Attached to the Federal Chamber of Commerce of Yugoslavia in 1946.
2. Jordan Investments, Ltd. v. Soiuznefteksport (1958), reported in *The New York Times,* June 20, 1958.
3. See R.S.F.S.R. Code of Civil Procedure Sec. 117 and Genkin, "Pravovoe Polozhenie Vsesoiuznykh Vneshnetorgovykh Ob'iedinenii," in Genkin (ed.), *Pravovye Voprosy Vnesnei Torgovli SSSR* (Moscow 1955), p. 53, at 87 (in Russian).
4. See Entreprise Populaire "F.E.B." Fabrique de films Volfen v. Firme Gevaert AGFA N.V., Soviet Supreme Court (Civil Chamber), April 28, 1966, in Boguslavsky, *Journal du droit international,* 1967, p. 718 (in French).
5. R.S.F.S.R. Sup. Ct., Plenary Session, Ruling of Feb. 3, 1932, Protocol No. 1, R.S.F.S.R. Code of Civil Procedure Sec. 171 annot. (1943).
6. See, generally, Korolenko, *Torgovye Dogovory i Soglasheniia SSSR s Inostrannymi Gosudarstvami* (Moscow 1953) (in Russian).
7. R.S.F.S.R. Code of Civil Procedure Sec. 433. See also Sec. 59.

8. An interesting attempt to circumvent this prohibition is the Cooperation Agreement of Nov. 23, 1963, between the Polish Chamber of Foreign Commerce and the Italian Arbitration Association. See *Il Diritto negli Scambi Internazionali,* 1966, pp. 123–126 (in Italian).
9. See V. H. Li, "Legal Aspects of Trade with Communist China," *Columbia Journal of Transnational Law,* Vol. 3, 1964, p. 63.
10. E.g., Treaty Between the USSR and Germany, Oct. 12, 1925, *League of Nations Treaty Series,* Vol. 53, 1926, p. 7.
11. See Schaub & Matic, "Legal Aspects of United States Trade With Yugoslavia," *The Business Lawyer,* Vol. XX, 1965, p. 727, at 737–8.
12. See *S.I.M.,* Vol. XIII, 1962, p. 33. See also Indian Society of International Law, *International Commercial Arbitration,* 1964, pp. 379–385.
13. See Crespi-Reghizzi, "Legal Aspects of Trade with China: The Italian Experience," *Harvard International Law Journal,* Vol. 9, 1968, p. 85, at 124–5. See also V. H. Li, *op. cit. supra* note 9, pp. 63–64, and Fellhauer, "Foreign Trade Arbitral Jurisdiction in the People's Republic of China," Recht im Aussenhandel, in *Der Aussenhandel,* Vol. 12, 1960 (in German).
14. See, e.g. Sino-Czech Trade and Payments Agreement of 1955, which incorporates by reference the Comecon arbitral provision; see also Remer, *The Trade Agreements of Communist China* (1961), pp. 97 and 103.
15. See Benjamin, "The Work of the Economic Commission for Europe in the Field of International Commercial Arbitration," *International and Comparative Law Qtly.,* Vol. 7, 1958, p. 22.
16. See *op. cit. supra,* note 8.
17. Appeals from quality arbitrations held by the Gdynia Cotton Tribunal lie to the Le Havre Cotton Association. See also Lebedev, *Mezhdunarodnyi Torgovyi Arbitrazh* (Moscow 1965), p. 187 (in Russian), and Jakubowski, "The Settlement of Foreign Trade Disputes in Poland," *The International and Comparative Law Qtly.,* Vol. 11, 1962, p. 806, at 818–20.
18. Romanoeksport v. Albimport, Case No. 39/61, in *S.I.M.,* Vol. XVII, 1965, p. 35.
19. Decision No. 47/59, in Kojouharoff, p. 155.
20. Oscar Mayer (Zurich) v. Cogis (Milan), Decision No. 40/1963, April 17, 1963, "Iz Praktiki Vneshnetorgovoi Arbitrazhnoi Komissii," *S.I.M.,* Vol. XIX, 1965, pp. 45–47. See Fabbia, in *Il Diritto negli Scambi Internazionali,* 1964, pp. 193–95 (in Italian). See also Nestor, "De Quelques Problèmes Relatifs à la Compétence de l'Arbitrage Commercial," in *Rechtsfragen der Kooperation zwischen Unternehmen in Ost und West* (Munich 1967), p. 107, at 110–111 (in French).
21. See Hungarian Rules, Arts. 18–19.
22. See Keilin, "Morskoi arbitrazh v. SSSR za poslednie gody," *Torgovoe moreplavanie i morskoe pravo: sbornik statei i materialov,* No. 1, 1963, pp. 12–14 (in Russian).

23. Sovfrakht v. Soiuzpromeksport and Promsyr'eimport, April 28, 1964, *Bulletin of the Supreme Court of the U.S.S.R.*, 1964, No. 4, pp. 32–5, in Boguslavsky, *Journal du droit international,* No. 3, 1967, p. 708 (in French and Russian).
24. Decision No. 16/64, in Kojouharoff, pp. 153–4.
25. See generally, King-Smith, "Communist Foreign Trade Arbitration," *Harvard International Law Journal,* Vol. 10, No. 1, 1969, p. 34, at 45 *et seq.*
26. See, e.g., Genkin, in *S.I.M.*, Vol. XIV, 1963, pp. 3–5, reporting the activity of the January 1963 Moscow Conference of Presidents of the Foreign Trade Arbitration Commissions of the member countries of Comecon.

CHAPTER 21
EASTERN FOREIGN TRADE TRIBUNALS IN ACTION

1. E.g., Polish Rules Sec. 25; Czech Rules Arts. 8(4), 9(2); Bulgarian Rules Sec. 11–13.
2. In 61 of the 84 cases brought before the Moscow tribunal from 1957 through 1959 the parties reportedly waived their right to choose arbitrators and allowed, instead, the President of the Commission to make the selection. See Genkin, "O Rabote Vneshnetorgovoi Arbitrazhnoi Komissii pri Vsesoiuznoi Torgovoi Palate za 1957–1959," *S.I.M.*, Vol. XI, 1961, p. 4.
3. Hungarian Rules Art. 4(1); Czech Rules Sec. 10(2); see also Firma Ligna v. Baumgartner & Co. A.G., II Zivilkammer des Obergerichtes des Kantons Zürich, No. 125 A. (R.), March 15, 1957, *revised,* Urteil des Schweizerischen Bundesgerichtes, Staatsrechtliche Kammer, Feb. 12, 1958 (in German).
4. See King-Smith, "Communist Foreign-Trade Arbitration," *Harvard International Law Journal,* Vol. 10, 1969, 34 at pp. 52–53 and the Eastern authorities cited therein.
5. "The Law of Foreign Trade in the Legal Systems of the Countries of Planned Economy," in Schmitthoff (Sources) 41 at pp. 45–46.
6. Art. 1 of the Charter of the U.S.S.R. All-Union Chamber of Commerce states that the Ministry of Foreign Trade "exercises general supervision" over its activities. The statute of the East German Chamber of Foreign Trade states that "general supervision over the Chamber is exercised by the Minister for Foreign and Intra-German Trade," *Satzung der Kammer für Aussenhandel der D.D.R.* Sec. 1(4) (1954).
7. E.g., In re "King Edgar" (1932), in *S.R.M.A.K.*, 1934, p. 9; Gebreders Kats v. Eksportkhleb (ca. 1936), in *V.T.P.V.A.*, 1941, p. 34, "Z Orzecznictwa Kolegium Arbitrazowego Przy PIHZ," *Handel Zagraniczny,* No. 3, 1958, p. 36 (in Polish).
8. See Amtorg Trading Corp. v. Camden Fibre Mills, Inc., 197 Misc. 398,

94 NYS 2d 651 (Sup. Ct.), *modified,* 277 App. Div. 531, 100 NYS 2d 747 (1950), *aff'd,* 304 N.Y. 519, 109 NE 2d 606 (1952).

9. E.g., *ibid.* See also Leff, "The Foreign Trade Arbitration Commission of the U.S.S.R. and the West," *The Arbitration Journal,* Vol. 24, No. 1, 1969, 1 at 24 *et seq.*

10. Eksportles v. Compagnie Commerciale de Bois à Papier (1939), in Ramzaitsev (1957), p. 32 and Eksportles v. Oesterreichische Chanvertretung (1957), in Ramzaitsev, "Voprosy Mezhdunarodnovo Chastnovo Prava v Praktike Vneshnetorgovoi Arbitrazhnoi Komissii," *Sovetskoe Gosudarstvo i Pravo,* Sept. 1957, p. 50, at 59–60 (in Russian).

11. Treaty of Commerce and Navigation Between the USSR and Austria, Oct. 17, 1955; see also cases cited in Chapter XXIV *infra.*

12. See Pisar, "The United Nations Convention on Foreign Arbitral Awards," *The Journal of Business Law,* July 1959, p. 219.

13. See Khrushchev's famous report to the 20th Congress of the Communist Party, *The New York Times,* June 5, 1956.

14. See Pisar, "Treatment of Communist Foreign Trade Arbitration in Western Courts," in Domke (ed.), *International Trade Arbitration* (1958), p. 107. See also Berman, "Soviet Justice and Soviet Tyranny," *Columbia Law Review,* Vol. 55, 1959, p. 795.

15. See Berman, "Force Majeure and the Denial of an Export License Under Soviet Law," 73 *Harvard Law Review,* 1959, 1128, at 1140.

16. See e.g., Eksportkhleb v. Société Commerciale de la Seine (1950), in Ramzaitsev (1957), p. 26; Eksportles v. Compagnie Commerciale de Bois à Papier (1939), in *ibid.*, p. 32; Soiuzugleeksport v. Legeta (1938), in Ramzaitsev (1952), p. 42. In this connection, it is interesting to note that in the famous Lena Goldfields arbitration of 1930, which was boycotted by the U.S.S.R., Soviet experts insisted that the arbitrators had no capacity to determine their own competence. See Nussbaum, "The Arbitration Between the Lena Goldfields, Ltd., and the Soviet Government," *Cornell Law Qtly.*, Vol. 36, 1950, p. 31, at 41.

17. See, e.g., Sovfrakht v. Soiuzpromeksport and Promsyr'eimport, April 23, 1964, *Bulletin of the Supreme Court of the U.S.S.R.*, 1964, No. 4, pp. 32–5, reported by Boguslavsky in *Journal du droit international,* No. 3, 1967, p. 708 (in French), where the tribunal's determination of its own competence was overruled by the Soviet Supreme Court for lack of party consent.

18. International Chamber of Commerce, *Rules of Conciliation and Arbitration* Sec. 10(3) (1947).

19. Decision No. 56/66, in Kojouharoff, p. 156. See also the Moscow tribunal's decision in Soiuzpromeksport v. Pintus (1939), in Ramzaitsev (1952), p. 15.

20. Dossier 322/1965, Decision No. 28, March 19, 1966, in Nestor, "De

Quelques Problèmes Relatifs à la Compétence de l'Arbitrage Commercial," *Rechtsfragen der Kooperation Zwischen Unternehmen in Ost und West* (Munich 1967), p. 107, at pp. 117–8 (in French).

21. See Ramzaitsev, "The Law Applied by Arbitration Tribunals," in Schmitthoff (Sources), p. 141.
22. Decision No. 10/66, in Kojouharoff, p. 153.
23. Artia v. Mercantile Corporation of New York, Decision No. 16/67, in E. Kafajova, "Chronique de Jurisprudence Tchécoslovaque," *Journal du droit international,* Vol. 96, No. 1, 1969, p. 176, 181 (in French); see also *Prawo w Handlu Zagranicznym* No. 3, 1963 pp. 88–97 (in Polish).
24. See Rumanian Decision No. 7/1955, in Nestor, *op. cit. supra* note 20, p. 115; see also Soviet Rules Sec. 1.
25. In Société d'Avance Commerciale v. Soiuzpromeksport (1940) in Ramzaitsev (1952), p. 51, plaintiff sought to join as codefendant the Soviet insurance agency Gosstrakh, with which it had no arbitration agreement. The request was granted upon receipt from Gosstrakh of an intimation that it was not opposed to being joined. A similar request was granted in Stefenson v. Soiuzpromeksport (1938), in *ibid.*
26. In Eksportles v. Compagnie Commerciale de Bois à Papier, (1939), *op. cit. supra* note 16, the tribunal stated: "In the absence of such a system the agreement to refer to arbitration would have been a dead letter, since the party wishing for some reason to sabotage the arbitral proceedings could always render the arbitral agreement incapable of being performed."
27. Decision No. 32/62, in Kojouharoff, p. 158.
28. E.g. Soviet Rules Sec. 20; Chinese Rules Sec. 18; Czech Rules Art. 14(15).
29. Shär, "Bericht über die Durchführung eines Schiedsverfahrens vor der Aussenhandels-Arbitragekomission bei der Handelskammer der UdSSR in Moskau," *Recht der Internationalen Wirtschaft,* July 1956, p. 75 (in German). Israeli counsel were Messrs. Schlossberg and Argaman of the Tel-Aviv bar. The Israeli case has, however, been criticized on procedural, as well as substantive grounds. See Eisemann, "Keine Haftung des FOB-Verkäufers für die Beschaffung der Ausfuhrgenehmigung nach Sowjetischem Recht," *Verkehr,* Jan. 10, 1959, p. 41 (in German).

CHAPTER 22
THE CONTROLLING LEGAL SYSTEM

1. Ramzaitsev, *Morskoi Arbitrazh v Sovetskom Soiuze* (Moscow 1956), p. 18 (in Russian); *cf.* Firma Ligna v. Baumgartner & Co. A. G., II Zivilkammer des Obergerichtes des Kantons Zürich, No. 125 A. (R), March 15, 1957. Sec. 10(2) of the current Czech Rules specifically provides that citizenship is not a prerequisite.

2. See Kojouharoff, p. 159; New York Convention Art. V and Geneva Convention Art. IV (1) (b).
3. Czech Rules, Sec. 31; Rumanian Rules, Sec. 43.
4. Decision No. 32/62, in Kojouharoff, p. 158.
5. Lunz, *Mezhdunarodnyi Grazhdanskyi Protsess,* 1965, p. 165 (in Russian).
6. See King-Smith, "Communist Foreign Trade Arbitration," *Harvard International Law Journal,* Vol. 10, 1969, p. 34, at 70–71.
7. See Art. 27; see also Jakubowski, "The Settlement of Foreign Trade Disputes in Poland," *The International & Comparative Law Qtly.,* Vol. 11, 1962, p. 806, at 820.
8. Decision of May 7, 1963, of the District Court of Zürich, Switzerland, reported in *Handel Zagraniczny,* No. 9, 1964, p. 552 (in Polish).
9. See Goikhbarg, Preface to Pereterskii, *Otcherki Mezhdunarodnovo Chastnovo Prava RSFSR* (Moscow 1925), p. 5 (in Russian); see also Rink, *Sovetskoe Mezhdunarodnoe Chastnoe Pravo i Vneshnetorgovye Sdelki* (Moscow 1954) p. 13 (in Russian).
10. See Chapter 13 *supra.*
11. Basic Principles (Legislation) Art. 18; see also Lunts (1949), p. 35.
12. Both prescribe six-month periods for the presentation of claims, but the former is tolled by the buyer's demand and the latter by the seller's refusal of the demand.
13. See Lunts, "Conflict of Laws in International Sales: Theory and Practice of Socialist Countries," *Recueil des cours de l'Académie de droit international de la Haye* (1965), p. 23.
14. E.g., Decision No. 41/64, in Kojouharoff, pp. 178–9.
15. See Comecon Conditions of 1968, Art. 110.
16. Soviet Basic Principles (Legislation) Art. 129; Basic Principles (Procedure) Art. 64. *Cf.* Levin, *Osnovye Problemy Sovremennovo Mezhdunarodnovo Prava,* 1958, p. 128 (in Russian); see also Polish Private International Law Art. 1(2) (1965).
17. E.g., Pereterskii & Krylov, *Mezhdunarodnoe Chastnoe Pravo* (Moscow 1940), p. 109 (in Russian).
18. By joint operation of Secs. 565 and 45.
19. USSR Laws, 1929, Ch. 697. USSR Laws, 1937, Ch. 221. After a 1930 decree, bills of exchange retained their use only for foreign trade purposes and were not employed in the public sector of domestic commerce. The U.S.S.R.'s acceptance of the provisions of the Uniform Law thus served to facilitate foreign commerce without affecting internal economic activity. Locally, Soviet enterprises use drafts similar to bills of exchange as a form of payment. See Kharkov Office of Paper Sales v. Gosbank, in Konstantinovsky, *Soviet Law in Action* (Berman, ed.), 1953, p. 42.

20. See *S.R.M.A.K.* 1937, p 10.
21. Arts. 14–15. See also Quigley, "New Soviet Merchant Shipping Code," *The American Review of East–West Trade,* Dec. 1968, p. 64.
22. See R.S.F.S.R. Code of Civil Procedure Secs. 50 and 74.
23. Czech Rules, Sec. 16; Polish Rules, Sec. 10(4) (b).
24. This method was authorized under Sec. 8 of the former Code of Procedure. The new Code, which provides merely that "the court applies rules of foreign law in accordance with the law," offers less helpful guidance. See R.S.F.S.R. Code of Civil Procedure Sec. 10; East German Code of Civil Procedure Sec. 293; Hungarian Code of Civil Procedure Art. 200; Polish Code of Civil Procedure Art. 1143.
25. Levitin, "Voprosy Publichnovo Poriadka v Mezhdunarodnom Chastnom Prave," in *Problemy Mezhdunarodnovo Chastnovo Prava* (Moscow 1960), p. 224 (in Russian); see also Basic Principles (Legislation) Art. 128; R.S.F.S.R. Civil Code Sec. 568.
26. See Mádl, *Foreign Trade Monopoly: Private International Law* (Budapest 1967) p. 156.
27. Lunts (1959), pp. 235–6.
28. See Lebedev, *Mezhdunarodnyi Torgovyi Arbitrazh* (Moscow 1965), p. 189 (in Russian). See also Boguslavsky, "Arbitrazhnoe rassmotrenie sporov vo vneshnei torgovle SSSR s evropeiskimi stranami narodnoi demokratsi," in *Pravovye voprosy vneshnei torgovli SSSR* (Moscow 1955), p. 261 (in Russian).
29. See the remarks of Prof. Knapp at the Colloquium on the Sources of the Law of International Trade, Sept. 24, 1962, reported by Sarre, in Schmitthoff (Sources), p. 270; see also Ramzaitsev, "The Law Applied by Arbitration Tribunals," in *ibid.*, pp. 150–51.
30. In re Estate of Larkin, 416 P. 2d 473 (California 1966, Opinion by Tobriner, J.); *cf.* Zschernig v. Miller, 412 P. 2d 781 (Oregon 1966), reversed on appeal to U.S. Supreme Court, 389 U.S. 429, 88 S. Ct. 664 (Jan. 15, 1968), in regard to East German law; see, in general, Ehrenzweig, *Private International Law* (Leyden 1967), pp. 157–58. See also Lunts, *op. cit. supra* note 27.
31. See Pisar, "Soviet Conflict of Laws in International Commercial Transactions," *Harvard Law Review*, Vol. 70, 1957, pp. 597, 621–2, 656; *cf.* Lunts (1959), p. 236; Levitin, *op. cit. supra* note 25, pp. 224–25.

CHAPTER 23
LAW SELECTION METHODS

1. See Bulgarian Law on Obligations and Contracts Art. 9(1). See also Mádl, *Foreign Trade Monopoly: Private International Law* (Budapest 1967), p. 103.

2. Decision of Dec. 5, 1956, cited by Ionasco and Nestor, "The Limits of Party Autonomy," in Schmitthoff (Sources), p. 188.
3. Decision No. 16/64, in Kojouharoff, pp. 169–71.
4. In re "Phoenix" (1936), *S.R.M.A.K.*, 1937, p. 143.
5. Soiuzugleeksport v. Legata (1938), *V.T.P.V.A.*, 1941, p. 21.
6. Incomar v. Raznoeksport (1954), in Ramzaitsev, "Problems of Private International Law in the Jurisprudence of the Arbitration Commission for Foreign Trade," *Sovetskoe Gosudarstvo i Pravo,* No 9, 1957, p. 85 (in Russian).
7. See *Prawo w Handlu Zagranicznym* No. 4, 1963, p. 73 (in Polish). See also King-Smith, "Communist Foreign-Trade Arbitration," *Harvard International Law Journal,* Vol. 10, 1969 p. 34, at 58 and 88.
8. Limited Company C. of Tangiers v. Motokov (Nov. 2, 1954), in *Journal du droit international,* 1956, p. 458 (in French).
9. See, e.g., Lunts (1949), p. 227.
10. Cosmos v. Motokov (Nov. 2, 1954), in Kojouharoff, p. 172, and in Szászy, *Private International Law in the European People's Democracies* (Budapest 1964), p. 278. See also Lunts (1963), p. 141.
11. See Mora, The "Applicable Law" in Hungarian Commercial Arbitration. *Questions of International Law,* Hung. Branch of International Law Assn. (Budapest 1964), pp. 140–42.
12. See Decisions of June 6, 1961, and Dec. 19, 1960, in Jakubowski, "The Settlement of Foreign Trade Disputes in Poland," *International and Comparative Law Qtly.,* Vol. 11, 1962, p. 814.
13. Centrotex v. M. K. Co. of Pakistan (Mar. 1, 1954), in *Journal du droit international,* 1956, pp. 468–72 (in French).
14. Kojouharoff, p. 186.
15. Schaub & Matic, "Legal Aspects of United States Trade with Yugoslavia," *The Business Lawyer,* 1965, p. 736.
16. Haidar Ali v. Mezhdunarodnaia Kniga (ca. 1938), *V.T.P.V.A.*, 1941, p. 22.
17. Respectively, Hollis Bros., Ltd., v. Eksportles (1957), in Lunts (1963), p. 152; Nekon v. Prodintorg (1957), *ibid.,* p. 151; DIA-Bergbau v. Soiuzpromeksport (1956), in Ramzaitsev (1957), p. 64; Tekhnopromeksport v. Nikeksport (1956), *ibid.*
18. Metalimex v. Rudmetal (1956), in Ramzaitsev (1957), p. 65.
19. Oscar Mayer (Zürich) v. Cogis (Milan), Decision No. 40/1963, April 17, 1963, in Shpektorov, "Iz Praktiki Vneshnetorgovoi Arbitrazhnoi Komissii," *S.I.M.,* Vol. XIX, Moscow 1965, pp. 45–47; see also Fabbia, in *Il Diritto Negli Scambi Internazionali,* 1964, p. 193 (in Italian).
20. Decision No. 56/66, May 26, 1966, of the Bulgarian tribunal.

21. Decisions of Sept. 19, 1958, and Nov. 29, 1958, in Ionasco and Nestor, *op. cit. supra* note 2, p. 193.
22. Decision of Feb. 11, 1957, *ibid.*, p. 194.
23. Raznoimport v. Mussalla & Serdika (1941), in Ramzaitsev (1952), pp. 34–5.
24. A & P Import Co. v. Raznoeksport (1938), *V.T.P.V.A.*, 1941, p. 24.
25. USSR Trade Delegation in Turkey v. Khaki Sheshbesh (1937), in Ramzaitsev (1952), p. 43.
26. See comments of Professor Stalev, quoted by Ionasco and Nestor, *op. cit. supra* note 2, p. 195.
27. See Fellhauer, "Drei Jahre Schiedsgericht bei der Kammer für Aussenhandel der deutschen demokratischen Republik," *Der Aussenhandel,* 1957, p. 19 (in German).
28. See Kemper & Wiemann, "Die Bestimmungen des auf Aussenhandelskaufverträge anwendbaren Recht durch das Schiedsgericht bei der Kammer für Aussenhandel," Recht im Aussenhandel, *Der Aussenhandel,* No. 6, 1961 (in German).
29. Société M. N. v. Koospol S. A. (1953), "Notes on Czechslovakian Judicial Decisions," *Journal du droit international,* Vol. 83, 1956, p. 453. See also Centrotex v. M. K. Co. of Pakistan (March 1, 1954) in *ibid,* No. 2, 1956, p. 470.
30. Decision No. 244/57 reported in *Prawo w Handlu Zagranicznym,* No. 8, 1964, pp. 59–63 (in Polish).
31. Hollis Bros. Ltd. v. Eksportles (no date given), in Ramzaitsev (1952), p. 36; Simon Frères v. Soiuzpushchina (1951), *ibid.* (1957), p. 66.
32. Respectively, Skembri (Turkey) v. Roskombank (1940), in Ramzaitsev (1952), p. 37; Eksportles v. Lemay Frères (1952), *ibid.* (1957), p. 67; Isaiev v. Iransovtrans (1947), *ibid.*, p. 66.
33. Ariovich & Jacob Fur Co. v. Soiuzpushchina (1951), in *ibid.* (1952). p. 89.
34. Decision No. 67/64, Feb. 5, 1966; see also, Decisions Nos. 1/56, 5/55, 2/56, 16/56, 10/56, 17/56, 9/56 and 67/64, in Kojouharoff, pp. 171–3.
35. Decision No. 565/56, in Reczei, *Die Anknüpfung des Obligationenstatus im Internationalen Privatrecht: Fragen des Internationalen Privatrechts* (Berlin 1958), p. 175 (in German); see also Mádl, *op. cit. supra* note 1, pp. 135–36.
36. WMW Export v. Tekhnoimport (1959), in Lunts, "Conflict of Laws in International Sales: Theory and Practice of Socialist Countries," Recueil des cours de l'Académie de droit international de la Haye (1965), p. 23.
37. Ramzaitsev (1952), p. 32.
38. Pereterskii & Krylov, *Mezhdunarodnoe Chastnoe Pravo* (Moscow 1940), p. 177 (in Russian).

39. See Szászy, *op. cit. supra* note 10, p. 297; *cf.* Reczei, *Nomzetkozi Maganjog* (Private International Law) (2d ed., Budapest 1959), p. 226 (in Hungarian).

40. See Lunts (1963), pp. 31 *et seq.*

41. See Batiffol, *Droit International Privé* (4th ed., Paris 1967), pp. 224–25 (in French).

42. Soiuzneftեksport v. Moroni & Keller, *S.p A.* (1960), in Ramzaitsev, "The Law Applied by Arbitration Tribunals," in Schmitthoff (Sources), p. 145. See also Mádl, *op. cit. supra* note 1, p. 210, where it is contended that the rule of *siège social* is predominant.

43. Decision No. 11/64, April 18, 1964, in Kojouharoff, pp. 159–160.

CHAPTER 24
ENFORCEMENTS OF ARBITRATION CLAUSES AND AWARDS

1. Soviet Basic Principles (Procedure) Art. 64; Rumanian Code of Civil Procedure, Arts. 166 and 135, Czechoslovak Act on International Arbitration—Enforcement of Arbitration Awards, of December 4, 1963, Art. 29. Polish Code of Civil Procedure Art. 1146 (1964); see also Lasok, "The Polish System of Private International Law," *The American Journal of Comparative Law,* Vol. 15, 1967, pp. 337–38.

2. See Nussbaum, "The Arbitration Between the Lena Goldfields, Ltd., and the Soviet Government," *Cornell Law Qtly.,* Vol. 36, 1950, p. 31 at 41, For the text of the ignored award which held the Soviet government liable for 12,965,000 pounds sterling, see *The Times* (London), Sept. 3, 1930.

3. See UNECE Ad Hoc Group on Arbitration, National and International Institutions Active in the Field of International Commercial Arbitration, *Trade/WP 1/5, Note by Secretariat* (1955), p. 14.

4. Legeta v. Soiuzugleeksport (1938), in Ramzaitsev (1957), p. 13.

5. R.S.F.S.R. Code of Civil Procedure. See 437; see also Secs. 340, 357 and 358.

6. Vedomosti Verkhovnovo Sovieta SSSR, No. 6, 1960, p. 421; see Lebedev, *Mezhdunarodnyi Torgovyi Arbitrazh* (Moscow 1965), p. 196 (in Russian).

7. *Ibid.,* pp. 193–94.

8. See generally Pisar, "The Treatment of Communist Foreign Trade Arbitration in Western Courts," in *International Trade Arbitration* (Domke, ed., 1958), p. 101, and in *Aspects Juridiques du Commerce avec les Pays d'Economie Planifiée* (Paris 1961), p. 163 (in French).

9. Respectively, Legeta v. Soiuzugleeksport (1938); in re Sheshbesh (1940), in Ramzaitsev (1957), p. 13; and May & Hassell, Ltd. v. Vsesoiuznoe Ob'edinenie "Eksportles" 66 *Lloyd's List L.H.* 103 (K.B. 1940).

10. Amtorg Trading Corp. v. Camden Fibre Mills, Inc., 304 N.Y. 519, 521, 109 NE 2d 606 (1952). The first-instance decision, rendered by the Supreme Court of New York, Special Term, New York County, Part 1, 197 Misc. 398, *94 NYS 2d 651* (1950), stated: "For it is axiomatic that an arbitrator and a party may not be fused into one. Stated differently, there can be no arbitrator in the person of a party. When, therefore, an arbitrator and a party are separate entities the inquiry is as to the intangible ties between them which, although they do not unite them corporeally, preclude an impartial adjudication or might justify an inference of partiality."
11. It can hardly be assumed that the court ignored this approach because Amtorg's complete subservience to the Soviet government made it doubtful whether it could be considered an American corporation in the proper sense. The same formalistic considerations which prompted it to conclude that the Moscow trade tribunal was a juridically independent entity ought to have prevented it from questioning Amtorg's New York status and its separateness in point of law from the Soviet state.
12. I.e., Gilbert v. Burnstine, 255 N.Y. 348 (1931).
13. The Fehmarn (1958), *Weekly Law Review* 159 (C.A.).
14. See respectively, 2 L.I. Rep. 147 (1958) and Ibrahim & Co. v. Promsyr'e-import and Ingostrakh (1959), in Lebedev, *op. cit. supra* note 6, pp. 199–200.
15. See respectively India Hide and Wool Export Co. v. Raznoeksport (1961), in *ibid.,* pp. 198–99, Handel Zagraniczny No. 9, 1964, p. 552, and *Prawo w Handlu Zagranicznym,* No. 8, 1964, p. 64 (in Polish).
16. See respectively Lebedev, *op. cit. supra* note 6, p. 183, in re Chanakchili (1946), in Ramzaitsev (1952), p. 29, and Exportles v. Intercontinental de Bois Rufin P'erar (1950), in *ibid.,* p. 30. See also Saymen, "Notes on Turkish Court Decisions," *Journal du droit international,* Vol. 84, 1957, p. 1037, at 1061 (in French).
17. Ligna v. Baumgartner & Co. S. A., Urteil des Schweizerischen Bundesgerichtes, Staatsrechtliche Kammer, Feb. 12, 1958 (in German); see also *Recueil Officiel des Arrêts du Tribunal Fédéral Suisse,* No. 1, 1958, p. 39 (in French). The first-instance decision is reported in II *Zivilkammer des Obergerichtes des Kantons Zürich,* No. 125 A. (R.), March 15, 1957 (in German).
18. See Mezger, "Die Anerkennung Jugoslawischer und Anderer Osteuropäischen Schiedsprüche in der Bundesrepublik," *Neue Juristische Wochenschrift,* No. 7, 1962, pp. 278–83 (in German).
19. Soviet-German Agreement on Arbitral Tribunals for Commercial and Other Civil Matters, Part VI; see also Czechoslovak-Soviet Agreement of June 5, 1922, Art. 15; Italian-Soviet Agreement of Feb. 7, 1924, Art. 12.
20. E.g., Treaty of Commerce and Navigation between the U.S.S.R. and Austria, Oct. 17, 1955; Treaty of Commerce between the U.S.S.R. and

Finland, Dec. 1, 1947; Treaty of Commerce and Navigation between the U.S.S.R. and Italy, December 11, 1948. See "Arbitrato," *Enciclopedia del Diritto,* Vol. 2, 1958, p. 893, at 965–75 (in Italian).

21. E.g., Convention Concerning the Exchange of Goods and Payments between the U.S.S.R. and Sweden, Sept. 7, 1940.

22. E.g., Treaty of Commerce and Navigation between the U.S.S.R. and Denmark, Aug. 17, 1946; Agreement between the U.S.S.R. and France on Commerce and the Status of Soviet Trade Delegations in France, Sept. 3, 1951, Art. 11.

23. Czech Rules Art. 13(2) expressly requires the court to ensure that the award is substantiated and formulated so as to be enforceable abroad.

24. E.g., French Code of Civil Procedure Art. 1006. Italian legislation is exorbitantly severe, nullifying attempted ousters of state jurisdiction where one party is a resident Italian national. See Italian Code of Civil Procedure Art. 2.

25. See Stankoimport v. Swisstool (1950), in Ramzaitsev (1952), p. 25, and Lebedev, *op. cit. supra* note 6, p. 178.

26. Metalimport v. Soc. Interferros, April 23, 1965, Milan Ct. of Appeals, in *Il Diritto negli Scambi Internazionali,* 1965, pp. 52–3 (in Italian). Rumania, Albania, Czechoslovakia, Germany and Poland were signatories of the Protocol; Rumania, Czechoslovakia and Germany ratified the convention.

27. See Convention between Switzerland and Czechoslovakia Concerning Reciprocal Judicial Assistance in Civil and Commercial Matters, Dec. 21, 1926, *Recueil Officiel des Lois,* Vol. 43, 1927, p. 536 (Switz.).

28. See generally Bredin, "La Convention de New York," *Journal du droit international,* 1960, p. 1002 (in French) and Mezger, "Das Europäische Übereinkommen über die Handelschiedsgerichtsbarkeit," Rabel, *Zeitschrift für Ausländisches und Internationales Privatrecht,* No. 2, 1965, p. 232 (in German).

29. See U.N. Economic and Social Council, Conference on International Commercial Arbitration, Provisional Summary Records of the Eighth Meeting 4–5, U.N. Doc. No. E/Conf. 26/S.R. 8 (1958). See also Pisar, "The United Nations Convention on Foreign Arbitral Awards," *Journal of Business Law,* 1959, pp. 219–33.

CHAPTER 25

CONCLUSION: A PROPOSED CODE OF FAIR PRACTICES

1. See *L'Actualité Economique*, No. 81, June 14, 1967, p. 39; *Correspondance Economique,* January 10, 1968, p. 4; and *Le Monde* (Paris), January 8, 1969 (in French).

2. See *Aspects Juridiques du Commerce avec les Pays d'Economie Planifiée* (Paris 1961) (in French); *The Sources of the Law of International Trade* (Schmitthoff, ed.) (London 1964); and *Unification of the Laws Governing International Sales of Goods* (Honnold, ed.) (Paris 1966).
3. See Erosi, "Measures for Unifying the Rules on Choice of Laws," in Honnold, *op. cit. supra* note 3, pp. 297 and 304; see also Rubanov and Tschikvadze, "Some Aspects of the Unification of the Law of Sales" in *ibid.*, p. 344.
4. See Pisar, "Practical Problems of Commercial Dealings Between Private Parties and Communist-Owned Business Enterprises," *Testimony before the Committee on Interstate and Foreign Commerce, U.S. Senate, 1959.*
5. Sir McKenzie Chalmers, "Codification of Mercantile Law," *Law Quarterly Review,* Vol. 19, 1903, p. 10; see Schmitthoff, "The Risk of Loss in Transit in International Sales," in Honnold, *op. cit. supra* note 3, pp. 198–9.

ABOUT THE AUTHOR

Samuel Pisar is a prominent international lawyer, a member of the Washington, D.C., and California Bars and a Barrister-at-Law of Gray's Inn, London. He heads the European office of an American law firm specializing in trade and investments between the United States and the Common Market, and serves on the Boards of several banks and multinational corporations. Mr. Pisar, who is fluent in seven languages, received his education in a number of countries and has been awarded Doctorates in law from Harvard and the University of Paris. Throughout his academic and professional career he has published articles on legal, economic and financial subjects. As an acknowledged authority in his field, he has testified before Committees of the U.S. Senate and House of Representatives, chaired international conferences and lectured extensively on both sides of the Atlantic. Made a citizen of the United States by special Act of Congress, Mr. Pisar was a member of President Kennedy's Task Force on Foreign Policy as well as an adviser to the Department of State and a counsel to UNESCO. A frequent traveler both West and East, he works mainly out of his Paris office.

INDEX